Excel 97 for Windows

Concepts & Examples

Karen Jolly
Portland Community College

Franklin, Beedle & Associates, Incorporated
8536 SW St. Helens Drive, Suite D
Wilsonville, Oregon 97070
503/682-7668

President and Publisher	Jim Leisy (jimleisy@fbeedle.com)
Production	Susan Skarzynski
	Tom Sumner
	Stephanie Welch
Cover Design	Susan Skarzynski
Marketing Group	Victor Kaiser
	Cary Crossland
	Carrie Widman
	Sue Page
Order Processing	Chris Alarid
	Ann Leisy

Printed in the U.S.A.

Names of all products herein are used for identification purposes only and are trademarks and/or registered trademarks of their respective owners. Franklin, Beedle & Associates, Inc., makes no claim of ownership or corporate association with the products or companies that own them.

© 1998 Franklin, Beedle & Associates Incorporated. No part of this book may be reproduced, stored in a retrieval system, transmitted, or transcribed, in any form or by any means—electronic, mechanical, telepathic, photocopying, recording, or otherwise—without prior written permission of the publisher. Requests for permission should be addressed as follows:

Rights and Permissions
Franklin, Beedle & Associates, Incorporated
8536 SW St. Helens Drive, Suite D
Wilsonville, Oregon 97070
http://www.fbeedle.com

Library of Congress Cataloging-in-Publication Data

Jolly, Karen
   Excel 97 for Windows : concepts and examples / Karen Jolly.
      p.   cm.
   Includes index.
   1. Microsoft Excel for Windows. 2. Business--Computer programs.
3. Electronic spreadsheets.   I. Title.
HF5548.4.M523J638 1997
005.369--dc21
                                                           97-28521
                                                              CIP

Preface

Excel 97 for Windows: Concepts & Examples enables you to master Excel in a short period of time. The central concepts of electronic worksheets are covered—workbooks, functions, charts, databases, templates, and macros. Exercises throughout the textbook help clarify complex Excel features; the exercises provide immediate practice and reflect the most common spreadsheet uses.

This textbook is intended for a beginning Excel course that spans either a semester or a quarter. The clear explanations, helpful illustrations, and thorough index make the text an excellent reference. The exercises and end-of-chapter study questions have been carefully tested and proofread to ensure accuracy.

Students using this textbook should have a basic understanding of the Windows 95 operating system (how to open and save documents, manage files, and use the mouse). This textbook is not devoted to basic computer operations since computers can be configured to meet different personal needs.

Presented in Small Units

This book presents Excel features in a concise manner, allowing the reader to start working at the computer almost immediately. Frequently used Excel features are covered early in the book and serve as a basis of knowledge for the more advanced concepts. Emphasis is placed on using the mouse and menus, but Power User tips introduce keyboard shortcuts.

Practice Is Essential to Mastery

Practice is essential in mastering any skill; this especially applies to using computer software. The introduction of each Excel feature is followed by an exercise that provides step-by-step instruction. The integration of theory and practice ensures learning.

The Student Data Disk contains documents for use in completing the assignments. With these files, the students can practice skills without having to create a worksheet from scratch, and can thereby devote more time to learning.

Written So Students Retain Knowledge

This textbook's design allows each instructor to tailor the course to ensure retention and conceptual understanding. The numerous exercises and assignments can be customized to meet students' needs. The textbook is divided into two sections, beginning and intermediate, which allows for further flexibility in course content. The beginning chapters (Chapters 1–8) build on concepts introduced sequentially, and should therefore be completed in the order presented; the intermediate chapters (Chapters 9–17) may be presented in any order desired by the instructor.

Assignments at the end of each chapter augment the chapter exercises with more in-depth practice. The assignment instructions test the students' understanding of the chapter by omitting specific "how-to" instructions. Chapters 2–17 end with case problems that present real-world business situations. The students call on prior knowledge to plan, design, and prepare the required project.

The end-of-chapter reference material is especially helpful. A summary provides an abstract of the chapter material; a list of terminology contains terms defined within the chapter; and pictures of toolbar buttons introduced in the chapter provide a visual review.

Supplementary Material

An instructor's manual—including an outline for each chapter, completed worksheets for all exercises and assignments, and answers to all study questions—is available upon adoption of this textbook. Sample tests covering theory and application are provided, along with answer keys. There are tests for each chapter, so instructors can schedule exams at any time.

Acknowledgments

Special thanks need to be expressed to the many people who have encouraged and supported me in writing this textbook. They include:

Paul Jolly, my husband, for his love, encouragement, patience, and ability to fully support this project. Without his understanding, this book would still be a dream.

Kevin and Trista Jolly, my children, for their continual encouragement and pride in this project.

To my parents, Maynard and Leora Johnson, for their patience, understanding, and support.

To my colleagues at Portland Community College for their support, patience, and suggestions. A special thanks to Vicky Charlston, Cheryl Owings, and Art Schneider.

To my publisher, Jim Leisy, for his encouragement. A special thanks to Tom Sumner, Susan Skarzynski, and Stephanie Welch for their developmental editing and production efforts on behalf of the manuscript. Thanks also to everyone else at Franklin, Beedle & Associates—Vic, Sue, Cary, Carrie, Chris, and Ann.

Thanks to all the reviewers of this textbook. Their suggestions and insights provided valuable additions.

Contents

Chapter 1 Getting Acquainted with Microsoft Excel — 1

Orientation to Electronic Spreadsheets 1	Exercise 1.4 Selecting Ranges 24
Communicating Tools 3	Using Help 26
Excel Basics 5	Exercise 1.5 Using Help 28
Exercise 1.1 Becoming Familiar with Excel 12	Summary 29
Exercise 1.2 Exploring Dialog Boxes 16	Study Questions 31
Getting Around in Excel 18	Assignments 33
Exercise 1.3 Moving Around a Worksheet 20	

Chapter 2 Creating a Worksheet — 36

Entering Information 36	Exercise 2.6 Quitting Excel and
Exercise 2.1 Adding Text to a Worksheet 38	Retrieving a Workbook 52
Exercise 2.2 Adding Data to a Worksheet 40	Printing a Workbook 52
Simple Formatting Techniques 41	Exercise 2.7 Printing a Workbook 53
Exercise 2.3 Formatting a Worksheet 43	Exercise 2.8 Editing and Printing
Exercise 2.4 Formatting Numbers and	a Workbook 58
Adding a Border 45	Summary 59
Exercise 2.5 Saving a Workbook 49	Study Questions 61
	Assignments 62

Chapter 3 Entering Basic Formulas — 70

Introduction to Formulas 70	Exercise 3.7 Entering Data by Range 86
Exercise 3.1 Calculating Numbers 72	Exercise 3.8 Using AutoCalculate 87
Entering Formulas 74	Exercise 3.9 Looking at Error Messages 88
Exercise 3.2 Entering and Editing Formulas 76	Printing Formulas 89
Exercise 3.3 Using the Point-and-Click	Exercise 3.10 Printing Formulas 89
Method 77	Planning a Worksheet 90
Exercise 3.4 Using AutoSum 81	Exercise 3.11 Planning a Worksheet 91
Exercise 3.5 Adding a Grand Total 83	Summary 92
Exercise 3.6 Using AutoSum for	Study Questions 93
Nonadjacent Cells 85	Assignments 95

Chapter 4 Moving and Copying Information — 101

Moving Cell Contents 101	Related Commands 115
Exercise 4.1 Moving Cells 105	Exercise 4.5 Using Undo and Repeat 117
Exercise 4.2 Inserting Cells between	Exercise 4.6 Using Paste Special 118
Other Cells 108	Exercise 4.7 Transposing a Worksheet 120
Copying Techniques 109	Exercise 4.8 Copying and Applying Formats ... 122
Exercise 4.3 Copying Cells 111	Summary 122
Exercise 4.4 Copying and Inserting	Study Questions 124
between Cells 114	Assignments 126

Chapter 5 Working with Formulas — 135

Moving and Copying Formulas	135	
Exercise 5.1	Using Relative References	137
Exercise 5.2	Using Absolute References	139
Exercise 5.3	Understanding Formulas	140
Exercise 5.4	Using Mixed References	144
Exercise 5.5	Understanding Mixed References	145
A Preview of Functions		146
Exercise 5.6	Using the Paste Function Dialog Box	149
Using Statistical Functions		150
Exercise 5.7	Completing an Average	152
Exercise 5.8	Using the Maximum and Minimum Functions	153
Exercise 5.9	Using the COUNT and COUNTA Functions	156
Logical Functions		156
Exercise 5.10	Using the IF Function	159
Exercise 5.11	Additional Uses of the IF Function	160
Summary		161
Study Questions		162
Assignments		164

Chapter 6 Multiple-Sheet Workbooks and Other Time Savers — 173

Using Workbooks		173
Exercise 6.1	Using Multiple-Sheet Workbooks	176
Exercise 6.2	Printing a Workbook	178
Shortcut Menus		179
Exercise 6.3	Using Shortcut Menus	181
Copying between Worksheets and Workbooks		182
Exercise 6.4	Copying Information into Worksheets	182
The Fill Commands		182
Exercise 6.5	Using Fill to Copy	185
Exercise 6.6	Using Fill Across Worksheets	187
Exercise 6.7	Using AutoFill	189
Exercise 6.8	Using the AutoFill Shortcut Menu	191
Exercise 6.9	Using Fill Justify	193
Exercise 6.10	Creating a Custom List	195
Other Automatic Excel Features		196
Exercise 6.11	Using AutoFormat	197
Exercise 6.12	Centering Worksheet Titles	198
Exercise 6.13	Using AutoComplete	200
Exploring Toolbars		201
Exercise 6.14	Using Toolbars	204
Using the Spelling Checker		205
Exercise 6.15	Using Spelling Checker	207
Summary		208
Study Questions		210
Assignments		211

Chapter 7 Additional Formatting Techniques — 219

Changing the Size of Cells		219
Exercise 7.1	Adjusting Cell Widths and Heights	222
Hiding and Unhiding Columns and Rows		223
Exercise 7.2	Hiding and Unhiding Columns	224
Exercise 7.3	Hiding and Unhiding Rows	226
Inserting and Deleting Cells in a Worksheet		227
Exercise 7.4	Inserting Rows and Columns	228
Exercise 7.5	Deleting Rows and Columns	230
Using the Format Cells Dialog Box		231
Exercise 7.6	Formatting Numbers	234
Exercise 7.7	Formatting Date and Time	237
Exercise 7.8	Formatting for Alignment	242
Exercise 7.9	Working with Fonts	245
Exercise 7.10	Shading, Borders, and Color	249
Exercise 7.11	Using WordArt	252
Summary		252
Study Questions		255
Assignments		257

Chapter 8 Large Worksheet Tips, Page Setup, and Printing Techniques — 265

Working with Worksheet Windows		265
Exercise 8.1	Opening and Arranging Workbooks	268
Exercise 8.2	Viewing Workbook Windows	270
Exercise 8.3	Using Split Panes in a Large Worksheet	272
Exercise 8.4	Freezing Panes	274
The Page Setup Dialog Box		274
Exercise 8.5	Using the Page Tab of the Page Setup Dialog Box	276
Exercise 8.6	Using the Margins Tab of the Page Setup Dialog Box	277
Exercise 8.7	Customizing Headers and Footers	281
Exercise 8.8	Using the Sheet Tab of the Page Setup Dialog Box	283

Additional Printing Techniques		284	Summary		289
Exercise 8.9	Using the Print Dialog Box	285	Study Questions		291
Exercise 8.10	Using Page Breaks and Printing Sections of a Worksheet	288	Assignments		293

Chapter 9 Creating Charts   304

Placing a Chart on a Worksheet		304	Exercise 9.6	Creating a Column Chart	323
Exercise 9.1	Creating a Chart	308	Exercise 9.7	Creating an Area Chart	324
Exercise 9.2	Editing a Default Chart	309	Exercise 9.8	Creating a Line Chart	325
Exercise 9.3	Using the Chart Wizard	315	Exercise 9.9	Creating a Pie Chart	327
Editing Chart Data		316	Summary		327
Exercise 9.4	Editing a Chart	318	Study Questions		329
What Type of Chart to Use?		319	Assignments		330
Exercise 9.5	Creating a Bar Chart	321			

Chapter 10 Using Built-in Functions   333

Exploring the Power of Functions		333	Exercise 10.7	Using the Declining-Balance Function	354
Using Mathematical Functions		337	Exercise 10.8	Using Sum-of-Years' Digits Depreciation	357
Exercise 10.1	Using Mathematical Functions	339			
Using Financial Functions		340	LOOKUP Functions		358
Exercise 10.2	Using the Payment Function	343	Exercise 10.9	Using a Vertical Lookup Table	360
Exercise 10.3	Determining an Amount of Interest	345	Exercise 10.10	Using a Horizontal Lookup Table	361
Exercise 10.4	Determining an Amount of Principal	347	Summary		362
			Study Questions		364
Exercise 10.5	Preparing a Payment Chart	349	Assignments		367
Depreciation Functions		350			
Exercise 10.6	Using Straight-Line Depreciation	352			

Chapter 11 Using Excel to Manage Lists   375

Basics of List Management		375	Using Filters		387
Exercise 11.1	Preparing a List	376	Exercise 11.6	Filtering and Printing a List	388
Rearranging a List		377	Exercise 11.7	Filtering, Sorting, and Printing a List	392
Exercise 11.2	Sorting a List	380			
Exercise 11.3	Using a Custom Sort	381	Summary		392
Maintaining a List		382	Study Questions		394
Exercise 11.4	Using a Data Form	383	Assignments		395
Exercise 11.5	Searching a Database	386			

Chapter 12 Using Macros   403

Using Macros		403	Introduction to Visual Basic		410
Exercise 12.1	Recording a Macro	406	Exercise 12.5	Printing a Macro	412
Exercise 12.2	Running a Macro	407	Summary		412
Exercise 12.3	Using Shortcut Keys	408	Study Questions		413
Exercise 12.4	Preparing a Library Sheet	410	Assignments		414

Chapter 13 Creating Formulas from Labels 419

Using Natural-Language Formulas 419
Exercise 13.1 Using Natural-Language Formulas 420
Using Cell Names in Formulas 421
Exercise 13.2 Defining Names 423
Exercise 13.3 Pasting Names in a Formula 424
Automatic Features for Naming Cells 425
Exercise 13.4 Creating Names 426
Exercise 13.5 Applying Names in a Worksheet 427
Exercise 13.6 Pasting a List of Cell Names 429
Summary 429
Study Questions 430
Assignments 431

Chapter 14 Linking and Embedding 436

Linking Excel Data 436
Exercise 14.1 Linking Excel Worksheets 438
Exercise 14.2 Linking Workbooks 440
Copying between Software Applications 440
Exercise 14.3 Copying Data between
              Applications 442
Exercise 14.4 Using Drag and Drop
              between Applications 443
Object Linking and Embedding (OLE) 444
Exercise 14.5 Embedding Information 445
Exercise 14.6 Changing an Embedded
              Document 446
Exercise 14.7 Linking Information between
              Two Applications 448
Summary 449
Study Questions 450
Assignments 451

Chapter 15 Using Templates 455

Excel Templates 455
Exercise 15.1 Creating a Template 456
Exercise 15.2 Using a Template 457
Using Spreadsheet Solutions Templates 457
Exercise 15.3 Customizing and
              Saving a Template 460
Exercise 15.4 Using a Customized Template 462
Summary 462
Study Questions 463
Assignments 463

Chapter 16 Additional Worksheet Topics 477

The Drawing Toolbar 477
Exercise 16.1 Using Drawing Tools 481
Using Maps in a Worksheet 482
Exercise 16.2 Placing a Map in a Worksheet ... 483
Creating an Organizational Chart 484
Exercise 16.3 Creating an
              Organizational Chart 485
Protecting a Worksheet 485
Exercise 16.4 Protecting a Worksheet 487
Exercise 16.5 Protecting Cells and Worksheets 488
Additional Editing Techniques 489
Exercise 16.6 Using Find and Replace 491
Exercise 16.7 Adding Cell Comments 492
Summary 493
Study Questions 494
Assignments 495

Chapter 17 Excel and the Internet 499

The World Wide Web 499
Navigating the Web 500
Exercise 17.1 Exploring the World Wide Web 501
Querying the Web 501
Exercise 17.2 Querying the Web 504
Exercise 17.3 Finding a Stock Symbol 505
Exercise 17.4 Refreshing a Query 506
Creating a Web Page 506
Exercise 17.5 Creating a Web Page 509
Summary 510
Study Questions 511
Assignments 511

Appendix A Managing Documents 513
Appendix B Shortcuts 515
Appendix C Toolbars 518
Glossary 522
Index 533

Chapter 1

Getting Acquainted with Microsoft Excel

Objectives

1. Describe an electronic worksheet.
2. Open and close the Excel program.
3. Identify the parts of an Excel worksheet.
4. Move around a worksheet by using menu commands and dialog boxes.
5. Select cells and ranges of cells.
6. Use online Help.

Introduction

Spreadsheet programs are some of the most frequently used computer programs. A spreadsheet computer program is used primarily for organizing numeric information. Its major advantage is ease in manipulating numbers. The Excel program does all this as well as quickly and easily completes tasks that include designing a complex worksheet, reporting financial information, and preparing impressive and informative charts.

This text is designed to give students hands-on practice working with Excel spreadsheets. After a concept is presented, a short computer exercise designed to reinforce the learning objective is provided. These exercises contain full step-by-step instruction for practice using Excel. At the end of each chapter is a set of assignments designed for additional practice. These assignments will reinforce the learning objectives of each chapter. Also, one case problem presenting a real-life business situation is provided at the end of each chapter beginning with Chapter 2. (If you are not familiar with Windows, you should read through Appendix A.)

The first chapter is an orientation to the Excel spreadsheet program and will review some of the basic Windows operations.

Orientation to Electronic Spreadsheets

What Is a Spreadsheet?

A *spreadsheet*, also called a *sheet* or *worksheet*, is used to organize numerical data. Before computers, accountants and other business people used columnar paper consisting of rows and columns to organize data into business reports such as budgets, financial analyses, and sales projections. This data was then used to report financial information to the firm and to help make decisions.

Figure 1.1 shows a portion of a budget prepared using columnar paper. This budget consists of columns and rows and is presented in a way that easily identifies the expenses budgeted for each month.

Figure 1.1   Columnar Paper Used for Preparation of a Budget

		JAN	FEB	MAR
8	Expenses			
9	Rent	250 00	250 00	250 00
10	Bus Fare	35 00	35 00	35 00
11	School Exp.	500 00	20 00	20 00
12	Food	100 00	100 00	100 00
13	Entertain.	50 00	50 00	50 00
14	TOTAL	935 00	455 00	455 00

In a typical spreadsheet, a *column* may represent a period of time, such as a day, a month, or a year. The *rows* may represent items such as product quantities, types of expenses, or revenues. The columns in the spreadsheet in Figure 1.1 represent months of the year (January, February, and March), and the rows represent a specific type of expense (rent, bus fare, etc.). Totals and other calculations are completed using a calculator, and the amounts are then written in the appropriate place on the spreadsheet.

What Is an Electronic Spreadsheet?

The computer has changed the way work is completed in business. Just as word-processing programs have nearly replaced the typewriter, spreadsheet programs have virtually replaced the pen, pencil, calculator, and columnar paper for organizing financial information. An *electronic spreadsheet* is a worksheet created with a computer, providing greater accuracy and flexibility in making changes quickly.

Like columnar paper, a computerized spreadsheet consists of a grid of rows and columns that are used to store data for numeric reports. All types of information can be entered into this electronic spreadsheet—*text* (words), numbers (data), mathematical formulas, dates, and times. Figure 1.2 shows the same budget as in Figure 1.1, this time using Excel.

Figure 1.2   Budget Prepared Using an Electronic Worksheet

	A	B	C	D
	Expenses	January	February	March
8	Expenses	January	February	March
9	Rent	$ 250	$ 250	$ 250
10	Bus Fare	35	35	35
11	School Expenses	500	20	20
12	Food	100	100	100
13	Entertainment	50	50	50
14	Total Expenses	$ 935	$ 455	$ 455

What Is the Advantage of an Electronic Spreadsheet?

There are many reasons why spreadsheet programs have become popular. One reason is accuracy of calculating numbers. A spreadsheet is used primarily to store numeric data and to make calculations using that data. When a spreadsheet is created using paper and pencil, a great deal of time is spent manually completing calculations and checking their accuracy. With the use of the computer, calculations are completed quickly and accurately, eliminating the chance of error. When changes in data are made, the computer automatically corrects the calculations and displays the correct amounts. Making changes, whether in the data entered or in the appearance of a spreadsheet, is called *editing* a spreadsheet.

In addition to making accurate calculations, spreadsheet programs do much more than just compute data. Graphs and charts are easily created using data in a worksheet. Complex formulas can be completed after only two or three data entries. Making business decisions by analyzing financial information is done quickly. Quick access to the Internet and the ability to retrieve data for a worksheet allows flexibility for Excel users. File sharing within a company is also enhanced with this quick access, and a completed document may be formatted and presented as an attractive report.

Communicating Tools

Data is entered, then the numbers are calculated. There are two basic *tools* used to communicate with Excel—the keyboard and the mouse.

Using the Keyboard

The *keyboard* is the most frequently used communicating tool, used to enter both text and data. A computer keyboard is shown in Figure 1.3. The *Enter key* is located at the right edge of the keyboard and is used to complete an entry of information.

The keyboard consists of the standard alphabetic keys, a numeric keypad on the right side of the keyboard, arrow keys, and a set of 12 to 15 *function keys* across the top. The function keys are identified by the letter F before the number, such as F1, F2, F3, etc.

Arrow keys are usually to the right of the alphabetic keys. A *numeric keypad* is available on the right side of the keyboard and is used as a 10-key data entry keypad.

Figure 1.3   Computer Keyboard

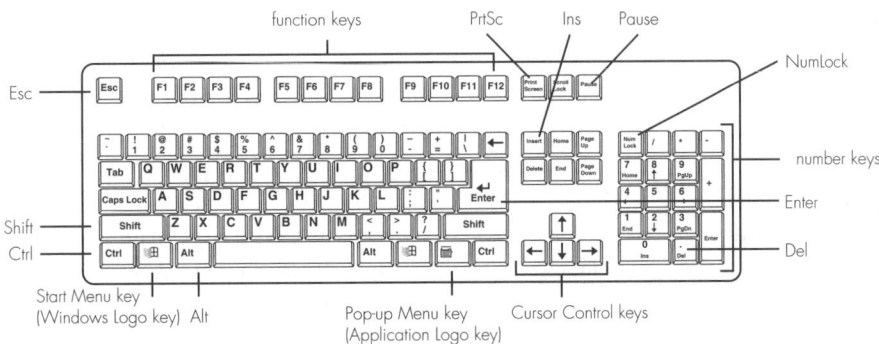

Using the Mouse

The *mouse* is used to identify where data will be entered, select commands, make editing choices, move information, move and size windows, select graphics, and perform many other tasks.

The mouse has two buttons that are used to select information. To select an *icon* (a picture that represents a command), move the mouse arrow to the icon. Then click the left mouse button once to select the item or double-click (clicking twice quickly) to view or open the icon. The contents are then shown in a window. The right mouse button is used for special tasks that are explained later in this text.

In Excel, the mouse pointer takes on different shapes in a worksheet depending on the activity or function performed. The following guide illustrates these shapes:

Shape	Where Used	How to Use Mouse
↖	Menu bar, scroll bars, toolbar	Point and select cells or drag cells to a new location.
✛	Inside a worksheet	Select a cell or cells.
+	Inside a worksheet after selecting a drawing tool	Drag crosshair to draw an object or define an area.
I	In the formula bar and in a text box within a dialog box	Click to place the insertion point where editing will begin.
✛🖌	Inside a worksheet when formatting cells	Click and drag across cells where format will be applied.
╪	Between row headings on the left border	Click and drag to adjust row height.
╫	Between column headings on the top border	Click and drag to adjust column width.
+	On a worksheet when creating a series	Click and drag to create the series.
╪	At horizontal split bar	Click and drag to split worksheet horizontally.
╫	At vertical split bar	Click and drag to split worksheet vertically.
↖?	Within the Help dialog box and when What's This? is selected in the Help menu	Within a dialog box, click on the area in question. When using What's This?, move to the area where help is desired and click the mouse button.
🔍	In Print Preview	Click the mouse to enlarge a portion of the page.
⌛	Whenever Excel is working and cannot accept data	Indicates that Excel is calculating, saving a document, printing, or otherwise busy. No other action can be completed.
☝	In the Help window and the Internet	Point the mouse on the item and click to see a definition, access the next command, or to access a link.

Excel Basics

Starting the Program

The instructions in this book are written for Excel programs installed on the hard drive of a computer rather than on a network. If the program is installed on a network, check with your classroom instructor to find the specific method used for starting Excel.

Opening Excel

After Windows is open, move the mouse to the *Start button* on the left side of the taskbar at the bottom of the screen. Using the Start button is a fast way to open programs or documents. Click on Start; the Programs menu appears, shown in Figure 1.4.

Point to the Programs selection in the menu; a submenu opens listing available program choices on your computer. This is shown in Figure 1.5.

Figure 1.4   Start Menu for Windows 95

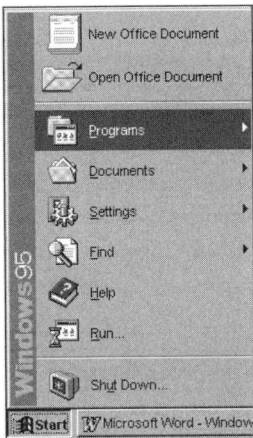

Figure 1.5   Opening the Excel Program

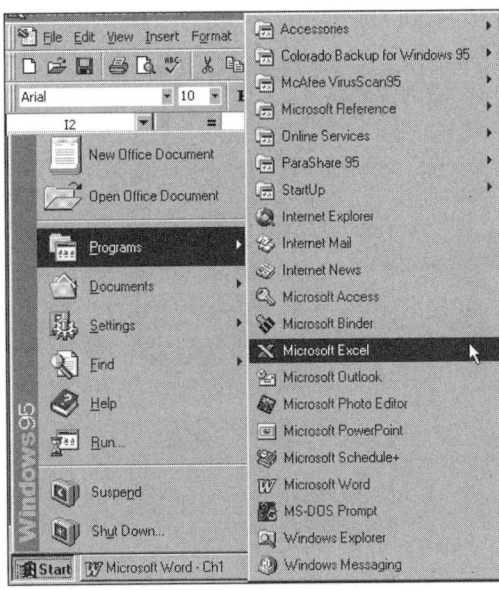

Point to Microsoft Excel and click the left mouse button to open the program; it will begin to load into the active memory (RAM) of the computer. After Excel is open, its identification appears in the taskbar along with other open programs, as shown in Figure 1.6.

Figure 1.6   Excel Program Button

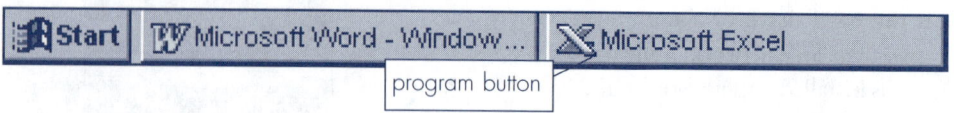

Excel opens as a workbook. Each **workbook** is a collection of worksheets like the one shown in Figure 1.7. A new workbook containing three separate worksheets opens each time Excel is started. They are numbered using tabs at the bottom of the worksheet. You may click on a tab to access a different worksheet of the workbook. The use of workbooks and worksheets will be discussed further in Chapter 6.

Figure 1.7   Workbook in Excel

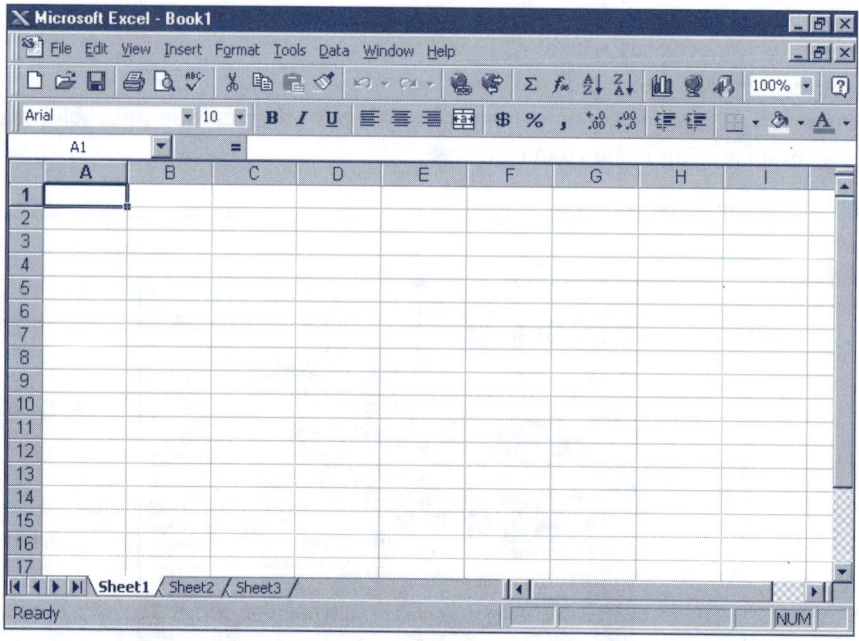

The worksheet window may be enlarged by clicking the **Maximize button** in the upper-right corner of the window, shown in Figure 1.8.

Figure 1.8   Window Control Buttons

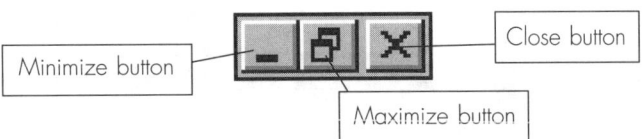

The window size is decreased by clicking in the **Minimize button**, reducing the open sheet to a button in the taskbar. The **Close button** closes the worksheet window.

The Excel Worksheet

An Excel worksheet, also called a sheet, is a grid of horizontal rows and vertical columns on the computer screen. (The amount of the worksheet that is visible on the screen varies slightly depending on the size of the monitor used.) These rows and columns are only a part of a total worksheet. The portion of the worksheet visible on the computer screen is called the *worksheet window*. The total size of the worksheet is actually large enough to accommodate 256 columns and 65,536 rows. Figure 1.9 gives a perspective of the size of the worksheet compared to the worksheet window.

Figure 1.9   Worksheet Size

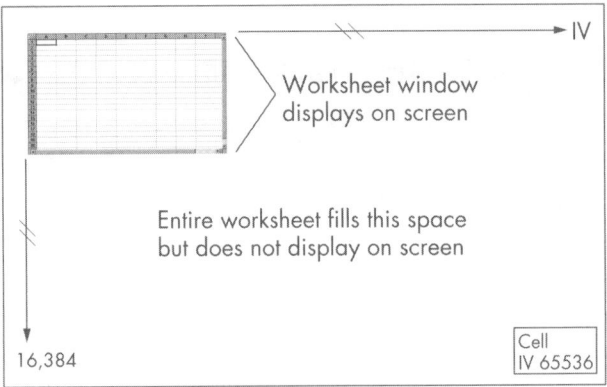

Each row and column of a worksheet has its own identification. Rows are identified by numbers ranging from 1 to 65,536—called row headings. Columns are identified by letter, starting with A and continuing through Z, called column headings. As more columns are used, additional letters are added. After Z comes AA–AZ, then BA–BZ, etc. IV is the last column available.

The place where a row and a column intersect is called a cell. Each cell is identified by a *cell reference*, formed by the letter of its column followed by the number of its row. For example, the cell at the intersection of column E and row 27 has the cell reference E27, which identifies the location of the cell in the worksheet. Some spreadsheet programs use the term *cell address* rather than *cell reference*.

Figure 1.10 shows cells A1, B1, C1, A2, B2, C2, A3, B3, and C3. Cell C3 has a heavy line around it, indicating that it is the active cell. The active cell is the only cell where information can be entered. Any cell may be the active cell, but only one cell at a time can be active.

Figure 1.10 Active Cell

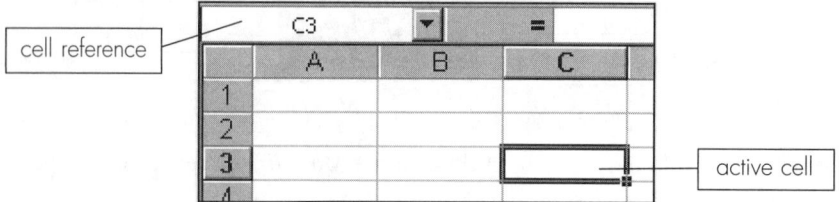

Each cell in a worksheet can store information. This information is usually a number, but it can also be text. Text is information that describes or identifies part of the worksheet and is a combination of letters, symbols, numbers, and spaces.

Identifying the Parts of the Excel Worksheet

Figure 1.11 shows an Excel worksheet with different sections identified, followed by a brief description of each section.

Figure 1.11 Excel Worksheet

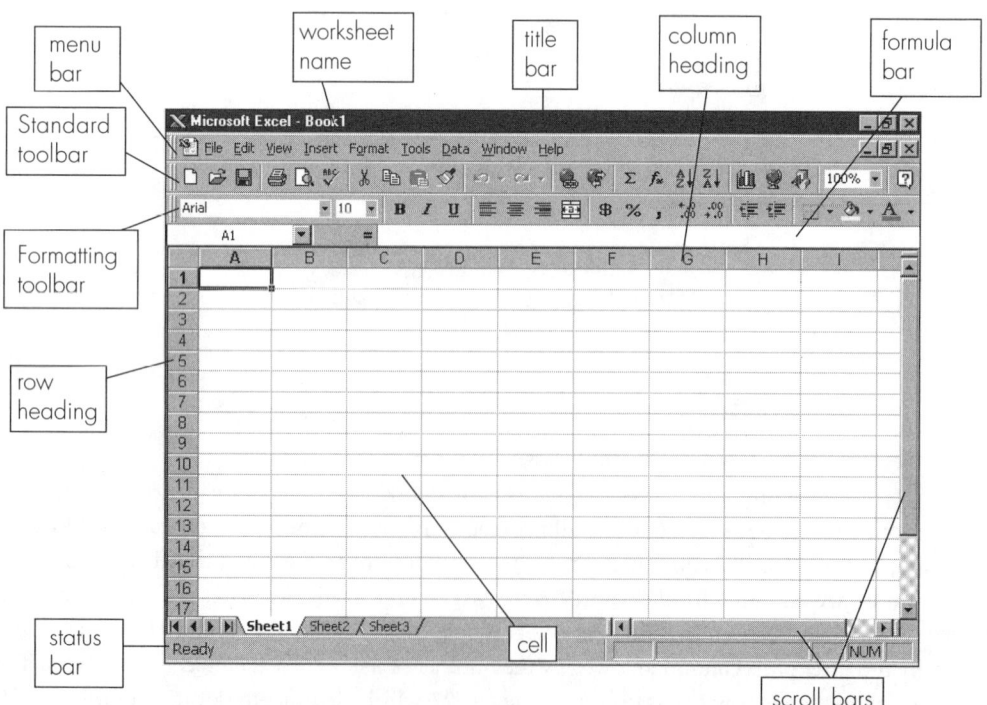

- The title bar is at the top of the worksheet window. It identifies the software and the file name of the document. If the open document has not been saved, the title bar indicates Book1, Book2, etc. to identify unnamed open documents. The title bar is recognized by its shading.

The first four lines after the title bar are used for communicating with the computer. These areas are called the menu bar, Standard toolbar, Formatting toolbar, and formula bar.

- The *menu bar* (Figure 1.12) is the first line below the title bar and displays choices such as File and Edit. These choices are used to interact with Excel. The menu bar always displays when Excel is active.

Figure 1.12   Menu Bar

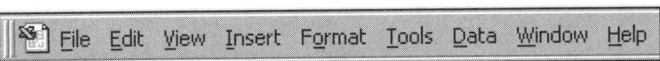

- The *Standard toolbar* is the next line, shown in Figure 1.13, and is used to execute frequently used commands and actions. The *buttons* or icons on the toolbar represent commands such as printing, copying information, or opening a new workbook.

Figure 1.13   Standard Toolbar

To see what a button does, move the mouse pointer near the tool button; a ScreenTip opens that identifies the button. (Do not click the mouse button.) Figure 1.14 shows the label attached with the Paste button.

Figure 1.14   Paste ScreenTip

- The *Formatting toolbar* is the third line (Figure 1.15) and contains buttons used to quickly format the worksheet. These buttons are used for commands such as bolding text (so it prints darker) or italicizing it.

  The toolbars can be arranged in different order depending on user preference. On your screen, the Formatting toolbar may appear above the Standard toolbar.

Figure 1.15   Formatting Toolbar

- The *formula bar* is on the fourth line and is used to enter or change values in cells. It is divided into three sections. The *Name box* is at the left side of the formula bar and identifies the cell reference of the active cell. The *entry area* is at the right side and is used to display the data or formula as it is entered. The small area between the reference area and the data display area sometimes displays buttons used in the worksheet.

Figure 1.16 shows the formula bar when it is active, which is when entries are being made in the worksheet. When it is inactive, only the Name box will have text displayed in it. The formula bar will be discussed further in Chapter 2.

Figure 1.16   Formula Bar

The area below the formula bar is the worksheet where text, numerical data, and calculation results are entered. The Excel worksheet window is shown in Figure 1.17; a description of its parts follows.

Figure 1.17   Worksheet Window

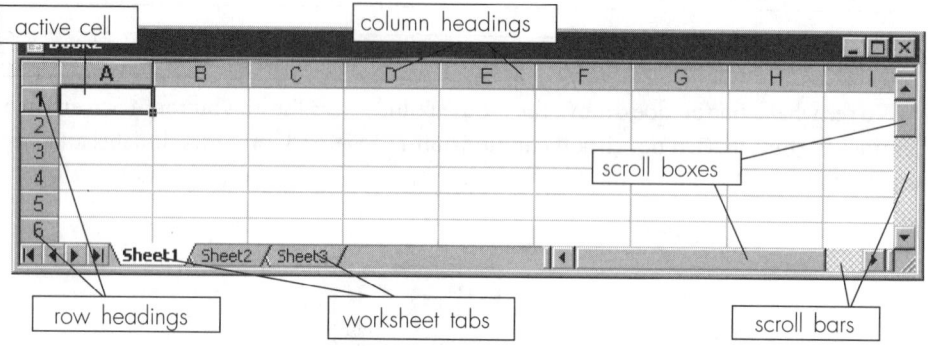

- The *row* and *column headings* in the top and left borders indicate which worksheet rows and columns are currently visible in the worksheet window. In the worksheet shown in Figure 1.17, columns A through I are displayed, as are rows 1 through 6. The number of columns and rows displayed will vary.
- A grid of *cells* is visible as the main framework of the worksheet. Each cell is used to store a single piece of information (text, numbers, or formulas) used in the worksheet.
- The *active cell* (also called *selected cell*) is identified by the dark border surrounding it. Text or data may be entered into the active cell. In Figure 1.17, cell A1 is the active cell.
- The *scroll bars* are located along the right side and the bottom of the worksheet. As with other Windows programs, the scroll bars and *scroll boxes* allow access to all parts of the worksheet. In a scroll box, the mouse is used to click and drag to a new location of the worksheet.
- The *worksheet tabs* access other worksheets in the workbook; they are on the same line as the bottom scroll bar. These tabs are described in Chapter 6.
- The *status bar* is at the bottom of the screen (Figure 1.18). This area displays information about the current command or operation of Excel. Most of the time the status bar displays Ready.

Figure 1.18   Status Bar

- The *mode indicator* at the right side of the status bar gives information about the working conditions of the program.

Using the Menu Bar

The menu bar, shown in Figure 1.19, is the primary source for entering commands that instruct the computer to carry out an action.

Figure 1.19   Menu Bar

Each menu topic in the menu bar has a pull-down menu listing several available choices. To access the pull-down menu, click on one of the menu topics. The pull-down menu opens, listing the related choices; move the mouse to the desired choice and click once to select that command.

The File menu is used to create a new workbook, as well as retrieve an existing workbook or close one that is open. Figure 1.20 shows the pull-down File menu.

Figure 1.20   Pull-down File Menu

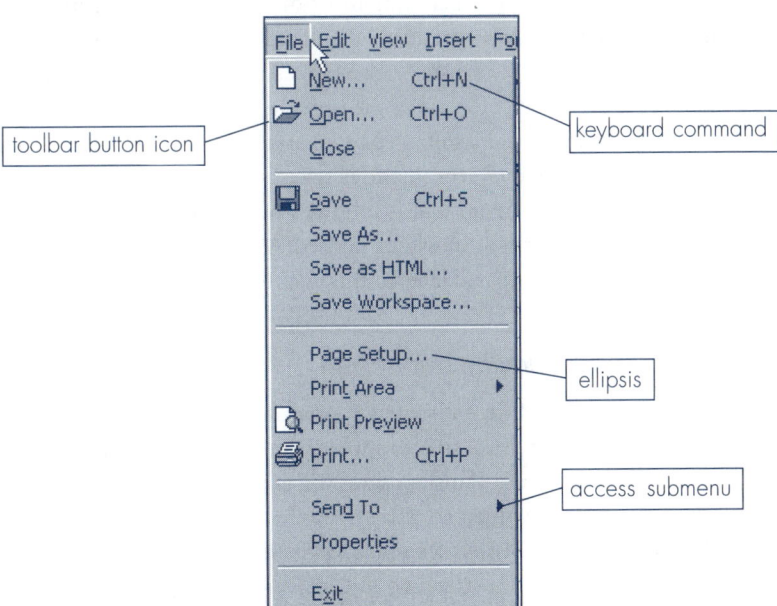

Commands in the pull-down menu are selected by pointing the mouse to the command and clicking once on the left mouse button. In this text, selecting a menu command will be stated as "select File, then Open," which means first click on the File menu and then click on the Open command.

On the left side of the pull-down menu, the corresponding toolbars buttons are pictured. It is usually faster to use the toolbar buttons than the pull-down menus to access commands, so these icons serve as reminders.

Some commands can also be accessed by using the keyboard and are called ***keyboard commands*** or ***shortcuts***. The keyboard command is displayed at the right side of the pull-down menu. The keyboard command is usually a combination of the Ctrl key and an alphabetic key. The keyboard command at the right side of the menu for New reads Ctrl+N. When using the keyboard to access a new Excel worksheet, hold down Ctrl while keying N on the keyboard. Throughout the text, these keyboard command instructions will be presented as Ctrl+N.

Power Users

To access menu commands from the keyboard (without using the mouse), press **Alt** or the slash (**/**) key plus the underlined letter on the menu selection to access the pull-down menu. For instance, to access the File menu, press **Alt** (or **/**) while keying **F**. Then select the underlined letter from the desired command. For instance, use **N** for New.

The right and left arrow keys can also be used to move from one pull-down menu to another. Use the up and down arrows to select commands in the pull-down menu.

For experienced Excel users, using keyboard commands saves time. In this text, the commands accessed through the toolbars and menus are emphasized; the keyboard commands will be mentioned. A list of keyboard commands, including function keys, appears in Appendix B.

Most commands in the pull-down menu are displayed in black. Some, however, may be dimmed. Excel monitors the status of your worksheet and makes available only applicable commands. The dimmed commands are unavailable for use at the time the menu is accessed.

A command in a pull-down menu followed by an arrow (▶) indicates that a submenu with a few additional choices will open when the command is selected.

A command in a pull-down menu that is followed by ellipsis (…) indicates that after the command is selected, additional information will be needed. A dialog box will open to request additional information. Dialog boxes are discussed later in this chapter.

Exercise 1.1   Becoming Familiar with Excel

You will open Excel, explore the different shapes the mouse takes, and look at pull-down menus.

Complete the following exercise at the computer. The instructions in italics are provided to help you understand what the next group of instructions will accomplish. Some questions require that you write the answers in the space provided.

Open Excel to a new workbook (if instructions for your classroom are different, check with your instructor).

1 Click on the **Start** icon at the bottom-left corner of the Windows screen.

2 Point to **Programs**. A submenu appears. In the submenu, select **Microsoft Excel**. (On some computers, you may need to select **MS Office** and then **Excel**.)

A new Excel worksheet opens on the screen.
Practice using the mouse and become familiar with its different shapes.

3 Point to cell E5. The shape ✥ is used to indicate the mouse pointer.

4 Move the mouse pointer to the entry area of the formula bar. It becomes an I-beam $\rm I$. The entry area is shown in the following illustration:

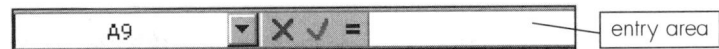

5 Move the mouse pointer between the numbers on rows 4 and 5 to see the double-sided arrow.

6 Move the mouse pointer between the letters of columns D and E to see the double-sided arrow.

7 Click on **Help** in the menu bar, then select **What's This?**. Move the mouse back to the worksheet. The mouse indicator takes the shape.

8 Cancel the Help request by pressing Esc on the keyboard, usually located in the upper-left corner of the keyboard.

9 Click the mouse on the **File** menu. What command will access a submenu? _____

10 Name one selection in the **File** menu that has an ellipsis following it, indicating it will open to a dialog box. _____

11 Move the mouse pointer to the **Edit** menu.

12 What are the symbols at the right edge of the pull-down menu by **Cut**? _____

13 What symbol is at the left edge of **Cut**? _____

Exit Excel if you do not have time to continue with Exercise 1.2.

14 From **File**, select **Exit** to quit Excel.

Using Dialog Boxes

When an Excel command in a pull-down menu is followed by an ellipsis, a ***dialog box*** will be used to gather additional information. In the Format menu, shown in Figure 1.21, Cells, AutoFormat, Conditional Formatting, and Style will access dialog boxes. (Row, Column, and Sheet will access submenus.)

Figure 1.21   Accessing the Format Cells Dialog Box

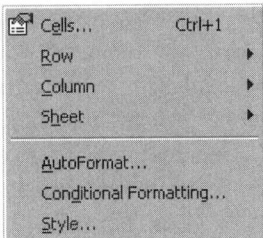

Figure 1.22 shows the dialog box that opens when the Cells command is selected, allowing for additional format choices. The dialog box for Format Cells is a ***tabbed dialog box***, which presents additional sets of options. The Font tab has been selected in this dialog box, as it illustrates several of the different options available.

Figure 1.22   Font Tab in Format Cells Dialog Box

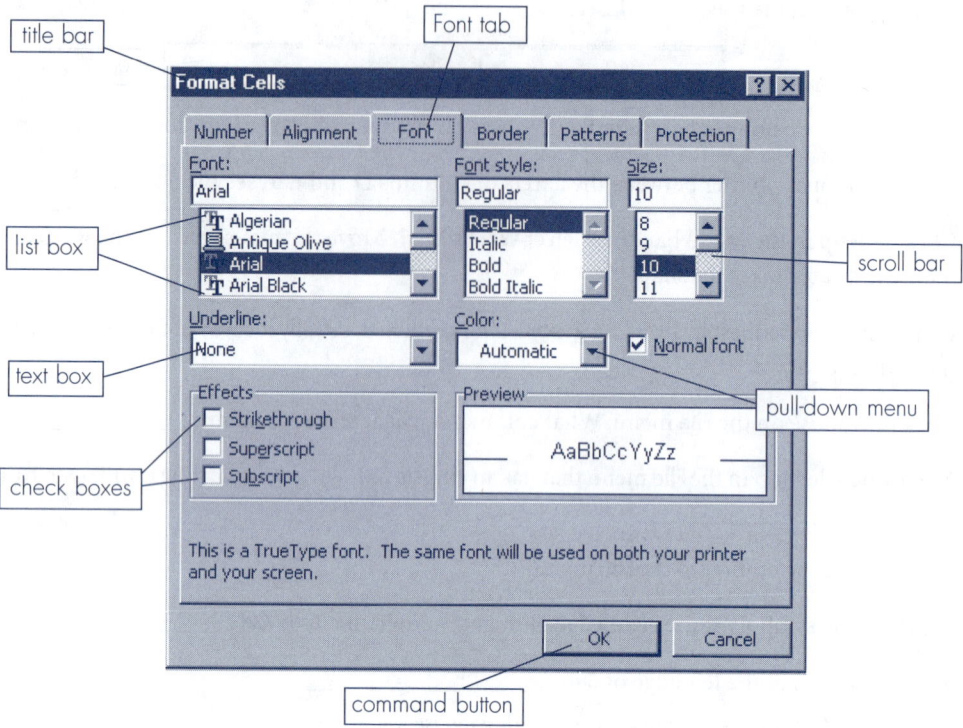

- *Title bar*—Each dialog box has a title bar identifying it. The title of the dialog box is located at the left side of the title bar. The title in Figure 1.22 is Format Cells.
- *Tabs*—Tabs are located along the top edge of some of the dialog boxes and are used to move quickly between available choices. In the Format Cells dialog box, the tabs are Number, Alignment, Font, Border, Patterns, and Protection.
- *List box*—A list box provides several available choices. Sometimes scroll bars are needed so all the choices can be accessed. In Figure 1.22, the Font, Font style, and Size sections use list boxes and have scroll bars indicating that more choices are available.
- *Text box*—A text box provides an area to key in additional information needed to carry out the command. Underline and Color use text boxes.
- *Pull-down menu*—A pull-down menu is recognized by the small arrow pointing downward ▼. Click on the arrow to display a list of additional choices.
- *Check box*—A check box may be turned on or off; more than one choice in the group may be selected. When a check box is selected, a ✓ appears in the box. Figure 1.23 shows the check boxes in the Effects section of the Font tab of the Format Cells dialog box; Strikethrough and Superscript are selected.

- *Option button*—Option buttons are used for related choices; only one option may be selected at a time. When an option is selected, a black dot appears in the small round button preceding the option. Option buttons are shown in Figure 1.24 with Bottom selected. (This is not found in the Format Cells dialog box.)
- *Command button*—A command button is a rectangular button labeled with the action it carries out, most often OK or Cancel.

A dark border around the button indicates it is the **default command.** The default command is the command that is most often used and can be executed by pressing Enter on the keyboard as well as clicking on it.

In Figure 1.25, OK is the default command. The Cancel button is used to close the dialog box when you've made no changes. If changes have been made, they will not apply if the dialog box is closed using Cancel.

Opening a New Workbook

There are several ways to open a new workbook. First, select the New command from the File menu. The New dialog box opens, pictured in Figure 1.26.

Figure 1.23   Check Boxes

Figure 1.24   Option Buttons

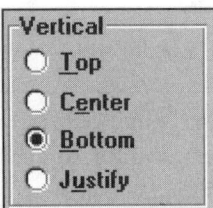

Figure 1.25   Command Button

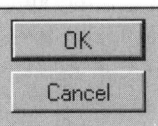

Figure 1.26   New Dialog Box

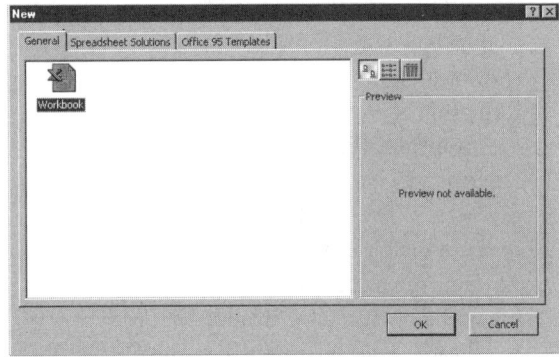

The workbook icon is selected. Click OK and a new worksheet titled Book2 will open.

The second way to open a new workbook is to select the New button  in the toolbar. This button is located on the left side of the Standard toolbar, shown in Figure 1.27. The shortcut to access a new workbook is Ctrl+N.

Figure 1.27   Buttons for New, Open, and Save

Although several commands are presented in the text to accomplish the same task, select the one method you prefer and use it. As you become experienced with Excel, you may choose another method to accomplish the same task.

Exiting Excel

Exit Excel by selecting Exit from the File menu.

Power Users

Use **Alt**+**F4** to exit Excel.

Before Excel quits the program entirely, it recognizes which workbooks have been saved and which have not. Saving a workbook (or worksheet) stores it electronically so it can be used again. A *warning box* may open, shown in Figure 1.28, as a reminder to save a workbook.

In this box, the choices are Yes (save it), No (don't save it), or Cancel (I've changed my mind and don't want to quit using Excel). If Yes is selected, a dialog box opens asking you to name the worksheet. For now, it will not be necessary to save worksheets; Chapter 2 describes this process in more detail.

If Office Assistant is active, the dialog box will look like the one shown in Figure 1.29. The same information is provided in this box.

Sometimes Excel recognizes that an error will occur if a command is executed. When this happens, Excel opens a dialog box that provides a warning. An example of such a warning would be that another worksheet has already been saved using the same name.

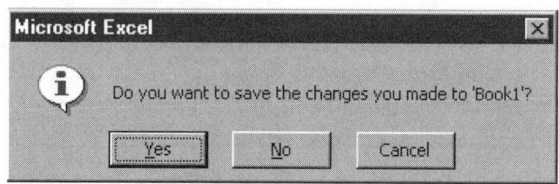

Figure 1.28   Warning Box

Figure 1.29   Warning Box with Clippit, the Office Assistant

Exercise 1.2   Exploring Dialog Boxes

Complete this exercise at the computer. You will be looking at several different Excel dialog boxes. The information in italics tells you what the next set of instructions will do; the specific instructions follow.

1 Open a new Excel workbook if one is not already open on your screen.

2 Key your first name in cell A1. Press **Enter** on the keyboard.

Note: If the active cell does not move to cell A2, your instructor should review the setup instructions section of the instructor's manual.

3   From **File**, select **Print** to open the **Print** dialog box.

4   Press `Tab` several times to see how the active area changes as you move through the dialog box. You may also click the mouse in an area to make it active.

5   Notice that one copy is selected. This is the default. If you want to print more than one copy of the worksheet, key in the number desired.

6   Click **Cancel** to exit the dialog box without making changes.

7   From the **Edit** menu, select **Delete**. The **Delete** dialog box opens; it uses buttons to communicate with Excel.

8   Click **OK**. This closes the dialog box and accepts any changes that you have made.

9   From the **Format** menu, select **Cells**. The tabs across the top of the dialog box indicate additional choices: **Number, Alignment, Font, Border, Patterns,** and **Protection**.

10 Click on the **Border** tab.

11 Click on the arrow next to **Automatic** in the **Color** section. A palette of available colors opens.

12 Click **OK** to exit the dialog box.

Explore a pull-down menu.

13 From the **View** menu, select **Toolbars**. A submenu opens. Two of the listed toolbars are active, indicated by the check boxes.

14 From **Tools**, select **Options**. Then click in the **View** tab. Check boxes are used to gather information. Click **OK**.

Open new workbooks.

15 From the **File** menu select **New**. In the **New** dialog box, make sure the workbook icon is selected, then click **OK**. A new workbook opens, titled **Book2**.

16 Click on the New button in the toolbar. A new workbook opens, titled **Book3**.

17 Hold down `Ctrl` while keying **N** (`Ctrl`+N). A new workbook opens, titled **Book4**.

Quit Excel if you are not completing Exercise 1.3.

18 From the **File** menu, select **Exit**.

19 A warning box opens asking if you want to save changes. Click **No**. This may happen once for each open workbook.

Getting Around in Excel

Moving Around the Worksheet

Because a worksheet is large and only a small portion of it shows on the computer screen, Excel provides several methods to move quickly to other parts of the worksheet.

Figure 1.30   Scroll Bars

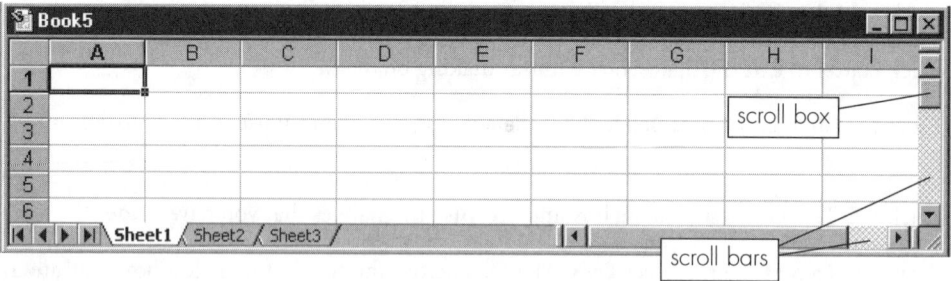

One way to access parts of a worksheet that are not on the screen is to use the scroll bars and scroll boxes, located at the bottom and right edges of the worksheet. They allow movement through a large worksheet. To scroll one row at a time, click the arrow at the end of the scroll bar that points in the direction you want to move.

Power Users

To quickly scroll to the last row containing data, hold down **Ctrl** while dragging the scroll box to the bottom of the scroll bar. In the same way, to scroll to the last column containing data, hold down **Ctrl** while dragging the scroll box to the right.

A quick way to return to the beginning of the worksheet, cell A1, is to hold down **Ctrl** and press **Home**. The **Home** key is located above the arrow keys, between the alphabetic keys and the numeric keypad.

The arrow keys on the keyboard may also be used to move between cells in the worksheet. When used, they move one cell at a time in the direction of the arrow.

When the scroll box is moved, a *ScrollTip* shows the column or row location of the visible area of a worksheet. The worksheet shown in Figure 1.31 is at row 8, indicated by the ScrollTip. This feature is particularly useful when moving through a large worksheet.

Figure 1.31   ScrollTip Identifies the Row

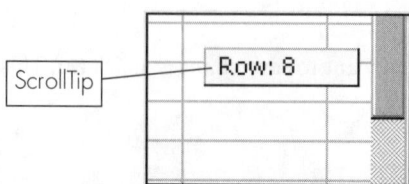

Moving Within a Block of Cells

To quickly move to the edge of a large worksheet, Excel has a handy move technique. Double-click on the cell directly beside the active cell that is in the direction in which you want to move. For instance, to activate a cell in the last row of the block of used cells, position the mouse at the bottom of the cell and double-click. The active cell is now the last cell of that block of the worksheet. Any blank lines below it are not selected.

Using the Go To Command

The *Go To command* found in the Edit menu is used to move to a specific cell that is distant from the active cell. The Go To dialog box is shown in Figure 1.32.

Figure 1.32   Go To Dialog Box

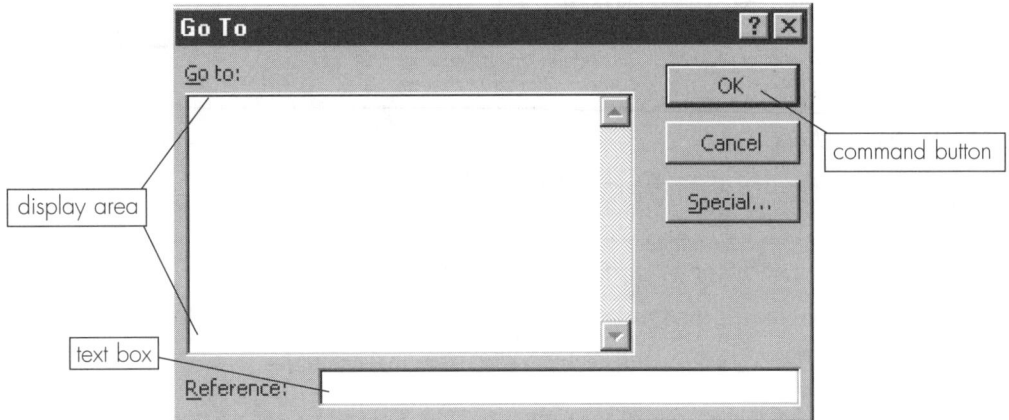

A blinking cursor, called the *insertion point*, is in the Reference text box where the cell reference is entered. Key the reference of the new cell location and click OK; the requested cell becomes active. For instance, key D141 and click OK; cell D141 becomes the active cell.

The display area of the Go To dialog box shows a list of recent cell references that have been accessed through the Go To command. (They usually have a dollar sign before them; cell A1 is referenced $A$1. The meaning of the $ will be discussed in Chapter 5.)

To return to a cell previously accessed, click on the cell reference in the list box, then click OK; the requested cell is now active. Figure 1.33 shows that cells A1, B302, and DE217 have already been accessed. To return to a cell, highlight the cell reference and click OK. In Figure 1.33, cell A1 is highlighted; cell A1 will become the active cell when OK is selected.

Figure 1.33   Using the Go To Dialog Box

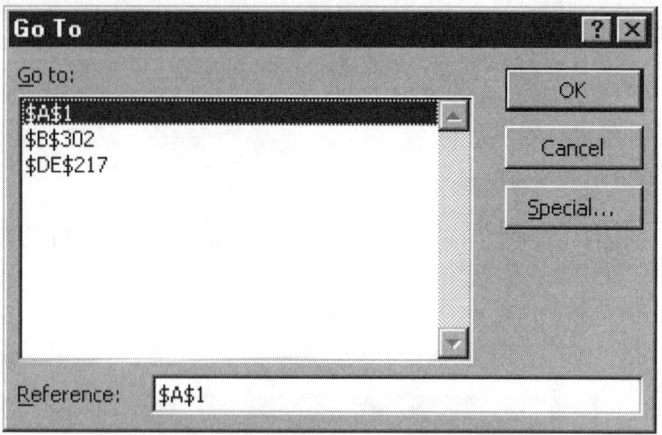

Power Users

To access the Go To dialog box, use **F5** or **Ctrl**+**G**.

Exercise 1.3   Moving Around a Worksheet

You will explore the different methods of moving around the worksheet window.

1 Open a new Excel worksheet and click in cell D10 to make it active.

2 Click once on the down arrow of the right scroll bar. This moves the window down one row. Row 2 is the first row in the worksheet window.

3 Click once on the right arrow of the bottom scroll bar. This accesses the next column to the right; column B is now the first column in the worksheet window. Note the last column displayed on the screen.

4 Click on the left arrow on the bottom scroll bar to return to column A.

5 Click once on the up arrow of the right scroll bar. Row 1 is again visible in the window.

Move through the worksheet using keyboard arrows. The active cell is still cell D10.

6 Press the up arrow ⬆ on the keyboard. Cell D9 is active and is listed in the Name box at the left edge of the formula bar.

7 Press the left arrow ⬅ on the keyboard. Cell C9 is active and is listed in the Name box of the formula bar.

8 Press the down arrow ⬇. Cell C10 is active.

9 Press the right arrow ➡. Cell D10 is active.

10 Press the up arrow two times. Cell D8 is active.

11 Press the right arrow three times. Cell G8 is active. If you are at the right edge of the screen, the window will automatically move so the active cell is visible.

12 Click on the right scroll bar in the light gray space between the scroll box and the down arrow. Excel moves down one full screen.

13 Click in the scroll box, continue to hold down the mouse button, and drag it back to the top of the screen. Row 1 is again the first row of the sheet.

Move through the worksheet using the Go To command.

14 From the **Edit** menu, select **Go To**. The **Go To** dialog box opens.

15 Key **J30**. Click **OK**. Cell J30 is the active cell.

16 From the **Edit** menu, select **Go To**. In the **Reference** section, key **AL445**. Press **Enter** on the keyboard to execute the default command of OK. Cell AL445 becomes active.

17 From the function keys, press **F5** to open the **Go To** dialog box. In the **Reference** section, key **DC300**. Press **Enter**.

18 Press **F5** to open the **Go To** dialog box or select **Go To** from the **Edit** menu. The dialog box that opens looks similar to the illustration at the right

19 Click on **$J$30** to select it. Then click **OK**. J30 is again the active cell.

20 Press **Ctrl**+**Home** to return to cell A1.

21 Exit Excel if you are not continuing with Exercise 1.4.

Selecting Cells and Ranges of Cells

A group of cells is called a *range of cells*. When a range is selected, a command can be applied to the entire range. Only one cell of a worksheet is the active cell, although a range is selected. The active cell reference is displayed in the Name box.

Figure 1.34 shows B3 as the active cell; its cell reference is displayed in the Name box and the cell is surrounded by a heavy border.

Figure 1.34   Active Cell B3

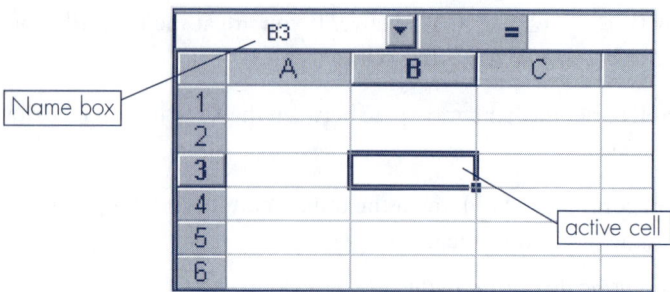

To select an entire column, click on the column heading (A, B, C, etc.). The entire column is highlighted, showing it has been selected. In Figure 1.35, column B is selected.

An entire column can also be selected from any location on the worksheet by holding the Ctrl key and pressing the Spacebar.

Similarly, to select an entire row, point and click on the row heading (1, 2, 3). In Figure 1.36, row 5 is selected.

Figure 1.35   Column B Selected

Figure 1.36   Row 5 Selected

A range is identified by its first and last cells; a colon is placed between the cell reference of the first cell and the cell reference of the last cell. The term A1:C3 indicates that the range begins with cell A1 and includes all the cells through C3.

You can select ranges with the mouse. Place the mouse pointer in the first cell of the range; the pointer takes the ✥ shape. The first cell of a range is the cell in the upper-left corner of the range. Hold down the mouse button and drag the mouse through the rest of the cells you want to select. Release the mouse button after the range is selected. The active cell may be any cell within the range and can be moved using the Tab key.

Figure 1.37   Selected Range of A1:C3

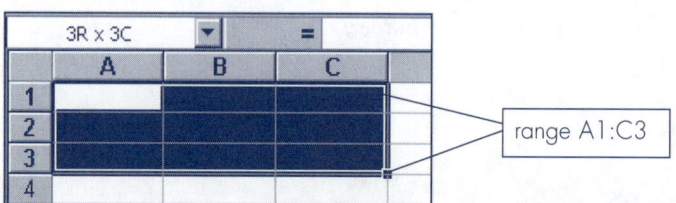

In Figure 1.37, the range A1:C3 is selected. Cell A1 is the active cell. As you hold down the mouse button and select a range, the range size displays in the Name box (3R × 3C in Figure 1.37, indicating the size is three rows by three columns). Once you release the mouse button, the Name box displays the active cell reference, A1 (Figure 1.38).

Another way to select a range is to select the first cell of the range, hold down the Shift key, and click in the last cell of the range. This method, called *extending a selection*, is especially useful with large worksheets. An existing range can also be extended by clicking in the new cell while pressing the Shift key. For instance, to extend an existing range of A1:C3 to A1:F10, hold down the Shift key while clicking in cell F10.

Figure 1.38 Selected Range with Active Cell Identified in Name Box

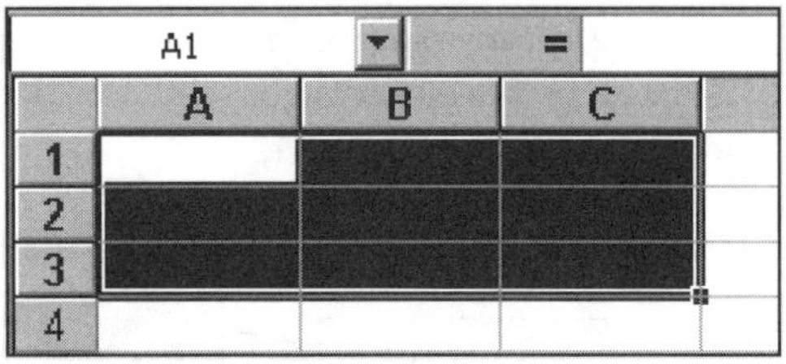

Power User

A range can also be selected by keying the range into the Name box. Click in the Name box to make it active and then key in the range. In Figure 1.39, the range of B3:E11 will be selected. This method is useful when large ranges are selected.

Figure 1.39   Keying In a Range

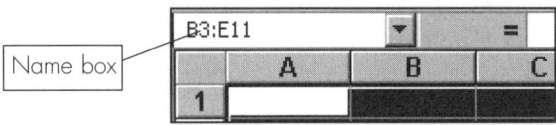

For very large ranges, select the left corner of the range. Then access the Go To dialog box and key the reference of the last cell in the Reference text box. Then hold down the Shift key as you click OK. The large range is selected.

It is also possible to select more than one range of cells at the same time. These ranges do not need to be adjacent. To select additional ranges, hold down the Ctrl key and drag the mouse through the cells of the additional ranges.

Figure 1.40   Multiple Ranges of A1:B3 and B6:C8 Selected

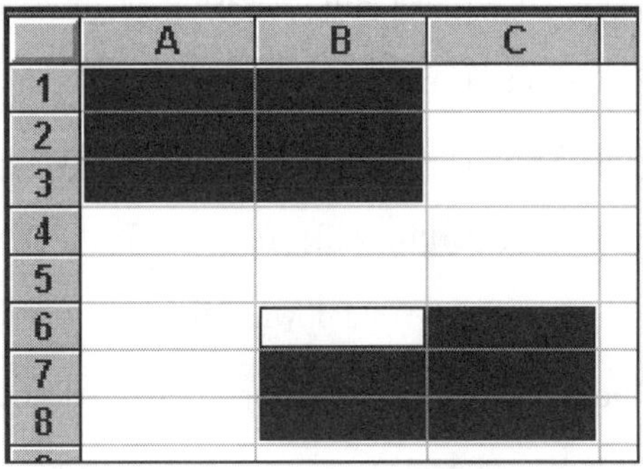

Figure 1.40 shows two selected ranges. One range is A1:B3; the other range is B6:C8. The active cell is B6.

To move the active cell within the selected range, press the Tab key on the keyboard. This moves the active cell one cell to the right; if the active cell is the last cell in that row, the Tab key will move the active cell to the first selected cell in the next row. Holding down the Shift key while pressing Tab reverses the direction of the move.

To deselect any range of cells, click the mouse button anywhere in the worksheet.

The entire worksheet can be selected. Click in the *Select All button* between the row and column headings, shown in Figure 1.41.

Figure 1.41   Select All Button

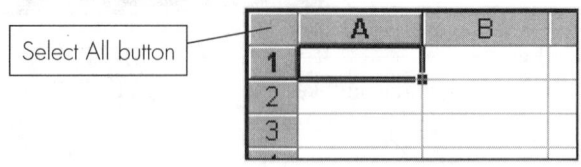

Power Users

The keyboard command to select the entire worksheet is **Ctrl**+**Shift**+**Space Bar**. You may also use the shortcut of **Ctrl**+**A**.

Exercise 1.4   Selecting Ranges

This exercise will give you practice selecting cells and ranges of cells.
Select ranges of cells.

1. Open to a new Excel worksheet if one is not already on your screen.

2. Place the mouse pointer on cell B7. Hold down the mouse button and drag to cell E14 (before releasing the mouse notice the range size of **8R × 4C** displays in the Name box). The range B7:E14 has been selected.

3. Click on the **C** column heading. The Name box reads **1C** (before releasing the mouse) to show one column is selected. After releasing the mouse, column C is selected; cell C1 is the active cell.

4. Press **Tab**. The active cell moves to cell C2.

5. Press **Tab**. The active cell moves to cell C3.

6. Hold down **Shift** while you press **Tab**. The active cell moves "backward" to cell C2.

7. Click in cell C4. Hold down **Ctrl** while pressing **Space Bar**. Column C is selected.

8. Click on the row heading for row 8 to select that row.

9. Click in cell D10. Hold down **Shift** while pressing **Space Bar**. Row 10 is selected.

10 Click on cell A3 and drag a range of four rows and four columns. *Do not release the mouse button.* Read what is in the reference area (**4R x 4C**). When the mouse is released, the range A3:D6 is selected.

11 Release the mouse button.

12 Press **Tab**. The active cell is B3.

13 Press **Tab**. The active cell is C3.

14 Hold down **Shift** and press **Tab**. The active cell returns to cell B3.

15 Press the down arrow on the keyboard. The range is deselected. Use **Tab** to move within a selected range of cells.

16 Select the range A3:C6. (Click in cell A3, hold down the mouse button, and drag to cell C6. The range is selected when the mouse button is released.)

17 Hold down **Ctrl**. With the mouse, select the range of C10:E14. Release **Ctrl**. Two ranges are now selected; the active cell is C10.

18 Press **Tab**. The active cell is D10.

19 Press **Tab**. The active cell is E10.

20 Press **Tab**. The active cell is C11.

21 Click in the worksheet to deselect the range.

> *Power Users*
> - Click in the Name box in the formula bar. Key **B3:D12**. Then press **Enter**. The range B3:D12 is selected.
> - Click in the worksheet to deselect the range.

22 Click in the Select All button at the upper-left corner of the worksheet.

23 Click in the worksheet to deselect the range.

24 Hold down **Ctrl** and **Shift**; tap **Space Bar** once. The entire worksheet is selected.

25 Click in the worksheet to deselect the range.

26 Hold down **Ctrl** and key **A**. The entire worksheet is selected.

27 Click in the worksheet to deselect the range.

Select a large range.

28 Click in cell C3.

29 Hold down **Shift** while you click in cell M12. The range C3:M12 is selected.

30 Scroll so cell T15 is visible. Hold down [Shift] while clicking in cell T15. The selection is extended.

31 Exit Excel if you are not continuing with Exercise 1.5.

Using Help

It is almost impossible to learn everything about Excel and all that it can do. Many times assistance is needed to understand how to complete a task, to try to discover the appropriate command or calculation to perform, or to just learn more about an Excel feature. For that reason, help is provided through Excel's *Help* feature. This *online Help* is fast and convenient. Online refers to features built into a program and designed to provide assistance while working within a program.

Using the Office Assistant

Office 97 has a new feature called *Office Assistant*, which provides tips about the program. It sits on the screen and is by default an animated paper clip, pictured in Figure 1.42, although a different assistant may be selected. This assistant is shared by all Office programs.

The Office Assistant answers questions, offers tips, and provides additional help. Tips point out how to use features or keyboard shortcuts in the program more efficiently. Suggested help is provided for a specific task you are performing and appears even before Help is accessed.

Figure 1.42   Office Assistant, Clippit

Office Assistant may be turned off so it is not displayed.

Figure 1.43   The Help Menu in Excel

There are eight other assistants to choose from. Each makes its own unique sounds and can be animated. To animate *Clippit* the paper clip (and other Office Assistants), click the right mouse button on its window and then select Animate.

Microsoft Excel Help

The Help menu provides several additional Help options, shown in Figure 1.43.

Selecting Microsoft Excel Help opens Office Assistant, if it is available. The Contents and Index command opens a full-range Help file. Clicking on What's This? accesses the pointer shown at the left of the pull-down menu. The pointer becomes a question mark when moved into the worksheet. Move the pointer to the area where help is needed and click the mouse button to display a ScreenTip.

A *ScreenTip* shows information about the different parts of the screen and identifies them. An information box opens on the screen describing the topic.

Help Contents and Index

From Help, select Contents and Index to open the Help Topics dialog box, shown in Figure 1.44.

There are three tabs across the top of the Help dialog box: Contents, Index, and Find. Each tabbed section provides access to help in a specific way.

Figure 1.44   Help Dialog Box

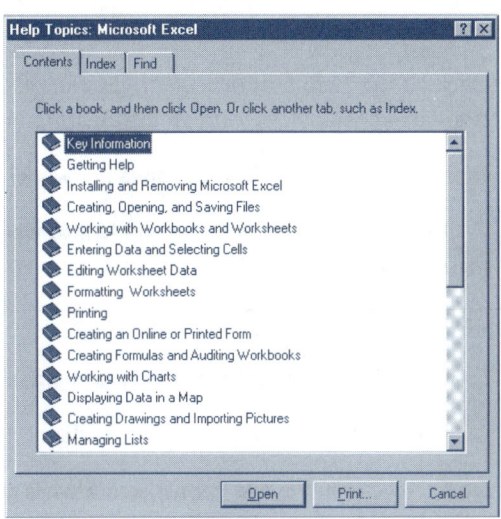

The dialog box looks like Figure 1.44 when the Contents tab is selected. General topics are listed in this section. A closed book icon indicates more information within a topic is listed. Double-click on the closed book to open it and view the additional subtopics.

Figure 1.45 shows the contents of the Index tab. This lists Help by available topics. Scrolling through the lengthy list accesses all choices, so it is often easier to key in the desired topic. As you key each letter, Help automatically advances to words matching the keyed letter or letters, making it quick to access topics in Help.

Figure 1.45   Index Tab in Help

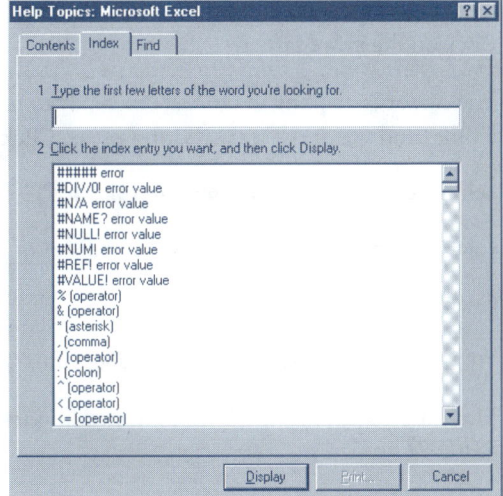

The Find tab allows you to search in Help for specific words and phrases of Help topics instead of searching for information by category.

> *Power Users*
>
> To quickly access Help, press **F1**.

Exercise 1.5 Using Help

This exercise will give you practice using Help in the Excel program.

1. If you do not have an open Excel worksheet on your computer screen, start Excel and open to a new workbook.

2. Click on the Help button at the right end of the Standard toolbar. Clippit (or the installed Office Assistant) opens, along with an information box.

3. In the text box, enter **How do I save my work?** Then click **Search**. Additional choices open.

4. Click on the top bullet, **Troubleshoot template problems**. A dialog box opens providing specific information about the topic.

5. Click on the dialog box's Close box; then close Clippit.

6. From the **Help** menu, select **Contents and Index**.

7. Click on the **Contents** tab, then double-click on the **Getting Help** book.

8. Double-click on **Ways to get assistance while you work**.

9. Click on the **ScreenTips** box and read the pop-up explanation. Continue to explore this box on your own.

10. Click on **Help Topics** in the upper-left corner until you return to the original **Help Topics** dialog box.

11. Click on the **Index** tab.

12. The cursor is blinking in the text box ready to receive information. Key **formatting cells** (one letter at a time) and watch the text selection move. Click on **Display**.

13. Select **Clear or delete cells, rows, or columns**. Then click on **Display**. Information opens on the screen.

14. Click on **Help Topics** in the upper-left corner of the dialog box.

15. Click **Cancel**.

16. From **Help** on the menu bar, select **What's This?**.

17. Move the pointer to the B column heading in the main worksheet. The pointer takes the arrow shape.

18. Click in the **B** heading. An information box opens providing additional information.

19. Click outside the text box to deselect the Help topic.

20. Exit Excel.

Summary

- A worksheet consists of rows and columns. Columns are identified by letters across the top of the worksheet. Rows are identified by numbers on the left side of the worksheet.
- *Worksheet* and *spreadsheet* are terms that are used interchangeably for a grid used to organize numerical data. Excel uses the term *worksheet*.
- Making changes to a worksheet is called editing a worksheet.
- Both the keyboard and the mouse are used to interface with the computer. The mouse is used to point, click, and drag.
- Most keyboards include a numeric keypad to enter numbers.
- The mouse indicator takes different shapes in Excel depending on the activity performed.
- In addition to entering alphabetic and numerical data, the keyboard may be used to move around an Excel worksheet and to choose commands.
- Only a small portion of the total worksheet can be seen at one time in the worksheet window.
- A cell is the intersection of a row and column. It is identified by the row and column headings, and is called the cell reference.
- A cell that is selected or active has a heavy border surrounding it.
- Any cell of a range may be the active cell, but only one cell may be active at a time.
- The title bar is the first line of the worksheet screen. It displays the name of the program and the workbook.
- The menu bar is the second line on the screen. It lists the major categories of choices used to interact with the computer.
- The Standard toolbar is the third line on the screen. It is used to execute frequently used commands.
- The Formatting toolbar is the fourth line of the screen and is used to quickly change the format of a selection.
- The formula bar is the fifth line of the screen. The Name box displays the reference of the active cell; the entry area displays data as it is input in the cell.
- A command instructs the computer to carry out an action.
- A pull-down menu appears when a menu topic is selected. The pull-down menu lists the related commands that are available.
- The Control key (Ctrl) on the keyboard may be used in conjunction with another key(s) for selecting commands.
- A dialog box is used when Excel needs additional information before carrying out a command.
- The default command button can be selected either with the mouse or with the Enter key on the keyboard. The default command is identified by the bold border around it.
- To open a new workbook, select the New command from the File menu or click on the New button ▢ in the toolbar. Power users may use the keyboard command of Ctrl+N.
- To quit Excel, select Exit from the File menu. Excel reminds the user to save changes to all unsaved worksheets.
- Scroll bars are used to move line by line, screen by screen, or from beginning to end of a worksheet. They are located at the right edge and bottom of the worksheet window.
- The Go To command is especially helpful when working with large worksheets.
- Cells may be selected individually, as a range, or as multiple ranges.

- A range of cells is a group of adjacent cells.
- To select more than one range of cells, hold down Ctrl while selecting additional ranges.
- To select an entire worksheet, click in the Select All button, which is located in the upper-left corner of the worksheet at the intersection of the row and column headings.
- Excel provides extensive online Help using the Help menu.
- Office Assistant, viewed by default as Clippit, provides intuitive, animated assistance.

Important Terminology

active cell	Help	scroll box
button	icon	ScrollTip
cell	insertion point	Select All button
cell reference	keyboard	selected cell
check box	keyboard command	sheet
Clippit	list box	shortcut
Close button	Maximize button	spreadsheet
column	menu bar	Standard toolbar
column heading	Minimize button	Start button
command button	mode indicator	status bar
default command	mouse	tabbed dialog box
dialog box	Name box	tabs
edit	numeric keypad	text
electronic spreadsheet	Office Assistant	text box
Enter key	online Help	title bar
entry area	option button	tool
exit Excel	pull-down menu	warning box
extend a selection	range of cells	workbook
Formatting toolbar	row	worksheet
formula bar	row heading	worksheet tab
function keys	ScreenTip	worksheet window
Go To command	scroll bar	

Buttons to Know

Study Questions

True-False

Place a T in the space if the statement is true; place an F if the statement is false.

_____ 1. The terms *spreadsheet* and *worksheet* describe a form used to organize numerical data.
_____ 2. An electronic spreadsheet refers to a computerized spreadsheet.
_____ 3. A spreadsheet consists of a grid of rows and columns.
_____ 4. A disadvantage of using spreadsheet software is the difficulty in making changes.
_____ 5. Editing is adding formulas to a worksheet.
_____ 6. An entire worksheet is visible on the screen at one time.
_____ 7. Cells can hold only numeric values.
_____ 8. The cell that is the intersection of row 10 and column C uses a cell reference of Row 10 Column C.
_____ 9. The toolbar is used to execute frequently used commands.
_____ 10. The Name box of the formula bar displays the active cell reference.
_____ 11. Row headings are letters and column headings are numbers.
_____ 12. Scroll bars are used to view other sections of a worksheet.
_____ 13. A menu instructs the computer to carry out an action.
_____ 14. The entry area of the formula bar shows the cell reference.
_____ 15. The status bar gives a brief description of choices available in the currently highlighted selection.
_____ 16. On a pull-down menu, a selected command is highlighted.
_____ 17. The buttons in the menu bar are identified by holding the mouse pointer near the button to display its name. This feature is called ButtonTip.
_____ 18. Commands are sometimes accessed by using the keyboard.
_____ 19. A command in a pull-down menu followed by an ellipsis (...) indicates there is no keyboard command available.
_____ 20. In dialog boxes, only one option button and one check box may be selected at once.
_____ 21. A check box is selected when a ✔ is placed in the box.
_____ 22. The default command button has a heavy border surrounding it.
_____ 23. To open to a blank worksheet, use the Open command in the File menu.
_____ 24. The button in the toolbar used to open a new workbook is ▢.
_____ 25. To end an Excel work session, select the Exit command from the File menu.
_____ 26. When a cell is active, the cell reference displays in the status bar.
_____ 27. The command that moves to a specific cell is the Jump command, found in the Edit menu.
_____ 28. Only one cell may be selected at one time.
_____ 29. To select an entire row, click the mouse in the row heading of the row you want selected.
_____ 30. The term A1:B5 defines the range of cells that begins with cell A1 and includes all cells through cell B5.
_____ 31. When a range of cells is selected, every cell is active.
_____ 32. The Help feature is available at the computer.
_____ 33. Office Assistant may provide animated help.

Chapter 1 Getting Acquainted with Microsoft Excel

Fill-In

In the space provided, write the answer that completes the statement.

1. Little pictures that identify parts of the computer and software program are called _____ .
2. The portion of a worksheet that is shown on the computer screen is called the _____ .
3. The intersection of a row and a column is called a(n) _____ .
4. Each cell in a worksheet is identified by the cell _____ .
5. The cell reference for the intersection of row 12 and column J is _____ .
6. The first line on an Excel screen is called the _____ .
7. The _____ is divided into the Name box and the entry area.
8. The _____ cell is the cell into which data may be entered.
9. The name of the open worksheet shows in the _____ .
10. An instruction to Excel that carries out an action is a(n) _____ .
11. When the mouse is held on a menu item, a(n) _____ opens that lists related commands.
12. The symbol and letter combination that follow a command on a pull-down menu is the _____ .
13. When additional information is needed before a command can be executed, a(n) _____ box opens.
14. A default command button may be selected by pressing the _____ key on the keyboard.
15. A cell that displays a heavy border around it is called the _____ cell.
16. In a pull-down menu, some commands have an icon at the _____ side as a reminder of the toolbar button.
17. The place where the data entry begins displays a blinking cursor and is called the _____ point.
18. A range of cells is selected when the cells are _____ .
19. Any rectangular section of a worksheet that is larger than a single cell is called a(n) _____ of cells.
20. A range of cells can be selected by holding the mouse button down and _____ through the area.
21. In a highlighted range of cells, the active cell can be moved one cell to the right by pressing the _____ key.
22. Multiple ranges are selected by holding the _____ key while making each selection.
23. The feature that allows the row number to be seen on the screen while scrolling through a worksheet is called a(n) _____ .

Assignments

Assignment 1.1

Identify the parts of an Excel worksheet.

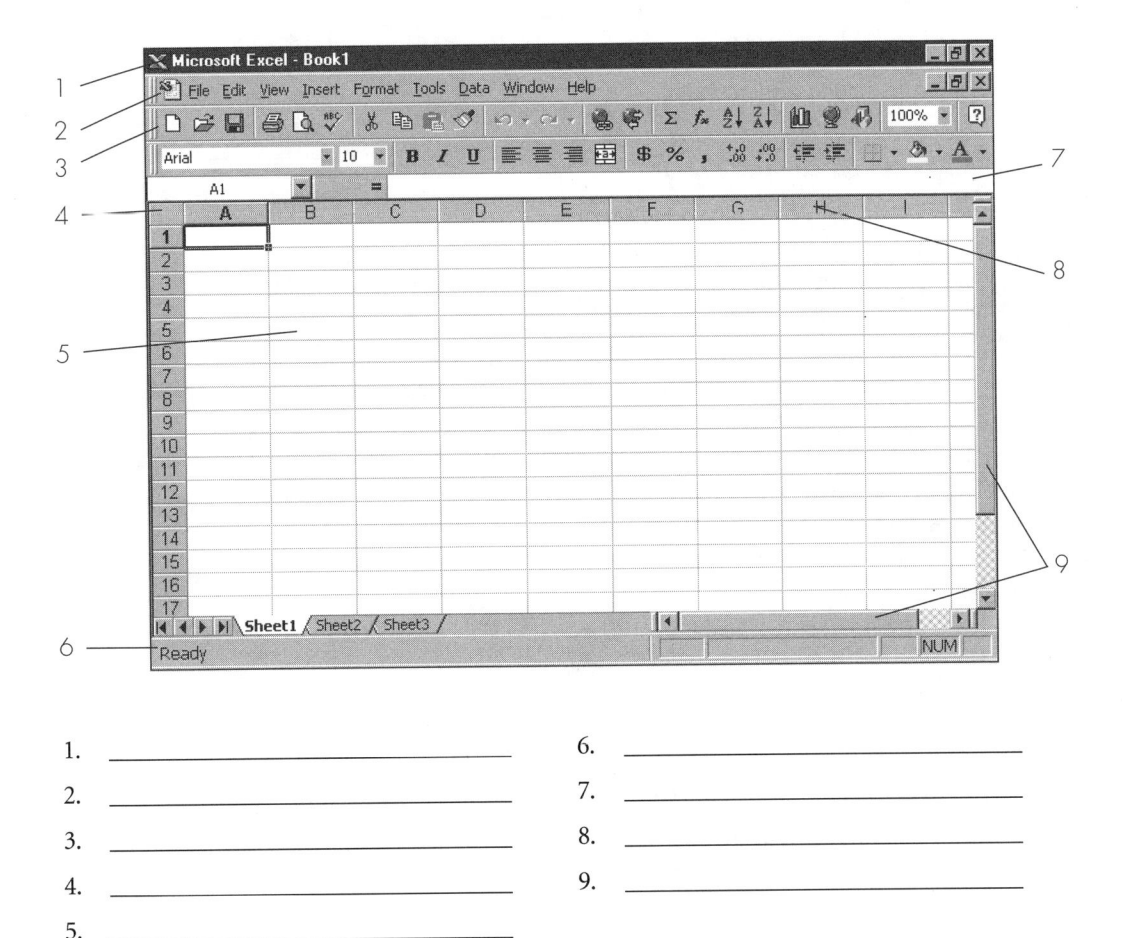

1. _____   6. _____
2. _____   7. _____
3. _____   8. _____
4. _____   9. _____
5. _____

Assignment 1.2

Complete the following assignment at the computer. It provides practice in moving around the Excel worksheet.

1. Open Excel.
2. The active cell is _____ .
3. Move to cell Z391. The fastest method is to use _____ .
4. Move one window to the left. Do this by _____ .
5. Go to cell A1. The fastest method is _____ .
6. Go to cell Z391 again. The fastest method is to use _____ .

7. Return to cell A1.
8. Click on the number **15**. _____ is the selected row. The active cell is _____ .
9. Click on the letter **E**. _____ is the selected column. The active cell is _____ .
10. Click on cell D3 and drag to D8. The _____ of D3:D8 has been selected.
11. Click in cell A1. The range _____ is deselected. Cell _____ is active.
12. Click in cell D10. Hold down **Shift** and press **Space Bar** once. _____ is selected.
13. Click in cell F4. Hold down **Ctrl** and press **Space Bar** once. _____ is selected.
14. Click in the Select All button. _____ is selected.

Use the menu bar to complete the next set of questions.
15. The Cut command is in this menu topic: _____
16. The Print command is in this menu topic: _____
17. The Go To command is in this menu topic: _____
18. The Cells command is in this menu topic: _____
19. The Sort command is in this menu topic: _____
20. The Macro command is in this menu topic: _____
21. The Print Preview command is in this menu topic: _____
22. The Exit command is in this menu topic: _____
23. Select the range of cells B7:D11 by dragging through them.
24. Hold down **Ctrl** and select the range C14:F17. The active cell is _____ .
25. Press **Tab**. The active cell is _____ .
26. Press **Tab** three times. Cell C15 is active.
27. Hold down **Shift** and press **Tab**. The active cell is _____ .
28. Hold down **Shift** and press **Tab**. The active cell is _____ .
29. Click in cell A1 to make it the active cell and deselect the ranges.
30. Click in the Name box. Enter **P37:U45**. The active cell is _____ .
31. Click in the Name box. Enter **L20:N22,P25:S27**. _____ (one or two) ranges are selected.
32. To exit Excel, select **File**, then **Exit** or press _____ on the keyboard.
33. Exit Excel. Do not save your work.

Assignment 1.3

You will make a working or backup copy of the Student Data Disk provided with this textbook. After making the copy, store the original disk and use the copy for all classwork. You will need a formatted 3.5" high-density disk as well as the Student Data Disk for this assignment.
You should have Windows 95 running.
The Student Data Disk is a high-density disk. Be sure the disk you have is also a high-density disk.
1. From **Start** (in the lower-left corner), select **Programs**, then **Windows Explorer**.
2. Click on **My Computer** (you may need to scroll to the top of the section to find this selection).
3. In the right section, click on **3½ Floppy (A:)** (the disk to copy).

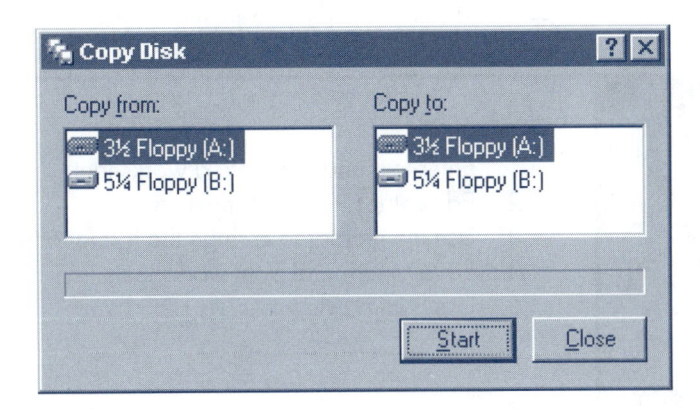

4. From the **File** menu, select **Copy Disk**. A dialog box opens, similar to the one shown below:

5. Within the dialog box, be sure **3½ Floppy (A:)** is selected in both the **Copy from** and the **Copy to** boxes. If it is not, click on it to select it (as illustrated above).
6. Click **Start**. Follow the instructions on the computer screen to copy the disk. You will eventually insert the new disk, the destination disk, and the information will be written to it.
7. Close the **Copy Disk** dialog box.
8. Write **Student Data Disk Copy** and your name on a label and affix it to the disk. This is the disk you will use to save documents when completing textbook exercises and assignments. It will be referred to in the textbook as the Student Data Disk.
9. Remember to place the original disk in a safe place. This can be used as a backup disk in case there is a problem with the copy you just made.

A Note about the Student Data Disk

The disk that accompanies this book contains compressed files. As you work through this text, you will need to delete work as it is completed to allow room for additional work. If you do not want to delete your work, you will need seven additional disks. Copy the data from the Student Data Disk in the following order: Chapters 1–4, Chapters 5–6, Chapters 7–8, Chapters 9–10, Chapters 14 and 17, and Chapters 15–16. You will now have space to store all completed work.

Chapter 2

Creating a Worksheet

Objectives

1. Enter text and data into a worksheet.
2. Edit entries in a worksheet.
3. Use the toolbar to change the format of a worksheet.
4. Save, open, and print worksheets.
5. Use Print Preview.

Introduction

A worksheet contains millions of cells, any of which can store information. The three types of information that Excel uses are data (numbers), text (words), and formulas (mathematical statements). Creating a simple worksheet consists of entering information into cells, creating formulas with that information, formatting the worksheet, and saving it for future use.

In this chapter, a simple worksheet will be completed. Each exercise in this chapter builds on the previous exercise. For this reason, the first six exercises in this chapter should be completed at the computer in one sitting.

Entering Information

Books, Workbooks, and Worksheets

When Excel is started, a worksheet opens on the computer screen. Its title in the title bar is Book1. A *book*, or workbook, is a group of worksheets saved as one file. The use of workbooks and worksheets will be further explained in Chapter 6.

The Formula Bar

When data is entered, the formula bar becomes active. When the formula bar is active, the Cancel and Enter boxes appear in the formula bar between the Name box and the entry area. Figure 2.1 shows both an inactive and active formula bar.

Figure 2.1 Active and Inactive Formula Bar

Inactive Formula Bar

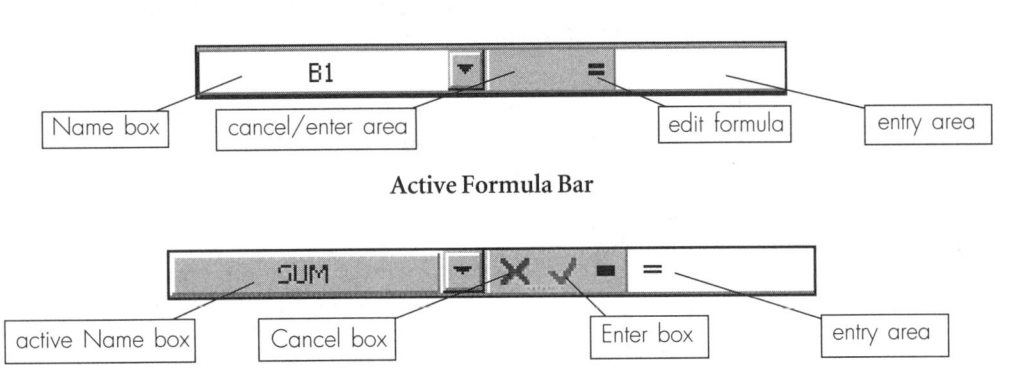

(Name box | cancel/enter area | edit formula | entry area)

Active Formula Bar

(active Name box | Cancel box | Enter box | entry area)

Entering Text

Excel recognizes the difference between text and numbers and automatically aligns text at the left of the cell and numbers at the right. *Text* is generally used for labels that identify the data in the worksheet. *Labels* are usually the first entry in a row or column. Excel allows up to 32,000 characters in any one cell.

When entering text, use capital letters and punctuation marks as needed, but do not be concerned with other formatting styles. To *complete an entry*, press either the Tab or the *Enter key* on the keyboard, or click the mouse on the *Enter box* in the active formula bar. Pressing Tab enters the information and activates the cell to the right. Pressing the Enter key enters the information and activates the cell below. Using the Enter box in the formula bar enters the information but does not change which cell is active.

Note: If the current cell remains active when you press Enter, choose the Options command from the Tools menu, select the Edit tab, and then select the Move selection after Enter check box.

Figure 2.2 shows A1 as the active cell. The formula bar is active; the reference to the active cell (A1) is displayed in the Name box and the cell contents, Enter, are displayed in the entry area. The Cancel and Enter boxes are active.

Figure 2.2 Cell Reference and Formula Bar

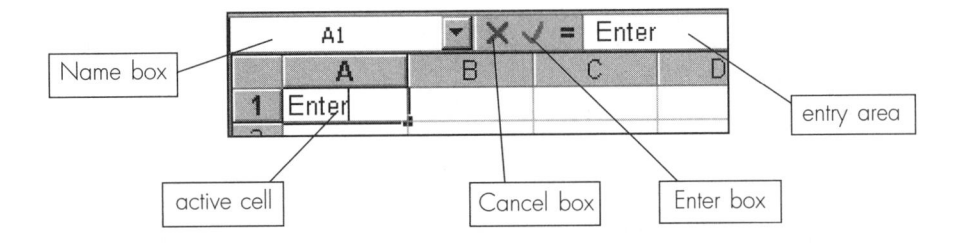

(Name box | active cell | Cancel box | Enter box | entry area)

Editing Text

The ease of correcting errors is a major benefit of using a spreadsheet program. To correct an entry as it is being keyed, use the Backspace key to delete the last keystroke; it is identified with a left-pointing arrow (←). Then rekey the correct information. To replace the cell's entire contents, click in the cell and key the new information.

A completed entry can be edited or corrected within the cell or in the entry area of the formula bar. Double-click in the cell to edit information. An *insertion point*, indicating placement for entering information, displays in the cell as shown in Figure 2.3.

Pressing Backspace removes one letter to the left of the insertion point. Pressing Delete will delete one character to the right of the insertion point.

Figure 2.3   Insertion Point in a Cell

Incorrect data may be selected by clicking and dragging the mouse over the data to highlight it. To correct the information, just key it in. In Figure 2.4, the next keystroke will replace the selected text "nt."

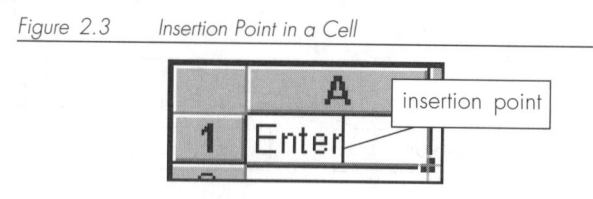

Figure 2.4   Data Display Area Ready for Correction

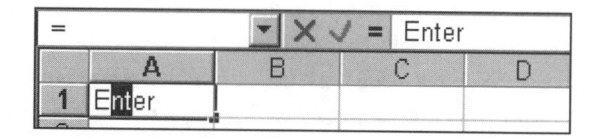

To insert a character, double-click in the cell to select it. Position the insertion point where additional information will be added. Then key the additional information.

The *Cancel box* ☒ is used to cancel the entry and return to the data stored in the cell *before* the cell editing began.

Exercise 2.1   Adding Text to a Worksheet

You will create a worksheet that will summarize the inventory of three different locations in a company. The first six exercises in Chapter 2 should be completed in one work session at the computer.

Complete the numbered instructions as you do each exercise and assignment. Italicized text previews the instructions that follow.

1 Open Excel to a new sheet.

2 Click the mouse in cell B1. Key **Inventory** in cell B1. Press **Enter**.

Identify the column and row labels.

3 Click the mouse in cell A2 to make it active.

4 Key **Plant** in cell A2. Press **Tab**. B2 is the active cell.

5 Key **Widgets** in cell B2. Press **Tab**. C2 is the active cell.

6 Key **Sprocks** in cell C2. Press **Tab**. D2 is the active cell.

7 Key **Cubes** in cell D2. Click in the Enter box ✓ in the formula bar. D2 remains the active cell.

8 Key **Boise** in cell A4; press **Enter**. A5 is the active cell.

9 Key **Denver** in cell A5; press **Enter**. A6 is the active cell.

10 Key **Portland** in cell A6; press **Enter**. A7 is the active cell.

11 Key your name in cell A10. Click in the Enter box ✓ in the formula bar. The name may extend beyond the cell.

Edit the worksheet.

12 Click in cell A4 to make it active. Press **Backspace** on the keyboard. The contents of cell A4 are deleted.

13 Key **Spokane**. Click on the Cancel box ✗. This cancels the entry and returns to the original entry.

14 Key **Seattel**. Press **Enter**.

15 Double-click in cell A4 to make it active. Position the insertion point between the **e** and **l**. You may need to use the arrow keys to move to the correct spot.

16 Press **Backspace** on the keyboard. The **e** is erased.

17 Press the **Delete** key on the keyboard. The **l** is erased.

18 Key **le**. The entry now reads **Seattle**. Press **Enter**.

Your worksheet should look like the following:

	A	B	C	D
1		Inventory		
2	Plant	Widgets	Sprocks	Cubes
3				
4	Seattle			
5	Denver			
6	Portland			
7				
8				
9				
10	Student's Name			

(A5 = Denver)

19 Continue with Exercise 2.2.

Entering Numbers

Numbers are entered into the worksheet using either the top row of the keyboard or the ***numeric keypad*** (if the NUM indicator is on). The numeric keypad is turned on and off with the Num Lock button above the numbers. The entry is completed using either the Tab key, the Enter key on the numeric keypad, the cursor movement keys (arrows), or the Enter box ✓.

When a number is entered, Excel recognizes it as a number and automatically aligns it at the right side of the cell. To indicate a negative number, type a minus sign as the first character.

Chapter 2   Creating a Worksheet

When the numeric keypad is used, the Enter key to the right of the keypad completes the entry and activates the cell below. Using the numeric keypad will speed up data entry in the worksheet.

When a number is longer than the cell width, Excel will sometimes display the number in scientific notation (7.3938E+10 displays for 73938485784). This is the *General number format* that Excel uses as the default. If this happens, do not be alarmed. The number format may be changed later.

The method for editing numbers and text is the same: double-click on the cell with the error, and make the correction in the cell.

Exercise 2.2   Adding Data to a Worksheet

You will add data to the worksheet you created in Exercise 2.1. Be sure the numeric keypad is turned on and use it to enter numbers.

1 Click in cell B4. Key **13325**. Press **Enter** on the numeric keypad.

2 Key **22117** in cell B5; press **Enter**.

3 Key **32115** in cell B6. Press **Enter**. Position the mouse at the top edge of the active cell and double-click it. It moves to the top of the range (cell B4). Press **Tab** to move to cell C4.

4 Click in cell C4. Key **48897**, then press **Enter**.

5 Key **34432** in cell C5, then press **Enter**.

6 Key **32258** in cell C6. Click in the Enter box ☑ in the formula bar.

7 Double-click at the top of the active cell to activate the cell at the top of the column.

8 Activate cell D4. Key **49831**, then press **Enter**.

9 Key **42279** in cell D5; press **Enter**.

10 Key **39998** in cell D6; press **Enter**.

Your worksheet should look like the following:

	A	B	C	D
1		Inventory		
2	Plant	Widgets	Sprocks	Cubes
3				
4	Seattle	13325	48897	49831
5	Denver	22117	34432	42279
6	Portland	32115	32258	39998
7				
8				
9				
10	Student's Name			

11 Continue with Exercise 2.3.

Simple Formatting Techniques

Excel is preset to use a certain font style and font size; the cells are a predetermined width; the margins around the worksheet are also preset. These settings are called *defaults*.

Making a change that affects the way a worksheet looks is called *formatting*. Excel provides easy ways to make format changes. Formatting choices include making type bold or italic, enlarging the size of the type, using an underline for accent, or changing the way the numbers are displayed.

Changing Text Style

The text in a worksheet may be displayed in bold, italic, underline, or in a combination such as bold italic. It may also be enlarged or made smaller. Some of these formatting features are available in the *Formatting toolbar*, the second toolbar on the Excel screen, shown in Figure 2.5.

Figure 2.5   Formatting Toolbar

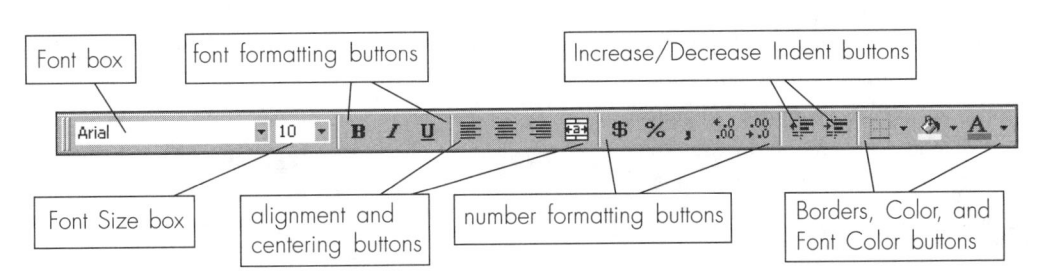

To change the format of text or data, first select the cell or cells. To format the selected cells for *bold*, click the *Bold button* **B** in the toolbar. Use the *Italic button* *I* for *italics* and the *Underline button* **B** to underline cell contents. The font formatting buttons are shown in Figure 2.6.

Figure 2.6   Font Formatting Buttons

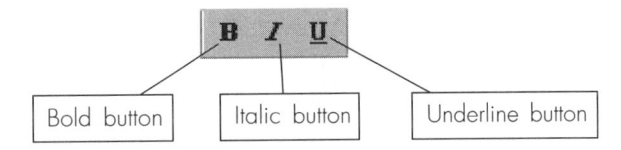

The *font*, which is the style of type, can be changed as well as its size. The font size is shown in the Font Size box, shown in Figure 2.7. The arrow to the right of the box accesses a pull-down list, showing additional sizes you can select.

Changing Alignment

Alignment describes the place where the data or text lines up. The *alignment buttons* are located in the middle of the Formatting toolbar, shown in Figure 2.8.

To format the cell contents for *center alignment*, first select the cells. Then click the *Center Align button*. To format the cell contents for *left alignment*, click the *Left Align button*. To format the cell contents for *right alignment*, click the *Right Align button*. Unless centered or right alignment is chosen, Excel automatically aligns cell contents so text aligns at the left and numbers align at the right. The Merge and Center button will be discussed in Chapter 6.

Indenting Text within a Cell

As text is entered into the cell, it begins at the left edge of the cell. Using alignment buttons, it can be centered or aligned at the right. Using the indent buttons, the text can also be indented from the left gridline. To indent cell information, click on the Increase Indent button. Figure 2.9 shows a worksheet with rows 2–4 and 6–8 indented.

To decrease the indent, click on the Decrease Indent button.

Figure 2.7   Font Size List Box

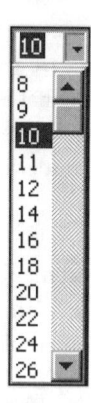

Figure 2.8   Alignment and Centering Buttons

Left Align button

Right Align button

Center Align button

Merge and Center button

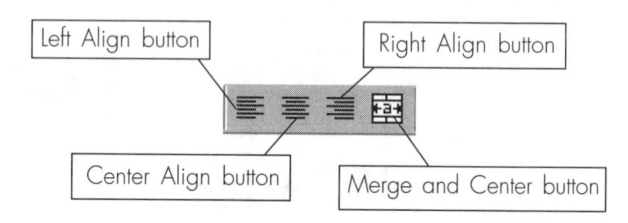

Figure 2.9   Using Increase Indent

	A
1	**Word**
2	Daily Work
3	Quizzes
4	Tests
5	**Excel**
6	Daily Work
7	Quizzes
8	Tests

Exercise 2.3 Formatting a Worksheet

You will format the worksheet you used in Exercise 2.2.

1 Click in cell B1 to select it. The word **Inventory** is in this cell.

2 In the toolbar, click the Bold **B** and Italic *I* buttons.

3 Click on the arrow beside the Font Size box. Select **14**. The cell contents have increased in size.

Format the column labels.

4 Select the column labels located in the range A2:D2. (Do this by clicking in cell A2 and dragging through D2.) Format the range for bold. Click on the Center Align button.

Format the row labels.

5 Select the row labels located in the range A4:A6. Then click on the Increase Indent button.

6 In cell A10, change the font size to **9**.

Your worksheet should look like this:

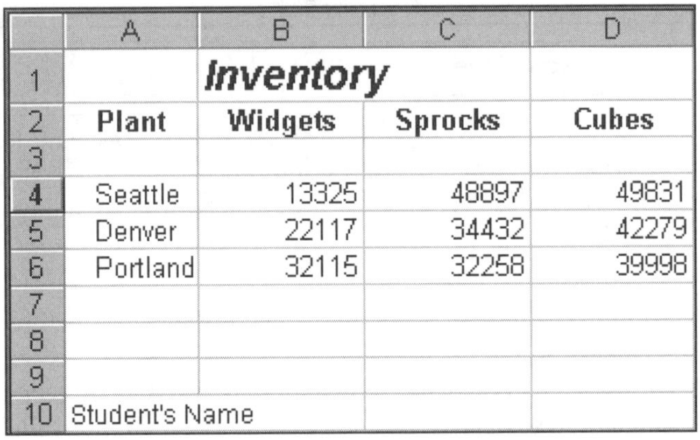

	A	B	C	D
1		*Inventory*		
2	Plant	Widgets	Sprocks	Cubes
3				
4	Seattle	13325	48897	49831
5	Denver	22117	34432	42279
6	Portland	32115	32258	39998
7				
8				
9				
10	Student's Name			

7 Continue with Exercise 2.4.

Using Borders

Borders are horizontal and vertical lines that are used for emphasis or style, to make the worksheet attractive, and to clarify data. Borders can surround the entire worksheet, one cell, or a range of cells. Double lines, dotted lines, dashed lines, and thick and thin lines are available.

The *Borders button* is at the right side of the Formatting toolbar and is shown in Figure 2.10.

Figure 2.10 Borders Button on the Formatting Toolbar

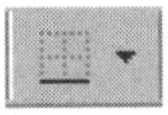

The arrow to the right of the Borders button indicates the ***Borders palette***, a pull-down menu that provides additional border choices. This menu shows a grid of border placement and style choices, shown in Figure 2.11. Clicking on a border style will apply it to the selected cells.

A border extends the entire width of the cell. When the Underline button U is selected, however, only the *contents* of the cell are underlined.

Figure 2.11   Borders Palette

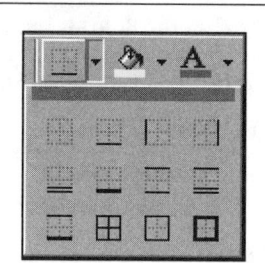

Formatting Numbers

Numbers are entered in Excel using the General number format. This format enters numbers without commas or dollar signs. However, by using the ***number format buttons*** (Figure 2.12) on the Formatting toolbar, numbers can be formatted to show commas with the ***Comma Style button***, dollar signs with the ***Currency Style button***, and percentages with the ***Percent Style button***. The number of decimal places in a number can be increased or decreased using the ***Increase Decimal button*** or the ***Decrease Decimal button***.

Figure 2.12   Number Format Buttons on the Formatting Toolbar

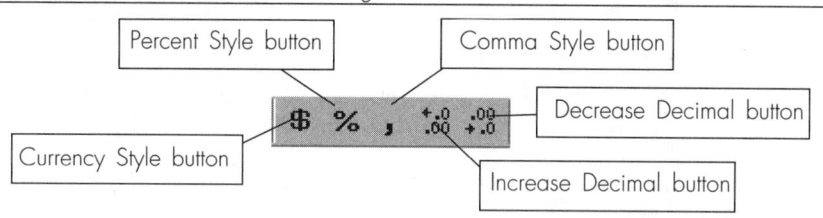

When entering numbers, key only the number and the decimal. Formatting choices can be applied later to all selected cells as a group.

After numbers are entered, there are several formats that may be applied. The following chart shows a number and how it is displayed with some of the most common number styles:

Number Entered	Number Format	Decimals	Appearance
2700	Currency	2	$2,700.00
2700	Comma	0	2,700
.267	Percent	0	27%
.267	Percent	1	26.7%
3.256	Currency	2	$3.26

When formatting numbers in a range of cells, it is important that the decimals align. As numbers are entered, Excel aligns the entries at the right edge of the cell. When either the Currency or Comma style is applied, the data moves slightly to the left. Proofreading for decimal alignment is important. Figure 2.13 illustrates how decimals align with Excel.

Sometimes text entered into a cell is too long for the width of the cell. To increase a cell's width, position the mouse in the column heading to the right of the column letter and double-click the mouse. Figure 2.14 shows where to place the mouse and the shape it takes to increase the width of column C. Double-click the mouse to automatically adjust the width of the column to allow space for the longest entry in that column.

Using Currency Format

In preparing worksheets, use the correct style for formatting currency. Dollar signs are placed on the first line of a column of money amounts and again in the total. Other numbers in the list do not use a dollar sign. Underlines are used to indicate the cells that are to be added; the total usually has a bold or double underline. Decimals are aligned. Currency usually contains two decimals but can also be expressed with no decimals. Figure 2.15 shows the correct number style used for dollar amounts, called the *Currency format*.

Figure 2.13   Number Formats and Their Alignment

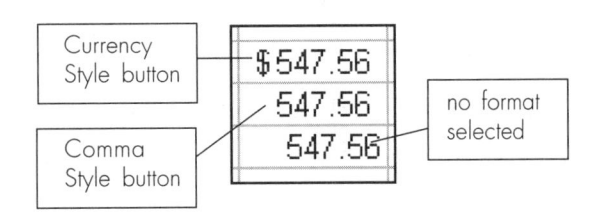

Figure 2.14   Increase Cell Width

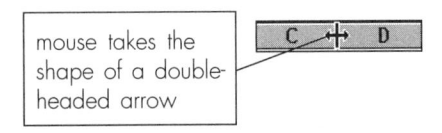

Figure 2.15   Correct Dollar Sign Placement and Use of Underlines

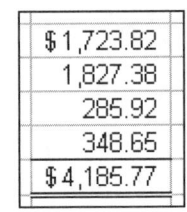

Exercise 2.4   Formatting Numbers and Adding a Border

You will format the worksheet used in Exercise 2.3.

1 Select the range B4:D4.

2 Click the Currency Style button. The columns automatically adjust to accommodate the longer numbers.

3 Click the Decrease Decimal button two times so no decimals are included in the numbers.

4 Select the range B5:D6 and click the Comma Style button. Format the range so no decimals are displayed in the cells.

5 Select the range B6:D6. Click on the Bottom Border button in the Formatting toolbar. A line appears beneath the items in columns B, C, and D. (You may need to access this button in the Borders palette.)

6 Select the range A2:D2. Click on the arrow beside the Borders button ▣▾. The Borders palette opens showing the available choices.

7 Select the Surround Border button ▣ located in the lower-right corner.

8 Click in any empty cell to deselect the range of cells.

Your worksheet should look like this:

	A	B	C	D
1		*Inventory*		
2	Plant	Widgets	Sprocks	Cubes
3				
4	Seattle	$ 13,325	$ 48,897	$ 49,831
5	Denver	22,117	34,432	42,279
6	Portland	32,115	32,258	39,998
7				
8				
9				
10	Student's Name			

9 Continue with Exercise 2.5.

Opening and Closing Worksheets

Your Student Data Disk stores documents in a subdirectory. If you are unfamiliar with file management, you may want to work through Appendix A, "Managing Documents Using Windows."

Saving a Workbook

The book or workbook that is currently displayed on the computer screen is referred to as the *active book*. The information for this book includes every sheet in the book and is stored as one file in the memory of the computer (RAM). This memory is temporary and will be erased when the computer is turned off or when you end the Excel work session.

A workbook will usually be saved for later use. This provides the opportunity to edit the data or the format or complete a workbook.

A workbook may be saved to the hard drive of the computer or on a floppy disk. The instructions in this textbook assume that the workbook will be saved to a floppy disk in the A drive.

To save a completed workbook, select the Save As command from the File menu, shown in Figure 2.16.

If Office Assistant appears, the warning shown in Figure 2.17 opens asking which software version of Excel you wish to use. Each version of any software is identified by a number, such as 5.0, 6.0, or 95. The higher the number, the more recent the version. As each new version is released, additional features and enhancements are added. Documents created with older versions may generally be read by newer versions, but the reverse is not always true. This is the case with Excel 97 for Windows. However, it is possible to save the document so it may be read by the two previous versions (5.0 and 95) as well as the

Exercise 2.4—Formatting Numbers and Adding a Border 47

current version for Office 97; the format suggested by Office Assistant saves the workbook as versions read by 97 as well as 5.0/95. Some of the enhancements specific to Office 97 are lost, but these are usually not the fundamental features. For this text, save workbook in the suggested format unless otherwise specified.

The dialog box that opens looks similar to Figure 2.18.

The Save in text box displays a folder icon followed by the folder's name and a down arrow. Click on the arrow to view the directory of the computer. Locate the drive you used to save your work—usually the 3½ Floppy (A:)—and click once on it to select it. Figure 2.19 shows the file structure in Explorer used to access data.

Figure 2.16   Save As Command in File Menu

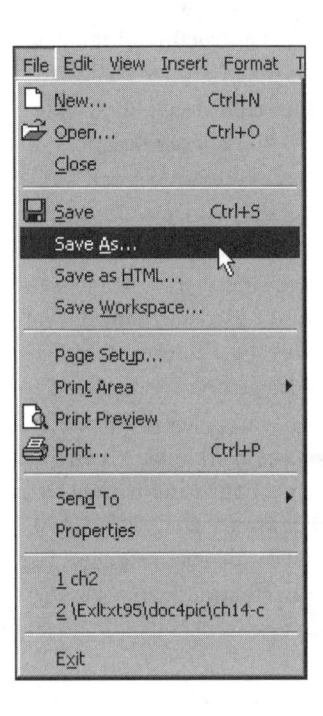

Figure 2.17   Office Assistant for Saving Work

Figure 2.18   Save As Dialog Box

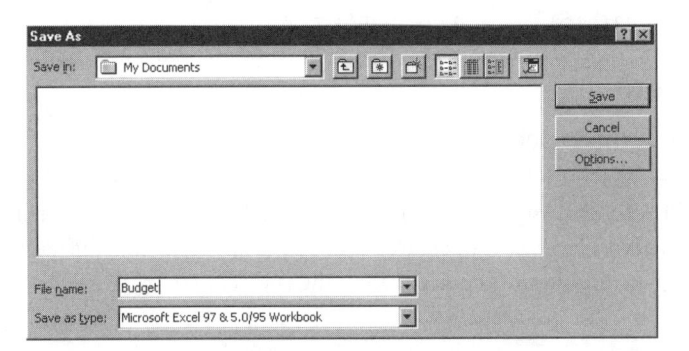

Your Student Data Disk is divided into subdirectories, which are shown as folders. The structure of the data disk is shown in Figure 2.20. Each folder represents a section of work, usually one for each chapter.

To access the correct subdirectory, double-click on it. When the subdirectory is open in the Save in box, you are ready to name the worksheet. The text box used for naming the workbook is at the bottom of the dialog box. A suggestion is highlighted in the text box. Simply key in the new file name for the workbook; the highlighted suggestion is automatically replaced. *File names* can contain up to 218 characters and may include spaces but not punctuation marks. Select a file name that describes the document so that it is easy to locate for later use.

Click on the Save button to save the workbook to the data disk. (The Save button is the default command and can also be executed by pressing Enter on the keyboard.) The name in the title bar of the workbook changes to reflect the saved name of the book.

Figure 2.19   File Structure Used for Saving Documents

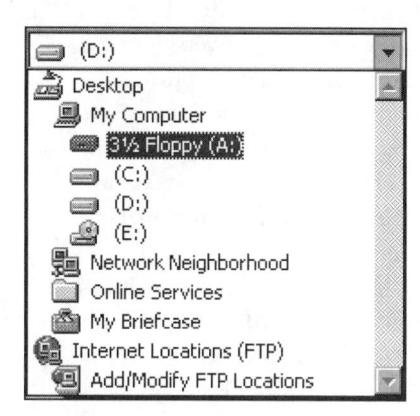

Figure 2.20   File Structure of the Student Data Disk

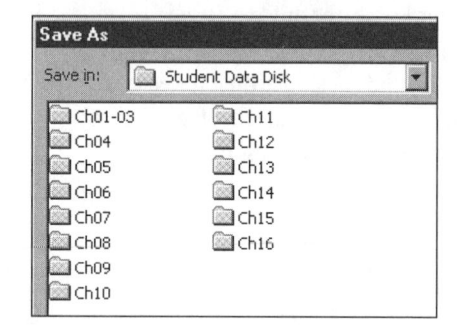

Use Save or Save As?

Clicking on the *Save button* will also save a book. If a book has not been saved before, clicking on the Save button opens the Save As dialog box. If a book has been saved previously, the Save button saves the document using the file name already assigned to it.

Frequent saving is important, especially when working on large, complicated worksheets. Power failures or errors can quickly destroy a worksheet. Saving often is protection from having to redo hours of work, and using the Save button makes it easy.

Power Users:

The keyboard command for a quick save is **Ctrl**+**S**.

Excel will not allow two workbooks to be saved under the same name. If a file name has already been used, a warning box like the one in Figure 2.21 opens, explaining that the name has already been used. Options to replace the old workbook or cancel the save request are given.

Figure 2.21 Replace File Warning Box

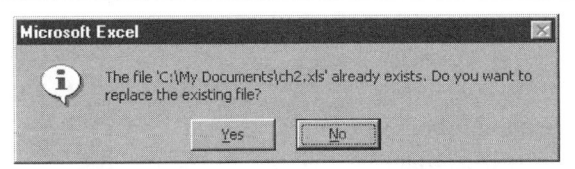

If the new workbook is to replace the previous one, click Yes; if not, click No. Then scroll to Save As from the File menu to save the workbook under a different name.

Save and Save As Commands

Both the *Save* and *Save As commands* save new Excel worksheets. Use Save As the first time a document is saved (when it is being named). Then use the Save command or the Save button when a document is changed or edited (all other times). Using this rule of thumb helps to avoid replacing a needed document.

Exercise 2.5   Saving a Workbook

You will save the workbook you have been working on through Exercise 2.4. If you are saving work to your Student Data Disk, be sure it is in the disk drive of your computer. This data disk will be used to access files and to save new ones.

1   From **File** select **Save As**.

2   If Office Assistant opens, select to **Use suggested format**. The **Save As** dialog box opens.

Determine the disk drive and subdirectory you will use to save your data.

3   If your disk is in drive A, be sure that drive is indicated in the **Save in** text box. Then select the **Ch01-03** subdirectory by double-clicking on it.

4   In the **File name** text box, key **Ch2 Exer**. Do not enter a period in the **File name** box. Even though the text box has a suggestion in it, it will be replaced by the new text because it was highlighted.

5   Click on the **Save** button.

6   The workbook stays open on the screen. The title bar displays the file name, **Ch2 Exer**.

7   Continue with Exercise 2.6.

Closing a Book

More than one file or book can be open at the same time. The names of all open files display in the Window menu. The active book is indicated by the checkmark in front of its title. Figure 2.22 shows the Window menu with Book1, Book4, and ch2 open. Ch2 is active and displayed on the screen, as is indicated by the checkmark.

Think of these open windows as a stack of papers on your desk; only the top one is seen and is active. To view the one below, you would move the top paper. To view another book, select it and it will move to the top and become visible on the screen.

All open books in the Window menu can be arranged so each is visible. However, only the top one is active and is identified by the colored title bar.

Figure 2.22   Window Menu

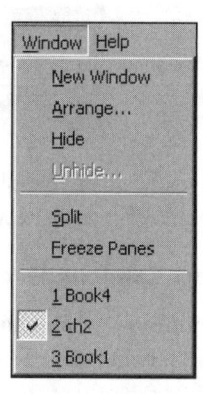

Figure 2.23   Open Excel Workbooks

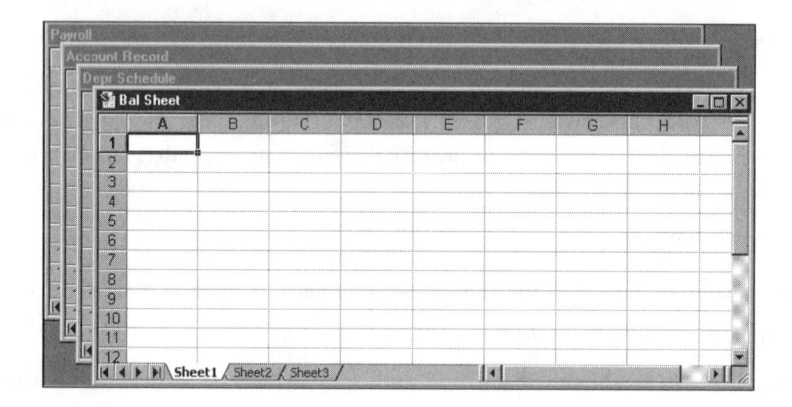

In Figure 2.23, four books are open. They are named Payroll, Account Record, Depr Schedule, and Bal Sheet. Bal Sheet is the active book, as is indicated by the colored title bar.

To close a book so it is no longer in the current memory of the computer, use the ***Close command*** from the File menu. The book closes but Excel remains open. To close all open books at the same time, hold down the Shift key before selecting the Close command in the File menu.

To end Excel, select the Exit command from the File menu. All books are closed when you select the Exit command. If any changes have occurred in the books since they were last saved, a dialog box will open for each book as a reminder to save it.

Power Users

To quit Excel, double-click on the Control-menu box at the left side of the title bar or the ***Close box*** at the right side of the title bar. These boxes are identified in Figure 2.24.

Figure 2.24   Control-menu and Close Boxes

Opening a New Book

There are several ways to create a new worksheet. When Excel is started, a new book automatically opens; one worksheet is displayed on the screen and is ready to accept data.

Clicking on the *New button* 🗋, located at the left side of the toolbar, opens a new book. In the File menu, the New command will also access a new book.

Power Users

The keyboard command **Ctrl**+**N** can be used to open to a new book.

Opening a Saved Book

Workbooks are stored so they may be edited and used again. Once a book has been designed, businesses often use the same style and information for other reports. For example, an old book may be updated so it includes information for the current month, or the information in the book may be used later to prepare a chart. Accessing a previously saved book is also called *retrieving the book*.

To open an existing book, select the Open command from the File menu. Locate and select the directory or disk in which the workbook was stored. The names of all the documents saved in this disk or directory are displayed in the list box. Double-click on the name of the book to open it, or click the selection once to highlight it and then click Open. Figure 2.25 shows the *Open dialog box* with available choices in the list box.

Figure 2.25   Open Dialog Box

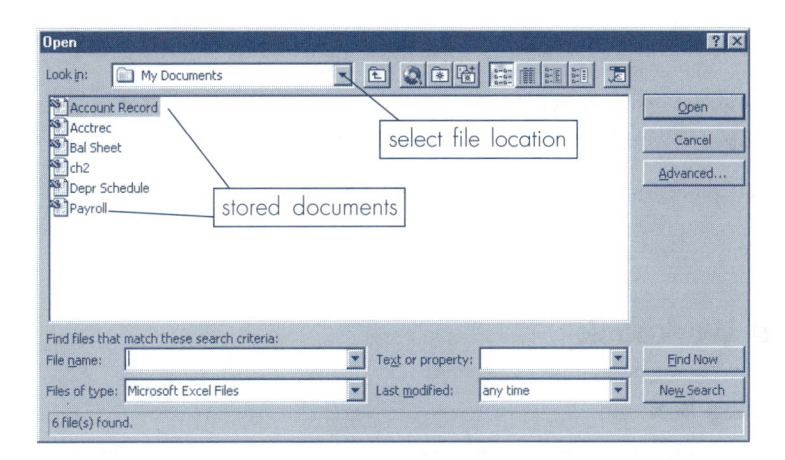

The Open dialog box may also be accessed by clicking on the *Open button* 📂 at the left end of the toolbar.

After the book has been opened, Excel remembers the name and file location of the book. As changes are made, Excel will save these changes to the original book by completing a quick save when the Save button 💾 is used.

Power Users
For a quick save, use the keyboard command **Ctrl**+**S**.

The difference between the File Open and File New commands can be confusing. When a workbook has already been saved, use the Open command from the File menu. When a *new workbook* will be created, select the New command from the File menu. When the text instructs you to "open a new workbook," select the New command from the File menu.

Exercise 2.6   Quitting Excel and Retrieving a Workbook

You will exit Excel and open the workbook you previously saved in Exercise 2.5.

1. From the **File** menu select **Exit**.
2. After Excel closes, open it again.
3. Excel opens to a new workbook titled **Book1**.
4. From the **File** menu, select **Open**.
5. Locate the workbook saved as **Ch2 Exer**. It will be in the disk/folder to which you saved it during the last exercise, probably in the **Ch01-03** folder.
6. Double-click on **Ch2 Exer** to open the saved book.

Move between books.

7. Click the New button. A new book will open on the screen, named **Book2**.
8. From the **Window** menu, select **Ch2 Exer**. This book is now active and visible. This is like having two pieces of paper in your hand and moving one on top of the other.
9. Leave Excel open with the **Ch2 Exer** book on the screen.
10. Continue with Exercise 2.7.

Printing a Workbook

The Print Dialog Box

The Print command is accessed in the File menu or by using the *Print button* on the Standard toolbar. Choosing Print from the file menu opens the *Print dialog box* shown in Figure 2.26.

Figure 2.26   Print Dialog Box

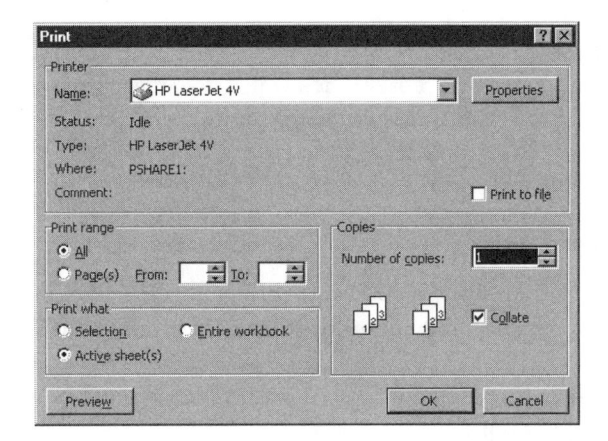

The selected printer is displayed in the dialog box. This illustration shows the HP LaserJet 4V printer. If a different printer is available in the classroom, its name will appear in this dialog box.

The Print dialog box may also be used to instruct Excel how many copies or what portion of the workbook to print. Click OK to print the worksheet.

Power Users

The keyboard command to print is **Ctrl**+**P**.

Time Saver

The **OK** button in the **Print** dialog box is the default button; it can be executed by clicking on it or pressing **Enter** on the keyboard.

Additional information on printing is found in Chapter 8.

Exercise 2.7   Printing a Workbook

You will print the workbook used in Exercise 2.6.

1 Open workbook **Ch2 Exer** if it is not already open.

2 From the **File** menu, select **Print**. The **Print** dialog box opens on the screen. Click **OK**.

Chapter 2 Creating a Worksheet

3 Retrieve the printed document from the printer.

4 At the top of the worksheet, write "Ch 2, Exercise 7, first print."

5 Click the Print button and retrieve the printed document from the printer. At the top of the worksheet, write "Ch 2, Exercise 7, second print."

6 Continue with Exercise 2.8.

A Brief Look at Page Setup

Excel provides flexibility in the way a workbook is printed on the page. Some options are listed in the *Page Setup dialog box*, shown in Figure 2.27, which is accessed by executing the Page Setup command from the File menu.

Most of the information about the Page Setup dialog box will be given in Chapter 8; at this time we will consider only how to change margins and add a header or footer.

Changing the width of the *margins* changes the amount of white space on the sides of the printed worksheet. Across the top of the Page Setup dialog box are four tabs labeled Page, Margins, Header/Footer, and Sheet. Click on the Margins tab to open the Margins section, shown in Figure 2.28.

Figure 2.27   Page Setup Dialog Box

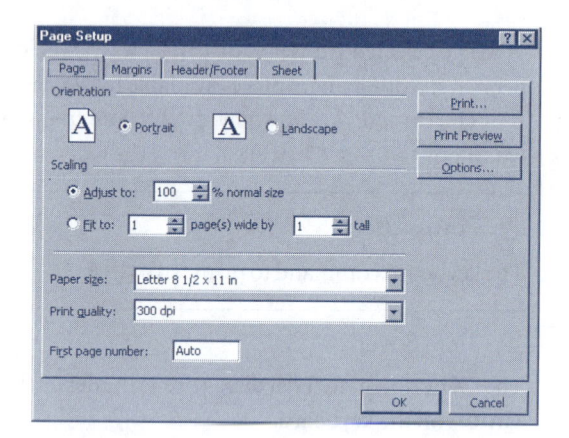

Figure 2.28   Margins Tab in Page Setup Dialog Box

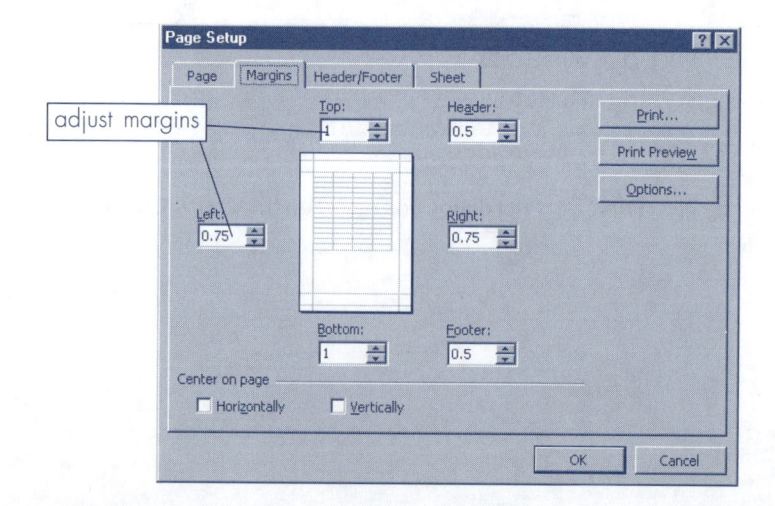

Excel uses preset (default) 1" margins at the top and bottom of the page and .75" (¾") on the sides. These margin settings are listed at the edges of the sample document. Excel defaults to letter size (8½" by 11") paper with the short side as the top of the paper (portrait style).

The arrows beside each margin measurement can be used to adjust margins in .25" (¼") increments. If you need to enter smaller units for margins, key a new margin setting in the text box. The worksheet margins are adjusted on the page when the Page Setup dialog box is closed. To make changes in the Page Setup dialog box, highlight a text box and key in the correct information or click the arrows. The Tab key can be used to move between areas.

To save a workbook so it can be recalled and edited, it is necessary to know the file name and the saved location of the workbook. The file name is the saved name of the workbook; it can be printed on every worksheet page by using the Header/Footer tab located in the Page Setup dialog box, shown in Figure 2.29. Printing the file name on a worksheet helps identify it so it will be easy to locate later.

Figure 2.29   Header/Footer Tab in Page Setup Dialog Box

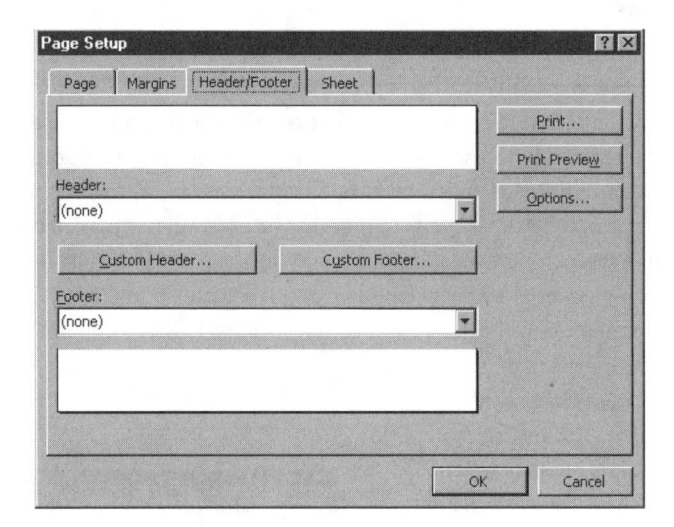

A *header* prints specified information at the top of every page; a *footer* prints specified information at the bottom of the page. The header information is entered at the top of the dialog box; the footer information at the bottom. The white area displays the current header and footer. Just below this display box is a text box titled Header, which is followed by a down arrow. Click on the arrow to access some built-in choices, as shown in Figure 2.30.

Figure 2.30   Header Choices for Windows

```
Header:
(none)
─────────────
(none)
Page 1
Page 1 of ?            header selection arrow
Sheet1
Confidential, 3/21/97, Page 1
ch2
```

Selecting one of these choices displays it in the header display area. The active scroll bar to the right of the selections indicates that more choices are available. In addition to the page number, selections include the file name and date.

Using Print Preview

A miniature picture of the worksheet may be viewed in ***Print Preview***. There are three ways to access Print Preview. One way is to use the Print Preview command in the File menu. Print Preview can also be accessed by clicking Print Preview in the Page Setup dialog box. You may also use the ***Print Preview button*** on the Standard toolbar. When Print Preview is selected, a reduced version of the worksheet opens on the screen. This helps in determining the placement of the worksheet on the page, the exact width of the columns, etc. Adjustments to margin and column widths can be made in Print Preview.

When Print Preview is active, a toolbar opens across the top of the page. The toolbar is used to access several dialog boxes so format changes can be made while the worksheet is fully visible on the screen. When Margins is selected, the Print Preview window looks like Figure 2.31.

Although the purpose of Print Preview is to provide a full view of the worksheet in order to make some formatting changes, it is possible to enlarge a section of the sheet so it can be read and edited. When the mouse pointer is moved onto the sheet, it changes to a magnifying glass. Move the magnifying glass indicator to the part of the worksheet you want to read and click the mouse; the sheet will enlarge so you can read the spot where you placed the magnifying glass. To return to full-page view, click again in the worksheet.

Figure 2.31   Print Preview

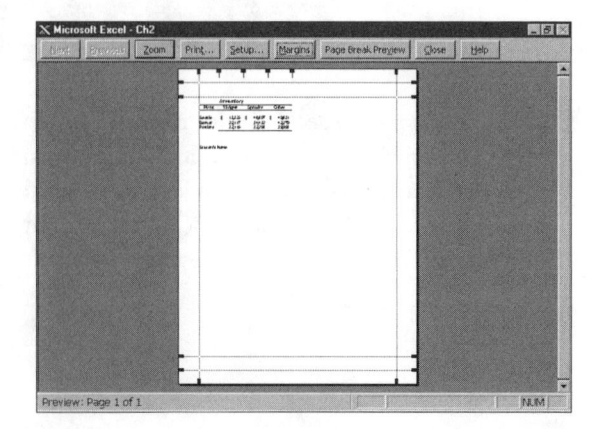

To print directly from Print Preview, click the Print button to open the Print dialog box.

Margins and column widths may be adjusted in Print Preview. To display the margins in Print Preview, click on the Margins button in the Print Preview toolbar. This displays the ***margin handles*** located at the top and bottom of the page and the ***column handles*** located at the top of the worksheet (Figure 2.32). The margin and column handles are used to adjust the margin and column widths in the Print Preview window. When the cursor is placed over one of the margin or column handles, the mouse takes the shape of a double-headed arrow.

Figure 2.32   Margin Handles in Print Preview

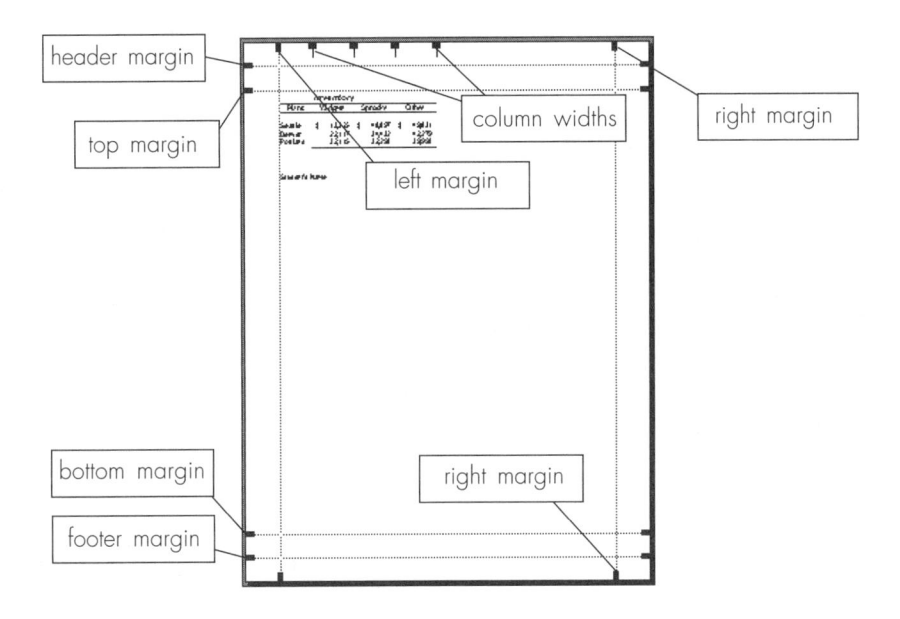

The margin handles at the left and at the right of the screen adjust the top and bottom margins and the placement of headers and footers. The handles at the top and bottom adjust the right and left margins, as shown in Figure 2.32.

To adjust margins, click on the margin or header/footer handle and drag the mouse. The width of the margin displays in the status bar at the bottom left of the screen, as shown in Figure 2.33. The measurement disappears when the mouse button is released.

Figure 2.33   Print Preview Status Bar

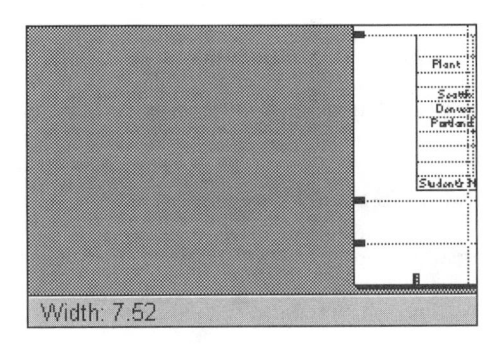

Column widths are changed using the column handles, shown in Figure 2.34. Move the mouse pointer to the column handle; it changes to a double-headed arrow. Then click the mouse and drag the column handle to the desired column width. The status bar displays the width of the column as the handle is moved, and a dotted line (the move line) appears onscreen to show the new placement.

Figure 2.34   Column Guides in Print Preview

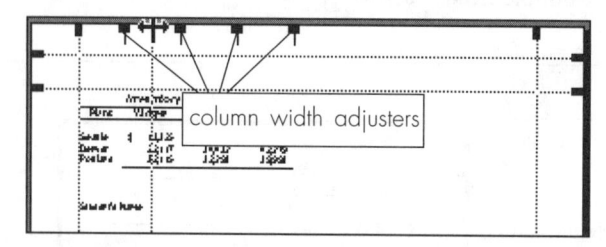

To remove the column and margin handles from the screen, click on the Margins button.

To view the next page, click Next in the toolbar. To view the previous page, click Previous. If a choice is dimmed in the toolbar, it is not currently available.

For larger worksheets, use the scroll bars along the right edge to view additional pages. As the screen scrolls through the worksheet, the current page numbers display in the status bar.

The Setup button opens the Page Setup dialog box (discussed in Chapter 8). Page breaks can be adjusted with Page Break Preview. Help can also be accessed from Print Preview. The Close button is used to return to the regular worksheet window.

Exercise 2.8   Editing and Printing a Workbook

You will change the margins on the worksheet used in Exercise 2.7 and print from the Print Preview window. Be sure the Ch2 Exer worksheet is open.

1   From **File** select **Page Setup**.

2   In the **Page Setup** dialog box, click on the **Margins** tab. Set a top and bottom margin of 2". (Click in the arrow by the text box until you reach **2**.) Set a left and right margin of 1.5".

3   Click on the **Header/Footer** tab of the dialog box.

4   Click on the arrow by the **Header** text box, then click on the file name, **Ch2 Exer**.

5   Click on the **Print Preview** button of the dialog box (on the right side).

6   Click on **Margins** to see the margin and column handles.

7   Move the mouse to the worksheet area. The mouse takes the shape of a magnifying glass. Click an area in the worksheet to enlarge it.

8   Click again to return the worksheet to full-page view.

9   Move the mouse to any margin handle to see the double-headed arrow shape.

10 Move the mouse to the column width handle. A double-headed arrow appears.

11 Click on the **Print** button at the top of the screen. The **Print** dialog box opens. Click **OK**.

12 Retrieve the document from the printer. At the top of the worksheet, write "Chapter 2, Exercise 8."

13 Click on the Save button 🖫 to quickly save the changes made in the workbook.

14 End the Excel program if you are not going to continue working at the computer. From the **File** menu, select **Exit**.

Summary

- Text automatically aligns at the left side of the cell and numbers automatically align at the right side of the cell.
- As information is entered into a cell, the entry is displayed in the cell and in the formula bar.
- Errors are corrected in the cell or in the formula bar.
- An entry is complete when the formula bar displays only the cell reference.
- To complete an entry and move down one cell, press the Enter key.
- To complete an entry and move to the right one cell, press the Tab key.
- To complete an entry and remain in the same cell, click the Enter box ✓ in the active formula bar.
- Use the numeric keypad to enter numbers.
- A default is a preset choice built into the software.
- Changing the way a worksheet looks is called formatting a worksheet.
- Simple formatting can be done with the toolbars.
- Alignment refers to the location of text within a cell in relation to its borders.
- Borders are horizontal and vertical lines used for emphasis and style.
- Numbers may be displayed in many ways. Some changes to number formatting can be made in the Formatting toolbar.
- Columns can be increased or decreased in size by clicking on the line between the column headings and dragging the mouse to a new size.
- In a column of money amounts, the dollar sign ($) is used only in the first entry of the column and in the total.
- To save a new workbook, select Save As from the File menu.
- When Save is selected, Office Assistant opens and suggests a format for saving work.
- To make intermediate saves as you create a workbook, select Save from the File menu or use the Save button 🖫 in the toolbar. Using the shortcut Ctrl+S also saves work.
- Closing the workbook removes it from the memory of the computer (and the screen) but does not quit Excel.
- Moving between open workbooks is done by accessing the Window menu.
- When more than one workbook is open, the active workbook is identified by its colored title bar.
- To open a new workbook, use the New command from the File menu or click on the New button 🗋.
- Saved workbooks may be retrieved for later use. From File, select Open or click the Open button 📂 in the toolbar. The Open dialog box shows accessible saved workbooks.
- To print the workbook, select the Print command from the File menu or click the Print button 🖨 in the toolbar.

- The Margins tab of the Page Setup dialog box is used to change the margins of the workbook.
- Headers print at the top of every page; footers print at the bottom. The settings can be changed in the Header/Footer tab of the Page Setup dialog box.
- Print Preview shows the full worksheet prior to printing. Changes in margins and column widths may be made from Print Preview.

Important Terminology

active book	default	new workbook
alignment	Enter box	number format buttons
alignment buttons	Enter key	numeric keypad
bold	file name	Open button
Bold button	font	Open dialog box
book	footer	Page Setup dialog box
Borders palette	format	Percent Style button
borders	Formatting toolbar	Print button
Borders button	General number format	Print dialog box
Cancel box	header	Print Preview
center alignment	Increase Decimal button	Print Preview button
Center Align button	insertion point	retrieve a book
Close box	Italic button	right alignment
Close command	italics	Right Align button
column handles	label	Save button
Comma Style button	left alignment	Save command
complete an entry	Left Align button	Save As command
Currency format	margin handles	text
Currency Style button	margins	Underline button
Decrease Decimal button	New button	

Buttons to Know

Study Questions

True-False

Place a T in the space if the statement is true; place an F if the statement is false.

_____ 1. Text automatically aligns at the left and numbers automatically align at the right of the cell.
_____ 2. The formula bar is active at all times.
_____ 3. Double-click in a cell to edit its contents.
_____ 4. When an entry is complete, the formula bar is active and the Enter ✓ and Cancel ✗ boxes are visible.
_____ 5. Formatting is used to change the data contents of a cell.
_____ 6. Alignment refers to the type size used in a worksheet's title.
_____ 7. To underline the entire width of a cell, use the Borders palette.
_____ 8. The Borders palette is used to change the placement of a line around a cell.
_____ 9. Numbers may be entered on the numeric keypad or by using the top row of the alphabetic keyboard.
_____ 10. When numbers are formatted, dollar signs and commas may be added to the numbers in a range of cells.
_____ 11. In a column of money amounts, a dollar sign ($) is included in every cell.
_____ 12. If a number is too long for a cell, the width automatically adjusts to fit the entry.
_____ 13. When saving a worksheet, enter the name to be saved in the File name section of the Save As dialog box.
_____ 14. No two files may be saved using the same name.
_____ 15. When a worksheet is closed, it is erased.
_____ 16. To end Excel, select Close from the File menu.
_____ 17. To retrieve a worksheet, use the New command from the File menu.
_____ 18. To print a document, select the Print command in the Format menu.
_____ 19. A footer cannot be changed.
_____ 20. To change margins, use the Page Setup dialog box.
_____ 21. The file name is the name of the subdirectory (folder) where the worksheet will be stored.
_____ 22. To add a border, access the Borders palette from the File menu.
_____ 23. Print Preview allows you to see how a worksheet will look on the printed page.
_____ 24. Margins and column widths may be adjusted in Print Preview.
_____ 25. The width of a cell cannot be changed.
_____ 26. A header is the first line of a worksheet, usually entered in cell A1.
_____ 27. When saving a document, Office Assistant suggests a format. Accepting the suggestions automatically saves the document to the A drive.
_____ 28. Printing the file name on a worksheet is useful when the worksheet needs to be edited.

Fill-In

Place the word in the space that correctly completes the statement.

1. The ✓ is used to _____ an entry.
2. The Name box of the _____ toolbar displays the reference of the active cell.

3. If an entry is edited incorrectly and the original entry is desired, click in the _____ box in the formula bar to return to the original contents to the cell.
4. Changing the appearance of a worksheet is called _____ .
5. The _____ is the saved name of a workbook.
6. The **B** button is the _____ button.
7. The *I* button is the _____ button.
8. Using the ▤ button aligns text from the _____ .
9. Using the ▤ button aligns text from the _____ .
10. Using the ▤ button aligns text from the _____ .
11. Use the _____ menu to move between several open workbooks.
12. To save a new workbook, use the _____ command from the File menu.
13. The 🖫 button is the _____ button, used to do a quick save of a worksheet.
14. When several worksheets are open, the _____ worksheet has a solid colored title bar, indicating it is active.
15. A _____ prints at the top of every page of a workbook.
16. Reopening an existing workbook so it can be edited is called _____ the workbook.
17. To print the saved name of a worksheet at the top on every page, select the Header/Footer tab in the _____ dialog box.
18. Use the ⬚ button to _____ the number of decimals in a worksheet.
19. Use the ⬚ button to _____ the number of decimals in a worksheet.
20. To open to a blank workbook and begin a new worksheet, use the _____ command from the File menu.
21. The 📂 button is used to _____ a workbook.
22. The ▯ button is used to open to a _____ workbook.
23. The 🖨 button is used to _____ a workbook.
24. The 🔍 button is used to _____ a worksheet.
25. To _____ an indent within a cell, use the ⬚ button.
26. To _____ an indent within a cell, use the ⬚ button.

Assignments

Assignment 2.1

You will enter text and numbers into a worksheet that will be saved and printed. This worksheet summarizes the sales of different types of merchandise.

Instructions for assignments and exercises are numbered in the order in which they must be completed. Each numbered instruction gives a general instruction; the bulleted instructions that follow provide specific instructions.

1. Open Excel to a new worksheet. If Excel is already open, click on the New button ▯ in the toolbar.

2. Enter the following data:

	A	B
1	Merchandise	Sales
2		
3	Sheets	340
4	Towels	530
5	Rugs	275
6	Blinds	620
7	Pillows	200
8		
9	Total	

3. In cell A12, enter your name. Double-click on the top border of the active cell to activate the cell at the top of the range.
4. Format the worksheet.
   - Format the row titles (cells A1 and B1) for bold text and center alignment.
   - You may need to adjust column widths so all data will fit.
5. Save the worksheet. It is important to save your work often.
   - From the **File** menu, select **Save As**.
   - Accept the suggestion of Office Assistant if it is activated.
   - Check the path to be sure you will be saving to the **Ch01-03** subdirectory on your Student Data Disk.
   - In the **File name** text box, type **Assig 2-1**. Click **Save**.
6. Change the way numbers are displayed.
   - Format cells B3 and B9 for currency. Nothing happens in cell B9 because there is not yet a number in the cell. When a number is entered, it will be formatted for currency.
   - Format the range B4:B7 for commas.
7. Add underlines to cells.
   - Underline cell B7. (Click on the Bottom Border button .)
   - Select cell B9. Click on the down arrow by the Borders button to access the Borders palette and select the Double Underline button .
8. Place your name on the worksheet.
   - Double-click in cell A12 to edit it. Position the cursor in front of your name.
   - Key **Prepared by**. The entry will be longer than the cell width and will extend into the next column. Press **Enter**.

Your worksheet should look like this:

	A	B
1	Merchandise	Sales
2		
3	Sheets	$ 340.00
4	Towels	530.00
5	Rugs	275.00
6	Blinds	620.00
7	Pillows	200.00
8		
9	Total	
10		
11		
12	Prepared by Student's Name	
13		

9. Make changes in Page Setup.
   - In **Page Setup**, change the top and left margin margins to 2.5".
   - Click in the **Header/Footer** tab. Select a header that displays the file name (**Assig 2-1**).
   - Close the **Page Setup** dialog box.
10. Click on the Save button in the toolbar to do a quick save. This saves changes made to the worksheet.
11. Print the worksheet.

Assignment 2.2

You will create a worksheet, change margins, and print the worksheet from Print Preview.

Instructions are numbered in the order in which they will be completed. Specific instructions are given for entering and formatting the worksheet; however, you will need to recall specific information to complete the worksheet.

1. Open to a new worksheet and enter the data shown in the following illustration. Format as shown:

	A	B
1	Student's Name	
2		
3	Toy	Number
4	Bicycles	183
5	Dolls	537
6	Games	472
7	Trucks	312
8	Books	718
9	Models	1010
10	Blocks	487

2. Save the worksheet as **Assig 2-2** to the **Ch01-03** folder of your data disk.
3. Change the header.
   - Access the **Header/Footer** section of the **Page Setup** dialog box.
   - Change the header to include the file name. Then click on **Print Preview**.
4. Make changes using Print Preview.
   - Click on the **Margins** button in the toolbar if the margin lines are not visible.
   - Select the margin icon at the top of the screen that is used to adjust the top margin (shown below). Hold down the mouse button and drag to *about* 1.5". Read the status bar (at the bottom left of the screen) to determine exact width. This leaves a top margin of about 1.5". Because of monitor size, type styles, and other factors, your display may not show *exactly* 1.5". Get as close to 1.5" as possible.

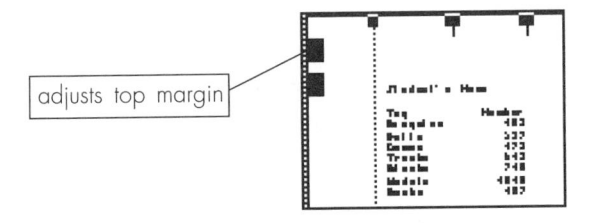

adjusts top margin

- Move to the margin icon on the top-left side of the screen that adjusts the left margin (see illustration). Click and drag to 2.5"; check the width in the status bar for the left margin.

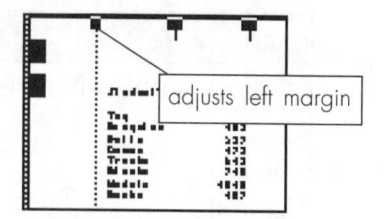

- Print the worksheet from Print Preview.
5. Complete a quick save.

Assignment 2.3

You will create and format a worksheet that summarizes the expenses of a business trip.
1. Open to a new worksheet and enter the following information. Replace **Student's Name** with your name.

	A	B
1	Student's Name	
2	Trip Expenses	
3		
4	Expense	Amount
5	Lodging	250
6	Food	203.75
7	Tips	43.45
8	Air Fare	228.75
9	Taxi	33.8
10	Other	21.6

2. Format the worksheet.
   - Format the two-line title (in rows 1 and 2) for bold and italic.
   - Format the column labels for bold and center alignment.
   - Format the numbers correctly for currency. Remember to place the dollar sign ($) in the first line only.
3. Adjust the margins and column widths using Print Preview. Try to place the worksheet so it is near the center of the page.
4. Place the file name in the header.
5. Save the worksheet as **Assig 2-3**. Be sure to save it in the **Ch01-03** subdirectory.
6. Print the worksheet. (Use the Print button.)

Assignment 2.4

A small food store has prepared an inventory. They have asked you to enter the inventory in an Excel worksheet, and to then format and print the worksheet.

1. Open to a new workbook. Create the worksheet in the following illustration. Format as shown.

	A	B
1	Grocers Inc.	
2	Food	1997
3		
4	Bakery	2,580.00
5	Canned Goods	1,875.00
6	Cereal	2,280.00
7	Dairy	995.00
8	Frozen Food	2,091.00
9	Produce	1,578.00 ← single underline

2. Enter your name in cell A13.
3. Adjust the columns so all text fits, if needed.
4. Adjust the margins to 2.5" at each side and 2" at the top.
5. Place the file name in the header.
6. Save the worksheet as **Assig 2-4** in the **Ch01-03** folder and print the sheet.

Assignment 2.5

Your instructor has asked you to create a worksheet that will be used for determining students' grades. You will format and print the worksheet.

In this worksheet, the test scores for a class are summarized for each student.

1. Set up a new worksheet like the following example:

	A	B	C	D	E
1	First Quarter Test Scores				
2					
3	Student	Test 1	Test 2	Test 3	Total
4	DeBord	87	92	75	
5	Douglas	83	85	98	
6	Gilliam	86	93	85	
7	Heider	90	75	75	
8	Holm	85	62	82	
9	McNerney	96	95	92	
10	Reardon	92	83	81	
11	Schoesler	87	90	93	
12	Wilhite	75	87	100	
13	Wilson	82	91	79	

2. Complete the worksheet.
   - Enter your name in cell A14. Enter your test scores: **98**, **99**, and **100**.
   - In cell A7, replace **Heider** with your instructor's name.
3. Save the worksheet as **Assig 2-5** in the **Ch01-03** folder.
4. Change the way the worksheet will be printed.
   - Place the file name in the header.
   - In Print Preview, change the widths of columns B, C, and D to about **6.0**. Refer to the width in the status bar. Change column A so each individual's entire name fits within the cell.
   - Change the margins so the worksheet is centered on the page. (Don't try to be exact at this time!)
5. Save and print the worksheet.

Assignment 2.6

You have been asked to create a worksheet that summarizes magazine sales for the year. You will also format and print the worksheet. You will use this completed worksheet in Assignment 3.6.

1. Set up a new worksheet like the following example:

	A	B	C	D	E	F
1	Trista's Publishing Company					
2						
3		Mac's Big Magazine	Great Housekeeping	Sunrise	Great Food	Total
4						
5	1st Qtr	3300	3847	4293	2380	
6	2nd Qtr	4503	5834	5837	2384	
7	3rd Qtr	5725	4853	4859	3382	
8	4th Qtr	4735	5928	4985	3756	
9	Total					

2. Enter your name at the bottom of the worksheet.
3. Adjust the column widths so all text fits in the cells.
4. Place the file name in the header.
5. Use Print Preview to adjust the placement of the worksheet.
6. Save the worksheet as **Assig 2-6** in the **Ch01-03** folder.
7. Print the worksheet.

Case Problem 2

You have been asked to prepare a report for the Squire Shoe Shop that shows shoe sales for the first quarter of this year.

Squire Shoe Shop sells four different types of shoes: dress shoes, walking shoes, sports shoes, and casual shoes. Sales in dollars are as follows:

Dress shoes:	January, $287.85; February, $300.28; March, $299.75.
Walking shoes:	January, $366.20; February, $408.16; March, $387.50.
Sports shoes:	January, $297.30; February, $375.25; March, $348.24.
Casual shoes:	January, $338.56; February, $583.26; March, $491.25.

You have decided to prepare a spreadsheet that will show this information in a way that is easy to see and understand. Place this information on an Excel worksheet in a style and format of your choice. Be sure that the numbers are correctly formatted for currency in the worksheet. Check that each amount is labeled.

It is important to know who prepared any worksheet. In a cell at the bottom of the worksheet key **Prepared by** and then your name. Save this worksheet as **Case 2** and be sure the file name prints on the worksheet.

Chapter 3

Entering Basic Formulas

Objectives
1. Enter formulas using the keying and the pointing methods.
2. Enter addition formulas using AutoSum.
3. Print a worksheet so that it displays formulas.
4. Use automatic features to enter subtotals and grand totals.
5. Recognize error messages.
6. Plan the design of a worksheet.

Introduction

Electronic spreadsheets effectively arrange data in columns and rows. However, the real advantage of spreadsheet software is its ability to store formulas that use cell contents to perform calculations. When changes are made to data, Excel automatically recalculates the results, saving time in checking, rechecking, and proofreading long lists of numbers. Excel's computations are always accurate.

Printing a worksheet's formulas helps facilitate the proofreading process. It is often easier to see relationships and make corrections on paper than on a computer screen.

This chapter will explain how to enter and edit data to ensure its accuracy and how to create formulas that use this data. Included will be steps to printing a worksheet with the formulas displayed.

Note that at the end of this chapter you may delete the Ch01-03 folder from your Student Data Disk.

Introduction to Formulas

About Formulas

Worksheets contain words and numbers entered in cells. Formulas are entered to perform mathematical operations using the data in the cells. As in math, a *formula* is a sequence of instructions used to complete a mathematical problem. An amount entered in a cell is a value that doesn't change. A formula in a cell also remains the same, but the results will change if any of the values in the formula change.

For instance, consider the formula A + B. If A represents 7 and B represents 5, the result of the formula is 12. If the value of A changes from 7 to 8, the result of A + B becomes 13 (8 + 5). The formula remained the same (A + B) but the result of the formula changed because the variable (A) changed.

Entering Numbers in Excel

Excel automatically aligns numbers at the right as they are entered. Key a decimal point when entering numbers. Other symbols used in numbers, such as the comma or dollar sign, can be added later by formatting an entire group of numbers at the same time.

Making Calculations

The speed and 100 percent accuracy of making calculations with a computer are advantages of using an electronic spreadsheet. A formula instructs Excel what numbers to use and what calculation to make. After a formula is entered, the results of the calculation appear almost instantly in the cell. The symbols used in these formulas, called *arithmetic operators*, are shown in Figure 3.1.

Figure 3.1   Arithmetic Operators

Arithmetic Operator	Action Excel Will Take
+	Add
-	Subtract
*	Multiply
/	Divide

An Excel formula begins with an equal (=) sign. When the = sign is entered, Excel changes to *Enter mode*, which is indicated in the status bar. The formula bar becomes active and the Cancel and Enter boxes appear in the formula bar. Figure 3.2 shows the active formula bar.

Figure 3.2   Buttons in Active Formula Bar

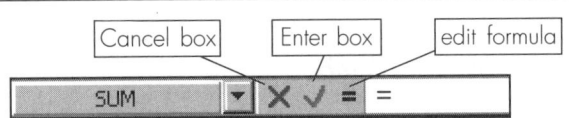

The chart in Figure 3.3 explains some basic formulas and mathematical operators used in Excel formulas.

Figure 3.3   Creating Formulas

Formula	Instructions for Excel
=10+12	Add 10 to 12
=12-10	Subtract 10 from 12
=10*12	Multiply 10 by 12
=12/6	Divide 12 by 6

When the formula entry is complete, calculations are performed and the results are almost instantly placed in the active cell. As a formula is entered, it displays both in the cell and in the entry area of the formula bar.

Figure 3.4 shows a simple formula as it is entered into a cell (the figure on the left) and after the entry has been completed (the figure on the right). As the formula is entered, the formula bar is active; the formula displays both in the entry area and in the active cell. After the entry has been completed, the formula bar is inactive; the result displays in the cell while the formula still displays in the entry area.

Chapter 3 Entering Basic Formulas

Figure 3.4 Entering a Formula

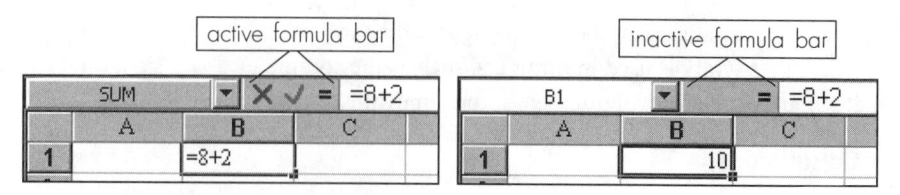

In a formula, the mathematical operations are performed in the same order as they are in algebra. Follow these rules when entering formulas:
- Instructions within parentheses are completed first.
- Multiplication and division are performed before addition and subtraction.
- Operations at the same level are completed from left to right.

The chart in Figure 3.5 shows how changing the placement of parentheses in a formula that uses the same numbers will obtain differing results.

Figure 3.5 Order of Operations

Formula	Result
=4*8+15/5-3	32
=(4*8)+15/(5-3)	39.5
=4*(8+15)/5-3	15.4
=(4*8+15)/5-3	6.4
=4*(8+15/(5-3))	62

Exercise 3.1   Calculating Numbers

You will write Excel formulas and then use Excel as a calculator.
Section A   Compete this section without using the computer.

1 Write the formula Excel will use to add 360, 382, 953, and 923.

2 Write the formula Excel will use to subtract 285 from 902.

3 Write the formula Excel will use to multiply 17 by 36 by 2.

4 Write the formula Excel will use to divide 147 by 13.

5 Write the formula Excel will use to add 36 to the result of 25 divided by 5.

6 Write the formula Excel will use to divide the sum of 36 and 25 by 5.

7 Write the formula Excel will use to multiply 3 by 5 and then divide the product by 2. To that answer, add 8.

_____

8 Write the formula Excel will use to add 10 to the product of 26 and 8; then add 4 and subtract 34.

_____

Now use these formulas to complete Section B.

Section B   You will use the computer to complete this section of the exercise.

9 Open Excel to a new workbook.

10 In cell B1, enter the formula you wrote in number 1. (It should be **=360+382+953+923**.) The numbers are shown in cell B1 as well as in the formula bar. Press **Enter** to complete the entry. The sum, **2618**, is in cell B1. Cell B2 is the active cell.

11 In cell B2, enter the formula you wrote for number 2. (It should be **=902-285**.) Press **Enter** to complete the entry. The amount, **617**, displays in cell B2. Cell B3 is the active cell.

12 In cell B3, enter the formula you wrote for number 3. (It should be **=17*36*2**.) Press **Enter** to complete the entry. The product, **1224**, displays in cell B3. Cell B4 is the active cell.

13 In cell B4, enter the formula you wrote for number 4. (It should be **=147/13**.) Press **Enter** to complete the entry. The amount, **11.3076923**, displays in cell B4. Your answer may show a different number of decimals. Cell B5 is the active cell.

14 In cell B5, enter the formula you wrote for number 5. (It should be **=36+25/5** or **=25/5+36**.) Press **Tab** to complete the entry. The amount, **41**, displays in cell B5. Cell C5 is the active cell.

15 In cell C5, enter the formula you wrote for number 6. (It should be **=(36+25)/5**.) Press **Tab** to complete the entry. The amount, **12.2**, displays in cell C5. The formulas in cells B5 and C5 are the same. Notice how the parentheses change the results. The active cell is D5.

16 In cell D5, enter the formula you wrote for number 7. (It should be **=3*5/2+8**.) With the mouse, click the Enter box ☑ in the formula bar. The amount, **15.5**, displays in cell D5. Cell D5 remains active.

17 In cell A8, enter the formula you wrote for number 8. (It should be **=10+26*8+4-34**.) Press **Tab** to complete the entry and move the active cell to B8. The result, **188**, displays in cell A8.

18 Print the worksheet.

19 Close the workbook without saving changes. From the **File** menu, select **Close**. A dialog box will open asking if you want to save changes. Select **No**.

Entering Formulas

Usually a formula will be entered using cell references rather than exact numbers. This links the formula to specific cells in the worksheet and provides speed and accuracy when editing the worksheet because if a number value is changed in a cell, the formula does not need to be changed.

Keying in Formulas

Let's start by entering simple numbers to see how Excel performs mathematical operations. The spreadsheet in Figure 3.6 shows a list of numbers in the range A1:A5. The illustration at the left shows the way a formula is entered into cell A6. As it is being entered, the formula is displayed both in the cell and in the entry area; the formula bar is active. In the illustration at the right, the result of the formula, 30, is shown in cell A6. The formula is displayed in the entry area of the active cell; the formula bar is inactive.

Figure 3.6   Cell Entry and Formula Bar

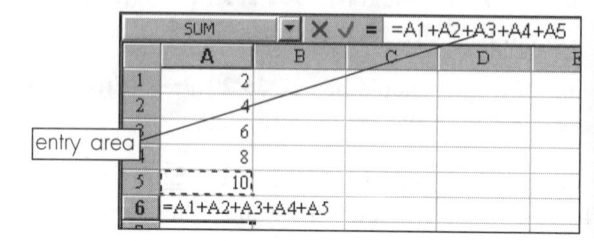

When any number in the range A1:A5 changes, the results of the formula will also change because the formula is linked to the cell contents. Figure 3.7 shows the result when cell A5 is changed from 10 to 20. The result changes, but the formula (displayed in the entry area) remains the same.

To multiply numbers, again use cell references to link the formula to the cells. Figure 3.8 illustrates multiplication using cell references.

Figure 3.7   Changes in a Result

Figure 3.8   Multiplying in Excel

Using a worksheet for an invoice and cash discount is shown in Figure 3.9. The formula in B5 multiplies the invoice amount by the discount rate. Because the formula is linked to the cells, the values entered in the cells are used to complete the multiplication.

Figure 3.9 Formula Using Cell References

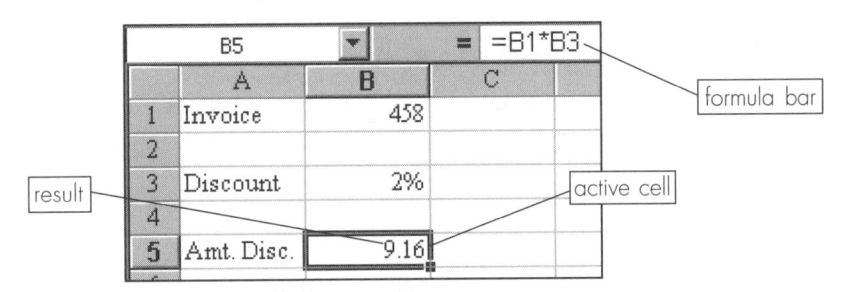

Figure 3.10 Changes in a Cell Affect Formula's Result

When a formula is linked to specific cells, altering the contents of a cell will change the result of the formula, as shown in Figure 3.10.

Figure 3.11 shows a change when the discount rate increases to 5%. While the formula does not change, the amount of the discount does. The advantage of using cell references is evident when changes are made.

Figure 3.11 Formula Remains Constant, Result Changes

All formulas are stored in Excel. If an error is made that Excel recognizes (usually in the way a formula is built), the computer will beep to alert the user that the formula is invalid. A warning box explaining the error may open on the screen. This allows a formula to be corrected before continuing with the worksheet.

If a formula is entered incorrectly but is still a valid formula, it will be stored and used as if it were correct, causing an error in the worksheet. It is important, therefore, to carefully proofread all formulas and data entered in a worksheet to ensure the total accuracy of the worksheet.

Remember, calculations will not be completed until the entry is completed with the Tab key, Enter key, or the *Enter box* .

Because Excel is so speedy and accurate, careful preparation of a worksheet is important. Plan the design of a worksheet before beginning work at the computer. Use cell references in formulas rather than the constant values and proofread the formulas carefully on the screen before completing them. While it is easy to make changes, a complex worksheet should be constructed accurately rather than edited later.

Editing a Formula

When a formula needs editing, double-click on the cell that contains the formula. A cell reference in a formula is color coded to correspond to the actual cell in the worksheet. This easily identifies the variables used in the formula to simplify proofreading and increase the accuracy of editing.

Exercise 3.2 Entering and Editing Formulas

You will enter amounts and formulas in worksheet cells and then make changes in the cell values to see how quickly Excel completes the new calculations.

1. Open a new workbook.

2. Enter the following information into the worksheet:

	A
1	15
2	3
3	20

3. In cell B1, enter the formula **=A1+A2+A3** and complete the entry. The result, **38**, displays in cell B1.

4. Double-click in cell B1. Notice how each cell reference in the formula is color coded to match that cell in the worksheet. Press **Enter**.

5. Change A2 to **7**. Complete the entry. The result in cell B1 also changes to reflect the new value for cell A2.

6. In cell B2, enter the formula **=A3-A2**. Complete the entry. The result, **13**, displays in cell B2.

7. Double-click in cell B2 to edit it. Notice how each cell reference in the formula is color coded to match that cell in the worksheet.

8. In cell A3, change the amount from **20** to **35**. Complete the entry. The values change in both cells B1 and B2 to reflect the new value for cell A3.

9. Close the document without saving it.

Creating Point-and-Click Formulas

Large worksheets may contain hundreds of formulas and thousands of data cells. Since the process of creating a worksheet requires a high degree of accuracy, cell references can be entered by using the mouse rather than keying them in. This is called the *point-and-click method* of entering a formula.

After keying the equal (=) sign, click the mouse in the cell which will be entered in the formula. The cell reference is shown in the entry area and a moving border, called a *marquee*, surrounds the selected cell and provides a visual reminder that the cell will be used in the formula. Figure 3.12 shows the marquee surrounding cell A1 while entering a formula in cell A4.

Figure 3.12   Creating a Formula—Cell A1 Entered in a Formula

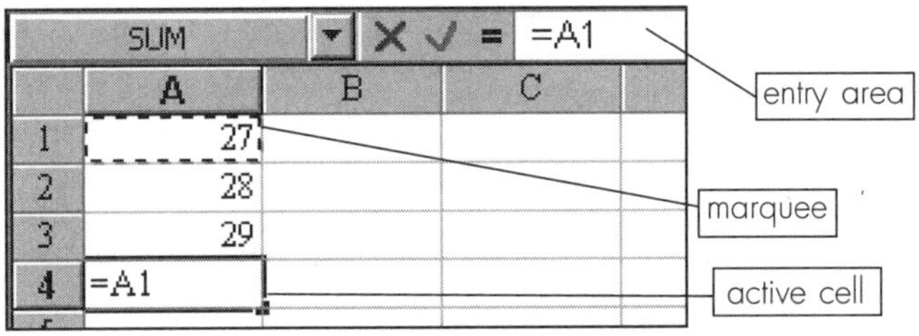

As additional cells are selected, Excel includes those references in the formula; an arithmetic operator (+, -, *, or /) must be entered between cell references.

After the formula is entered, complete it by pressing the Tab or Enter key on the keyboard, or click in the Enter box in the formula bar. Figure 3.13 shows the completed formula and its results.

Figure 3.13   Completed Formula

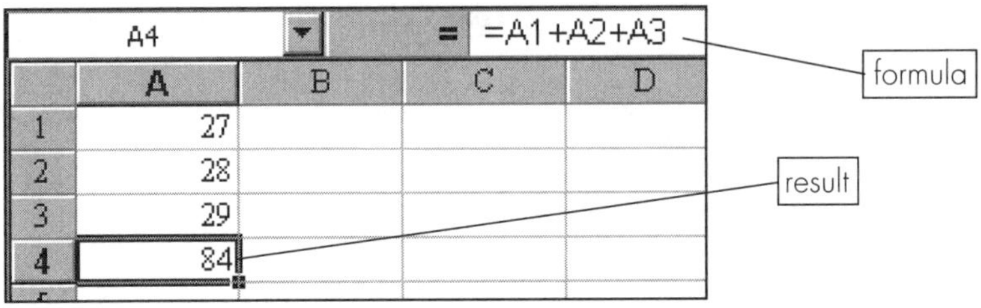

An entry can be erased by clicking in the *Cancel box* or by pressing the *Escape key* (Esc) on the keyboard. Corrections to a formula are made either in the cell or in the entry area of the formula bar.

Exercise 3.3   Using the Point-and-Click Method

You will create a worksheet using the point-and-click method to enter cell references. This worksheet summarizes the sales of three products in three different plant locations. The instructions are numbered. The words in italics tell you what the following set of numbered instructions will accomplish.

1   Open the workbook you saved as **Ch2 Exer** on your Student Data Disk.

2   Save the workbook as **Exer 3-3**. Since this is a new file name, be sure to select the **Save As** command from the **File** menu. Remember to save it to the **Ch01-03** folder on the Student Data Disk.

Enter formulas.

3   Click in cell E4 to make it active.

4   Key **=** then click in cell B4. The formula bar reads **=B4**. A marquee surrounds cell B4.

5. Key **+** then click in cell C4. The formula bar reads **=B4+C4**. A marquee surrounds cell C4.

6. Key **+** then click in cell D4. The formula bar reads **=B4+C4+D4**.

7. Press **Enter** to complete the entry. The total is displayed in cell E4. Cell E5 is active.

8. Use the point-and-click method to enter **=B5+C5+D5** in cell E5.

Correct an entry.

9. In cell E6, key **=** then click in cell B6. The formula bar reads **=B6**.

10. Enter **+** then click in cell B6 again. The formula bar reads **=B6+B6**.

11. You have made a mistake. Click on the Cancel box **X** in the formula bar. The formula is removed from the formula bar; cell E6 is still active.

12. Key **=** then click in cell B6.

13. Key **+** then click in cell C6. The formula bar reads **=B6+C6**.

14. Key **+** then click in cell D6. The formula bar reads **=B6+C6+D6**.

15. In the formula bar, click on the Enter box ✓ to complete the entry. The total is displayed in cell E6, and the formula displays in the formula bar. Cell E6 remains active.

16. Place a border at the bottom of cell E6.

Complete and print the worksheet.

17. In cell A7, enter **Total**. Format it for bold and center alignment.

18. In cell E7 key **=** then click in cell B7 and enter **+**. (Do not key the period.)

19. Click in cell B4. This was an error! Press the **Esc** key to cancel the formula.

20. With cell E7 still active, key the formula **=B7+C7+D7**.

21. Click on the Enter box ✓ in the formula bar. A **0** displays in cell E7. As formulas are entered into cells B7, C7, and D7, the amount in cell E7 will change.

22. In cell E2, key **Total**. Format it for bold and center alignment.

23. In cell B7 use the point-and-click method to enter the formula **=B4+B5+B6**. (Remember all formulas begin with an equal sign.)

24. In cell C7, use the point-and-click method to enter the formula **=C4+C5+C6**. Press **Tab**.

25. In cell D7, use the point-and-click method to enter the formula **=D4+D5+D6**.

26. Be sure row 7 is formatted for currency.

27. Place a double line at the bottom of the total range (B7:E7).

28 Place the file name in the header.

Your worksheet should look like this:

	A	B	C	D	E
1		***Inventory***			
2	Plant	Widgets	Sprocks	Cubes	Total
3					
4	Seattle	$ 13,325	$ 48,897	$ 49,831	$ 112,053
5	Denver	22,117	34,432	42,279	98,828
6	Portland	32,115	32,258	39,998	104,371
7	Total	$ 67,557	$ 115,587	$ 132,108	$ 315,252
8					
9					
10	Student's Name				

29 Do a quick save and print the worksheet.

Using AutoSum

Any adjacent range of cells can be added quickly by using *AutoSum*. The *AutoSum button* Σ is located on the Standard toolbar. AutoSum instructs Excel to add every cell in a range. The range of cells to be added may be either horizontal or vertical. For example, using AutoSum with the range A2:A5, the automatic formula to add cells is =SUM(A2:A5). The formula could also be entered without AutoSum as =A2+A3+A4+A5.

Refer to Figure 3.14. To enter a formula in cell D1, click on the cell and click AutoSum Σ. The adjacent range, A1:C1 is automatically selected as the sum range. A marquee surrounds the range.

Figure 3.14   Formula Built Using AutoSum Button

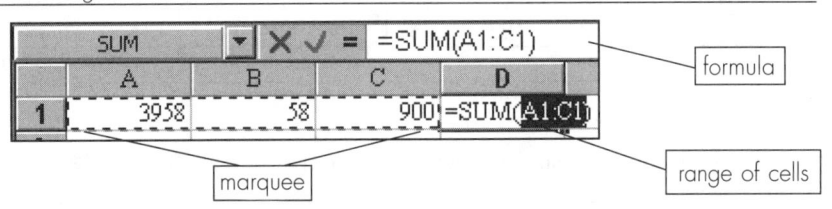

To extend a selected range of cells, click the mouse and drag it through the additional cells to be included in the range. The range in the formula will change to reflect the selected range.

Several AutoSum formulas may be entered in adjacent cells at the same time. In Figure 3.15, the sum of the rows is placed in column D. The range D1:D3 was selected and AutoSum Σ was clicked. Formulas are entered in column D to add the rows. This completed worksheet is illustrated in Figure 3.15, showing both the totals and the formulas used.

Chapter 3   Entering Basic Formulas

Figure 3.15   Using AutoSum to Add Rows

Totals

	A	B	C	D
1	25	30	33	88
2	26	31	34	91
3	27	32	35	94

Formulas

	A	B	C	D
1	25	30	33	=SUM(A1:C1)
2	26	31	34	=SUM(A2:C2)
3	27	32	35	=SUM(A3:C3)

To add the columns in the worksheet and place the totals in row 4, select the range A4:C4. Then click AutoSum [Σ]. Formulas are entered in row 4, as illustrated in Figure 3.16, which shows both totals and formulas.

Figure 3.16   Using AutoSum to Add Columns

Totals

	A	B	C
1	25	30	33
2	26	31	34
3	27	32	35
4	78	93	102

Formulas

	A	B	C
1	25	30	33
2	26	31	34
3	27	32	35
4	=SUM(A1:A3)	=SUM(B1:B3)	=SUM(C1:C3)

To add both rows and columns in one step, select the range A1:D4; this range includes both the column and the row needed for the totals. Using AutoSum [Σ], formulas are entered into both the row and the column in one step. Figure 3.17 shows the completed worksheet and its formulas.

Figure 3.17   Using AutoSum for Adding Rows and Columns

Totals

	A	B	C	D
1	25	30	33	88
2	26	31	34	91
3	27	32	35	94
4	78	93	102	273

Formulas

	A	B	C	D
1	25	30	33	=SUM(A1:C1)
2	26	31	34	=SUM(A2:C2)
3	27	32	35	=SUM(A3:C3)
4	=SUM(A1:A3)	=SUM(B1:B3)	=SUM(C1:C3)	=SUM(A4:C4)

Power Users

The keyboard command to enter an AutoSum formula is [Alt]+[Enter].

Exercise 3.4   Using AutoSum

A firm's first quarter sales report needs to be completed. You will complete the report several times using different methods to enter the AutoSum total.

1   Open the workbook saved as **Ch3 Ex4** from the Student Data Disk. Resave it as **Exer 3-4**.

Complete the totals in column E in the first worksheet.

2   Select cell E5 (January total). Click on AutoSum [Σ]. Excel selected the adjacent range of B5:D5. Because this is correct, press **Enter**.

3   Repeat using AutoSum for the February and March totals (E6:E7).

Complete the totals in row 8.

4   Click in cell B8. Click on AutoSum [Σ]. Excel selected the adjacent range of B5:B7.

5   Repeat the totals in row 8 using AutoSum [Σ].

Complete the second worksheet.

6   In the second worksheet, select the cells in row 19 where the totals are needed (B19:E19). Click AutoSum [Σ]. Totals for the columns are added with one click!

7   Select the cells in columnE where totals are needed (E16:E18); click AutoSum [Σ]. The worksheet is complete.

Complete the third worksheet.

8   In the third worksheet, select the range A26:E30, which includes the total row and column (four rows and four columns). Click AutoSum [Σ]. All totals are entered. Are the references correct?

9   You have three identical worksheets. Save and print the entire workbook.

Determining a Grand Total

A *grand total* is determined by adding individual totals. Using AutoSum makes this nearly automatic. Figure 3.18 shows a worksheet with data entered; totals are needed in rows 4 and 8 and the grand total (the total of rows 4 and 8) will be entered in row 9.

Figure 3.18   Completing a Worksheet

	A	B	C	D
1	Store A	Item 1	Item 2	Total
2	North	450	360	
3	South	835	755	
4	Total			
5	Store B			
6	North	725	920	
7	South	839	385	
8	Total			
9	Grand Total			

To complete the totals in row 4 and column D in one step, highlight the range B2:D4, then click AutoSum ∑. Then complete the totals in row 8 and column D in the same way. The worksheet now looks like Figure 3.19.

Figure 3.19 Totals Added for a Worksheet

	A	B	C	D
1	Store A	Item 1	Item 2	Total
2	North	450	360	810
3	South	835	755	1590
4	Total	1285	1115	2400
5	Store B			
6	North	725	920	1645
7	South	839	385	1224
8	Total	1564	1305	2869
9	Grand Total			

Next place the grand totals in row 9. Highlight the range B2:D8, which is the numerical data of the worksheet. Use AutoSum ∑, and the grand totals (the sum of the totals in row 4 and row 8) are entered into row 9. The completed worksheet is shown in Figure 3.20.

Figure 3.20 Using AutoSum for a Grand Total

	A	B	C	D
1	Store A	Item 1	Item 2	Total
2	North	450	360	810
3	South	835	755	1590
4	Total	1285	1115	2400
5	Store B			
6	North	725	920	1645
7	South	839	385	1224
8	Total	1564	1305	2869
9	Grand Total	2849	2420	5269

Figure 3.21 shows the formulas that were entered using AutoSum. Notice that the formula for the grand total in cell B9 reads =SUM(B8,B4), indicating it is the sum of cells B8 and B4. Compare the formulas in cells B8 and C8 with those in cells B9 and C9.

Figure 3.21 Viewing Formulas for Grand Total

	A	B	C	D
1	Store A	Item 1	Item 2	Total
2	North	450	360	=SUM(B2:C2)
3	South	835	755	=SUM(B3:C3)
4	Total	=SUM(B2:B3)	=SUM(C2:C3)	=SUM(B4:C4)
5	Store B			
6	North	725	920	=SUM(B6:C6)
7	South	839	385	=SUM(B7:C7)
8	Total	=SUM(B6:B7)	=SUM(C6:C7)	=SUM(B8:C8)
9	Grand Total	=SUM(B8,B4)	=SUM(C8,C4)	=SUM(B9:C9)

Using AutoSum is a speedy way to enter formulas, but careful proofreading remains essential. It is easy to accidentally include a cell that is not wanted in a formula.

Exercise 3.5 Adding a Grand Total

A firm's annual sales report needs to be completed. You will use AutoSum to complete the report.

1. Open workbook **Ch3 Ex5** from the **Ch01-03** folder on the Student Data Disk. Resave it as **Exer 3-5**.

2. Select the range B5:E8 and use AutoSum to add the range. Totals appear in row 8 and column E.

3. Select the nonadjacent ranges of the other three quarters: B11:E14, B17:E20, and B23:E26. (Use the **Ctrl** key to select nonadjacent ranges.) Click on the AutoSum button. All three ranges are added with only one mouse click.

Complete the grand total.

4. Highlight the worksheet range B5:E28.

5. Click on AutoSum. The totals appear in row 28. Each element in the formula is separated by commas, indicating the addition of separate cells. Check the accuracy of the formulas.

6. If totals are also included in column F, highlight the column then press **Delete** on the keyboard.

7. Increase cell widths if needed.

8. Save and print the worksheet. Write your name and **Ch3 Ex5** on the worksheet.

Adding Nonadjacent Ranges

AutoSum can also be used to add nonadjacent ranges. It is important to understand the way these formulas are written.

AutoSum uses cell ranges in its automated formula and an example of a written formula is =SUM(A1:A4). This instructs Excel to add every cell between A1 and A4. However, if nonadjacent cells are to be added, the cell references will be separated by a comma. The formula =SUM(A1, B2, C3) instructs Excel to add cells A1, B2, and C3. This formula could also be written =A1+B2+C3.

Both ranges and individual cell references can be used in a formula. The formula =SUM(A1:A4, B5:B6, C8) instructs Excel to add the two ranges to cell C8. This formula could also be written =A1+A2+A3+A4+B5+B6+C8.

The worksheet in Figure 3.22 will be used to illustrate this concept.

Figure 3.22 Using AutoSum for Nonadjacent Ranges

	A	B	C	D
1	Store A	Item 1	Item 2	Total
2	North	450	360	810
3	South	835	755	1590
4	Total	1285	1115	2400
5	Store B			
6	North	725	920	1645
7	South	839	385	1224
8	Total	1564	1305	2869
9	Grand Total	2849	2420	5269
10				
11				
12	Summary			
13		Item 1	Item 2	Total
14	Total North			
15	Total South			

A summary is needed for the total items for North and South. Item 1 from both stores needs to be added together with the total placed in cell B14. Likewise, the total for Item 2 for both North and South needs to be calculated. Figure 3.23 shows the completed worksheet; the second illustration displays the formulas used.

Figure 3.23   Using AutoSum for Nonadjacent Cells

	A	B	C	D
1	Store A	Item 1	Item 2	Total
2	North	450	360	810
3	South	835	755	1590
4	Total	1285	1115	2400
5	Store B			
6	North	725	920	1645
7	South	839	385	1224
8	Total	1564	1305	2869
9	Grand Total	2849	2420	5269
10				
11				
12	Summary			
13		Item 1	Item 2	Total
14	Total North	1175	1280	2455
15	Total South	1674	1140	2814

	A	B	C	D
1	Store A	Item1	Item 2	Total
2	North	450	360	=SUM(B2:C2)
3	South	835	755	=SUM(B3:C3)
4	Total	=SUM(B2:B3)	=SUM(C2:C3)	=SUM(B4:C4)
5	Store B			
6	North	725	920	=SUM(B6:C6)
7	South	839	385	=SUM(B7:C7)
8	Total	=SUM(B6:B7)	=SUM(C6:C7)	=SUM(B8:C8)
9	Grand Total	=SUM(B8,B4)	=SUM(C8,C4)	=SUM(B9:C9)
10				
11				
12	Summary			
13		Item 1	Item 2	Total
14	Total North	=SUM(B2,B6)	=SUM(C2,C6)	=SUM(B14:C14)
15	Total South	=SUM(B3,B7)	=SUM(C3,C7)	=SUM(B15:C15)

To complete the sum for cell B14, click on the cell and click AutoSum, then click in cells B2 and B6. Remember to key a comma between the cell references.

Exercise 3.6 Using AutoSum for Nonadjacent Cells

A small hardware firm prepares its annual sales report, broken into quarterly totals. They would now like to see how each product sold during the year.

1. Open workbook **Ch3 Ex6** and resave as **Exer 3-6**.

At the bottom of the worksheet (rows 28–30) a total for each type of product is needed.

2. In cell B28, use AutoSum to enter the total number of hammers sold during the year. Click on AutoSum, then click in cells B8, B14, B20, and B26. Be sure to place a comma after each cell entry. The formula reads **=SUM(B8,B14,B20,B26)**.

3. In cell B29, use AutoSum to enter the total number of levels sold during the year. Follow the same procedure as in Step 2.

4. In cell B30, enter the total number of drills sold during the year. Follow the same procedure as in Step 2.

5. Save and print the worksheet. Write your name and **Ch3-6** on the printout.

Entering Data by Range

When entering numbers in a range, highlight the range you want to use for the data. Then enter the numbers in cells, pressing the Enter key after each entry. Excel will move down the column to the next cell; in the last cell of the column, pressing the Enter key will activate the cell at the top of the next column. Figure 3.24 illustrates this concept. After the amount is entered in cell B5 and the Enter key is pressed, the active cell became C3.

Figure 3.24   Entering Data by Range

	A	B	C	D
1				
2		January	February	March
3	Item A	3254		
4	Item B	5784		
5	Item C	2547		

Identifying Numbers in a Worksheet

In a worksheet, all numbers listed must be identified or explained. Use row and column text *labels* to explain the numbers so the reader can easily determine their relationship. All numbers in a worksheet must be identified by a row and/or column label.

Exercise 3.7 Entering Data by Range

Reader's Book Store has branches in four cities. You will enter the sales data for two months, using the range method for entering the data.

1. Open workbook **Ch3 Ex7** and resave it as **Exer 3-7**.

2. In the **January** section, highlight the range B4:D7. Enter the following data and press **Enter** after each entry.

	A	B	C	D	E
3	January	Books	Magazines	Gifts	Total
4	Boston	3,857	3,841	225	
5	New Orleans	6,094	5,947	265	
6	Portland	3,948	6,284	485	
7	Seattle	9,694	2,256	558	

3. In the **February** section, highlight the range B11:D14. Enter the following data, and press **Enter** after each entry.

10	February	Books	Magazines	Gifts	Total
11	Boston	4,838	4,056	475	
12	New Orleans	5,969	7,853	855	
13	Portland	2,039	4,852	548	
14	Seattle	4,968	1,056	721	
15	Total				

4. Complete the totals needed in rows 8 and 15 and in column E.

5. In cell A19, replace **Student's Name** with your name.

6. Save and print the worksheet.

Using AutoCalculate

The *AutoCalculate* feature enters temporary formulas on the worksheet so the totals can be checked quickly without entering formulas. These temporary totals are displayed in the status bar at the bottom of the screen. In Figure 3.25, the maximum number listed, 25, is displayed.

Figure 3.25 *AutoCalculate Displayed in Status Bar*

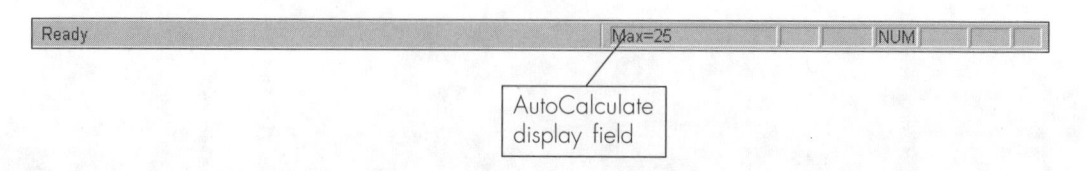

Ready		Max=25		NUM	

AutoCalculate display field

Exercise 3.8—Using AutoCalculate

To use AutoCalculate, select a range of cells, as shown in Figure 3.26.

Figure 3.26   Using AutoCalculate

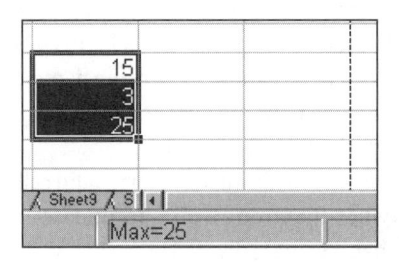

With the mouse pointer on the AutoCalculate field, click the right button to display a list of available options and select the one you want, as shown in Figure 3.27. The AutoCalculate feature is great to quickly determine an average, to count the number of entries, to count the number of numeric entries, to determine the maximum (largest number) and minimum (smallest number), and to determine the sum of the numbers.

Figure 3.27   AutoCalculate Choices

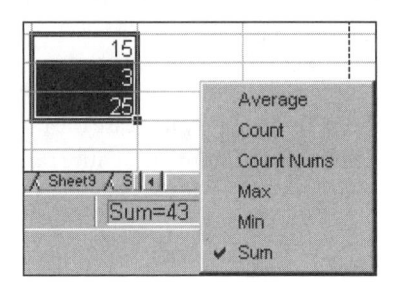

Exercise 3.8   Using AutoCalculate

You will open a workbook and use the AutoCalculate feature to determine the average, sum, and other statistics of the workbook.

1. Open workbook **Ch3 Ex8** and resave it as **Exer 3-8**.

2. Select the range A2:A4. In the status bar, click the right mouse button and select **Average**. The average is _____ .

3. Click the right mouse button and select **Min**. The minimum number is _____ .

4. Select the range A2:C2. Click the right mouse button to see the sum. It is _____ .

5. The average is _____ .

6. Select the range C2:C4. The count is _____ . The maximum is _____ .

7. Close the worksheet without saving.

Error Values

When Excel cannot properly calculate the formula that is entered in a cell, it displays an *error value*. These messages begin with the number sign (#). Some error values are given below:
- **#N/A**—Stands for "No value is available." This helps to ensure a blank cell is not used in a formula.
- **#NAME?**—Appears when Excel cannot recognize a name. It may be that the name was misspelled or a colon was omitted when defining a range (A10A33).
- **#NUM!**—Indicates a problem with a number.
- **#REF!**—Displays when reference is made to an invalid cell.
- **#VALUE!**—Displays when the wrong type of formula is entered.
- **#DIV/0**—Displays when a value is divided by zero.

While error values are confusing now, they are helpful in warning the user of a potential error. As worksheets are created, it is not unusual for an error to be made. Recognizing these messages helps in understanding how to create a worksheet and how to edit the worksheet so it is accurate.

Exercise 3.9   Looking at Error Messages

You will open a worksheet and create formulas that contain errors.

1 Open workbook **Ch3 Ex9** and resave it as **Exer 3-9**.

Increase an AutoSum range.

2 Select cell E2, then click AutoSum. Immediately increase the range by dragging through A2:D2. Once you press the mouse button do not release it until the entire range is selected.

3 Complete the entry.

Select AutoSum ranges that will not work.

4 In cell E3, enter **3852** and complete the entry.

5 Select cell F3, then click on AutoSum. Only cell E3 is in the sum range. Complete the entry.

Enter formulas that cause error messages.

6 In cell A5, key **=SM(A2:A5)**. Complete the entry. The **#NAME?** error message is shown in cell A5. The function name, SUM, was misspelled.

7 In cell B6 key **=SQRT(-1)**. Press **Enter**. The **#NUM!** error message is shown in cell B6. An unacceptable formula was entered.

8 In cell C6, key **=D11*(4**. Press **Enter**. A warning box opens because of the incomplete parenthesis and suggests a correction. You may choose to accept this correction or not. Click **No**.

9 Click **OK**, then on the Cancel box **X** to cancel the entry.

10 Close the worksheet without saving changes.

Printing Formulas

Proofreading a worksheet is perhaps the most important step in its preparation. Every data and text entry, as well as all formulas, must be checked for errors. Because one error in a formula may cause the entire worksheet to be incorrect, it is especially important to have accurate formulas. You can print an Excel worksheet showing the formulas entered; this worksheet can then be proofread on paper.

To print formulas, the formulas must first be displayed in the worksheet. To do this, select Options from the Tools menu. The Options dialog box opens, and is shown in Figure 3.28.

Across the top are a group of tabs labeled View, Calculation, Edit, General, etc. The View tab is used to change the way worksheets, objects, and windows are displayed. When Formulas is selected (under Window options), cells increase in width and formulas are displayed in the cells. When worksheet formulas are displayed, they will print instead of the results.

To display the results instead of the formulas, again open the Options dialog box from the Tools menu. Deselect the check box by clicking Formulas, then click OK to close the dialog box.

Figure 3.28   View Tab of Options Dialog Box

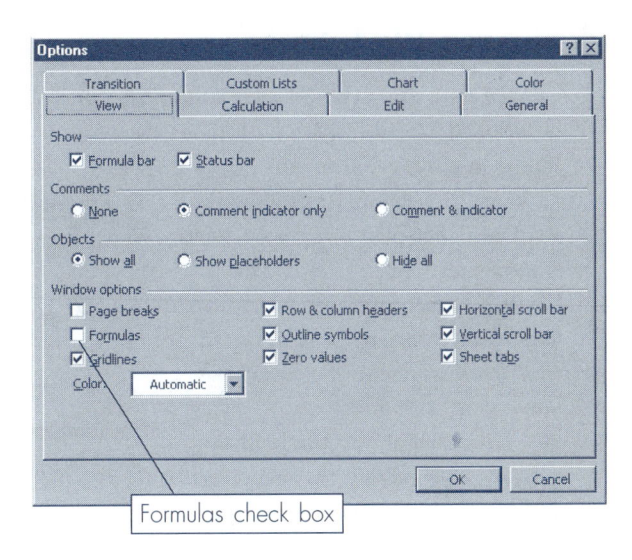

Power Users

The shortcut to show formulas is **Ctrl**+~; the tilde (~) is located on the top row at the left edge of the keyboard. When formulas are displayed, this shortcut also returns the view to display the results.

Exercise 3.10   Printing Formulas

You will retrieve a workbook, rename it, and print the formulas.

1   Open the workbook you saved as **Exer 3-6**.

2   In the **Tools** menu, select **Options**. The **Options** dialog box opens.

Choose to have the worksheet display and print the formulas.

3   Click in the **View** tab to open it on the screen. Click in the **Formulas** check box, then click **OK**.

4   Print the worksheet. This worksheet may take two pages. Write your name at the top.

Turn off the Formulas option.

5. In the **Tools** menu, select **Options**. Then click in the **Formulas** check box to deselect the option, then click **OK**.

6. Hold down `Ctrl` and press ~ (tilde). The worksheet changes to display formulas.

7. Hold down `Ctrl` and press ~ (tilde). The worksheet changes to display results.

8. Close the worksheet without saving changes.

Planning a Worksheet

The planning stage of a worksheet is the most critical step in its preparation. All needed information must be included. The worksheet must convey the information concisely and in an easy-to-understand format. It must be attractive in design.

For this section, let's follow the steps needed to plan a worksheet that summarizes weekly sales (by day of the week) for the Johnson Appliance Company. Johnson's sells refrigerators, freezers, dishwashers, washers, and dryers.

When beginning the planning stage, it is a good idea to use a pencil and paper to design the worksheet. List all items of information to be included; these will become the labels. The labels needed for the Johnson Appliance Company would be a list of the appliances and the days of the week. Your worksheet may look like Figure 3.29.

Next, determine the type of information that the worksheet will convey. Our worksheet summarizes weekly sales. List the information the worksheet will show. You will want to know the total sales for each day of the week and the total weekly sales for each appliance as well as the total sales for the week.

Figure 3.29 Determining Labels

Sun. Mon. Tues. Wed. Thurs. Fri.
Refrigerators
Freezers
Washers
Dryers
Total

Figure 3.30 Determining Formulas Needed

Sales for each day
Weekly sales for each appliance
Total Sales for the week

Now include this additional information and your formulas in your written worksheet plan. It may look like the following:

Figure 3.31   Planning Formulas

```
                    Sun.  Mon.  Tues.  Wed.  Thurs.  Fri.  Sat.  Total=Sum
Refrig.
Freezers
Dishwashers
Washers
Dryers
Total=Sum
```

Be sure the worksheet includes title information. The title answers who, what, and when. This is the place to enter the name of the company (or the department if this is a large firm). Include what the report does and the date. Because so many worksheets report similar information, the date is critical to identify the specific period of any report. For the Johnson illustration, the heading may be

Figure 3.32   Planning a Title

```
Johnson Appliance Company
Sales Report
For the Week of June 2, 1998
```

After carefully planning the worksheet and preparing a handwritten draft, check to be sure all parts are included. You are then ready to complete the worksheet at the computer.

Exercise 3.11   Planning a Worksheet

This is *not* a computer exercise.

On a separate sheet of paper, plan the following worksheet. Your worksheet should include the worksheet title, column and row titles, and any needed formulas.

Prepare a worksheet that shows the projected income for John Adams. John is a college student who needs to plan his finances carefully. He currently has a summer job. His financial package includes student work-study income as well as a grant. In addition, he will earn a minimal amount of income from investments.

Plan the worksheet so there is enough room to enter the income by month. Include each income source and a grand total showing annual income. Your plan will be handwritten.

Summary

- A formula is used to instruct the computer which calculations will be performed.
- Formulas are prepared using constant values and mathematical operators.
- Keyboard symbols are used as arithmetic operators. They are addition (+), subtraction (-), multiplication (*), and division (/).
- As numbers are entered, they automatically align at the right of the cell; as text is entered, it automatically aligns at the left of the cell.
- When a cell is active, the formula displays in the entry area of the formula bar. The results display in the cell. The formula appears in the cell only when it is first being entered or if the Formulas check box has been selected.
- All formulas begin with an equal sign (=).
- Multiplication and division operations are completed first, beginning with those at the left. Then the addition and subtraction operations are completed.
- When parentheses are included in a formula, the mathematical operation within the parentheses is completed first. Parentheses may be nested within each other; the mathematical operation in the innermost parentheses is the first operation performed.
- To complete an entry, press Tab or Enter on the keyboard, or click the mouse on the Enter box ✓ in the formula bar.
- Formulas should be prepared using cell references rather than the specific numeric values.
- Formulas are entered by keying cell references or by pointing and clicking in the cells you want to use as references. Pointing and clicking provides more accuracy.
- Excel automatically recalculates formulas when the number in a cell changes.
- An entry can be erased by clicking in the Cancel box ✗ or by pressing Esc on the keyboard.
- To add an adjacent range of cells, use the AutoSum button Σ. The formula automatically appears in the cell and in the data display area of the formula bar.
- When using the AutoSum button Σ, the cells to be added are expressed as a range. For example, the range A2:A9 indicates all cells beginning with A2 and ending with A9. The contents of each cell within that range will be included in the sum. The formula could also be expressed as =A2+A3+A4+A5+A6+A7+A8+A9.
- The AutoSum button Σ can be used for adding horizontal or vertical ranges of cells. It adds the cells just to the left or just above the active cell.
- A marquee surrounds the range of cells included in an AutoSum formula.
- Excel will enter a SUM formula in one step when adding adjacent ranges.
- A grand total can be added automatically with Excel. Highlight the entire worksheet; only the values that are derived from a formula are used to determine the grand total.
- An error value may open when an error is made. This gives information about the error so it can be corrected.
- Use column and row labels to identify all numbers in a worksheet.
- The accuracy of a worksheet is important. Careful proofreading of data entries and formulas is critical.
- A worksheet may be printed showing the formulas used in a worksheet. Activate the Formulas check box in the View tab of the Options dialog box (this is accessed from the Tools menu), or use the shortcut command of Ctrl+~.

- AutoCalculate is used to quickly determine a sum or average without entering formulas.
- AutoCalculate is accessed by clicking the right mouse button in the AutoCalculate field in the status bar.
- A worksheet should be well planned to determine the data and results needed.

Important Terminology

arithmetic operators	Enter box	grand total
AutoCalculate	Enter mode	label
AutoSum	error value	marquee
AutoSum button	Escape key	point-and-click method
Cancel box	formula	

Buttons to Know

Study Questions

True-False

Place a T in the space if the statement is true; place an F if the statement is false.

_____ 1. A constant value is a number, date, time, or text.
_____ 2. A formula may produce different results if a part of it changes.
_____ 3. The : is Excel's symbol for division.
_____ 4. Key = to begin a formula.
_____ 5. The formula bar is active when ✕ ✓ = is displayed.
_____ 6. An entry must be completed before calculations will be performed.
_____ 7. Formulas may be entered only in inactive cells.
_____ 8. The result of the formula =18(4/2)+2*2 is 40.
_____ 9. In a formula, use cell references rather than exact amounts.
_____ 10. The formula =B5/C3 tells Excel to divide the contents of cell B5 by the contents of cell C3.
_____ 11. In the formula =B3+B4, the results will change if the number in cell B3 changes.
_____ 12. A warning box will open if the formula =B4(B3 is entered.
_____ 13. The marquee surrounding a cell indicates that it is the active cell.
_____ 14. The AutoSum button Σ is used to automatically add an adjacent range of cells.
_____ 15. The formula =SUM(B3:B8) can also be written as =B4+B5+B6+B7.
_____ 16. The procedure to add a range of cells using Σ is to enter = then click Σ in the toolbar.
_____ 17. Formulas created by AutoSum can be entered in only one cell at a time.
_____ 18. An example of an error message is #REF!.
_____ 19. A worksheet may print formulas instead of values in the cells.
_____ 20. When entering formulas, the preferred method is to key in all cell references.
_____ 21. AutoCalculate is used to quickly enter formulas in a worksheet.

Fill-In

Place the word in the space that correctly completes the statement.
1. The symbols +, -, *, and / are _____ operators in Excel.
2. An Excel formula must begin with a(n) _____ .
3. Use the ☑ box in the formula bar to _____ an entry.
4. When an entry is complete, the formula displays in the entry area of the formula bar, and the results display in the _____ cell.
5. The formula used to add the contents of cells B7, D8, and C11 is _____ .
6. The three ways to complete an entry are to click ☑ on the toolbar, press _____ , or press the Enter key on the keyboard.
7. The method of entering a formula that includes clicking on a cell is called the _____ method.
8. Pressing _____ on the keyboard is used to stop the marquee from displaying.
9. The Σ button is used for the _____ function.
10. To print a worksheet displaying the formulas, select the _____ tab in the Options dialog box.

Writing Formulas

Write the formula Excel would require to complete the mathematical statement.

Example
Add 36 to 45 and subtract 17.   =36+45-17
Add 25 to the product of 36 and 7.   =25+(36*7)
Add 4 to 2 and then multiply by 36. To this number add 2 and then subtract 5.
=2+(36*(4+2))-5

1. Add 17 to 36. _____
2. Subtract 37 from 91. _____
3. Multiply 91 by 36 by 2. _____
4. Divide 459 by 3. _____
5. Add 379 to 376 and then subtract 597. _____
6. Divide 793 by 16 and add 20 to that amount. _____
7. Multiply 19 by the sum of 36 and 27; then divide by 27. _____
8. Subtract 107 from the product of 47 and 19. Add to that the product of 18 and 3. _____
9. Divide 16 by 8 and then multiply the quotient by 4. Multiply the resulting product by 7. _____
10. Calculate the sum of the contents of cells A3, A4, and A5. (Use cell references in the formula.) _____
11. Subtract the contents of cell B5 from the contents of cell B3. (Use cell references in the formula.) _____
12. Multiply the contents of cell C3 by the contents of cell D4. _____

Assignments

Note: After completing all work in Chapter 3, you may delete the Ch01-03 directory from your Student Data Disk if you are using one data disk.

Assignment 3.1

In this assignment, you will create a worksheet, use Excel as a calculator, and create formulas.
1. Open Excel to a new workbook.
2. Enter your name in cell A1.
3. Enter data in the worksheet.
   - In cell B2, add **471** and **657**.
   - In cell B3, subtract **197** from **993**.
   - In cell B4, multiply **35** by **3** by **25**.
   - In cell B5, divide **107** by **4**.
4. Save the workbook as **Assig 3-1** in the **Ch01-03** folder.
5. Enter the following amounts in row 9:

	A	B	C
8			
9	8	19	5
10			

6. Use cell references to enter formulas.
   - In cell A11, calculate the sum of cells A9, B9, and C9, using cell references. The result in cell A11 is **32**.
   - In cell A12, calculate the sum of B9 and C9, then subtract cell A9. The result in cell A12 is **16**.
   - In cell A13, multiply cell B9 by cell C9. The result in cell A13 is **95**.
   - In cell A14, divide the sum of A9 and B9 by C9. The result in cell A14 is **5.4**.
   - In cell A15, subtract C9 from B9 and multiply by A9. The result in cell A15 is **112**.
7. Save and print the worksheet.
   - Place the file name in the header.
   - Print the worksheet.
   - Print the worksheet showing formulas.
8. Save changes and close the workbook.

Assignment 3.2

Bacha Foods would like you to complete the sales report that was started for the first quarter sales. They have four districts and group their products into three categories: canned goods, frozen foods, and toiletries. Information has been entered for January and February.

You will complete the sales report for Bacha Foods. Selected answers (a Checkpoint) are provided at the end of this assignment.
1. Open workbook **Ch3 As2** in the **Ch01-03** folder on the Student Data Disk.

To prevent accidentally saving the workbook on the original disk, save it as your working copy.

2. Save the workbook as **Assig 3-2**.

3. Look at the worksheet to determine what needs to be completed. Note that totals for each month are missing, the data for March is not entered, and some formatting is not complete.
   - Complete the totals for January and February. In addition to the total for each food product, a total amount is needed for each state in the district (column E).
   - Enter the March information into the worksheet and provide totals. Highlight the data range (B23:D26) before entering the data. The March information is given below:

March			
District	Canned Goods	Frozen Foods	Toiletries
Oregon	389562.38	583762.2	182658.4
Washington	348561.2	385617.69	228593.48
Idaho	385729.12	1295683.92	283956.66
Montana	99872.03	87928.02	128738.22
Total			
Quarterly Total			

4. Do a quick save to prevent loss of work.
5. Complete the **Quarterly Total** section (row 28) using the AutoSum feature.
6. Complete the worksheet.
   - Format the quarterly total amounts for bold (row 28).
   - Format the worksheet for currency.
   - Adjust cell widths if necessary.
   - Place a single underline above the total rows. Place a double underline under the row for the quarterly totals.
7. Complete an analysis of sales at the bottom of the worksheet.
   - Beginning with cell A30, enter the following:

30	Total Oregon
31	Total Washington
32	Total Idaho
33	Total Montana

   - Use AutoSum to enter the formula in cell B30 to add the canned goods sold in Oregon. Repeat with the rest of the states and for the rest of the products.
8. Change the top margin to 2" and the left margin to 1.25". Place the file name in the header.
9. In cell A36, key **Prepared by** followed by your name.
10. Save and print the worksheet. (This worksheet may print on two pages.)
11. Print the worksheet showing formulas. If needed, adjust the margins and column widths in Print Preview so it prints on two (not three) pages.
12. Close the worksheet. Do not save changes.

   Checkpoint:

January Total Sales	$3,045,593.08
Total Canned Goods in February	$1,145,375.12
Quarterly Total of Toiletries	$2,623,859.29

Assignment 3.3

Best Software, Inc., is completing its annual sales report. The basic worksheet has been planned, created, and the data has been entered. You are to complete the worksheet totals and format it. Remember to save often to avoid loss of work.

A Checkpoint is provided at the end of the assignment to check your accuracy.

1. Open workbook **Ch3 As3** and save it as **Assig 3-3**.
2. Print the workbook so you can refer to it as you are completing it. This helps in planning your work.
3. Complete the worksheet.
   - Complete the first quarter totals, including the total sales for each month (column E). Use the AutoSum button Σ.
   - Complete the second quarter totals using AutoSum.
   - Complete the third and fourth quarter totals.
   - Complete the annual sales amount in row 25.
4. Format the worksheet.
   - Enter a label for column E (**Total**).
   - Format the column labels for bold and center alignment.
   - Bold the row labels that contain the quarterly and annual sales.
   - Indent all row labels except the labels for the total lines.
   - Format for currency.
   - Select the border that places a single line at the top and a double line at the bottom for each total row.
   - For the annual sales, place a bold border under the amounts, and format the amounts in bold.
   - Adjust column widths, if needed.
5. Set the top margin at 2.25" and the left margin at 1.5".
6. Place the file name in the header of the worksheet.
7. Put your name in cell A28.
8. Save and print the worksheet and also print a copy showing the formulas. If needed, adjust the margins and column widths in Print Preview so it prints on two (not three) pages.

   Checkpoint:
First Quarter Word Processing	$13,761.02
Second Quarter Total	$52,269.05
Annual Utilities	$56,239.66

Assignment 3.4

Chang Yeung Manufacturing is preparing its January 30 payroll. You will complete the worksheet for this payroll, determining the amount of net pay for each employee.

A Checkpoint is provided at the end of the assignment to check your accuracy.

1. Prepare a worksheet that shows the following information:

	A	B	C	D
1	Chang Yeung Manufacturing			
2	Payroll Report			
3	30-Jan-98			
4				
5	Employee	Gross Pay	Deductions	Net Pay
6				
7	Anderson	386.28	121.38	
8	Binh	393.85	135.65	
9	Collins	188.38	87.92	
10	Downey	583.95	195.13	
11	Emory	283.37	101.22	
12				
13	Total			

2. Save the workbook as **Assig 3-4**.
3. Complete the worksheet. The formula for net pay is gross pay less deductions.
4. Format the worksheet.
   - Format the three-line title and the column labels for bold.
   - Format column labels for right alignment.
   - Format for currency.
   - Indent the employees' names.
   - Place underlines in the correct places.
   - Adjust column widths, if necessary.
   - Enter your name in cell A15.
5. Adjust placement on the page.
   - Place the file name in the header.
   - Use Print Preview to adjust the margins; attempt to place the worksheet in the center of the page.
6. Save and print the worksheet.
7. Print a copy displaying the formulas. Adjust the margins and column widths so this worksheet fits on one page. Remember, the total page count is given in the status bar.

   Checkpoint:
   Net Pay, Anderson $ 264.90
   Total Gross Pay $1,835.83

Assignment 3.5

First Rate Book Store has branches in four cities. The basics of a worksheet have been entered. You will enter data and complete the worksheet.
1. Open workbook **Ch3 As5** and save it as **Assig 3-5**.
2. Enter the following November and December sales. Always highlight a range before entering data to save entry time.

	A	B	C	D	E
3	November	Books	Magazines	Gifts	Total
4	Boston	3,857	3,841	225	
5	New Orleans	6,094	5,947	265	
6	Portland	3,948	6,284	485	
7	Seattle	9,694	2,256	558	
8	Total				
9					
10	December	Books	Magazines	Gifts	Total
11	Boston	4,838	4,056	475	
12	New Orleans	5,969	7,853	855	
13	Portland	2,039	4,852	548	
14	Seattle	4,968	1,056	721	
15	Total				
16	Grand Total				

3. Complete the totals.
   - Complete the totals in rows 8 and 15 and column E.
   - Complete the grand total. If column F shows totals, delete them.
4. Complete the summary section for books and magazines sold at each store during November and December. Use the section at the bottom of the worksheet that is prepared for the summary information.
   - In cell B19, enter the formula to add the sales of books and magazines in Boston.
   - In cell B20, enter the formula to add the sales of books and magazines in New Orleans.
   - Add the books and magazines sales in Portland and Seattle.
5. Check the worksheet for proper format. Amounts are not currency.
6. Adjust placement on the page.
   - Print the file name in the header.
   - Use Print Preview to adjust the margins; attempt to place the worksheet in the center of the page.
7. At the bottom of the worksheet, key **Prepared by** followed by your name.
8. Save and print the worksheet.
9. Print a second copy that shows the formulas used.

   Checkpoint:
November Total, Boston	7,923
Total Books in December	17,814
Grand Total Magazines	36,145

Assignment 3.6

This worksheet summarizes a publishing firm's magazine sales for a year. The sales are listed by magazine and by quarter.
1. Open the workbook you saved as **Assig 2-6**.
2. Save the workbook as **Assig 3-6**.
3. Complete the worksheet by entering the formulas for the total column (column F) and the total row (row 9). Be sure to place a formula in cell F9, too.
4. Format the worksheet correctly. Look at numbers, underlines, column widths, etc. (The numbers in this worksheet are not dollar amounts.)
5. Adjust margins in Page Setup or Print Preview.
6. Print the worksheet.
7. Proofread carefully to check for accuracy.
8. Make needed corrections and save the completed worksheet.
9. Print a copy of the worksheet that displays formulas. Double check the accuracy. Be sure this worksheet takes only one page.

Case Problem 3

World's Best Electronics has asked you to prepare a report that lists the sales, returns, and net sales of their electronic equipment for the current month.

Use an Excel spreadsheet to report this information. For each product, show the sales and returns, as well as the net sales. Also include total sales, returns, and the net total.

It is important to know who created each worksheet. At the bottom of the worksheet enter **Prepared by** and your name. Place the file name in the header.

Prepare a written plan of the worksheet and submit it with the completed worksheet.

Format the worksheet appropriately. Print it close to the center of the page. Print a report showing the formulas that were used. Be sure each number listed in the worksheet is labeled.

Save the workbook as **Case 3**.

The specific information follows:
- Sales of VCRs were $11,038.56 with $854.28 returned.
- TV sales were $42,986.37 with $1,006.89 returned.
- There were $1,056.25 worth of CDs sold with $36.29 returned.
- Sales of cameras were $33,281.56 with $802.58 returned.
- Tape sales were $558.29 with $97.65 returned.
- There were $1,866.28 worth of tape players sold with $100.69 returned.

Checkpoint:

Total Sales	$90,787.31
Net Sales of Tape Players	$1,765.59

Chapter 4

Moving and Copying Information

Objectives

1. Move and copy cells using menu commands, keyboard commands, the toolbar, and the drag-and-drop technique.
2. Move and copy cells and insert them between existing cells.
3. Use commands and buttons for Undo, Repeat, and Paste Special.
4. Use Format Painter to copy formats.

Introduction

After a worksheet is complete, information may need to be changed, added, deleted, or rearranged. These changes are easy to make with Excel.

Information can be copied and used in several different locations in a worksheet, or it can be moved to a new location. Copying saves time and helps ensure the accuracy of a worksheet. The format of one cell can be copied to other cells.

This chapter covers moving and copying cell contents, using the Undo and Repeat commands, and using other related commands.

At the end of this chapter, you will delete the Ch04 directory from your Student Data Disk.

Moving Cell Contents

Techniques for Moving Data

While editing, the contents of cells can be moved to new locations in a worksheet. There are two ways to move a cell. The first is called the ***cut-and-paste method***. Think of this as physically "cutting" out the cells and "pasting" them to a new location. The second method of moving information, called the ***drag-and-drop method***, uses the mouse to drag cells to a new location. This method will be discussed in the next section.

To move a cell or a range of cells, first select the cells you want to move. The selected cells are called the ***move area***; in Figure 4.1 the move area is the range A1:D1.

Figure 4.1   Range of Cells Selected to Move

	A	B	C	D
1	January	February	March	April

Next, select the ***Cut command*** from the Edit menu. A *marquee*, used as a visual reminder of the move area, surrounds the range of cells, shown in Figure 4.2. The status bar reads "Select destination and press ENTER or choose Paste."

Figure 4.2   Move Area Surrounded by Marquee

	A	B	C	D
1	January	February	March	April

The ***destination***, also called the ***paste area***, is the cell or range of cells where the data will be placed. Figure 4.3 shows cell A4 selected as the ***destination cell***, which is the upper-left cell of the destination.

Figure 4.3   Copy Area A1:D1 with Marquee; Paste Area Begins with Cell A4

	A	B	C	D
1	January	February	March	April
2				
3				
4				

destination cell

Select the ***Paste command*** from the Edit menu to relocate the cell contents. The destination matches the size and shape of the move area, although only one cell was selected. All contents, formats, and formulas are included with the cells when they are moved. Cell contents that were previously in the destination cells are deleted. Figure 4.4 shows the completed move.

Figure 4.4   Move from Row 1 to Row 4 Completed

	A	B	C	D
1				
2				
3				
4	January	February	March	April

It is not necessary to select the entire range as the destination. Select only the destination cell, which is the upper-left or first cell of the range.

The toolbar provides buttons for copying and moving cells, as shown in Figure 4.5. It is usually faster to use these buttons than the commands in the pull-down menus.

Figure 4.5   Cut and Paste Buttons

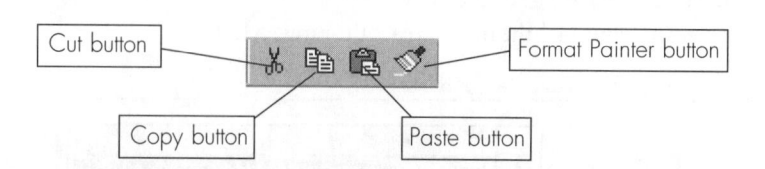

After the cut area is selected, click on the *Cut button* 🔲. Move the mouse to the destination cell and click on the *Paste button* 🔲.

Power Users

The shortcut command for cut is **Ctrl**+**X** and for paste is **Ctrl**+**V**. The Paste command can also be completed by pressing the **Enter** key.

Drag-and-Drop Moves

Another way to move cells is by the drag-and-drop method. In this method, the mouse pointer is used to "grab" the move area. The cells are then "dragged" to the new location and "dropped" into place.

Note: Be sure the settings in the Options dialog box allow for drag-and-drop editing. This can be done by selecting the Tools menu, then Options. Then open the Edit tab, and select Allow Drag and Drop.

First, select the cell or the range of cells in the move area. In Figure 4.6, the move area is B3:B6. Position the mouse pointer over any section of the gray border surrounding the move area (except the box in the lower right corner). The shape of the mouse pointer changes to an arrow. (It may seem difficult to get the mouse pointer to change to an arrow. Use a steady hand and keep moving in slow, small motions around the border until it changes shape.) Figure 4.7 shows the arrow at the border of the move area.

Hold down the mouse button and drag the selection to the new location. During the move, the status bar reads "Drag to move cell contents."

As the mouse moves across the screen, a border appears indicating the shape and position of the selection, and a ScreenTip identifies the range (B8:B11) where the cells will be placed, as shown in Figure 4.8.

Figure 4.6   Move Area Selected

	A	B	C
1		January	February
2			
3	One	38382	38383
4	Two	2983	2839
5	Three	28735	29839
6	Four	58438	57438
7			

Figure 4.7   Mouse Is Active to Begin Move

	A	B	C
1		January	February
2			
3	One	38382	38383
4	Two	2983	2839
5	Three	28735	29839
6	Four	58438	57438
7			

Figure 4.8   Move Border with ScreenTip

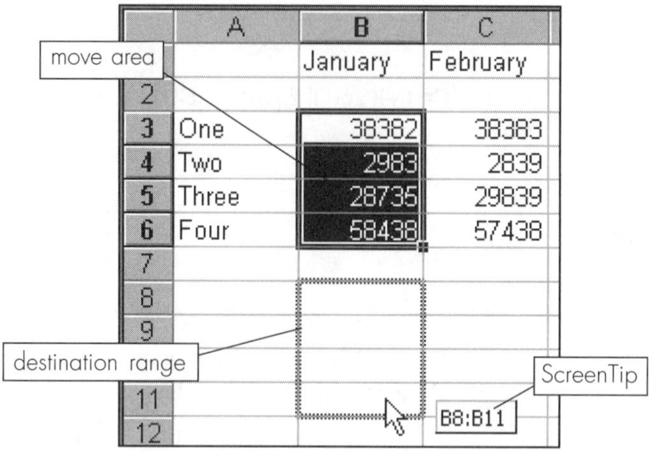

When the border surrounds the destination area, release the mouse button to drop the contents into the paste area. The cell contents are now relocated and all information previously contained in the range B8:B11 is deleted. Figure 4.9 shows the results of moving the range B3:B6 to the range B8:B11.

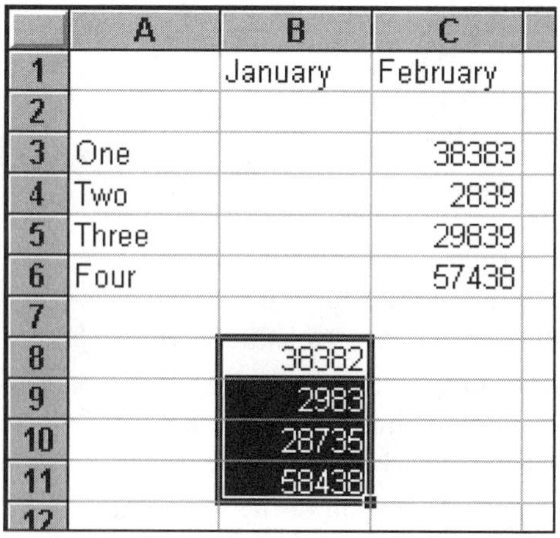

Moving cell contents to a location not currently visible on the screen is also possible. Move the mouse to the edge of the screen until the worksheet begins to scroll to new columns or rows. For short moves, the drag-and-drop method will probably be faster; however, in large worksheets where a distant move is needed, the cut-and-paste method is recommended.

Figure 4.9   Move Completed

Why So Many Choices?

Today, software developers recognize that people work in different ways and prefer different techniques to accomplish their work. As software has become more sophisticated, choices have been built into it to accommodate the preferences of each user. You may find that one method of cut and paste works best for you, but try all the methods so you understand each one. Then use the method you prefer, although it may be different from the one used by the person sitting next to you or your instructor. As you become more proficient with Excel, you may decide to use a different method than the one you first selected.

Exercise 4.1   Moving Cells

You will rearrange a worksheet using several methods of moving information.

1   Retrieve document **Ch4 Ex1** and save it as **Exer 4-1**.

You will arrange the days of the week in row 1 and the months of the year in row 2 using the Edit menu.

2   Click the mouse in cell A1. From **Edit**, select **Cut**. A marquee surrounds cell A1.

3   Select cell A4, the destination. From **Edit**, select **Paste**. The contents of cell A1 are now in cell A4.

4   Select the range B1:C1. From **Edit**, select **Cut**.

5   Select cell B4, the destination cell. From **Edit**, select **Paste**.

Move cells using the Cut and Paste buttons on the toolbar.

6   Select the range D1:D2. Click on the Cut button in the toolbar.

7   Select cell B5, the destination cell. Click on the Paste button in the toolbar.

8   Use the toolbar to move the cell contents of A2 to A1.

Select either the instructions for Regular Users or for Power Users.

Regular Users

9a   Move the cell contents of C4 to cell B1.

9b   Move the cell contents of E2 to C1 using a method of your choice.

Power Users (Use the keyboard Copy and Paste commands)

9a   Select cell C4.

9b   Hold down **Ctrl** while pressing **X**. A marquee surrounds cell C4.

9c   Select cell B1, the destination.

9d   Hold down **Ctrl** while pressing **V**.

Move cells using drag and drop.

10   Select cell E1. Move the mouse to the border of the active cell until it takes the shape of an arrow. Press and hold down the mouse button. The status bar reads **Drag to move cell contents**.

11   Drag cell E1 to cell A2. A ScreenTip identifies the destination cell. Release the mouse button when the border surrounds cell A2.

12   Use the drag-and-drop method to move the range B2:C2 to C4:D4. A ScreenTip identifies the destination range.

Move cells to a destination not on the screen.

13 Select cell B5. Use the drag-and-drop method to move it to cell L4. (Column L may not be on the screen.) Continue to hold down the mouse button and move cell B5 to the right scroll bar. The screen will begin to scroll; to stop the scroll, move the mouse just to the left of the right scroll bar.

14 Select cell L4 and release the mouse button.

15 Move cell L4 back to cell E1.

Complete the worksheet.

16 Complete the worksheet by moving, in the correct order, the days of the week in row 1 and the months of the year in row 2. Use the method you prefer.

17 Enter your name in cell A5.

18 Place the file name in the header.

19 Save and print the worksheet.

Moving between Existing Cells

You may move and insert cells between other cells without deleting information. When cells are inserted between other cells, the original cells shift to make room for the new ones with no data loss.

To use the drag-and-drop technique for moving data between cells, hold down the Shift key while moving the cells. First select the move area, B4:B5, as shown in Figure 4.10.

Move the mouse close to the border of the move area; the mouse will change to an arrow. Hold down the Shift key first, then the mouse button. In the status bar, Excel provides a reminder that reads "Drag to Cut and Insert cell contents."

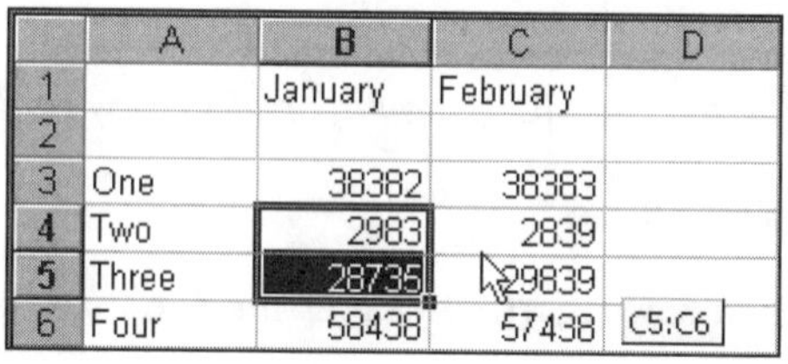

Now drag the cells to their new location. A bold, jagged line, called the *insertion border*, appears between cells C4 and C5 and the ScreenTip identifies the destination (see Figure 4.11).

Figure 4.10   Move Range of B4:B5 Selected

Figure 4.11   Insertion Border between Cells C4 and C5

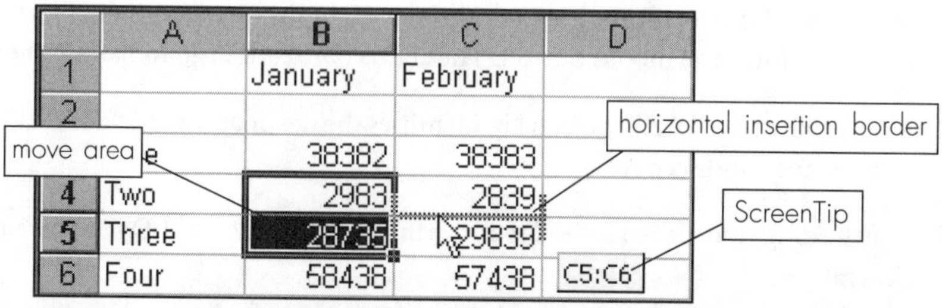

Release the mouse button first and then the Shift key. The range of cells, B4:B5, is placed within the range C5:C6. The cells that were previously in this range have shifted down to the range C7:C8, shown in Figure 4.12.

A vertical insertion border appears when cells are to be inserted between columns. In Figure 4.13, the range B4:B5 is the move area. The vertical insertion border is between the range A6:A7 and B6:B7.

When the move is complete, the contents of cells B6 and B7 automatically shift to the right to make room for the new cells. Cell B7 was empty, so no cells were shifted in row 7, shown in Figure 4.14.

If you want to move to an area off the screen, move the mouse pointer to the edge of the screen and scroll to the destination. However, it is usually easier to use the cut-and-paste method rather than the drag-and-drop method when the destination is not visible on the screen.

Figure 4.12   Insertion Move Complete

	A	B	C
1		January	February
2			
3	One	38382	38383
4	Two		2839
5	Three		2983
6	Four	58438	28735
7			29839
8			57438
9			

Figure 4.13   Vertical Insertion Border with ScreenTip

	A	B	C
1		January	February
2			
3	One		38382	38383
4	Two	2983	2839
5	Three	28735	29839
6	Four	58438	57438
7			
8		B6:B7	
9			

ScreenTip — move area — vertical insertion border

Figure 4.14   Vertical Drag-and-Drop Move

	A	B	C	D
1		January	February	
2				
3	One	38382	38383	
4	Two		2839	
5	Three		29839	
6	Four	2983	58438	57438
7		28735		
8				

Exercise 4.2 Inserting Cells between Other Cells

You will practice moving cells and inserting them between existing cells. When this exercise is complete, the numbers will be arranged in order, counting by 5.

1. Open workbook **Ch4 Ex2** and save it as **Exer 4-2**.

2. Select cell D3 (the number **5**). Hold down **Shift**.

3. Position the mouse pointer near the border of cell D3 so it changes to an arrow. Hold down the mouse button. Check the status bar to be sure it reads **Drag to Cut and Insert cell contents**.

4. Move to the left of cell A1. A vertical insertion border should appear at the left edge of the cell and the ScreenTip should read **A1**. Release the mouse button first, and then release **Shift**; the existing cells in row 1 shift one cell to the right.

5. Select cell A3 (the number **10**). Hold down **Shift** while you position the mouse near the cell border so the mouse changes to an arrow.

6. Hold down the mouse button while moving above cell B1; a horizontal border is placed above cell B1 and the ScreenTip reads **B1**. Release the mouse button first, then release **Shift**; the cells in column B shift down.

If a warning box opens that asks, "Do you want to replace the contents of destination cells?" click on Cancel. The Shift key is not held down throughout the entire process.

7. Select cell C3. Hold down **Shift**. Drag C3 so that a vertical border appears between cells B1 and C1. The remaining cells shift one column to the right.

8. Select the range F2:G2. Hold down **Shift**. Move the range so that a horizontal border appears above cells D1 and E1; the ScreenTip reads **D1:E1**. Release the mouse and then the **Shift** key; the remaining cells move down one row.

9. The number **30** is in cell F1; no changes need to be made in this cell.

10. Select cell J1. (You may need to scroll to the right to locate it.) Hold down **Shift**. Place the horizontal border above cell G1 and enter data in cell G1. The other cells in column G move down one row.

11. Select cell B2. Hold down **Shift**. Place a horizontal insertion border above cell H1 and replace the contents of cell H1. The other cells in column H move down one row.

The numbers in row 1 are in increments of 5, beginning with 5 and ending with 40. Row 2 will now be arranged from 45–80 in increments of 5.

12. Select the range E3:E4. Hold down **Shift**. Place a horizontal border between cells A1 and A2; the ScreenTip reads **A2:A3**. The other cells in column A move down two rows.

13. Continue using the drag-and-drop and insert-paste methods to complete the worksheet. Row 1 begins with 5 and ends with 40. Row 2 will begin with 45 and end with 80; row 3 will begin with 85 and end with 120. If the destination cell is empty, an insert paste will not be needed.

14. In cell A5, key your name.

15 Place the file name in the header.

16 Save and print the worksheet.

Copying Techniques

Copying Cell Contents and Formats

Cell contents (both data and formulas) can be copied to other locations of the worksheet. The format (bold, italics, etc.) of a cell can also be copied to another cell without copying the numeric value or the text entry.

There are two basic methods used for copying. The first uses the Edit menu commands of Copy and Paste or the Copy and Paste buttons on the toolbar; the second uses the drag-and-drop technique.

As with moving cells, the first step is to select the *copy area*—the cell or range of cells you want to copy. Then select the *Copy command* from the Edit menu. A marquee surrounds the copy area, and the status bar reads "Select destination and press ENTER or choose Paste." In Figure 4.15, the copy area is the range A1:A3.

Figure 4.15   Copy Range of A1:A3 and the Paste Range of C1:C3

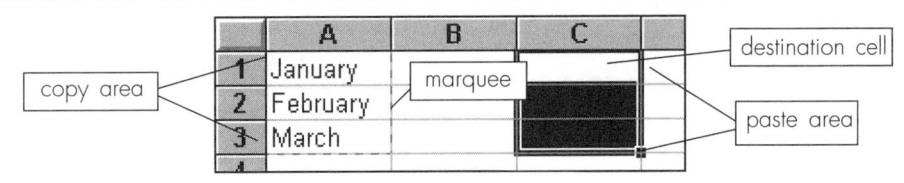

	A	B	C
1	January		
2	February		
3	March		

copy area — marquee — destination cell — paste area

Next, select the destination cell. Excel automatically fills in the range. The destination cell in Figure 4.15 is cell C1 for the range C1:C3. Then select Paste from the Edit menu.

Figure 4.16 shows the completed copy. The cell contents from the copy area are also in the destination, including all formats and formulas. Copying cells overwrites previous contents.

Because formulas or data may be copied to several locations, the copy area remains active, allowing for cell contents to be pasted to more than one destination. The marquee surrounding the copy area serves as a visual reminder of the active copy area.

Figure 4.16   Paste Completed

	A	B	C
1	January		January
2	February		February
3	March		March

The marquee disappears when another entry is made or when you press the Esc key.

The *Copy button* and Paste button on the toolbar can also be used. First, select the copy area, then click on the Copy button. Next, select the destination cell and click the Paste button.

Power Users

The keyboard command for copying is **Ctrl**+**C**. The keyboard command for pasting is **Ctrl**+**V**.

When selecting the destination area, select only the destination cell. If the destination area is selected, it must match the copy area exactly. If it does not, a warning box like the one in Figure 4.17 opens, explaining the error and suggesting possible solutions.

Figure 4.17   Copy/Paste Warning Box

Drag-and-Drop Copying

The drag-and-drop method for copying cell contents is similar to the drag-and-drop method for moving cells. First, select the copy area; in Figure 4.18 it is B4:B5.

Move the mouse to the border of the range. When the mouse pointer becomes an arrow, hold down the Ctrl key. The arrow now displays a small plus sign beside it.

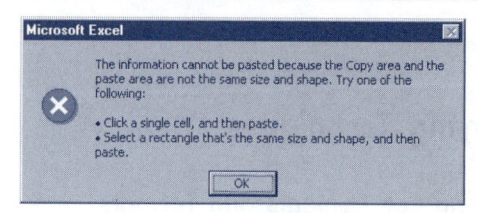

Figure 4.18   Copy Range of B4:B5

	A	B	C	D
1		January	February	March
2				
3	One	38382	38383	8375
4	Two	2983	2839	39835
5	Three	28735	29839	6948
6	Four	58438	57438	67748
7				
8		128538	128499	122906

The status bar reads "Drag to copy cell contents, use Alt key to switch sheets." Do not release the Ctrl key or the mouse button until the copy procedure is completed.

Drag the cells to the destination (C11:C12). As the cells are moved, a gray border that is the exact size of the copy area also moves so you can visualize the size of the paste area and the ScreenTip shows the destination range. Figure 4.19 shows the copy area and the destination.

Figure 4.19   Copying Cells

	A	B	C	D
1		January	February	March
2				
3	One	38382	38383	8375
4	Two	2983	2839	29835
5	Three	28735	29839	6948
6	Four	58438	57438	67748
7				
8		128538	128499	112906
9				
10				
11				
12				
13				
14				

When the gray border surrounds the destination, release the mouse button and then the Ctrl key to complete the copying process. All cell contents previously in the destination area will be deleted. The cell contents, the formulas, and the formats from the copy area are now copied into another location. The completed copy is shown in Figure 4.20.

If the paste area is located in a part of the worksheet that is not currently visible on the screen, use Copy and Paste from the Edit menu, the toolbar, or the keyboard commands.

Figure 4.20   Cells B4:B5 Copied to the Range C11:C12

	A	B	C	D
1		January	February	March
2				
3	One	38382	38383	8375
4	Two	2983	2839	29835
5	Three	28735	29839	6948
6	Four	58438	57438	37748
7				
8		128538	128499	112906
9				
10				
11			2983	
12			28735	

Exercise 4.3   Copying Cells

You will practice copying and pasting using several techniques.

1   Open to a new workbook and enter the following information:

	A
1	Rogers
2	Sampson
3	Tweet
4	Uriah
5	Vector

2   Save the workbook as **Exer 4-3**.

3   Select the copy range of A1:A5. From **Edit**, select **Copy**.

You will paste to the range C4:C8.

4   Select the destination cell C4.

5   From **Edit**, select **Paste**. The marquee surrounds the copy area after the paste is complete, indicating an active copy area.

6   Select cell B6. From **Edit**, select **Paste**. The contents in the active copy area are copied again.

7   Select cell C7. From **Edit**, select **Paste**. The original cell contents are replaced with the new cell contents.

8   Select the range D4:D5. From **Edit**, select **Paste**. A warning box opens stating the problem and suggesting solutions. Click **OK**.

Chapter 4   Moving and Copying Information

9   Stop the marquee from displaying by pressing **Esc**.

Regular Users

10a Copy the range B8:C8 to the range beginning with cell C1.

10b Select cell A13. Press **Enter** to complete the second paste and to stop the marquee.

Power Users (Use the keyboard Copy command)

10a Select the range B8:C8. Use the keyboard command of **Ctrl**+**C**. A marquee surrounds the copy area.

10b Select cell C1. Use the keyboard command of **Ctrl**+**V** to paste the cells.

11 Select the range B10:C10. Click on the Copy button.

12 Select cell C7. Click on the Paste button.

13 Select cell B14. Click on the Paste button.

14 Stop the marquee from displaying by pressing **Esc**.

15 Select the range A3:A5. Move the mouse to the border. Hold down **Ctrl**; a plus appears by the arrow. Drag the cells to E6:E8. The ScreenTip reads **E6:E8**. Release the mouse button. Cell contents have been copied.

16 Repeat the process to copy the range B9:C10 to C13:D14.

17 Place the file name in the header.

18 Place your name in cell A16.

19 Save and print the worksheet.

Copying between Existing Cells

Cells can be copied and inserted between existing cells; the information previously stored in those cells will then shift its location to allow room for the insertion of new cells.

To use the drag-and-drop technique for inserting copied cells, hold down the Ctrl and Shift keys while moving cells.

First select the copy area; in Figure 4.21, the copy area is the range A6:D6.

Place the mouse pointer near the copy border so it takes the arrow shape. Hold down the Shift and Ctrl keys along with the mouse button. The status bar reads "Drag to Copy and Insert cell contents."

Continue to hold down the keys as the cells are moved to the paste area. An insertion bar indicates the placement in the worksheet; a ScreenTip identifies the range. In Figure 4.22, the insertion border is the horizontal border between rows 3 and 4 and the ScreenTip identifies the cells that will be filled. Release the mouse button before releasing Shift and Ctrl; the cell contents are copied.

Figure 4.23 shows the information in row 6 copied and inserted into row 4. The remaining rows shift down. No cell contents are deleted. The totals in the range B8:D8 move to B9:D9.

This technique is also used to copy and paste cells between columns. The insertion border takes a vertical shape to indicate pasting between columns, as shown in Figure 4.24. The cells will be pasted between C4:C5 and D4:D5.

Figure 4.21   Copy Area Selected

	A	B	C	D
1		January	February	March
2				
3	One	38382	38383	8375
4	Two	2983	2839	29835
5	Three	28735	29839	6948
6	Four	58438	57438	67748
7				
8		128538	128499	112906

Figure 4.22   Horizontal Copy Insertion Border

	A	B	C	D
1		January	February	March
2				
3	One	38382	38383	8375
4	Two	2983	2839	29835
5	Three	28735	29839	A4:D4
6	Four	58438	57438	67748
7				
8		128538	128499	112906

Figure 4.23   Copy Complete

	A	B	C	D
1		January	February	March
2				
3	One	38382	38383	8375
4	Four	58438	57438	67748
5	Two	2983	2839	29835
6	Three	28735	29839	6948
7	Four	58438	57438	67748
8				
9		186976	185937	180654

Figure 4.25 shows the completed worksheet. The contents of the range B4:B5 have been copied into D4:D5, and the previous cell contents have shifted to the right. The column totals adjust to reflect the change in cell contents.

When a cell is copied between columns, a vertical insertion border is used and the remaining cells move to the right. If cells are copied between rows, a horizontal insertion border is used and the remaining cells shift down. Cell contents are not deleted when copied this way.

Figure 4.24   Insertion Border between Rows C and D

	A	B	C	D
1		January	February	March
2				
3	One	38382	38383	8375
4	Two	2983	2839	29835
5	Three	28735	29839	6948
6	Four	58438	57438	6718
7				
8		128538	128499	112906

Figure 4.25   Completed Vertical Drag-and-Drop Copy

	A	B	C	D	E
1		January	February	March	
2					
3	One	38382	38383	8375	
4	Two	2983	2839	2983	29835
5	Three	28735	29839	28735	6948
6	Four	58438	57438	67748	
7					
8		128538	128499	107841	

Exercise 4.4   Copying and Inserting between Cells

Cells will be copied and inserted between existing cells.

1 Open workbook **Ch4 Ex4** and save it as **Exer 4-4**.

2 In cell A2, key **City**; in cell B2, key **State**. Format for bold and center alignment.

3 Copy the range A2:B2 to C2:D2.

The cities and states will be placed in cells next to each other. Remember to hold down the Ctrl and Shift keys when copying cells and inserting them between existing cells.

4 Select cell C3 (**Texas**). Move the mouse pointer to the border of the active cell so it takes an arrow shape. Hold down the **Ctrl** and **Shift** keys. Click the mouse button and drag the vertical insertion border between cells A3 and B3. The ScreenTip reads **B3**.

5 Release the mouse button and then the **Ctrl** and **Shift** keys. Cell C3 is copied into cell B3; the contents of cells B3 and C3 shift one column to the right.

Copy cell C5 to cell A4.

6 Select cell C5 (**New York**). Move the mouse to the border of the active cell to get an arrow shape. Hold down **Ctrl** and **Shift**. Click the mouse button and drag the vertical insertion border between cells A4 and B4. The ScreenTip reads **B4**.

7 Release the mouse button and then the **Ctrl** and **Shift** keys.

8 Copy cell D4 (**Washington**) and insert it between cells A5 and B5.

9   Copy cell C7 (**Illinois**) and insert it between cells A6 and B6.

10 Copy cell D6 (**Virginia**) and insert it between cells A7 and B7.

11 Copy cell C8 (**Florida**) and insert it between A8 and B8. Columns A and B now list the cities and states; column C lists cities.

Copy cells using a horizontal insertion border.

12 Select cell D6 (**Virginia**). Hold down **Ctrl** and **Shift**. Click the mouse button. Move the cell between D2 and D3 to use a horizontal insert paste and enter it in cell D3. Release the mouse, then the **Ctrl** and **Shift** keys. The remaining cells have shifted down one row.

13 Insert cell D6 (**New York**) between the range D4 and D5 for a horizontal insert paste.

14 Select cell D9 (**Illinois**). Move it to cell D8 (do not hold down keys). A warning box opens that asks **Do you want to replace the contents of the destination cells?**

15 Click **OK**. You have moved cell D9 to cell D8.

16 Move cell D10 to D7. You will replace the contents of D7.

17 Enter your name in cell A10.

18 Place the file name in the header.

19 Save and print the worksheet.

Related Commands

The Undo and Redo Commands

The *Undo command*, located in the Edit menu, reverses the last entry. The words used in the Undo command change depending on the action to be reversed. For instance, if a cell has been pasted, the Undo command reads "Undo Paste" (Figure 4.26). If a drag-and-drop move is completed, the Undo command reads "Undo Drag and Drop" (Figure 4.27). The shortcut button is shown at the left of the command.

Figure 4.26   Undo Command after a Paste Command

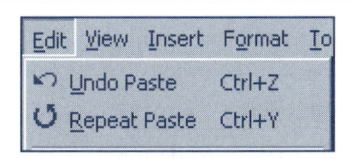

Figure 4.27   Undo Command after a Drag-and-Drop Move

Power Users

The keyboard command for Undo is **Ctrl**+**Z**.

Undo remembers the sequence of commands used in a worksheet. They are listed in a drop-down menu by the Undo button, shown in Figure 4.28. Select the actions you wish to undo by clicking on them. The worksheet returns to its previous form. Undo remembers the last 16 entries.

The *Redo command* is available after an Undo command has been used. It "redoes" what was undone.

Figure 4.28   Undo Selections

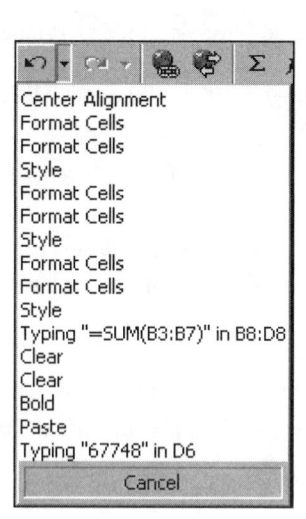

The Repeat Command

Excel will repeat the last command entered into a worksheet when the *Repeat command* on the Edit menu is selected.

The Repeat command changes to reflect the last action performed. If right alignment has just been applied, the Edit menu will read "Repeat Right Alignment." It will read "Repeat Paste" if the last command was to paste cell contents (Figure 4.29). Repeat can be used for repeating format choices.

Figure 4.29   Undo and Repeat Commands

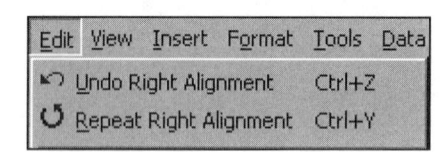

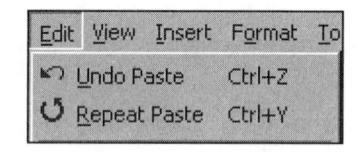

Repeat will repeat the last command. Redo is available only after Undo is used; it will perform a command that has been undone.

Power Users

The keyboard command for Repeat is the **F4** function key.

Exercise 4.5 Using Undo and Repeat

You will practice using the Undo and Repeat commands.

1 Open workbook **Ch4 Ex5** and save it as **Exer 4-5**.

2 Select the range A6:A7. Copy and paste it to the range beginning with cell A11.

Undo this command.

3 From the **Edit** menu, select **Undo Paste**.

4 Select cell C11 and click on the Paste button. The contents are pasted to the range C11:C12.

5 Click on the Undo button to undo the last command.

Power Users

5a Select cell E4 and click on the Paste button.

5b Undo the Paste command using the keyboard. Press **Ctrl**+**Z**.

---

6 In cell B8 use AutoSum to add the column and complete the entry.

7 Click on the Undo button.

8 Click on the Redo button.

9 Highlight the range C3:C9. Format the range for bold and right alignment.

10 Click on the Undo button. Only the last format choice is undone.

Use the Repeat command.

11 Select the range A3:A7. Format for bold.

12 Select the range D3:D5; then select **Repeat Font** from the **Edit** menu.

13 Repeat the format in cell D8.

14 Select the range B3:B7.

15 Select the Comma button.

16 Select the range D5:D9.

17 From **Edit**, select **Repeat Style**.

18 Access the drop-down list next to the Undo button.

Chapter 4   Moving and Copying Information

19 To select the first three commands, scroll down and click on the third. The formats for comma and bold are undone.

20 Access the Redo drop-down list next to the Redo button.

21 Select the first choice. Bold is repeated.

22 Place your name in cell A1.

23 Place the file name in the header.

24 Print and save the worksheet.

Using Paste Special

When cells are copied, all contents, formats, or formulas are also copied. However, it is sometimes useful to copy only the format, borders, or values of a cell. The *Paste Special dialog box*, shown in Figure 4.30, allows copying only parts of the cell contents.

Choices about pasting cell contents are listed in the Paste section at the top of the dialog box. To paste only the formula, select the Formulas option. Only the formula is copied; no formats will be copied.

To paste only the values of a cell, select the Values option. This is useful when a cell contains a formula, but you want to copy only the result.

Select the Formats option to paste only the formats from the copied cell or cells. The formats in the copied cell will be applied to all cells in the paste area. This is useful when repeating a format throughout a worksheet. When a cell contains a border, its format minus the border may be copied.

Figure 4.30   Paste Special Dialog Box

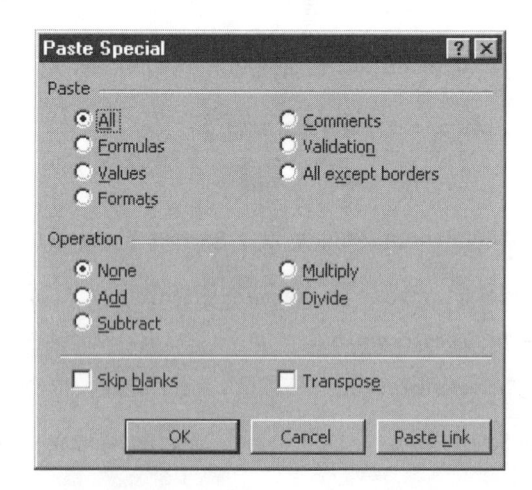

The Operation section of the Paste Special dialog box is used to combine the copy and paste areas. For instance, if you select the Subtract option button, the formula or value that is copied will be subtracted from the paste area formula or value.

Exercise 4.6   Using Paste Special

You will create a simple worksheet and copy format and formula information in the worksheet.

1 Open a new Excel workbook.

2 In cell A1, key your name.

Exercise 4.6—Using Paste Special

3   In the range A2:C2, key **January**, **February**, and **March**.

4   In cell A3, key **1**. In cell A4, enter a formula to add 1 to the contents of cell A3. Copy this formula through the range to cell A14.

5   Format the range A4:A14 for bold, italic, and center alignment.

Copy only the format of a cell.

6   Select cell A4. From **Edit**, select **Copy**.

7   Select the range A1:C2. From **Edit**, select **Paste Special**.

8   In the **Paste** section, select **Formats**, then **OK**. The format you applied to the numbers was copied to the column titles.

9   Select cell A3. From the **Edit** menu, select the **Repeat Paste Special** command (at the top of the pull-down menu).

10 In cell B3, key **10**.

Copy only the formula of a cell.

11 With cell A4 active, select a copy command.

12 Select the range B4:B14. Select a paste command. Note that the format was also copied to the new range.

13 Select the Undo button from the toolbar to undo the Paste command.

14 The marquee should still be surrounding cell A4. If so, from **Edit**, select **Paste Special**. (If the marquee is not surrounding cell A4, select A4 and a copy command. Then repeat this instruction.)

15 In the **Paste** section, select **Formulas**, then **OK**. Notice that only the formula was copied and not the format. Click in cells B4 and B6 to view the formula.

Copy only the numeric value of a cell.

16 Select a copy command for the range A8:A10.

17 Select the range C12:C14. From **Edit**, select **Paste Special**.

18 In the **Paste** section, select **Values**, then **OK**. Notice that only the value of the range A8:A10 was copied. Click in the cells to see that neither the format nor the formula was copied.

19 Format cell A1 for left alignment.

20 Place the file name in the header.

21 Save this workbook as **Exer 4-6** and print the worksheet.

Transposing a Worksheet

At the bottom of the Paste Special dialog box are two check boxes: Skip blanks and Transpose. The Skip blanks check box is used so blank cells in the copy area will not replace cell values previously located in the paste area. The *Transpose* check box is used when the labels of the rows and columns should change places—the column labels will become row labels and the row labels will become column labels. Look at the row and column labels in the worksheet shown in Figure 4.31.

In Figure 4.31, Item, January, and February are column labels, but they will be transposed with the row labels; Lamps, Tables, and Pictures will become column labels.

Highlight the portion of the worksheet that will be transposed. From the Edit menu, select Copy. Then select the destination cell. Select Paste Special from the Edit menu. When the dialog box opens, click the mouse pointer in the Transpose box to select it; a ✓ in the box indicates it is selected (Figure 4.32).

The result of transposing cells in this worksheet is shown in Figure 4.33. The values in the cells associated with each column and row also move so the worksheet values are still correct. Notice the value of lamps in February to see how it changed position.

Figure 4.31 A Simple Worksheet

	A	B	C
1	Item	January	February
2	Lamps	273	382
3	Tables	139	374
4	Pictures	293	282

Figure 4.32 Paste Special Dialog Box with Transpose Selected

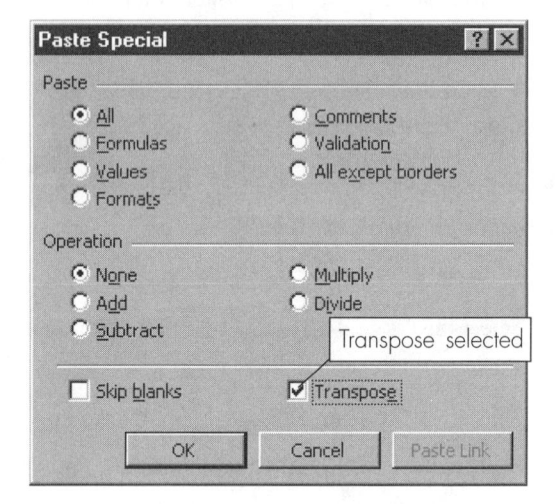

Figure 4.33 Worksheet with Transposed Cell Locations

	A	B	C	D	E
1	Item	January	February		
2	Lamps	273	382		
3	Tables	139	374		
4	Pictures	293	282		
5					
6					
7					
8		Item	Lamps	Tables	Pictures
9		January	273	139	293
10		February	382	374	282

Exercise 4.7 Transposing a Worksheet

You will open a worksheet, transpose its contents, and print it.

1 Open workbook **Ch4 Ex7** and save it as **Exer 4-7**.

2 In cell A10, replace **Student's Name** with your name.

3   Complete the worksheet with the totals in row 7. Format cell A7 for bold and center alignment. Place a double border under the totals in row 7.

4   Highlight the range A2:D6 and select a copy command.

5   Select cell C12 as the destination cell. From the **Edit** menu, select **Paste Special**.

6   Click the **Transpose** box (at the bottom of the dialog box), then click **OK**.

7   Look at the worksheet. Notice that the numbers and formulas remain accurate and have moved in relation to the column labels. Also notice how the border choices have remained after transposition.

8   Place the file name in the header.

9   Save and print the worksheet.

Copying to Many Locations

A cell or range of cells may be copied in one step to more than one area of a worksheet by making *multiple paste* selections for the destination.

First, highlight the copy area and select a copy command. (In Figure 4.34, the copy area is A1:C1.) Next, select the destination cell. Then hold down Ctrl and select each additional destination cell. With the destination cells highlighted, select a paste command. The information is now copied into all selected paste areas. Figure 4.34 shows the paste completed into three separate ranges of A9:C9, B11:D11, and C13:E13.

Figure 4.34   Multiple Paste Areas

	A	B	C	D	E
1	**Item**	**January**	**February**		
2	Lamps	273	382		
3	Tables	139	374		
4	Pictures	293	282		
5					
6	**Total**	705	1038		
7					
8					
9	**Item**	**January**	**February**		
10					
11		**Item**	**January**	**February**	
12					
13			**Item**	**January**	**February**

Figure 4.35   Using Format Painter

Using the Format Painter

Copying the format from one cell to another is quickly done by using the *Format Painter button*, located on the Standard toolbar. After a cell is formatted, highlight the cell, and then click on the Format Painter button. The mouse pointer takes this shape:

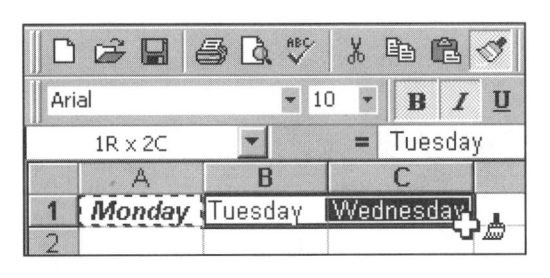

Click in the cell or drag through the range you want to format, as shown in Figure 4.35. When the mouse button is released, the format is applied to the cells selected with the Format Painter.

Using the Format Painter is especially useful when several format choices are applied in a cell—such as bold, italics, and alignment—providing a quick and easy way to apply the format to additional cells.

The Format Painter can also be used for formatting multiple ranges. Double-click the Format Painter button . Then select each cell or range of cells where the format will be applied. When formats are applied in all the cells that require the same format, click again on the Format Painter button to stop the Format Painter.

Exercise 4.8   Copying and Applying Formats

You will create a worksheet and then copy and format information in multiple locations.

1. Open workbook **Ch4 Ex8** and save it as **Exer 4-8**.
2. Select the range A1:E4. Then select a copy command.
3. Select cells A7, A12, and A17. (Hold down **Ctrl** to select multiple cells.) Then select a paste command.
4. Highlight the column titles (B1:E1). Format for bold, italic, right alignment, and underline.
5. Click on the Format Painter button . Drag the mouse through B7:E7 (column titles of second area).
6. With B7:E7 still highlighted, double-click on the Format Painter button . Drag it through the ranges B12:E12 and B17:E17. Click again on the Format Painter button to stop the command.
7. Select cell A2. Format it for bold, underline, and center alignment.
8. Double-click the Format Painter button . Click in cell A3, then cell A4. Drag through the ranges A8:A10, A13:A15, and A18:A20. Stop the Format Painter.
9. Adjust column widths if needed.
10. Enter your name in an empty cell.
11. Copy the format in cell B1 to the cell containing your name. Format for left alignment.
12. Place the file name in the header.
13. Save and print the worksheet.

Summary

- Cell contents can be moved to a new location on a worksheet through a process of cutting and pasting.
- The move area is the cell or range of cells that will be move to a new location.
- The paste area, or destination, is the cell or range of cells to where the cell contents will be moved.
- The destination cell is the upper-left cell of the paste area.
- To move cells, highlight the move area; then select the Cut command from the Edit menu. Select the destination cell; then select the Paste command from the Edit menu.

- The keyboard command for Cut is Ctrl+X. The keyboard command for Paste is Ctrl+V.
- The Cut button is ![cut]. The Copy button is ![copy].
- A marquee surrounds the active move or copy area.
- Cells can be copied to a new location. To do this, select a cell or range of cells. Then paste them to the destination.
- The Copy command can be accessed in the File menu or by clicking the Copy button ![copy]. The keyboard command for Copy is Ctrl+C.
- The marquee disappears when a new selection is made. It can also be stopped from displaying by pressing the Esc key on the keyboard.
- The drag-and-drop technique uses the computer screen to visualize the placement of the paste area. Hold down the mouse button near the cell border until it takes the shape of an arrow, then move the cell or range of cells to a new location.
- To use the drag-and-drop method, the mouse must take the shape of an arrow. A box the size of the move area then moves with the mouse pointer around the screen as a visual indicator for placement of the paste area. A ScreenTip identifies the destination cell or range.
- When cells are moved, the contents of any cells already in the paste area are deleted.
- Copying cells using the drag-and-drop method uses the same technique as moving cells. The Ctrl key must be held down to copy.
- To move cells and insert them between existing cells, use the drag-and-drop method and hold down the Shift key during the process.
- To copy cells and insert them between existing cells, use the drag-and-drop method and hold down the Ctrl and Shift keys during the process.
- To insert cells between existing cells, hold down the Shift key while using the drag-and-drop method of moving cells. The remaining cells move to make room for the new cells.
- When inserting cells between existing cells, the existing cells shift down or to the right.
- When text is copied to a new location, all previous contents of that location are replaced.
- The Undo command will erase the last entries and return the worksheet to its previous condition.
- The keyboard command for undo is Ctrl+Z. The button is ![undo].
- Use the Undo command to undo several commands or entries; access the drop-down menu and select the command(s) to undo.
- The Repeat command repeats the last entry. The keyboard command for repeat is F4.
- Use the Redo command to redo commands previously undone; select the drop-down menu and select the command(s) to redo. The Redo button is ![redo].
- Column and row labels can be exchanged on a worksheet by using Transpose in the Paste Special dialog box.
- Multiple paste areas can be selected. Hold down the Ctrl key while selecting additional paste ranges.
- Paste Special allows only formulas, cell values, or formats of a cell or range of cells to be copied to a new location.
- Use the Format Painter button ![fp] to copy a format. Click once on the Format Painter button ![fp] to copy the format to one location; double-click to copy the format to multiple locations.

Important Terminology

copy area
Copy button
Copy command
cut-and-paste method
Cut button
Cut command
destination
destination cell

drag-and-drop method
Format Painter button
insertion border
marquee
move area
multiple paste
paste area

Paste button
Paste command
Paste Special dialog box
Redo command
Repeat command
Transpose
Undo command

Buttons to Know

Study Questions

True-False

Place a T in the space if the statement is true; place an F if the statement is false.

_____ 1. To move cell contents, first select the cells, then choose the Paste command from the Edit menu.

_____ 2. When pasting cells, only the data is pasted.

_____ 3. The destination cell is any cell in the paste area.

_____ 4. When using the drag-and-drop method to move cells, first select the cells from the move area.

_____ 5. One way to move a cell is to first select the Cut command, then the Paste command.

_____ 6. When copying cell contents, select only the destination cell before pasting.

_____ 7. When using the drag-and-drop method to move cells across the screen, a border will appear to visually indicate the size of the move area.

_____ 8. Cell contents can be moved only to cells that are visible on the computer screen and not to other parts of the worksheet.

_____ 9. When cells are moved, the contents of the cells in the paste area automatically adjust to new positions to make room for the new cells.

_____ 10. When using the drag-and-drop copy technique, a ScreenTip indicates the cells in the destination range.

_____ 11. To insert cells between existing cells, hold down the Ctrl key while completing a drag-and-drop move.

_____ 12. When inserting cells between existing cells, an insertion border visually shows where the insertion of cells will take place.

_____ 13. The Copy and Paste commands are found on the File menu.

_____ 14. When copying cells, all contents in the paste area are eliminated.

_____ 15. To use the Copy button 📋 in the toolbar, the paste area must first be selected.
_____ 16. When using the Copy button 📋 in the toolbar, select the paste range and click on the Copy button to paste the cells.
_____ 17. When moving cells to a destination that is in the center of cells that contain data, the data in those cells is replaced.
_____ 18. To reverse the last entry made in a worksheet and return the previous contents to the cells, select the Cancel command from the Edit menu.
_____ 19. When the Repeat command is used, the information may be repeated only one time.
_____ 20. The Paste Special dialog box allows choices about pasting that may include only formats or formulas.
_____ 21. When you want to switch the headings so row labels become column labels, select the Change Places command in the Paste Special dialog box.
_____ 22. Cells may be pasted to multiple ranges with one Paste command.
_____ 23. Undo is used to cancel all changes made to a worksheet.
_____ 24. The Format Painter button 🖌 is used to copy formats to different sections of a worksheet.
_____ 25. The Repeat command is used to repeat the last command; it can be used only once.
_____ 26. The Paste button 📋 is used when cutting cells; it is different from the Paste button used for copying cells.

Fill-In

Place the word in the space that correctly completes the statement.
1. The area of the worksheet where moved cells will be placed is the _____ area.
2. The area of the worksheet that includes the cells to be moved is called the _____ area.
3. The upper-left cell of the paste area is called the _____ cell.
4. When a horizontal insertion border is used in a drag-and-drop move, the existing cells shift _____ .
5. The area that contains the cell or range of cells to be copied is called the _____ area.
6. To copy cells using the drag-and-drop method, hold down the _____ key while completing the copy.
7. To complete one paste and turn off the marquee, press the _____ key.
8. To use the drag-and-drop method for copying cells and insert them between existing cells, hold down the _____ and _____ keys while copying.
9. An entry can be repeatedly placed in a new location by using the _____ command in the Edit menu.
10. To copy a format to several cell ranges in a worksheet, select the _____ and drag the mouse through the range.
11. To copy only the formula of a cell, use the _____ command from the Edit menu.

Assignments

Note: After completing all work in Chapter 4, you may delete the Ch04 directory from your Student Data Disk if you are using one disk.

Assignment 4.1

The City's Best Newspaper is preparing a statement of revenue and expenses for a month. They have listed all the entries, but the order needs to be rearranged. You will rearrange the order of the row labels and then complete the statement.

1. Open workbook **Ch4 As1** and save it as **Assig 4-1**.
2. Use move commands to rearrange the worksheet in the correct order, shown in the following illustration. Format as shown, and enter the amounts in column B.

	A	B	C
1	City's Best Newspaper		
2	Statement of Revenue and Expenses		
3	January, 1996		
4			
5			
6	Revenue		
7	Advertising Revenue	20547	
8	Circulation Revenue	18745	
9	Classified Ad Sales	11347	
10	Expenses		
11	Labor	15574	
12	Office Supplies	7574	
13	Paper & Supplies	10578	
14	Transportation Expense	8475	
15	Utilities	4476	
16	Miscellaneous Expense	1057	

3. Complete the worksheet.
   - After the revenue and expense sections, enter row labels for **Total Revenue** and **Total Expenses**. You will need to insert the labels between existing data.
   - Total the revenue and the expenses.
   - Leave a blank row after **Total Expenses**, and make a title for **Net Income**.
   - Complete the formulas needed. Net income is total revenue less total expenses.
4. Format the worksheet.
   - Format numbers correctly for currency.
   - Place border lines where needed.
   - Place your name in cell A24.

5. Format placement on the page.
   - Place the file name in the header.
   - Use a top margin of 2".
6. Save and print the worksheet. Print a copy that shows the formulas used.

Assignment 4.2

You will complete a weekly payroll for Lewis Manufacturing. This large worksheet is completed faster by copying text and formulas. The Undo and Repeat commands will also be used.

1. Open a new workbook and enter the following:

	A	B
1	Lewis Manufacturing	
2	Payroll Report	
3		
4	Week 1	
5	Week 2	
6	Week 3	

2. Move data to new locations.
   - Move the range A5:A6 to A11:A12.
   - Move cell A12 to cell A18.
3. Enter the following data in row 5:

	A	B	C	D
5	Name	Rate	No. Hours	Gross Pay

4. Format title and labels.
   - Format all entries in column A for bold.
   - Format the column labels for bold and center alignment.
   - Copy the column labels (A5:D5) to cells A12 and A19. The column labels and format are copied to the new location.
5. Save as **Assig 4-2**.
6. Enter the following employees and their rate of pay:

	A	B
6	P. Bacha	6.25
7	V. Charlston	8.75
8	S. George	6.5
9	C. Owings	7.25

7. Complete the format and correct an error.
   - Format the employees' names for right alignment. Then click the mouse in any empty cell.
   - A mistake was made. From **Edit**, select **Undo Right Alignment**. The names are again aligned at the left.
   - Copy the employees' names and pay rates (including the format) to A13:B16 and A20:B23. Can you do this in one step?

8. Save the worksheet.
9. Using this worksheet, enter the number of hours each employee worked each week. When you are finished, your worksheet will look like the following:

	A	B	C
1	Lewis Manufacturing		
2	Payroll Report		
3			
4	Week 1		
5	Name	Rate	No. Hours
6	P. Bacha	6.25	39
7	V. Charlston	8.75	40
8	S. George	6.5	37
9	C. Owings	7.25	39
10			
11	Week 2		
12	Name	Rate	No. Hours
13	P. Bacha	6.25	40
14	V. Charlston	8.75	39
15	S. George	6.5	40
16	C. Owings	7.25	38
17			
18	Week 3		
19	Name	Rate	No. Hours
20	P. Bacha	6.25	27
21	V. Charlston	8.75	39
22	S. George	6.5	40
23	C. Owings	7.25	40

10. Complete the gross pay in column D. Gross pay is the rate multiplied by the number of hours.
11. Format numbers.
    - Format the rate for Comma style, two decimal places. Use right alignment.
    - Format the number of hours for Comma style, zero decimal places. Use right alignment.
12. Adjust the column widths.
13. Complete the totals.
    - Insert a blank row after the entry for C. Owings in Weeks 1 and 2.
    - On the line below C. Owings (last entry), key **Total**. Format for bold and center alignment (this is the same format you used for **Name**).
    - Place a total after the payroll for each week.
    - After the Week 3 total, key **Grand Total** and format it as you did **Total**.
    - Complete the total formulas using AutoSum. Total only the amount of gross pay each week. Also use AutoSum to complete the grand total.
14. In cell A30, key **Prepared by** followed by your name.
15. Select a top margin and left margin of 2". Place the file name in the header.
16. Save and print the worksheet.

17. Print a second copy that shows formulas. Adjust the margins and column widths so the worksheet fits on one page. Use Print Preview to view these adjustments.
18. Close the worksheet without saving changes.

Assignment 4.3

Kevin's Den of Electronics has started preparing a quarterly report for sales. You will complete the report showing the actual sales amount and compare that with the forecast amount.

A Checkpoint is provided at the end of the assignment.

1. Open workbook **Ch4 As3** and save it to your disk as **Assig 4-3**.
2. Add the following information beginning with row 14:

	A	B	C	D	E
13					
14		Forecast	Actual	Difference	%Forecast
15		800			
16		800			
17		1200			
18		900			
19		1200			
20					

3. Copy formats and ranges.
   - Format column labels for bold and right alignment. Then copy the format of the column labels to the totals and to the column labels of the second part of the worksheet.
   - Copy the range A5:A10 to A15:A20.
4. In cell A24, key **Prepared by** followed by your name.
5. Remember to save often.
6. Complete the worksheet.
   - Place totals in row 10 and in column E.
   - Place a sum formula in row 20 that will add the range B15:D20. (You will later replace the numbers in columns C and D in the bottom section of the worksheet.)
   - Copy only the value of the totals in column E to cell C15. (Use Paste Special.)
   - In column D, enter the formula to determine the difference. It is the actual sales less the forecast amount. You may have some negative amounts.
   - In column E, enter the formula to determine the percentage of difference. It is Actual divided by Forecast.
7. Format the worksheet.
   - Format the **% Forecast column** column for percentages.
   - Format other numbers for comma style with zero decimal places.
   - Format the total amounts for bold. Place a single underline above the range and a double underline beneath it.
   - Copy the format for the total amounts to the totals in the second section.
   - Adjust the column widths so all data shows in the cells. You may use Print Preview.
8. Format for a top margin of 2" and a left margin of 1.5". Place the file name in the header.
9. Save and print the worksheet.

10. Check the worksheet to see how it looks. Are all amounts entered and formatted correctly? Are underlines used correctly? Does it have a professional appearance? If needed, make changes and print a corrected copy.
11. Display the formulas in the worksheet and print it on one page. (Use Print Preview.)
12. Close the workbook without saving changes.

Checkpoint:

Cell E5	824
Cell B10	1,527
Cell D15	24
Cell E15	103%
Cell B20	4,900

Assignment 4.4

K. P. Sound Shop has started a worksheet to report the value of the inventory for May. You will complete the worksheet and format it. You will then complete the inventory worksheet for June.

1. Open to workbook **Ch4 As4** and save it as **Assig 4-4**.
2. Complete the worksheet.
    - Rearrange the inventory in alphabetic order.
    - Enter the value of the inventory in column B using the following data:

	A	B
1	K. P. Sound Shop	
2	Inventory - Valued	
3	May 30, 1998	
4		
5	CD Player	2258.64
6	Clock	335.87
7	Clock/Radio	905.84
8	Radio	567.76
9	Stereo	3540.25
10	Tape Deck	1907.54
11	Television	7521.25
12	VCR	2847.37

3. Format the worksheet.
    - Format the three-line title for bold.
    - Format column B for currency.
    - Total the worksheet in row 13. In cell A13, key **Total** and format it for bold and center alignment.
    - Place correct borders around the total amounts.
4. In cell A15, enter your name. In cell A16, enter today's date.
5. Format the placement of the worksheet.
    - Place the file name in the header.
    - Set a top margin of 2.5" and a left margin of 2".

6. Save and print the worksheet. At the top, write "Print 1."
7. Print a copy that shows the formulas used.
8. Complete the worksheet for the month of June.
   - Copy the entire worksheet and place it beginning in cell A20.
   - Change the heading to read **30-June-1998**.
   - Change the data in column B as listed below:

	A	B
23	CD Player	3518.44
24	Clock	385.91
25	Clock/Radio	1155.84
26	Radio	3476
27	Stereo	354.25
28	Tape Deck	1627.14
29	Television	6921.05
30	VCR	3147.57

   - In Print Preview, adjust the margins so that both worksheets remain on the same page.
9. Save and print the worksheet. At the top, write "Print 2."

Assignment 4.5

Bill's Round Specialties sells balls used for sporting events, such as golf balls and tennis balls. They have branches in major cities throughout the country. They prepare a quarterly report summarizing the sales by ball type for their branches.

The first report is completed, but lacks totals and formatting. You will finish the first quarter report and prepare reports for the other three quarters. You will also determine the total annual sales for each ball type and the total sales of all balls.

1. Open workbook **Ch4 As5** and save it as **Assig 4-5**.
2. Complete the worksheet.
   - In cell A11, key **Total**. Format it for bold and right alignment.
   - In cell G4, key **Total**.
   - Use AutoSum to place totals in row 11 and column G.
3. Format the worksheet.
   - Bold the three-line worksheet title and the column labels.
   - Format column labels for bold italics.
   - Place a border beneath the column labels.
   - Format for currency.
   - Place underlines correctly. Place a double underline under the totals.
4. Save the worksheet often.
5. Complete the worksheet for the second quarter.
   - Copy the worksheet (not including the two-line heading). Begin with **First Quarter**. Leave two blank lines under the first worksheet.
   - Change the title from **First Quarter** to **Second Quarter**. The Second Quarter worksheet is below the First Quarter worksheet.

- Enter the following amounts:

Second Quarter					
	Footballs	Baseballs	Volleyballs	Golf Balls	Tennis Balls
Miami	3541.11	789.57	667.77	325.58	158.35
Philadelphia	257.25	513.14	587.85	695.47	1057.68
Omaha	1057.95	1537.54	675.12	2035.68	687.54
Austin	1125.68	1105.68	1457.3	1157.65	598.65
New Orleans	489.65	587.65	1157.96	254.68	486.24
Seattle	1247.25	953.24	678.95	1058.67	665.37

- Place totals in the last row and in column G and format as you did for the First Quarter worksheet.
- Format **Second Quarter** for bold.
- Check other formats; the Second Quarter worksheet should have the same format as the First Quarter worksheet.

6. Complete the third and fourth quarter worksheets as you did the second quarter worksheet. The information is provided below:

Third Quarter					
	Footballs	Baseballs	Volleyballs	Golf Balls	Tennis Balls
Miami	1105.68	1457.3	2035.68	687.54	486.24
Philadelphia	1058.67	158.35	257.25	675.12	665.37
Omaha	1157.96	254.68	1057.95	667.77	325.58
Austin	1125.68	678.95	1057.68	489.65	587.65
New Orleans	587.85	695.47	513.14	1157.65	598.65
Seattle	3541.11	789.57	1537.54	1247.25	953.24

Fourth Quarter					
	Footballs	Baseballs	Volleyballs	Golf Balls	Tennis Balls
Miami	678.95	1157.96	489.65	1457.3	254.68
Philadelphia	513.14	953.24	257.25	675.12	587.85
Omaha	486.24	1125.68	695.47	1157.65	1105.68
Austin	667.77	3541.11	1057.95	1247.25	1057.68
New Orleans	598.65	1058.67	789.57	1537.54	158.35
Seattle	325.58	687.54	665.37	587.65	2035.68

7. Use AutoSum to place a grand total in the last row of the worksheet. Be sure to place the label **Grand Total** in the row. Format the row for bold.
8. Place the file name in the header.
9. In cell A48, enter **Prepared by** followed by your name.
10. Use Print Preview to print each worksheet on one page and to adjust the margins so it is centered.
11. Save and print the worksheets. Print a copy that shows the formulas used.

Checkpoint:

First Quarter Football Total	2,807.61
Second Quarter Total	27,612.22
Grand Total Volleyball	19,207.92

Assignment 4.6

Skrib's J Corporation is completing a worksheet that shows a retail employee's sales for two months. You will complete and format the report. Some summary information regarding each salesperson's productivity will also be completed.

1. Open to workbook **Ch4 As6** and resave it as **Assig 4-6**.
2. Enter the following amounts for the sales report:

	A	B	C	D
4	January	Area A	Area B	Area C
5	Bill	3857	3841	225
6	John	6094	5947	265
7	Susan	3948	6284	485
8	Krista	9694	2256	558
9	Total			
10				
11	February	Area A	Area B	Area C
12	Bill	4838	4056	225
13	John	5969	7853	855
14	Susan	2039	4852	548
15	Krista	4968	1056	721

3. Complete the worksheet.
   - Enter the totals needed in row 9, row 16, and column E, and label column E **Total**.
   - Enter the grand total in row 17.
   - In the section beginning with row 19, enter the total for each salesperson. Use AutoSum and nonadjacent ranges. The formula for Bill will be **=SUM(B5:D5,B12:D12)**.
4. Format the worksheet. Use Format Painter whenever possible.
   - Format the title for bold and italics.
   - Format the column labels for bold and right alignment. Left align the names of the months.
   - Format the grand total for bold, including the total amounts. Center the words **Total** and **Grand Total**.
   - In column A, indent the labels that contain the names.
   - Place borders correctly.
   - Format correctly for currency. Do not include decimal places.
5. Enter your name in cell A25.
6. Place the file name in the header of the worksheet.
7. Use Print Preview to center the worksheet on the page. (It does not need to be exact.)
8. Save and print the worksheet. Print a copy showing the formulas used.

   Checkpoint:
January Total	$43,454
Bill January Total	$7,923
Grand Total Area A	$41,407

Case Problem 4

Lee and Stephen's Ice Cream Shoppe prepares a quarterly report for sales of their ice cream products.

Prepare a report that summarizes the sales information for the first quarter of the current year. Use the information provided below:

	January	February	March
Cones	1238	1938	2283
Shakes	885	730	1058
Sundaes	957	1154	2004

Use a three-line title that includes the name of the firm, **Quarterly Report**, and the date (use March 30 of the current year). Provide product totals for the quarter and for each month.

Plan the worksheet using pencil and paper. Turn in your plan along with your completed Excel documents.

Format the worksheet correctly. The numbers given are the actual number of products sold and not money amounts. You will find AutoSum techniques helpful in preparing this worksheet. Save the worksheet as **Case 4**. At the bottom of the worksheet key **Prepared by** followed by your name. Place the file name in the header.

Print the worksheet. Check to see how it looks. Are all amounts entered and formatted correctly? Are underlines used correctly? Does it have a professional appearance? Is it centered and have you included the file name in the header? If needed, make changes and print a corrected copy. Also print a copy that shows the formulas you used.

Add the information for the second quarter. Copy the original information to new cells in the worksheet. Change the months to **April, May,** and **June**. Change the title from **First Quarter** to **First and Second Quarters**. Enter the following information:

	A	B	C	D
1		April	May	June
2	Cones	2783	3382	3092
3	Shakes	1872	2039	1753
4	Sundaes	2001	2563	2172

Change the date to **June 30** of the current year. In addition to the monthly totals, include grand totals for both quarters. Readjust columns and margins if needed. Save as **Case 4, June**.

Checkpoint:

Total January	3,080
Total Shakes First Quarter	2,673
Total Sundaes Second Quarter	6,736
Total June	7,017
Grand Total	33,904

Remember to delete the **Ch04** directory if you are using one disk.

Chapter 5

Working with Formulas

Objectives

1. Use relative cell references when moving and copying formulas.
2. Use absolute and mixed cell references.
3. Understand how functions are created.
4. Use basic statistical functions.
5. Use IF statements in formulas.

Introduction

Much of Excel's power is in its ability to copy formulas accurately and quickly. As a formula is moved in a worksheet, the cell references within the formula adjust to the new location. Understanding the concept of these adjusted cell references, called relative references, is critical for the Excel user. There are occasions, however, when a specific cell will be referred to in the worksheet, and its reference should not change when the formula is copied. These references are called absolute references.

Excel provides functions to easily create complex formulas. A preview of functions is given in this chapter. The student will use statistical functions including average, minimum, and maximum.

One function often used in creating formulas is the IF function. This allows choices to be made when creating a formula. Stated simply, the IF function states, "If this is the result, then enter this amount in the box. If the result is different, then enter another amount."

Moving and Copying Formulas

Cells containing formulas can be moved or copied like cells that contain data. However, the reference to particular cells in a formula is important. In order to build error-free worksheets, it is important to understand what happens to cell references in formulas as they are moved or copied to new locations in a worksheet.

Using Relative References

When cells are moved or copied all cell contents are also moved, including any cell reference used in a formula. However, the cell reference in a formula automatically adjusts to its new location. This type of changeable reference is called a *relative reference*. Relative references may require additional study at the computer for full understanding of their use.

Look at the worksheet in Figure 5.1. The formula to subtract A2 from A1 is entered in cell A3.

Formulas should be copied whenever possible. This is faster and safeguards against error. The formula in cell A3 will be copied into cells B3 and C3, providing totals for those columns.

The formula in cell A3 reads =A1-A2 (Figure 5.1). When it is copied into cell B3, the formula automatically adjusts the cell references to column B; it reads =B1-B2, as shown in Figure 5.2. The formula for cell B3 is shown in the entry area and the results are in cell B3.

The references adjusted from column A to column B and are relative references. As their position on the worksheet moves, references adjust to reflect their new location, in this case a different column.

Figure 5.3 shows the same formula copied into cell C3. Again, the references automatically change to reflect their new location in column C.

Likewise, when a cell is copied to a new row, the reference to the row changes. In Figure 5.4, the formula =A1+10 is entered in cell A2.

When the formula was copied into cell A3, the cell reference automatically changed to the next row, reflecting its new position; the result of 30 is entered into the cell (Figure 5.5).

Copying formulas speeds up the creation of a worksheet. Relative references assure that a formula will change relative to its new location.

Figure 5.1   Subtracting Numbers

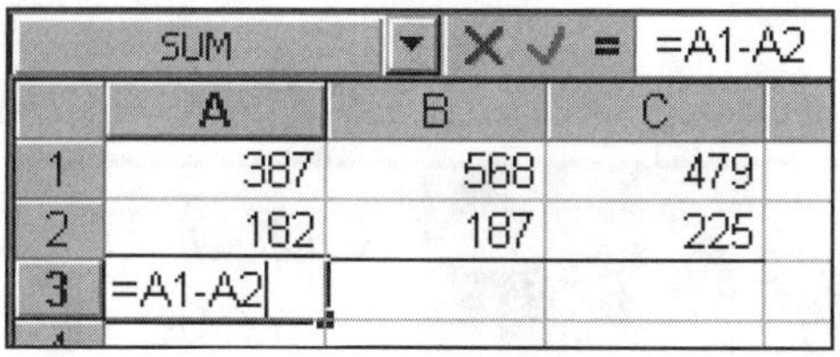

Figure 5.2   Formula Copied to Show Relative References

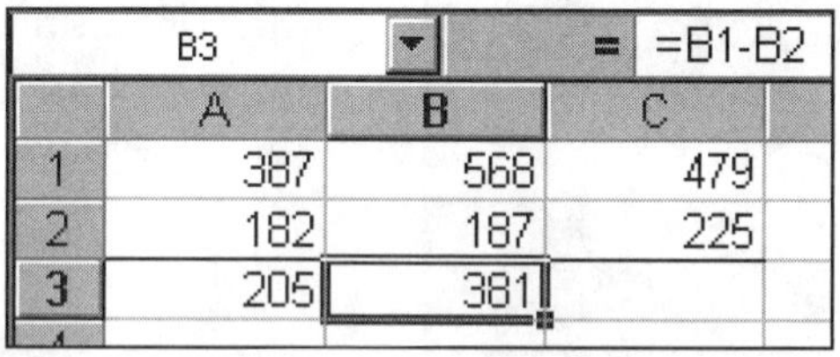

Figure 5.3   Copy Complete with Additional Relative References

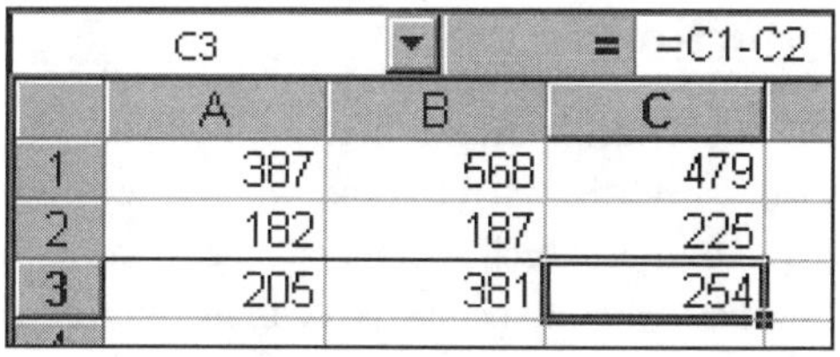

Figure 5.4   Entering a Formula

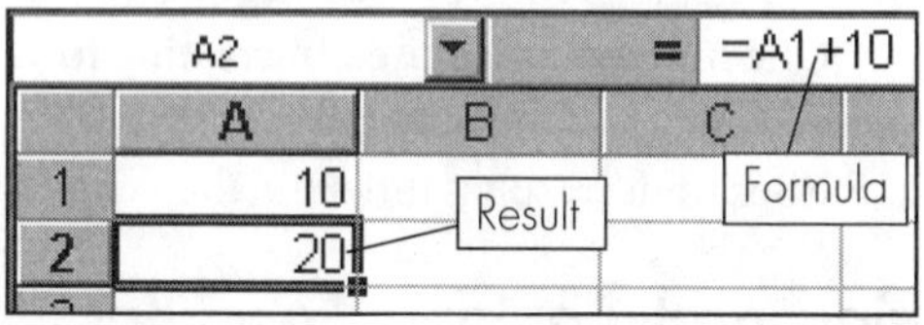

Figure 5.5   Cell Copied; Reference Changed

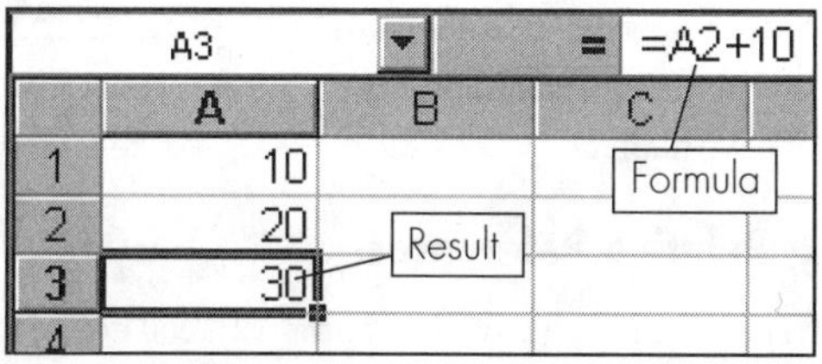

Exercise 5.1   Using Relative References

You will retrieve a worksheet and copy formulas to new locations to see how relative references adjust to new locations.

Note: Before completing the exercises and assignments in this chapter, you will need to expand the Chapter 5 files on your Student Data Disk. In Windows Explorer, locate the Chapter 5 file and double-click on it. When the files have been expanded, you will be able to access them from Excel.

1. Open workbook **Ch5 Ex1** and save it as **Exer 5-1**.

2. Enter an AutoSum total in cell B8.

3. With cell B8 active, select a copy command. Then click in cell C8 and select a paste command. Notice how the cell references have changed to reflect the change in column.

4. Click in cell D8 and select a paste command. The formula is copied into cell D8; the references to the column change to reflect the new location in column D.

5. In cell E5, enter a point-and-click formula to add the cells in row 5. The formula will read **=B5+C5+D5**.

6. With cell E5 active, select a copy command.

7. Highlight the range of column E that needs a total (E6:E8). Select a paste command. A range of cells is pasted at one time. In each cell reference, notice how the row number has changed to reflect the new location of the formula.

8. Enter your name in cell A11.

9. Place the file name in the header.

10. Save and print the worksheet. Print a second copy showing formulas.

Using Absolute References

It is preferable to use cell references in formulas so that changes made in one cell can automatically be reflected in other cells. When formulas are copied, the cell references change to reflect their new location because they are relative references.

There are times when a formula contains a cell reference that should always remain the same. This is called an *absolute reference*; the contents of this specific cell will be used in several formulas and copied to other cells. An absolute reference in a formula is identified by a dollar sign ($) in front of both the column and row headings.

For example, $C$8 is an absolute reference and C8 is a relative reference. Both refer to the same cell. The difference comes when the cell is moved or copied. A formula using the absolute reference ($C$8) instructs Excel to always use the contents of cell C8 no matter where the reference is located in the worksheet. A formula using the relative reference (C8) instructs Excel to adjust the cell reference to new locations.

Let's look at an example of how an absolute reference is used. The worksheet in Figure 5.6 is designed to show the commissions earned on sales. The commission rate is 8.5%, located in cell B8.

The amount of commission in column C is determined by multiplying the total sales by the commission rate. The formula used in cell C2 is =B2*B8. Because the commission rate in cell B8 is to be multiplied by each sales amount, the commission rate must be an absolute reference. Use the dollar signs ($) in the formula to show the absolute reference for cell B8 ($B$8). Then as the formula is copied, the reference to cell B8 does not change.

Figure 5.7 shows the formula for Randall's commission entered in cell C2.

Figure 5.8 shows the copied formula. The relative reference (B2) changes to cell B3, but the absolute reference ($B$8) remains the same. (If cell B8 were not absolute, it would have changed to B9. Since cell B9 is empty, the result would have been an error.) In Figure 5.8, the formula in cell C3 instructs Excel to multiply cell B3 by cell B8.

The completed worksheet is shown in Figure 5.9. The worksheet at the top shows the results; the bottom worksheet displays the formulas. Study the formulas in column C to see how the relative and absolute references are used.

Figure 5.6   Commissions Worksheet

	A	B	C
1	Salesman	Total Sales	Commission
2	Randall	10,563	
3	Swanson	12,857	
4	Thompson	19,257	
5	Wilson	15,230	
6			
7			
8	Commission Rate	8.5%	

Figure 5.7   Absolute Reference

	A	B	C
1	Salesman	Total Sales	Commission
2	Randall	10,563	=B2*$B$8
3	Swanson	12,857	
4	Thompson	19,257	
5	Wilson	15,230	
6			
7			
8	Commission Rate	8.5%	

Figure 5.8   Copying an Absolute Reference

C3   =   =B3*$B$8

	A	B	C
1	Salesman	Total Sales	Commission
2	Randall	10,563	897.855
3	Swanson	12,857	1092.845
4	Thompson	19,257	
5	Wilson	15,230	
6			
7			
8	Commission Rate	8.5%	

Figure 5.9   Worksheet Using Absolute References

Completed Worksheet

	A	B	C
1	Salesman	Total Sales	Commission
2	Randall	10,563	897.855
3	Swanson	12,857	1092.845
4	Thompson	19,257	1636.845
5	Wilson	15,230	1294.55
6			
7			
8	Commission Rate	8.5%	

Formulas Displayed

	A	B	C
1	Salesman	Total Sales	Commission
2	Randall	10563	=B2*$B$8
3	Swanson	12857	=B3*$B$8
4	Thompson	19257	=B4*$B$8
5	Wilson	15230	=B5*$B$8
6			
7			
8	Commission Rate	0.085	

The dollar signs in absolute references can be entered quickly using the F4 function key. First key the cell reference, then press F4. The dollar signs are placed around the reference to indicate that it is an absolute reference.

As with relative references, it takes practice at the computer to fully understand the concept of absolute references.

Exercise 5.2   Using Absolute References

Ace Store completes a daily sales record. The amount for the state sales tax needs to be entered and the worksheet completed. As formulas are entered, you will use both relative and absolute references.

1   Open workbook **Ch5 Ex2** and save it as **Exer 5-2**.

2   Change the date in cell A3 to today's date.

Complete the sales tax column. This is the amount of the sale times the tax rate.

3   In cell C8, enter the formula to determine the tax (**=B8*B5**). Press F4 to change cell B5 to an absolute reference (**$B$5**).

4   Copy the formula of cell C8 to the range C9:C11.

5 Click in cell C9. Notice the change in the formula. The reference to the customer changed but the reference to the sales tax rate in cell B5 remained the same because it was entered as an absolute reference.

Complete the received column.

6 In cell D8, enter the formula for the amount received. It is the amount of the sale plus the sales tax.

7 Copy the formula of cell D8 to the range D9:D11. Then deselect the range.

8 Complete the daily totals in row 12.

9 Format the worksheet for currency.

10 Place the file name in the header.

11 Replace **Student's Name** in cell A16 with your name.

12 Save and print the worksheet.

13 Print a copy that shows the formulas.

Change the tax rate.

14 Change the tax rate to **7%**. Watch the changes in the worksheet as you complete the entry.

15 Print the worksheet.

16 Close the worksheet. Do not save changes.

Exercise 5.3   Understanding Formulas

Do not use the computer to complete this exercise. It is designed to help you understand what happens to formulas when they are copied to new locations.

Part 1

	A	B	C
1	17	21	=A1*B1
2	15	22	3)
3	16	38	4)
4	32	58	5)
5	=A1+A2+A3+A4	1)	2) and 6)

Write the formulas that will reside in the cells when formulas are copied.
Copy the formula in A5 to cells B5 and C5.
   1. The formula in cell B5 will read _____ .
   2. The formula in cell C5 will read _____ .

Exercise 5.3—Understanding Formulas

Copy the formula in cell C1 to the range C2:C5.
3. The formula in cell C2 will read _____.
4. The formula in cell C3 will read _____.
5. The formula in cell C4 will read _____.
6. The formula in cell C5 will read _____.

Part 2

	A	B	C	D	E	F
1	ABC Company					
2						
3	Tax Rate	0.05				
4						
5	Invoice	Sales	Returns	Amount Due	Tax Due	Total Due
6	Andrews Co.	2453.25	385.38	=B6-C6	=D6*$B$3	=D6-E6
7	Graves Co.	4245.25	457.65	1)	4)	7)
8	Pearson Co.	5327.25	257.58	2)	5)	8)
9	Schatz Co.	2478.25	62.17	3)	6)	9)
10	Total	=SUM(B6:B9)	10)	11)	12)	13)
11						

Copy the formula in D6 to the range D7:D9.
1. The formula in cell D7 will read _____.
2. The formula in cell D8 will read _____.
3. The formula in cell D9 will read _____.

Copy the formula in E6 to the range E7:E9.
4. The formula in cell E7 will read _____.
5. The formula in cell E8 will read _____.
6. The formula in cell E9 will read _____.

Copy the formula in F6 to the range F7:F9.
7. The formula in cell F7 will read _____.
8. The formula in cell F8 will read _____.
9. The formula in cell F9 will read _____.

Copy the formula in cell B10 to the range C10:F10.
10. The formula in cell C10 will read _____.
11. The formula in cell D10 will read _____.
12. The formula in cell E10 will read _____.
13. The formula in cell F10 will read _____.

Using Mixed References

A formula may also contain a *mixed reference*. This is a reference in which either the column or the row is absolute. The cell reference $B3 is a mixed reference; the reference to column B always remains column B, but the row reference adjusts when copied to a new location. The reference B$3 is also a mixed reference. In this case, column B adjusts to reflect the new location and the reference to row 3 remains constant.

Illustrating mixed references requires creating a more complex worksheet than the previous worksheets used in this text. The following worksheet (Figure 5.10) shows how expenses are distributed in three divisions of a business. The total expenses for the firm were $516,745 and are entered in cell B4.

The share of expenses for each division is given in cells C4, D4, and E4 respectively, and the expenses are distributed according to the percentage rates listed in column B.

Figure 5.10   Distributing Expenses

	A	B	C	D	E
1	Distributing Expenses				
2					
3	Expenses		Division A	Division B	Division C
4	Total Expenses	516,745.00	102,938.00	283,954.00	129,853.00
5					
6	Expenses				
7	Rent	38%			
8	Utilities	21%			
9	Advertising	15%			
10	Insurance	12%			
11	Miscellaneous	14%			

To distribute expenses, multiply the expenses for each division by the percentage rate for each expense type. The total expense in division A is $102,938. To determine the expense for rent, multiply $102,938 by 38%; for utilities, multiply by 21%; etc.

Figure 5.11 shows the formula entered in cell C7 for rent expense. The total expense for Division A is in cell C4, and the rate for rent is in cell B7, so the formula is =C4*B7. However, mixed references should be used in the formula so it remains accurate when copied.

The first cell reference is C$4. As this reference is copied to columns D and C, the column reference changes but the row remains constant (row 4). The second cell reference in the formula is $B7. As this reference is copied, the column reference remains B, but the row adjusts for each type of expense. Figure 5.11 shows the correct formula in cell C7.

Figure 5.11   Mixed Reference

	A	B	C
1	Distributing Expenses		
2			
3	Expenses		Division A
4	Total Expenses	516,745.00	102,938.00
5			
6	Expenses		
7	Rent	38%	=C$4*$B7

The formula needed to determine the utilities expense for Division A is =C4*B8. In Figure 5.12, the formula in cell C7 has been copied to cell C8. The formula in cell C8 is =C$4*$B8. Compare it with =C$4*$B7 in cell C7. As the formula moved from row 7 to 8, the relative reference adjusted to row 8. In the cell reference C$4, the row remained 4 because it used an absolute reference ($4), but the column reference C remained the same.

Figure 5.12   Mixed Reference Copied to New Location

C8		=	=C$4*$B8	
	A	B	C	D
1	Distributing Expenses			
2				
3	Expenses		Division A	Division B
4	Total Expenses	516,745.00	102,938.00	283,954.00
5				
6	Expenses			
7	Rent		38%	39,116.44
8	Utilities		21%	21,616.98
9	Advertising		15%	

If a relative reference were used, the formula in cell C8 would be =C5*B8. Because cell C5 is empty, an error message would appear and no value would be entered.

In Figure 5.13, the formula in cell C7 (C$4*$B7) has been copied to cell D7. The formula in cell D7 reads =D$4*$B7. As the formula moved from column C to D, the relative reference to that column changed in the formula. The reference to row 4 remained the same because it was an absolute reference.

Figure 5.13   Mixed Reference Copied to New Location

D7		=	=D$4*$B7	
	A	B	C	D
1	Distributing Expenses			
2				
3	Expenses		Division A	Division B
4	Total Expenses	516,745.00	102,938.00	283,954.00
5				
6	Expenses			
7	Rent		38%	39,116.44	107,902.52
8	Utilities		21%	21,616.98	
9	Advertising		15%	15,440.70	

The completed worksheet is shown at the top of Figure 5.14; the formulas are displayed in the bottom worksheet. Study the way the formulas change to reflect the absolute and relative references.

Figure 5.14   Distribution Worksheet Completed

Completed Worksheet

	A	B	C	D	E
1	Distributing Expenses				
2					
3	Expenses		Division A	Division B	Division C
4	Total Expenses	516,745.00	102,938.00	283,954.00	129,853.00
5					
6	Expenses				
7	Rent	38%	39,116.44	107,902.52	49,344.14
8	Utilities	21%	21,616.98	59,630.34	27,269.13
9	Advertising	15%	15,440.70	42,593.10	19,477.95
10	Insurance	12%	12,352.56	34,074.48	15,582.36
11	Miscellaneous	14%	14,411.32	39,753.56	18,179.42
12	Total	100%	102,938.00	283,954.00	129,853.00

Formulas Displayed

	A	B	C	D	E
1	Distributing Expe				
2					
3	Expenses		Division A	Division B	Division C
4	Total Expenses	516745	102938	283954	129853
5					
6	Expenses				
7	Rent	0.38	=C$4*$B7	=D$4*$B7	=E$4*$B7
8	Utilities	0.21	=C$4*$B8	=D$4*$B8	=E$4*$B8
9	Advertising	0.15	=C$4*$B9	=D$4*$B9	=E$4*$B9
10	Insurance	0.12	=C$4*$B10	=D$4*$B10	=E$4*$B10
11	Miscellaneous	0.14	=C$4*$B11	=D$4*$B11	=E$4*$B11
12	Total	=SUM(B7:B11)	=C$4*$B12	=D$4*$B12	=E$4*$B12

Cell references can be quickly changed from absolute to mixed by using the F4 key. Each time you press F4, the reference type changes in the following order: first relative (A1), then absolute ($A$1), then mixed (A$1), then mixed ($A1).

Through practice, using absolute and mixed references in formulas will become clearer. This may take trial and error. When creating a worksheet, try a formula one way. Look carefully at the cells to see if they are performing the correct calculations. Any incorrect amount should be recognized. Then go back, edit the formula, and try again. With experience, the structure of formulas will be easy to determine, and the references will be correct the first time.

Exercise 5.4   Using Mixed References

You will complete a worksheet that shows the distribution of expenses for a firm with three branches. Mixed references will be used. You will also enter incorrect references to see the results when a relative rather than a mixed reference is used.

1. Open workbook **Ch5 Ex4** and save it as **Exer 5-4**.

You will enter the formula to multiply the total for Branch A (103,285.50) by the rent percentage (36%).

2. In cell C6, key **=C4**. Press F4 two times until **C$4** is entered.

3. Key ***B6**. Press F4 three times until the reference is **$B6**. Complete the entry and keep cell C6 active. The number in cell C6 should be **37,182.78**.

4. Copy C6 to the range D6:E9. Compare the formulas and references in cells C6, D6, and E6, and in the range D7:E9.

5. Compare the references in rows 7, 8, and 9. Try to understand what the formula calculated.

6. Use AutoSum to complete the totals in row 10.

7. Format the worksheet accurately for currency.

8. Replace **Student's Name** in cell A13 with your name. Remember, double-click in a cell to edit its contents.

9. Set margins for 2.5" at the top and .75" on the right and left margins. Place the file name in the header.

10. Save and print the worksheet.

11. Print a copy that displays the formulas. Adjust the column widths and margins so the worksheet prints on one page.

12. Return to the regular view of the worksheet that displays results.

Change some mixed references to relative references to see the results in the worksheet.

13. Change the formula in cell C6 to read **=C4*B6**. Copy it to the range C7:C9. Click in cell C7 to read the formula. It now reads **=C5*B7**. Study the results. Because these are relative references, they automatically adjusted to the new location but produced inaccurate results. Can you figure out why?

14 Change the formula in cell D6 to read **=D4*B6**. Copy it to the range D7:D9. Click in cell D7 to study the formula. It now reads **=D5*B7**. Because these are also relative references, they adjusted to the new location but again produced inaccurate results. Can you figure out why?

15 Close the workbook, but do not save these changes.

Exercise 5.5   Understanding Mixed References

Do not use the computer to complete this exercise. It is designed to help you understand what happens to formulas when copied to new locations.

The worksheet will determine how much attendance must increase at each location to meet several different rates of increase.

	A	B	C	D	E	F
1	Determining Increasing Attendance					
2						
3	Location	Rate of Increase	5%	10%	15%	20%
4	Downtown	13,500	675			
5	East Mall	9,385				
6	West Mall	12,385				
7	South Mall	18,385				
8	North Mall	22,583				

The formula entered in cell C4 is shown in the next illustration. You will write the new formulas that will result when the formula in cell C4 is copied to different cells.

MAX = =$B4*C$3

	A	B	C	D	E	F
1	Determining Increasing Attendance					
2						
3	Location	Rate of Increase	5%	10%	15%	20%
4	Downtown	13,500	=$B4*C$3	1)	2)	3)
5	East Mall	9,385	4)	8)	12)	16)
6	West Mall	12,385	5)	9)	13)	17)
7	South Mall	18,385	6)	10)	14)	18)
8	North Mall	22,583	7)	11)	15)	19)

Copy the formula in cell C4 to D4:F4.

　　1. The formula in cell D4 will read _____ .
　　2. The formula in cell E4 will read _____ .
　　3. The formula in cell F4 will read _____ .

Chapter 5 Working with Formulas

Copy the formula in cell C4 to C5:C8.
  4. The formula in cell C5 will read _____.
  5. The formula in cell C6 will read _____.
  6. The formula in cell C7 will read _____.
  7. The formula in cell C8 will read _____.

Complete the worksheet by copying the formula in cell C4 to D5:F8.
  8. The formula in cell D5 will read _____.
  9. The formula in cell D6 will read _____.
  10. The formula in cell D7 will read _____.
  11. The formula in cell D8 will read _____.
  12. The formula in cell E5 will read _____.
  13. The formula in cell E6 will read _____.
  14. The formula in cell E7 will read _____.
  15. The formula in cell E8 will read _____.
  16. The formula in cell F5 will read _____.
  17. The formula in cell F6 will read _____.
  18. The formula in cell F7 will read _____.
  19. The formula in cell F8 will read _____.

A Preview of Functions

Functions are used to take the place of long, complex formulas. There are many types of functions included with Excel; some are used for specific business, engineering, and math computations. A few basic statistical functions will be introduced in this chapter. Functions are covered in depth in Chapter 10.

What Is a Function?

A worksheet often requires using a complex formula. Complex, built-in formulas are called *functions*. By entering only a few variables, called *arguments*, the complex formula is completed and the result is displayed in the cell.

Using the AutoSum button Σ is a shortcut for the SUM function. The formula that is entered into the cell shows the function name (SUM) immediately following the equal sign. A list or a range of cell references (the arguments) follows. By entering a function command and arguments, Excel makes the necessary calculations. In the formula =SUM(B1:B6), the name of the function is SUM. The argument is the range B1:B6. The user needs to understand the result of the function but not necessarily the mathematical formula used.

Using Functions

The Paste Function button *fx* in the Standard toolbar accesses the *Paste Function dialog box*, used to access functions.

A Preview of Functions

🅿 Power Users

Use **Shift**+**F3** to access the **Paste Function** dialog box.

All functions are listed by category at the left side of the dialog box, as shown in Figure 5.15.

Select the Function category from the list on the left and a Function name from the list on the right. Click OK to open a specific function box and enter arguments. For the SUM function, select Math & Trig from the Function category list and then SUM from the Function name list. Then select OK. Figure 5.16 shows the selection of the SUM function.

Click OK to open the SUM Formula Palette. The function name is displayed at the top-left corner. Suggested arguments, such as a cell reference or data, are entered. All text boxes identified in bold must be used in order to complete the function; those shaded may be used but are not necessary. In the bottom half of the palette, the action of the SUM function is described as "Adds all the numbers in a range of cells." The SUM Formula Palette is shown in Figure 5.17. A *Formula Palette* opens when you are completing a function. It displays the name of the function, its arguments, a description of the arguments, and the results of the function and formula.

Figure 5.15   Paste Function Dialog Box

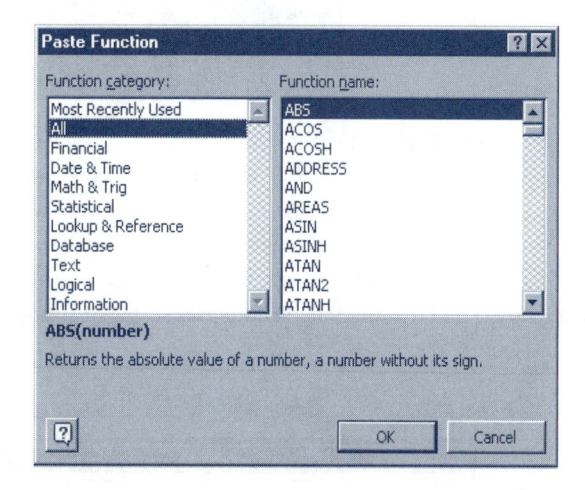

Figure 5.16   Paste Function Dialog Box with SUM Selected

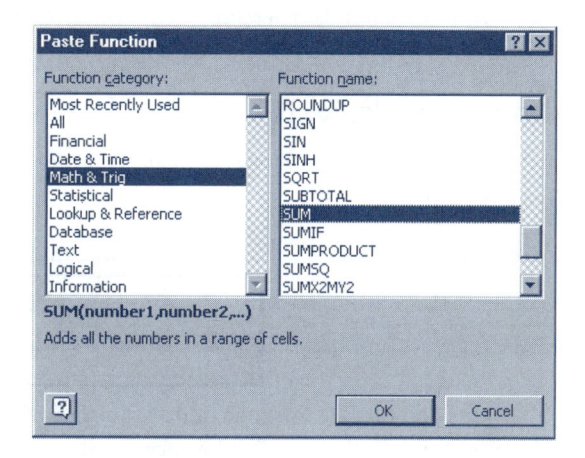

Figure 5.17   Using a Formula Palette

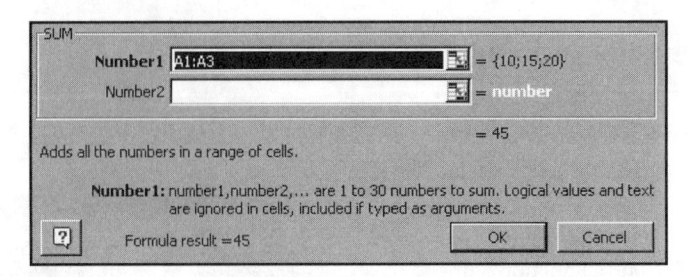

This function will add the range A1:A3; the exact numbers in the cells—10, 15, and 20—are displayed after the text box. The result, 45, is given at the bottom of the dialog box.

If there is an error in the formula, a blue dot will appear in the cell containing the result. Use Office Assistant to help determine the cause of the error.

If the suggested range is not correct, click the ***Collapse Dialog button*** at the right of the text box. The Formula Palette collapses so the entire worksheet is visible and a text box opens, shown in Figure 5.18.

Figure 5.18   Correcting a Function Range

Drag through the correct range on the screen (or key in the correct range in the text box), then click on the *Expand Dialog button* to return to the Formula Palette and complete the function.

As in formulas, cell references are always preferred in functions. However, individual numbers can be entered. As the numbers are entered, additional text boxes open to allow more entries.

Using the Formula Palette

The formula bar contains the Edit Formula button; it is the equal sign shown in the inactive formula bar, pictured in Figure 5.19.

Figure 5.19   Edit Formula Button

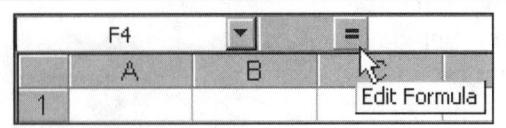

Click on the Edit Formula button. The ***Function box*** lists the SUM function (or the last function selected) and the Formula Palette opens, as shown in Figure 5.20.

Figure 5.20   Formula Palette Accessed from the Formula Bar

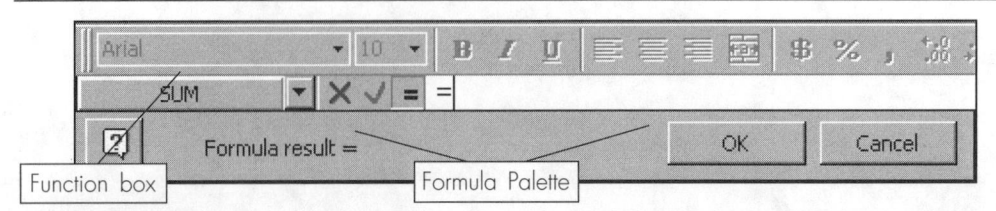

If the SUM function is the one needed, click on it and the Formula Palette opens for SUM.

The down arrow by the Function box accesses additional common functions. If the suggested function is not the one needed, click on the down arrow to view the list of other functions, shown in Figure 5.21.

Figure 5.21   Accessing Functions Using a Shortcut

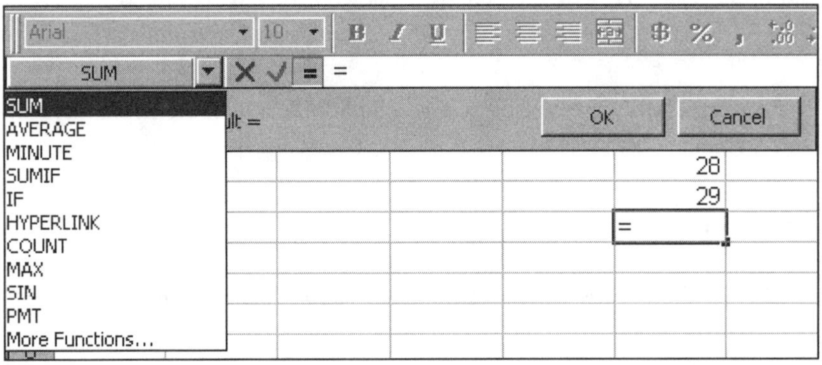

Click on the needed function to select it. The Formula Palette for that function opens. The last selected function is the one shown in the Function box.

Exercise 5.6   Using the Paste Function Dialog Box

You will use the Paste Function dialog box to complete a SUM function in a worksheet.

1   Open a new workbook. Save it as **Exer 5-6**.

2   Select cell A1.

Enter a SUM function using the Paste Function dialog box.

3   Click on the Paste Function button [f_x]. The **Paste Function** dialog box opens.

4   In the **Function category** section, select **Math & Trig**. Click in the **Function name** section. Press **S** (the first letter of SUM). In the **Function name** section, the choices that begin with **S** are displayed. Scroll to **SUM**. Click once to select it.

5   Click **OK**. The cursor is blinking in the **Number1** box. Key **10**. Press [Tab]. Another number box opens and the cursor blinks in the **Number2** box.

6   In the **Number2** box, key **15**. Press [Tab]. The results of the formula are shown at the bottom of the dialog box (**25**).

7   In the **Number3** box, key **20**. Then click **OK**. The total, **45**, is entered in cell A1.

8   In the range C1:C4, key **104**, **36**, **27**, and **130**.

9   Select cell C5. Select the **SUM** function from the **Math & Trig** category. Click **OK**.

10 In the **SUM** Formula Palette, the range C1:C4 is suggested. Click **OK** to complete the function.

Enter the SUM function by selecting a range.

11 Click in cell D5. Click on the Paste Function button.

12 Select **Math & Trig** and then the **SUM** function. Click **OK**.

13 In the Formula Palette, click on the Collapse Dialog button. The dialog box collapses.

14 Click and drag through the range C1:C4.

15 Click on the Expand Dialog button to access the **SUM** Formula Palette. Check to see that the correct range was suggested; then click **OK**.

Use a shortcut to edit the function.

16 In the range E1:E4, key the following numbers: **362**, **47**, **91**, and **89**.

17 Click in cell E5. Click on the Edit Formula button in the formula bar. The Function box shows the function name.

18 If **SUM** is the suggested formula, click on it and continue with Step 20. If **SUM** is not the suggested formula, click on the down arrow to access additional functions. Click on **SUM**.

19 Use the dialog boxes to complete the function.

Copy a function.

20 In the range F1:F4, key the following numbers: **36**, **45**, **136**, and **27**.

21 Copy the formula from cell E5 to cell F5. Notice how functions can be copied and the relative references will adjust.

22 Place your name in cell A12.

23 Place the file name in the header.

24 Resave the worksheet and print a copy. Print a copy that shows the formulas.

Using Statistical Functions

Statistical functions are used for statistical analysis such as average and count. A few of the statistical functions will be covered in this section.

The AVERAGE Function

The *AVERAGE function* is a statistical function, accessed through the Statistical category in the Paste Function dialog box. To determine an average, enter the numbers or cell references in the text boxes.

To access the AVERAGE function, select the Statistical category in the list box on the left and the AVERAGE function from the list box on the right. Function names are listed in alphabetical order. The Paste Function dialog box is shown in Figure 5.22 with the AVERAGE function selected.

Figure 5.22   Accessing a Statistical Function

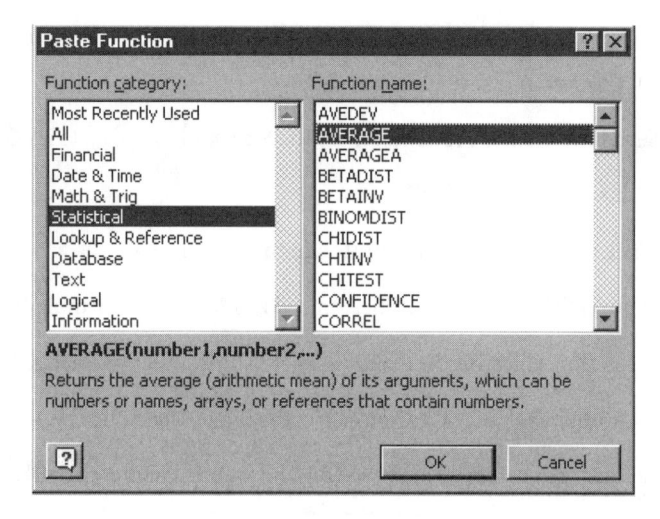

After the function is selected, click on OK; the AVERAGE Formula Palette opens, shown in Figure 5.23.

Figure 5.23   The AVERAGE Formula Palette

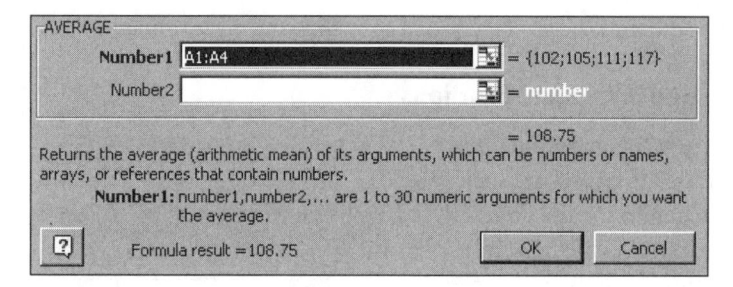

When all arguments (numbers or cell references) are entered, click OK. The average is placed in the active cell. Figure 5.24 shows a worksheet with a list of numbers. The AVERAGE function (shown in the formula bar) is used to complete the average and place the result, 108.75, in cell A5. The range of cells used in this function (shown in the formula bar) is A1:A4.

Figure 5.24   Determining an Average

The AVERAGE function can also be accessed by clicking the Edit Formula button on the formula bar, which opens the Formula Palette.

Chapter 5   Working with Formulas

Exercise 5.7   Completing an Average

You will use statistical functions in a worksheet. In this exercise, you will enter the AVERAGE function.

1 Open workbook **Ch5 Ex7** and save it as **Exer 5-7**.
2 Select cell B8. Select the **AVERAGE** function from the **Statistical** category. Click **OK**.
3 The range B1:B7 is suggested. Click **OK**.
4 Select cell C8. Click on the Edit Formula button in the formula bar.
5 In the Function box, **AVERAGE** is listed. Click on it. The AVERAGE Formula Palette opens.
6 Cell B8 is the suggestion. Click on the Collapse Dialog button in the **AVERAGE** Formula Palette.
7 Drag the mouse through the range C1:C6 to select the range. Then click on the Expand Dialog button.
8 When the range is entered correctly in the **AVERAGE** Formula Palette, click **OK**.
9 Copy cell C8 to D8. Look at the function in D8. Is it accurate?
10 Place your name in cell A12.
11 Place the file name in the header.
12 Save and print the worksheet. Then print a copy showing the formulas.

The Maximum and Minimum Functions

The *maximum (MAX)* and *minimum (MIN) functions* are statistical functions used to determine the largest (maximum) or smallest (minimum) value in a group of numbers. To access the MAX and MIN functions, select the Statistical category in the Paste Function dialog box, as shown in Figure 5.25.

Figure 5.25   Selecting Statistical Functions

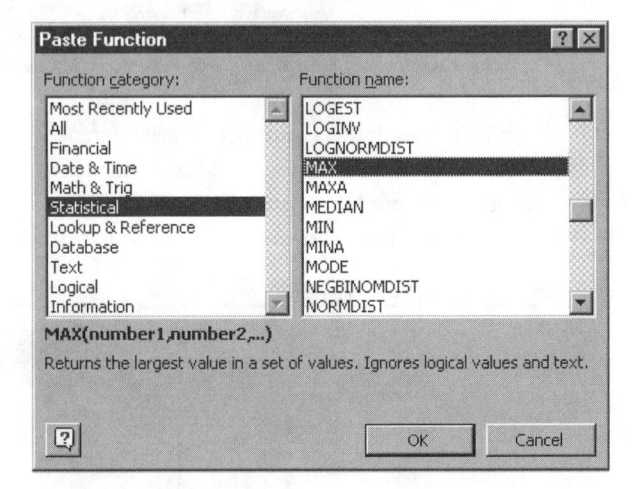

The Maximum feature is illustrated in Figure 5.26; random numbers are listed in cells B1:B7. The function used in cell B8 resulted in the maximum (largest) number of the range; the function used in cell B9 resulted in the minimum (smallest) number of the range. The results of the functions are shown in the worksheet at the left; the functions are displayed in the worksheet at the right.

Figure 5.26   Maximum and Minimum Functions

	A	B		A	B
1		389	1		389
2		2857	2		2857
3		38	3		38
4		192	4		192
5		385	5		385
6		9283	6		9283
7		7385	7		7385
8	Maximum	9283	8	Maximum	=MAX(B1:B7)
9	Minimum	38	9	Minimum	=MIN(B1:B7)

Once the maximum or minimum function is selected, the Formula Palette opens and displays a suggested range of cells. The function is completed in the same way as the other functions.

Exercise 5.8   Using the Maximum and Minimum Functions

You will enter maximum and minimum functions in the statistical spreadsheet previously created.

1   Open workbook **Exer 5-7** and save it as **Exer 5-8**.

2   Select cell B9. Choose the **MAX** function from the **Statistical** category.

3   Because the suggested cell is not correct, click in the Collapse Dialog button and drag through the range B1:B6.

4   Click on the Expand Dialog button. Check to be sure the range is correct, then click **OK**.

5   Select cell C9. Use the shortcut to choose the **MAX** function from the formula bar.

6   Copy cell C9 to D9. Look at the function in D9. Is it accurate?

7   In cell B10, enter a **MIN** function and copy it to C10 and D10.

8   Save and print the worksheet. Then print a copy with the formulas displayed.

Using the COUNT Function

The *COUNT function* is a statistical function that counts the cells that contain numbers in a list. Both numerical values and dates are counted; however, text is not. In the Paste Function dialog box, the COUNT function is accessed from the Statistical category (Figure 5.27).

Figure 5.27   Accessing the COUNT Function

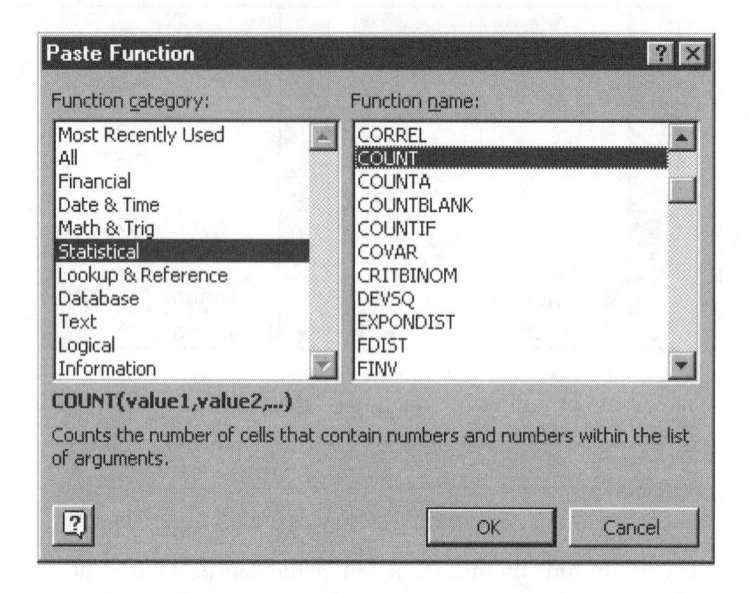

The COUNT Formula Palette opens (Figure 5.28); it is completed in the same way the other Formula Palettes are completed.

Figure 5.28   The COUNT Formula Palette

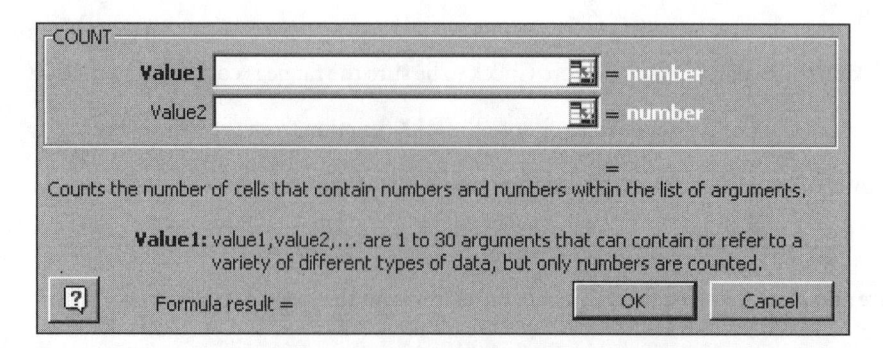

Figure 5.29 shows the result of the COUNT function; the results are shown at the left, the functions at the right. The range B1:B8 was selected for the count. The result is 4; the text in cell B1 was not counted.

Figure 5.29 Example of COUNT Function

	A	B
1	Text	Data
2		
3	Date	3/9/94
4		
5	Value	268
6	Value	28.38
7		
8	Sum Func	296.38
9		
10	Count	4

	A	B
1	Text	Data
2		
3	Date	34402
4		
5	Value	268
6	Value	28.38
7		
8	Sum Function	=SUM(B5:B7)
9		
10	Count	=COUNT(B1:B8)

Using the Count All Function

The *count all function*, named *COUNTA*, is also accessed from the Statistical category and is similar to the COUNT function; it counts how many cells in the selected range are not empty. All cells in the range except the blank ones are counted using the COUNTA function. The COUNTA Formula Palette is shown in Figure 5.30.

Figure 5.30 The COUNTA Formula Palette

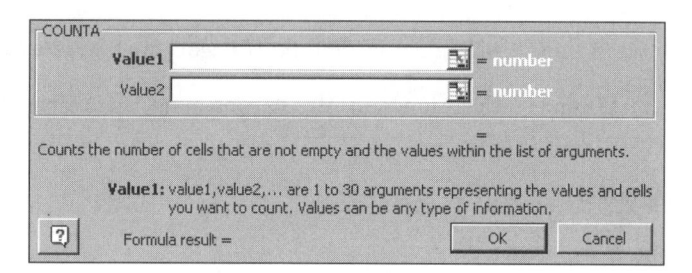

COUNTA
Value1 [ ] = number
Value2 [ ] = number
=
Counts the number of cells that are not empty and the values within the list of arguments.

Value1: value1,value2,... are 1 to 30 arguments representing the values and cells you want to count. Values can be any type of information.

Formula result =   OK   Cancel

The completed worksheet is shown in Figure 5.31. The result displays in cell B12 with the function displayed in the entry area of the formula bar.

Figure 5.31 Completing the COUNTA Function

B12		=	=COUNTA(B1:B11)
	A	B	C	D
1	Text	Data		
2				
3	Date	3/9/98		
4				
5	Value	268		
6	Value	28.38		
7				
8	Sum Func	296.38		
9				
10	Count	4		
11				
12	Count All	6		

All cells containing information are counted, including cell B1, which contains text.

Summary of Statistical Functions Introduced

AVERAGE	Calculates the average of the selected cells.
COUNT	Counts how many number entries are in the selected range.
COUNTA	Counts all cells that contain data. Empty cells are not counted.
MAX	Displays the maximum value in the selected range.
MIN	Displays the minimum value in the selected range.

Exercise 5.9 *Using the COUNT and COUNTA Functions*

You will use the COUNT and COUNTA functions to count the entries in an existing worksheet.

1. Open workbook **Ch5 Ex9** and save it as **Exer 5-9**.

2. Select cell E4. Choose the **COUNT** function (**Statistical** category) in the **Paste Function** dialog box.

3. In the **COUNT** Formula Palette, click the Collapse Dialog button. Drag through the range A1:A16. Then click the Expand Dialog button, then **OK**.

4. There are seven cells that contain numerical information. Click in cell A13. **1/2** is entered there, but notice the apostrophe before it. The apostrophe instructs Excel to treat this as text. Therefore, it is not counted in the COUNT function.

5. Click in cell E5. Access the **COUNTA** function (**Statistical** category) in the **Paste Function** dialog box.

6. Select the range A1:A16 and finish the function. All cells containing data are included and the result is **12**. Excel does not count blank cells.

7. Enter your name in cell D1.

8. Place the file name in the header.

9. Save and print the worksheet.

Logical Functions

Logical functions are used to make a conditional test in a formula that can be answered only with true or false. While there are many logical functions available, only the IF function will be discussed in this text.

The IF Function

IF functions are often used when certain conditions must be met. For instance, a bonus is provided to salespeople selling more than $1,000 worth of products. The IF function will compare the actual sales of each person and enter the appropriate bonus, if earned.

An IF function must be able to have a true or false answer (true the employee earns a bonus, or false he or she does not). If a bonus is earned, one entry is placed in the cell; if the bonus is not earned, a different entry is placed in the cell.

The first item to be determined in an IF function is the value that is tested. The result must be answered either true or false. This test is called a *logical test*. Then you must determine what will be entered in the cell if the test result is true and what will be entered if the test result is false.

The IF Formula Palette is shown in Figure 5.32. Be sure to read the description of the logical test in the bottom half of the Formula Palette.

As an example, a commission rate is based on the amount of sales made during one month. For salespeople whose total sales is equal to or greater than $10,000, a 15% commission will be earned. Those whose total sales are less than $10,000 will earn a 10% commission.

The first step is to enter the logical test. This is what will be compared. A sample worksheet is shown in Figure 5.33.

In this example, the amount in column B (the amount of sales) will be compared for the logical test. A logical question is posed—are the sales equal to or greater than $10,000? That question is entered in the Logical test box, as shown in Figure 5.34.

Then enter the additional arguments—what will be entered if true (15%) and what will be entered if false (10%)? Once all arguments are entered, click OK and complete the IF function. The completed sheet is shown in Figure 5.35, with the results of the IF function in column C and the IF function shown in the formula bar.

Figure 5.32   IF Formula Palette

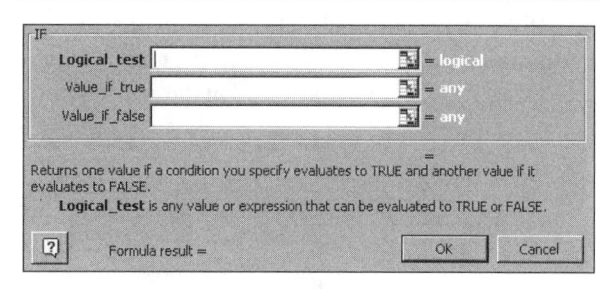

Figure 5.33   Using an IF Function

	A	B	C
1		Sales	Commission Rate
2	Candi	$15,784	
3	Elsie	10,154	
4	Kathleen	9,587	
5	Mary	10,057	
6	Mike	8,045	
7	Ron	9,950	
8	Sue	10,487	

Figure 5.34   Completing an IF Function

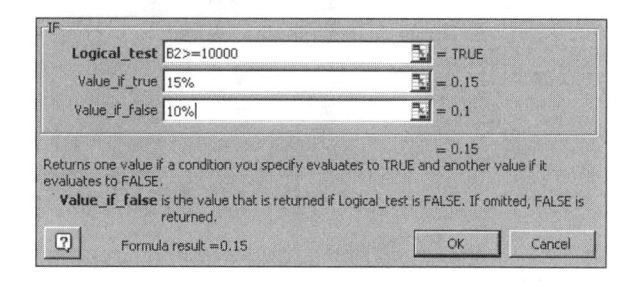

Figure 5.35   An IF Function in a Worksheet

C2		=IF(B2>=10000,15%,10%)	
A	B	C	D
	Sales	Commission Rate	
Candi	$15,784	15%	
Elsie	10,154	15%	
Juen	9,587	10%	
Kathleen	10,057	15%	
Mary	8,045	10%	
Ron	9,950	10%	
Sue	10,487	15%	

When the function is complete, 15% is entered in cell C2 (Figure 5.35). The completed formula in the entry area of the worksheet reads =IF(B2>=10000,15%,10%). Any sales not meeting the condition are false; those sales would be multiplied by 10%.

Text, rather than formulas, can also be used in an IF function. For example, the IF function of IF(B2<=10,000,"Goal Met", "Goal Not Met") would evaluate the condition in B2 to see if it is less than or equal to 10,000. If it were true, the text Goal Met would be placed in the cell; if it were false, the text Goal Not Met would be placed in the cell. Figure 5.36 shows a worksheet using this IF function.

Figure 5.36 Entering Text in an IF Function

	A	B	C	D	E	F
1		Sales	Commission Rate	Goal Met?		
2	Candi	$ 15,784	15%	Goal Met		
3	Elsie	10,154	15%	Goal Met		
4	Juen	9,587	10%	Goal Not Met		
5	Kathleen	10,057	15%	Goal Met		
6	Mary	8,045	10%	Goal Not Met		
7	Ron	9,950	10%	Goal Not Met		
8	Sue	10,487	15%	Goal Met		
9						

D2 =IF(B2>=10000,"Goal Met","Goal Not Met")

The completed IF Formula Palette is shown in Figure 5.37. As text is entered into the Formula Palette, quotation marks are automatically placed around the text.

Figure 5.37 Entering Text in a Function

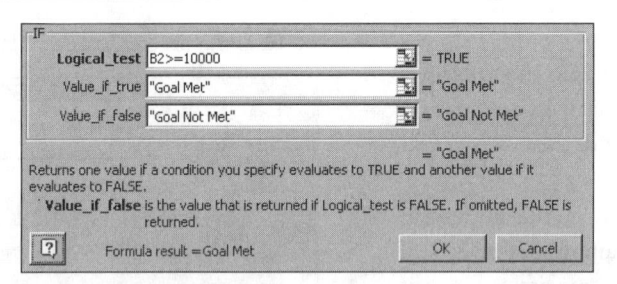

IF
Logical_test B2>=10000   = TRUE
Value_if_true "Goal Met"   = "Goal Met"
Value_if_false "Goal Not Met"   = "Goal Not Met"

= "Goal Met"
Returns one value if a condition you specify evaluates to TRUE and another value if it evaluates to FALSE.
  Value_if_false is the value that is returned if Logical_test is FALSE. If omitted, FALSE is returned.

Formula result =Goal Met   OK   Cancel

The following table provides additional examples of the IF function and how it is applied:

IF(Logical_test, Value_if_true, Value_if_false)		
IF(A24<=25,A4*E4,A4*B4)		
IF (logical value)	True—do this	False—do this
If A24 is less than or equal to 25	Multiply the value in A4 by the value in E4	If A24 is greater than 25, multiply the value in A4 by the value in E4
IF(G7=A4,G7/8,0)		
If the value in G7 equals the value in A4	Divide the value in G7 by 8	If G7 does not equal A4, place a zero in the cell
IF(C>=50,"OK","Reorder")		
If the value in C3 is greater than or equal to 50	Place OK in the cell	If C3 is less than 50, place Reorder in the cell

As worksheets are prepared, IF statements are often used. Because of their extensive use, they require a thorough understanding.

If an error is made in the argument of a function, a message immediately appears indicating it is invalid. Invalid arguments are often caused because the formula is not properly constructed. A common error is the order of the equal and greater than/less than symbols. In Excel, the greater than or less than symbol must appear first. The statement in Figure 5.38 indicates that the formula is invalid because the equal sign comes before the greater than symbol.

Figure 5.38   An Invalid IF Statement

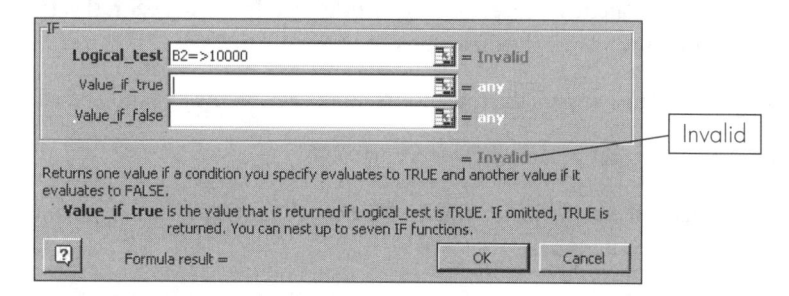

Exercise 5.10   Using the IF Function

SunShine Realty provides a basic salary for their employees. They also offer a $100 bonus for sales of $12,000 or more. A worksheet for the March bonus has been started. You will complete the worksheet.

1 Open the **Ch5 Ex10** workbook and save it as **Exer 5-10**.

2 In cell D6 select the **IF** function from the **Logical** category.

The IF function is used to add a $100 bonus to all sales equal to or greater than $12,000.

3 In the **IF** Formula Palette, complete the logical test. Key **B6>=12000**. In the **Value_if_true** box, key **100**; in the **Value_if_false** box, key **0**. Then click **OK**.

4 Copy the function in D6 to the range D7:D12.

5 Complete the worksheet. Salary is the base salary plus the bonus. Complete the totals in row 14.

6 Save the workbook.

7 In cell F6, select the **IF** function from the **Logical** category and click **OK**.

This IF function will enter a comment in the cell. If a bonus is received, enter Good Job; if not, enter Work Harder.

8 In the **IF** Formula Palette, enter the logical function **D6=100**. In the **Value_if_true** box enter **Good Job**. In the **Value_if_false** box enter **Work Harder**.

9 Place the file name in the header.

10 Place your name in cell A17.

11 Save and print the worksheet.

Exercise 5.11 Additional Uses of the IF Function

You will complete the hours worked section of a worksheet, using IF functions.

1. Open to the **Ch5 Ex11** workbook and save it as **Exer 5-11**.

Complete the regular work section. The logical function for regular hours is all hours less than or equal to 40. Enter that logical function.

2. In cell C7, access the **Paste Function** dialog box and select the **IF** function from the **Logical** category.
3. The **IF** Formula Palette is placed over the worksheet. In the **Logical_test** variable, click on the Collapse Dialog button to collapse the dialog box.
4. Click in cell B7 to compare the total hours, then click on the Expand Dialog button.
5. Complete the logical statement by entering **>=40**.
6. Enter the **Value_if_true** variable, which is **40**. Forty hours is the maximum number of hours that can be worked at the regular rate.
7. Enter the **Value_if_false** variable, the contents of cell B7. Then click **OK**. The number **40** is entered in cell C7.
8. Copy the formula in cell C7 to the rest of the regular hours range.

Complete the overtime hours section of the payroll. Overtime is all hours greater than 40. The logical function compares the value in cell C7; if it is greater than 40, enter the difference; if it is less than 40, enter 0.

9. Click in cell D7 and access the **IF** function from the **Logical** category.
10. For the **Logical_test**, click on the Collapse Dialog button.
11. Click in B7, then on the Expand Dialog button.
12. Complete the **Logical_test**, which is **B7>=40**.
13. For the **Value_if_true** variable, click on the Collapse Dialog button.
14. Click in cell B7, enter a minus (-) sign, then click in C7. Restore the dialog box.
15. For the **Value_if_false** variable, enter **0**.
16. Copy the formula in cell D7 to the range containing the rest of the overtime hours.
17. Enter your name in cell A14.
18. Place the file name in the header.
19. Resave the worksheet and print it. Then print a copy with formulas displayed.

Summary

- A relative reference in a formula adjusts cell references when the formula is copied to a new location. The references adjust relative to the new location of the cells.
- An absolute reference is used when a specific cell will be used in several formulas that will later be copied. An absolute reference does not change when the formula is copied.
- An absolute reference is identified by the dollar signs ($) in the cell reference. $A$1 is an absolute reference.
- In a mixed reference, one part of the reference remains absolute and does not change while the other part of the reference is relative and will adjust a to new location. $A1 and A$1 are mixed references.
- A cell reference can be made absolute ($B$1) by pressing F4 immediately after the cell reference is entered.
- Press F4 several times to see all the options for changing references from absolute to mixed.
- A function is a built-in formula to automatically complete a series of mathematical calculations.
- Functions are available and selected in the Paste Function dialog box, which is accessed by clicking the Paste Function button f_x.
- Arguments are the variable information used in a function. They can be numbers or cell references.
- A Formula Palette is used to enter the arguments (variables) of a function.
- A Formula Palette can be collapsed so data in a worksheet can be accessed while a function is being completed.
- Statistical functions are used for statistical analysis, such as the AVERAGE and COUNT functions.
- The AVERAGE function is used to average a series of numbers.
- The maximum (MAX) and minimum (MIN) functions are used to find the largest and smallest number within a defined range of numbers.
- The COUNT function is used to determine the number of entries in a range of cells. It counts numbers and dates but ignores text.
- The count all (COUNTA) function determines the total number of cells that contain information in a given range. Empty cells are not counted, but cells that contain text are.
- The IF function determines if a logical test is true or false. If it is true, one value will be entered; if it is false, a different value is entered.
- The logical test of an IF function must be answered true or false.
- The Value if true box contains the cell entry if the Logical test is true; the Value if false box contains the result if the Logical test is false.
- Numbers or text may be entered in a worksheet with the IF function.

Important Terminology

absolute reference
argument
AVERAGE function
Collapse Dialog button
count all (COUNTA) function
COUNT function
Expand Dialog button
Formula Palette
function
Function box
IF function
logical functions
logical test
maximum (MAX) function
minimum (MIN) function
mixed reference
Paste Function dialog box
relative reference
statistical functions

Chapter 5 Working with Formulas

Buttons to Know

Study Questions

True-False

Place a T in the space if the statement is true; place an F if the statement is false.

_____ 1. When moving or copying cells, all formulas in the cells change to reflect the new location of the cell.
_____ 2. A relative reference to a cell does not change when the cell is moved to a new location.
_____ 3. An absolute reference is identified by the percent signs in its reference. %A%3 is the absolute reference for cell A3.
_____ 4. The reference $A$5 is absolute; when it is copied, it will read $A$5.
_____ 5. The reference $A7 is mixed. When it is copied to the next row, it will read $A8.
_____ 6. When $A7 is copied to the next column, it will read $B7.
_____ 7. When the cell reference A8 is moved to the next column, it reads A9.
_____ 8. The Paste Function button is used to easily enter functions.
_____ 9. A function is a special type of formula that automatically completes a series of mathematical calculations.
_____ 10. A function palette is used to enter arguments in a function.
_____ 11. The button in the Formula Palette that temporarily shrinks the box to provide access to the worksheet is called the Shrink button.
_____ 12. A function is entered into only the active cell and cannot be copied.
_____ 13. Arguments of a function are the math symbols = and >, and they are used in the logical test of a function.
_____ 14. To average cell contents, select AVERAGE from the Financial category.
_____ 15. The MIN and MAX functions are found in the Math & Trig category in the Paste Function dialog box.
_____ 16. The COUNT function counts all cells that contain data in the specified range.
_____ 17. The IF function is used to enter a function that may return different results depending on a logical test.
_____ 18. The IF statement =IF(B2>1000,15,10) instructs Excel to enter 15 if the value in B2 is 800.
_____ 19. IF functions are used for only true or false tests.

Fill-In

Place the word that correctly completes the statement in the space provided.

1. The cell reference A$4 is an example of a(n) _____ reference.
2. The _____ Dialog button restores a Formula Palette to its original size so the function can be completed.
3. The _____ function is used to determine the average of a group of numbers.
4. The _____ function is used to determine the largest number in a group of numbers.
5. The _____ function is used to determine the smallest number in a group of numbers.

6. In an IF function, the logical test must have either a true or _____ answer.
7. The Value if _____ entry places the result in the cell if the logical test is met.
8. An IF function reads =IF(B7=10,"Great","OK"). The value in B6 is 7. _____ will be entered in the active cell.

Formulas

Worksheet 1

Practice building formulas using relative, absolute, and mixed references. Fill in references as if the formulas will be copied to new locations.

	A	B	C
1	Discount Rate	3%	
2			
3	Invoice Amount	Discount Amount	Amount of Payment
4	$450		

1. Enter the formula that would be placed in cell B4 for the amount of the discount. It is the amount of the invoice times the discount rate. _____
2. Enter the formula that would be placed in cell C4 for the amount of the payment. It is the amount of the invoice less the amount of the discount. _____

Worksheet 2

Determine the amount of income to be spent on each of the expense categories. Assume the formula will be copied, so absolute and relative references must be used accurately.

	A	B	C	D	E
1	Annual Income	$ 28,000			
2					
3					
4			Annual	Quarterly	Monthly
5	Housing	30%			
6	Food	20%			
7	Transportation	10%			
8	Other	40%			

Enter the formulas for the amount of the annual and quarterly housing expenditures.
1. Enter the formula for the annual housing expenditure into cell C5. It is 30% of the annual income. The formula is _____ .
2. Enter the formula for the annual food expenditure into cell C6. The formula is _____ .
3. Enter the formula for the annual transportation expenditure into cell C7. The formula is _____ .
4. Enter the formula for the other expenses into cell C8. The formula is _____ .
5. In cell C9, enter the formula for the total of column C. _____
6. Enter the amount of the housing expenditure on a quarterly basis. It will be entered into cell D5. It is 30% of the annual income divided by 4. Use the result of cell C5 divided by 4. _____
7. The formula in cell D6 is _____ .
8. The formula in cell D7 is _____ .
9. The formula in cell D8 is _____ .

10. In cell D9, enter the total of column D. _____

Enter the amount of the monthly housing expenditures.

11. In cell E5, enter the formula for the monthly housing expenditure. It is 30% of the annual income divided by 12. _____
12. The formula in cell E6 is _____.
13. The formula in cell E7 is _____.
14. The formula in cell E8 is _____.
15. In cell E9, enter the total of column E. _____

Worksheet 3

Use Excel functions to determine the amounts placed in columns B and C. The sales quota is $4,000. If the quota is met, the commission rate is 10%; if it is not met, the commission rate is 6.5%. The comment for meeting the quota is Goal Met. If the quota is not met, place a minus sign in the cell.

	A	B	C
1			
2	Sales	Commission Rate	Comment
3			
4	4,500		
5	3,850		
6	4,001		

1. In cell B4, enter the IF function for the commission rate.
   a. The Logical test is _____.
   b. The Value if true is _____.
   c. The Value if false is _____.
2. In cell C4, enter the comment.
   a. The Logical test is _____.
   b. The Value if true is _____.
   c. The Value if false is _____.

Assignments

Assignment 5.1

Data has been entered in an inventory worksheet for Heather's Sales, but it needs to be completed and formatted. This inventory worksheet will show a projected sales increase of 4% and the percent of total inventory each product represents.

1. Open the **Ch5 As1** workbook and save it as **Assig 5-1**.
2. Complete the basic worksheet.
   - Complete the sums to show total amounts in the total row and column.
   - Adjust column widths if needed.
3. Complete the formulas.
   - In cell B13, enter a formula to multiply the total of widgets by the rate of increase. Be sure the cell representing the rate of increase is entered as an absolute reference.

- Copy the formula in cell B13 to C13:E13.
- Enter a formula to reflect the amount of increase to the total. In cell B15, enter the formula to add the total of widgets to the projected amount of increase for widgets. Copy this formula to the appropriate cells in row 15.
- Determine the percent of total in row 16. The formula is the total of each product divided by the total products. In cell B16, enter the formula to determine the percentage of the total the widgets represent. Divide the total projected (B15) by the total of all products after the projection (E15). One cell reference must be absolute.
- Copy this formula to the appropriate cells for sprocks and cubes.
4. Complete the statistical information in the section beginning with row 18.
   - In row 19, determine the average sales of each product sold.
   - In row 20, determine the minimum sales for each type of product.
   - In row 21, determine the maximum sales for each type of product.
5. Complete the ordering information in the section beginning with row 26 using an IF statement.
   - Access the **IF** function. It is in the **Logical** category of the **Paste Function** dialog box.
   - For the **Logical_test**, enter a statement that identifies sales as equal to or greater than **$100,000**.
   - For the **Value_if_true** variable, key **Reorder**. (You will reorder all products where sales are greater than $100,000.)
   - For the **Value_if_false** variable, key **No Order**. (You will not reorder products where sales are less than $100,000.)
6. Format the worksheet.
   - Format numbers correctly including those that represent dollar amounts.
   - Place a single line above and a double line below row 9.
   - Format percents using the Percent Style button in the toolbar.
   - Place the file name in the header.
   - Indent all labels in column A in the **Projections** section (A12:A29) except the label **Order Information**.
7. Place your name in a cell at the bottom of the worksheet.
8. Save and print the worksheet.
9. Check the worksheet to see how it looks. Are all amounts entered and formatted correctly? Are underlines used correctly? Does it have a professional appearance? If needed, make changes and print a corrected copy.
10. Print a copy that shows the formulas.

   Checkpoint:
Cell B13	$3,902.16
Cell C15	$120,210.48
Cell B16	28%

Assignment 5.2

Ace Paper Supplies uses an Excel spreadsheet to keep track of its inventory in actual numbers, in dollar value, and in percentages of the total for each product. The inventory data has been entered. You are asked to format a worksheet.

Use some of the shortcuts you learned to complete and format the worksheet.
1. Open the **Ch5 As2** workbook and save it as **Assig 5-2**.

2. Complete the worksheet.
   - Copy the items in the range A7:A11 to the range A16:A20.
   - Complete the number of items sold in column E. This is calculated by adding the beginning inventory to the purchases and subtracting the ending inventory.
   - Complete the **$ Sold** column (beginning with cell B16). This is the number of items sold times the price of each. Copy the formula from cell B16 to the range B17:B20.
   - Complete the **$ Ending** column (beginning with cell D16). This is the total number of units in the ending inventory multiplied by the price of each.
   - In cells B21 and D21, enter the formula to add the total of the **$ Sold** column and the total the **$ Ending** column.
   - Complete the **% Total Sales** column. In cell C16, enter a formula to show the percent of total sales. This is the **$ Sold** divided by the total sold (cell B21). One cell reference is absolute. Copy the formula where needed. (Formulas are not needed in the total row; they will be 100 percent.)
   - Complete the **% Total End** in column E. It is the amount of ending inventory for each product divided by the total of ending inventory. One cell reference is absolute.
3. Determine whether products need to be reordered. Prepare a section at the bottom of the worksheet (beginning with cell A24) and title it **Order Information**. Prepare an IF statement for this information.
   - Copy the list of products to this section, beginning with row 26.
   - In cell B26 enter an IF statement. The **IF** function is in the **Logical** category.
   - For the **Logical_test**, enter a statement that identifies ending inventory less than **200**.
   - For the **Value_if_true** variable, key the term **Reorder**. (You will reorder all products with an inventory of less than 200.)
   - For the **Value_if_false** variable, key the term **No**. (You will not reorder items with an inventory of greater than 200.)
4. Format the worksheet.
   - Format column labels in row 14 as the labels in row 5 are formatted. (*Hint:* Use the Format Painter to copy the format.)
   - Format currency correctly.
   - Use the Percent Style button in the toolbar to format percentages. Format for one decimal place.
   - Format the section heading in A24 as bold.
5. Be sure the file name is in the header.
6. Place your name in a cell at the bottom of the worksheet.
7. Save and print the worksheet.
8. Check the worksheet to see how it looks. Are all amounts entered and formatted correctly? Are underlines used correctly? Does it have a professional appearance? If needed, make changes and print a corrected copy.
9. Print a copy of the worksheet showing the formulas you entered.

   Checkpoint:

Cell E7	350
Cell B16	$1,249.50
Cell D16	$417.69
Cell C16	52.5%
Cell E16	39.2%

Assignment 5.3

Maynard's Furniture wants to compare what the selling price of furniture will be using two markup methods. One method is based on the selling price; the other method is based on cost.

You will prepare a worksheet that provides markups using two different bases.
1. Open Excel to a new workbook.
2. Enter the following information into your worksheet:

	A	B	C	D	E
1	Maynard's Furniture				
2	Feb, 1998				
3					
4		Cost	Markup	Selling Price	
5	Chairs	119.5			
6	Desks	179			
7	Lamps	37.8			
8	Waste Baskets	3.5			
9	Computer	1315			
10	Telephone	85			
11					
12	Markup Rate	40%		Markup Rate	60%
13	based on Selling Price			based on Cost	

3. Save the workbook as **Assig 5-3**.
4. Move the range D12:E13 so it begins at cell A27.
5. Complete the first section. It will show both the markup and the selling price; the markup rate is based on the selling price.
   - In column D, enter the formula for the selling price. For cell D5, it is **=B5/(100%-40%)**.
   - In column C, enter the markup. It is the selling price less cost.
6. Add information to the worksheet.
   - Copy the range A4:C10 to the range beginning at cell A18.
   - Copy cell D4 to cell D18.
7. Complete the second section. It will show the markup and selling price; the markup rate is based on cost.
   - In column D (beginning with cell D19), enter the formula for the selling price. For cell D19, it is **=B19+(60%*B19)**.
8. Format the worksheet.
   - Format the name of the firm for bold and italic.
   - Format the date for bold.
   - Format column labels for bold and right alignment.
   - Format numbers correctly for currency. Use two decimals for all numbers.
   - Adjust margins and column widths in Print Preview.
   - Include the file name in the header.
9. Enter your name in cell A31.

10. Save and print the workbook.
11. Check the worksheet to see how it looks. Are all amounts entered and formatted correctly? Are underlines used correctly? Does it have a professional appearance? If needed, make changes and print a corrected copy.
12. Print a copy that displays the formulas.
13. Close without saving changes.

Checkpoint:

Cell C5	$79.67
Cell D5	$199.17
Cell C19	$71.70
Cell D19	$191.20

Assignment 5.4

You will complete a payroll register for a pay period.

1. Input the payroll register so it looks like the following example. Key the date as **June 30, 1997**; Excel may change it to another date style.

	A	B	C	D	E	F	G
1	Payroll Register						
2	30-Jun-97						
3							
4		FICA Rate	Income Tax				
5		7.50%	Less than $350	20%			
6			$350 plus	30%			
7							
8	Name	Pay Rate	No. Hours	Regular Hours	Overtime Hours		
9							
10	K. Kendall	9.5	43				
11	J. Marsh	5.75	40				
12	A. Newton	8.25	39				
13	L. Owens	7.5	42				
14	R. Parsons	6.35	48.5				
15	B. Smith	8.45	38				
16							
17							
18		Regular Pay	Overtime Pay	Gross Pay	FICA Tax	Income Tax	Net Pay

2. Save the workbook as **Assig 5-4**.
3. Complete the payroll.
   - Regular hours are all hours worked up to 40. Use an IF function to determine regular hours.
   - Overtime hours are all hours over 40. Use an IF function to determine the overtime hours.

- Copy the employees' names to the range beginning with row 20.
- The regular pay is the amount of regular hours multiplied by the pay rate.
- Overtime pay is the amount of overtime hours times the pay rate times 1.5. (Employees earn one and one-half time for all hours over 40 per week.)
- Gross pay is the regular pay plus the overtime pay.
- FICA is the gross pay times the FICA rate in cell B5.
- Income tax uses two tax rates. For employees earning less than **$350** a week, use a **20%** tax rate (cell D5). For employees earning **$350** or more, use a **30%** rate (cell D6). Use an IF statement for this formula.
- Net pay is gross pay less FICA and less income tax.
- Total all columns except the pay rate.
- Be sure the total rows are labeled.

4. Complete some statistical analysis.
   - At the bottom of the worksheet, include headings and formulas to include the average number of hours worked and the maximum hours worked by one employee.
   - At the bottom, include a section of information that shows the average net pay, the maximum net pay, and the minimum net pay.
5. Format the worksheet.
   - Format the two-line heading for bold and italics.
   - Format the column titles for bold and center alignment. Place a single underline beneath the titles.
   - Format the word **Total** for bold and right alignment.
   - Indent the names of the employees in column A.
   - Format the statistical information at the bottom in a style of your choice.
   - Include the file name in the header.
   - Format the numbers for money amounts *except the following*: number of hours, regular hours, and overtime hours. Format those for Comma style and one decimal.
   - Adjust column widths if needed.
   - Use Print Preview to place the worksheet in the center of the page.
6. Place your name in a cell at the bottom of the worksheet.
7. Save and print the worksheet.
8. Check the worksheet to see how it looks. Are all amounts entered and formatted correctly? Are underlines used correctly? Does it have a professional appearance? If needed, make changes and print a corrected copy.
9. Print a copy of the worksheet showing the formulas. Select a left margin of .5". This worksheet will print on two pages.
10. Close without saving changes.

    Checkpoint:

    | Cell D21 | $230.00 |
    | Cell E21 | $17.25 |
    | Cell G21 | $166.75 |

Assignment 5.5

You will use the payroll register you completed in Assignment 5.4 to prepare a payroll report for the next week. By changing the variables (the number of hours worked), the payroll report will be complete.
1. Retrieve the **Assig 5-4** workbook and save it as **Assig 5-5**.
2. Change the employees' hours worked. As the new hours are entered, watch as Excel automatically adjusts the amounts in the cells that contain formulas.

Kendall	44
Marsh	42.5
Newton	39
Owens	41
Parsons	43
Smith	40

3. Do a quick save.
4. Is the statistical section correct? Are all other amounts in the worksheet correct?
5. Print a copy of the worksheet.

Assignment 5.6

First Charity in your city is completing its campaign for contributions. Many businesses within the community have donated awards to be provided to contributors of different levels. All contributors will receive a mug; those contributing $150 or more will receive a T-shirt.

The worksheet shows the names of those contributing and the amount of the contributions. You are to use an IF function to determine whether the contributors will receive a mug or a T-shirt.
1. Open workbook **Ch5 As6** and save it as **Assig 5-6**.
2. Complete the worksheet.
   - In cell C6, enter the IF function.
   - The **Logical_test** is contributions of $150 or greater. If true, key **T-Shirt**. If false, key **Mug**.
   - Copy the function to the appropriate range of the worksheet and center align the information.
   - Include the file name in the header.
   - If desired, add formatting choices.
3. In cell A19, enter **Prepared by** followed by your name.
4. Save and print the worksheet.
5. Print a copy that shows the formulas used. Use landscape style and fit it on one page.

Assignment 5.7

Home Appliance Company is determining the forecast of appliance costs in the next 5 years. Each year they predict the price increase, although the increase will not be the same each year.

You will complete a worksheet to help determine the cost of appliances.
1. Open to a new workbook and enter the following data:

	A	B	C	D	E	F	G
1	Home Appliance Company						
2	Cost Forecast						
3							
4			3%	3.5%	5%	4%	5%
5		1997	1998	1999	2000	2001	2002
6	Freezer	147,895					
7	Range	98,657					
8	Refrigerator	125,794					
9	Dishwasher	136,589					

2. Complete the worksheet.
   - In column C, enter the forecast cost with a 3% increase in costs. Use 1997 as the base year.
   - In column D, enter the forecast cost with a 3.5% increase over 1998 prices.
   - Complete the forecast for 2000, 2001, and 2002.
   - Place totals in row 10.
3. Format the worksheet.
   - Format the two-line title for bold.
   - Format the column labels for bold and right alignment. Place a line under the years.
   - Format correctly for currency. Do not use decimals.
   - Format the total row in bold. Use underlines correctly.
   - Adjust column widths if necessary.
   - Place the file name in the header.
   - Use Print Preview to center the worksheet on the page.
4. Place your name in a cell below the main body of the worksheet.
5. Save the worksheet as **Assig 5-7** and print it.
6. Print a second copy showing the formulas. Adjust the margins in Print Preview so it stays on one page.

Assignment 5.8

Sumartra Gift Distributors records sales on a daily basis in an Excel spreadsheet. They provide various discounts based on the sales amount. If the sale is greater than $150, a 3.5% discount is awarded. For sales of $150 or less, a 2% discount is awarded.

The amount of the sale has been recorded in a worksheet. You will use an IF function to determine the amount of the discount and complete the worksheet.

1. Open workbook **Ch5 As8** and save it as **Assig 5-8**.
2. Complete the formulas needed.
   - In cell C7, enter the IF function needed to determine the discount rate.
   - In cell D7, enter the formula to determine the amount of the discount.
   - In cell E7, enter the formula to determine the amount due.
   - Copy formulas as needed throughout the worksheet.
   - Provide totals in row 16.

3. Format the worksheet.
   - Format for currency and percentages. Round percents to one decimal.
   - Place underlines correctly in the worksheet. Place emphasis on the total line.
   - Place the file name in the header.
   - Complete additional format choices so you have a professional-looking worksheet.
4. Place your name in a cell at the bottom of the worksheet.
5. Save and print the worksheet.
6. On one page, print a copy that shows the formulas.

Case Problem 5

You have been asked to prepare a worksheet that summarizes the commissions earned for the employees of Givensky and Culbertson, a furniture store. The commission is based on amount of sales. There is also a sales goal of $10,000 each month; you will indicate which employees have met this goal.

Set up the worksheet. Include a three-line heading that includes the name of the firm, the name of the report, **Earnings Summary**, and **For the Week Ending (current date)**. Include your handwritten draft used in planning the worksheet. Include a worksheet that shows the formulas you used. Save this workbook as **Case 5**.

Nguyan Tran sold $10,500 worth of furniture. Kathy Larson sold $13,350. Rex Shahbazi sold $9,750. $12,030 is Mac Wilcox's sales amount. Linda Shockman sold $14,080 and Jennifer Kendall sold $9,070.

In the worksheet, include the sales amount for each employee, the amount of commission earned, and whether or not the goal has been met. The commission rate is 4%.

Print the worksheet and be sure to check it to see how it looks. Are all amounts entered and formatted correctly? Are styles and underlines used effectively? Does it have a professional appearance? All worksheets need labels to identify the data. Did you include the needed labels? Also, be sure to identify the worksheet with your name and the file name. If needed, make changes and print a corrected copy.

As a means to planning, Givensky and Culbertson asks you to prepare the same worksheet using a commission rate of 3.25% and a sales goal of $12,500. This "what if" example provides information for the firm to use in planning for the future. Name this sheet **Case 5a**. Print the worksheet and a copy that shows the formulas.

Checkpoint (for Case 5):
Tran's Commission $420.00
Total Commissions $2,751.20
The sales goal was met for all employees except Shahbazi and Kendall.

Multiple-Sheet Workbooks and Other Time Savers

Objectives

1. Use workbooks to save related worksheets.
2. Use shortcut menus for selecting commands.
3. Move and copy data between worksheets.
4. Use AutoFill to create a series.
5. Format a worksheet using the AutoFormat feature.
6. Center a title over adjacent columns.
7. Open, size, and relocate specialized toolbars.

Introduction

Excel opens to a new workbook each time it is started. Each new workbook opens with three worksheets, allowing a group of related worksheets to be saved in one file.

Excel provides shortcuts that enable speedy creation of worksheets. This unit covers fast ways to format worksheets and labels and center worksheet titles.

Toolbars provide a fast and easy method to access frequently used commands. In addition to the Standard and Formatting toolbars that open with Excel, other specialized toolbars are available.

At the end of this chapter you may delete the Ch05 and Ch06 folders from your Student Data Disk.

Using Workbooks

When an Excel workbook opens, it contains three individual worksheets that all have unique names. A workbook is saved under one file name.

At the bottom of an Excel workbook is a series of tabs that are labeled Sheet1, Sheet2, and Sheet3. Each tab accesses a different worksheet. Three or more related worksheets may be saved as one **workbook** file. The *active sheet* is indicated by a lighter tab and is the sheet displayed on the screen; the tabs of the other sheets are dimmed. A workbook may contain over 5,600 sheets.

Figure 6.1 shows the worksheet tabs for an open workbook with the Jan Sales sheet active.

Figure 6.1   Worksheet Tabs

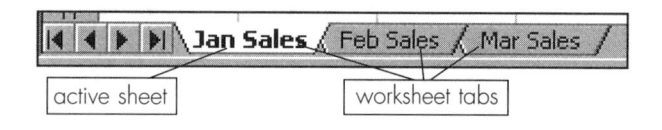

To select a different sheet, click on the *sheet tab* of the worksheet you want to view, and it becomes the active sheet. Although Excel workbooks open with three sheets, more may be added.

Using workbooks that contain multiple worksheets is a convenient way to organize work. For example, a workbook is a useful way to save monthly sales reports because all related reports are open at the same time. It is easier to move between worksheets in the same file (workbook) than to work with several open workbooks.

Throughout the rest of the text all of the exercises for a chapter will be saved in one workbook with each exercise on an individual worksheet.

Inserting a New Worksheet

Although Excel workbooks open with three sheets, additional ones can be added by selecting the Worksheet command on the Insert menu. New worksheets are inserted to the left of the active worksheet and are automatically numbered, beginning with Sheet4.

To add several worksheets at once, hold down the Shift key and select as many worksheet tabs as you want added. With several worksheet tabs highlighted, select Worksheet from the Insert menu. The number of tabs highlighted indicates the number of new sheets that will be added.

Selecting a Worksheet Group

Text and data can be added to several sheets at the same time. To select two or more adjacent sheets, click the tab of the first sheet, hold down the Shift key, and click the tab of the last consecutive sheet you want to select. To select nonadjacent sheets, click the tab of the first sheet, hold down the Ctrl key, and click the tabs of the other sheets you want to select. A *worksheet group* is a group of sheets that may be active simultaneously.

When a group is active, entries made in one active sheet are made in all active sheets. For instance, to place the name of a firm at the top of all worksheets in one step, select the worksheets, then enter and format the company name. Figure 6.2 shows the information that was entered only in the Jan Sales sheet displayed on all three worksheets. In each window, a white tab indicates which sheet is active.

Figure 6.2   Entering Information on Multiple Sheets

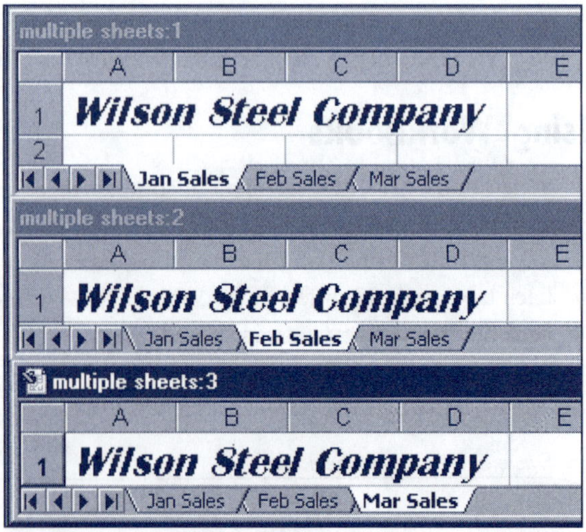

Ungrouping Worksheets

To *ungroup worksheets* from an adjacent group, hold down the Shift key and click in the sheet tab of the first sheet you selected; it displays in bold.

To ungroup worksheets from a nonadjacent group, hold down the Ctrl key and click in each sheet tab you want deselected.

Renaming a Worksheet

To rename a worksheet, double-click on its tab. The sheet name becomes active (highlighted) and can be changed. In Figure 6.3, the first sheet has been named Jan Sales. The second sheet is selected; its tab is highlighted, indicating that it is ready to be renamed. A sheet name can be up to 31 characters long, including spaces. Select a descriptive name for each worksheet.

Figure 6.3   Renaming a Sheet

The name of a sheet may be printed as a header or footer in a worksheet. To select the sheet name, access the Header/Footer tab of the Page Setup dialog box. Then click in the down arrow at the right of the Header or Footer text box. In the drop-down menu, select the sheet name, as shown in Figure 6.4.

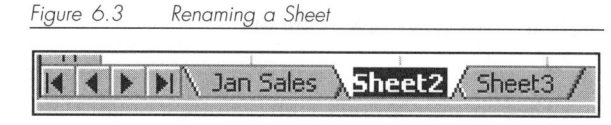

Figure 6.4   Selecting the Sheet Name

When the name of a sheet is changed, it is automatically updated in the header or footer.

Figure 6.5   Move or Copy Dialog Box

Moving and Copying a Worksheet

The Move or Copy dialog box is used to change the order of worksheets or to copy a sheet. It is accessed from the Edit menu and is shown in Figure 6.5.

The file name, move sheets.xls, is shown in the first text box. The names of the individual sheets in the workbook are shown in the bottom text box. The active sheet of the workbook will be placed before the sheet that is highlighted in the dialog box. In Figure 6.5, the selected sheet will be placed before the Jan Sales sheet.

Another method to move a sheet is to click on the sheet tab and drag the sheet to its new location. Figure 6.6 shows the active Jan Sales sheet as it is moved to its new location between Sheet2 and Sheet3. The document icon illustrates a worksheet's placement as it is moved.

Figure 6.6   Moving a Worksheet Tab

To copy a worksheet, hold down the Ctrl key while dragging the sheet to its new location. As the sheet icon is moved, a + appears in it, indicating it is being copied to the new sheet.

Scrolling between Worksheets

To access other worksheets, use the ***tab scrolling buttons*** (Figure 6.7) on the bottom left of the screen. The two outer buttons scroll to the first or last worksheet. The two in the center move one worksheet at a time in the direction of the arrow.

Figure 6.7   Tab Scrolling Buttons

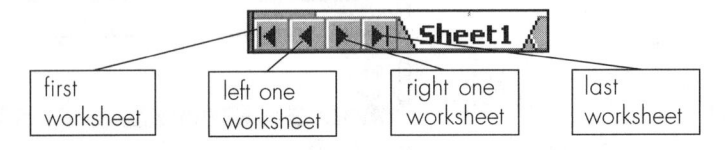

Deleting a Worksheet

To ***delete a worksheet*** from a workbook, select the sheet or sheets you want to delete. Then select Delete Sheet from the Edit menu.

Exercise 6.1   Using Multiple-Sheet Workbooks

A workbook that contains several worksheets has been developed for you to use when completing the exercises for Chapter 6. You will open the workbook and rename the worksheets. You will also rearrange the worksheets.

This exercise *must* be completed before doing the other exercises in this chapter. Each instruction must be followed exactly as stated because the other exercises in the chapter are dependent on the correct completion of this exercise.

1   Open the **Ch6 Exer** workbook. It is located in the **Ch06** folder.

Save the workbook.

2   Save the workbook as **Exer 6**.

Change the names on the tabs.

3   Double-click on the **Sheet1** tab and change the selected name to **Shortcut Menus (3)**. The (3) indicates that this sheet will be used in Exercise 3. Click in the worksheet.

4 Double-click on the **Sheet2** tab and rename it **Fill (5)**.

5 Rename each sheet as follows: (You may need to use the tab scrolling buttons to access unnamed sheets.)
        Sheet3   ShortFill (8)
        Sheet4   AutoFormat (11)
        Sheet5   Center (12)
        Sheet6   Spell (15)

6 Click in each worksheet to end the editing of each sheet name.

Insert a new sheet.

7 Click on the **Spell (15)** tab to make it the active sheet.

8 From the **Insert** menu, select **Worksheet**. A new worksheet is inserted and becomes the active sheet.

9 Rename the new worksheet **Justify (9)**.

10 Click once on the sheet named **ShortFill (8)** and insert another worksheet. Name the new sheet **AutoFill (7)**.

Move worksheets.

11 Select **Justify (9)**. Click on its tab and drag it before **AutoFormat (11)**.

12 Insert a sheet before **AutoFormat (11)**. Rename it **Custom List (10)**.

13 Select **Center (12)** and **Spell (15)**. (Hold down the Shift key to select consecutive worksheets.) From **Insert**, select **Worksheet**. Two additional worksheets are inserted, probably named **Sheet4** and **Sheet5**.

14 Rename the first new sheet **AutoComplete (13)**; rename the second new sheet **Toolbars (14)**.

15 Select both **AutoComplete (13)** and **Toolbars (14)** and move them before **Spell (15)**.

16 Your worksheets should be in the following order. If they are not, close the workbook and complete the entire exercise again.
Shortcut Menus (3), Fill (5), AutoFill (7), ShortFill (8), Justify (9), Custom List (10), AutoFormat (11), Center (12), AutoComplete (13), Toolbars (14), Spell (15)

17 Save the workbook.

Printing a Workbook

Only the active worksheet prints when you select the Print button. However, the entire workbook can be printed from the Print dialog box in the File menu, shown in Figure 6.8.

Figure 6.8   Print Dialog Box

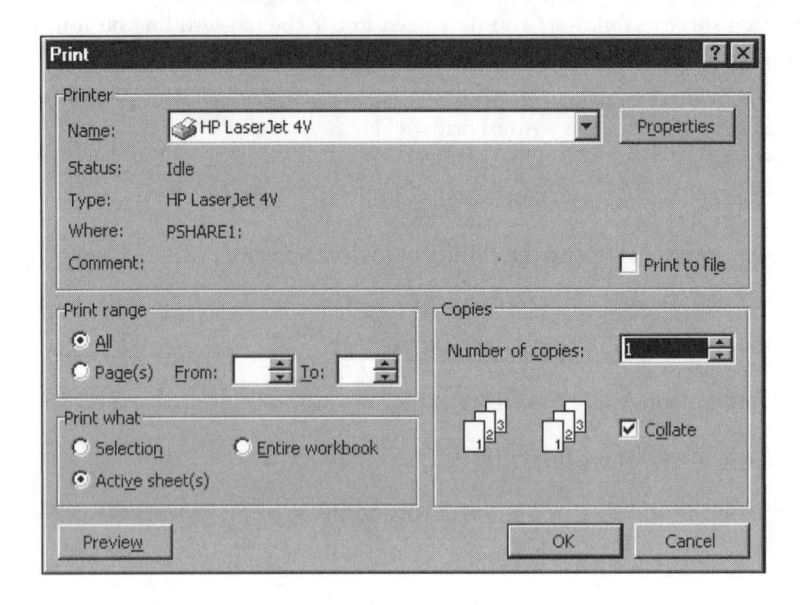

The Printer section indicates the selected printer. In some businesses and classrooms, more than one printer may be available. If a different printer is to be used, it can be selected in the drop-down menu that opens when the down arrow is selected.

The Print range section indicates how much of the selected sheet is to be printed. If desired, only one or two pages of a multiple-page worksheet can be printed.

In the Print what section are choices to print the selection (part of the worksheet), the active sheet, or the entire workbook. Selecting Entire workbook prints all sheets containing data in the open workbook.

The Copies section is used to determine the number of copies to be printed.

Exercise 6.2   Printing a Workbook

You will enter information on several sheets of a workbook and then print the entire workbook.

1 Open to a new workbook.

2 Select **Sheet1**. Hold down the [Shift] key and select **Sheet3**. Three sheets are selected.

3 Enter and format your name in cell A1. Click in all three sheets to verify that the contents of cell A1 have been entered in each sheet.

4 In **Page Setup**, set top and left margins for 3".

5 In the **Header/Footer** tab, access the header selections and select the file name.

6 Access the footer selections and select the sheet name. The selected sheets will print the file name in the header and the sheet name in the footer.

7. Hold down **Shift** and click in **Sheet1** to ungroup the sheets.
8. From **File** select **Print**. In the **Print** dialog box, select to print the **Entire workbook**.
9. Do not save the changes.

Shortcut Menus

Shortcut menus were developed to put the most frequently used commands in a single menu that can be accessed anywhere in a worksheet window. A shortcut menu opens near the mouse when the right mouse button is clicked. Figure 6.9 displays a shortcut menu with many frequently used commands listed.

Commands listed on a shortcut menu are executed the same way as commands accessed from a menu bar. The shortcut menu in Figure 6.9 lists the frequently used commands Cut, Copy, and Paste in the top section. Access to several frequently used dialog boxes is available in the bottom section of this shortcut menu and is indicated by an ellipses following a command.

The choices on shortcut menus change depending on the status of a worksheet. For instance, if a column is highlighted when a shortcut menu is accessed, a choice of Column Width appears on the shortcut menu, although it is not usually available. Figure 6.10 shows a shortcut menu when a column is selected. Notice the additional choices of Column Width, Hide, and Unhide.

Figure 6.9   Shortcut Menu

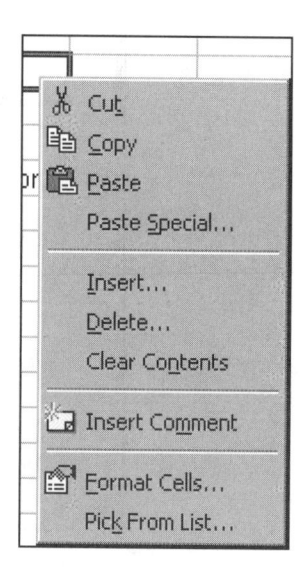

Figure 6.10   Changing Shortcut Menus

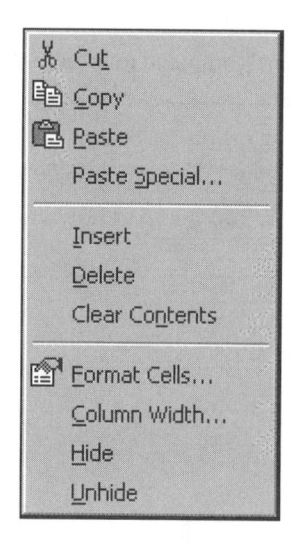

Shortcut menus can be used for drag-and-drop moving and copying. Hold down the right mouse button while dragging the cell contents during the copying or moving process. When the mouse button is released, the drag-and-drop shortcut menu opens. The menu shown in Figure 6.11 opens, allowing the cells to be moved or copied.

Figure 6.11   Shortcut Menu for Drop and Drag

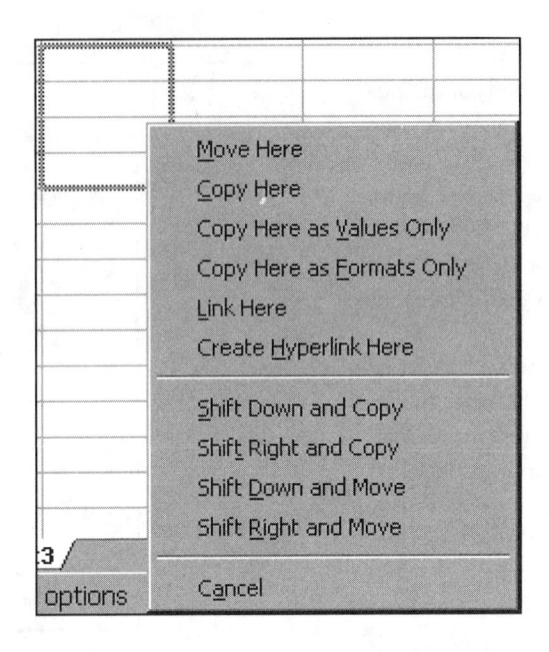

Power Users

The keyboard command to access a shortcut menu is **Shift**+**F10**.

Shortcut menus can be used to move or copy worksheets within a workbook. Click the right mouse button on a sheet tab to open a shortcut menu, shown in Figure 6.12.

Figure 6.12   Shortcut Menu for Worksheets

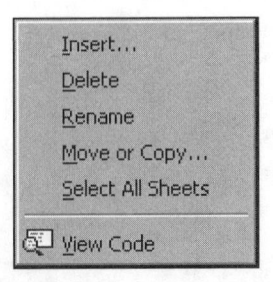

Exercise 6.3 Using Shortcut Menus

Data is entered into a worksheet showing the sales results for a six-month period for Smith Brothers and its stores in Boston, Dallas, Miami, and Chicago. You will complete and format the worksheet using shortcut menus.

1 Open the **Exer 6** workbook to the worksheet titled **Shortcut Menus (3)**.

2 Format cell A1 for bold and italic.

3 In cell A1, click the right mouse button to access the shortcut menu. Select **Copy**.

4 Highlight the range B3:E3 and access the shortcut menu.

5 Select **Paste Special**, then **Formats**. Click **OK**.

6 Select cell B3 and a copy command.

7 Click in cell A11 and open the shortcut menu. Select the **Paste Special** command, then **Paste Formats**.

8 Highlight the cells in column E that contain data (E3:E9).

9 Move the mouse to the edge of the range to get the arrow shape. Click on the right mouse button and drag to column C. The ScreenTip reads **C3:C9**.

10 Release the mouse button. The shortcut menu opens.

11 Select the command to **Shift Right and Move**. The labels for the cities are now listed in alphabetic order.

Move the April data in the worksheet.

12 Highlight the range A17:E17.

13 Access the shortcut menu. Select **Cut**.

14 Paste this in cell A7 using a shortcut menu.

Prepare header/footer information for all sheets in the workbook.

15 Move the mouse to the **Shortcut Menus (3)** tab. Click the right mouse button to access the shortcut menu. Then click on **Select All Sheets**.

16 From **File** select **Page Setup**. Place the sheet name in the header and the file name in the footer. Verify that all of the selected worksheets have correct header/footer settings.

17 Hold down the [Shift] key and click again in **Shortcut Menus (3)** to deselect sheets.

18 Replace **Student's Name** in cell A14 with your name.

19 Save and print the worksheet.

Copying between Worksheets and Workbooks

Any information in an Excel worksheet may be copied to other worksheets or workbooks. Copying between worksheets and workbooks is like copying within a worksheet. First select the copy area. Then select the destination. The destination may be another worksheet or workbook. If a group of worksheets is selected as the destination, the data will be copied into all of the worksheets in the group.

Exercise 6.4   Copying Information into Worksheets

You will create a new worksheet and then copy and move information into other worksheets and workbooks.

1   Open Excel to a new workbook.

2   In cell A1, enter your name. Place your address in cell A2 and your city, state, and zip code in cell A3.

3   Format this information for bold.

4   In row 5, enter the labels **Monday, Tuesday, Wednesday, Thursday,** and **Friday**.

5   Select the cells containing your address; then select a copy command.

6   Click in **Sheet2**. Position the mouse in cell A1 and select a paste command.

7   Return to **Sheet1** and select the column labels. Then select a copy command.

8   Select **Sheet2** and **Sheet3** as a group. (Hold down [Shift] to select the two sheets.)

9   In the active sheet, select cell A5 and then a paste command. The labels have been copied into the two sheets. The copy area is still active.

10 Open a new workbook. In cell A1, select a paste command. The information has been pasted into a new workbook.

11 Close the new workbook without saving it.

12 In the first workbook, click in the sheets to see how the information was copied.

13 Print the workbook, then close without saving it.

The Fill Commands

Copying cell contents using the Copy and Paste commands is convenient, but using the *fill commands* will copy and paste in one step. These fill commands are used to copy data and formulas, create a series of data, and create a custom series in two adjacent cells.

Using Fill to Copy

In the Edit menu, select the Fill command. A submenu opens providing choices to copy (fill) the selected cells Down, Right, Up, or Left. This submenu is shown in Figure 6.13.

Figure 6.13   Fill Menu

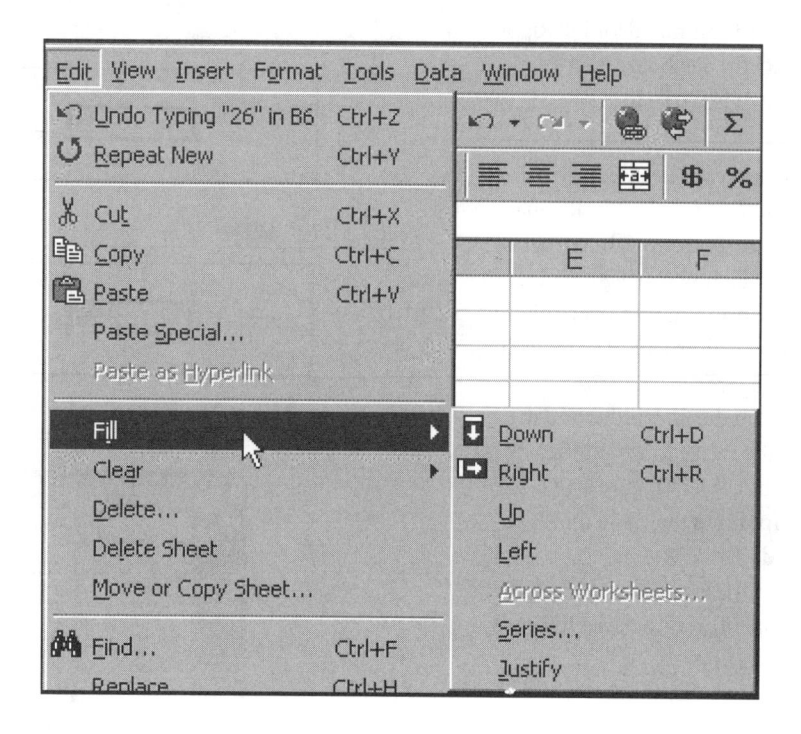

First enter data in a cell. Then highlight that cell and the adjacent range of cells, called the *fill range*, as shown in Figure 6.14. The fill range can extend either vertically or horizontally.

Figure 6.14   Using the Fill Command

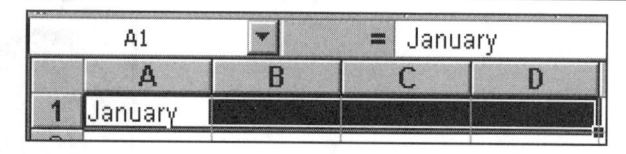

From Edit, select Fill, then Right; the contents are copied into the selected range, shown in Figure 6.15.

Figure 6.15   Using Fill to Copy

℗ Power Users

The keyboard command for Fill Right is **Ctrl**+**R**; the keyboard command for Fill Down is **Ctrl**+**D**.

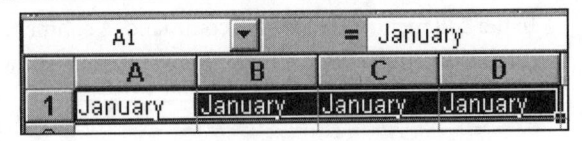

Figure 6.16   Fill Handle

Contents can also be copied using the *fill handle*. It is the black square located at the bottom-right corner of the active cell, shown in Figure 6.16.

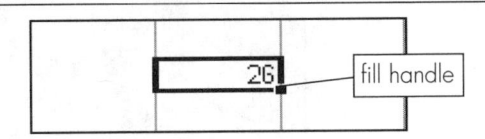

Figure 6.17   Mouse Shape with the Fill Handle

Position the mouse over the fill handle; it takes the shape of a crosshair, shown in Figure 6.17.

Click on the fill handle, and drag to select the range to which the contents will be copied (Figure 6.18). The ScreenTip shows the value that is being copied.

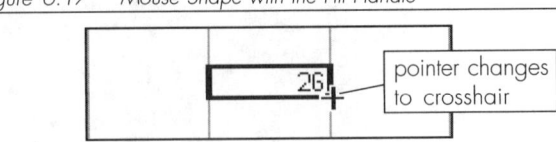

Figure 6.18   Fill Area Highlighted

When the mouse is released, the data is copied into the selected cells (Figure 6.19).

Figure 6.19   Completed Fill

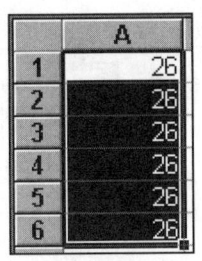

Fill commands can be used to copy formulas. Accessing the Fill submenu from the Edit menu is one way. Figure 6.20 shows a quarterly report; an AutoSum formula is entered into the total for the first quarter. The fill range (C6:E6) and the cell containing the formula (B6) are then selected.

From the Edit menu, select Fill, then Right. The completed worksheet is shown in Figure 6.21.

Formulas may also be copied using the fill handle. Select the cell containing the formula, click on the fill handle, and drag across the paste area.

Figure 6.20   Fill Right for Formulas

B6			=SUM(B2:B5)	
	A	B	C	D	E
1		Quarter 1	Quarter 2	Quarter 3	Quarter 4
2	North	458	358	784	348
3	South	548	687	167	574
4	East	578	157	586	198
5	West	487	689	178	785
6		2071			

Figure 6.21   Worksheet Completed Using the Fill Handle

C6			=SUM(C2:C5)	
	A	B	C	D	E
1		Quarter 1	Quarter 2	Quarter 3	Quarter 4
2	North	458	358	784	348
3	South	548	687	167	574
4	East	578	157	586	198
5	West	487	689	178	785
6		2071	1891	1715	1905

Exercise 6.5   Using Fill to Copy

You will use fill commands to copy cell contents and formulas.

1 Open **Exer 6** to the worksheet **Fill (5)**.

2 Select the range A1:E1. From the **Edit** menu, select **Fill**, then **Right**. **January** is copied into the selected range.

3 Select the range A2:A8. From the **Edit** menu, select **Fill**, then **Down**. **February** is copied into the selected range.

4 Select cell A11. Move the mouse to the fill handle to get the crosshair shape. Hold down **Ctrl**, then click and drag to cell E11. **March** is copied into the range.

5 Select cell A12. Move the mouse to the fill handle to get the crosshair shape. Hold down **Ctrl** and click and drag to cell A15. **April** is copied into the range.

6 Use the fill handle to copy the range B4:B6 to the range D4:D6.

7 Enter an AutoSum formula in cell C17 and complete the entry. Click on the fill handle and drag through E17. The formula is copied. Click in cells D17 and E17 to see the references in the formulas.

8 Save and print the worksheet.

Using Fill Across Worksheets

The Fill command can be used across different worksheets in a workbook. First select the sheets to which you want data copied. Then select the copy range. The data you want to copy must be in the active worksheet.

From the Edit menu, choose Fill. When the submenu opens, shown in Figure 6.22, choose Across Worksheets.

Figure 6.22   Selecting Fill Across Worksheets

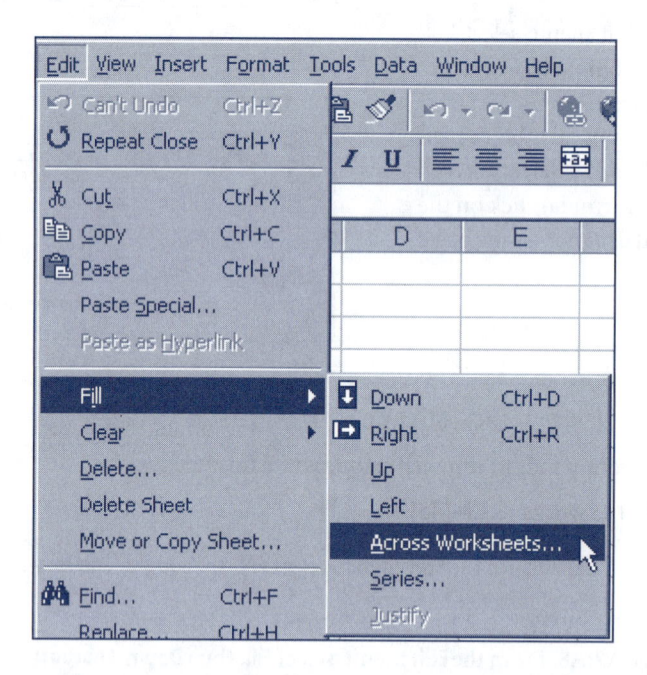

The ***Fill Across Worksheets*** dialog box opens, shown in Figure 6.23. You may select to copy the contents of the cells or only the formats. Both contents and formats are copied when All is selected.

Figure 6.23   Fill Across Worksheets Dialog Box

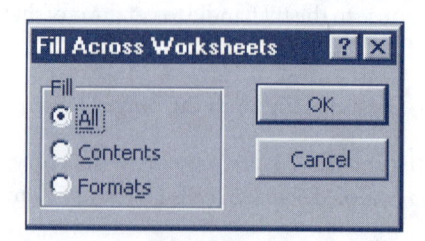

Exercise 6.6   Using Fill Across Worksheets

You will use the Fill Across Worksheets feature.

1 Click on the **AutoFill (7)** sheet. From **Insert**, select **Worksheet**. The new sheet is the active sheet.

2 Rename the sheet **Across Worksheet (6)**.

3 In A22 enter the name of your school. Format it for bold.

4 In A23 enter the city of your school. Format it for italic.

5 Select all of the sheets from **Across Worksheet (6)** to **Spell (15)**.

6 Hold down the [Alt] key and select **Across Worksheet (6)** to make it the active sheet.

7 Select the range A22:A23.

8 From **Edit**, select **Fill**, then **Across Worksheets**.

9 When the dialog box opens, be sure **All** is selected. Then click **OK**.

10 Ungroup the sheets. Click in several of the sheets to see that the information and formatting have been copied.

11 Save the workbook. Print the **Across Worksheet (6)** sheet.

Creating a Series

Excel can automatically create a series such as months of the year, days of the week, quarters of the year, or a series of numbers. This feature is called *AutoFill*, and it automatically completes a series after entries have been keyed in only one or two cells.

Excel recognizes and completes some series after only one or two entries are made. Figure 6.24 indicates the series that Excel will complete after the initial entries indicated.

Figure 6.24   Series Recognized in Excel

Initial Entries	Series Completed with
Mon	Tue, Wed, Thu, etc.
Monday	Tuesday, Wednesday, Thursday, etc.
Jan	Feb, Mar, Apr, etc.
January	February, March, April, etc.
Quarter 1	Quarter 2, Quarter 3, Quarter 4, etc.
Q1	Q2, Q3, Q4, Q1, etc.
10:00 AM	11:00 AM, 12:00 PM, 1:00 PM, etc.
Salesman 1	Salesman 2, Salesman 3, etc.
1997, 1998	1999, 2000, 2001, etc.
1, 2	3, 4, 5, 6, etc.
2, 4	6, 8, 10, 12, etc.

The fastest way to complete a series is with the fill handle. For example, a worksheet requires column labels consisting of the months January through June. First enter January and complete the entry (Figure 6.25).

Figure 6.25   First Cell Selected

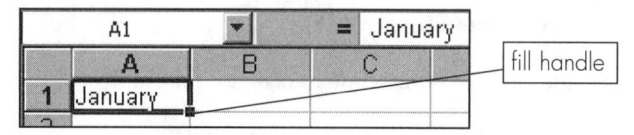

Then move the mouse pointer to the fill handle (Figure 6.26). It takes the shape of a crosshair.

Figure 6.26   Handle Selected for AutoFill

Hold down the left mouse button and drag the mouse over the fill range. A border surrounds the range to provide a visual indicator of its size. A ScreenTip shows the entry of the last cell selected (it is June in Figure 6.27).

Figure 6.27   Selected Fill Range

Release the mouse to complete the fill, shown in Figure 6.28. The months January through June are entered on the worksheet after only January was keyed.

Figure 6.28   AutoFill Selection Complete

Excel provides circular dates. For instance, after December comes January, and after Saturday comes Sunday and then Monday. Excel understands there are four quarters in a year and continues from Q4 to Q1.

A series of incremental numbers, such as 1, 2, 3 or 10, 20, 30, can also be extended using AutoFill. Enter the first two values in the series, and then highlight those cells. Click on the fill handle and drag the mouse over the fill range; the incremental value of the series displays in the entry area (Figure 6.29).

Figure 6.29   AutoFill with a Numeric Series

If a series has been extended too far, cells can be cleared. Click on the fill handle and drag in the direction of the last desired cell. The cells that will be cleared appear in gray (Figure 6.30). When the mouse button is released, the contents in the grayed cells are deleted.

Figure 6.30   Clearing AutoFill Cells

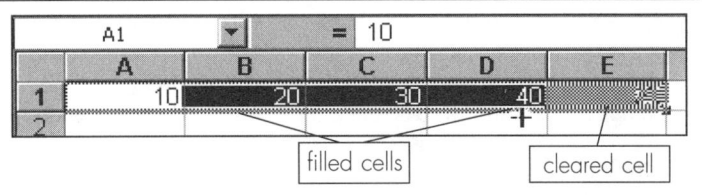

Series Dialog Box

Using the fill handle, you can quickly create a series of numbers, but the Series dialog box provides additional choices. The dialog box is shown in Figure 6.31. It is accessed by selecting Edit, then Fill, then choosing the Series command.

Figure 6.31   Series Dialog Box

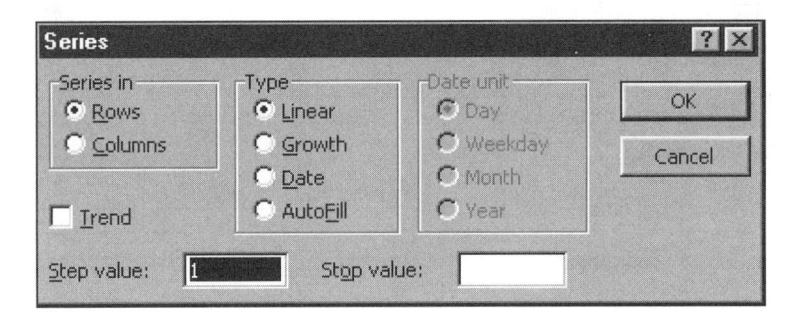

First, indicate if the series is to be in rows or columns. If Rows is selected, the series will fill the cells to the right. If Columns is selected, the series will fill the cells below. Figure 6.31 shows Rows selected.

Next select the type of series. The data series is created based on the starting values (usually in cells A1:A2) and the value in the Step value text box. When the Growth option is selected, the first value is multiplied by the step value. When the Date option is selected, the Date unit section becomes active to determine how dates are entered.

The AutoFill option in the Series dialog box is used exactly the same as using the fill handle to drag to create a predetermined series.

Exercise 6.7   Using AutoFill

You will practice using AutoFill.

1   Open the **AutoFill (7)** sheet in the **Exer 6** workbook.

2   In cell A1, key **January** and keep the cell active. Move the cursor to the fill handle; it changes to a crosshair.

3. Click and hold the mouse on the fill handle and drag through the range A1:F1. As the mouse button is dragged through the cells, the original entry is displayed in the reference area; at cell F1 **June** is displayed in the ScreenTip. Release the mouse; the first six months of the year are entered.

4. In cells A2 and A3, key **1** and **2** respectively. Then select the range. Click on the fill handle and drag through the range A2:A7. The number **6** is displayed in the ScreenTip. Release the mouse; the numbers **1** through **6** are entered.

5. In cell B2, key **Monday**. Use AutoFill to create a series on row 2 from **Monday** to **Friday**.

6. In cell A9, key **Feb 98**. Use AutoFill to create a series in column A that ends with **Jan-99**. (Excel may automatically change the format in which the number is displayed.)

7. In cells B6 and B7, key **1998** and **1999** respectively. Then select this range. Use AutoFill to create a range that extends through **2003**.

8. In cells C3 and C4, key **Product 1** and **Product 2** respectively. Then select the range. Use AutoFill to extend the series through **Product 6** in cell C8.

Clear part of the series.

9. Select the range A1:F1.

10. Click on the fill handle and drag to the left to C1. Cells D1 through F1 are gray. Release the mouse to clear the cell contents.

11. In cell A24, enter your name.

12. Save and print the worksheet.

AutoFill Shortcut Menus

Data can also be entered using the AutoFill shortcut menu. Place data in a cell, and then hold down the right mouse button while dragging through the fill range. When the mouse is released, the AutoFill shortcut menu opens, shown in Figure 6.32.

Figure 6.32   AutoFill Shortcut Menu

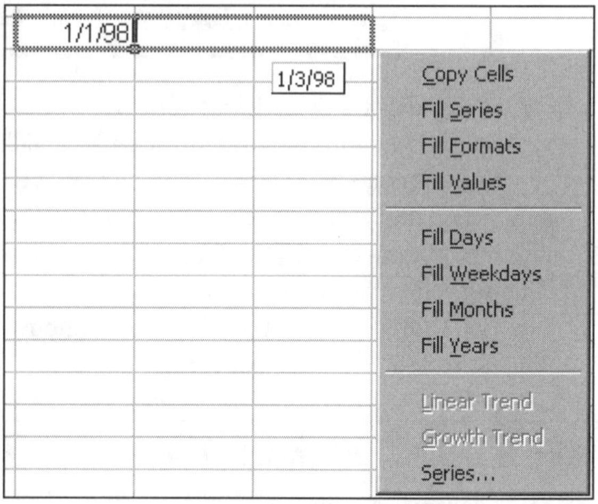

Click on the type of fill wanted, and the data is entered. A completed fill is shown in Figure 6.33 when Fill Months is selected. Notice that the months increased by one month in each cell entry and retained the format of the original entry.

Figure 6.33   AutoFill Completed with Shortcut Menu

| 1/1/98 | 2/1/98 | 3/1/98 | 4/1/98 |

AutoFill not only saves time in keying entries, but also ensures accuracy. Excel does not make spelling errors. If in doubt, try it. Software programs are learned best through trial and error.

Exercise 6.8   Using the AutoFill Shortcut Menu

You will use shortcut menus to fill and format several series.

1 Open the **Exer 6** workbook and then the **ShortFill (8)** worksheet.

2 Select cell B1. Move the mouse to the fill handle and hold down the right mouse button; drag through cell H1. The ScreenTip reads **Sunday**. When you release the mouse button, the shortcut menu opens. Select **Fill Weekdays**. Days of the week, excluding weekends, are entered in the cells.

3 In cell B2, enter **Monday**. Move the mouse to the fill handle and hold down the right mouse button; drag through cell H2. The ScreenTip reads **Sunday**. When you release the mouse button, the shortcut menu opens. Select **Fill Days**. Days of the week are entered in the cells.

4 Select the range A3:A7. Move the mouse to the fill handle, hold down the right mouse button, and drag through cell A17. From the shortcut menu, select **Copy Cells**.

5 Format cell A1 for bold. Move the mouse to the fill handle, hold down the right mouse button, and drag through cell A17. From the shortcut menu, select **Fill Formats**. Only the format was copied.

6 In cell B4 key **25**; in cell B5 key **26**. Select both cells. Move the mouse to the fill handle, hold down the right mouse button, and drag through cell G5. From the shortcut menu, select **Fill Series**. The series has been extended.

7 Put your name in cell C9.

8 Save and print this worksheet.

Fill Justify

The *Fill Justify command* is used to split the contents of a cell into several cells. When a long cell entry is made, it can automatically be distributed into two or more cells, depending on the length of the entry. Figure 6.34 shows a long entry in cell A1.

Figure 6.34   Using Fill Justify

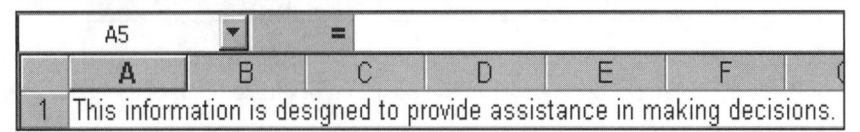

Select the cell with the data entry (A1). Then select Edit, then Fill, then Justify (Figure 6.35).

Figure 6.35   Selecting Fill Justify

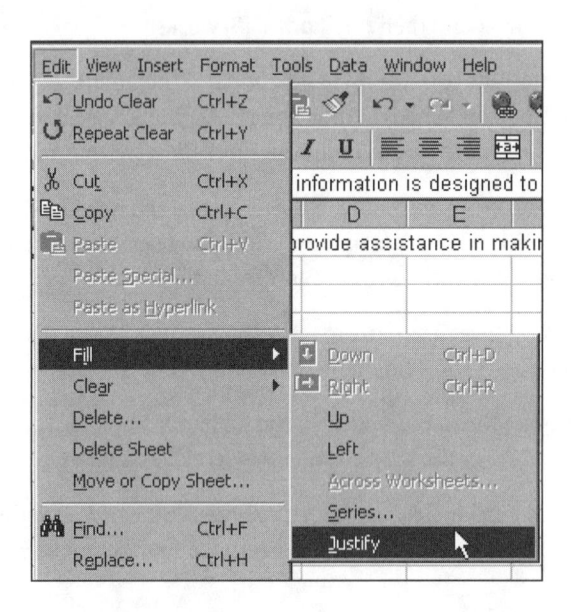

A warning message appears that reads "Text will extend below selected range." This warns that the cell contents will fill more than one cell. Selecting OK places the contents in the range just below the first cell; any contents already in the range will be deleted. The result is shown in Figure 6.36.

Figure 6.36   Text Formatted for Fill Justify

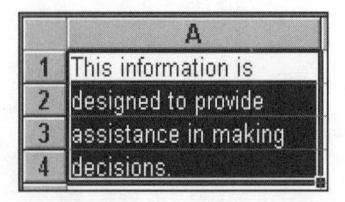

If the column width is altered, the Fill Justify command must again be used to distribute the text across the entire width of the cell.

Exercise 6.9   Using Fill Justify

You will enter a long entry and use Fill Justify to move it to several cells. You will also adjust column size.

1. Select the sheet **Justify (9)** from the **Exer 6** workbook.

2. In cell A1 key the following statement and complete the entry:
   This class is extremely fun. I enjoy learning Excel.

3. With cell A1 active, select **Edit**, then **Fill**, then **Justify**. A warning box opens stating, **Text will extend below selected range**. Click **OK**. The entry has extended into several cells.

4. Move the mouse between the headings of columns A and B. It takes the shape of a double-headed arrow. Click and drag so column A is wider.

5. Select the range of the column that includes the statement. Then choose **Edit**, then **Fill**, then **Justify**. The entry has now adjusted to occupy fewer cells.

6. Place your full name (including first, middle, and last) in cell A6. Format it for bold and **Fill Justify**.

7. Save and print the worksheet.

Creating a Custom List

When completing spreadsheets, businesses often use the same list over and over. It may be a list of products, cities where manufacturing plants are located, or salespeople. A list can be created, saved, and then entered using Excel's AutoFill feature. These lists are called *custom lists*.

To create a custom list, key in a list on a worksheet and highlight it. A custom list is shown in Figure 6.37.

Figure 6.37   Custom List

	A
1	Butter Dish
2	Cup
3	Dessert Bowls
4	Dessert Plates
5	Dinner Plates
6	Oval Platter
7	Oval Serving
8	Round Serving
9	Salad Plates
10	Sauce Dish
11	Saucer
12	Soup Bowls

To enter a new list, select Options from the Tools menu. When the Options dialog box opens, click on the Custom Lists tab, shown in Figure 6.38. The built-in choices are displayed in the Custom lists section at the left side of the dialog box.

Figure 6.38   Custom Lists Tab in Options Dialog Box

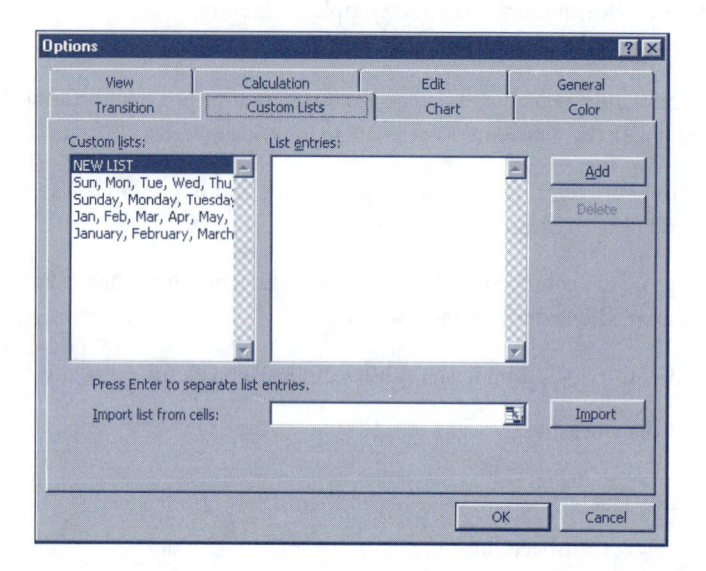

Click on the Collapse Dialog button at the right side of the Import list from cells text box. This collapses the dialog box so the text in the worksheet becomes visible. Drag through the range of the new list, shown in Figure 6.39. The selected list is indicated by a marquee and a ScreenTip indicates the range of the selection. When the list is selected, click the Expand Dialog button.

Figure 6.39   Range Selected for a Custom List

Click on the Import button. In the Custom Lists tab, the new list is displayed in the List entries box at the right of the dialog box. Click OK to save the list and exit the box.

To insert a custom list, key the first item on the list in a worksheet and drag the fill handle over the range. Although a custom list may have been created using a vertical range of cells, it can be inserted into any selection in a worksheet; it makes no difference whether the range is vertical or horizontal. A horizontal range is shown in Figure 6.40.

Figure 6.40   Custom List Inserted Horizontally into a Worksheet

| Butter Dish | Cup | Dessert Bowls | Dessert Plates | Dinner Plates | Oval Platter | Oval Serving | Round Serving |

A custom list can be deleted in the Custom Lists tab of the Options dialog box. Choose the list you want to delete, then select Delete. A warning box opens reminding you that the list will be permanently deleted.

Exercise 6.10   Creating a Custom List

You will open a new worksheet and create a custom list.

1 Open to the **Custom List (10)** worksheet tab in the **Exer 6** file.

2 In cell A1, key your first name.

3 In row B starting with cell B1, key the names of your family members or close friends. Enter four to eight names.

4 From the **Tools** menu, select **Options**, then **Custom Lists**.

5 When the dialog box opens, click on the Collapse Dialog button . The dialog box collapses.

6 Click and drag through the range of names. Then click the Expand Dialog button . Check the range in the text box.

7 Click on the **Import** button. In the **Custom Lists** tab, the names will be listed in the right box. Then click **OK** to save your list.

Enter the custom list in the worksheet.

8 In cell C3, key your first name.

9 Click on the fill handle and extend the range so all names entered in Step 3 appear in the worksheet. Your custom list is entered.

10 Click in cell A1 to deselect the cells.

11 Save and print the worksheet.

Custom lists are saved as part of Excel. Because you are probably in a shared environment (classroom), the custom list will be deleted so the program remains as defaulted and your list is not saved with Excel.

12 From **Tools**, select **Options**, then **Custom Lists**.

13 Click in your name in the **Custom lists** box and then **Delete**. Click **OK** to the warning box. The custom list is permanently deleted. Click **OK** to close the **Options** dialog box.

Other Automatic Excel Features

Using AutoFormat

Preparing a worksheet that has a professional appearance is an important feature of any spreadsheet software. Formatting a worksheet can take as much time as entering data, even with a powerful program like Excel. As a way to increase the speed of creating a worksheet and still maintaining a professional appearance, Excel uses a feature called *AutoFormat*.

AutoFormat automatically applies a built-in format to a worksheet with over a dozen different format styles to select from. Titles, subtitles, money amounts, labels, and summary rows and columns are recognized and formatted appropriately.

To apply AutoFormat, highlight the worksheet range to be formatted. After the range is highlighted, select AutoFormat from the Format menu. The AutoFormat dialog box opens, shown in Figure 6.41.

Figure 6.41   AutoFormat Dialog Box

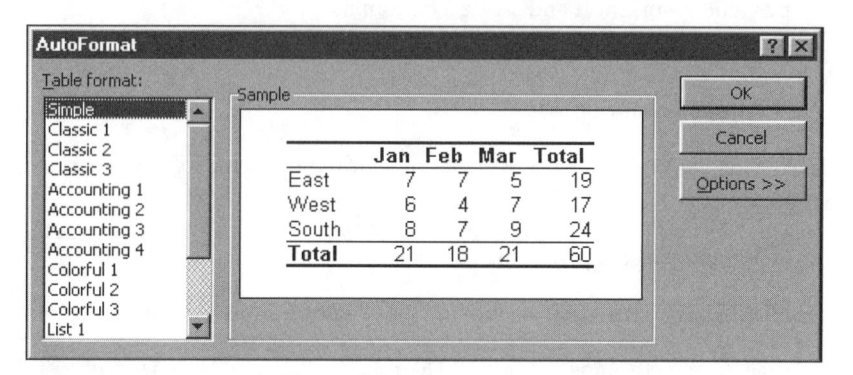

At the left of the dialog box is the Table format section, listing the 16 format choices available. When a choice is selected, a sample format is displayed in the Sample box. Selecting OK applies the displayed format.

Use the Options button at the right side of the dialog box to add choices about which format attributes to apply. When you click the Options button, the dialog box enlarges to show the Formats to apply section, shown in Figure 6.42.

Figure 6.42   Formats to Apply in AutoFormat Dialog Box

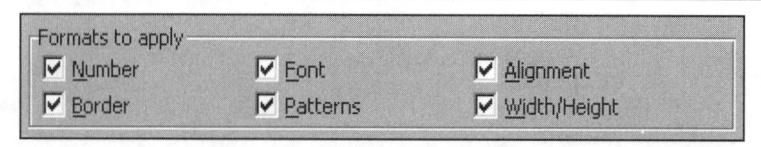

To retain formats that are already applied, clear the check boxes for the formats that AutoFormat should not change.

Exercise 6.11 Using AutoFormat

An inventory worksheet has been completed, which you will format using AutoFormat.

1 Open the **Exer 6** workbook if it is not already open and select the **AutoFormat (11)** worksheet.

2 Highlight the used portion of the worksheet. From **Format**, select **AutoFormat**.

3 Click on **Classic1** to view the style.

4 Click on **Colorful2** to view the style.

5 Click on a **List** and a **3D Effects** format to view their styles.

6 Click through the four **Accounting** choices.

7 Select one of the **Accounting** choices. Then click **OK**. The worksheet is formatted.

8 In cell A10, replace **Student's Name** with your name.

9 Save the changes and print the worksheet.

Centering Titles

Centering text over several adjacent columns is easy using the *Merge and Center button*. Select the range of cells over the columns. Then key the information in the first cell. Click on the Merge and Center button and the information is centered within the selected range of cells. (The text can be entered first, the range selected, and then the Merge and Center button selected.) Merge and Center merges the selected cells into one cell.

Figures 6.43 through 6.46 show the procedure for centering a title over the entire worksheet range (columns A through E). Figure 6.43 shows the selected range.

Key the text in the first cell—A1 in this example. Then click the Enter box to complete the entry (Figure 6.44).

Figure 6.43   Selected Range of Title

	A	B	C	D	E
1					
2					
3			Jan	Feb	Mar	Q Total
4	Product 1		235	295	364	894
5	Product 2		385	403	437	1225
6	Total		620	698	801	2119

Figure 6.44   Title Entry Completed

	A	B	C	D	E
1	Wonderful Products				
2					
3			Jan	Feb	Mar	Q Total
4	Product 1		235	295	364	894
5	Product 2		385	403	437	1225
6	Total		620	698	801	2119

Click on the Merge and Center button. The contents in the cell are automatically centered over the selected range (Figure 6.45). Additional format choices, such as bold and italic, can be added.

Figure 6.45   Title Centered over Range

	A	B	C	D	E
1		Wonderful Products			
2					
3		Jan	Feb	Mar	Q Total
4	Product 1	235	295	364	894
5	Product 2	385	403	437	1225
6	Total	620	698	801	2119

Figure 6.46 shows the labels North Territory and South Territory centered over two columns. This is done by selecting a two-cell range and using the Merge and Center button.

Figure 6.46   Worksheet with Centered Cell Contents

	Best Example of a Great Worksheet			
	North Territory		South Territory	
	Smith	Brown	Adams	Jackson
Dolls	38	28	18	30
Trains	48	39	51	45
Trucks	28	30	24	31
Bicycles	27	22	19	28
Total	141	119	112	134

Exercise 6.12   Centering Worksheet Titles

You will format a worksheet that shows the Northwest's Bests.

1 Select the worksheet tab **Center (12)** in the **Exer 6** workbook.

2 Select cell A1. Format for bold and italic and a font size of **14**.

3 Highlight row 1 through column I (A1:I1). Click on the Merge and Center button.

4 With cell A1 still active, select a copy command.

5 Click in cell A2 and access the shortcut menu (click the right mouse button). Select **Paste Special**.

6 In the **Paste Special** dialog box, select **Paste Formats**. Then click **OK**. The format was copied and the text is centered over the range of cells.

7 Format B4:I5 for italic.

8 Highlight row 5, columns B through I. Select a bold underline to be placed under this range and use center alignment.

9 Highlight B4:D4 and click on the Merge and Center button.

10 Highlight E4:G4 and format it to be merged and centered.

11 Center H4:I4 across columns.

12 In cell A12, replace **Student's Name** with your name.

13 Click in cell D2, then G2. Because this is a merged cell, it is active whenever the mouse is clicked in any part of it.

14 Change the month and year to the current month and year.

15 Save and print the worksheet.

Using AutoComplete

When entering text, Excel fills in suggested text based on entries previously made in the column. This feature is called *AutoComplete*. When the first few characters entered match an existing entry in the same column, a suggestion is provided. To accept the entry, press Enter. An exact copy of the entry is placed in the active cell. If this entry is not correct, simply continue entering the text.

In the highlighted cell in Figure 6.47, "The Best R" was keyed. Excel then entered "estaurants" to complete the entry and to match the one already entered in the column. If the entry is not wanted, continue keying the correct entry.

Figure 6.47   AutoComplete Enters Text

	A
1	The Best Restaurants
2	The Best Convention Centers
3	The Best Hotels
4	The Best Restaurants
5	The Best Restaurants

Excel completes entries that contain text or text combined with numbers. AutoComplete does not complete entries containing numbers, dates, or times.

Pick From List

Often the same item is repeated several times in a column. To lessen the amount of keying required, a feature called *Pick From List* allows any of the previously entered labels to be entered into a cell without rekeying. To repeat a cell entry, access the shortcut menu. The last choice on the menu is Pick From List (Figure 6.48).

Figure 6.48   Shortcut Menu to Access Pick From List Command

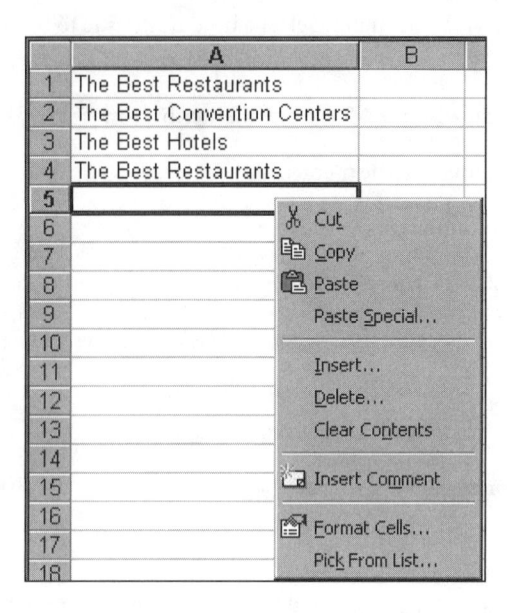

Select Pick From List to access a list of all cell entries entered in that column (Figure 6.49). Select the cell entry you want, and it is entered.

Figure 6.49   Using Pick From List

AutoComplete and Pick From List are useful tools for entering long row labels in a worksheet and preventing spelling errors.

Exercise 6.13   Using AutoComplete

You will practice using AutoComplete and the Pick From List selection on the shortcut menu.

1   Open the **Exer 6** workbook to the **AutoComplete (13)** sheet.

2   Enter the following information into the worksheet. Key the information in columns A and C. Adjust the column widths.

	A	B	C
1	Wyatt Company		Anderson Windows
2	Leong Group		Burchfield Doors
3	Sunomo Associates		Schneider and Sons and Daughters
4	Rogers Incorporated		Burns Interiors

3 In cell A5, key **W**. Notice that Excel enters **Wyatt Company**. Continue keying the entry **un Foundation** (creating Wun Foundation).

4 In cell A6, key **S**. **Sunomo Associates** is suggested. Press [Enter].

5 In cell A7, key **W**. Because two firms begin with a W, Excel makes no suggestion. Now key **y**. **Wyatt Company** is now suggested; accept the entry.

6 Click in cell C5. Access the shortcut menu, then select **Pick From List**.

7 Select **Schneider and Sons and Daughters**.

8 In cell C6, use **Pick From List** to enter **Burchfield Doors**.

9 Enter your name in cell A10.

10 Save and print the worksheet.

Exploring Toolbars

The two toolbars that are usually displayed in an Excel worksheet are the Standard toolbar and the Formatting toolbar. They contain buttons for the most commonly used actions. In addition, several other toolbars are available. Each of these toolbars contains buttons corresponding to a specific task such as formatting or charting. Some toolbars, such as the Chart toolbar, automatically display when you are working with the corresponding feature.

Standard Toolbar

The *Standard toolbar* is shown in Figure 6.50 with the buttons identified. Those buttons that have not already been introduced will be covered in later chapters. The toolbar on your computer may be slightly different. Because it is easy to personalize Excel, your toolbar buttons may have been customized.

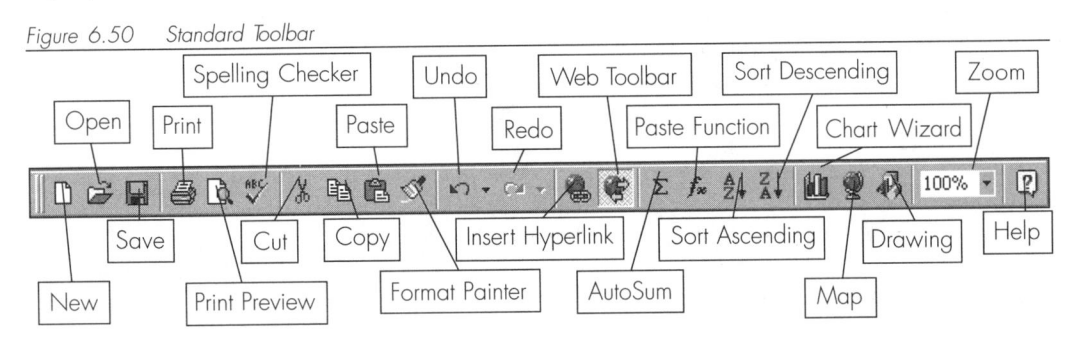

Figure 6.50   Standard Toolbar

Formatting Toolbar

Excel opens with the **Formatting toolbar** as the second toolbar on the screen (Figure 6.51) and is used primarily to format a worksheet.

Figure 6.51   Formatting Toolbar

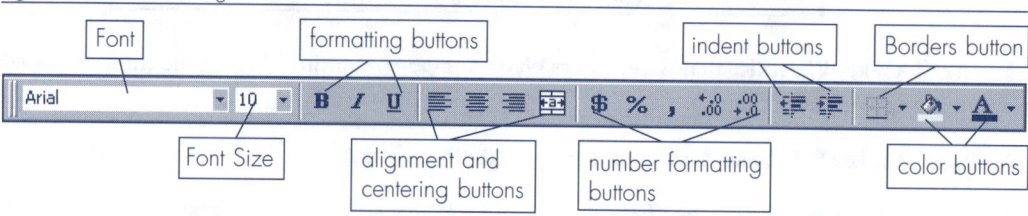

[Formatting toolbar diagram with labels: Font, formatting buttons, indent buttons, Borders button, Font Size, alignment and centering buttons, number formatting buttons, color buttons]

Toolbar Basics

Specialized toolbars provide additional buttons to use for specific activities such as creating charts or simple drawings. A toolbar can also be customized to contain frequently used tools. As topics are covered in this text, specific toolbars will also be discussed. For instance, the Chart toolbar will be introduced in Chapter 9 when charts are presented.

To access other toolbars, select Toolbars from the View menu. A submenu opens showing the available toolbars, shown in Figure 6.52. The toolbars that are opened are indicated by checkmarks. (In Figure 6.52 the Standard and Formatting toolbars are marked as open.)

A toolbar also can be accessed by moving the mouse to an open toolbar and clicking on the right mouse button.

The most often used toolbars are displayed in the drop-down menu. However, additional toolbars can be accessed by selecting Customize. Toolbars can be customized for individual preferences; you can place additional command buttons on the toolbar and remove those that you do not use.

Figure 6.52   Toolbar Menu

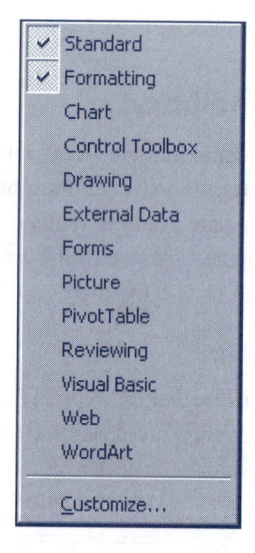

[Toolbar menu showing: ✓ Standard, ✓ Formatting, Chart, Control Toolbox, Drawing, External Data, Forms, Picture, PivotTable, Reviewing, Visual Basic, Web, WordArt, Customize...]

A toolbar may open as a *floating toolbar* that can be positioned over any part of a worksheet and moved around the screen. Toolbars can also be positioned at the edges of a worksheet screen in a ***toolbar dock***, which is any location at the four sides of a worksheet. To move a toolbar, click in its title bar. Its size and shape may also be changed by moving to an edge of the toolbar; the mouse takes the shape of a double-headed arrow. Then click and drag the toolbar to its desired shape.

Using a toolbar dock reduces the work area of a worksheet. Figure 6.53 shows a worksheet with additional toolbars opened; there are five toolbars residing in toolbar docks surrounding the workspace, and the Web toolbar is floating in the middle of the screen.

Figure 6.53   Toolbar Docks

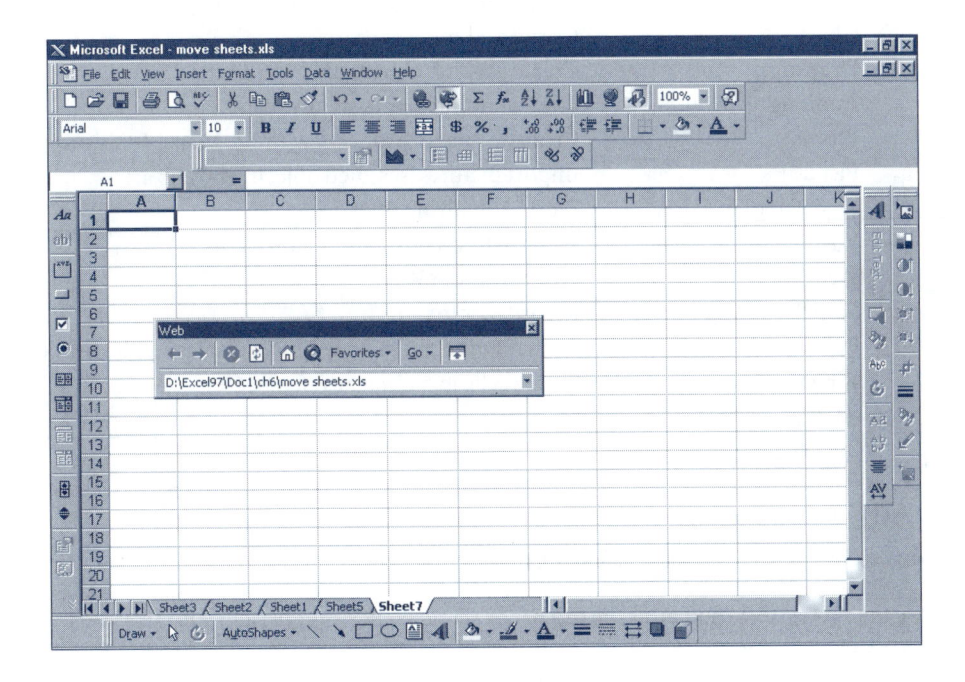

To move a toolbar from a floating to a docked position, double-click on an empty spot in the toolbar. To move a toolbar from a docked to a floating position, click the mouse in the double line at the left side of the toolbar as shown in Figure 6.54, and drag it from the dock.

Figure 6.54   Moving a Docked Toolbar

To hide a floating toolbar, click in the Close box in its upper-right corner. Docked toolbars can be closed using the Toolbar submenu, accessed from the View menu, or by clicking the right mouse button in a toolbar to access the shortcut menu.

Chapter 6   Multiple-Sheet Workbooks and Other Time Savers

Note: It is important to hide all toolbars except the Standard and Formatting toolbars when leaving the classroom. Once a toolbar is open, it remains open until it is manually closed. If Excel is quit and restarted, any open toolbar will again open on the screen.

Other Toolbars

A list of some available toolbars and their uses is shown below. All toolbars are illustrated in Appendix C, with each button identified.

Toolbar Name	What It Is Used for
Standard	Complete basic worksheet tasks
Formatting	Format characters, numbers, and cells
Chart	Create and modify charts
Drawing	Create graphic objects and WordArt
Auditing	Trace and find errors in formulas
Forms	Create forms for working with the Visual Basic program
Picture	Import pictures, scanned objects, and clip art
PivotTable	Work with pivot tables
Visual Basic	Work with the Visual Basic program
Web	Work with the Web
Stop Recording	Record macros
Full Screen	Return to the normal view after displaying the full screen
Circular Reference	Locate cells in a circular reference

Exercise 6.14   Using Toolbars

You will practice working with different toolbars.

1 Open the **Exer 6** workbook to the **Toolbars (14)** worksheet.

2 Move the mouse to a toolbar at the top of the screen. Click on the right mouse button to access the toolbar shortcut menu.

3 Select the **Drawing** toolbar. It may open as a floating toolbar. If it doesn't open as a floating toolbar, click in the double lines at the top or left of it and drag it onto the worksheet. The double lines look like .

4 Move the **Drawing** toolbar around the screen. (Click in its title bar and drag the toolbar to a different location.)

5 Size the toolbar. (Move the mouse to the right edge of the toolbar. A double-headed arrow appears. Click on the mouse button and drag the arrow to the left, making the toolbar narrower.) Resize the toolbar so that all of the buttons are in one row.

6 Click in the title bar of the **Drawing** toolbar and drag it to the bottom edge of the screen. It will rest in a toolbar dock.

7 Again access the Toolbar shortcut menu by moving the mouse to a toolbar and clicking the right mouse button. Select the **Forms** toolbar.

8 Click in the title bar of the **Forms** toolbar and drag to an edge of the screen to place it in a toolbar dock.

9 Access the Toolbar shortcut menu. Click on **Customize**.

10 Click in the check box beside **Full Screen**. (You may need to use the scroll bar to access the Full Screen option.) Then click **Close**. The **Full Screen** toolbar has only one button.

11 Click in the **Full Screen** button. Notice that the screen fills the entire monitor. Some toolbars are not available; the title bar is hidden.

12 Click in the **Close Full Screen** button to return the worksheet area to its original size. Then close the **Full Screen** toolbar (click in its Close box).

13 Access the Toolbar shortcut menu and select **Customize**.

14 Click in any empty box to show a new toolbar. Close the **Customize** dialog box and place the toolbar in a toolbar dock.

15 Double-click in the double line at the end or top of the toolbar and drag it back onto the worksheet area. It again becomes a floating toolbar.

16 Close the **Drawing** toolbar.

17 Remove all toolbars from toolbar docks (except the Standard and Formatting toolbars).

18 Close the worksheet without saving it.

Using the Spelling Checker

The *spelling checker* in Excel helps you maintain accuracy by avoiding misspelled words. Excel shares the same dictionary with the other Office programs and uses it to check for spelling errors. Because many words used in a worksheet may be specialized and may not be listed in the standard dictionary, the dictionary can be customized.

Excel normally checks an entire worksheet for spelling errors, beginning with the selected cell. To check only a part of the worksheet, highlight the range to be checked. To begin the spelling checker, choose Spelling from the Tools menu or click on the Spelling button in the Standard toolbar.

Power Users

The spelling checker can also be accessed by pressing the F7 function key.

When Excel finds a spelling error (or a word that is not in the standard dictionary), it displays the word in the Spelling dialog box, shown in Figure 6.55.

Figure 6.55   Spelling Dialog Box

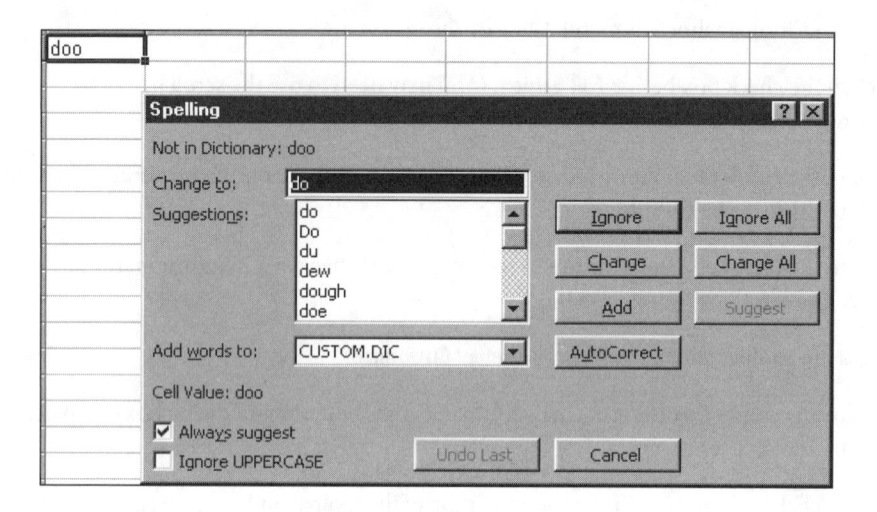

In Figure 6.55 the misspelled word is "doo," shown at the top of the dialog box. Excel recommends a replacement in the highlighted Change to box. If this suggestion is correct, click on the Change button. Other suggestions are listed below in the Suggestions list box. When the scroll bar is shaded, additional suggestions can be accessed by scrolling. If you want to choose one of these suggestions, select the correct word and then select Change; the correctly spelled word is inserted into the worksheet. Keying the correct word in the Change to box and clicking on Change also changes the spelling. The Change All button is used to change the spelling in all occurrences of the word.

Excel may display "No Suggestions" in the Suggestions list box. If that is the case, simply key the correct spelling in the Change to box. If the word displayed is spelled correctly, click Ignore.

Using AutoCorrect

The *AutoCorrect* feature corrects errors as they are entered into a worksheet. For instance, if you enter "teh" instead of "the," AutoCorrect will automatically correct the error and enter "the" into the cell. The AutoCorrect dialog box (Figure 6.56) is accessed in the Tools menu. While you can set Excel to ignore the AutoCorrect feature, it is usually preferable to use AutoCorrect to help prepare an error-free worksheet.

Figure 6.56   AutoCorrect Dialog Box

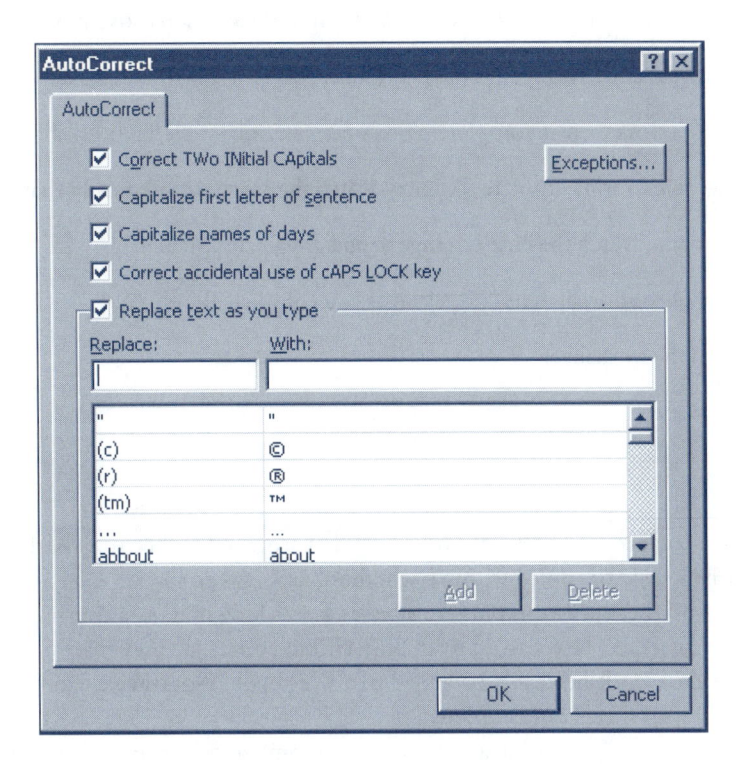

AutoCorrect is now available in the entire suite of Office products. Because most classrooms share computers, AutoCorrect will not be customized in this text.

Exercise 6.15   Using Spelling Checker

Several spelling errors have been placed in a worksheet to provide practice using Excel's spelling checker.

1 Open the workbook **Exer 6** and then select the **Spell (15)** worksheet.

2 Key your name in cell A3.

3 Click in cell A1. From **Tools** select **Spelling** or click on the Spelling button. The **Spelling** dialog box opens.

4 The spelling checker indicates that the footer, **Exer 6**, is misspelled. Click **Ignore**.

5 The next word displays in the spelling checker. The suggested word, **January**, is correctly spelled in the **Change to** text box. Click on **Change**.

6. The next misspelled word appears. The suggestion is correct, so click **Change**.
7. **Marh** is the next word to be checked. Click **March** in the **Suggestions** box, and then click on **Change**.
8. Continue until the entire worksheet has been checked. (Cell A2 is **Time**; cell B2 is **Month**.)
9. When the entire worksheet is complete, a box opens stating that it has been checked. Click **OK**.
10. In cell A5, key **teh**. As you complete the entry, watch the entry automatically change to **the**.
11. In cell A6, key **adn**. Watch the entry change to **and** as you complete it.
12. In cell A7, key **ahve** and watch its correction as you complete the entry.
13. Save and print the worksheet.
14. Close the worksheet.

Summary

- A workbook contains several worksheets that are saved in the same file. Individual worksheets may be moved or copied within a workbook or between workbooks.
- Each worksheet in a workbook is accessed by clicking in its tab.
- A worksheet can be renamed by double-clicking on its tab and entering its new name.
- Additional worksheets can be added to a workbook. Worksheets can be rearranged and unneeded worksheets can be deleted.
- Shortcut menus put the most frequently used commands in a single menu that is accessible from any location on a worksheet screen.
- Access shortcut menus by clicking on the right mouse button.
- Use the right mouse button to access the Drag-and-Drop shortcut menu.
- AutoFill is used to copy data. Click on a cell's fill handle and drag through the desired range. Information in the first cell is copied to all of the selected cells.
- AutoFill is used to enter a series after information is entered into only one or two cells.
- AutoFill automatically recognizes days of the week, months of the year, and number patterns. When one item is entered, the series is completed automatically.
- The fill handle is used to select a range for AutoFill.
- A series command can be selected from the Edit menu. First select Fill, then select Down, Up, Right, or Left.
- Cell contents that are entered in one worksheet may be copied to other worksheets by selecting the Fill Across Worksheets command.
- A custom list can be saved for the needs of an individual business. It is created using the AutoFill feature.

- AutoFormat is used to apply a built-in format to a worksheet.
- The Options button accesses the Formats to apply section of the AutoFormat dialog box and is used to apply only parts of the AutoFormat choices. Format choices include alignment, borders, font, number styles, patterns and shading, and column width and row height.
- The Merge and Center button allows a title or heading to be centered across two or more adjacent columns.
- The Merge and Center button is on the Formatting toolbar.
- The Standard toolbar contains buttons commonly used when working with Excel.
- The Formatting toolbar contains frequently used formatting buttons.
- Specialized toolbars can be used with Excel. They are accessed from the shortcut menu, which is accessed by clicking the right mouse button on any toolbar.
- A floating toolbar is located in the worksheet screen. It can be sized or moved.
- Toolbar docks are located along the four edges of the worksheet screen where a toolbar can be placed. A toolbar must be undocked before it can be moved.
- AutoComplete is used to automatically complete a cell entry to match a previous entry in the column.
- Excel provides a listing of cell contents previously used in a column. The Pick From List command quickly accesses that list for use in a worksheet.
- AutoCorrect corrects misspelled words that are listed in the AutoCorrect dialog box.
- The spelling checker uses a standard Microsoft dictionary to check spelling in a worksheet.
- Misspelled words can be changed individually or as an entire group.
- The spelling checker also checks words in headers and footers.

Important Terminology

active sheet	fill handle	shortcut menu
AutoComplete	Fill Justify command	spelling checker
AutoCorrect	fill range	Standard toolbar
AutoFill	floating toolbar	tab scrolling buttons
AutoFormat	Formatting toolbar	toolbar dock
custom list	Merge and Center button	ungroup worksheets
delete a worksheet	Pick From List	workbook
Fill Across Worksheets	sheet tab	worksheet group
fill commands		

Buttons to Know

Study Questions

True-False

Place a T in the space if the statement is true; place an F if the statement is false.

_____ 1. A workbook contains only one worksheet.
_____ 2. The tabs at the bottom of a workbook read Sheet1, Sheet2, etc. and cannot be changed.
_____ 3. A worksheet can be moved only within its workbook.
_____ 4. More than one worksheet may be selected at a time.
_____ 5. You may print only one copy of a worksheet at a time.
_____ 6. A shortcut menu is used to eliminate steps in the cut-and-paste process.
_____ 7. Shortcut menus can be accessed only in the menu bar.
_____ 8. Use the Fill Across Worksheets command to copy a sheet name to the tabs of the other sheets in a workbook.
_____ 9. The fill handle of an active cell is located in the upper-left corner.
_____ 10. When using AutoFill, the fill range is the range of cells that will be used in the AutoFill process.
_____ 11. AutoFill can be used to copy a cell entry.
_____ 12. When using AutoFill to fill in the days of the week, the last day selected displays in the Name box of the formula bar.
_____ 13. AutoFill works only for built-in lists. A business cannot create a specialized list.
_____ 14. AutoFormat will apply a format to a selected part of a worksheet when the AutoFormat command is selected from the Format menu.
_____ 15. The Center Align button is used to center the title of a worksheet over several columns.
_____ 16. To create a custom list, use the Custom Lists tab, found in the Options dialog box.
_____ 17. The fastest way to make entries to several worksheets of a workbook is to enter data in one worksheet and then copy it to the others.
_____ 18. When text is centered over columns, the cells it occupies are merged into one cell.
_____ 19. The commands available in a shortcut menu change depending on how a worksheet is being used.
_____ 20. When a toolbar is placed at the edge of the screen, it is in a toolbar home.
_____ 21. Toolbars cannot be moved or sized.
_____ 22. The feature that makes sure all words are correctly spelled is the Spell-It-Right feature.
_____ 23. Excel may complete cell entries after only one letter of the entry is keyed.
_____ 24. The feature that repeats a cell entry is Choose The Entry.

Fill-In

Place the word in the space that correctly completes the statement.

1. To move a worksheet to a different workbook, open the _____ or _____ dialog box.
2. Access a shortcut menu by _____ .
3. The command that automatically places days of the week or months of the year in a worksheet is called _____ .

4. The feature that formats a worksheet is called _____ .
5. To copy cell contents in one worksheet to other worksheets, use the Fill _____ feature.
6. Change the name of a worksheet tab by clicking _____ (one, two, or three) times on the tab.
7. To quickly access a menu, click on the right mouse button to open a(n) _____ .
8. A toolbar that can be moved is a(n) _____ toolbar.
9. To place a title of a worksheet over several columns, use the _____ and _____ feature.
10. The _____ toolbar contains formatting buttons such as Italic or Merge and Center.
11. The feature that allows an entry to automatically be entered into a cell is _____ .
12. The feature that allows a choice of previous entries to be entered in a cell is _____ From List.
13. When a word like "teh" is entered in Excel, it is corrected through a feature called _____ .
14. This button is the _____ and _____ button and is used to center titles.

Assignments

Note that you will delete the Ch05 and Ch06 directory when you have completed all of the work in Chapter 6.

Assignment 6.1

Cross Country Sales Firm, a regional company, prepares sales reports on a quarterly basis. It uses a multiple-sheet workbook for this information. The sales data for each salesperson is placed on a separate sheet.

You will complete the sales reports for a quarter. The actual sales amounts have been entered in the workbook, but you will need to complete and format the documents.

1. Open the workbook **Ch6 As1** and save it as **Assig 6-1**.
2. Rename the sheets as follows:

Sheet Name	Renamed to
Sheet1	B. Johnson
Sheet2	L. Huong
Sheet3	D. Thomas
Sheet4	F. Kenady

3. Select the four sheets and enter the following information at one time.
   - Key the following two-line heading in cells A1 and A2:

     Cross Country Sales Firm
     Quarterly Report
   - In A6, key **Goal**.
   - In B7, key **April**; use AutoFill to extend the months through **June** on row 7.
   - In cell E7, key **Total**.

- In cells A8:A11, key the following row titles:

    Desks
    Side Tables
    Chairs
    File Cabinets

- In cell A12, key **Total**.
- In cell A13, key **Goal Met?**.

4. Ungroup the worksheets. In cell A3 of each sheet, key the name of the salesperson. Place the sales territory in cell A4 and the amount of the goal in cell B6. The following chart provides the individual information:

Sales Person	Territory	Goal
Bruce Johnson	North	15,000
Luong Huong	South	18,000
Dennis Thomas	East	20,000
Flora Kenady	West	21,500

5. Complete the formulas in the worksheets.
    - Group all of the worksheets.
    - In each worksheet, complete the formula to enter the totals in row 12 and column E.
    - Ungroup the sheets. Click in the tab for **B. Johnson**.
    - In cell B13, enter an IF function to determine whether the sales goal was met. If it was met, key **Yes**; if it was not met, key **No**. Use an absolute reference for the goal so the function may be accurately copied.
    - Copy the formula to the range C13:E13.
    - Group all sheets with **B. Johnson** on top.
    - Select the range B13:E13. Then from **Edit**, select **Fill**, then **Across Worksheets**.

6. Format the worksheets. It may be quicker to group the worksheets to format all of them at the same time.
    - Format the four-line heading for bold and merge and center it. Increase the font size of the title to **16** points. Merge and center the rows individually.
    - Indent the row labels.
    - Format the column labels for bold and right alignment.
    - Format the total row for bold. Place the word **Total** in italics.
    - Bold the row that indicates whether or not the goal was met. Center the results (**Yes** or **No**).
    - Format for Comma style with zero decimals.
    - Place underlines correctly around the total row.
    - In Page Setup place the sheet name in the header and the file name in the footer. Set a top margin of 2.5" and a left margin of 1.5".
    - Place your name in cell A18.
    - Insert a blank row after the totals and before the **Goal Met** row.
    - Adjust the column widths if needed.

7. Print the worksheet and check to see how it looks. Are all amounts entered and formatted correctly? Are underlines used correctly? Does it have a professional appearance? Are all words correctly spelled? If needed, make changes and print a corrected copy.

8. Save and print the entire workbook.

9. Print one worksheet showing the formulas.

   Checkpoint:
B. Johnson grand total	57,629
L. Huong	Goal met in May

Assignment 6.2

Plains Paper Company asks you to prepare a worksheet listing current sales. From these sales you are asked to make quarterly sales projections for the next year. You will complete and format the worksheet.

1. Open a new workbook and enter the following information:

	A	B	C	D	E	F
1	Plains Paper Company					
2	Sales Projections					
3	For Year of 1998					
4						
5						
6			1997	1998		
7			4th Q Sales	1st Quarter		
8	No. Dakota	108562				
9	So. Dakota	148569				
10	Nebraska	205784				
11	Kansas	199847				
12	Colorado	532587				
13	Wyoming	175486				
14	Total					
15						
16						
17						
18	Rate of Increase		3%	3.50%	4%	5%

2. Complete the worksheet.
   - Use AutoFill to extend the labels in row 7 through the **4th Quarter**.
   - Copy the row labels in row 7 to row 17.
   - Save the worksheet as **Assig 6-2** in the **Ch06** folder.
3. Enter the sales projections for the first quarter of 1998. The sales projection for the first quarter is 3% greater than the sales of the fourth quarter of 1997.
   - In cell C8 enter a formula that determines the amount of projected increase in sales for 1998 and adds it to the fourth quarter sales of 1997. This formula will be copied down and across the columns. Some cell references are mixed. (Remember to use **F4** to change cell references to mixed references.)
   - Copy the formula in cell C8 to the ranges C9:C13 and D8:F13. Click in some cells to be sure the formula copied the way you planned.
   - Complete the totals in row 14 and place appropriate underlines (borders).
4. Format the worksheet.
   - Format the range A1:F3 for bold and merge and center. Increase the font to **12** points.
   - Format rows 6 and 7 for bold and center alignment. Place a bold underline below both rows.
   - Center and merge C6 over the range C6:F6.

- Format the word **Total** in column A for bold and center alignment.
- Format correctly for currency.
- Copy the format in cell C7 to the range C17:F17.
- Adjust the column widths if necessary.
- Adjust the margins so labels are easy to read and the worksheet is centered on the page. Also be sure the worksheet name is in the header and the file name is in the footer.
- Check spelling.

5. Rename **Sheet1** to **Sales Proj**.
6. Enter your name in cell A21.
7. Save and print the worksheet.
8. Check the worksheet to see how it looks. Are all amounts entered and formatted correctly? Are underlines used correctly? Does it have a professional appearance? Are all words correctly spelled? If needed, make changes and print a corrected copy.
9. Print a second copy that shows the formulas used. Adjust margins and column widths to keep it on one page.

Checkpoint:
    Cell C8 $111,818.86
    Cell D11 $213,046.89
    Cell E14 $1,519,833.80

Assignment 6.3

Vicky's Victorian Shoppe is a gift shop. They always prepare a report showing the units sold for each quarter of the year. You are to complete this worksheet. Please show the percentage of total sales per group of items for each of the three months. Use the following information to complete the worksheet.

1. Key the following information in the worksheet. Use the following shortcuts:
   - Key **January** in cell B5. Use AutoFill to extend the series.
   - Key **Group 1** and **Group 2** in cells A6 and A7. Use AutoFill to extend the series.
2. Format the worksheet as shown. The title is in **12** point.

	A	B	C	D	E	F
1	Vicky's Victorian Shoppe					
2	Units Sold					
3						
4						
5		January	February	March	Total	Average
6	Group 1	183	377	395		
7	Group 2	385	286	787		
8	Group 3	218	354	192		
9	Group 4	281	179	305		
10	Group 5	309	284	267		
11	Group 6	168	259	178		
12	Total					
13	Average					

3. Save the workbook as **Assig 6-3** in the **Ch06** folder.
4. Complete the worksheet.
   - In one step, complete the totals in column E and row 12. Remember, highlight B6:E12 and click AutoSum. Format the range for Comma style with zero decimals.
   - Use a function to complete the averages in column F and row 13. Format the averages for two decimals.
5. Format the worksheet.
   - Add underlines and other format choices, if you wish.
   - Indent the label **Total** and right align the label **Average**.
   - In Page Setup, set a top margin of 2.5" and a left margin of 2".
   - Place the sheet name in the header and the file name in the footer.
6. Change the sheet name to **Units Sold**.
7. Place your name in cell A16.
8. Save and print the worksheet.
9. Check the worksheet to see how it looks. Are all amounts entered and formatted correctly? Are underlines used correctly? Does it have a professional appearance? Are all words correctly spelled? If needed, make changes and print a corrected copy.
10. Print a second copy that shows the formulas. Adjust margins and column widths so it fits on one page.
11. Prepare a worksheet that shows the same information for the next quarter.
    - Name the second sheet of the workbook **2 Quarter**.
    - Use the Fill Across Worksheets command to place the title, column labels, row labels, and formulas in the second sheet.
    - Print a copy of this sheet.

   Checkpoint:
Total Group 1	955
Total January	1,544
Average Group 1	318.33
Average January	257.33

Assignment 6.4

Wilhite Sports Equipment has branches in several large cities. Its sales are reported monthly. It is now preparing sales projections for each of the branches and has asked you to complete the worksheet information for them. You will create and use custom lists that will be used in future documents.

1. Create the two custom lists shown below:

Chicago	Baseball
Dallas	Basketball
Denver	Football
Los Angeles	Golf
New Orleans	Soccer
Omaha	Tennis
Portland	Track
San Antonio	Wrestling
San Francisco	
Seattle	
St. Louis	

2. Create a new worksheet.
   - In the three-line heading, include the name of the company, **Annual Sales Report**, and the date. For the date, key **December 31** and the current year.
   - Enter the custom list of cities in column A.
   - Enter the custom list of equipment in row 5.
   - Save the worksbook as **Assig 6-4**.
   - Open the workbook **Ch6 As4**. Copy the sales amounts from this worksheet into your new worksheet. (This saves you time from entering this large amount of data.)
3. Complete the worksheet.
   - Complete the totals in row 17 and column J.
   - In row 20, enter the custom list for the equipment beginning with column B.
   - In cell A21, key **Projection %**. Enter the following percents for the individual products:

Baseball	Basketball	Football	Golf	Soccer	Tennis	Track	Wrestling
1.50%	1.15%	0.75%	2%	1.50%	2%	2.50%	1.25%

   - In cell A22, key **Projections**. In cell B22 enter the formula to increase the total sales by the projected percent.
4. Format the worksheet using AutoFormat. Be sure currency is correctly formatted. Merge and center the three-line title across the worksheet.
5. Rename this worksheet **1998**.
6. Place the file name in the header and the sheet name in the footer.
7. Place your name in cell A25.
8. Print the worksheet and check to see how it looks. Are all amounts entered and formatted correctly? Are underlines used correctly? Does it have a professional appearance? Are all words correctly spelled? If needed, make changes and print a corrected copy.
9. Save the worksheet.
10. Print a second copy showing the formulas used.
11. Delete the custom lists in the **Options** menu.

   Checkpoint:
Total Chicago	116,228
Total Golf	72,469
Projections Soccer	117,468

Assignment 6.5

Sharon's Secretarial Service is preparing a depreciation schedule. Some data has been entered, but you need to complete and format the worksheet.
1. Open the workbook **Ch6 As5** and save it as **Assig 6-5**.
2. Complete the worksheet.
   - The formula for the annual depreciation is cost less trade-in divided by years of service.
   - The formula for the per month amount is annual depreciation divided by 12.
   - Only the annual depreciation and the per month columns need totals in row 12.
   - Place the sheet name in the header and the file name in the footer.

3. Replace **Student's Name** with your name.
4. Use AutoFormat to format this worksheet. Select any format style. Do not AutoFormat the Width/Height of the cells and the Number. Be sure currency is correctly formatted. In Print Preview, place the worksheet in the center of the page.
5. Save and print a copy.
6. Check the worksheet to see how it looks. Are all amounts entered and formatted correctly? Are underlines used correctly? Does it have a professional appearance? Are all items correctly spelled? If needed, make changes and print a corrected copy.
7. Print a copy showing the formulas used.
8. Close the worksheet.

   Checkpoint:
Copier per Month	$300.00
Desk Annual	75.00
Chair per Month	1.04

Assignment 6.6

Wilson's Grocers summarizes the sales made at each cash register on a daily basis. The report includes sales, returns, and the amount of sales tax.

Some data has been entered into a worksheet. You are to complete the worksheet, enter formulas, and format the worksheet.

1. Open the **Ch6 As6** workbook and save it as **Assig 6-6**.
2. Complete the worksheet.
   - In cell A12, key **Total**.
   - Sales tax is determined by sales less returns times the tax rate.
   - Total receipts are determined by sales less returns plus sales tax.
   - Percentage of the total is determined by total receipts for each register divided by total of all receipts.
   - Enter a total in row 12.
3. Determine and enter an appropriate sheet name.
4. Replace **Student's Name** with your name.
5. Format the worksheet. You may use AutoFormat or format it yourself using the formatting techniques you have learned. Adjust the margins and column widths for attractive placement. Place the sheet name in the header and the file name in the footer.
6. Save and print a copy of the worksheet.
7. Check the worksheet to see how it looks. Are all amounts entered and formatted correctly? Are underlines used correctly? Does it have a professional appearance? Are all words correctly spelled? If needed, make changes and print a corrected copy.
8. Print a copy showing the formulas. Try to keep it on one page.
9. **Sheet2** shows the amounts for February 11.
   - Use the Fill Across Worksheets command to enter the title, labels, and formulas from Feb 10 in **Sheet2**.
   - Rename **Sheet2** to **Feb 11**.

10. Close the worksheet.

Checkpoint:
Feb 10

CR1 Tax	$33.11
CR1 Total Receipts	768.93
CR1 % Total	18.5%
Total Sales	$4,141.89

Feb 11

Total Sales	$4,491.78

Case Problem 6

L & N Furniture Company has three branches in the city: Broadway, Central, and Main. Each branch records its sales figures on a quarterly basis; the home office also keeps those records.

You have been asked to prepare a sales report for each branch and to prepare a statistical analysis of sales for the three stores. Because these are similar worksheets, you decide to use a multiple-worksheet document. Use the current year for the worksheet.

First, plan the worksheet. Each branch manager arranges his or her sales report using different formats. Be sure to plan your worksheets so all branches have the same format.

Complete and format the worksheet for each branch. The data section of each branch's reports is given below. Use this information in preparing your reports. Be sure to print a worksheet showing the formulas. You may want to create a custom list for this worksheet.

Broadway	Quarter 1	Quarter 2	Quarter 3	Quarter 4
Living Room	35847	56897	70458	43025
Bedroom	21457	28475	30214	27415
Dining Room	46850	32541	55456	40547
Accessories	10658	9987	13574	7541

Central	Bedroom	Living Room	Dining Room	Accessories
Quarter 1	30547	48756	35897	8547
Quarter 2	37415	50147	48740	10557
Quarter 3	29874	48751	39854	9586
Quarter 4	38540	55687	40057	11547

Main	Quarter 1	Quarter 2	Quarter 3	Quarter 4
Accessories	8569	10057	9987	8007
Bedroom	35254	31427	40154	36874
Living Room	48756	50078	60478	50147
Dining Room	50470	41058	47884	34478

On a separate worksheet, summarize the data and provide the following statistical information:
- the amount of the largest total branch sales for each quarter
- the average of the quarterly sales and the average for the year

Format the worksheet in an appropriate style. Print the worksheet and check it to see how it looks. Are all amounts entered and formatted correctly? Are underlines used correctly? Does it have a professional appearance? Are all words correctly spelled? If needed, make changes and print a corrected copy.

Chapter 7

Additional Formatting Techniques

Objectives

1. Adjust the column widths and row heights of a worksheet.
2. Insert and delete cells, rows, and columns.
3. Hide rows and columns.
4. Format a worksheet using the Format Cells dialog box.
5. Use graphics, WordArt, color, and other enhancements.

Introduction

First impressions are lasting. Because the information presented in a worksheet contains important business data, a professional appearance is vital. Excel provides many ways to enhance the appearance of a worksheet. This is called formatting a worksheet.

In Excel, the width and height of rows and columns may be adjusted to accommodate the cell contents. Lengthy labels can be adjusted to fit on two or more lines. Numbers may be displayed in various styles. The font style, the font size, and the way text is displayed can be altered. The use of shading and borders enhances the appearance of a worksheet. WordArt and graphics add style to a worksheet.

This chapter provides tools you can use to make changes in a worksheet and to format a worksheet so it presents a professional appearance.

Changing the Size of Cells

Formatting Column Widths

When entering data in a cell, the preset column width will often be too wide or too narrow for the data. When an entry is longer than the width of the column, scientific notation (for example, 2.09E+09) or ####### displays in the cell. All of the numbers entered in the cell are stored in memory but do not show. Increasing the column width displays all of the data entered in a cell. In the same way, columns can be made narrower. Some methods have already been used to change column widths, but several others are available.

To change *column width*, select a column or any cell within the column. Then select the Column command from the Format menu. A submenu opens, shown in Figure 7.1.

To set a standard width for a column, select Width. The Column Width dialog box opens, as shown in Figure 7.2.

The default width of a column is 8.43 points. Selecting **Standard Width** in the Column submenu adjusts a column width to this default (8.43 points). Entering a different width in the text box changes the column width for the selected column or columns.

Choosing *AutoFit Selection* in the Column submenu provides a column width adjusted to fit the longest entry in a column. This selection allows some columns to be wider than others. This is the fastest way to ensure column widths are appropriate for all data in a worksheet.

Column widths can also be changed using shortcut menus. Highlight a column, then access the shortcut menu. The choices Column Width, Hide, and Unhide appear, as shown in Figure 7.3.

Column widths can also be changed using "click and drag." When the mouse is between column letters, it takes the shape of a double-headed arrow. Hold down the left mouse button and drag the mouse to the left or the right. As the mouse moves, the width of the column to its left changes. A dotted line, called the *move line*, shows the new width of the column. The exact width is displayed in a ScreenTip above the column. Release the mouse button to adjust the column to the width indicated by the move line. Moving the mouse to the right increases the width of the column; moving to the left decreases the width (Figure 7.4).

Column widths can also be adjusted in Print Preview. Click on the Margins button to show the margins and column handles. Clicking and dragging on the handles ( ) at the top of the screen adjusts the widths of margins and columns. Figure 7.5 shows column and margin handles used to adjust a worksheet.

Figure 7.1   Format Column Submenu

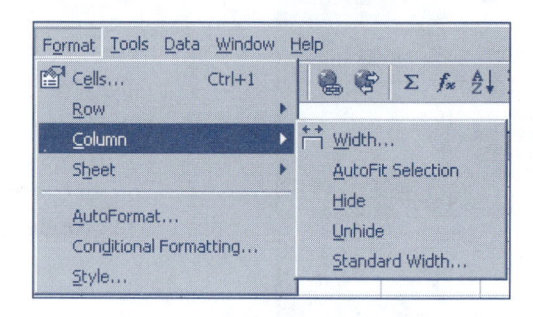

Figure 7.2   Column Width Dialog Box

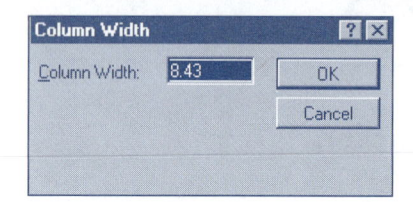

Figure 7.3   Shortcut Menu for Changing Column Width

When working with a small worksheet, adjusting column widths on the worksheet screen is fast and convenient. However, in a very large worksheet, AutoFit Selection or Print Preview may be the most efficient method of changing column widths.

Changing Row Heights

There are several methods to change *row height*. When Row is selected in the Format menu, a submenu opens, as shown in Figure 7.6.

Select Height to access the Row Height dialog box (Figure 7.7). Excel defaults to a height of 12.75 points. The height of a row may be changed by keying in a new number.

Use AutoFit to adjust the height to accommodate the largest entry in a row.

Another way to change row heights is to use the mouse; when it is between row numbers, it takes the shape of a double-headed arrow. Click the mouse button and drag up or down to adjust the row above to a new height. While you are dragging the mouse, the row height changes; a dotted line moves with the mouse to indicate the new row height. The height is displayed in a ScreenTip. When the mouse is released, the row adjusts to its new height.

A quick way to adjust the height to accommodate the largest font of a row is to double-click on the mouse while it is on the line below the row to be adjusted; this automatically accommodates the tallest entry in the row.

Like column widths, row heights can also be changed by using shortcut menus or Print Preview.

Figure 7.4   Changing Column Width

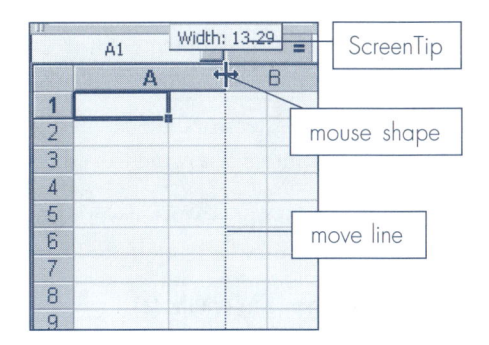

Figure 7.5   Column and Margin Handles in Print Preview

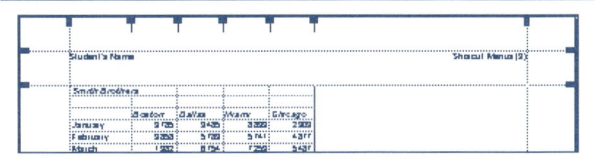

Figure 7.6   Format Row Submenu

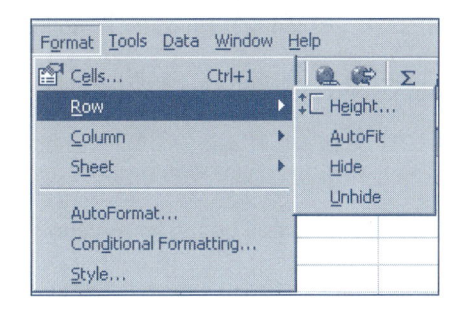

Figure 7.7   Row Height Dialog Box

Exercise 7.1 Adjusting Cell Widths and Heights

You will prepare cell contents that are too long, then adjust the column widths to accommodate the data using several methods. You will also adjust the height of rows.

1 Open the **Ch7 Exer** workbook. (This file opens to a blank screen but other tabs of the workbook contain saved worksheets.) Save the worksheet as **Exer 7**.

2 This workbook opens with ten worksheets prepared. Select all of the worksheets that contain data (through **Sheet11**). Place the file name in the footer and the sheet name in the header. Then ungroup the worksheets.

3 Rename **Sheet1** to **Widths (1)**.

4 In cell A1, key **123456**; in cell A2, key **678901**. In cell A3, key the formula **=A1*A2**. The result is too large for the cell, so it displays in scientific notation. (This will be changed later.)

5 Highlight columns A:D. Format for currency. Cells A1:A3 display ####### because their contents are too large for the column width.

6 In cell B1, key **987654321** and complete the entry. The entry is too long. A string of number symbols (####) displays in the cell.

7 In cell B2, key **87654320**. The entry is too long.

8 In cell B3, enter a formula to add B1 and B2. Again, the entry is too long.

9 In one step, copy the range A1:B3 to the following ranges: C1:D3, E1:F3, A5:B7, C5:D7, and E5:F7. (You will have a worksheet filled with number signs.)

10 In cell A9, key **Prepared by** and your name.

11 Move the mouse cursor to the line between columns A and B. The double-headed arrow appears. Click and drag to the right until all the numbers in column A show. You may need to experiment to find the correct width. Your name will still be too long to fit into the cell.

12 Highlight column B. From **Format**, select **Column**, and then click on **AutoFit Selection**. Column B is now wide enough to accommodate its largest entry.

13 Highlight columns C, D, and E. Use the shortcut menu to select **Column Width**. Change the width to **5**. Click **OK**. The selected column width is too narrow.

14 Double-click on the column line between columns E and F. The selected columns have adjusted to fit the longest entry in each column. Deselect the range.

15 Use any method to adjust column F so that all of the numbers show.

16 Move the cursor to the line between rows 4 and 5. Click and drag upward until **4.5** is in the ScreenTip (or until the row is close to the desired height). Row 4 is now narrower.

17 Move the cursor to the line between rows 8 and 9. Access the shortcut menu. Select **Row Height**. Key **4.5**, then click **OK**. Row 8 is now narrower.

18 Save and print the worksheet. The worksheet may print on two pages.

Hiding and Unhiding Columns and Rows

Hiding Columns

Worksheets provide a large amount of important information and are often used to generate reports. These reports serve different purposes and may be prepared for different people. Some of these reports may need only a portion of the information from the original worksheet.

Instead of preparing an entirely new worksheet, you can hide columns and rows. A report can then be printed from the portion that is displayed. Hiding columns and rows retains their contents in memory, but they are not displayed and will not print.

There are several methods to *hide columns*. The quickest method is to position the mouse pointer on the line to the right of the column heading that will be hidden; the pointer takes the shape of the double-headed arrow . Click the left mouse button and drag the column to the left until the move line covers the column or columns to be hidden. The column headings remain the same; the hidden ones do not show on the screen.

For example, a sales report is completed that shows the amount of sales for each salesperson on a monthly basis and includes a quarterly total (Figure 7.8).

Now a report is needed that shows only the total sales; the individual monthly amounts are not needed (Figure 7.9). Hiding columns B:D provides this report, showing only the salespeople and the total sales, columns A and E. The hidden columns reside in memory; they do not appear on the screen and will not print.

Another way to hide columns is to select the columns you want to hide, then select Column and then Hide from the Format menu. The Hide command is also available in the shortcut menu when the mouse is right-clicked in the column headings.

Figure 7.8   Sales Report

	A	B	C	D	E
1					
2	Sales Person	Jan	Feb	Mar	Total
3					
4	Anderson	875	958	728	2,561
5	Mason	283	584	983	1,850
6	Smith	598	872	789	2,259

Figure 7.9   Hidden Columns

	A	E
1		
2	Sales Person	Total
3		
4	Anderson	2,561
5	Mason	1,850
6	Smith	2,259

Unhiding Columns

Again, there are several methods to **unhide columns**. Position the mouse in the column heading just to the right of the hidden cells. The mouse takes the shape of a double-headed arrow with a double line, as shown in Figure 7.10. It takes careful control of the mouse to obtain this shape; keep the mouse movements short. When the double-headed arrow shape is obtained, click and drag the move line to the right to reveal the hidden columns.

Selecting Format, then Column, and then Unhide also reveals hidden columns. For instance, if column B is hidden, select a range of cells (or column headings) through columns A:C and choose Unhide. Column B reappears.

Sometimes unhiding a column can be tricky. You may need to try several methods to unhide it.

Figure 7.10   Revealing Hidden Columns

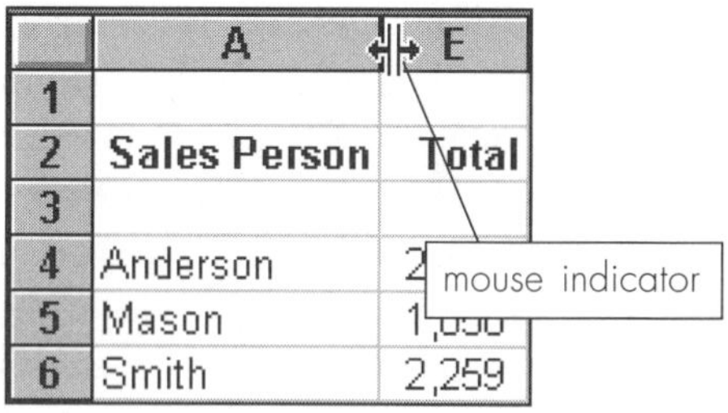

Power Users

The shortcut to Hide Columns is **Ctrl**+**0**. The shortcut to Unhide Columns is **Shift**+**Ctrl**+**)** (right parenthesis).

Exercise 7.2   Hiding and Unhiding Columns

West Coast Sales completes quarterly reports showing its entire sales information. The data has been entered into a worksheet and formatted. However, the worksheet needs to be completed. In addition, sales reports are needed; you will print these reports from the worksheet. You will hide columns that contain information not needed for the reports before you print them.

1 Open **Sheet2** of the **Exer 7** workbook and rename it **Hide and Unhide (2)**.

2 Place totals in row 13 and column E. Adjust the column widths so the contents of the columns show.

3 Move the mouse to the line between columns B and C until the mouse takes the shape of the double-headed arrow. Hold down the left mouse button and drag to the left until the move line is over the line at the right edge of column A.

4 Release the mouse. The worksheet now shows columns A, C, D, and E.

5 Move the mouse to the line between columns D and E until the mouse takes the shape of the double-headed arrow. Hold down the left mouse button and drag to the left until the move line is over the right edge of column A. Release the mouse button. The worksheet now shows columns A and E.

6 Key your name in cell A17.

7 Save and print the worksheet. At the top write "Print 1."

8   Move the mouse to the right of the line between columns A and E; it takes the shape of the double-headed arrow with a double line. This takes a steady hand. Move the mouse to the right; column D reappears.

9   Move the mouse to the right of the line between columns A and D; it takes the shape of the double-headed arrow with a double line. Double-click on the left mouse button. Column C reappears.

10 Repeat until all columns are visible. Adjust the widths of all columns.

11 Save and print the worksheet. At the top write "Print 2."

12 Highlight the range B4:D4. From the **Format** menu, select **Column**, then **Hide**. Columns are hidden.

13 Highlight the column headings A:E. Access the shortcut menu and select **Unhide** at the bottom of the list of commands. The columns reappear.

14 Close the worksheet without saving changes.

Hiding Rows

Just as it is possible to hide columns, it is also possible to *hide rows*. Again, this is useful when a report is prepared from an existing worksheet, but the report will not include all of the information in the worksheet.

To hide a row, position the mouse on the line below the row to be hidden. The mouse takes the shape of the two-sided arrow. Click and drag upward until the move line is over the rows you want to hide. The row headings remain the same; the headings of the hidden rows do not show on the screen.

To illustrate hiding rows, a company will prepare a sales report that provides information on total sales for all areas but not the individual sales information. Using the worksheet shown in Figure 7.11, the report is generated by hiding the rows containing individual sales information.

After hiding rows 5, 6, 9, and 10, the report will be ready. Place the mouse pointer on the line between rows 6 and 7. When the mouse changes to the two-sided arrow, click and drag upward until the move line is on the bottom line of row 4. Repeat with rows 9 and 10. Figure 7.12 shows the completed worksheet. The rows remain in the worksheet but are not visible and will not print.

Figure 7.11   Sales Report

	A	B	C
1			
2			
3	Sales	Week 1	Week 2
4			
5	Person 1	368	859
6	Person 2	587	812
7	Total North	955	1,671
8			
9	Person 3	586	776
10	Person 4	839	837
11	Total South	1,425	1,613
12			
13	Total Sales	2,850	2,850

Rows may also be hidden by selecting the Format menu, then Row, and then Hide. In addition, the shortcut menu can be used to access the Hide command when a row is selected.

Unhiding Rows

Unhide rows is similar to unhiding columns. Rows can be unhidden by using the Format menu or by clicking and dragging.

To unhide rows by clicking and dragging, position the mouse in the row heading just above the hidden row(s). The mouse takes the shape of the double-headed arrow with a double line. It requires a steady hand to get this arrow shape. Figure 7.13 shows the mouse shape and its position as rows are unhidden.

With the mouse pointer displayed as a double-headed arrow, click and drag downward until the move line is over the line of the row directly below it. Because the row heights may not be the same after the rows are unhidden, it may be necessary to readjust them.

You may also unhide rows from the menu bar by selecting Format, then Row, and then Unhide. The Unhide command is also available on the shortcut menu when rows adjacent to a hidden row are selected.

Figure 7.12   Hidden Rows

	A	B	C
1			
2			
3	Sales	Week 1	Week 2
4			
7	Total North	955	1,671
8			
11	Total South	1,425	1,613
12			
13	Total Sales	2,850	2,850

Figure 7.13   Unhiding Rows

	A	B	C
1			
2			
3	Sales	Week 1	Week 2
4			
	Person 2	587	812
7	Total North	955	1,671
	Person 3	586	776
10	Person 4	839	837
11	Total South	1,425	1,613
12			
13	Total Sales	2,850	2,850

Power Users

The shortcut to hide rows is **Ctrl**+**9**. The shortcut to unhide rows is **Shift**+**Ctrl**+**(** (left parenthesis).

Exercise 7.3   Hiding and Unhiding Rows

United States Sales has prepared a semiannual report using an Excel worksheet. Data has been entered, but the rest of the worksheet needs to be completed. Then reports must be generated that summarize the sales for the six-month period. Because not all information is pertinent to the report, some rows will need to be hidden.

1 Open the workbook **Exer 7**. Rename **Sheet3** to **Hide Rows (3)**.

2 Complete the totals for the four regions, including the grand total. Adjust column widths if needed.

Prepare a report that shows only the totals for the regions.

3   Position the mouse below row 6. Click on the mouse button and drag upward over row 6. Row 6 is now hidden.

4   Position the mouse below row 8. Click on the mouse button and drag upward over row 7. Rows 6, 7, and 8 are now hidden.

5   Highlight rows 12:14. From the **Format** menu, select **Row**, then **Hide**. Rows 12:14 are hidden.

6   Highlight rows 18:20. Access the shortcut menu and select **Hide**.

7   Highlight rows 24:26. Select a method to hide the cells.

8   In cell A32, key your name.

9   Print the worksheet. At the top write "Print 1."

Unhide the rows to return the worksheet to its original format.

10 Move the mouse to below row 5. The mouse takes the double-headed arrow shape with a double line ↕. Remember to use steady, short movement with the mouse. Click and drag down. Row 8 reappears.

11 Move the mouse to below row 5 and double-click. Row 7 appears.

12 Move the mouse to below row 5 and double-click. Row 6 appears.

13 Highlight rows 11:15. From the **Format** menu, select **Row**, then **Unhide**. Rows 12:14 reappear.

14 Highlight rows 17:21. Access the shortcut menu, then select **Unhide**.

15 Unhide rows 23:27 using a method of your choice.

16 Save the worksheet.

Inserting and Deleting Cells in a Worksheet

Inserting Cells, Rows, and Columns

Figure 7.14   Insert Menu

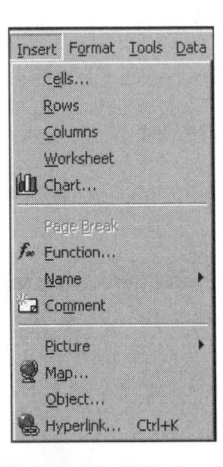

In order to have flexibility in worksheet preparation, additional cells, rows, or columns may be inserted into a worksheet. Maybe another product was added to the inventory and needs to be listed in the worksheet or an additional blank line should be added to further separate items. The Insert menu, shown in Figure 7.14, has separate commands for inserting cells, rows, and columns.

When cells are inserted, Excel shifts the existing cells in the worksheet to make room for the inserted cells; relative references are also adjusted to reflect new locations of cells.

To *insert a row*, highlight a cell in the row below the desired location for the new row. (Clicking on the row heading selects the entire row.) Then select Row from the Insert menu; a new row is inserted above the selected row. To *insert a column*, click on the column heading or a cell within the column to select the column; then select Column from the Insert menu. A new column is inserted to the left of the selected column.

When a row is inserted, existing rows move down one row; when a column is inserted, existing columns move to the right one column. The number of rows or columns selected indicates the number of rows or columns that will be inserted. If two rows are selected, two new rows will be inserted.

To *insert cells*, select Cells from the Insert menu; the Insert dialog box opens, as shown in Figure 7.15. This dialog box provides choices for shifting the existing cells around those to be inserted. The cells may be moved to the right or down to the next row. Click OK when the choice is complete. You can also insert an entire row or column using this dialog box. The shortcut menu can also be used to access the Insert dialog box.

In Figure 7.16, a new cell was inserted at cell A2; the existing cells shifted to the right.

Figure 7.15   Insert Dialog Box

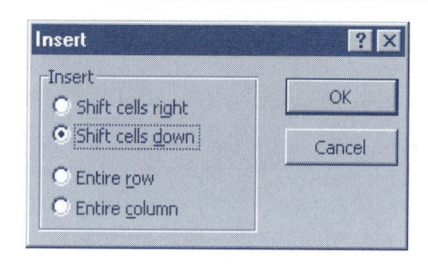

Figure 7.16   Cell Inserted at A2

	A	B	C	D
1	5	15	25	
2		10	20	30
3	15	25	35	
4	20	30	40	
5	25	35	45	

Exercise 7.4   Inserting Rows and Columns

You will complete and edit a worksheet showing the inventory for a small firm. Both a product and a city location have been added, making it necessary to insert cells in the worksheet.

1   Open the **Exer 7** workbook if it is not already open. Select **Sheet4** and rename it **Insert (4)**.

2   Click on a cell in row 2. From the **Insert** menu, select **Rows**. One row is inserted between rows 1 and 2.

3   In cell A2, key **Plant C**. Format for bold and italic, and merge and center the cells.

4   Select rows 3 and 4. From the **Insert** menu, select **Rows**. Two rows were selected, so two rows are inserted.

5   In cell A3, key **June 1998**. Notice that the format of the surrounding rows is automatically applied. Then center the contents across columns.

6 Format the column labels for bold and italics with a bottom border.

7 Select a cell in column D. From the **Insert** menu, select **Columns**. Note that the title lines of the worksheet automatically adjust to center over the inserted column, too. Notice that the underlines have also been copied.

8 In cell D5, key **Doodads**. Before this was entered, the format for the column titles was already in place. When inserting a column, the format of the surrounding cells is automatically applied to the new cells.

9 Enter the numeric values for cells D7:D9. In cell D7, key **63852**; in cell D8, key **83952**; and in cell D9, key **38487**. Be sure there is a formula in the total row.

10 Select rows 8 and 9, then access the shortcut menu. Select **Insert**. Two rows were selected so two additional rows are inserted.

11 In cell A8, key **Dallas**. In cells B8:E8, enter the following numbers: in cell B8, key **30283**; in cell C8, key **51829**; in cell D8, key **58372**; and in cell E8, key **30594**. These cells are not already totaled, so enter a formula to provide a total.

12 In cell A9, key **Minneapolis**. In cells B9:E9, key **40362**, **42291**, **73091**, and **38875**.

13 Format the title in cell A1 for bold and merge and center the cells.

14 Complete the worksheet. Be sure formulas are placed in the cells as required. Place your name in a cell at the bottom of the worksheet. Check the format. Be sure money amounts are correctly formatted. Adjust the column widths if needed. Use Print Preview to adjust the margins so the worksheet is in the center of the page.

15 Save and print the worksheet.

16 Print a copy that shows the formulas.

Deleting Cells, Rows, and Columns

Use the *Delete command* to delete cells, rows, or columns from a worksheet. When cells are deleted, they are removed and the remaining cells shift to fill the space. Think of this as physically cutting and removing cells from a worksheet.

To delete a row or column, click the mouse in the row or column heading. Then select Delete from the Edit menu.

To delete a cell or range of cells, first select the range. Then from the Edit menu, select the Delete command. The Delete dialog box opens, shown in Figure 7.17, requesting information about how to adjust the remaining cells.

Figure 7.17 Delete Dialog Box

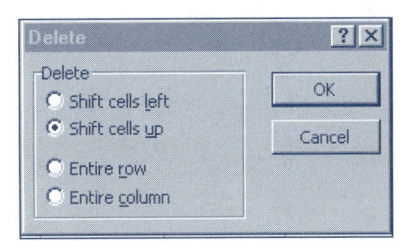

When cells are deleted, all contents in the cells are eliminated. Relative references adjust to new locations. If a remaining cell contains a formula that refers to a deleted cell, an error message of *#REF!* appears in the cell containing the formula, indicating the reference has been deleted.

The Delete command is available on the shortcut menu when cells, columns, or rows are selected.

The Clear Command

The *Clear command* is accessed from the Edit menu. Using the Clear command can eliminate cell contents but leave the surrounding cells in place, or it can leave a formula but eliminate the format or data.

First highlight the cell or range of cells to be cleared. Then select Clear from the Edit menu. A submenu opens with choices for clearing cells, shown in Figure 7.18.

Figure 7.18   Clear Submenu

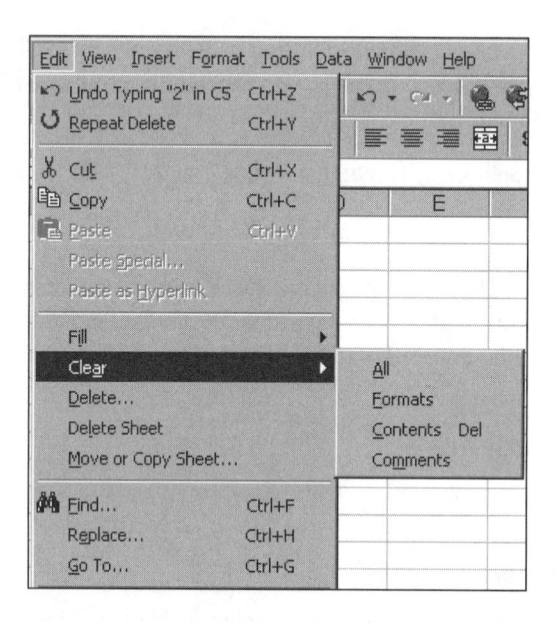

To clear all parts of the cell, select All. You may also clear only formats, contents (formulas and data), or notes. Selecting Contents clears formulas and data but leaves formats. Pressing Delete on the keyboard also clears the contents but leaves the formats.

Exercise 7.5   Deleting Rows and Columns

In this exercise you will practice deleting and clearing rows, columns, and cells. Several error messages will appear.

1   Open the **Exer 7** workbook if it is not already open. Open **Sheet5** and rename it **Delete (5)**.

2. Select the range A5:D5. From the **Edit** menu, select **Clear**, then **Formats**. The contents remain, but they are not formatted.

3. Select cell A1. Access the shortcut menu and select **Clear Contents**.

4. Key your name in cell A1. The format remains. Undo this action.

5. Select B8:D8. From the **Edit** menu, select **Clear**, then **Contents**.

6. In cell B8, key **438.72**. The format remains.

7. In cell C8, key **102.50**.

8. In cell D8, enter the formula to determine the net pay. Clearing contents also clears a formula.

9. Select the range A9:D9. Use the shortcut menu to select **Delete**. The **Delete** dialog box opens. Select **Shift cells up**.

10. Key your name in cell A14, replacing **Student's Name**.

11. Change the margins to 2" at the top and left.

12. Save and print the worksheet.

Delete unusual ranges to see how Excel responds.

13. Select the range B8:B9. From the **Edit** menu, select **Delete**.

14. In the **Delete** dialog box, select **Shift cells left**. Notice the error messages for column C, the column that contains the formula.

15. Click on the Undo button .

16. With the range B8:B9 still selected, access the shortcut menu. Select **Delete**.

17. In the **Delete** dialog box, select **Shift cells up**. Then click **OK**. Again notice the error messages.

18. Click on the Undo button .

19. Close the worksheet without saving changes.

Using the Format Cells Dialog Box

When the Cells command is selected from the Format menu, the *Format Cells dialog box* opens, providing many formatting choices. Along the top of the dialog box are tabs used to access different types of formatting choices. The tab choices are Number, Alignment, Font, Border, Patterns, and Protection. Click on the tabs of the dialog box to move from one group of formatting choices to another. The Format Cells dialog box is shown in Figure 7.19 with the Number tab selected. This section describes the formatting choices available with each tab.

While the Standard toolbar is used to make simple formatting choices such as bold, italic, Currency number style, or underlines, there are additional, more complex formatting choices available in the Format Cells dialog box.

Formatting Numbers

The *Number tab* of the Format Cells dialog box is shown in Figure 7.19.

A Category list is displayed in the dialog box with a sample of the *number format* in the Sample section. Because numbers are so common in spreadsheets and because so many different formats are available, indicating the exact format for each number is a useful Excel feature.

Figure 7.19   Format Cells Dialog Box

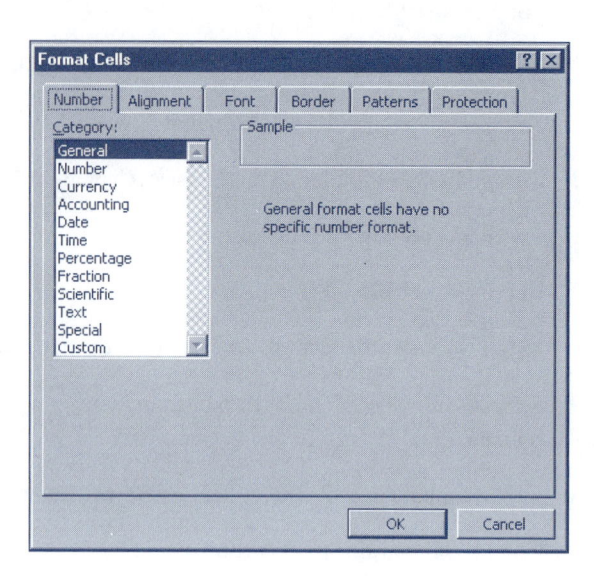

Sometimes when a category is selected, an additional group of choices becomes available, as with the Currency selection, shown in Figure 7.20.

Figure 7.20   Currency Formatting Choices

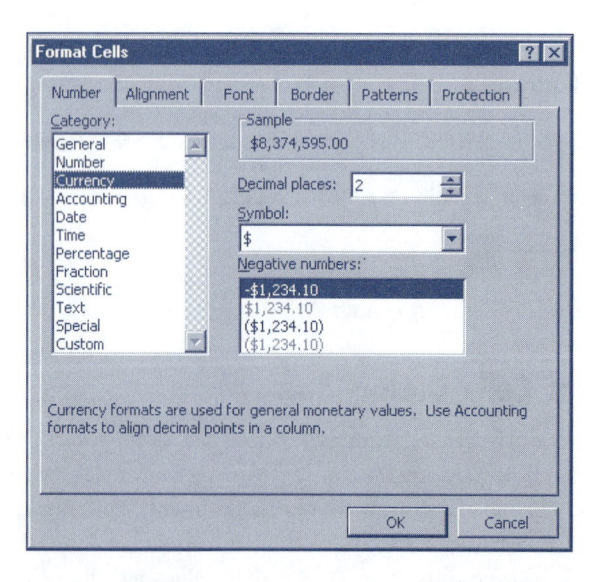

When a *Currency style* is selected, the format choices are displayed. Negative numbers may be displayed in black or red, and with minus signs (–) or parentheses indicating they are negative. A Symbol box is provided to determine whether or not dollar signs ($) should print in these cells. The number of decimals may also be changed.

When a dollar sign is placed in a worksheet using the Format Cells dialog box, it becomes a floating symbol and is immediately placed to the left of the first digit of the number. When the Currency style is accessed from the toolbar and the Currency Style button [$] is used, the dollar sign is placed at the far left of the cell. Figure 7.21 illustrates the difference between these styles.

Figure 7.21   Placing the Dollar Sign

```
Formatted with          $   3.48        Formatted in
Currency button             $3.48       Format Cells menu
```

The Special category is used to format cells for zip code, zip code + 4, telephone numbers, and social security numbers. This is shown in Figure 7.22.

Figure 7.22   Special Number Formatting Choices

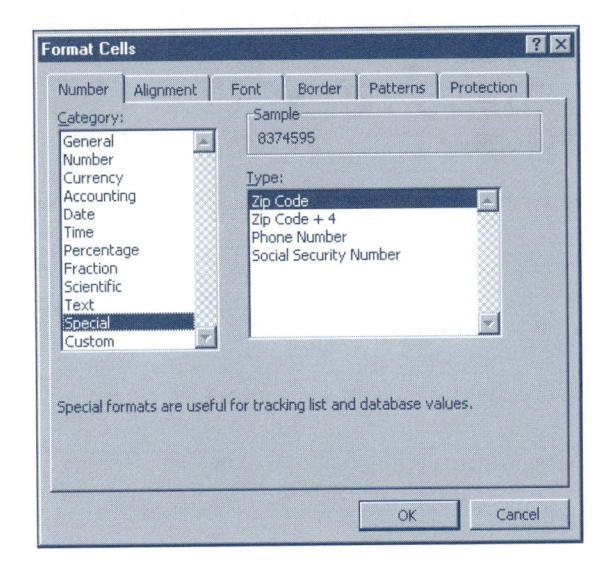

If a percent sign (%) or dollar sign ($) is entered as a number is typed, Excel automatically changes the format of the cell from the General number format to Percent or Currency style. Excel also adjusts the decimal when Currency or Percent style is used. A dollar amount or percentage entered with no decimal displays as a whole number. But if a number has two decimal places, it will be entered into the worksheet with two decimal places.

When formatting a number, only its appearance in the worksheet changes. A number entered with five decimal places (6.38941) still contains five decimal places in memory even when it is formatted to display two decimal places (6.39 when rounded to two decimal places).

Exercise 7.6 Formatting Numbers

You will use the Number tab of the Format Cells dialog box to select and change the format of several numbers.

1 Open **Sheet6** of the **Exer 7** worksheet. Rename the sheet **Format Numbers (6)**.

2 Highlight A1:A2. From **Format**, select **Cells** and then the **Number** tab if it is not open.

3 Select the **Number** category. Select **2** decimal places and to have negative numbers display in red and with parentheses. Use a comma separator for four-digit numbers. Then click **OK**.

4 Select cells A3:A4 and access the shortcut menu. Select **Format Cells**, then select the **Number** tab.

5 Select the **Number** category and format for **3** decimal places with negative numbers displayed with the minus (–) sign.

6 Select cells B1:B2. In the **Number** tab of the **Format Cells** dialog box, select the **Currency** category with **2** decimal places and negative numbers displayed in red.

7 Select cell C1. In the **Number** tab of the **Format Cells** dialog box, select the **Percentage** style. Select to format with two decimal places.

8 Select cell C2. In the **Number** tab of the **Format Cells** dialog box, select the **Percentage** style. Format for percentages with **1** decimal place.

9 Enter the following information in the worksheet, including the dollar ($) and percent (%) signs.

	C
3	$65
4	4.60%
5	$36.40

10 In cell C6, key **$36.4**. Notice that the number is entered as currency and shows two decimal places although you entered only one. Now click on the Currency button in the Formatting toolbar [$]. Notice that the dollar sign aligns at the left border of the cell.

11 Place your name in cell A7.

12 Save and print the worksheet.

Using the Date Function

To enter a date, use the *Paste Function button* [fx] on the toolbar to open the Paste Function dialog box, shown in Figure 7.23.

From the Function category, select Date & Time. Then from the Function name list on the right side of the Paste Function dialog box, select the style wanted. Then click OK.

Today's date can be entered into a cell using the *Date & Time function* of TODAY. This date is entered as a *volatile* date, which means it automatically changes to the current date each time the worksheet is opened. For instance, a date entered today (March 12, 1998) will show on the worksheet as tomorrow (March 13, 1998) if the worksheet is opened tomorrow. A date that does not change is called a *static* date.

Figure 7.23 Paste Function to Enter the Current Date

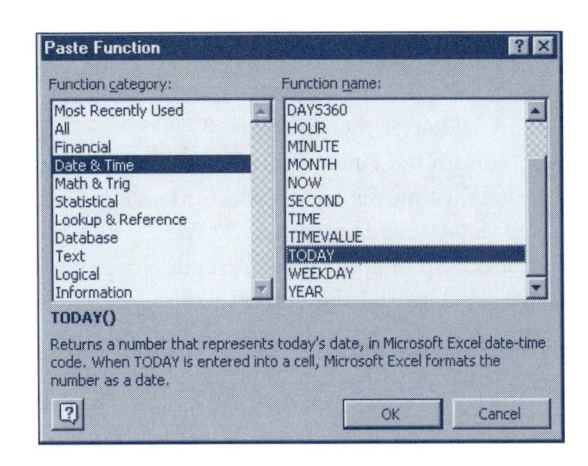

Power Users

The current date is used frequently in worksheets. To enter today's date, enter **Ctrl**+; (semicolon).

Formatting Dates

Figure 7.24 shows choices for formatting dates.

Dates are recognized as numbers and must be formatted for dates. The format applied to the cell determines the way the date is displayed. If Mar 30, 1998 is entered, Excel will display the entry as 30-Mar-98. If a date is entered as 8-30-98 or 8/30/98, Excel recognizes the number pattern and changes the cell to a date format.

All dates are stored as serial numbers. Days are numbered from the beginning of the century, with January 1, 1900 being day number 1.

Sometimes a number that looks like a date is entered, but you want it to remain a number, such as 8-9-10. Key an apostrophe (') before the number; the number will display as text and align at the left edge of the cell.

Figure 7.24 Date Formatting Choices

Using the Time Function and Format

To enter the time, use the Paste Function dialog box and select the Date & Time category, as shown in Figure 7.25.

From the Function name list, select the time wanted. To select the current date and time, select NOW. Click OK to complete the entry; both today's date and the current time appear in the cell as a volatile date and time.

Figure 7.25 Selecting Date & Time in Paste Function

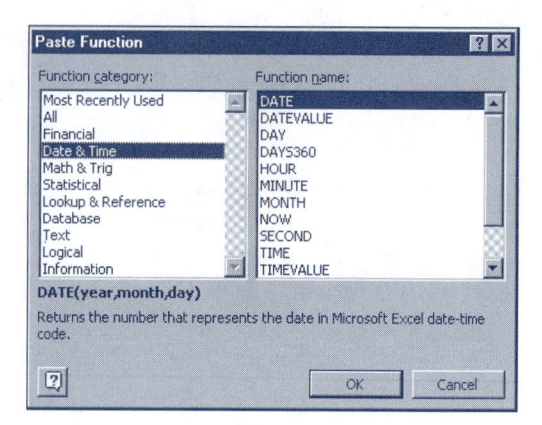

Power Users

To enter the current time, enter **Ctrl**+**Shift**+: (colon).

Choices for formatting time include the hour, minute, and second, with or without the AM or PM notations. The Time formatting choices available in the Format Cells dialog box are shown in Figure 7.26.

Figure 7.26 Formatting Time

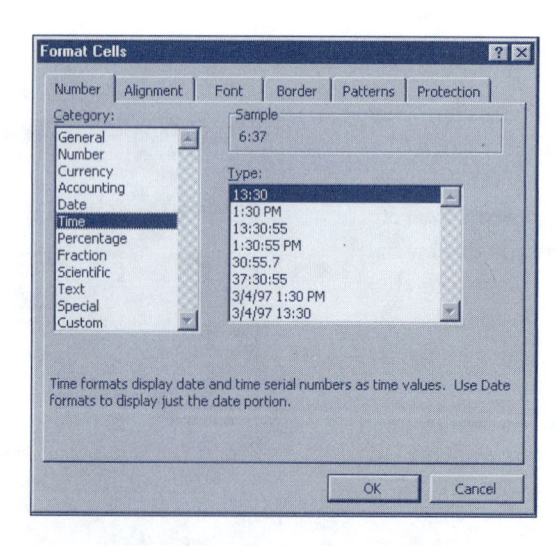

Figure 7.27 shows a time choice with 9:01:14 entered into the cell.

Figure 7.27 Inserting Time in a Cell

Exercise 7.7 Formatting Date and Time

You will use the Number tab in the Format Cells dialog box for practice in formatting the date and time in a worksheet.

1. Change the name of **Sheet7** in the **Exer 7** workbook to **Date and Time (7)**.

2. Select cell A1. From the **Format** menu select **Cells**, then choose the **Number** tab. Click on **Date**.

3. In the **Type** area, notice the choice that is selected. Click **OK** to see what the formatted choice looks like.

4. Select cell A2. Access the shortcut menu. Select **Format Cells**. Be sure the **Date** category is selected in the **Number** tab.

5. Select a choice where the month is the middle item (**4-Mar-98**). Click **OK**.

6. Select cell A3 and then select a format where the month is first (**March 4, 1998**). Excel adjusts the column width to accommodate this entry.

7. In cell A8, key **3-8-98**. Notice how Excel changes the format to its standard format, **3/8/98**.

Enter the current date.

8. Click in cell A9 and access the **Paste Function** dialog box. Select the **Date & Time** category and then choose the **TODAY** function. Click **OK**. A dialog box opens reminding you this is a volatile date. Click **OK**.

Format a cell for 10-20-30. It is not a date.

9. In cell A11, key **10-20-30**. Notice that Excel formats it as a date.

10. In cell A12, key **'10-20-30**. The apostrophe before the number tells Excel that this is a text entry.

11. In cell A13, key **'35.17**. The number is formatted as text and aligns at the left.

Format time.

12. In cell B1, select the **Time** category in the **Number** tab of the **Format Cells** dialog box. Notice the choice selected. Click **OK**.

13. In cell B2, select the Time format that displays AM or PM.

14. In cell B3, select the Time format that displays hours, minutes, and seconds with AM or PM. Excel automatically adjusts the column width.

15. In cell B4, select the Time format that displays only hours, minutes, and seconds.

16. In cell B5, select the Time format that displays the month, the day, and the year as well as the time. Make the date today's date.

Enter the current date and time.

17 In cell B1 access the **Paste Function** dialog box and select the **Date & Time** function **NOW** and click **OK**. A dialog box opens reminding you this is a volatile date. Click **OK**.

18 Place your name in cell A16.

19 Save and print the worksheet.

Formatting for Alignment

Alignment refers to the placement of information within a cell. As information is entered into cells, the information is aligned at the bottom of the cells. Text is aligned at the left and numbers are aligned at the right; this is called the *general alignment*. You have used the toolbar buttons to change alignment to the left, center, or right of a cell, and to merge and center cell contents over a group of cells. The *Alignment tab* of the Format Cells dialog box provides additional alignment choices, as shown in Figure 7.28. There are three main areas of this dialog box: Text alignment, Orientation, and Text control.

Text alignment allows for both horizontal and vertical alignment. *Horizontal alignment* is the horizontal placement of data within a cell. A drop-down list contains choices for horizontal alignment and is shown in Figure 7.29. All choices except Fill, Justify, and Center Across Selection are also available on the Formatting toolbar.

Justify adjusts text so it spans the entire width of a cell. *Fill* repeats an entry in a cell until it completely fills the width of the cell, a useful technique for making borders such as *** or —. In Figure 7.30, only three asterisks were entered in the cell; when Fill was selected, the asterisks automatically filled the width of the cell.

Figure 7.28   Alignment Tab

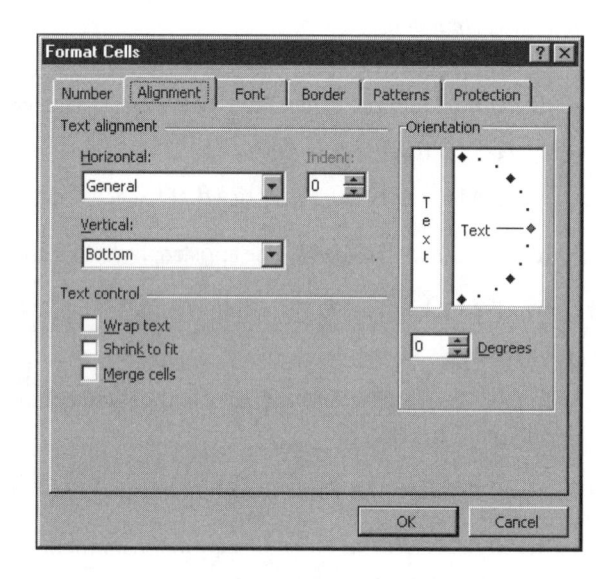

Figure 7.29   Selecting Horizontal Alignment

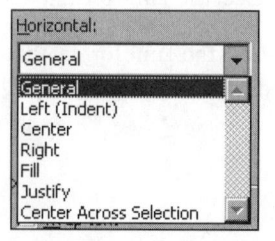

Center Across Selection is similar to the Merge and Center button in the Formatting toolbar. When Center Across Selection is used, text centers across the selected cells, but they are not merged into one cell.

Figure 7.30   Using Fill Alignment

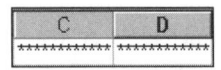

C	D
***********	***********

Vertical alignment refers to the vertical placement of data in a cell. Text automatically aligns at the bottom of a cell, even when the height of the cell has increased. Additional choices for vertical alignment are displayed in the drop-down menu shown in Figure 7.31. When vertical alignment is justified, cell contents adjust to completely fill the cell height; the contents will begin at the top of the cell and end at the bottom.

In Figure 7.32, the formats show the alignments within the cells. Cell A1 is formatted to be horizontally aligned at the left and vertically aligned at the top. Cell B2 is formatted to be horizontally and vertically aligned from the center. Cell C3 is formatted to be horizontally aligned at the right and vertically aligned at the bottom. Study this figure to see where cell contents are placed as different formats are selected.

Figure 7.33 shows different justified alignment formats. The long column titles are automatically wrapped to more than one line. The vertical alignment changes in this illustration to show where the text is placed when Horizontal Justify is selected and the Vertical alignment is Top, Center, Bottom, and Justify.

Text may be indented within a cell so it doesn't align at the left border; this is called *indent alignment*. An example is shown in Figure 7.34.

Figure 7.31   Choices for Vertical Alignment

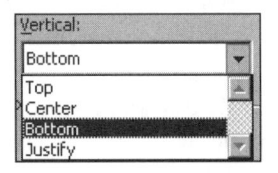

Vertical:
Bottom
Top
Center
Bottom
Justify

Figure 7.32   Formatting for Alignment

	A	B	C
1	Left/Top	Left/Center	Left/Bottom
2	Center/Top	Center/Center	Center/Bottom
3	Right/Top	Right/Center	Right/Bottom

Figure 7.33   Justify Formats

	A	B	C	D
1	Justify at the top	Justify at the Center	Justify at the bottom	Justify both Vertically and Horizontally

Use the Increase Indent and Decrease Indent buttons on the Formatting toolbar to increase or decrease the indent, shown in Figure 7.35.

If the width of an indent needs to be adjusted, change the amount in the Indent selection box in the Alignment tab, shown in Figure 7.36. The indent defaults to 2.

Text orientation refers to the way text is displayed in a cell and may be changed in the Orientation section of the Alignment tab, shown in Figure 7.37.

If text is to be displayed in a vertical position, click in the vertical Text box (Figure 7.38).

Text can also be aligned at any angle within a cell. The Orientation section shows the selected angle of the ***rotated text***. Click in the angle box and drag the mouse to the angle desired for the cell. The angle can also be selected by degrees. Figure 7.39 previews the cell alignment.

Figure 7.34   Indent Alignment

	A
1	**Days**
2	Monday
3	Tuesday
4	Wednesday
5	Thursday
6	Friday
7	Saturday

Figure 7.35   Indent Alignment Buttons

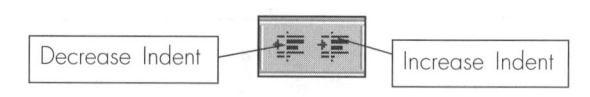

Figure 7.36   Altering the Amount of Indent

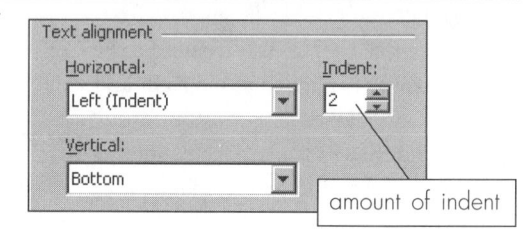

Figure 7.37   Text Orientation

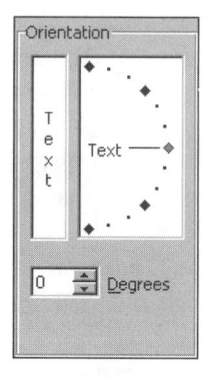

Figure 7.38   Selecting Vertical Text Alignment

Figure 7.40 shows cells containing text rotated to several different angles. The vertical alignment box was selected for the first cell.

The third section of the Alignment tab is Text control. The choices are Wrap text, Shrink to fit, and Merge cells.

The check box by **Wrap text** is used when text is to be placed on two or more lines within one cell. If a label or cell entry is too long or unbalanced, selecting Wrap text will place text on more than one line. An example of wrapped text within a cell is shown in Figure 7.41. The row height automatically adjusts to accommodate the entry. Text can also be decreased in size to fit the current size of a cell. An example of **Shrink to fit** is shown in Figure 7.42. In this sample, the text on the first row was copied to the second row; then Shrink to fit was selected.

Entries that are longer than the current cell can also be made to fit by choosing *Merge cells*. The Merge and Center button has already been used to join the cells into one cell. This same format can be applied anywhere within a worksheet. Figure 7.43 illustrates this. Note that the headings of columns A, B, and C are highlighted, indicating that the data has been merged into one cell.

Figure 7.39   Selecting Text Angle

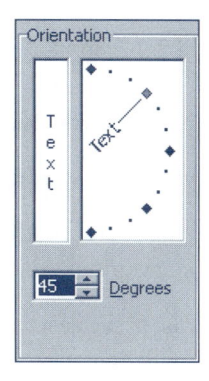

Figure 7.40   Rotated Text

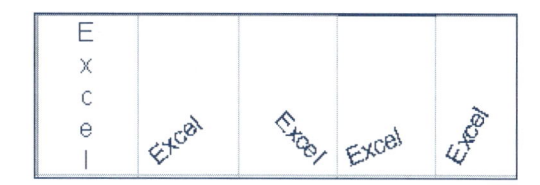

Figure 7.41   Using Wrap Text

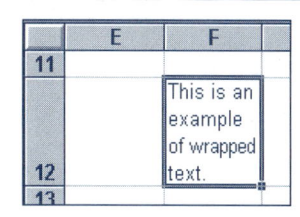

Figure 7.42   Shrink to Fit

Figure 7.43   Merge Cells

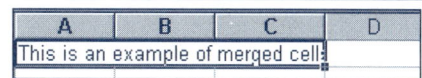

Exercise 7.8 Formatting for Alignment

You will apply alignment formats to various cells in a worksheet to see what different alignment styles are available.

1. Open the **Exer 7** workbook to **Sheet8** and rename it **Alignment (8)**.
2. Change the height of row 1 to **50**.
3. With cell A1 active, access the **Alignment** tab of the **Format Cells** dialog box and select to horizontally align at the left and vertically align at the top. Click **OK**.
4. Click in cell B1. Use the shortcut menu to access the **Format Cells** dialog box and open the **Alignment** tab. Select to horizontally and vertically align from the center.
5. Format cell C1 to horizontally align at the right and vertically align at the bottom.
6. Format cell D1 to horizontally align from the center and vertically align at the top.
7. Format cell E1 to horizontally align at the left and vertically align from the center.
8. Format cell F1 in a style you would like to try.
9. Format cell A3 for **Wrap text**.
10. Format cell B3 for justified alignment both horizontally and vertically.
11. Format cell C3 to justify the text horizontally and to vertically align at the top.
12. Format cell D3 to horizontally align from the center and to justify the text vertically.
13. Format cell D6 to fill the cell horizontally and to vertically align from the center. The text repeats itself to fill the cell.
14. Increase the width of column D to about **13**. The Fill command allows the entry to be adjusted to the new width.
15. Format cells A8 and B8 for **Merge cells**.
16. Try to select cell B8. It cannot be selected because it was merged with cell A8.
17. Format cell A10 using vertical text orientation ⟦Text⟧.
18. Format cell B10 for a rotated text orientation of 45 degrees.
19. Format cell C10 for a different rotated text orientation. Align it so it is centered both horizontally and vertically.

20 Click in cell F4. Click once on the Increase Indent button ![].

21 Click in cell F5. Click the Increase Indent button twice.

22 In cell F6, click on the Increase Indent button three times.

23 In cell F6, click once on the Decrease Indent button ![].

24 Click in cell F7. Access the **Alignment** tab of the **Format Cells** dialog box. Select an **Indent** amount of **1**. Then click **OK**.

25 In cell F8, click on the Increase Indent button three times. Adjust the column width, if needed.

26 Highlight A12:F12. Key your name and complete the entry using the ![] box, keeping the same range active.

27 In the **Alignment** tab of the **Format Cells** dialog box, select **Center Across Selection** in the Horizontal section and **Center** in the Vertical section.

28 Key your full name in cell A14. Select **Shrink to fit**.

29 Key your name in cell A16. Format it to justify text horizontally and vertically align from the center.

30 Save and print the worksheet.

Changing Font Styles

With today's computer technology, it is easy to select a different font. A *font* is a type style that is used in printing worksheets. For instance, this sentence is shown using a font named Tekton. And this sentence is entered using the Helvetica font. *And this style is Brush Script.* Changing the font changes the appearance of the worksheet.

In addition to changing the font style, you can also alter the font size so it is larger or smaller. Font sizes are measured in *points*, which is a measurement of the size of type. When Excel opens, it displays the *default font*, Arial 10 point.

Choices about a font can be changed in the *Font tab* of the Format Cells dialog box, shown in Figure 7.44.

Chapter 7 Additional Formatting Techniques

In the Font tab, the font, the size, and the style may be changed; additional enhancements such as bold or underline may be added. To select a different font, highlight the choice in the Font list box. The list box contains additional fonts that can be accessed using the scroll bar. A sample of the selected font is displayed in the Preview section of the dialog box.

Use the Size box to change the font size. The larger the number, the larger the font size. Excel defaults to a font size of 10 points. Different font sizes and styles may be used in the same worksheet, but use caution when applying different fonts and styles.

Figure 7.44   Font Tab in the Format Cells Dialog Box

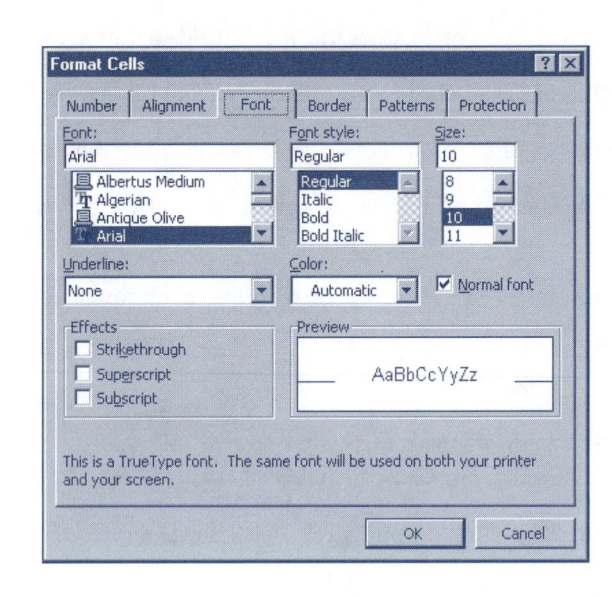

User's Tip

Use a maximum of two fonts for each worksheet. Vary their appearance in the worksheet by the size and styles applied to the fonts.

Underlines can be added in the Underline section. The choices in the Underline section are shown in Figure 7.45. The accounting styles place underlines under only the number; the borders in the toolbar place underlines across the entire width of a cell.

Figure 7.45   Underline Font Choices

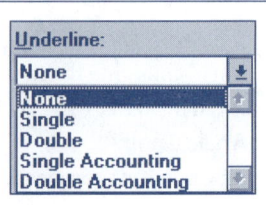

The Color section is used to add color to a cell. Strikethrough, Superscript, and Subscript can be selected in the Effects section.

In-cell editing allows different font styles and attributes to be applied to the contents of a cell. Figure 7.46 shows a company name entered in cell A1 using different fonts, sizes, and colors. Color and font attributes may also be changed for any one letter of a cell.

Figure 7.46   Editing Using Different Fonts within a Cell

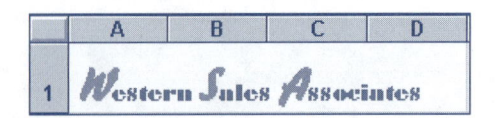

To change fonts and attributes within a cell, double-click on it. Then highlight the letter or figure that will have an attribute applied to it. Although each letter may have a different attribute, simplicity is recommended.

Font and font size may also be selected in the Formatting toolbar, as shown in Figure 7.47. The drop-down menus access the available styles and sizes.

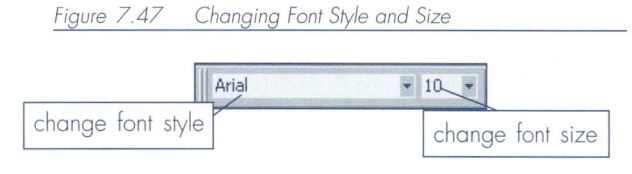

Figure 7.47   Changing Font Style and Size

Exercise 7.9   Working with Fonts

You will practice working with fonts, sizes, and enhancements. Some fonts used in this exercise may not be available on your computer. If the requested font is not available, substitute an available font.

1 Open the **Exer 7** workbook to **Sheet9** and rename it **Fonts (9)**. This worksheet is blank.

2 Enter your name in cell A1.

3 Use AutoFill to enter months in cells A3:E3, beginning with **January**.

4 Use AutoFill to enter days of the week in cells A5:E5, beginning with **Monday**.

Format individual cells.

5 Select cell A3. Open the **Format Cells** dialog box and choose the **Font** tab. Select a font different from the one highlighted. Format for **Italic** and **12** point. (Adjust column widths as needed in this exercise.)

6 Select cell B3. Access the shortcut menu and select **Format Cells**. Select the **Font** tab. Select a font not already used. Format for **Bold** and **14** point.

7 Format cell C3 in a font not already used, then select **Bold Italic** and **18** point.

8 Format cell D3 in an unused font, **Italic**, and **36** point. (Not all fonts will be available in a 36-point font size. Select a font that lists 36 point as an available option.)

9 Format cell E3 in an unused font and **12** point. Then select the **Alignment** tab. Format the cell so text is centered horizontally and vertically.

10 Use the Format Painter button to copy the format in cell E3 to cells A5 and E5.

Format additional cells.

11 Click in cell B5. Select a script font (such as Brush); then select 14 point. (A script font is somewhat like cursive handwriting.)

12 Click on the **Alignment** tab. Format the cell so text is centered horizontally and vertically. Select a rotated orientation.

13 Adjust the row height to between **60** and **70**.

14 Format cells C5 and D5 in a style of your choice.

Use superscript and subscript.

15. In cell A6, key **H20**. Double-click in cell A6 and highlight the **2** of **H20**. Open the **Format Cells** dialog box; the **Font** tab is the only available tab. Click the **Subscript** button in the **Effects** section.

16. In cell B6, key **'32**. The apostrophe must be entered before the number so Excel will read the number as text. (You will convert this to the math term of 3 squared.)

17. Double-click in cell B6 and highlight the **2** of **32**. Open the **Format Cells** dialog box; the **Font** tab is the only available tab. Click the **Superscript** button in the **Effects** section.

Use in-cell editing to format your name.

18. Double-click in cell A1. Highlight the first letter of your first name.

19. Open the **Font** tab of the **Format Cells** dialog box. Select the **Comic Sans** font, **22** point, **Regular** style (or a font you have available) and select a color.

20. Adjust the row height.

21. Repeat the font and attributes to the first letter of your last name.

22. Highlight the rest of your first name. Select **Bookman Old Style** font, **12** point, **Regular** style (or an available font).

23. Repeat the style with the rest of your last name.

24. Center your name over the columns of the worksheet.

25. Save and print the worksheet.

Adding Borders

Placing a *border* around a portion of a worksheet adds interest to the worksheet design and helps its readability. Borders have previously been added using the Formatting toolbar and AutoFormat.

The *Border tab* in the Format Cells dialog box is accessed from the Format menu or through shortcut menus and is shown in Figure 7.48.

Figure 7.48 Border Tab in Format Cells Dialog Box

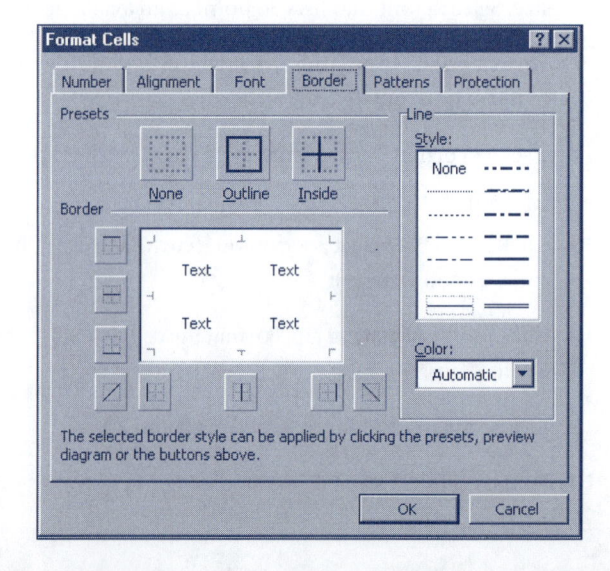

The sections in the Border tab are Presets, Line, and Border. The Presets section applies (or removes) borders to the selected cells. *Outline* places a border around the selected cells; *Inside* places borders around each individual cell.

The Border section illustrates the placement of borders. Around the edge of this section are the line angles that can be placed in the worksheet. Click either on the border, or the space within the viewing area. Borders are placed in the viewing area to help determine the look of the worksheet, as shown in Figure 7.49.

Figure 7.49 Placing Borders in a Worksheet

The *line style* is selected from the Line section, shown in Figure 7.50. First select the line style; then click in the Border section to determine the placement of that line.

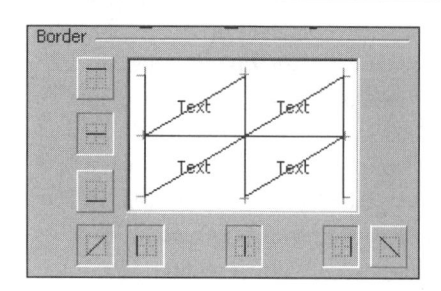

Figure 7.50 Selecting Line Style

The *Borders palette* is available in the toolbar. It is a *pull-away palette* and can be removed from the toolbar. It can then be moved around the worksheet as a floating palette and is pictured in Figure 7.51.

To move the pull-away palette from the toolbar, click in the shaded area at the top of the palette. Then drag the palette onto the worksheet.

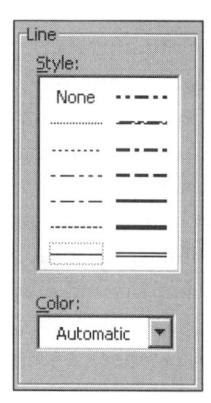

Figure 7.51 Pull-away Borders Palette

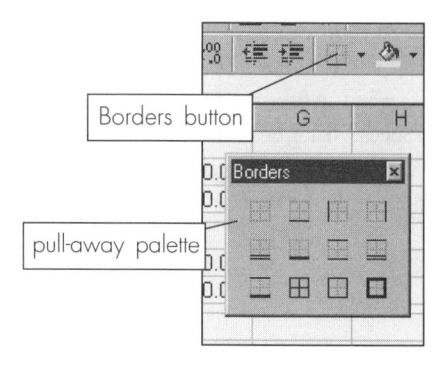

Color choices can be selected in the Format Cells dialog box or the toolbar. The two buttons on the toolbar used to add color to a cell are pictured in Figure 7.52. Click on the arrow beside each of these buttons to open a *color palette*. The button on the left (Fill Color) controls the background color of the cell; the button on the right (Font Color) determines the text color. The color palettes are also pull-away palettes.

Using Patterns

Patterns enhance the appearance of worksheets by adding color and shading or patterns to the background of a cell. To select patterns or other color choices, use the *Patterns tab* in the Format Cells dialog box, shown in Figure 7.53.

The color palette shown in the Patterns tab places a color in a cell. To place a pattern and pattern color in a cell, use the pull-down menu by Pattern, which accesses the color/pattern palette. This color and pattern palette is shown in Figure 7.54.

A word of caution when using worksheet enhancements: computers have made formatting easy and fun, and beginners often want to use all the capabilities available to them. However, worksheets can be overdone with too many different fonts, too many sizes, and too many borders and different patterns. Use these style techniques sparingly and for emphasis. Simple is often better!

Copying Formats

The *Format Painter button* is used to copy cell formats. You may also select Paste Special in the Edit menu to open the Paste Special dialog box, shown in Figure 7.55. Selecting the Formats option also copies only the format of a selected cell.

Figure 7.52   Color Tools

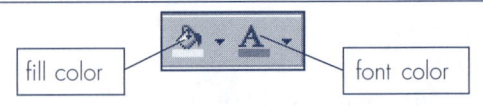

Figure 7.53   Patterns Tab in Format Cells Dialog Box

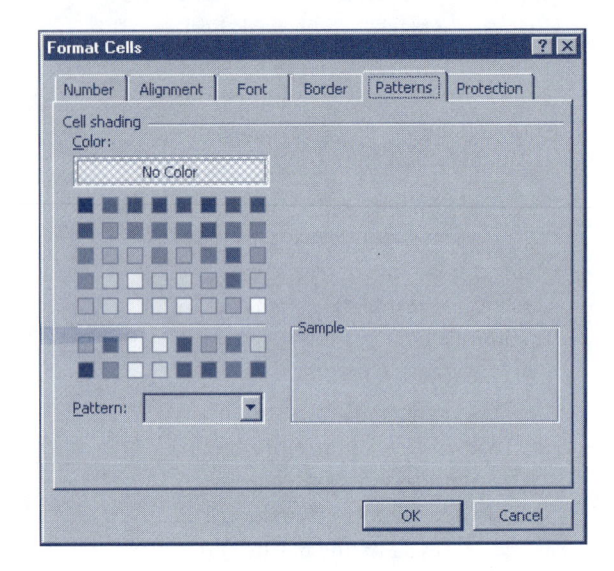

Figure 7.54   Patterns Available to Use

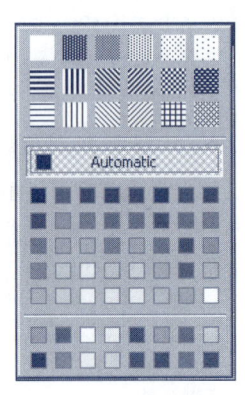

Figure 7.55   Using Paste Special Dialog Box to Copy Formats

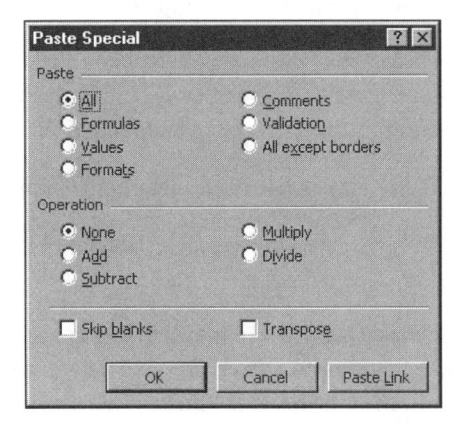

Formats may be copied between sheets of a workbook using either the Format Painter or the Paste Special dialog box.

Exercise 7.10   Shading, Borders, and Color

You will practice applying borders and patterns to a worksheet.

1   Open the **Exer 7** workbook to **Sheet10**. Change its name to **Borders (10)**.

2   Format cell A4 for bold. Open the **Patterns** tab in the **Format Cells** dialog box. Click on a gray shade at the right edge of the **Color** section. Click **OK**.

3   Format cell A6 for bold. Open the **Patterns** tab of the **Format Cells** dialog box. Click on a different gray shade at the right edge of the **Color** section. Click **OK**.

4   Format cell B4 for bold. Open the **Patterns** tab of the **Format Cells** dialog box, and then click on the arrow by **Pattern** to open the color/pattern palette. Select the pattern with darker diagonals that looks like . Click **OK**.

5   Select cell C4. In the Formatting toolbar, select the arrow next to the Fill Color button (with the paint bucket) and select a blue color. Then select the arrow next to the Font Color button and select white.

6   Format cell D4 for bold. Open the **Patterns** tab, then click on the **Pattern** arrow to open the color/pattern palette. Select the following lighter diagonal pattern: .

7   Format cell E4 for bold. Open the **Patterns** tab of the **Format Cells** dialog box. Click on the arrow by **Pattern**. Select the pattern with horizontal lines .

8   Select the range A6:F7. Open the **Border** tab of the **Format Cells** dialog box. Select a color for the border, and then select the **Outline** style in the **Preset** section. Click **OK**. The border is now displayed in color.

9   Copy the range A10:D10 to A11:D11. Press **Esc** on the keyboard to stop the marquee from displaying. Highlight the range A10:D11. Open the **Border** tab of the **Format Cells** dialog box.

10 In the **Style** section, select a dashed line. In the **Border** section, click the buttons that correspond to top and bottom. Click **OK**. A dashed line is at the top and bottom of the selection.

11 Select A11:D11. Open the **Border** tab of the **Format Cells** dialog box. A dashed line is at the bottom of the selection. In the **Line** section select a double-line style, and in the **Border** section click the button that corresponds to the top of the cells. Then select one of the angled lines. Click **OK** to close the dialog box.

12 With A11:D11 still selected, use the Formatting toolbar Font Color button to select red for the text.

13 In cell A1, enter your name. Merge and center it across the range A1:F1. Format it for a dark border and light (not white) text.

14 With A1 selected, open the **Border** tab of the **Format Cells** dialog box. In the **Style** section, select the bold line. In the **Border** section, click the button that corresponds to the top of the cells, then select a double-line style and click at the bottom of the cell area. Click **OK**. This places a bold line at the top of the range and a double line at the bottom.

Copy a format to another worksheet.

15 Save and print the worksheet.

16 Select cell A11, then click the Format Painter button.

17 Open the sheet named **Fonts (9)**.

18 Select the range A12:E12. The format is copied from one worksheet to another.

19 Save the workbook.

Using WordArt

WordArt is a quick way to add graphical text effects and is especially useful when formatting titles. WordArt is available on the Insert menu by selecting Picture, then WordArt, as shown in Figure 7.56.

Figure 7.56   Inserting WordArt

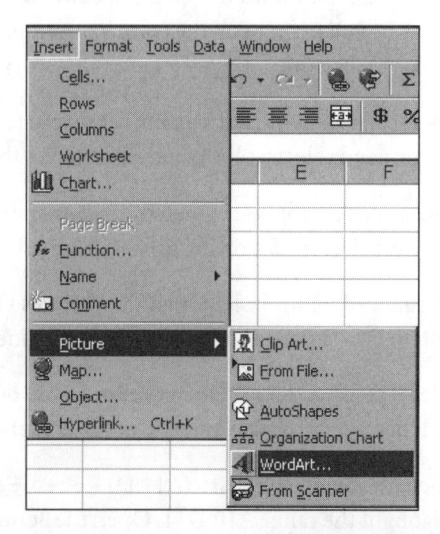

When WordArt is selected, the *WordArt Gallery* dialog box opens providing several choices for the shape of text, as shown in Figure 7.57.

Select a shape and click OK; then the Edit WordArt Text dialog box opens, shown in Figure 7.58.

Replace "Your Text Here" with the text needed. You may also select the font, font size, and attributes of bold or italics. When the text selections are complete, click OK to display the text on the screen. When the text appears on the screen, the WordArt toolbar opens. The white boxes around the WordArt are handles, which indicate that the WordArt object is active. Figure 7.59 shows a WordArt object inserted into a worksheet.

A WordArt object may be sized and moved (when it is active) in a worksheet. Click once in the WordArt object to activate it. Move the mouse to a white handle to size the WordArt object; position the mouse inside the art to move it.

When the Drawing toolbar is open, WordArt may be accessed from the Insert WordArt button. The Drawing toolbar is shown in Figure 7.60. The WordArt Gallery dialog box opens when the Insert WordArt button is selected.

Figure 7.57 WordArt Gallery Dialog Box

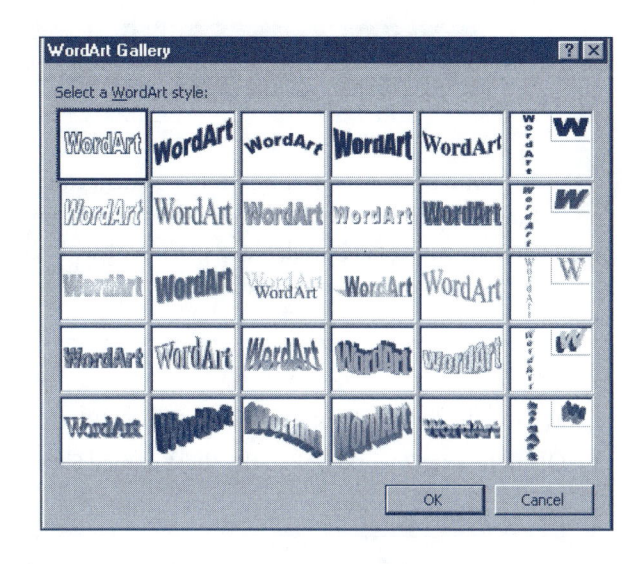

Figure 7.58 Edit WordArt Text Dialog Box

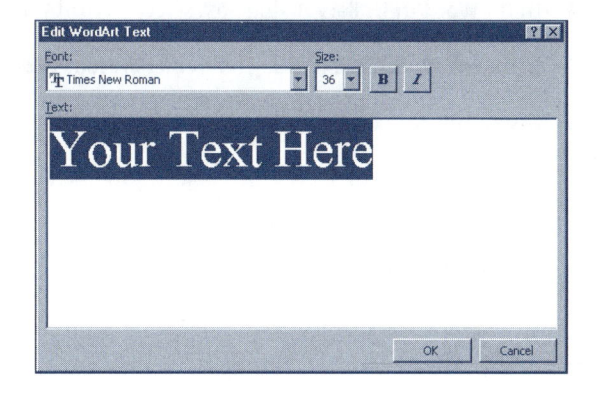

Figure 7.59 Inserting WordArt

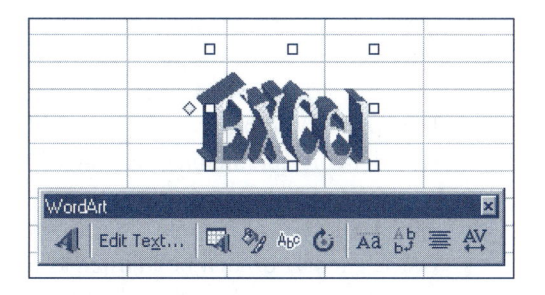

Figure 7.60   Inserting WordArt from the Drawing Toolbar

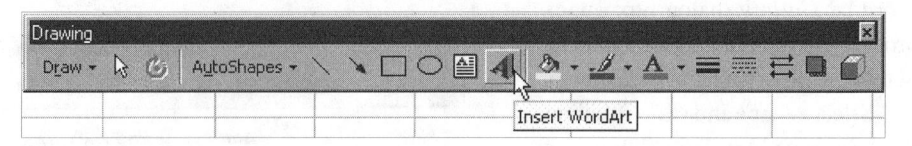

As with other Excel features, enhancements may be added to WordArt. The color of both text and outlines may be changed, text may be rotated within cells, use of all capitals is easily formatted, and alignment choices are available. Experiment with the features available in the Drawing toolbar for making creative, attractive worksheets.

Exercise 7.11   Using WordArt

You will use WordArt to enhance a worksheet title.

1. Open the **Exer 7** workbook to the sheet named **Sheet11**. Change its name to **WordArt (11)**.
2. Delete the title in cell A1.
3. Access the **WordArt Gallery** dialog box. To do this, select **Picture** from the **Insert** menu, then **WordArt**.
4. In the **WordArt Gallery** dialog box, select a WordArt pattern of your choice. Then click **OK**.
5. In the **Edit WordArt Text** dialog box, enter **Wilson's Grocers**. Choose a font size of **18** points. Then click **OK**.
6. Insert four to six rows at the top of the worksheet to allow room for the WordArt object.
7. Click in the center of the WordArt object. A four-sided arrow appears. Click and drag the art to the top of the sheet.
8. Save and print the document.

Summary

- The width of a column may be adjusted to accommodate the size of any entry.
- Select Column from the Format menu; a submenu opens with Width as a choice.
- Select AutoFit Selection to automatically adjust selected columns to accommodate their longest entries.
- AutoFit Selection is also selected by double-clicking on a column border.
- The Column Width command is available on shortcut menus.
- The width of a column may be changed by dragging the column border to a new width on the worksheet window. A ScreenTip shows its width. It may also be changed in the Print Preview window.
- The height of a row may be adjusted to accommodate any size of entry.
- To open the Row Height dialog box, select Row from the Format menu, then Height.
- The height of a row may be changed by dragging the row number to a new height on the worksheet window. A ScreenTip shows its height.
- Shortcut menus can be used to access the Row Height command.

- To insert rows, columns, or cells, select the Rows or Columns command from the Insert menu.
- When cells are inserted, the remaining cells move to the right or down. The relative references in the moved cells change to reflect their new location.
- Cells can be deleted in Excel. When a cell is deleted, the remaining space is closed up.
- The Delete command is in the Edit menu.
- When a cell or range of cells is deleted, the Delete dialog box opens with the choices of shifting the remaining cells up or to the left.
- Relative references automatically adjust when cells are deleted.
- If the cell reference in a remaining cell has been deleted, an error message such as #REF! appears.
- The Clear command is used when a part of a cell's contents is to be removed. Use Clear when formats, formulas, or contents need to be removed.
- The Clear command is found in the Edit menu. A submenu opens providing specific choices.
- Columns and rows can be hidden and neither printed nor shown on the screen; they are retained in the worksheet and in the memory of the computer.
- To hide a column, click to the right of the column heading and drag to the left over the columns to be hidden. Unhide the column by dragging to the right.
- To hide a row, click on the line below the row heading and drag up over the rows to be hidden. Unhide the row by dragging down.
- Select the Cells command from the Format menu to format information in a worksheet. The Format Cells dialog box opens with tab choices for individual types of formatting: Number, Alignment, Font, Border, Patterns, and Protection.
- To format numbers, select the Number tab of the Format Cells dialog box.
- Select the type of number to format from the Category section. Format choices are then displayed in the Type section.
- When a percent sign (%) or dollar sign ($) is entered, Excel automatically changes to the proper format.
- Using the Currency Style button places a dollar sign at the extreme left edge of a cell. Using the Format Cells dialog box to format for currency places a dollar sign immediately to the left of the first number in a cell.
- Enter an apostrophe (') before a number to display it as text.
- Dates are formatted in the Number tab. Select the Date & Time category.
- To enter the current date in a worksheet, press Ctrl+; (semicolon).
- Time is formatted by selecting the Number tab of the Format Cells dialog box, then choosing the Date & Time category.
- To enter the current time in a worksheet, press Ctrl+Shift+: (colon).
- The Alignment tab in the Format Cells dialog box is selected to format cell alignment within a worksheet, providing several options for aligning text within a cell.
- Text orientation can be controlled so it is rotated within a cell or printed in a vertical line.
- Use the Wrap text feature to place long titles onto two or more lines within the same cell.
- Cell contents that are longer than the cell width may be decreased in size to fit in the column. Use the Shrink to fit feature.
- Cells containing long entries can be merged into one cell.
- Using the Merge and Center button of the Formatting toolbar merges cells into one cell and centers their contents over the selected range of cells.

Chapter 7 Additional Formatting Techniques

- Cell contents may also be centered across several columns by selecting Horizontal alignment of Center Across Selection in the Format Cells dialog box. Cells do not merge.
- Font styles may be changed in the Font tab of the Format Cells dialog box.
- In addition to the font, the size and style may also be changed in the Font tab.
- The font size and style can be different for each letter of text within a cell.
- Color choices can be made for the letters and numbers within a cell.
- Border choices are available in the Border tab of the Format Cells dialog box.
- The style and placement of a border are controlled in the Border tab.
- Borders can be placed along the gridlines and diagonally within a cell. Line styles and color may be selected.
- The Patterns tab is accessed in the Format Cells dialog box.
- Shading intensity can be selected from the Patterns tab.
- To add interest to a worksheet, colors can be added to patterns.
- The palettes for color and borders are pull-away palettes; they can be moved from the toolbar to any location on the screen.
- The Format Painter button will copy only the format of a cell.
- A WordArt object may be used to add a graphical effect to text.
- WordArt is accessed from the Insert menu or the Drawing toolbar.
- A WordArt object may be sized and moved within a worksheet.

Important Terminology

#REF!	Format Cells dialog box	Paste Function button
alignment	Format Painter button	patterns
Alignment tab	general alignment	Patterns tab
AutoFit Selection	hide columns	points
border	hide rows	pull-away palette
Border tab	horizontal alignment	rotated text
Borders palette	indent alignment	row height
Center Across Selection	insert cells	Shrink to fit
Clear command	insert a column	Standard Width
color palette	insert a row	static
column width	Inside	text orientation
Currency style	Justify	unhide columns
Date & Time function	line style	unhide rows
default font	Merge cells	vertical alignment
Delete command	move line	volatile
Fill	number format	WordArt
font	Number tab	WordArt Gallery
Font tab	Outline	Wrap text

Buttons to Know

Study Questions

True-False

Place a T in the space if the statement is true; place an F if the statement is false.

_____ 1. It is impossible to change the width or height of cells.
_____ 2. If a column should not show in a printed worksheet, it must be deleted before printing takes place.
_____ 3. A column width may be changed by clicking and dragging the mouse to a new column width.
_____ 4. #### displays in a cell when an incorrect formula is entered.
_____ 5. If a column is hidden in a worksheet, its contents are deleted from the memory of the worksheet.
_____ 6. The Column Width command is available in shortcut menus.
_____ 7. Columns can be hidden by clicking and dragging the mouse over the columns to be hidden.
_____ 8. Double-click on the line between columns to select the best fit for the column to the left.
_____ 9. Column widths and margins may be adjusted in Print Preview.
_____ 10. The choices to adjust row height are accessed from the Format menu.
_____ 11. To insert a row, select Row from the Format menu.
_____ 12. When using the Insert command, the contents in a cell automatically adjust to allow room for inserted cells.
_____ 13. Row heights may be adjusted by double-clicking on the line between the row headings.
_____ 14. Once a row or column is hidden, it cannot be unhidden.
_____ 15. Deleting a cell or range of cells leaves a series of blank cells in the worksheet where the original cells were located.
_____ 16. When the Clear command is used, the cleared cells are removed from the worksheet and other cells move to replace the cleared cells.
_____ 17. The Format Cells dialog box is used to format only the font.
_____ 18. Alignment refers to the placement of a worksheet on the page.
_____ 19. If a dollar sign ($) is typed when a number is entered, it displays in the cell and the cell is automatically formatted to the Currency style.
_____ 20. The category of a number refers to the type of number displayed: currency, percents, fractions, etc.
_____ 21. When displaying money amounts, a dollar sign ($) must show in every cell.
_____ 22. Excel formats dates only in the 9/1/99 format style.
_____ 23. A volatile date will always print the current date.
_____ 24. Wrap text is selected for long labels that use more than one line of a cell.
_____ 25. Only row labels may be printed on more than one line.
_____ 26. Text within a cell may begin only at the left margin and align only at the bottom of the cell.
_____ 27. Orientation refers to the position of text in a dialog box.
_____ 28. Shrink to fit is used so a large worksheet can be printed on one page.
_____ 29. Text may be entered in a cell at a diagonal.
_____ 30. Some formatting tools are available on the toolbar.
_____ 31. A font is the type style used.

_____ 32. On the Font tab of the Format Cells dialog box, only the font and font size can be changed.
_____ 33. The color of a font cannot be changed.
_____ 34. In selecting a font size, the larger the number of the font, the smaller the font size.
_____ 35. Enhancements to fonts such as bold, italic, or underline are selected from the Enhancements tab in the Format Cells dialog box.
_____ 36. Font sizes cannot be increased or decreased.
_____ 37. Only the format of a cell will be copied if the Format Painter button is used.
_____ 38. A border can be placed around an entire worksheet or a single cell.
_____ 39. A pattern or shading can be applied to a cell by selecting the Patterns tab of the Format Cells dialog box.
_____ 40. The Font Color palette is used to change the color of a cell.
_____ 41. Copy only the format of a cell by selecting the Paste Special command on the Edit menu.
_____ 42. Using WordArt is a quick way to enlarge the title of a worksheet, change its font, and merge and center it in one step.
_____ 43. The Edit WordArt dialog box is used only to change text attributes.

Fill-In

Place the word in the space that correctly completes the statement.
1. The Column Width dialog box can be accessed from the _____ command in the Format menu.
2. The Row Height dialog box can be accessed from the _____ command in the Format menu.
3. To choose a column width that automatically adjusts to accommodate the longest entry in the column, use the _____ command.
4. When ####### displays in a cell, the _____ is too narrow.
5. The process of adding a blank row in a worksheet is called _____ a row.
6. The command used to remove cells from a worksheet is the _____ command.
7. The Format Cells dialog box has _____ to indicate the specific type of format to apply.
8. The Format Number dialog box is accessed by choosing the _____ command in the _____ menu.
9. To enter the current date, use _____ .
10. To enter the current time, use _____ .
11. To place a label on more than one line within a cell, use _____ .
12. The Wrap text command is found in the _____ tab of the Format Cells dialog box.
13. The section used to format labels so they are printed on their side or at an angle is called _____ .
14. To format for currency so a dollar sign is directly to the left of a number, use _____ .
15. A _____ changes the type style of a worksheet.
16. The font size and style that is preset with software is called the _____ .
17. A border may be applied to a cell by opening the Border tab of the Format Cells dialog box. It is accessed from the _____ command in the _____ menu.
18. To place a border at the bottom of a series of cells, first _____ the range of cells.
19. To place a border on all sides of a cell or range of selected cells, select _____ as the border style.

20. The color palettes are _____-away palettes.
21. The ◢ button is used to insert _____.

Assignments

Assignment 7.1

A small plant, Mills' Manufacturing Company, uses an Excel worksheet to track its inventory. A worksheet for the current inventory has been completed. The suggestion has been made that it could be more attractively presented. You will format the worksheet.

1. Open the **Ch7 As1** workbook and save it as **Assig 7-1**.
2. Format the title.
   - Insert three new rows at the top.
   - In cell B2, key **Mills' Manufacturing Company**.
   - In cell B3, key **Ending Inventory**.
   - In cell B4, key **March 30, 1996**.
   - Format cell B2 for **Brittanic Bold** font with a size of **14** points. Select the **M** of **Mills**. Format it for **Italic, 16** point. Repeat the same style for the **M** in **Manufacturing** and the **C** in **Company**. Format for white text and red fill color.
   - Format cells B3 and B4 for **Bold** with a font size of **12** points.
3. Format the worksheet.
   - Format the numbers in the worksheet for currency with zero decimals using the **Format Cells** dialog box.
   - Place the correct borders for the total row (row 11). Also format for bold and place a light gray color in the cells.
   - Place a bold border under the column labels and format the cells for the same shade of red used in the title.
   - Key the word **Total** in cell B11. Format for bold, center alignment, and shading to match the rest of the row.
4. Add style to the worksheet.
   - Adjust column widths if needed.
   - Click in cell A1. Key ** and complete the entry.
   - Format to fill the cell horizontally and vertically align from the center. Increase the height of row 1 to **30**.
   - With cell A1 selected, click on the fill handle and extend to column G.
   - Copy A1:G1 to cell A15. Adjust the height of row 15 to **30**.
   - Merge and center the cells of the three-line title.
5. In Page Setup, select a top margin of 2" and a left margin of 1.75". Replace **Student's Name** with your name.
6. Double-check the format of the worksheet for accuracy and attractiveness. Did you use the spelling checker?
7. Save and print the worksheet. At the top, write "Print 1."
8. Hide rows 8 and 10.
9. Print a copy. At the top, write "Print 2."
10. Print a worksheet that shows the formulas.

Assignment 7.2

Nevin's Grocery Store has completed its quarterly reports for 1999. Each report is a separate worksheet. You will format these quarterly reports and prepare an annual report that summarizes the sales for the year.

1. Open the **Ch7 As2** workbook and save it as **Assig 7-2**.
2. Change the name of **Sheet1** to **First Q**, **Sheet2** to **Second Q**, **Sheet3** to **Third Q**, and **Sheet4** to **Fourth Q**.
3. Insert a sheet at the beginning of the workbook. Name it **Annual**.
4. Prepare the **Annual** sheet for the quarterly reports.
   - In cell A3 of the **Annual** sheet, key **For year ending December 31, 1999**.
   - Select all worksheets in this workbook (five total).
   - In cell A1, key **Nevin's Grocery Store**. In cell A2, key **Sales Report**.
   - With all worksheets selected, double-click in cell A1 to edit the title.
   - Change the **N** of **Nevin** to **Brush** font **18** point. You may need to adjust the row height. Use the same format for the **G** of **Grocery** and the **S** of **Store**.
   - Click in the **First Q** sheet to make it active. Make sure the other sheets are still active.
   - On all of the sheets, format the column labels for bold italic with double border lines. Increase the row height to **20**. Center each heading both horizontally and vertically.
   - Format all of the sheets correctly for currency using the appropriate toolbar button. Use underscores correctly.
5. Complete the quarterly sheets.
   - Select all of the sheets with the **First Q** sheet active. (Hold down the Ctrl key to select nonadjacent sheets.)
   - Complete the formulas needed on the sheets. Adjust column widths if necessary.
   - Ungroup the sheets.
   - Copy the product names in column A (A7:A11) of the **First Q** sheet to the same range in the other four sheets. First select a copy command. Then select the other four sheets and use a paste command.
6. Complete the annual sheet.
   - Select only the **Annual** sheet.
   - In row 6, add the column titles of **First Quarter, Second Quarter, Third Quarter,** and **Fourth Quarter**. They are formatted like the column labels in the quarterly sheets; select to wrap the text. You may need to adjust row heights.
   - In the **First Q** sheet, select the total column (E7:E10) and copy the values only to the first quarter column of the **Annual** sheet (B7:B10).
   - Repeat copying the total values from the other three sheets to the correct columns in the **Annual** sheet.
   - Complete the totals needed on the **Annual** sheet and check the format.
7. On all sheets, format the three-line title for bold. On the quarterly sheets, merge and center each line of the three-line title. Put the text in a color of your choice.
8. Format the title of the **Annual** sheet.
   - On the **Annual** sheet, left align the three-line title.
   - On the **Annual** sheet, use WordArt to place **1999 Report** at the right side of the title area. Adjust the size and placement so it looks attractive.

9. Continue formatting the workbook.
    - On all of the worksheets, use Print Preview to set a top margin of 2" and a left margin of 1.75".
    - Place the file name in the header and the sheet name in the footer.
    - Place your name in a cell at the end of the worksheet.
10. Check the spelling in each worksheet.
11. Save and print the worksheets.

Assignment 7.3

Ryan's Manufacturing Company has completed the data for an inventory report, but the report needs to be formatted. Because this worksheet will be presented to the board of directors, special care must be taken to produce an attractive, professional appearance.

1. Open the workbook **Ch7 As3** and save it as **Assig 7-3**.
2. Complete the worksheet.
    - In cell A7, key **January**. Use AutoFill to extend the months down column A through **April**.
    - In cells A11 and E6, key **Total**.
    - In cell B6, insert **Product 1** before **Wondas**.
    - In cell C6, insert **Product 2** before **Transies**.
    - In cell D6, insert **Product 3** before **Zooms**.
    - Format the range B6:E6 for wrapped text and center the contents both horizontally and vertically.
    - Use AutoSum to add the cells.
3. Format the worksheet.
    - Insert a row at the top of the worksheet and a column at the left edge.
    - Double-click in cell B2 for in-cell editing. Change the format of the firm name using fonts and sizes (and color, if appropriate). At the very least, make the firm name bold and increase the font size. Experiment with fonts, font styles, etc.
    - Format cells B3 and B4 in a style of your choice.
    - In cell C6, key **South Division**. Merge cells and center it across the range C6:E6. Format for bold.
    - Format cell B12 for bold, center alignment, and italics.
    - Place a double line across the top of the range B6:F6 and a bold line across the bottom.
    - Select the range B6:E12. Place a medium-sized border at the left and right of this range.
    - Format borders on the total row.
    - Format all totals in bold. Select a light shading (or color) fill for the total row, including the label.
    - Place a double line under cell B12.
    - Place a double-line border to the right of the range F6:F12.
    - Place an X in cell E5 using borders. Use both diagonal borders (thin line) found in the **Border** tab of the **Format Cells** dialog box.
    - Format for the appropriate the numbers for commas with zero decimal places.
    - Highlight the ranges A1:G1 and A15:G15. Select the **Patterns** tab of the **Format Cells** dialog box, and select the pattern that looks like ▨. Apply a fill color if using a color printer.
    - Adjust rows 1 and 15 for a height of about **5.0**.
    - Select the ranges A2:A14 and G2:G14. Repeat the pattern format. Adjust the column widths to about **1.5**.
    - Highlight the range A1:G15 (the main body of worksheet). Place a bold border around the range.
    - Merge and center the three-line title across the columns.

4. In cell B14, place your name after the words **Prepared by**. Select a format of your choice.
5. Check the spelling in the worksheet.
6. In **Print Preview**, adjust for a top margin of 2.5" and a left margin of 2".
7. Place the file name in the header and the sheet name in the footer.
8. Save and print the worksheet.
9. Print a copy with the formulas displayed.

Assignment 7.4

Schneider & Schneider prepares a statement of income comparing income and expenses from the previous year. You will complete and format this worksheet.

1. Open Excel to a new workbook and enter the following data:

	A	B	C	D
1	Schneider & Schneider			
2	Statement of Income			
3	For Two Years Ended December 31, 1999			
4				
5			1999	1998
6	Net Sales		5029583	3538988
7	Costs and Expenses			
8		Costs of Sales	2503382	1938382
9		Research and Development	63283	83293
10		Marketing	583298	438905
11		Administrative	1205382	1029859
12	Total Expenses			
13	Income from Operations			
14	Other Income		43592	38683
15	Income Before Taxes			
16	Estimated Income Taxes			
17	Net Income			
18	Common Shares Outstanding		112590	110810
19	Earnings per Share			

2. Save the workbook as **Assig 7-4**.
3. Complete the worksheet.
   - Complete the total expenses in row 12. This is the total of costs and expenses, rows 8–11.
   - Complete the income from operations in row 13. This is net sales less total expenses.
   - Complete the income before taxes in row 15. This is income from operations plus other income.
   - Complete the estimated income taxes in row 16. This is income before taxes times a tax rate of 40%.
   - Complete the net income in row 17. This is income before taxes less estimated income taxes.
   - Complete the earnings per share in row 19. This is net income divided by common shares outstanding.
4. Format the worksheet.
   - Format the three-line title in a style you like. Use fonts, sizes, bold, italic, centering, and WordArt to add interest. Format all labels in the worksheet in the same font you select for the title.
   - Format the dates in cells C5 and D5 for center alignment, bold, and underline.
   - Bold rows 6, 12, 13, 17, and 19. (Can you do this in one step using multiple ranges?)
   - Place borders under the amounts in rows 6, 11, 12, 14, and 16.

- Place a double-line border under row 17.
    - Shade cells C17:D17 and C19:D19.
5. Format the numbers in columns C and D.
    - Format numbers for currency with negative numbers placed in parentheses and red color.
    - Format the rest of the numbers. Dollar signs should be placed in rows 6, 8, 12, 13, 15, 17, and 19.
    - Format row 18 for zero decimals.
    - Format row 19 for three decimals.
6. Adjust column widths.
    - Adjust the widths of columns A and B to **17.00**. Use the Wrap text feature in columns A and B.
    - Adjust the rest of the worksheet so the column widths are appropriate.
    - Format cell A7 for italic.
    - Change the height of rows 6, 14, and 17 to **30** points.
    - Add color to the worksheet if you are using a color printer.
7. Complete the format of the worksheet.
    - In Print Preview, select a top margin of 2" and a left margin of 1.75". Check to be sure that the placement is correct.
    - Place the file name in the header.
    - Merge and center each line of the three-line title.
    - Check the spelling in the worksheet.
8. Check the format and appearance of the worksheet. Make changes if they are needed.
9. Save and print the worksheet.
10. Print a second copy displaying formulas. After the formulas are on the screen, adjust the column widths.

    Checkpoint:
Cell C12	$4,355,345.00
Cell C15	$717,830.00
Cell C17	$430,698.00
Cell C19	$3.825

Assignment 7.5

The Moonbit Coffee Stand is a coffee shop with one location. The coffee shop has completed its monthly reports. You are to format those reports and use the data to prepare a quarterly report.
1. Open the **Ch7 As5** workbook and save it as **Assig 7-5**.
2. Click in the worksheet tabs to see the data that has been entered.
3. Complete and format the worksheets.
    - Click in the tab titled **Quarterly Report**. Hold down the **Shift** key and click in **December**. All four worksheets are selected.

- Enter the following information in the four worksheets:

	A
7	
8	Coffee
9	Flavored Coffee
10	Specialty Coffee
11	Iced Coffee
12	Flavored Soda
13	Total

- In cell A16, key **Prepared by** followed by your name.
- Format the two-line heading (in rows 2 and 3) for bold font, 14 point. Use in-cell editing to further enhance the title if you wish. (The name of company the will be added later.)
- Click in a monthly sheet since there are more columns to format in the monthly sheets than there are in the quarterly sheet. Format the column titles in row 7 for bold, wrapped text, and center alignment both vertically and horizontally. Place a bold border under the cells. Format the total in cell G7 for a 45-degree orientation and left alignment.
- With the four sheets still selected, place the file name in the footer.
- In Print Preview, set a top margin of about 2" and a left margin of about 1".
- Ungroup the sheets. Click in all of the worksheets to view the changes.
4. Format the quarterly sheet.
    - Use WordArt to enter the company name, **Moonbit Coffee Stand**, in row 1 of the Quarterly Report sheet. Adjust the row height so the art fits. Use a font size no larger than 20.
    - Copy the art to the other three sheets.
    - Group the three monthly worksheets.
    - Highlight the range to be added, B8:G13, and select AutoSum. The amounts on each worksheet are located in the same range and have been added in one step. Click in the worksheets to check their accuracy.
    - Format this range correctly for currency. Do not include decimals.
    - Format for appropriate borders on the total row.
5. Complete the quarterly report.
    - Select only the **October** sheet. Highlight the total column (G8:G12) and select a copy command.
    - Select the **Quarterly Report** sheet. Paste the October totals in the October column, beginning with cell B8. (Use Paste Special.)
    - Repeat with the November and December amounts.
    - Complete the totals in row 13 and column E.
    - Format the column labels in the Quarterly Report sheet for an angled orientation of about 45 degrees and left alignment.
    - Format the Quarterly Report sheet correctly. All amounts are currency and should be formatted for zero decimal places. Check the format for numbers, totals, and borders.
6. In cell A18 of the Quarterly Report sheet, key **Located in Seattle, Washington**. Use the Fill Across Worksheets feature to copy the information to the other sheets.
7. In the Quarterly Report sheet, merge and center the contents of rows 2 and 3 across all columns.
8. Group the three monthly sheets. Merge and center the contents of rows 2 and 3 across all columns.
9. Check to be sure all of the formats are accurate and appropriate and the spelling is correct.

10. Save and print all the worksheets.
11. Print a copy with the formulas displayed.

   Checkpoint:

Quarterly Report	Total of Totals	$236,241
October	Central Avenue Total	$12,744
November	Jefferson Square Total	$15,076
December	Total of Totals	$84,142

Assignment 7.6

You will prepare a mileage summary for a fleet of cars. You will determine the mileage of each car and the cost of gasoline used. You will then format the worksheet.

1. Open to a new Excel workbook.
2. Enter the following information:

	A	B	C	D	E
1	Fleet A				
2	Mileage Summary				
3	28-Jul-98				
4					
5	Price per Gallon	$1.27			
6					
7	Vehicle Number	Miles	Gallons Used	Miles Per Gallon	Cost
8					
9	30	387	16.5		
10	31	298	15.2		
11	32	283	12.6		
12	33	583	28		
13	34	192	10.5		

3. Save the workbook as **Assig 7-6**.
4. Complete the worksheet.
   - Complete the miles per gallon in column D. It is determined by dividing the miles by the gallons used.
   - Complete the cost in column E. This is the gallons used multiplied by the price per gallon.
   - In cell A15, key **Total**. In row 15, enter the totals for columns B, C, and E. Format the row in a style of your choice. Format cell A15 in a style of your choice.
5. Format the worksheet.
   - Place the current date in cell A3. Format it in the month, day, and year style.
   - Format the three-line heading in a style of your choice. At the very least, choose different fonts, sizes, alignment, borders, and patterns.
   - Format the labels for bold. Use wrapped text and a rotated orientation. Adjust column widths and row heights and alignment.
   - Use number formats appropriately. Display gallons used with one decimal place and miles per gallon with three decimal places.
   - The Cost column (E) should be formatted correctly for money amounts.
   - Use shading, borders, and colors of your choice.

- Adjust the column widths.
- Place your name in cell A18.
- Adjust the margins so the worksheet is centered on the page.
6. Check the format and appearance of the worksheet. Place the file name in the header.
7. Check the spelling in the worksheet.
8. Save and print the worksheet.
9. Print a copy with the formulas displayed.
10. Print a worksheet that shows only the vehicle number, the miles traveled, and the miles per gallon.

Checkpoint:
    Cell D9   23.455
    Cell E9 $20.96

Case Problem 7

Part 1

Your instructor has asked you to prepare a worksheet that will be used to enter grades for the class you are taking. Use a three-line title that includes the name of the class, your instructor's name, and the quarter/term you are taking the class.

You will have four tests and four quizzes to be entered. Each test has 100 possible points; each quiz has 25 possible points. You will want to show the total points earned on tests and quizzes. Your instructor also wants to know the percentage of total points each student earned.

Prepare a written plan of your worksheet to submit with the completed sheet.

The points each student earned are listed below. Enter your name for the student who is listed as **You**.

	Test 1	Test 2	Test 3	Test 4	Quiz 1	Quiz 2	Quiz 3	Quiz 4
Ron Jenson	87	90	84	96	22	24	23	19
Louis Langford	79	84	85	90	19	17	20	23
Paula Newton	69	77	88	76	23	23	24	20
Linda Paulson	90	84	93	83	20	24	17	23
You	98	89	97	100	24	23	20	25
Jackie Rush	97	84	73	80	17	23	23	17
John Twink	84	93	79	71	23	22	20	17
Jill Vincent	74	82	76	83	24	19	24	23
Bob Watson	82	96	82	90	22	24	22	24

Save the workbook as **Case 7**. Print the worksheet on one page. Check the format and appearance of the worksheet. Print another copy that shows the formulas you used so your instructor can proofread the accuracy of the worksheet.

Part 2

Your instructor was pleased with your worksheet. Now you are asked to print a summary report. Prepare a report that lists each student, the total number of points, and the percentage of total points. (Use Hide Columns.)

Checkpoint:
    Ron Jenson scores 89.0%.
    Bob Watson scores 88.4%.

Chapter 8

Large Worksheet Tips, Page Setup, and Printing Techniques

Objectives

1. Open several worksheets and arrange them on the screen.
2. Split a large worksheet into sections (panes) and freeze column and row labels.
3. Use the Page Setup dialog box to adjust the placement of a worksheet and create custom headers and footers.
4. Examine the print options in the Print dialog box.

Introduction

It is difficult to work with large worksheets when only a small portion of the worksheet is available on the screen. Excel allows you to manipulate windows so other sections of a worksheet or different worksheets can be viewed at the same time. By viewing two different sections of a large worksheet, it is easier to work with data that is widely separated on the worksheet.

The Page Setup dialog box provides several choices regarding the way a spreadsheet looks and its placement on the printed page. A worksheet can be printed with the wide side of the paper as the top, margins can be changed, and headers and footers can be customized. A worksheet may be printed in the center of the paper or with gridlines between cells. Large worksheets can be reduced in size to fit on one page. Labels can be printed on each page of a large worksheet, as can a header or a footer.

At the end of this chapter you may delete Ch06 and Ch07.

Working with Worksheet Windows

Excel provides several methods to make it easy to work in two or more worksheets or workbooks at the same time. The worksheets can be in the same workbook or in different workbooks.

Viewing Different Worksheets at the Same Time

Viewing different copies of the same workbook provides a way to work in different sections of a large worksheet or in different sheets of the book. When additional copies of the same workbook are accessed, Excel places a colon and a number after the title (:1, :2, :3, etc.). In Figure 8.1, the workbook titled Exer 7:1 has a checkmark before it in the Window menu, indicating it is the active workbook. While there are three copies of Exer 7 open, only one is active.

Figure 8.1   Window Menu

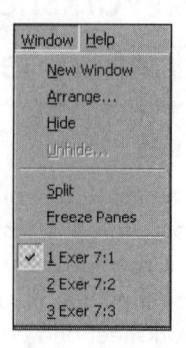

Copies of the same workbook are opened by selecting New Window from the Window menu. The copies may then be arranged by selecting Arrange from the Window menu. The *Arrange Windows* dialog box opens (Figure 8.2) providing arrangement choices for the open workbooks.

Figure 8.2   Arrange Windows Dialog Box

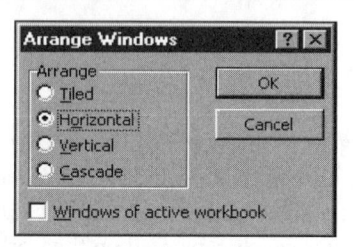

Selecting Tiled in the Arrange Windows dialog box arranges all the open workbooks so parts of each are seen (Figure 8.3). The tiled arrangement displays a section of each worksheet on the screen.

Figure 8.3   Tiled Windows; Copy Number 3 of the Workbook Is Active

Selecting Horizontal displays the open books horizontally. Figure 8.4 shows three workbooks arranged horizontally.

Figure 8.4   Horizontal Arrangement—Copy Number 3 of the Worksheet Is Active

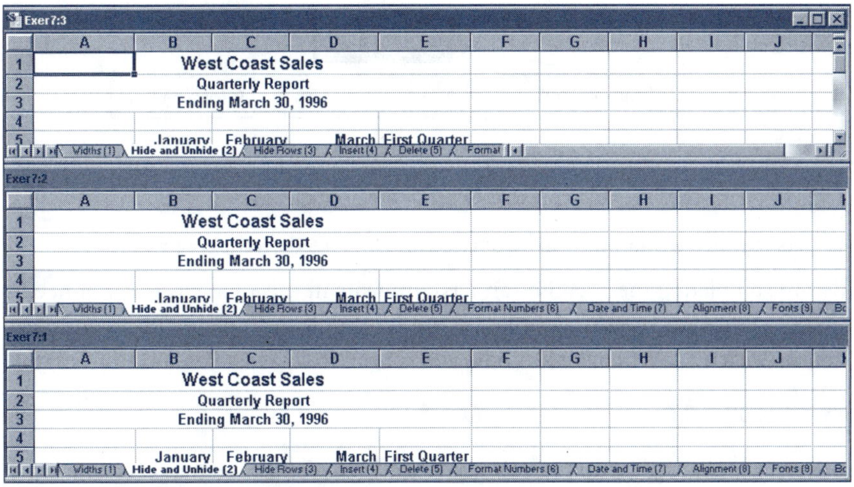

A Vertical arrangement shows the open windows vertically on the screen (Figure 8.5). To view different sheets of the same book, click in the sheet tabs at the bottom.

Figure 8.5   Vertical Arrangement; Copy Number 3 of the Workbook Is Active

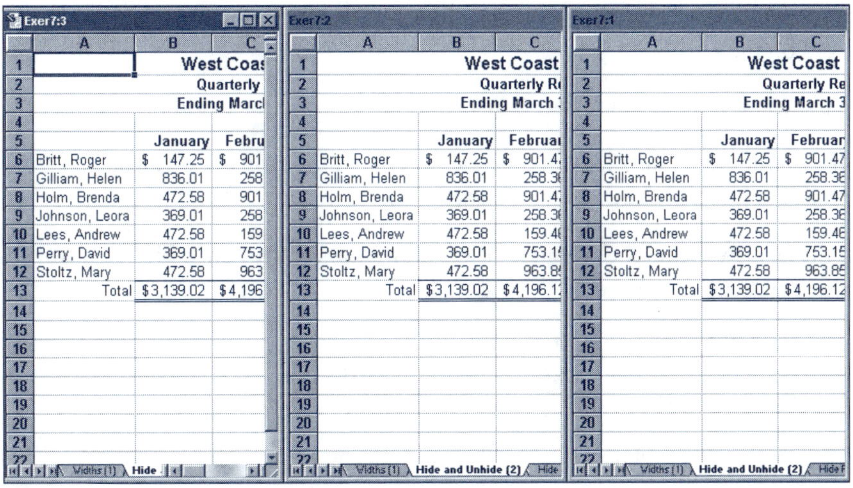

Although several copies of a workbook may be open at the same time, only one is active; the colored title bar indicates the active workbook. To select another copy, click anywhere in its window to activate it. In Figure 8.5, workbook Exer7:3 is the active workbook.

Closing Workbook Windows

To close one of the open workbooks, click the Close button (shown in Figure 8.6) in the upper-right corner of the title bar.

Figure 8.6   Minimize, Maximize, and Close Buttons

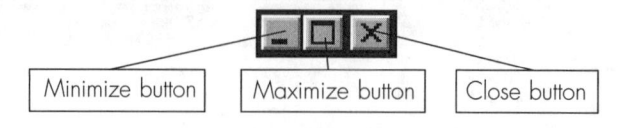

Exercise 8.1   Opening and Arranging Workbooks

Worksheets within a workbook will be opened and arranged on the screen.

Note: Before completing the exercises and assignments in this chapter, you will need to expand the Chapter 8 files on your Student Data Disk. In Windows Explorer, locate the Chapter 8 file and double-click on it. When the files have been expanded, you will be able to access them from Excel.

1   Open workbook **Ch8 Exer** and save it as **Exer 8**.

2   Select sheets 1–5. In Page Setup place the file name in the footer and the sheet name in the header.

3   Select **Sheet1**. This is a large worksheet and probably extends beyond what is displayed on the screen.

View two areas of the worksheet.

4   From the **Window** menu, select the **New Window** command. This opens a second copy of **Exer 8**. The title bar indicates that two workbooks are open, **Exer 8:1** and **Exer 8:2**.

5   From the **Window** menu, select **Arrange**. Click on **Tiled**, then **OK**. Two copies of the workbook are arranged on the screen.

6   From the **Window** menu, click **New Window**. A third copy of the workbook opens.

Note: If your monitor is small, each workbook may not have available scroll bars. If so, just click in the worksheets to activate them for instructions 7–13.

7   From the **Window** menu, click **Arrange**. Select the **Horizontal** view. Click **OK**. Three workbooks are open in horizontal view.

8   Click in workbook **:3** to activate it.

9   Use the scroll bars so rows 5 and 6 are visible.

10 Click in workbook **:2** to activate it. Scroll so rows 10 and 11 are visible.

11 Return to the **Arrange Windows** dialog box and select the **Vertical** view.

12 With workbook **:2** active, click on the **Sheet2** tab. Another worksheet of the same workbook opens.

Exercise 8.1—Opening and Arranging Workbooks   269

13 Click in workbook **:3** to make it active. Click on the **Sheet3** tab. (You may need to use the tab scrolling buttons to access it.)

14 Close workbooks **:2** and **:3** and maximize the remaining book.

15 Save and close the remaining book.

Opening Additional Workbooks

Several different workbook files may be open at the same time. A list of open workbooks is at the bottom of the Window pull-down menu, shown in Figure 8.7.

In this illustration, Ch7a3 is active, as is indicated by the checkmark. This is the workbook displayed on the screen. The other workbooks are open, but only the one with the checkmark is active.

Figure 8.7   List of Open Workbooks

To select a different workbook, click on the name of the workbook in the Window menu. Think of this as having several documents on your desk. Only the top document is seen. To see another document, move it to the top. Excel moves an active workbook to the top (screen) when you select it in the Window menu.

To open different workbooks, select Open from the File menu or click on the Open button and select the workbook. As additional workbooks are opened, they appear on the screen, covering those previously opened.

Figure 8.8   Showing Windows of an Active Workbook

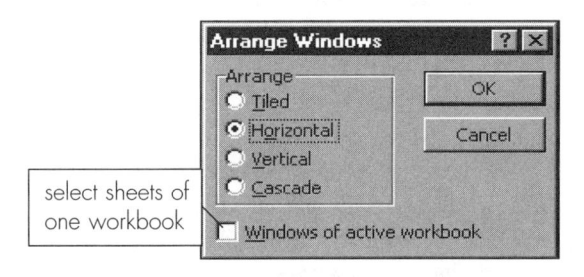

select sheets of one workbook

All open workbooks may be shown on the screen at the same time by selecting the appropriate option in the Arrange Windows dialog box. If only the worksheets of the active workbook are to be viewed, click in the check box at the bottom of the dialog box shown in Figure 8.8.

Exercise 8.2   Viewing Workbook Windows

Workbooks and worksheets will be opened and arranged on the screen.

1. Open workbooks **Exer 8** and **Ch8 As1**. Arrange the open documents in the tiled view.
2. Use the scroll bars in each open window to move horizontally and vertically in the workbook.
3. Open the workbook **Ch8 As2**. Arrange the open workbooks vertically.
4. Click in the **Exer 8** window to activate it. Select **New Window** from the **Window** menu.
5. Repeat step 4 to open a third copy of Exer 8. You have five workbooks open; three are copies of Exer 8.
6. Arrange the workbooks in tiled view.
7. Click in copy **:2** of **Exer 8**. From the **Window** menu, select **Arrange**; then click in the **Windows of active workbook** check box. This arranges the three copies of the Exer 8 workbook so they are the only ones visible on the screen.
8. Close all workbooks on the screen. Do not save changes.

Splitting a Worksheet Window into Panes

Worksheet windows may be split into *window panes* so that up to four different areas of a worksheet are visible at the same time. In working with large worksheets, it is easier to enter and edit data when the row or column headings can be seen. When the worksheet is split into panes, scroll bars are used to access different sections of the worksheet.

At the top right and bottom left of the scroll bars are the *split bars*. They are small rectangles by the scroll arrows, shown in Figure 8.9.

When moving the mouse to the split bar, the pointer becomes a double-sided arrow with a double line. Figure 8.10 shows the arrow in both the horizontal and vertical split bars.

Figure 8.9   Split Bars on Scroll Bars

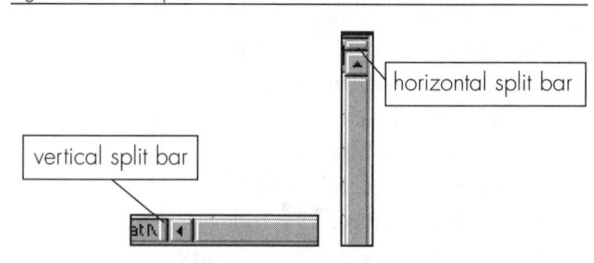

Figure 8.10   Double-Sided Arrows on Split Bar

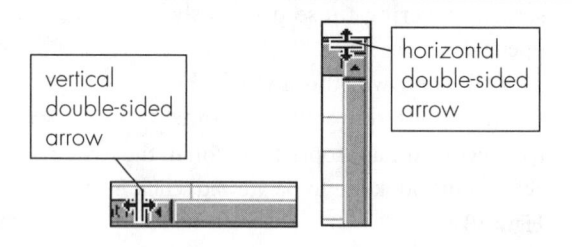

Click and drag the double arrow into the worksheet to split it into two panes. The split bar now extends through the worksheet.

Another method to split a worksheet into panes is to select the Split command from the Window menu, shown in Figure 8.11.

Figure 8.11   Selecting Split from the Window Menu

The worksheet splits into four panes, allowing editing in nonadjacent areas. Figure 8.12 shows a large worksheet split into panes.

Figure 8.12   Worksheet Split into Panes

The worksheet automatically splits in the middle. To rearrange the split area, move the mouse to the split bar and drag the bar to a new location. When the mouse is in the split bar, it takes the double-headed shape shown in Figure 8.13.

The window panes may be resized; click in the split bar and drag the pane to show a larger or smaller section of the worksheet. Move the mouse to the intersection of the split bars to resize both the horizontal and vertical splits at the same time.

To remove the split panes, select Remove Split from the Window menu, shown in Figure 8.14, or drag the split bars back to the top and left edges of the active worksheet. The fastest way to remove a split bar, however, is to double-click in it.

Figure 8.13   Split Bars

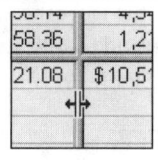

Figure 8.14   Remove Split Command on the Window Menu

Exercise 8.3   Using Split Panes in a Large Worksheet

You will work with a large worksheet, split it into panes, and scroll within each pane.

1   Open workbook **Exer 8**. Rename **Sheet1** to **Panes**. Resave **Exer 8**.

Split the worksheet into panes.

2   From the **Window** menu, select **Split**. The worksheet splits into four panes.

3   There are two scroll bars at the right side of the worksheet. In the top scroll bar, click once on the down arrow. Row 2 is now the first visible row. The section of the worksheet below the split line does not change.

4   There are two scroll bars at the bottom of the screen. In the left scroll bar, click once on the right arrow. Column B is now the first visible column; the section of the worksheet to the right of the split line does not change.

5   Use the scroll bars to view different areas of the worksheet. You can see how the scroll bars and split panes allow access to other areas of the worksheet.

6   Move the mouse to the horizontal split bar; click and drag the mouse up to hide two rows.

7   Scroll in the bottom worksheet so the first visible row is row 10.

8   Move the vertical split bar to the left edge of the worksheet. You now have two panes of the worksheet.

Exercise 8.3—Using Split Panes in a Large Worksheet

9 Use both the horizontal and vertical scroll bars of each pane to scroll to different areas of the worksheet.

10 Double-click on the split bar to remove the split.

11 From **Window**, select **Split**.

12 Move the mouse to the intersection of the split bars and drag to a new location.

13 From **Window**, select **Remove Split**. The original view of the worksheet appears on the screen.

14 Close the workbook without saving changes.

Freezing Panes

Cells may be "frozen" to remain on the screen at all times. The frozen area cannot be changed or moved, but the rest of the worksheet can be accessed by using the scroll bars. With a large worksheet, freezing cells containing labels is a good idea because this allows the labels to be visible at all times and makes it easier to enter information located far from the labels. Excel calls this process freezing panes.

To freeze panes, select the cell that is immediately below and to the right of the cells to be frozen. Then select the *Freeze Panes* command from the Window menu. Figure 8.15 shows a worksheet when the Freeze Panes command is selected. The frozen area is indicated by solid lines. Cell E7 is selected; rows 1–6 in columns A–D are frozen and will remain visible at all times. The rest of the worksheet will scroll, but the frozen area always remains on the screen and cannot be scrolled.

Figure 8.15   Pane Frozen at Cell E7

	A	B	C	D	E
1					
2					
3					
4					
5			Hours Worked		Pay Rate
6		Regular	Overtime	Total		Reg
7						
8		40	2	42	8.75

Figure 8.16 shows the entire worksheet. The labels in rows 5–6 in columns A–D are frozen and remain on the screen at all times. All rows below row 6 and all columns beginning with column E can be accessed. In Figure 8.16, notice that columns A:D show, but columns E:I do not; also, row 7 is not visible.

Figure 8.16   Worksheet with Panes Frozen at Cell E7 Scrolled to a Different Section

	A	B	C	D	J	K	L	M	N	O	P
3											
4											
5			Hours Worked			Deductions					
6	Name	Regular	Overtime	Total	FICA	Med Ins	Other	Tot Deductions			
8		40	2	42							
9											
10											
11	Dahl, Ashley	39.0	0.0	39.0	25.69	30	30	85.69			
12	Pudney, Joshua	40.0	4.0	44.0	31.19	30	30	91.19			

To return to a regular worksheet view, select Unfreeze Panes from the Window menu.

Exercise 8.4   Freezing Panes

Edit the worksheet by freezing panes and scrolling through the rest of the worksheet.

1 Open to the **Panes** worksheet of the **Exer 8** workbook.

Freeze labels.

2 Select cell A1 if not already selected. In the **Window** menu, select **Freeze Panes**. Note the row and column where the solid freeze lines are located.

3 Click on the down arrow. Notice that the rows below the solid horizontal line (indicating the freeze area) scroll while those above the line remain stationary.

4 Click once on the right arrow of the bottom scroll bar. Notice the columns to the right of the bold vertical freeze line move while those to the left remain stationary.

5 In the **Window** menu, select **Unfreeze Panes**. Then click in cell B7.

6 From the **Window** menu, click on **Freeze Panes**. Solid lines appear on the worksheet.

7 Use the horizontal and vertical scroll bars to access different parts of the worksheet.

Edit the worksheet.

8 Scroll in the worksheet so cell C10 is just below the freeze lines.

9 Change the **Overtime** entry for **K. Crewse** to **.5** and complete the entry.

10 In cell J16, change the **Federal Income Tax** for **K. Leendertse** to **79.50** and complete the entry.

Unfreeze panes.

11 From the **Window** menu, select **Unfreeze Panes**.

12 In cell A34 key **Prepared by** followed by your name. Format it for Arial font, left alignment, and not bold.

13 Save and print the worksheet. It may take more than one page to print the entire worksheet. At the top write "Exercise 8.4."

The Page Setup Dialog Box

Choices in the way a worksheet is printed on the page are made in the *Page Setup* dialog box, shown in Figure 8.17. It is accessed from the File menu.

Figure 8.17   Page Tab in Page Setup Dialog Box

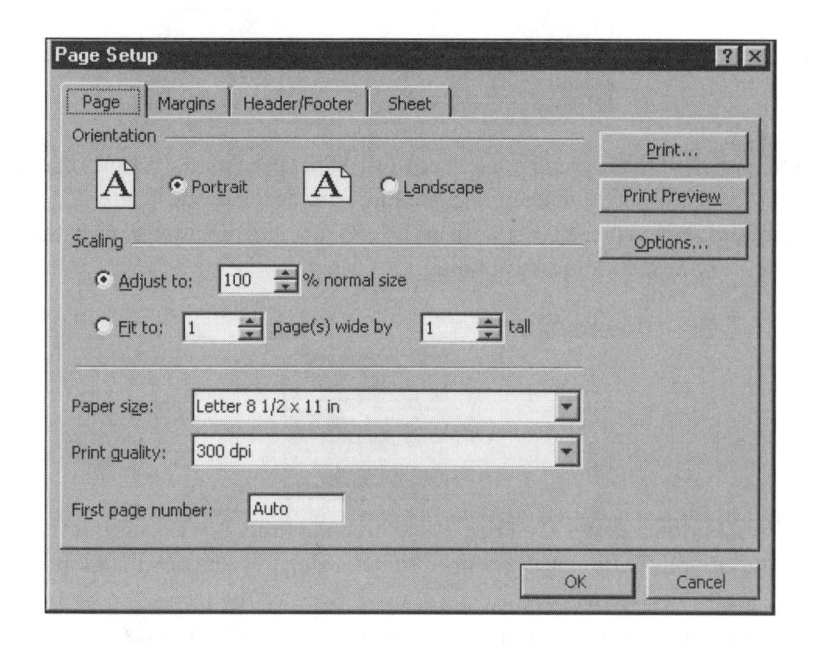

There are four tabs across the top: Page, Margins, Header/Footer, and Sheet. Each tab is used to adjust specific aspects of the worksheet.

Page Tab

In the *Page tab*, shown in Figure 8.17, choices are made for orientation, scaling, paper size, print quality, and page numbering.

The top section controls *orientation*. This refers to how the worksheet will be printed. An icon beside each button illustrates the way a worksheet will be placed on the page, shown in Figure 8.18. When Portrait is selected, the worksheet will print with the short side of the paper as the top (*portrait style*). When Landscape is selected, the worksheet will print with the long side of the paper as the top (*landscape style*).

Figure 8.18   Orientation Buttons in Page Tab of Page Setup Dialog Box

Scaling allows a worksheet to be adjusted so it prints on more or fewer pages than it would at normal size, or a certain number of pages can be specified for the printed work. By using the scaling feature, it is possible to place a rather large worksheet on one page. Select the Fit to option to automatically fit a worksheet on a specified number of pages. In Figure 8.19, the Scaling section shows the settings for a worksheet to be scaled to fit on one page.

Figure 8.19   Scaling Section in Page Tab of Page Setup Dialog Box

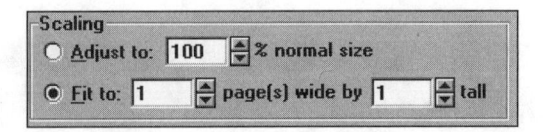

At the bottom of the Page tab is a text box titled First page number. Page numbers automatically begin at one, but if a different starting page number is needed, indicate it here.

The buttons at the right edge of the dialog box (Figure 8.20) are used to print the document, access Print Preview, or provide additional options.

Figure 8.20   Buttons in Page Setup Dialog Box

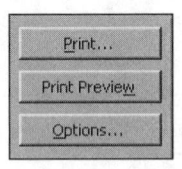

The Print button accesses the Print dialog box; the Print Preview button is used to open Print Preview. The Options button at the bottom of the dialog box accesses the Options dialog box. The options may vary depending on the printer used. Because the computers in most classrooms are defaulted for their particular setting, this text will not explore these options.

Exercise 8.5   Using the Page Tab of the Page Setup Dialog Box

You will print a worksheet and use Page Setup to change the orientation and scaling.

1   Open the **Panes** worksheet in the workbook **Exer 8**.

2   Click on the Print Preview button. Note that the worksheet will print on two or three pages (see the status bar). Close Print Preview.

3   Access the **Page** tab of the **Page Setup** dialog box. Click on the **Landscape** button, then select **Print Preview**. Notice that the worksheet still takes more than one page.

4   Click on **Setup** to return to the **Page** tab of the **Page Setup** dialog box.

5   In the **Scaling** section, click in the button by **Fit to**. Be sure it is **1 page(s) wide by 1 tall**.

6   Click **OK** to return to Print Preview. Now the worksheet fits on one page.

7   Close Print Preview.

Readjust the three-line title.

8   Merge and center the three-line title over the entire one-page worksheet.

Print the worksheet.

9   Print the worksheet. At the top of the worksheet write "Exercise 8.5."

10   Close the worksheet without saving changes.

Margins Tab

The *Margins tab* (shown in Figure 8.21) of the Page Setup dialog box is used to change the margins and placement of a worksheet.

Excel defaults to margins of 1" on the top and bottom and .75" on each side. Unless changed, these margins will be applied to all worksheets. To change the margins, simply key the desired size for the margin or click on the up or down arrows beside the margin numbers to select other sizes.

The margins for the header and footer are determined by using the Header and Footer boxes and control the width of the margin before the header or after the footer.

Figure 8.21   Margins Tab of Page Setup Dialog Box

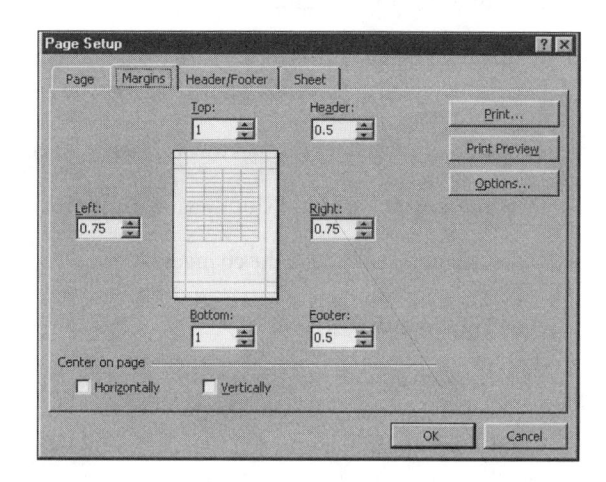

The Center on page section allows the worksheet to be centered horizontally or vertically between the margins. Checking both boxes will position the worksheet in the center of the page.

A preview of the worksheet placement is provided in the center of the Margins tab. As changes are made, an indicator in the preview area shows the place where the margins will change.

Exercise 8.6   Using the Margins Tab of the Page Setup Dialog Box

You will change the margins of a worksheet and print it with new margins. You will also use the Center on page feature.

1   Open workbook **Exer 8**. Rename **Sheet4** to **Margins**.

2   Select the **Margins** tab of the **Page Setup** dialog box. By the text box for the **Top** margin, click on the up arrow until **2.5** displays in the text box. Note in the preview area that a solid line at the top indicates the top margin.

3   Double-click in the text box for the **Left** margin. Key **2.5**.

4   In the **Header** and **Footer** boxes, change the settings to **1**. Either use the arrows or key the choice.

5   Click on the **Print** button, then **OK**. At the top write "Print 1."

6   Return to the **Margins** worksheet. Again open the **Page Setup** dialog box to the **Margins** tab.

7   Change the **Top** margin to **1**, the **Left** margin to **0.75**, and the **Header** and **Footer** margins to **0.5**.

8   In the **Center on page** section, click on **Horizontally**.

9 Click on the **Print Preview** button. Note that the worksheet is centered horizontally on the page but still has a one inch top margin.

10 Click on the **Setup** button and return to the **Margins** tab of the **Page Setup** dialog box. In the **Center on page** section, select **Vertically**. (Both **Horizontally** and **Vertically** are selected.) Then click **OK**.

11 Access Print Preview to see that the worksheet is centered.

12 Print the worksheet from Print Preview. At the top write "Print 2."

13 Close the workbook. Save the changes.

Header/Footer Tab

The *Header/Footer tab*, shown in Figure 8.22, is used to indicate the text for the header and/or footer. *Headers* print at the top of each page, and *footers* print at the bottom.

Although headers and footers have been used throughout this text, they can be customized. Below the Header and Footer sections is a text box and an arrow. The text box displays the selected header or footer; the arrow is used to access a list of built-in choices, shown in Figure 8.23. Although all choices are shown in the illustration, scroll bars are needed to access them in the Header and Footer sections.

Some of the choices for headers and footers include the page number, file name, worksheet name, or name of the preparer (determined by licensee of software). The same choices are available for both the header and the footer.

Figure 8.22 Header/Footer Tab of Page Setup Dialog Box

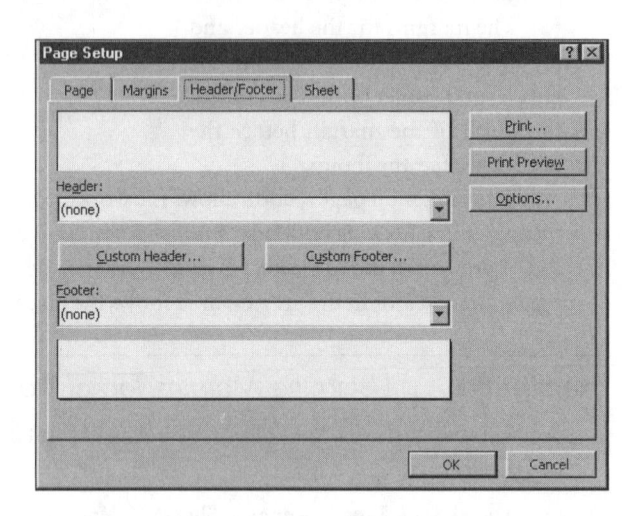

Figure 8.23 Header/Footer Built-in Choices

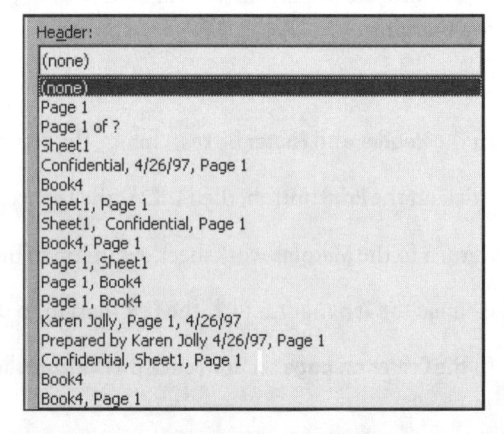

A customized header or footer is used so other information can be placed on a worksheet. The **Custom Header** and **Custom Footer** buttons are used for customization. Click on Custom Header; the Header dialog box opens (Figure 8.24). The Header and Footer dialog boxes are identical except for the title bar (Header or Footer).

Figure 8.24   Header Dialog Box

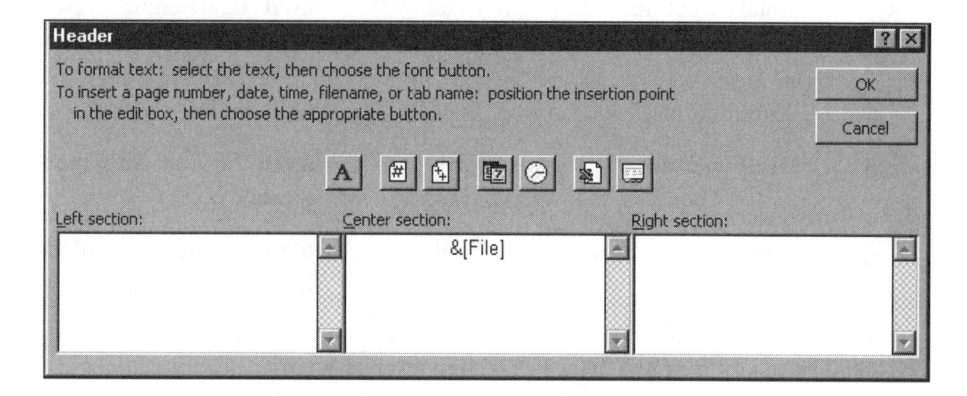

The Header (or Footer) dialog box contains three text boxes: Left section, Center section, and Right section. All text entered in the left box is aligned at the left margin; text entered in the right box is aligned at the right margin; and text entered in the center box is centered.

Headers and footers often include the date, the page number, the time, and/or the file name. These frequently used header/footer choices can be entered by using special *code buttons* available in the Header (or Footer) dialog box. Using a code button eliminates the need to manually key information into a worksheet. After a code button is selected, the code will appear in the text box beginning with an ampersand (&) and followed by the name. Code buttons are identified in Figure 8.25.

Figure 8.25   Header/Footer Code Buttons

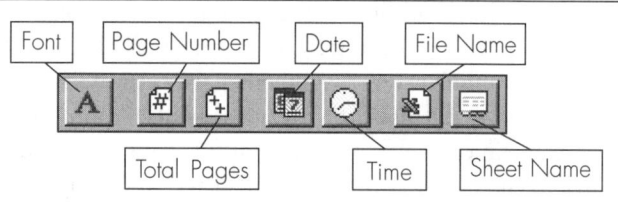

The chart in Figure 8.26 shows the Header/Footer code buttons, their names, the codes, and the actions they automate.

Figure 8.26 Header/Footer Buttons, Codes, and Actions

Button	Button Name	Code	Action
	Font button		Opens Font dialog box
	Page Number button	&[Page]	Inserts page number
	Total Pages button	&[Pages]	Inserts total number of pages
	Date button	&[Date]	Inserts current date
	Time button	&[Time]	Inserts current time
	File Name button	&[File]	Inserts the file name of the active workbook
	Sheet Name button	&[Tab]	Inserts the sheet name of the active worksheet

To insert the page number at the left margin of the header or footer, open the Header or Footer dialog box. Then click the mouse in the Left section text box; an insertion point blinks in the text box. Click on the Page Number button . The code, &[Page], appears in the text box. Figure 8.27 shows the page number code in the Left section box. If the word "Page" should be printed before the page number, key the word "Page" and a space before inserting the code.

Figure 8.27 Page Code in Left Section Text Box

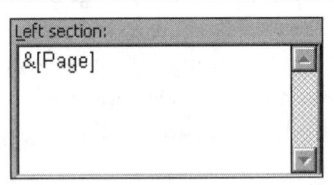

Left section:
&[Page]

The page number of the worksheet will now print on every page at the left margin of the header or footer. Pages are numbered consecutively when using the page code. If three pages are printed, the pages will automatically number 1, 2, 3, eliminating the need to manually number pages.

The ***Total Pages button*** inserts the code that prints the total number of pages of a worksheet. Page numbers are sometimes displayed as "Page 1 of 12," with 12 being the total number of pages. This page number style is entered by keying the word "Page" and a space, clicking on the ***Page Number button*** , then keying the word "of" with the appropriate spaces, and clicking on the Total Pages button . The header information will read "Page &[Page] of &[Pages]" and the codes indicate where the page numbers will be placed. The correct page numbers are substituted for the code as a worksheet is printed.

When the ***Time button*** and ***Date button*** are used, the current time or date prints in the header or footer as a volatile date. Using time and date is useful when printing drafts of a worksheet. Printing the date and time on each worksheet makes it is easy to determine which is most recent. To print a static time or static date, key it in as text; don't use the code buttons.

The ***File Name button*** is used to print the saved name of the workbook; the ***Sheet Name button*** is used to print the name of the worksheet tab.

To delete an entry in the header or footer, highlight the section and press the Delete key on the keyboard.

Figure 8.28 shows a header created in Excel. The page number and total pages are at the left side of the header; the sheet name is centered in the header; and the date and time are shown at the right side of the header.

Figure 8.28   Excel Header

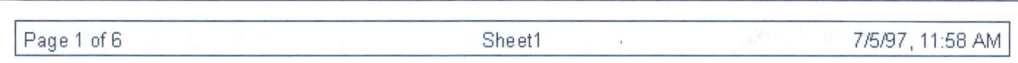

Page 1 of 6	Sheet1	7/5/97, 11:58 AM

Figure 8.29 shows the codes used to create the header in Figure 8.28.

Figure 8.29   Excel Header Codes

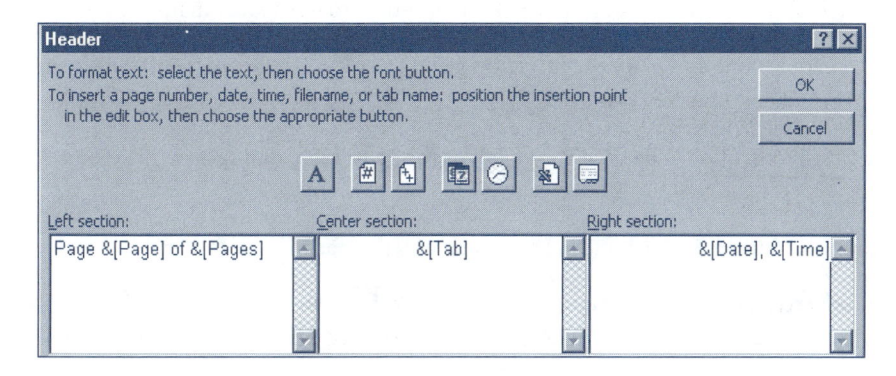

```
Header                                                        [?][X]
To format text: select the text, then choose the font button.        [  OK  ]
To insert a page number, date, time, filename, or tab name: position the insertion point
in the edit box, then choose the appropriate button.                 [Cancel]

                    [A] [#] [+] [🗐] [🕒] [📄] [📋]

Left section:              Center section:            Right section:
Page &[Page] of &[Pages]   &[Tab]                     &[Date], &[Time]
```

Text can be keyed into headers and footers. In the Header or Footer dialog box, click in any of the text boxes and key in the desired header or footer information.

The font or font style of header and footer information can be changed. Highlight the text or code to be formatted; then click the **Font button** [A] to open the Font dialog box. Select the fonts and styles for the text and click OK; these style changes will be applied to the selected text in each header or footer printed.

To add a second line to a header or footer, hold down Shift while pressing Enter on the keyboard. Then key the additional information on the second line.

Clicking OK sets the new header or footer choices. Cancel restores the header or footer to its previous settings.

Exercise 8.7   Customizing Headers and Footers

Custom headers and footers will be added to a worksheet. Because this exercise provides practice in using headers and footers, several different styles will be placed in the same worksheet. However, using a comparable number of formats in one worksheet is not recommended.

1 Open to the **Margins** worksheet in the **Exer 8** workbook.

2 Open the **Header/Footer** tab of the **Page Setup** dialog box.

Customize the header and the footer.

3. Click on the **Custom Header** button. The insertion point is blinking in the **Left section** text box.

4. Highlight the text in the **Center section** text box and press `Delete` on the keyboard to delete the text.

5. Click in the **Left section** text box. Click on the Date button. **&[Date]** is entered into the left text box.

6. Click in the **Center section** text box, then click on the Time button. **&[Time]** is entered in the text box. Press the `Space Bar` on the keyboard two times, then click on the File Name button. **&[File]** is entered in the text box.

7. Click in the **Right section** text box. Enter your name and then select it.

8. Click in the Font button `A` to open the **Font** dialog box. Format your name in **12** point type, **Bold Italic** (if available). Select a different font. Click **OK** to return to the **Header** dialog box.

9. Deselect your name and place the insertion point after it. Hold down `Shift` while pressing `Enter`. This begins a new line. Key **Exercise 8.7**.

10. Click **OK** to return to the **Header/Footer** tab of the **Page Setup** dialog box.

Customize the footer.

11. Click on the **Custom Footer** button. Delete any entries made in the footer.

12. In the **Left section** text box, key **Page**, press the `Space Bar`, then click on the Page Number button. Press the `Space Bar` once. Type **of** and press the `Space Bar` once. Click in the Total Pages button. The code **&[Pages]** is entered in the text box.

13. Click the mouse in the **Center section** text box. Type in the name of your instructor. Highlight the name. Click in the Font button `A` to open the **Font** dialog box. Format the name for **9** point **Italic**. Click **OK**.

14. Click in the **Right section** text box and then in the Sheet Name button. Highlight the sheet name code and click on the Font button `A`. Change the font to **18** point.

15. Close the Footer and Page Setup dialog boxes.

16. Save and print the worksheet.

Sheet Tab

The *Sheet tab*, shown in Figure 8.30, is used to provide additional instructions for printing. For example, only a section of a worksheet may be printed; labels may be printed on each page of multiple-page worksheets; specific formats such as gridlines, notes, etc. may be printed; and the printing order of multiple-page documents can be chosen.

At the top of the Sheet tab is the Print area section. When you want to print only a portion of a worksheet, indicate the print range in this area. You may also use the Collapse Dialog button to move the dialog box out of the way. Then drag through the print area and restore the dialog box to the screen.

Figure 8.30   Sheet Tab of Page Setup Dialog Box

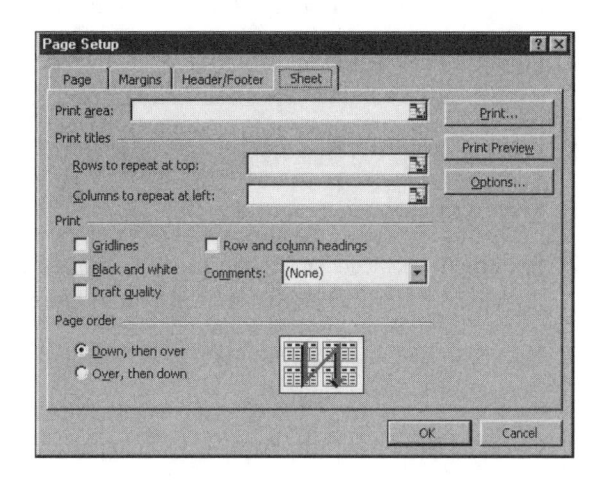

The Print titles section is used to print rows and columns on all pages. When a worksheet is longer than one page, reading the worksheet can be difficult if the column and row labels are not printed on each page. This makes the Print titles section extremely useful. To enter the range, click in the range box. Then click on the Collapse Dialog button and drag through the rows or columns. Then click on the Expand Dialog button. The range of the cells may also be keyed into the text box.

The Print section of the Sheet tab is used for specific print requests. *Gridlines* are the lines that separate cells and will be printed when this check box is selected. Black and white is an option used to print in black and white when a color printer is available. Draft quality is a quick way to print a worksheet for proofreading; gridlines and most graphics do not print when this option is selected. *Row and column headings* are the letters and numbers at the edges of a worksheet that identify the rows and columns, and they can also be printed on a worksheet.

Comments that provide further information about a sheet may be added to individual cells. They often provide specific information about the cell contents and may also be printed on a worksheet. Placement of these comments in a printed worksheet is indicated in the Comments drop-down menu. The two choices are at the bottom of the sheet or on the sheet.

The Page order section at the bottom of the Sheet tab gives instructions on the printing order of a large worksheet. A diagram by the choice indicates the selected printing order.

Exercise 8.8   Using the Sheet Tab of the Page Setup Dialog Box

Worksheets will be printed using some of the choices provided in the Sheet tab of the Page Setup dialog box.

1 Open workbook **Exer 8** to the **Margins** tab.

2 In the **Page Setup** dialog box, select the **Sheet** tab.

284 Chapter 8 Large Worksheet Tips, Page Setup, and Printing Techniques

3. Click on the Collapse Dialog button in the **Print area** section. When the dialog box collapses, drag the mouse through the range A1:E3. Then click on the Expand Dialog button.

4. From the **Page Setup** dialog box, click on the **Print Preview** button. Note that only the three-line title and the headers and footers would print if you selected to print it. Close Print Preview.

5. Rename **Sheet5** to **Large WS**.

6. In cell A55, enter your name.

7. Print the worksheet. Save the printout so you will be able to compare it with the other copies of the worksheet you will print that show row and column labels on every page.

8. Note that the column labels are on rows 5 and 6 and the names of the employees (the row labels) are in column A.

9. Open the **Sheet** tab of the **Page Setup** dialog box.

10. Click in the Collapse Dialog button by the **Rows to repeat at top** section. Drag through rows 5:6 (using the row headings at the left) in the worksheet, then click in the Expand Dialog button.

11. Repeat the procedure in the **Columns to repeat at left** section, and select column A.

12. In the **Page order** section, click **Over, then down**, then click **Down, then over** to see the different ways this worksheet may be printed. Select either of these choices.

13. Print gridlines. In the footer key this text: **Exercise 8.7**.

14. Print the worksheet. Notice that the labels are printed on every page.

15. In the **Page Setup** dialog box, select the **Sheet** tab. Format to print the row and column headings. Access **Print Preview** to see that the headings will print.

16. Save and print the worksheet.

Additional Printing Techniques

The Print Dialog Box

When the Print command is selected, the *Print* dialog box opens (Figure 8.31). Clicking OK immediately begins the printing process, but the Print dialog box provides other options as well.

The Print dialog box identifies the selected printer; the printer in Figure 8.31 is the HP LaserJet 4V. Each printer has its own Print dialog box; yours may look slightly different. However, the basic choices are the same in all Print dialog boxes. If your dialog box is different from the one illustrated, your instructor will provide additional directions.

The Print range section determines which pages to print. The default is to print all pages. In large worksheets, only one or two pages may be needed. Enter the page number of the first needed page in the From box and the page number of the last page needed in the To box. Use the Tab key or the mouse to move the insertion point to these boxes. To print pages 2 and 3, for example, enter 2 in the From box and 3 in the To box.

The Print what section provides choices for printing the Selection, Active sheet(s), or Entire workbook.

Figure 8.31   Print Dialog Box

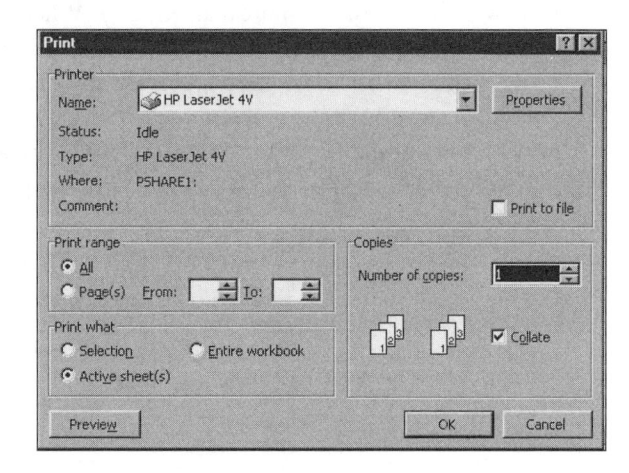

Choosing Selection prints the highlighted portion of the worksheet; Active sheet(s) prints the sheets that are selected; and Entire workbook prints all sheets in the workbook.

Excel prints one copy of a worksheet unless more are requested. The Number of copies box indicates how many copies to print. If more than one copy is needed, enter the number of copies in this box or use the up or down arrows to change the number of copies to print.

The Collate check box is used to organize pages when more than one copy of a document is printed. If this option is selected, a complete copy of one document is printed before the first page of the next copy is printed.

Exercise 8.9   Using the Print Dialog Box

You will use the Print dialog box to make choices about printing.

1 Open workbook **Exer 8** to the **Large WS** tab.

2 Access the **Print** dialog box. Change the **Number of copies** from **1** to **2**.

3 Click in the **From** box; enter **2**. Press `Tab`. A blinking cursor appears in the **To** box.

4 Key **2** in the **To** box. Two copies of page 2 will print.

5 Click on the **Preview** button. Select **Print** in the Print Preview window. At the top write "Print 1." Close Print Preview.

6 Select sheets **2** and **3**. Key your name in cell A2 (it is entered on both sheets). Ungroup the sheets.

7 Open the **Print** dialog box. In the **Print what** section, click on **Entire workbook**. Click **OK**. At the top write "Print 2."

8 Close this workbook without saving changes.

Printing Large Worksheets

Large worksheets print on more than one page. When a worksheet takes more than one page, a dashed line, called the *page break line*, indicates where each page ends. Excel automatically splits the pages between columns and rows; the page breaks are based on the paper size, margin settings, and scaling options. Figure 8.32 shows a vertical page break between columns H and I and a horizontal page break between rows 48 and 49. This worksheet is four pages (at least) long; cell H48 prints on page 1; cell I48 prints on a different page; cell H49 is in a different page; and cell I49 is on still another page.

Figure 8.32   Page Break Lines

	G	H	I	J
46	0.00	331.50	24.86	74.59
47	13.50	373.50	28.01	84.04
48	0.00	330.00	24.75	74.25
49	31.50	271.50	20.36	61.09
50	0.00	350.00	26.25	78.75
51	0.00	237.50	17.81	53.44
52	30.00	350.00	26.25	78.75

page break lines

Page break lines don't automatically show in a worksheet. When working with large worksheets, the page break lines should be made visible. To do this, open the Options dialog box from the Tools menu. Then select the View tab. In the Window options section, select Page breaks.

Adjusting Page Breaks

Page Break Preview offers a visual way to alter automatic page breaks. Access Page Break Preview in the View menu, as shown in Figure 8.33.

Figure 8.33   Selecting Page Break Preview from the View Menu

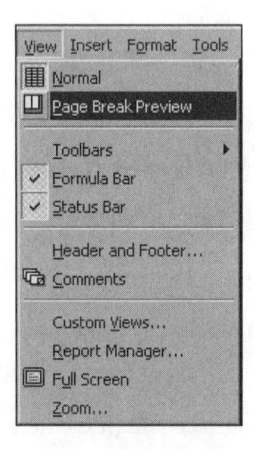

Page Break Preview opens, shown in Figure 8.34. The page breaks are indicated by blue lines on the screen, and each page is shown in reduced size.

Figure 8.34   Viewing Page Break Preview

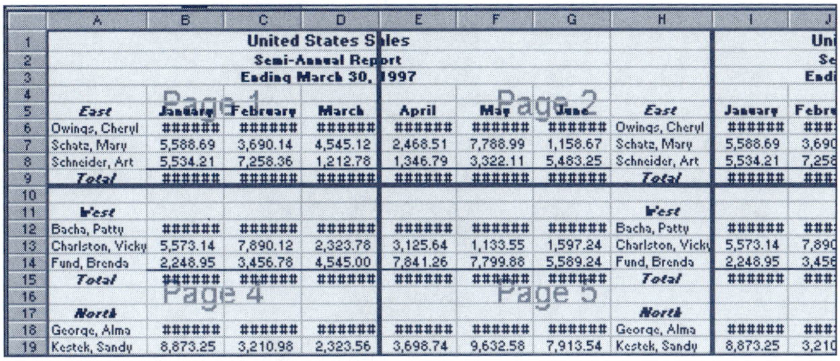

Page breaks can be adjusted by clicking and dragging the mouse. The page break lines move and the page indicators adjust. Page breaks indicated by a solid line like the ones in Figure 8.34 are manually adjusted page breaks; automatic pages breaks are indicated by a dashed line.

To remove a page break, drag the page break line outside the worksheet window. To remove all **manual page breaks**, right-click any cell of the worksheet and then click **Reset All Page Breaks** on the shortcut menu, shown in Figure 8.35.

Figure 8.35   Resetting All Page Breaks

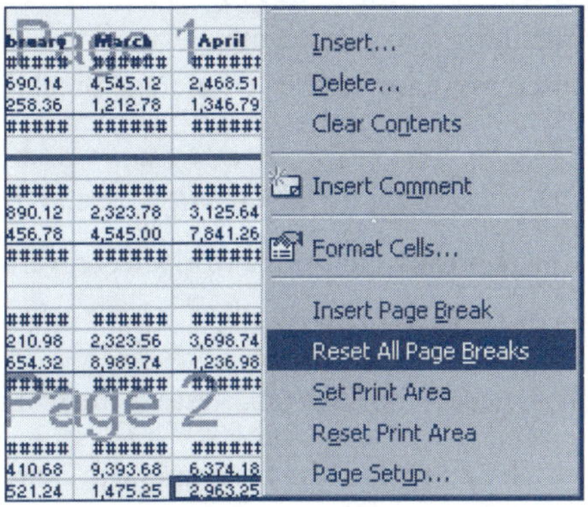

To view a worksheet without the page break lines, select Normal in the View menu.

Page breaks can also be set in the Normal view of a worksheet. To do this, select Page Break in the Insert menu, shown in Figure 8.36.

Figure 8.36 Inserting a Manual Page Break

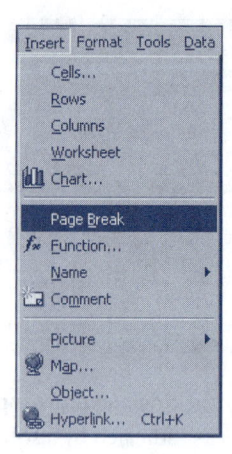

The page break is placed just above and to the left of the active cell.

Printing Part of a Worksheet

Defining a *print range* in the Sheet tab of the Page Setup dialog box is one way to print a portion of the entire worksheet. Using the Print dialog box provides another method. First, highlight the section to be printed, called the *print area*. Then, in the Print dialog box, click on the button by Selection, and then click OK. Only the highlighted section prints.

The section be to printed may also be selected in Page Break Preview.

Exercise 8.10   Using Page Breaks and Printing Sections of a Worksheet

You will place and remove page breaks and print a worksheet several different ways.

1   Open the **Panes** worksheet in the **Exer 8** workbook.

2   In the **Page Setup** dialog box, access the **Page** tab. Restore the scaling to **100%**.

3   Click on the **Header/Footer** tab and replace the file name with **Exercise 8.10** in the **Center section** of the footer.

Place page breaks.

4   From the **View** menu, select **Page Break Preview**. A dialog box may open indicating that the page breaks can be adjusted. If so, click **OK**.

5   A vertical page break is set between two columns. This worksheet is two pages wide and two pages long.

6   Move to the bottom of the screen. Click on the solid line at the bottom and drag it to the middle of the sheet. The grayed area at the bottom is blocked from the worksheet. It will not print at this time.

7   Move the horizontal page break line back to the bottom of the screen.

8   Move the vertical page break line to between columns H and I.

9   Click in cell A14. Click the right mouse button to access the shortcut menu. Select **Insert Page Break**. Now the worksheet is four pages long and all pages will be printed.

10 Click the Print Preview button and view the pages. Click in the **Normal View** button and view the page break lines on the actual worksheet instead of in Print Preview.

11 Return to **Page Break Preview** (**View** menu).

12 Click in cell F19 and insert an additional page break. Additional pages have been added.

13 Click in the uppermost horizontal page break line and drag it to the top of the worksheet. This removes the page break.

14 In the shortcut menu, select **Reset All Page Breaks**. Page breaks return to their original placement.

Print a range.

15 In Page Break Preview, highlight the range A5:H14.

16 Click the right mouse button and select **Set Print Area**. Click the Print button and only the highlighted section prints. On the printout, write "Print 1."

17 Access the shortcut menu and select **Reset Print Area**.

18 Return to the Normal view of the worksheet. Select the range J5:N10. Open the **Print** dialog box.

19 Check the box by **Selection**. Then print the selection. At the top write "Print 2."

20 Close the worksheet without saving changes.

Summary

- Worksheet windows can be sized and rearranged so that several may be viewed at the same time.
- To open copies of the same worksheet (so work can be done in different sections), select New Window from the Window menu.
- Windows are arranged by selecting Arrange from the Window menu. A small portion of each open workbook is displayed.
- Several copies of a worksheet may be open at the same time, but only one is active. Also, several copies of a workbook may be open at the same time.
- Worksheets may be split into panes, allowing different areas of the same worksheet to be viewed and edited.
- Split bars are placed between panes of a worksheet. They can be moved to adjust the size of the panes.
- Double-click on the split bar to remove a split.
- It is easier to complete and edit large worksheets if the labels are visible. The Freeze Panes command allows some rows and columns to remain on the screen as the rest of the worksheet is accessed.
- The Page Setup dialog box provides additional choices for the printing and placement of a worksheet.

- The Page tab of the Page Setup dialog box provides choices on orientation, scaling, paper size, and page numbering.
- A worksheet may be printed in landscape or portrait style. Landscape style uses the long side of the paper as the top. Portrait style uses the short side of the paper as the top.
- Scaling is used to reduce a large worksheet to fewer pages or to enlarge a small worksheet.
- Margins may be changed in the Margins tab of the Page Setup dialog box. Choices for centering the worksheet horizontally and vertically are also available here.
- The Header/Footer tab of the Page Setup dialog box is used to change the header and footer.
- Built-in choices for the header and footer are available, or they may be customized.
- Text that is frequently used in a header or footer can be quickly accessed by using the code buttons.
- Headers and footers can be formatted independently of the rest of a worksheet.
- The Sheet tab of the Page Setup dialog box provides a way to print labels on every page as well as other printing choices.
- To print column or row labels on all pages after the first, use the Print titles section of the Sheet tab.
- A worksheet may be printed with or without cell gridlines, which are the lines between cells.
- Row and column headings may be printed.
- The Print dialog box controls the number of copies to print, the specific pages to print, and the quality of the printed page.
- Excel automatically adds pages as needed; a page break line visually separates the pages.
- A manual page break can be inserted so pages can begin and end at any place in a worksheet.
- Use Page Break Preview to adjust page breaks. Page Break Preview is accessed in the View menu.
- It is possible to print only a portion of a worksheet. Highlight the portion of the worksheet to be printed and choose Selection in the Print dialog box or make the selection in Page Break Preview.

Important Terminology

Arrange Windows	landscape style	Print
code buttons	manual page breaks	print range
Custom Footer	Margins tab	Reset All Page Breaks
Custom Header	orientation	row and column headings
Date button	page break line	scaling
File Name button	Page Break Preview	Sheet Name button
Font button	Page Number button	Sheet tab
footers	Page Setup	split bars
Freeze Panes	Page tab	Time button
gridlines	portrait style	Total Pages button
headers	print area	window panes
Header/Footer tab		

Buttons to Know

Study Questions

True-False

Place a T in the space if the statement is true; place an F if the statement is false.

___ 1. Two or more worksheets may be open at the same time.
___ 2. Worksheet windows cannot be resized.
___ 3. Use the New Window command to open additional worksheets.
___ 4. Tiled arrangement refers to the placement of worksheets so that only the title bar of the inactive windows may be viewed.
___ 5. A window pane is the screen on the computer monitor.
___ 6. Different sections of one worksheet may be viewed at the same time.
___ 7. The split bars are used to adjust the sizes of the window panes.
___ 8. To work in different sections of a large worksheet, you can freeze panes so column and row labels may be viewed at all times.
___ 9. The Page Setup dialog box is accessed from the File menu.
___ 10. The Page tab is used to set margins and determine a header and footer.
___ 11. Landscape style prints a worksheet with the short side of the paper as the top.
___ 12. Margins may be changed only in the Edit dialog box.
___ 13. The only way to center a worksheet horizontally and vertically on a page is by making the adjustments in Print Preview.
___ 14. A worksheet may be printed showing the row and column headings.
___ 15. It is impossible to adjust a large worksheet so it fits on one page.
___ 16. Information that prints on the bottom of every page, such as the page number, is called a footnote.
___ 17. To change the margins of a worksheet, use the Sheet tab.
___ 18. The default header is the page number.
___ 19. A default header or footer automatically prints unless changes are made.
___ 20. The file name is the name of the user.
___ 21. The sheet name is the name of a saved workbook.
___ 22. There are several built-in headers/footers than can be easily inserted into a worksheet.
___ 23. Only built-in headers may be used in a worksheet.
___ 24. A header or footer code always begins with an ampersand (&).
___ 25. The Header dialog box can be accessed in the Page Setup dialog box.
___ 26. The header and footer codes supply the only information that can be used in a header or footer.

_____ 27. Headers and footers cannot be formatted for different fonts or sizes.
_____ 28. One way to print only a portion of a worksheet is to select the section to be printed and then click the Print button in the toolbar.
_____ 29. Labels may be printed on every page of a large worksheet.
_____ 30. Only one copy of a worksheet can be printed with each print command; to print three copies, the Print command must be selected three times.
_____ 31. It is possible to print only a page or two of a multiple-page worksheet.
_____ 32. Excel determines where page breaks will occur; the user has no control over page breaks.
_____ 33. Page Break Preview is accessed in the Tools menu.
_____ 34. A manual page break is set immediately above the selected cell.
_____ 35. Once a page break is set, it can be removed in Page Break Preview.
_____ 36. A vertical page break is set to the left of the selected column.
_____ 37. Horizontal and vertical page breaks can be set at the same time.
_____ 38. There is no visible difference between the manual page break lines and the automatic page break lines.
_____ 39. It is possible to highlight an entire worksheet by clicking in the Select All section of the worksheet.

Fill-In

Place the word in the space that correctly completes the statement.

1. To open a second copy of a worksheet, select _____ from the Window menu.
2. The fastest way to arrange open worksheets on the computer screen is to open all worksheets, then select _____ in the Window menu.
3. When several worksheets are open, only the _____ worksheet may be edited.
4. To split a window into panes, select _____ from the _____ menu.
5. Use the _____ to arrange the size of the panes on a worksheet.
6. Choices for printing labels or gridlines are made in the _____ tab of the _____ dialog box.
7. Printing a worksheet with the short side of the paper as the top is printing in _____ style.
8. The lines that separate cells on a printed worksheet are called _____.
9. Reducing a worksheet to fit on one page is called _____.
10. Information that prints at the top of every page is called a(n) _____.
11. Information that prints at the bottom of every page is called a(n) _____.
12. Text entered in the Left section text box of a header or footer is automatically aligned from the _____.
13. Text entered in the Right section text box of a header or footer is automatically aligned from the _____.
14. Text entered in the Center section text box of a header or footer is automatically aligned from the _____.

15. A commonly used header or footer element, such as page number, date, or time, can be entered by clicking on a(n) _____ button.
16. To use a page numbering style that includes the total number of pages in a worksheet, enter the _____ code in the header.
17. To change the header or footer in six sheets of a workbook at the same time, you must first _____ the sheets.
18. The place where one page ends and the next begins is called a(n) _____ .
19. In Page Break Preview, a(n) _____ line indicates a manually set page break.
20. When the user determines where pages end, a(n) _____ page break is set.
21. When the user wants to print part of a worksheet, the highlighted portion to be printed is called the _____ .
22. To print titles on each page, use the _____ tab in the Page Setup dialog box.

Identify the following icons:

[A] _____   [#] _____

[icon] _____ [icon] _____

[clock] _____ [$] _____

[icon] _____ [A] _____

[A] _____

Assignments

At the end of this chapter, you may delete the documents in Ch07 and Ch08.

Assignment 8.1

Lee has completed a comparison of grocery prices for six different grocery stores. She has entered the data on a worksheet. You will complete and format the worksheet. You will also create custom headers and footers.

1. Open to workbook **Ch8 As1** and save it as **Assig 8-1**.
2. In cell A15 enter the label **Total**.
3. Complete the totals needed in row 15 and in column H. Place the averages in column I.
4. Enter today's date in cell A2. Use a Date & Time function. Format it in the month, day, year style.
5. In cell A3, type **Prepared by** followed by your name.
6. Format the worksheet.
   - Format labels in row 5 for bold, center alignment, and a bottom border. Place at an angled orientation of your choice.
   - Format the worksheet correctly for currency.
   - Display the totals with the proper borders.

- Format the three-line title for bold type and increase the font size by one point for the name of the firm in row 1. Decrease the font size by one point for your name in row 3 and use italics.
- Format the totals in row 15 for bold with a surround border. Use a fill color for the row.
- Adjust the column widths appropriately.

7. Access the **Page Setup** dialog box and complete the following to change the placement of the worksheet:
   - Print **Gridlines** (found in the **Sheet** tab).
   - Center both **Horizontally** and **Vertically** (found in the **Margins** tab).
   - Print in **Portrait** style (found in the **Page** tab).
   - Scale to fit on one page (found in the **Page** tab).
8. Format the header as follows:
   - In the **Left section** text box, key **Page**, press **Space Bar**, then click on the Page Number button.
   - In the **Center section** text box, enter **Lee's Shopping Comparison**. Use the Font button to format it for **Italic**.
   - In the **Right section** text box key your name.
9. Format the footer as follows:
   - In the **Left section** text box, use the Date button to enter the date. The code **&[Date]** appears in the text box. Format it one font size smaller.
   - In the **Center section** text box, use the File Name button to enter the file name. The code, **&[File]**, appears in the text box. Press **Shift**+**Enter**; the insertion point moves to the next line. Use the Sheet Name button to enter the sheet name. The code **&[Tab]** appears on the second line of the text box.
   - In the **Right section** text box, use the Time button to enter the time. The code **&[Time]** appears in the text box. Format it one font size smaller.
10. For the three-line title, merge and center the cells. Use a fill color that matches that of the total row.
11. Do a quick save.
12. Check the worksheet to see how it looks. Are all amounts entered and formatted correctly? Are underlines used correctly? Have you used the spelling checker? Does it have a professional appearance? If needed, make changes and print a corrected copy.
13. Print the worksheet on one page. Write "Print 1" at the top of the worksheet.
14. Change to **Landscape** orientation and increase scaling to **100%**. Print a second worksheet. Write "Print 2" at the top of the worksheet. Which do you prefer?
15. Print a worksheet that shows the formulas. In the **Scaling** section of the **Page** tab (**Page Setup** dialog box), click in **Fit to 1 page(s) wide by 1 tall**.
16. Close the workbook without saving changes.

   Checkpoint:
Total Cost Eggs	$5.47
Average Eggs	$.91
Total Store 1	$13.19

Assignment 8.2

Austin's Hardware has retail outlets in different regions of the country. They are completing the revenue forecast for next year. You will complete and format this large worksheet using some of the techniques covered when working with large worksheets.

1. Open workbook **Ch8 As2** and save it as **Assig 8-2**.
2. Scroll the worksheet so row 5 is the first one visible at the top of the screen. Click in cell C6; then select **Freeze Panes** from the **Window** menu.
3. Complete the mathematical section of the worksheet. (Enter needed formulas.) Be sure column O shows the totals and the grand totals are in row 35.
4. Unfreeze the frozen panes.
5. Format the worksheet.
   - Format all numbers for Comma style with one decimal place.
   - Format row 5 so the labels are emphasized.
   - Align the word **Subtotal** in column A (cells A13, A20, A27, and A34) so it is right aligned and bold italic. Can you do this in one step by highlighting multiple cells?
   - Place border lines under the cells containing numbers in rows 12, 19, 26, and 33 to indicate where sums are located.
   - Place a wide border under row 34 and a double border under row 35. Format row 35 for bold.
   - Use color in the subtotal and total rows.
   - Check to be sure the columns widths are still appropriate.

   Adjust the subtotal row and the row just below the subtotal so they are separated.
   - Click on the line between rows 13 and 14 and drag to a height of **20** (from an original height of 13). If your original line is not 13 points high, drag the height so the row is 6 points larger than the original.
   - Repeat for rows 20, 27, and 34.
   - Format row 35 for a height of **27**.
   - Center the three-line title of the worksheet over the entire worksheet. Use font styles, color, and enhancements (bold, italics) of your choice.
6. Make the following adjustments for the printing and placement of the page.
   - Format for center placement (both vertical and horizontal).
   - In the header and footer include the name of the company (**Austin's Hardware Company**), the file name, the sheet name, your name, the page number, and the date and time of preparation. Format the header and footer appropriately.
   - Format for landscape style.
   - Use Page Break Preview to adjust the page breaks. If the worksheet doesn't print on one page, position the East division and the last quarter (October, November, December) so they print on the same page. Be sure the labels print on each page. You may need to adjust the three-line title so it is centered over only the first page. (Use the Format Cells dialog box to remove the Merge command.)
7. Check the format and appearance of the worksheet.
8. Save and print the worksheet.

9. Hide columns and rows.
   - Hide rows 7–12, 14–19, 21–26, and 28–33.
   - Insert a row before each of the subtotals.
   - Hide columns C–N.
10. Format the worksheet so it will print horizontally and vertically centered on the page in portrait style. Then print the worksheet.
11. Print a worksheet that shows the formulas. You may need to adjust it so it fits on one page.
12. Close the workbook without saving changes.

Checkpoint:

January Subtotal North	24.5
Total North Bolts	47.9
January Grand Total	94.6

Assignment 8.3

Kevin, the accountant at Peter and Paul's Outdoor Store, has started a comparative balance sheet and asks if you would complete it. In addition to completing the formulas, you will format the worksheet.

1. Open worksheet **Ch8 As3** and save it as **Assig 8-3**.
2. Complete the totals in columns B and C for the years 1997 and 1998. Use the following suggestions:
   - Place total current assets in row 13.
   - Place total fixed assets in row 19.
   - Subtract depreciation from total fixed assets for the subtotal in row 21.
   - Complete total assets in row 25. Add Fixed Assets less Depreciation and Other Assets to the Total Current assets.
   - Complete current liabilities in row 35.
   - Complete total liabilities in row 40. They are the total current liabilities plus the long-term liability.
   - Complete total equity in row 45. It is total assets less total liabilities.
   - Complete total liabilities and equity in row 47.
   - Determine the amount of equity for Peter and Paul. Peter receives 40% of the equity, and Paul receives 60%.
3. In column C, enter the percent of total the figure represents.
   - The total cash for 1998 represents 4.1% of the total assets. In cell D10 enter the formula that divides the amount of cash for 1998 by the total assets for 1998.
   - Complete the assets section.
   - Complete the percent of total liabilities and equity that each liability and equity amount represents of the total. For cell C31, enter the formula that divides the amount of accounts payable by the total liabilities and equity.
4. Format the worksheet.
   - Format row labels in column A (assets, liabilities, and equity) in bold, a larger font size, and center alignment. You may choose to angle the headings. Merge and center them across the worksheet. Add borders and color if you wish.
   - Format the total labels for bold and right alignment.

- Format the labels **1997**, **1998**, and **1998 Percent of Total** for bold and center alignment. Format **1998 Percent of Total** for wrapped text. Place a border at the bottom of the cells.
- Place appropriate underlines in the worksheet. You need an underline whenever a formula is completed. Place double underlines under total assets and total liabilities and equity.
- Place the worksheet in the center of the page and be sure it prints on only one page. Do not use a header. Place your name and the file name in the footer. You may also include additional information in the footer.
- Format correctly for currency. Round percents to one decimal. Format all total rows in bold.
- Remember to use the spelling checker for the worksheet and proofread each amount carefully.
- Adjust column widths and row heights if needed.
- Merge and center the three-line title over the columns of the worksheet and format it attractively.

5. Save and print the worksheet.
6. Print a second copy that shows only the title and the assets section.
7. Print a copy of the worksheet that displays the formulas. Print this copy in landscape style on one page.

Checkpoint:

1998 Total Current Assets	$199,865.00
1998 Total Assets	$373,335.75
1998 Total Liabilities	$229,353.00
1998 Equity, Peter Jackson	$57,593.10

Assignment 8.4

Andy Andrews has hired you to track the newspaper sales for News Distributors and to determine the profit made. This firm delivers seven newspapers to four newsstands in the city. You are asked to prepare a worksheet for each day of the week and record the information for the first day.

Create one worksheet for each day of the week and include all four stands on each worksheet.

1. Open a new workbook. Select seven worksheets and then enter the following information on all seven worksheets at the same time:

	A	B	C	D	E	F	G	H
1	News Distributors							
2	Seattle, Washington							
3	Monday, September 11							
4								
5	Stand 1							
6	Newspaper	Atlanta Globe	Boston Journal	Chicago Gazette	Denver Daily	New Orleans Cajun	Philadelphia Chronicle	Seattle Sun
7	Papers Delivered							
8	Papers Removed							
9	Papers Sold							
10	Profit per Paper	0.205	0.19	0.175	0.225	0.26	0.24	0.25
11	Profit from Sales							

2. Save the workbook as **Assig 8-4**.

3. Add a column title, **Total**, in column I.
4. Format this section of the worksheet as follows (keeping all seven worksheets active):
   - Cell A5, the stand name, should be bold, centered, underlined, and increased two font sizes.
   - The labels in row 6 should be bold, wrapped text, centered both vertically and horizontally, and have a border placed around them.
   - Adjust column widths, if necessary.
5. Copy this section three times on the sheet. Change the stand numbers so you have **Stand 1**, **Stand 2**, **Stand 3**, and **Stand 4**.
6. Make the following adjustments in Page Setup:
   - Center each sheet on the page vertically and horizontally.
   - Include the sheet name and your name in the header.
   - Include the page number and the file name in the footer.
   - Do not print gridlines.
   - Print the worksheet in landscape style. Be sure each worksheet fits on one page.
7. Formatting is complete and all information is entered that belongs on each sheet. Ungroup the sheets.
8. In the worksheets 2–7, change the dates so each day of the week has one sheet. You will have **Tuesday, September 12** through **Sunday, September 17**. Be sure to change the tab names to match the dates.
9. Enter the following information for Monday:

	D	E	F	G	H	I	J	K
1	Monday, September 11							
2	Stand 1	Atlanta Globe	Boston Journal	Chicago Gazette	Denver Daily	New Orleans Cajun	Philadelphia Chronicle	Seattle Sun
3	Papers Delivered	250	120	25	30	40	75	225
4	Papers Removed	13	14	8	5	7	9	14
5								
6	Stand 2							
7	Papers Delivered	150	175	160	85	40	45	400
8	Papers Removed	11	9	15	4	11	1	2
9								
10	Stand 3							
11	Papers Delivered	75	110	80	20	15	25	150
12	Papers Removed	7	3	2	0	0	9	1
13								
14	Stand 4							
15	Papers Delivered	110	125	120	50	40	30	210
16	Papers Removed	1	0	10	4	6	7	11

10. Complete the worksheet using the following steps:
    - Determine the number of papers sold each day. (Do you want to enter this formula on all sheets at the same time?)
    - Determine the profit from sales.
    - At the bottom of the worksheet, include a line that totals each paper's sales profit for each day and the grand total.
    - Make sure all totals are entered.
    - Format the profit from sales amounts for currency, and shade the rows.

- Format the other numbers for commas with zero decimals; format the profit per paper for three decimals.
- Merge and center the title across columns and make it bold. Increase the font size.

11. Print the entire workbook. Also, print a section of Monday's sheet that includes only data from Stand 1 (along with the worksheet title). Then print this worksheet with the formulas displayed on one page in landscape style.

Checkpoint:

All from Monday's sales
Profit in Sales, Stand 1, Atlanta Globe	48.59
Profit in Sales, Stand 3, Denver Daily	4.50
Total Profit, Seattle Sun, All Stands	239.25
Total Profit of All Stands	612.95

Assignment 8.5

Howard's Light Industrial has prepared a payroll report and made some entries. You will complete and format this payroll report.

1. Open the workbook saved as **Ch8 As5** and save it as **Assig 8-5**.
2. Complete the worksheet. When working with any large worksheet, you may want to freeze panes or split the worksheet into panes.
    - In column D, enter the regular hours worked; they are the first 40 hours worked. Use an IF statement for the overtime. Everything over 40 hours is paid at the overtime rate.
    - In column E, enter the formula to determine the overtime hours worked. Overtime hours are hours worked less regular hours (40). Use an IF statement.
    - In column F, enter the formula for the regular earnings. Regular earnings are regular hours times hourly rate.
    - In column G, enter the formula for the overtime earnings. Overtime earnings are overtime hours times hourly rate times 1.5.
    - In column H, enter the formula for total earnings. Total earnings are regular earnings plus overtime earnings.
    - In column I, complete the federal income tax. Use a **25%** rate for all employees, entered in cell F6.
    - In column J, complete the social security withheld. The rate, **7.5%**, is in cell C6.
    - Enter the insurance deduction in column K from the following list:

Dearborn, Andrea	$ 57.50
Ewert, Bob	38.75
Freeman, Connie	29.00
Gilliam, Helen	45.25
Gogham, Daniel	26.00
Hare, Martha	41.25
Hinton, Evelyn	55.00
Holm, Stanley	22.50
Lees, Beverly	27.85
Priesner, Andrew	41.00
Stultz, Richard	37.50

- Complete the total deductions in column L. It is federal income tax plus social security tax plus insurance.
- Complete the net pay in column M. It is total earnings less total deductions.
- Enter **Total** at the end of the worksheet and complete the totals. Do not total the column showing the hourly rate of pay.

3. Format the worksheet.
    - Format column labels for bold and wrapped text; center horizontally and place at the bottom of the cell. Place a bold border under this row.
    - Bold the identifying information: **Hourly Information**, **Earnings Information**, and **Deductions**.
    - Bold the row with the totals. Shade all cells in the total row that contain data.
    - Format for landscape style on one page with no gridlines. Center horizontally on one page with a 2" top margin. Place the file name, the sheet name, and your name in the footer.
    - Place an outline border around the main body of the worksheet (all cells containing data).
    - Place a border between columns E and F to separate the parts of the worksheet. Start the border at row 8 and extend it through the total. Repeat the border between columns A and B. Place the same border between columns H and I and between L and M.
    - Place a border under row 21 just before the totals.
    - Be sure numbers are formatted properly.
    - Check column widths and row heights.
    - Check the format and appearance of the worksheet.
    - Merge and center the title across the entire worksheet.
4. Rename **Sheet1** to **July 7**.
5. Save and print the worksheet. At the top write "Print 1."
6. Print a copy showing the formulas used. Adjust the column widths so the worksheet stays on one page. You may need to use Print Preview to determine the number of pages. You may adjust a column without a formula, such as column A, to be very narrow.
7. Return to the Normal view of worksheet.
8. Print a copy of the worksheet that shows only the names of the employees, the hours, and the earnings information. Adjust column widths. Center all column titles. Print in portrait style. At the top write "Print 2."
9. Close the worksheet without saving changes.

Checkpoint:

A. Dearborn Overtime Hours	3
A. Dearborn Regular Earnings	251.20
A. Dearborn Overtime Earnings	28.26
A. Dearborn Federal Income Tax	69.87
A. Dearborn Total Deductions	$148.32
Total Federal Income Tax	$836.85
Total Net Pay	$1,837.90

Assignment 8.6

Howard's Light Industrial has asked you to complete the payroll report for the week ending July 14. Use the original report from Assignment 8.5. Because that report is accurately completed, preparing another report is quick and easy.

1. Open the workbook saved as **Assig 8-5**.
2. Copy the **July 7** worksheet to a new sheet. (To copy a worksheet, hold the **Ctrl** key, click on the **July 7** tab, and drag to the next sheet tab.)
3. Rename the **July 7 (2)** tab to **July 14** and open that sheet.
4. Change the date in the title to **July 14**.
5. Change the information on the worksheet and check its accuracy.
    - Change the hours worked to the information provided below:

Dearborn, Andrea	38.0
Ewert, Bob	41.5
Freeman, Connie	38.5
Gilliam, Helen	42.0
Gogham, Daniel	41.0
Hare, Martha	40.5
Hinton, Evelyn	44.0
Holm, Stanley	41.0
Lees, Beverly	38.0
Priesner, Andrew	39.5
Stultz, Richard	41.0

   - Check the figures in the Overtime Hours column.
6. Look over the worksheet for format and content errors. Because the worksheet was correctly completed for July 7, it is now finished.
7. Save and print the worksheet.

Case Study 8

You have been asked to prepare a payroll report for Ellis Manufacturing Company, which employs nine people. The company has always completed the payroll information by hand because of its small size, but they realize that a computer can save considerable time and have hired you to design this report.

Prepare a payroll report that can be used for each weekly payroll. You will need to include space for the employee's name, rate of pay, regular hours worked, overtime hours worked, pay earned for the regular hours, pay earned for the overtime hours, and gross pay. You also need a section for deductions that include FICA tax, income tax, other deductions, and total deductions. Then include a place for the net pay.

Prepare a written plan of the worksheet before beginning to enter it. Turn your plan in with your computer work.

Use a separate worksheet for each weekly payroll. You will determine the payroll report for four weeks. You may want to enter information that is the same for all worksheets and format them at the same time.

The employees for this firm, their hourly pay rate, and the deduction information for the current week are provided. All hours over 40 are paid at 1.5 times the hourly rate. FICA (social security) tax is figured at a rate of 7.6%; income tax is figured at a rate of 24%.

Name	Rate of Pay	Other Deductions	Hours Worked Week 1	Hours Worked Week 2	Hours Worked Week 3	Hours Worked Week 4
Leslie Golden	7.90	33.00	42	38	44	46
Chang Hong	6.40	29.00	40	41	42	44
Kevin London	8.80	35.00	40.5	42	39	40
John Mason	7.25	30.00	46	41.5	43.5	40
Julie Otling	10.70	32.00	42	39	42	42.5
Michael Riley	9.45	28.00	40	44	40	40.5
Alan Thompson	7.35	20.00	38	42	40	32
Michelle Upton	12.50	25.00	43	39.5	40	41
Timothy Van Hoy	6.05	18.00	42	40	41	42.5

With each payroll report include the name of the firm, the fact that this is a payroll report, and the date of the report. It is important that the report be presented in an attractive manner. Be sure your name is placed in the sheet.

Save the workbook as **Case 8** and print it.

Check the appearance of the worksheet. Are all amounts entered and formatted correctly? Are underlines used properly? Does it have a professional appearance? If needed, make changes and print a corrected copy.

Checkpoint:
    Week 1 Regular Pay Total $3,041.30
    Week 1 Total Deductions $1,274.90

Intermediate Excel

The following chapters may be presented in any order desired by the instructor

Chapter 9

Creating Charts

Objectives

1. Identify the parts of a chart.
2. Prepare a default chart.
3. Prepare charts using the Chart Wizard.
4. Format, size, and place a chart.
5. Link worksheet data to a chart.
6. Determine the type of chart to use.

Introduction

A well-planned worksheet presents numerical data in an easy-to-read format. However, it is often easier to understand the relationship of the data with a chart or graph. A chart or graph provides a visual representation of the relationship of data presented in a worksheet. Excel uses the term "chart" whenever a chart or graph is prepared.

Excel provides options for many styles of charts. It is critical to choose the most appropriate style to display the relationship of the data. This chapter describes some of the different chart styles and provides tips on how to decide which style to use to display data.

Note that at the end of this chapter, you may delete the Ch09 directory from the Student Data Disk.

Placing a Chart on a Worksheet

What Is a Chart?

A *chart* is a graphic representation of worksheet data. Seeing a graphic display of data often makes it easier to compare information than seeing a page full of numbers. Charts are used in business to visually compare and evaluate data and then make decisions based on that data.

There are several chart types available with Excel. Charts show comparisons of one or more sets of data. Each chart type is useful for a business and the choice of chart type depends on the objective of the chart.

Figure 9.1 shows four of the many available chart types.

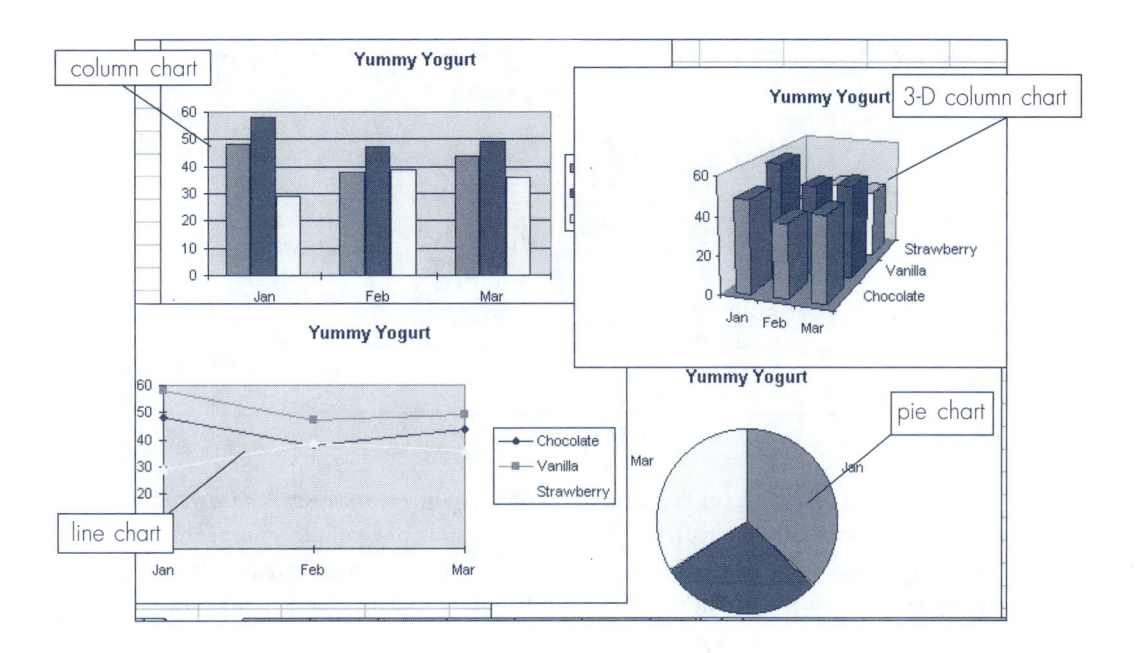

Figure 9.1   Some Chart Styles Available with Excel

The chart at the top left is a column chart. A variation of the column chart, the 3-D column chart, is at the top right. These charts compare sales of several different items (yogurt flavors, in this case) for several months. At the bottom left is a line chart, which shows the same data relationships as the column charts. The pie chart at the bottom right shows sales of one yogurt flavor over a period of three months. Pie charts show the relationship of one data field and are used for showing comparisons within that field.

Identifying Parts of a Chart

The parts of a chart are identified in Figure 9.2. The ***plot area*** is where values are plotted and represented by bars, lines, or pie slices. It is bordered by the ***value axis*** (y-axis) on the left and the ***category axis*** (x-axis) at the bottom. The labels in the value axis are determined by the values or numbers used in a worksheet. The names in the category axis are determined by the labels used in a worksheet. (The data in the axes can be edited later.)

Figure 9.2   Parts of a Chart

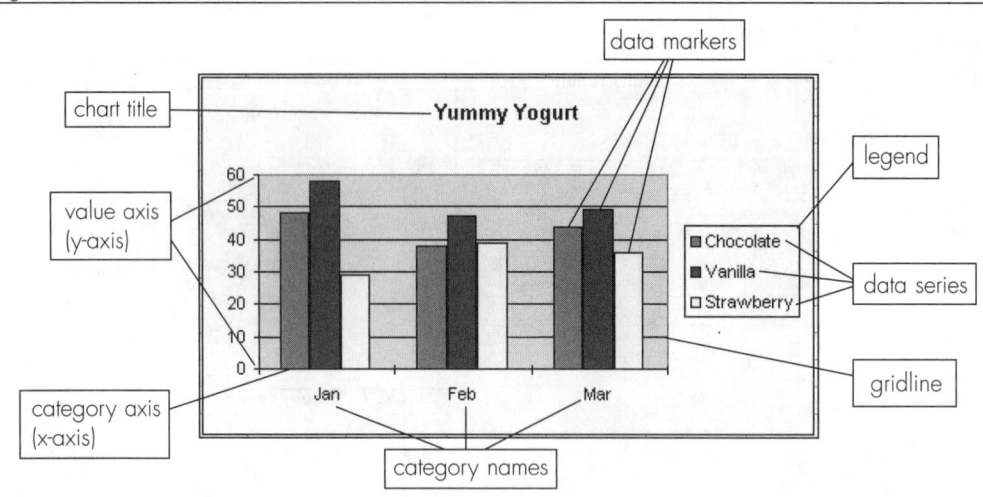

A ***data point*** is one value (or the contents of one cell) in a worksheet. A ***data marker*** is a graphic representation of that number, represented by a bar, column, piece of pie, or other marker in a chart. Data markers may be presented in different shades, colors, or patterns. The data in each row or column of a worksheet is a ***data series***. The chart in Figure 9.2 uses two data series: months and yogurt flavors. One data series is placed in the legend; the other is used for ***category names***. Each data series is identified by a unique color or pattern. In Figure 9.2, the category names (the months) at the bottom of the chart identify the groups of columns. A ***legend*** identifies the data markers and shows the pattern and color assigned to each data series of a chart. In Figure 9.2, the legend indicates that the light gray columns represent chocolate yogurt.

Creating a Chart

Excel uses the column chart as the ***default chart***; it is the quickest one to create. The first step to create a chart is to define what data will be charted. The data included in a chart is called the ***chart range***. To create a chart, the chart range must be selected on the worksheet, including the column and row labels. The title of a worksheet is not included in the chart range. Totals are rarely charted unless a chart is needed for a comparison of totals. If empty rows or columns are in a chart range, hide them prior to selecting the range. Figure 9.3 shows the chart range for a chart that will compare the sales of each yogurt flavor for three months.

Figure 9.3   Selecting a Chart Range

	A	B	C	D	E
1		\multicolumn{4}{c}{Yummy Yogurt}	
2		\multicolumn{4}{c}{Sales, First Quarter}	
3					
4	Flavor	Jan	Feb	Mar	Total
5	Chocolate	48	38	44	130
6	Vanilla	58	47	49	154
7	Strawberry	29	39	36	104
8					
9	Total	135	124	129	388

Placing a Chart on a Worksheet

After a chart range is selected, press F11 (in the function keys). A column chart is automatically placed on a new sheet in the workbook, called a *chart sheet*. This sheet is shown in Figure 9.4, in the sheet tab named Chart3. Each number in the chart range becomes a data marker and is represented by a chart column. The column labels become the category names and the row labels are placed in the legend. *Gridlines* are the horizontal lines in the plot area that represent values on the y-axis. Gridlines make it easier to view and evaluate data.

Figure 9.4   Creating the Default (Column) Chart

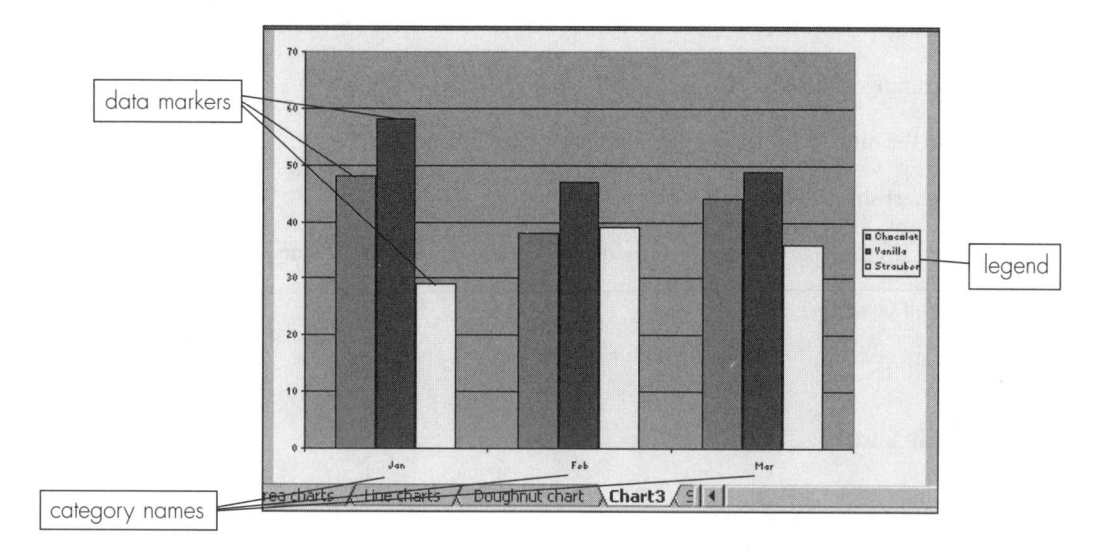

Once a chart is created, it can be edited. A *chart title* may be added. Colors may be changed. Data in the x-axis and y-axis may be transposed. The legend may be omitted. Text fonts and colors may be changed.

Printing a Chart Sheet

When a chart is on a separate chart sheet, it is printed as other worksheets are printed. With the chart sheet active, Active sheet(s) should be selected in the Print what section, as shown in Figure 9.5.

Figure 9.5   Printing a Chart Sheet

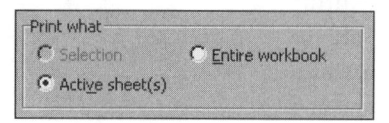

Chapter 9 Creating Charts

Exercise 9.1 Creating a Chart

You will create a chart for College Pizza Shop.

Note: Before completing the exercises and assignments in this chapter, you will need to expand the Chapter 9 files on your Student Data Disk. In Windows Explorer, locate the Chapter 9 file and double-click on it. When the files have been expanded, you will be able to access them from Excel.

1 Open the **Ch9 Exer** workbook and save it as **Exer 9**.

2 Open to the **Default Chart** sheet.

3 Select the chart range A4:D7.

4 Press **F11** (in the function keys). A chart sheet opens (in a separate sheet).

5 Rename the chart sheet as **Exer 9-1**.

6 Select all sheets. In the header, enter your name and the file name. In the footer, enter the sheet name.

7 Print the **Default Chart** sheet.

8 Save the workbook.

Editing a Default Chart

All sections of a chart can be made active. An *active chart area* is identified by the *handles* (black squares) at its edges. A section is made active by clicking in it. Once an area is active, it can be edited, moved, sized, or deleted. Figure 9.6 shows the legend as the active chart area.

To edit an active chart or area of a chart, double-click in the area; a dialog box opens providing editing choices. This dialog box can also be accessed in the shortcut menu, which opens when you point to the area and click the right mouse button.

The editing choices for a legend are found in the Format Legend dialog box, shown in Figure 9.7.

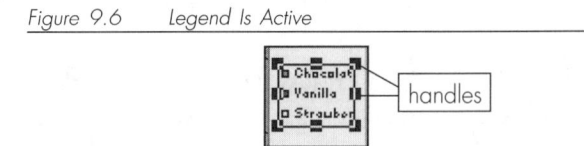

Figure 9.6 Legend Is Active

Figure 9.7 Format Legend Dialog Box

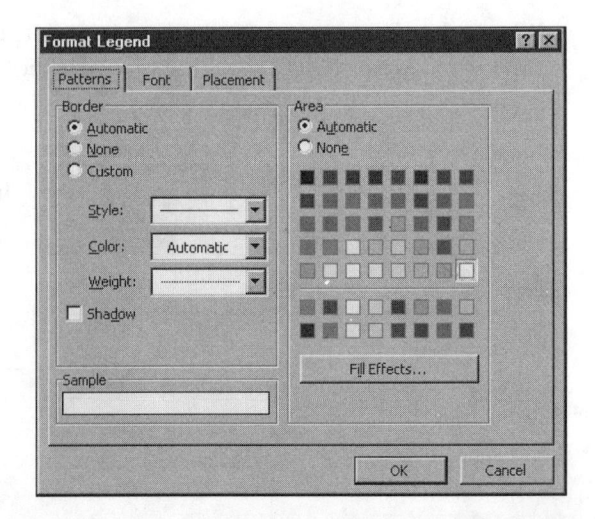

The tabs at the top of the dialog box indicate the formatting choices. For a legend, the editing choices are Patterns, Font, and Placement.

Patterns are used for the borders around a legend, and the Fill Effects button defines the area within a legend. *Fill effects* are the background, in this case the background color of the legend. Fill effects also include the color of the box, gradients of color, and texture or pictures as a background. There are several line styles and colors available for the border.

The font used in the legend may be changed. The dialog box that opens is the same Font dialog box used throughout Excel.

Placement of the legend is its location in a chart: at the bottom, corner, top, right, or left of the sheet.

Chart areas that may be edited include the plot area, data markers, x-axis, and y-axis. A title may be added and formatted.

Exercise 9.2 Editing a Default Chart

You will edit the chart created in Exercise 9.1. In this exercise, you will use many of the available editing choices; when creating charts, however, remember that a simple chart is often the most effective.

1 Open the **Exer 9** workbook to the **Exer 9-1** sheet.

2 Click in the plot area. The ScreenTip identifies it as the **Plot Area**.

3 Use the shortcut menu to access the **Format Plot Area** dialog box. Only patterns may be edited.

4 In the **Border** section, select a colored border.

5 In the **Area** section, click **Fill Effects**. Click in the tabs to see the choices available.

Choose the background for the plot area.

6 Click in the **Texture** tab and select a texture of your choice. Click **OK** two times.

Format the legend.

7 In the chart sheet, double-click in the legend. The **Format Legend** dialog box opens. The tabbed choices are **Patterns**, **Font**, and **Placement**.

8 Click in the **Font** tab. Select a different font in a larger size.

9 Click in the **Placement** tab. Select the **Bottom** placement. Click **OK**.

Format the labels in the category axis (x-axis).

10 Double-click in the category axis. The **Format Axis** dialog box opens with **Patterns**, **Scale**, **Font**, **Number**, and **Alignment** as the choices.

11 Click in the **Alignment** tab. Select an angle of your choice. Click **OK**.

Format a data marker.

12 Click in a marker for February and use the shortcut menu to access the **Format Data Series** dialog box. The formatting for one marker will affect all three February markers. The format choices are **Patterns**, **Axis**, **Y Error Bars**, **Data Labels**, **Series Order**, and **Options**.

13. Click in the **Patterns** tab and click **Fill Effects**. Click on the **Gradient** tab and select a gradient and color of your choice. Click **OK**.

14. Click in the **Data Labels** tab and select **Show value**. The numerical value of the data marker will be displayed above it.

15. Click in the **Series Order** tab. Rearrange the data markers so the order is **March**, **February**, **January**. Click **OK**.

Add a title to the chart and format it.

16. In the chart, access the shortcut menu and select **Chart Options**. Select the **Titles** tab.

17. In the **Chart title** text box, enter **Pizza Sales**. Click **OK**. The title appears on the chart.

18. Double-click on the title to access the **Format Chart Title** dialog box. The format choices are **Patterns**, **Font**, and **Alignment**.

19. Select an **Italic** font with a font size of **20**. Select a fill color or effect of your choice and a shadow border. (The **Shadow** option is selected in the **Border** section of the **Patterns** tab).

20. Print the sheet. At the top write "Exercise 9.2."

21. Save the workbook.

Using Excel's Chart Wizard

The *Chart Wizard button*, located on the right side of the Standard toolbar, creates charts quickly and easily. When the Chart Wizard button is used to place a chart in a worksheet, a series of dialog boxes gather information to determine the appropriate chart style.

The first step in preparing any chart is to select a chart range, including the row and column labels. Figure 9.8 shows a selected chart range.

Figure 9.8   Chart Range Selected

	A	B	C	D	E
1		Yummy Yogurt			
2		Sales, First Quarter			
3					
4		Jan	Feb	Mar	Total
5	Chocolate	48	38	44	130
6	Vanilla	58	47	49	154
7	Strawberry	29	39	36	104
8					
9	Total	135	124	129	388

After a chart range is selected, click on the Chart Wizard button. A series of dialog boxes opens. The first is the *Chart Type* dialog box, shown in Figure 9.9, where the type of chart is selected.

There are two tabs in the dialog box: Standard Types and Custom Types. The most common chart types are listed at the left side of the Standard Types tab. Each chart has several subtypes that may be selected; these are displayed at the right side of the dialog box. A description of the selected chart is found just below the illustrated chart types. To view the way a completed chart will look, click the mouse in the "Press and hold to view sample" box at the bottom right of the dialog box. A sample of the chart opens, shown in Figure 9.10; it includes data labels, title, legend, and other descriptors that are included with the chart.

In the Chart Type dialog box, select the Custom Types tab when specialized chart types are needed.

When the chart type is selected, click Next. The *Chart Source Data dialog box* opens, shown in Figure 9.11. There are two tabs in this dialog box: Data Range and Series. The *Data Range* tab identifies the location of the source data. The *Series* tab is used to alter the order of the series. Each charted series is identified and may be edited.

Figure 9.9   Step 1—Chart Type

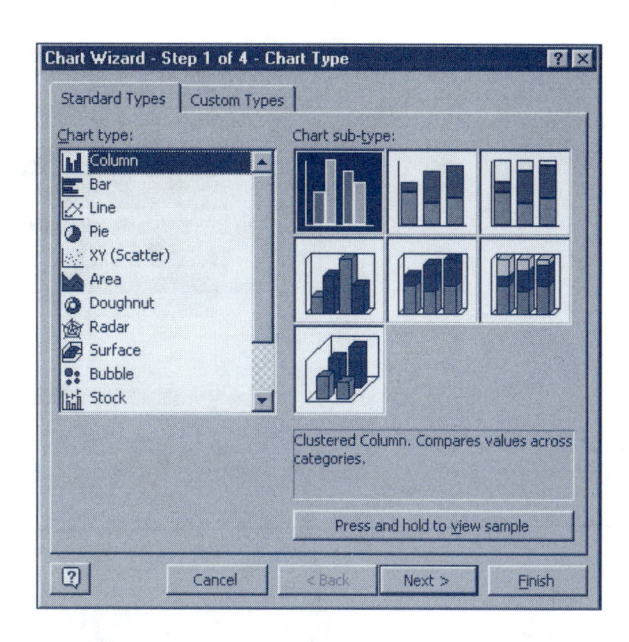

Figure 9.10   Viewing a Sample of the Chart

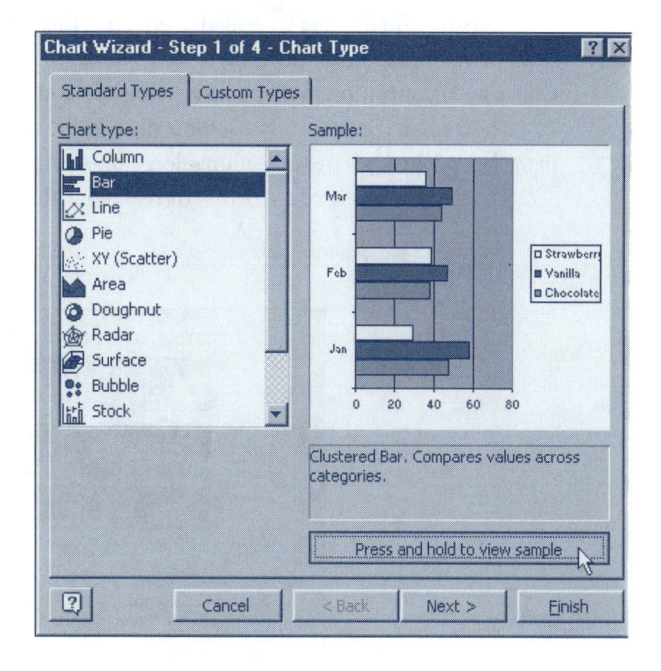

Figure 9.11   Chart Source Data Dialog Box

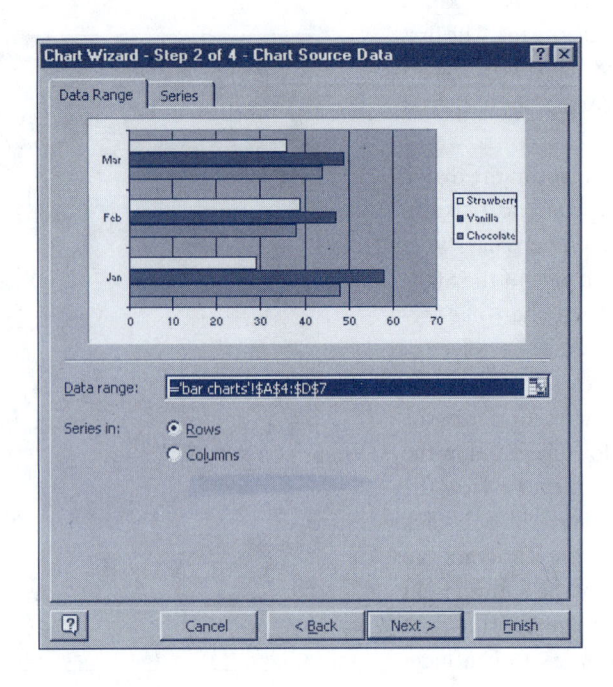

The source of the data is verified or edited in this step. The Data range text box identifies the data; the sheet name appears first; the range is identified as an absolute reference. If this range is incorrect, use the Collapse Dialog button to shrink the dialog box and select the correct range.

The chart in Figure 9.11 shows the series is in rows with the months in the y-axis and the yogurt flavors in the legend. In the Series in section select Columns to transpose the labels, as shown in Figure 9.12.

The Series tab is used to format or rearrange the data series.

Figure 9.12   Data Series in Columns

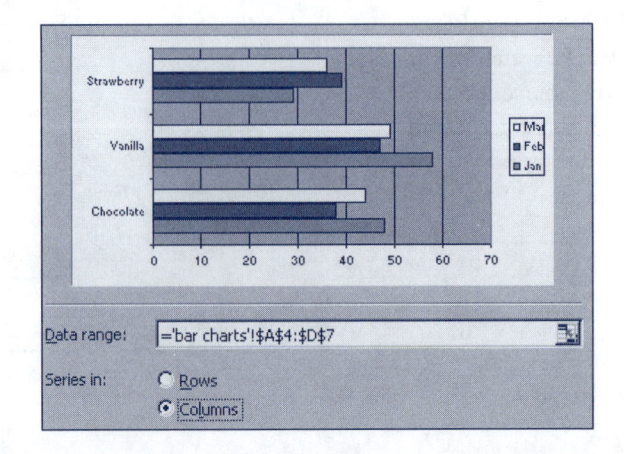

Click Next to open Step 3, the *Chart Options dialog box*, shown in Figure 9.13.

Figure 9.13   Chart Options Dialog Box

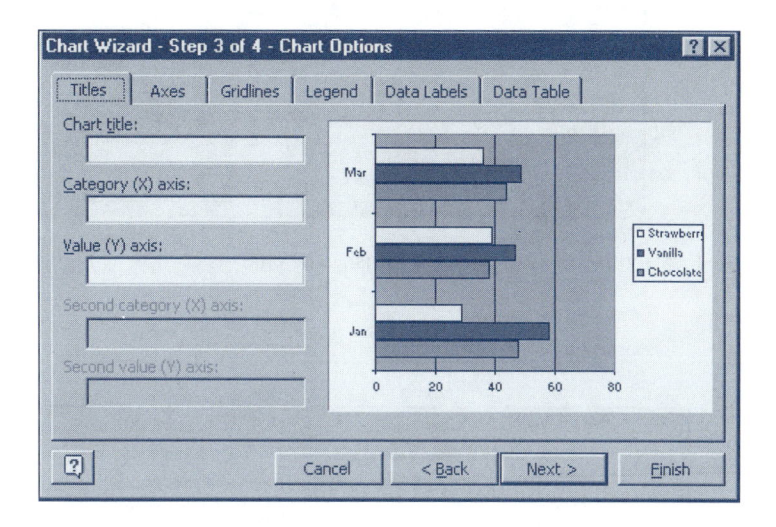

This dialog box includes tabs for Titles, Axes, Gridlines, Legend, Data Labels, and Data Table. Some formatting choices can be made here. A title may be added, gridlines added or omitted, legend placement determined, data labels added, or a data table inserted.

In the Titles tab, enter a chart title. If a label for the x- or y-axis is needed, enter it here. Figure 9.14 shows the resulting chart when labels are added.

Figure 9.14   Adding a Title and Labels

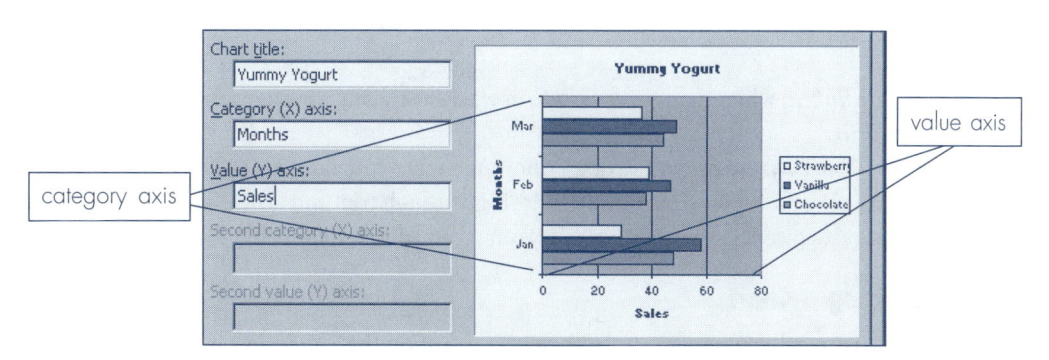

Click Next to open the *Chart Location dialog box*, shown in Figure 9.15. A chart may be placed within an existing worksheet or on a separate sheet. The chart may be placed in any sheet of the current book, which is selected by clicking the drop-down arrow next to the "As object in" box. When a chart is placed within a worksheet, it is an embedded chart. An ***embedded chart*** is printed within a worksheet rather than on a separate sheet.

Figure 9.15   Chart Location Dialog Box

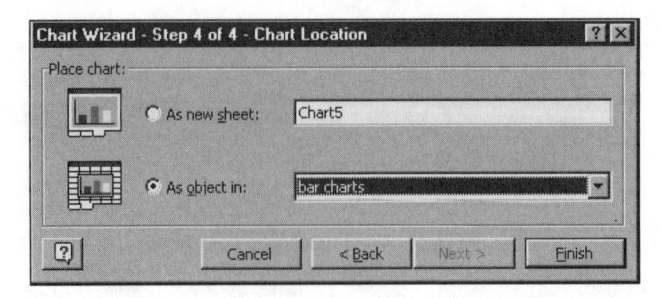

When the location is determined, click Finish. The chart is complete. Figure 9.16 shows the embedded chart.

Figure 9.16   Completing the Chart Wizard

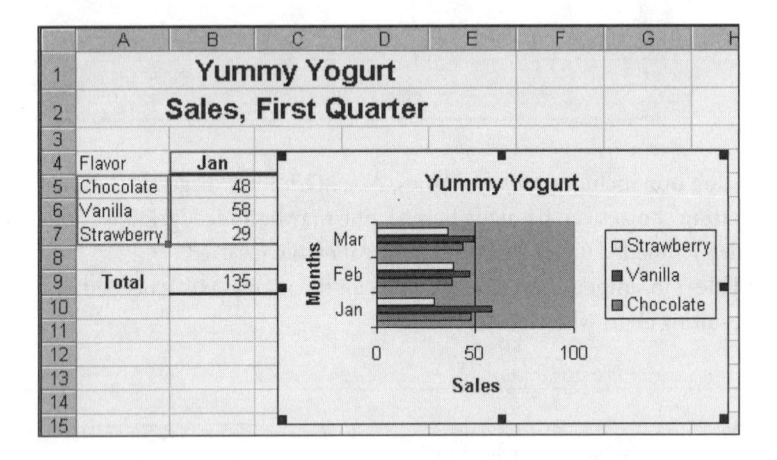

Charts are *linked*; when changes are made in worksheet data, the changes are automatically updated in the chart.

Using the *Chart Wizard* provides a quick, thorough way to prepare charts. Practice using the Chart Wizard and viewing the types of charts available. It is through trial and error that the proper charting choices will be recognized. Do not hesitate to try out several different possibilities.

Moving and Sizing a Chart

A chart may be moved to a new location. To do this, position the mouse in a white space in an active chart. Click on the mouse and drag the chart to a new position. When the mouse button is released, the chart will be relocated.

To change the size of a chart, position the mouse on a chart handle; the mouse shape becomes a double sided arrow. Click and drag the handles to the desired size and shape of the chart; a dotted line moves to indicate the new size of the chart. Dragging a corner handle adjusts the size in two directions; dragging a side handle adjusts the size in one direction. To resize the chart but maintain the same proportions, hold down the Shift key while adjusting the size of the chart.

Printing a Chart

A chart may be printed by itself. First select the chart, then select Print from the File menu. The Print what section has a Selected Chart button. Be sure it is selected, then click OK. The chart prints on its own page.

When a chart is selected, the tabs in the Page Setup dialog box change to include a Chart tab, shown in Figure 9.17.

Printing instructions about chart size, black and white printing, etc., are also located in this dialog box.

Figure 9.17   Chart Tab of Page Setup Dialog Box

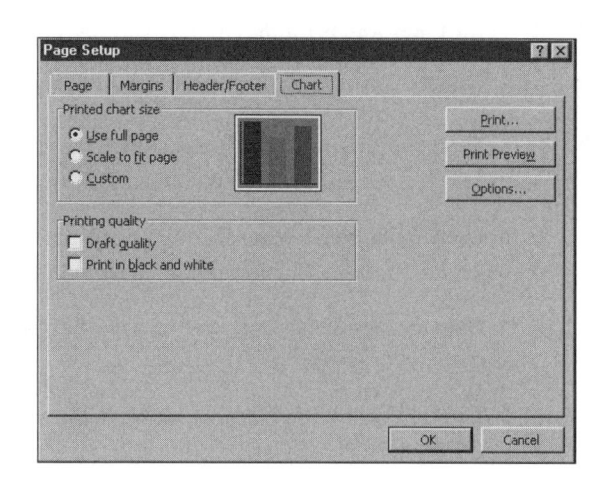

Exercise 9.3   Using the Chart Wizard

The College Pizza Shop has completed a worksheet for its first quarter sales. In order to compare the pizza sales and determine the most popular variety, the owner, Austin Nevin, would like to easily determine the relationship of pizza sales by variety and month. Because Excel is new to the Pizza Shop, Austin would like to experiment with several chart types.

You will create and print several charts that display the relationship of pizza sales each month.

1 Open to the workbook saved as **Exer 9** and select the sheet named **Default Chart**.

Create a chart using the Chart Wizard.

2 Highlight the range of the worksheet to be charted, A4:D7. Do not select totals when selecting a chart range.

3 Click on the Chart Wizard button . Select a bar chart of your choice. Then click on **Next**.

4 In the **Chart Source Data** dialog box, confirm the selected chart range as **$A$4:$D$7**. Be sure in the **Series in** section that **Rows** is selected. Click in the **Series** tab and be sure the series is in the order of **January, February, March**. Then click **Next**.

5 In the **Chart Options** dialog box, key the chart title **Pizza Choices**. In the **Category axis** section key **Types** and in the **Value axis** section key **Amount Sold**. Then click **Next**.

6 In the **Chart Location** dialog box, select to have the chart **As object in** the sheet. Then click **Finish**. The chart is inserted into the worksheet.

7 Click in the chart and move it below the cells containing data. You may need to adjust the size of the chart so all parts can be read.

Show the relationship of pizza varieties sold in January. Use a pie chart and place it in the sheet.

8. Select the range A4:D5 for the chart. Do not select totals.

9. Click on the Chart Wizard button. Select the first pie chart choice. Then click **Next**.

10. In the **Chart Source Data** dialog box, confirm the chart range. In the **Series in** section click the **Columns** button to view the difference, then return to **Rows**. Click **Next**.

11. In the **Chart Options** dialog box, be sure the title reads **January Sales**. Click in the **Legend** tab and move the legend to the **Left**. Click in the **Data Labels** tab and select **Show label and percent**. Then click **Next**.

12. In the **Chart Location** dialog box, select to have the chart **As object in** the sheet. Then click **Finish**. The chart is inserted into the worksheet.

13. Click in the chart and move it to a location in the worksheet where it will not cover the worksheet data or the other chart.

14. Click on the handle at the bottom center; a double-headed arrow appears. Drag the chart handle down to enlarge the chart.

15. Print the worksheet and the two charts. At the top write "Ex 9.3, Print 1."

Prepare another chart that displays the differences in the numbers of pizzas sold, and place it in a new sheet.

16. Highlight the range of the worksheet to be charted, A4:D7.

17. Click on the Chart Wizard button. Click in the **Custom Types** tab. Select the **cones** chart. Then click on **Next**.

18. In the **Chart Source Data** dialog box, confirm the selected data range as **$A$4:$D$7**. In the **Series in** section select **Columns**. Then click **Next**.

19. In the **Chart Options** dialog box, click in the **Titles** tab and name the chart **College Pizza Shop**. Click in the **Data Table** tab and select **Show data table**. Then click **Next**.

20. In the **Chart Location** dialog box, select to have the chart **As new sheet**. Then click **Finish**. The chart is inserted into a new worksheet.

21. Rename the sheet **Cones (9.3)**. Format the header to include your name and the file name; place the sheet name in the footer.

22. Return to the **Default Chart** sheet. Access **Page Break Preview** and adjust page breaks. You may print this information on one or two pages but be sure each chart fits entirely on one page.

23. Save and print the **Default Chart** sheet. At the top write "Ex 9.3, Print 2."

Editing Chart Data

Because a worksheet is linked to its chart, changing the data in a worksheet automatically changes its chart, keeping both current and accurate.

Adding New Data

When data is edited, the data markers in a chart immediately reflect the change. Rows or columns may be added; the chart again changes immediately. This is the value of creating linked charts; when information is changed in one place, Excel knows where the links occur and updates the chart.

Editing Data

Once a chart is completed, all parts of it may be edited. Select the section of the chart to be edited; a dialog box opens providing editing choices for that section. All formatting may be edited, including text and alignment, colors and patterns, borders and fonts, and orientation and rotation of a chart. The type of chart may also be changed.

The Chart Toolbar

The *Chart toolbar* places commonly used charting tools on the desktop. To access the Chart toolbar, move the mouse to any toolbar and click on the right mouse button. Then select Chart to open the Chart toolbar, shown in Figure 9.18.

Figure 9.18   Chart Toolbar

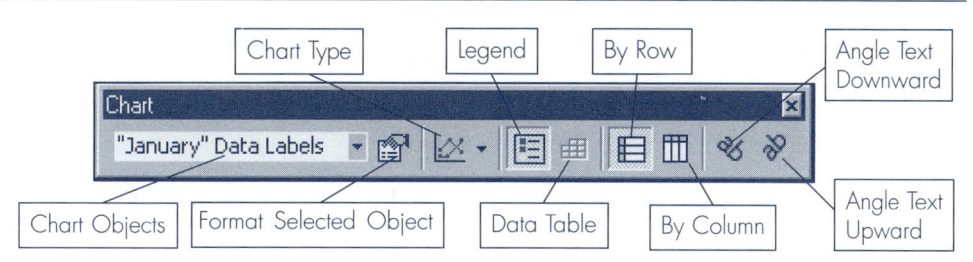

Select the down arrow next to the Chart Objects box to open a list of chart areas to be edited. The down arrow by the Chart Type button accesses a drop-down menu, shown in Figure 9.19, and allows quick selection of different chart types.

Figure 9.19   Selecting Chart Type from the Chart Toolbar

The other formatting tools on the Chart toolbar make it easy to add or remove objects (data table, legend), plot chart data series by row or column, or angle labels.

Exercise 9.4 Editing a Chart

College Pizza Shop finds information that is not accurate and wants to make changes in the original worksheet data. Notice how the charts change as the data changes.

1. Open the workbook saved as **Exer 9** to the **Changes** sheet. A chart is already prepared.

Prepare a chart on a separate sheet.

2. Highlight the range to be charted. Be sure to include row and column labels but not the totals.
3. Use the default chart to insert a chart into the workbook (press F11). Name the sheet **Exer 9-4**.

Change values in the worksheet to see how the chart and worksheet are linked.

4. Select both **Exer 9-4** and **Changes**. In the header, include your name and the file name. In the footer, include the sheet name.
5. In the worksheet, change the number of pepperoni pizzas in January to **47**. Notice how the charts also change.
6. Change the number of combo pizzas in February to **60**.
7. Change the number of cheese pizzas in February to **47**. Notice how these changes are reflected in both charts.
8. Change the number of cheese pizzas in March to **58**.
9. Save and print the **Changes** sheet and the **Exer 9-4** chart. At the top write "Exer 9-4, Print 1."

Insert new data.

10. In the **Changes** sheet, insert a column between columns C and D. (Select cell D3 before inserting the column.)
11. In cell D4 enter **C. Bacon**. Enter **36**, **42**, and **60** for **Jan**, **Feb**, and **Mar** respectively. As this data is entered, notice that the chart sheet automatically changes as each entry is made, but the embedded chart does not. Be sure totals are entered as needed.
12. Highlight the c. bacon column (D4:D8) and drag it to the embedded chart. In the Paste Special dialog box, check that the cells are added as a new series.
13. Print a copy of the **Exer 9-4** chart sheet. At the top write "Exer 9-4, Print 2."
14. Insert a row between rows 7 and 8.
15. In cell A8, enter **April**. Enter pizza quantities as follows: **pepperoni**, **70**; **cheese**, **83**; **c. bacon**, **28**; **combo**, **37**. Be sure the totals are included as needed. Note that this information is not reflected in either chart.

Change the chart range to display the new information in the chart.

16. Highlight the range of new information for April (A8:E8).

17 Click and drag the highlighted range to the chart on this sheet. Watch how the chart changes to reflect the additional data. The data is not updated in the chart sheet.

18 Copy the range (A8:E8) in the worksheet and paste it in the chart sheet. Select the chart before completing the paste.

19 Save changes.

20 Print a copy of the **Changes** sheet and the embedded chart. At the top write "Exer 9-4, Print 3."

Create a pie chart for the sales in March.

21 Select the nonadjacent ranges A4:E4 and A7:E7.

22 From the Chart Wizard, select a pie chart. Use the exploded 3-D style. Then click **Next**.

23 In the **Series in** section, select **Rows**. Then click **Next**.

24 In the **Chart Options** dialog box, include a title of **March Sales**. Do not include a legend. In the **Data Labels** tab, select **Show percent**. Then click **Next**.

25 Be sure the chart is on a separate sheet.

26 Name the chart sheet **Exer 9-4, Print 4**. Be sure the sheet name is in the footer. Print the sheet.

Use the Chart toolbar to edit the worksheet.

27 With **Exer 9-4, Print 4** open, access the Chart toolbar. To do this, position the mouse in any toolbar and click the right button. Select **Chart** in the drop-down menu.

28 From the drop-down menu for Chart Objects, select **Chart Title**.

29 Click on the Format Chart Title button in the Chart toolbar. Select a weighted line around the title and a shadow. Choose an angled orientation. Then click **OK**.

30 In the Chart toolbar, access the Chart Objects drop-down list. Then select **Plot Area**. Access the Chart Type drop-down menu and select the 3-D column chart. A legend is not needed.

31 Print the chart sheet and at the top write "Exer 9-4, Print 5."

32 Save the workbook.

What Type of Chart to Use?

The bar, column, area, line, and pie charts are the most commonly used chart types. Deciding which of these charts to use depends on the data and the purpose of the chart. Understanding the basics of each type of chart is important in deciding which chart best displays the data in question.

Using a Bar Chart

Bar charts compare individual figures over a specific period of time. These charts effectively compare sales figures by region, for example, or illustrate theater attendance for a season.

Yummy Yogurt charts their total sales for the quarter. The worksheet and bar chart are shown in Figure 9.20. This chart clearly shows the comparison of yogurt flavor sales each month.

Figure 9.20   Bar Chart Showing Quarterly Sales

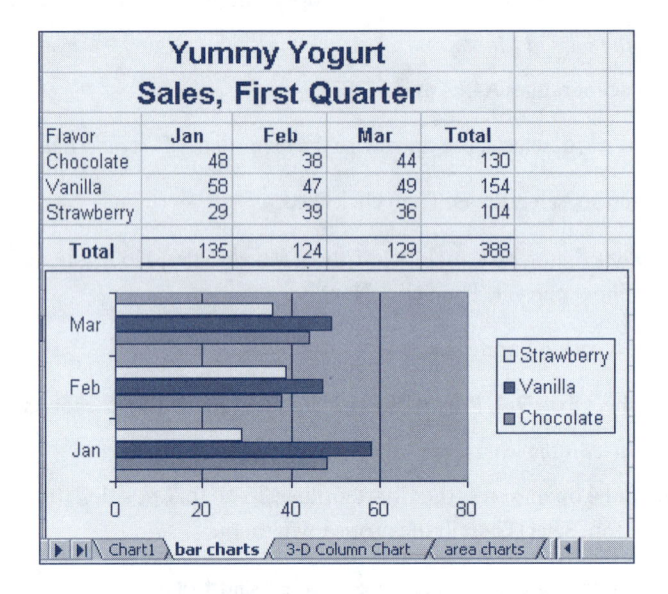

Flavor	Jan	Feb	Mar	Total
Chocolate	48	38	44	130
Vanilla	58	47	49	154
Strawberry	29	39	36	104
Total	**135**	**124**	**129**	**388**

A *stacked bar chart* is excellent for showing the relationship of individual items to the whole. The chart in Figure 9.21 shows the same information as Figure 9.20 in a stacked bar chart. Notice how easy it is to see the relationship of yogurt flavors sold each month and to see that January had the most overall sales, but the lowest amount of strawberry sales.

Figure 9.21   Stacked Bar Chart

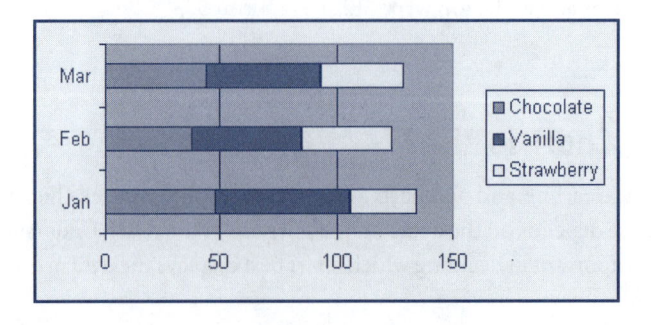

Exercise 9.5   Creating a Bar Chart

First Run Theaters has three movie houses in the city. They have completed an attendance report and would like to have charts prepared with this information.

Prepare a chart showing the total attendance for the three theaters. Arrange the chart so the weekly attendance figures for all the theaters are grouped together. Then create a stacked bar chart that shows the relationship of each week's attendance at each theater.

1   Open the **Exer 9** workbook to the worksheet named **Bar Chart**. This worksheet is already prepared and shows the daily attendance at the theaters.

2   Highlight the chart range A5:E8. Do not highlight the totals.

3   Click on the Chart Wizard button.

4   In the **Chart Type** dialog box, select the clustered bar chart.

5   In the **Chart Source Data** dialog box, select **Rows** in the **Series in** section. This compares the weekly attendance for each theater. (Click **Columns** in the **Series in** section to see its display.)

6   In the **Chart Options** dialog box, include a legend and a title of **First Run Theaters - August 1997**.

7   In the **Chart Location** dialog box, place the chart **As object in** the current sheet. Finish the Chart Wizard.

8   Position the chart just below the worksheet.

9   Check to be sure all category labels are correctly displayed. Adjust the size of the chart if necessary.

Prepare the stacked chart showing each week's attendance.

10   Again select the chart range A5:E8.

11   Click on the Chart Wizard button.

12   In the **Chart Type** dialog box, select a stacked bar chart.

13   In the **Chart Source Data** dialog box, select **Rows** in the **Series in** section.

14   In the **Chart Options** dialog box, include a legend. Title the chart **Weekly Attendance**.

15   In the **Chart Location** dialog box, place the chart **As object in** the current sheet. Finish the Chart Wizard.

16   Position the chart just below the first chart.

17   Print the **Bar Chart** sheet centered vertically and horizontally on one page. Save the workbook.

Using a Column Chart

Column charts show changes of data over a period of time, much like bar charts. A column chart that illustrates the Yummy Yogurt sales for the first quarter is shown in Figure 9.22. In this chart, emphasis is on the variation in sales during the quarter.

Figure 9.22 Column Chart Showing First Quarter Sales

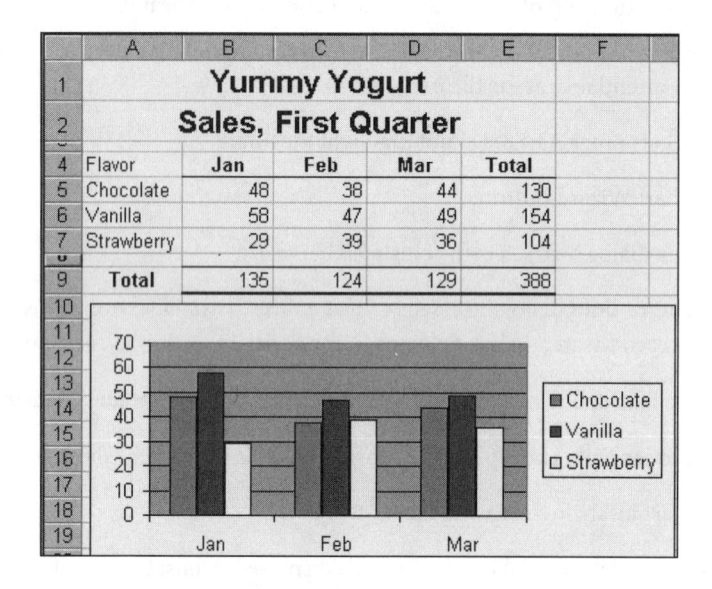

A column chart can also be presented in a 3-D format. A 3-D column chart shows two data series. The 3-D column chart in Figure 9.23 shows the yogurt sales both by flavor and month. In creating this style of 3-D chart, care must be taken to be sure all data series are visible in the chart. Because both data series are labeled, it is not necessary to include a legend.

It is easy to determine information just by looking at a chart. In Figure 9.23, how did the sales of strawberry yogurt compare with the other flavors for the three months?

Figure 9.23 3-D Column Chart

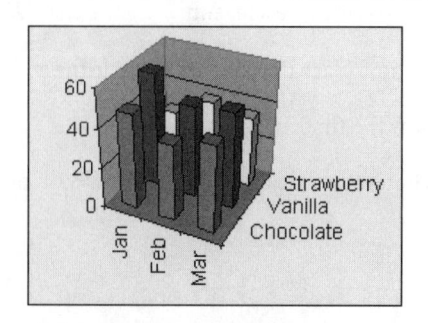

Exercise 9.6 Creating a Column Chart

First Run Theaters would like attendance information shown in column charts. They would like a chart showing the attendance differences by theater. Then they would like a 3-D column chart comparing the attendance by week and by theater.

1 Open the **Exer 9** workbook to the worksheet named **Col Chart**.

2 Select the chart range A5:E8. Access the Chart Wizard.

3 In the **Chart Type** dialog box, select the clustered column chart.

4 In the **Chart Source Data** dialog box, select the data so it is arranged by theater grouping.

5 In the **Chart Options** dialog box, add a title of **Theater Comparisons**. In the **Value axis** section key **Attendance**, and in the **Category axis** section key **Location**. Do not include a legend.

6 In the **Chart Location** dialog box, select to place the chart **As object in** the current sheet.

7 Move the chart just below the cells containing data. You may need to adjust the size.

Complete a 3-D column chart for the same data.

8 Select the chart range A5:E8 and access the Chart Wizard.

9 In the **Chart Type** dialog box, select the 3-D column chart.

10 In the **Chart Source Data** dialog box, select **Rows** in the **Series in** section.

11 In the **Chart Options** dialog box, include the title **August Attendance**. Do not include a legend. (It is not needed when both data series are charted.)

12 In the **Chart Location** dialog box, select **As object in** the current sheet.

13 Position the chart below the other chart in the sheet.

14 Check to be sure all category labels are correctly displayed. Adjust the size of the chart if necessary. You may need to format the text in the axis labels so the entire entry will display.

15 Format the worksheet so it will be centered on the page and it prints on one page.

16 Save and print the **Col Chart** worksheet.

Using an Area Chart

Area charts show a change that occurs over time. An area chart is helpful in showing the magnitude of a change. It also shows the relationship of each part to the whole.

The area chart in Figure 9.24 shows the yogurt sales for a quarter. This chart clearly shows the popularity of vanilla yogurt and the weaker sales of strawberry yogurt.

Figure 9.24   Using an Area Chart to Show Sales by Yogurt Flavors

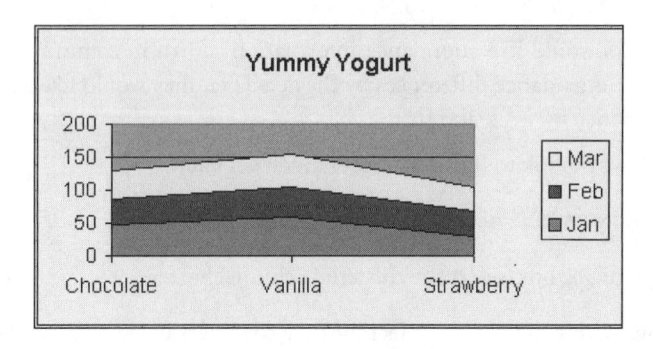

When charting by month, the area chart shows the consistency of sales for these three months, as shown in Figure 9.25.

Figure 9.25   Using an Area Chart to Show Sales by Month

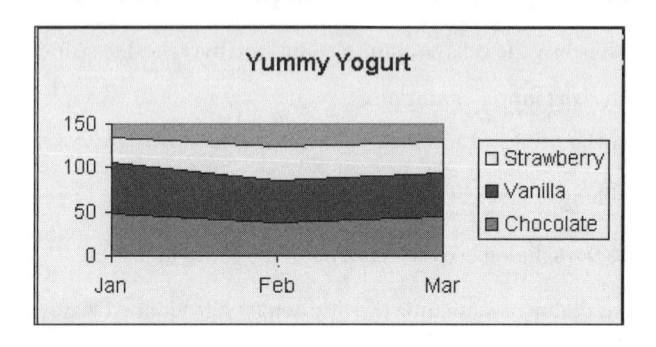

Exercise 9.7   Creating an Area Chart

The First Run Theaters would like to chart its attendance by week and would like to clearly see the changes in attendance over the month. Prepare an area chart for this information.

1. Open the **Exer 9** workbook to the sheet named **Area Chart**.
2. Select the chart range A5:E8. Click the Chart Wizard button.
3. In the **Chart Type** dialog box, select a stacked area chart.
4. In the **Chart Source Data** dialog box, select **Rows** in the **Series in** section.
5. In the **Chart Options** dialog box, enter a title of **August 1998 Attendance**. Include a legend if needed.
6. In the **Chart Location** dialog box, place the chart **As object in** the current sheet. Finish the Chart Wizard.
7. Move the chart so it is beside the cells containing data.
8. Look at the chart. Notice how easy it is to see that weeks 2 and 3 had the largest attendance.

9 Change the attendance at West Ridge Shows for week 2 to **3,707**. Notice the change in the chart.

10 Format the sheet so it is centered vertically and horizontally in landscape style.

11 Save and print the Area Chart sheet.

Using a Line Chart

Line charts are useful in tracking trends at even intervals over a period of time. It is similar to an area chart but emphasizes the rate of change over time rather than the magnitude of the change.

The data used for the chart in Figure 9.25 is also used for the chart in Figure 9.26. It is easy to see the drop in sales of vanilla yogurt and the increase in strawberry sales in the period from January to March.

Figure 9.26   Using a Line Chart

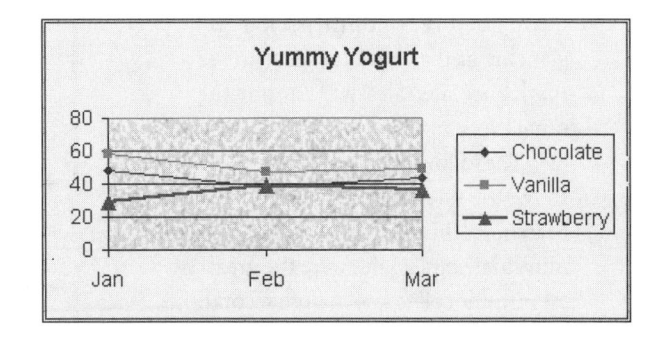

Exercise 9.8   Creating a Line Chart

The First Run Theaters would like to chart its attendance by week and would like to easily compare the attendance figures between the theaters. Prepare a line chart for this information.

1 Open the **Exer 9** workbook to the sheet named **Line Chart**.

2 Select the chart range A5:E8. Access the Chart Wizard.

3 In the **Chart Type** dialog box, select a line chart.

4 In the **Chart Source Data** dialog box, select **Columns** in the **Series in** section. (Notice that if **Rows** is selected, it is difficult to distinguish the data.)

5 In the **Chart Options** dialog box, enter a title of **August 1998 Attendance**. Include a legend if needed.

6 In the **Chart Location** dialog box, place the chart **As object in** the current worksheet. Finish the chart.

7 Position the chart below the cells containing data. Adjust the size of the chart, if needed, so all labels can be read.

8 Change the attendance at North Star Theater for week 3 to **2,987**. Notice the change in the chart.

9 Format so the sheet is centered both horizontally and vertically in portrait style.

10 Save and print the Line Chart sheet.

Using a Pie Chart

A *pie chart* shows the proportion of each part to the whole and contains only one data series. Pie charts are useful for comparing one figure to the whole.

The pie chart in Figure 9.27 shows the sales of chocolate yogurt during a three-month period. By glancing at the chart, it is easy to see that chocolate sales were about the same every month.

The following chart (Figure 9.28) shows the sales of each flavor during March. In this chart, you can determine that vanilla sales were the greatest with chocolate sales a close second.

Pie charts often have the pieces separated. When a piece is removed from the main area, it is called an *exploded pie chart*. An example of a 3-D exploded pie chart is shown in Figure 9.29.

Figure 9.27 Pie Chart for One Yogurt Flavor

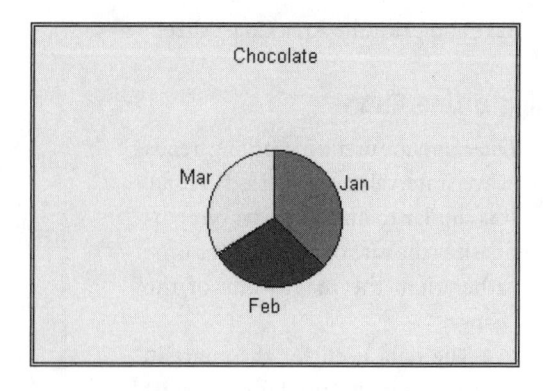

Figure 9.28 Pie Chart for One Month

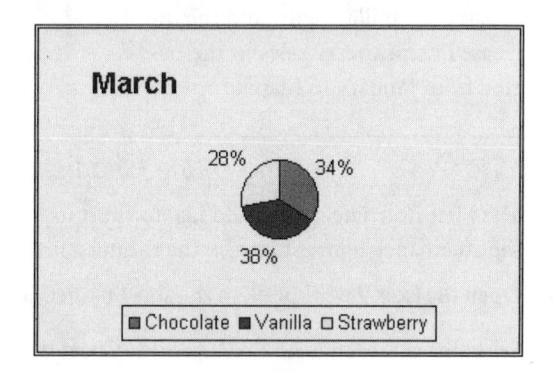

Figure 9.29 Exploded 3-D Pie Chart

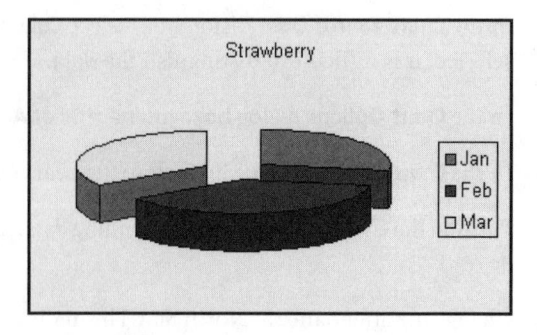

Exercise 9.9   Creating a Pie Chart

First Run Theaters would like to compare the attendance by theater and by week. They would like to compare the attendance at North Star Theater for each week. Then they would like to see the weekly attendance.

1. Open the **Exer 9** workbook to the sheet named **Pie Chart**.
2. Select the chart range. This chart compares only one data series, the weekly totals at North Star Theater, so select the range A5:E6.
3. Open the Chart Wizard.
4. In the **Chart Type** dialog box, select an exploded pie chart.
5. In the **Chart Source Data** dialog box, click in the **Columns** button. Select **Rows** in the **Series in** section. Because there is only one data entry in this column, the entire chart reflects that one entry.
6. In the **Chart Options** dialog box, provide a title if needed. Add a legend and data labels that show the value of each piece of pie.
7. In the **Chart Location** dialog box, select **As object in**. Position the chart below the cells containing data.
8. Check to be sure all category labels are correctly displayed. Adjust the size of the chart if necessary.

Provide a chart comparing week 4 attendance at all theaters.

9. Select the appropriate chart ranges. Select nonadjacent ranges of A5:A8 and E5:E8. Because only one data series can be charted, select only one column of data. Include the column labels for the chart.
10. Click in the Chart Wizard button.
11. Select any pie chart. You might like to use the 3-D pie chart.
12. Select a pie format of your choice. Select **Columns** in the **Series in** section.
13. In the **Chart Options** dialog box, key a title, legend, or data labels, if needed.
14. Place the chart in the same worksheet below the other data.
15. Check to be sure all category labels are correctly displayed. Adjust the size of the chart if necessary.
16. Save the workbook.
17. Print the worksheet so all charts are centered vertically and horizontally on the page.

Summary

- A chart is a graphic representation of data.
- The first step in completing a chart is selecting a chart range.
- Include row and column labels in the chart range. They will be used in the chart as data series that identify the charted data. Totals are not usually charted.

- The default chart is a column chart.
- To quickly create a chart, use the default chart.
- To create a default chart, press the F11 function key. The chart opens on a separate sheet.
- All chart elements may be edited. Text, color, font, and style are a few of the editing choices available.
- A chart sheet is a separate worksheet that contains only a chart.
- Handles are small black boxes along the sides of an active chart area. They are used in sizing a chart window or selected chart area.
- Click once to select a chart. A selected chart may be edited, moved, and sized.
- The Chart Wizard button opens a series of dialog boxes that helps prepare a chart. Several choices are provided in each dialog box.
- The column and row labels of a worksheet become the data series in a chart and are used for the legend and category labels.
- A chart is linked to a worksheet that contains the data. When the data in the worksheet changes, the new results are automatically entered in the chart.
- Additional data can be entered on a chart using the drag-and-drop method. Select the data in the worksheet and drop it into the chart. The chart is automatically updated to show the additional data.
- An embedded chart is placed on the same page as the worksheet data. It is saved and printed with the worksheet.
- The Chart toolbar is useful when editing a chart.
- Bar charts compare individual figures over a specific period of time. Use them for comparison of data.
- Column charts show variation of data over time. Use them when a relationship of an item is compared over a time period.
- Area charts show change over time. These charts effectively show the magnitude of that change.
- Line charts track trends of information at intervals of time.
- Pie charts show the relationship of one data series.

Important Terminology

active chart area	Chart toolbar	fill effects
area charts	Chart Type	gridlines
bar charts	Chart Wizard	handles
category axis	Chart Wizard button	legend
category names	column charts	line charts
chart	data marker	linked
Chart Location dialog box	data point	pie chart
Chart Options dialog box	Data Range	plot area
chart range	data series	Series
chart sheet	default chart	stacked bar chart
Chart Source Data dialog box	embedded chart	value axis
chart title	exploded pie chart	

Study Questions

True-False

Place a T in the space provided if the statement is true; place an F if it is false.

_____ 1. A graphic that shows the relationship between two sets of numbers is a chart.
_____ 2. The toolbar button used for creating charts is the Chart Wizard button.
_____ 3. The entire area for the chart is the plot area.
_____ 4. The value axis of a chart is at the bottom of the chart.
_____ 5. The range of data to be charted is called the chart selection.
_____ 6. Include column and row labels when selecting a chart range.
_____ 7. Always include totals in a chart range.
_____ 8. The first step in creating a chart is to select the Chart Wizard button.
_____ 9. A selected chart can be identified by the handles along the solid outline border.
_____ 10. The default chart type is a pie chart.
_____ 11. A column or pie chart can be expressed in several different styles.
_____ 12. All parts of a chart may be edited for color, font, text size, background, etc.
_____ 13. Once a chart is entered in a worksheet, it cannot be moved or sized.
_____ 14. There is no choice about the placement of row and column titles. A data series is always placed in columns.
_____ 15. A chart is always placed on the same sheet as its worksheet.
_____ 16. Special instructions for printing charts are available in the Print dialog box.
_____ 17. A special toolbar for charts is available.
_____ 18. An embedded chart is placed on the same sheet as its worksheet.
_____ 19. Data can be dragged and dropped into a chart to update the chart.
_____ 20. A chart added to a workbook on a separate sheet has its own tab, usually called Chart.
_____ 21. If changes are made in a worksheet, adjustments must be made manually in the corresponding chart.
_____ 22. A chart created in a separate sheet is not linked to its worksheet.
_____ 23. A chart in a separate document cannot be sized.
_____ 24. To change the size of an embedded chart, click in a handle and drag to the correct size.
_____ 25. A chart always contains a legend.

Fill-In

In the space provided, enter the word that correctly completes the statement.

1. In a chart, the bottom area is called the _____ axis.
2. In a chart, the left area is called the _____ axis.
3. Each plotted value of a chart is a(n) _____ marker and represents one number from a worksheet.
4. Data markers can be identified in the _____ of a chart.
5. The range of data to be charted is called the _____ .
6. The column chart is the _____ chart type because it is used most often.
7. A chart that is on the same sheet as the worksheet data is called a(n) _____ chart.

8. When changes are made in a worksheet, they are automatically reflected in the chart because they are _____ .
9. _____ around the edges of a chart indicate it is active and can be resized.
10. A(n) _____ chart shows the relationship of one variable.
11. Click _____ to select a chart.
12. The _____ contains the data series, legend, title, and labels.
13. When data is to be compared over a specific period of time, use a(n) _____ chart.
14. A(n) _____ chart displays only one data series.
15. To effectively show the magnitude of change over time, use a(n) _____ chart.
16. A(n) _____ chart shows trends of data over intervals of time.

Assignments

Note: The Ch09 subdirectory may be deleted from the Student Data Disk after completing Chapter 9.

Assignment 9.1

Matthew Gonzalez, president of S and G Theaters, has prepared a worksheet to indicate the total ticket sales at his three theaters. He would like to have charts created to show the relationships of this data.

You will prepare several charts to help Mr. Gonzalez plan for the future.

1. Open to the workbook saved as **Ch9 As1** and save the workbook as **Assig 9-1**.
2. Create an embedded bar chart that compares ticket sales by week at all three theaters. Title it **June Admissions**. Print the chart with the worksheet.
   - Do not print gridlines.
   - Include a legend if needed.
   - Format the chart. Look at fonts and font sizes, color, patterns, and fill.
   - Create a header and a footer. Be sure to include your name, the file name, and the sheet name.
   - Position the worksheet and chart on the page so they are centered horizontally and vertically.
   - Place an appropriate name on the sheet tab.
3. Prepare a line chart on a separate sheet so Mr. Gonzalez can easily see if ticket sales are low in a particular theater. Then print the chart.
   - Title it **June Admissions**.
   - Include a legend if needed.
   - Format the chart. Look at fonts and font sizes, color, patterns, and fill.
   - Place the chart on the page so it is centered horizontally and vertically.
   - Include your name in the header or footer. Also include the date, the file name, and the sheet name.
   - Rename the tab of the chart sheet appropriately.
4. Mr. Gonzalez would like to compare the ticket sales by week at each theater. Prepare embedded pie charts on Sheet2 that compare the admissions each week. Then print the charts. All charts will be placed on one sheet.
   - Indicate placement of charts on a separate worksheet in the **Chart Location** dialog box. As you select **As object in**, use the drop-down arrow to select **Sheet2**.

- Title each pie chart **Week 1**, **Week 2**, etc.
- Include legends if needed.
- Arrange and size the charts to maximize the use of the paper. Try either landscape or portrait style. Format the charts; use font and font size, color, borders, fill, and pattern.
- In the header, place **June Admissions** and format it for readability. In the footer, place your name, the file name, and the sheet name. Adjust the header margins so the title is closer to the charts. Header margins may be adjusted in Print Preview or the Page Setup dialog box.
- Rename the tabs in the workbook if necessary.
5. Save and print the workbook.

Assignment 9.2

Five years ago, Janice Bruce opened Bruce's Software Sales. She has prepared a worksheet comparing the total revenues, total sales, and net profits for the last five years. Now she would like to see the trend that has occurred over the last five years.

You will prepare charts for Janice that show this trend in the business.
1. Open to the workbook saved as **Ch9 As2** and save the workbook as **Assig 9-2**.
2. On a separate sheet, prepare an area chart that tracks the revenue, expenses, and profits over the five years.
   - Place the chart on a separate sheet.
   - Use a chart format that will easily show the increase in all areas, especially the net profit.
   - Title the chart **Profit Summary**.
   - Format the chart.
3. On a separate sheet, prepare a line chart that tracks the revenue, expenses, and profits over the five years.
   - Place the chart on a separate sheet.
   - Select an easy-to-read line chart format.
   - Title the chart **Profit Summary**.
4. Rename the sheet tabs appropriately.
5. Format the workbook so your name and the sheet name are in the header and the file name, time, and date are in the footer. Place the charts in the center of the page(s) on which they appear.
6. Save and print the workbook.

Assignment 9.3

Wilson's Clothing Store has branches located in five shopping malls. They are planning to expand some of their stores and would like to see how each store has done during September.
1. Open to the workbook saved as **Ch9 As3** and save the workbook as **Assig 9-3**.
2. Rename the **Sheet1** tab to **September**.
3. Prepare a 3-D column chart on a separate sheet. This chart should compare the sales of each department within the stores. Use a descriptive name to label the tab.
4. On a separate sheet, prepare a pie chart that compares the total sales of all stores. Title it **Total Sales**. Rename the sheet tab appropriately.
5. On a separate sheet, prepare a pie chart that compares the total sales of all departments. Label each data marker with its value. Title the chart **Departmental Sales**. Rename the sheet tab appropriately.

6. Format the four sheets at the same time. Create a header and footer. Be sure to include your name, the file name, the sheet name, and the page number. Format so it is centered both horizontally and vertically.
7. Save and print the entire workbook.

Assignment 9.4

Bev's Grocery Store has started a worksheet to show the revenue for 1998. This report shows the quarterly figures. You will complete the worksheet.

Bev would like charts created that show the relationships between the four quarters.

1. Open the workbook saved as **Ch9 As4** and save the workbook as **Assig 9-4**.
2. Complete all formulas in the worksheet. Use Currency style with zero decimals. Bold the figures in the net profit row.
3. In a separate sheet, prepare a column chart that compares the revenue, total expenses, and net profit for each quarter. Include the company name (**Bev's Grocery Store**) in the chart. Use a chart that will easily show the trend over the four quarters.
4. In a separate sheet, prepare another chart that shows the relationship of total expenses to the net profit. Provide all the information needed (title, legend, etc.).
5. Use descriptive names to rename the sheet tabs.
6. For the three sheets, create headers and footers. Include your name, the sheet name, the file name, and the page number. Format so all charts are centered both horizontally and vertically.
7. Save and print the entire workbook.

Case Problem 9

You have been asked to help Holm Steel Sales prepare the end-of-the-year sales report, which includes a worksheet and several graphs and charts. This portfolio of documents will be used for a report that will be submitted to the president of the company.

Design and prepare a worksheet that lists the salesmen, their territories, and their sales for each quarter. Use December 31 of this year as the report date. The amount of annual sales should also be listed, along with totals for the quarter. Provide a place in the worksheet that lists the amount of commission each salesman receives; each salesman is entitled to a 1.25% commission on all sales.

Be sure your name is in the worksheet. Include **Prepared by** followed by your name in the header or footer. Save the worksheet as **Case 9**.

The specific information is provided in the following list:

		Q1	Q2	Q3	Q4
Blake	West	$329,385	$229,859	$345,002	$398,395
Gilliam	Southwest	$385,221	$102,385	$338,298	$483,192
James	Midwest	$500,385	$332,185	$295,393	$431,835
Lees	Northeast	$128,593	$223,895	$430,198	$338,591
Stoltz	South	$498,383	$395,839	$339,583	$305,121

Prepare the following charts that compare this information. Prepare each chart as a separate sheet.
- Compare the annual sales by territory.
- Compare the sales of each salesman by quarter.
- Compare the quarterly sales by territory for all four quarters.

Chapter 10

Using Built-in Functions

Objectives

1. Identify a function in a worksheet and understand its terminology.
2. Use Paste Function to insert statistical, mathematical, financial, and depreciation functions into a worksheet and enter arguments.
3. Use lookup tables in a worksheet.

Introduction

Many formulas used in business contain complex and lengthy computations. To simplify the entry of some complex formulas, Excel provides built-in functions that replace common business and mathematical formulas. A function is a formula that has already been written and is completed by entering only a few variables.

Lookup tables use a table to insert matching information into a worksheet. For instance, a grading sheet may contain a table identifying a range of scores and the resulting letter grade. This table is used to place the letter grade in the worksheet that corresponds with a specific value in the lookup table.

Over 250 functions are available in Excel, and they perform many different types of complex calculations. Only a few of the basic business functions are covered in this text.

A brief introduction of functions was presented in Chapter 5. However, this chapter will provide a thorough discussion of functions, their use, and the terminology associated with them. In addition, several of the more common business functions will be covered.

Note that at the end of this chapter you may delete the Ch10 directory from your Student Data Disk.

Exploring the Power of Functions

What Is a Function?

Functions are used to quickly complete long, complex formulas by entering only a few variables. The SUM function is an example. Instead of entering individual variables such as =C1+C2+C3+C4+C5+C6+C7+C8+C9, you can obtain the same result when the SUM function enters the variable of C1:C9.

When a function is used, the formula to complete the complex math problem is built into the software. Excel provides functions that are useful for specialized fields such as mathematics and trigonometry, engineering, finance, and statistics. With a basic understanding of functions, it is easy to use the functions of Excel.

The Terminology of Functions

A formula that is entered with a function is written in a sequence called *syntax*. The formula is written internally and is understood by Excel although only the values, called *arguments*, are entered into the function.

The name of a function, such as SUM, is shown in all capital letters. Pieces of variable information, arguments, are shown in parentheses. Arguments are pieces of information used to produce a new value or to perform an action. The number value that is returned to a worksheet is called the *result*. Figure 10.1 shows an example of the SUM function and its syntax. The arguments, number 1 and number 2, will be replaced by values from a worksheet.

Figure 10.1   Function and Its Syntax

=SUM(number 1, number 2,...)

In Figure 10.2, the name of the function is SUM. Arguments are shown in parentheses. In this figure, the argument is the range C1:C10.

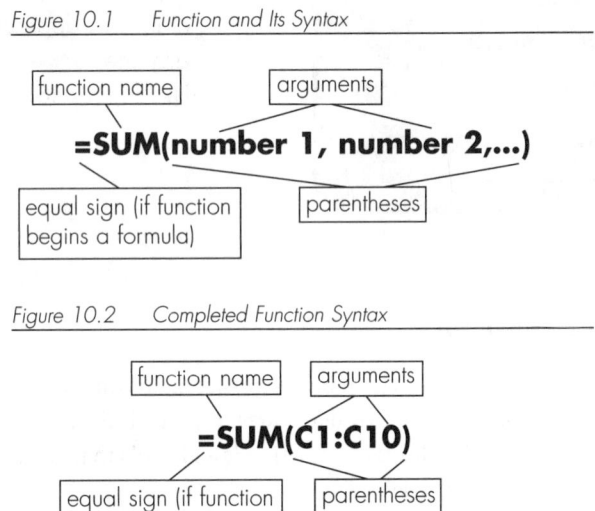

Figure 10.2   Completed Function Syntax

=SUM(C1:C10)

Arguments may be cell references, text, or numbers. An argument separated by a colon indicates a range of cells; an argument separated by a comma indicates nonadjacent cells. An argument may end with an ellipsis, indicating that additional arguments may be added.

Using Paste Function

Paste Function provides an easy way to enter a function without understanding all of the parts of its syntax. To access the Paste Function dialog box, select Function from the Insert menu or click on the *Paste Function button* in the Standard toolbar. All functions are available in the Paste Function dialog box, shown in Figure 10.3

Figure 10.3   Paste Function Dialog Box

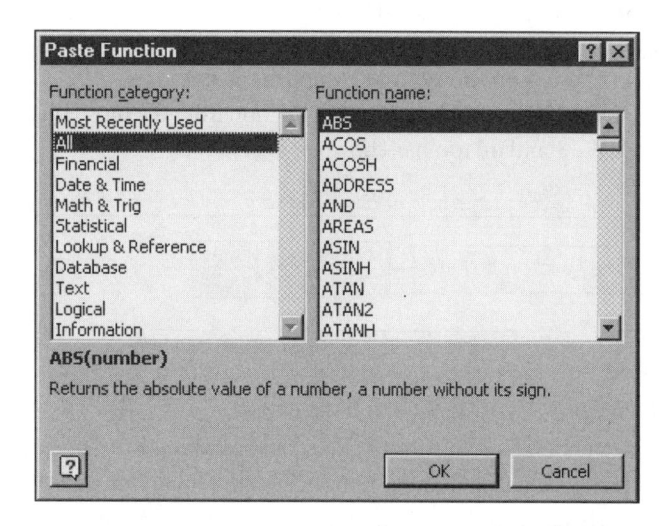

[Paste Function dialog box showing Function category list (Most Recently Used, All, Financial, Date & Time, Math & Trig, Statistical, Lookup & Reference, Database, Text, Logical, Information) and Function name list (ABS, ACOS, ACOSH, ADDRESS, AND, AREAS, ASIN, ASINH, ATAN, ATAN2, ATANH). Description: ABS(number) Returns the absolute value of a number, a number without its sign.]

Because of the number of functions available, the Paste Function dialog box organizes the functions into categories, such as Financial, Math & Trig, Statistical, and Database. They are listed at the left side under Function category. The functions of the highlighted category are shown at the right side in the Function name list.

When the All category is selected, every built-in function is listed. The Most Recently Used category lists the functions recently used on your computer.

When a function has been selected, click OK. The Paste Function dialog box closes and the *Formula Palette* opens. Figure 10.4 shows the SUM Formula Palette with the function entered and the parts of the dialog box identified.

Figure 10.4   Entering Arguments

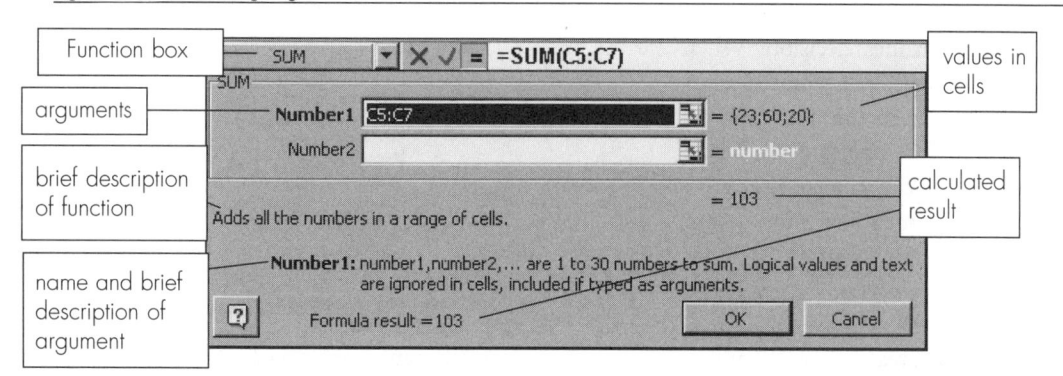

[Formula Palette dialog showing: Function box (SUM), =SUM(C5:C7), Number1 C5:C7 = {23;60;20}, Number2 = number, Adds all the numbers in a range of cells. Number1: number1,number2,... are 1 to 30 numbers to sum. Logical values and text are ignored in cells, included if typed as arguments. Formula result = 103. Labels: Function box, arguments, brief description of function, name and brief description of argument, values in cells, calculated result.]

A Formula Palette provides a description of the function, a description of the arguments, a place to show the results, and a place to enter the arguments. Some of the arguments are bold and some are not. The arguments displayed in bold must be entered to complete the function; the others are optional.

If cells have been selected before Paste Function is accessed, they will appear as arguments. If there is an error or if no cells were selected before accessing the Paste Function dialog box, click on the *Collapse Dialog button* to select the cell or range of cells that will be used in the function. Then click on the *Expand Dialog button* and complete the function.

Paste Function can be accessed by selecting Function from the Insert menu or by clicking the Paste Function button in the Standard toolbar, shown in Figure 10.5.

Figure 10.5   Accessing Paste Function in the Standard Toolbar

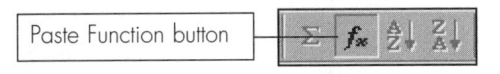

Power Users

Use **Shift**+**F3** to access the Paste Function dialog box.

Another method to access a function is to click on the equal sign in the formula bar. A box opens; the Name box has changed to the Function box, showing the last function selected, shown in Figure 10.6.

Figure 10.6   Accessing a Function in the Formula Bar

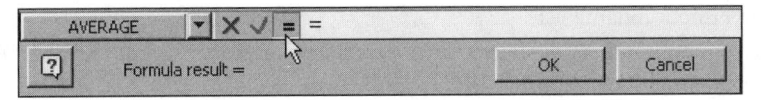

The down arrow to the right of the Function box is used to access other recently used functions, shown in Figure 10.7. This is helpful in quickly accessing functions that are used frequently.

What-if Analysis

Businesses often use spreadsheets to make business decisions. When a spreadsheet is accurately constructed, both the data and the formulas are accurate. Changing a number can change the result of a formula. For this reason, spreadsheets are often used for *What-if analysis*. Examples of this are: "What if the amount of sales were greater?" or "What if the interest rate were different?" or "What if the length of the loan were shorter or longer?"

Figure 10.7   Selecting Functions in the Drop-down List

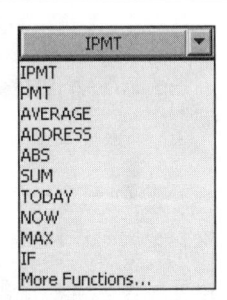

As work is completed in this chapter, several "What-if" questions will be asked. The answers can be found quickly because of Excel's speed and accuracy.

Using Mathematical Functions

Excel provides complex *mathematical functions* such as cosine, matrix determinant, and hyperbolic sine. However, some basic math functions are useful for general application. The function category that includes mathematical functions is Math & Trig; a few Math & Trig functions will be introduced in this chapter.

Figure 10.8 shows a small worksheet that illustrates mathematical functions. The top version shows the results of the functions; the bottom version shows the formulas used for the functions.

Figure 10.8   Results and Formulas of Mathematical Functions

	A	B	C	D
1		7.9276	1.85	4.586
2		7.82016	2.632	1.285
3		9.943399	6.3809	5.06
4		13.62	9.734	9.3812
5				
6	Product	8395.940305	302.4342	279.7345374
7	Round 5	8395.94031	302.4342	279.73454
8	Even	8396	304	280
9	Odd	8397	303	281

	A	B	C	D
1		7.9276	1.85	4.586
2		7.82016	2.632	1.285
3		9.943399	6.3809	5.06
4		13.62	9.734	9.3812
5				
6	Product	=PRODUCT(B1:B4)	=PRODUCT(C1:C4)	=PRODUCT(D1:D4)
7	Round 5	=ROUND(B6,5)	=ROUND(C6,5)	=ROUND(D6,5)
8	Even	=EVEN(B6)	=EVEN(C6)	=EVEN(D6)
9	Odd	=ODD(B6)	=ODD(C6)	=ODD(D6)

The SUM Function

The *SUM function* is a basic mathematical function used frequently in the creation of worksheets. Because it is used so often, the AutoSum button ∑ is located on the Standard toolbar for easy access.

The PRODUCT Function

The *PRODUCT function* multiplies arguments. In Figure 10.8, row 6 shows the results of multiplying the values in rows 1–4 (B1*B2*B3*B4). Arguments are entered in Paste Function in the same way the statistical functions were entered.

The ROUND Function

The *ROUND function* is used to round a number to a specified number of digits to the right or left of the decimal. The ROUND Formula Palette, shown in Figure 10.9, lists two variables, Number and Num_digits. Both variables are shown in bold and must be entered.

Figure 10.9   The ROUND Function

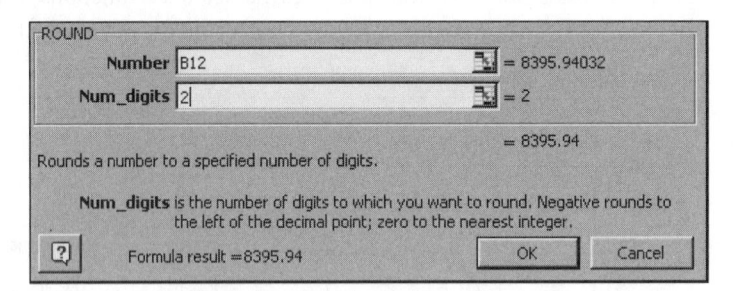

[Figure: ROUND Formula Palette dialog box showing Number = B12 (= 8395.94032), Num_digits = 2, Formula result = 8395.94]

The first variable, Number, asks for the cell reference of the number to be rounded (cell B12). Num_digits asks for the number of digits (decimals) to round to; in this example, it is two. (When the meaning of a variable is unclear, read the definition provided in the Formula Palette.) Notice that the calculated value shown after the Number text box is 8395.94032. The result (rounded to two decimal places) is 8395.94, shown at the bottom of the dialog box. This is the number entered into the cell; the unrounded number resides in the memory of Excel.

A Formula Palette can be positioned anywhere on the screen. Click in its title bar and drag it to an out-of-the-way location so a worksheet can be viewed better.

The EVEN and ODD Functions

Using the *EVEN function* results in a number that is the next higher even integer. Using the *ODD function* results in a number that is the next higher odd integer. The EVEN Formula Palette (shown in Figure 10.10) has one argument, Number. The ODD Formula Palette uses the same syntax.

Figure 10.10   The EVEN Function

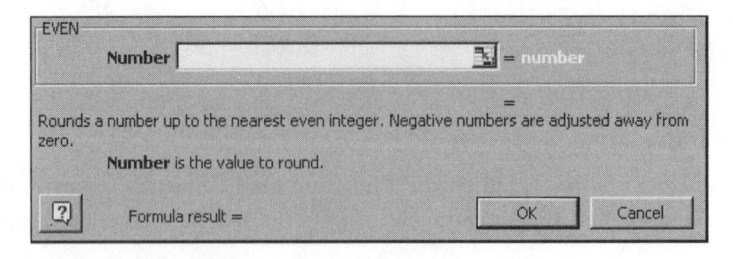

[Figure: EVEN Formula Palette dialog box with Number field empty, showing "Rounds a number up to the nearest even integer. Negative numbers are adjusted away from zero."]

Summary of Mathematical Functions Introduced

EVEN	Rounds a number up to the nearest even integer.
ODD	Rounds a number up to the nearest odd integer.
PRODUCT	Multiplies numbers.
ROUND	Rounds a number to a specified number of digits to the right or left of the decimal.
SUM	Adds numbers.

Exercise 10.1   Using Mathematical Functions

You will practice using mathematical functions in a worksheet.

Note: Before you can complete the exercises and assignments in this chapter, you need to expand the Chapter 10 files on your Student Data Disk. In Windows Explorer, locate the Chapter 10 file and double-click on it. When the files have been expanded, they will be listed in Windows Explorer, and you can access them from Excel.

1   Open **Ch10 Exer** and save it as **Exer 10**.

2   Select all of the sheets in this file. With them grouped, enter your name and the sheet name in the header. Enter the date and the file name in the footer. Format the sheet to be centered both horizontally and vertically.

3   Open the **Mathematical** sheet.

Enter a PRODUCT function.

4   In cell B5, access the **PRODUCT** function in the **Math & Trig** category.

5   The **PRODUCT** Formula Palette opens with a suggested range. Click in the Collapse Dialog button.

6   If the suggested range is incorrect, click and drag through the correct range. Then click on the Expand Dialog button.

7   Click **OK** to complete the function. The product, **39.44040919**, is entered in cell B5.

Enter a ROUND function.

8   In cell B6, access the **ROUND** function from the **Math & Trig** category.

9   The **ROUND** Formula Palette opens with a suggested cell or range. Click on the Collapse Dialog button.

10   Select cell B5. Then click on the Expand Dialog button.

11   In the **Num_digits** box, key **5** (to round to five decimal places). Notice that the calculated value **39.44040919** displays next to the **Number** text box (containing the reference to cell B5), but the value displayed as the result is rounded to five decimal places and reads **39.44041**. Click **OK**.

Enter an EVEN function.

12   In cell B7 access the **EVEN** function from the **Math & Trig** category.

13   Click on the Collapse Dialog button.

14   Click in cell B5 and complete the function. The result of cell B5 is rounded up to the next even whole number and displays in cell B7 as **40**.

Enter an ODD function.

15 In cell B8, access the **ODD** function in the **Math & Trig** category.

16 Click on the Collapse Dialog button ▦.

17 Click in cell B5 and complete the function. The result of cell B5 is rounded up to the next odd whole number and displays in cell B8 as **41**.

Enter additional math functions.

18 In cell C5, access the **PRODUCT** function from the **Math & Trig** category.

19 Cell B5 is the suggested cell. Click on the Collapse Dialog button ▦.

20 Click in cell C1 and then on the Expand Dialog button ▦. Press [Tab] to move to the **Number2** text box.

21 Again click on the Collapse Dialog button ▦. Select cell C2. Then restore the Formula Palette.

22 Complete the process to enter cell C3 as **Number3**. Then complete the function.

23 In cell C6, enter the function to round the amount in cell C5 to three digits to the right of the decimal.

24 In cell C7, enter the function to show the result in cell C5 as the next whole even number.

25 In cell C8, enter the function to show the result in cell C5 as the next whole odd number.

26 Save and print the worksheet.

27 Print a second copy of the worksheet that shows the formulas.

Using Financial Functions

Excel provides several *financial functions* for business use. Some of these functions are for simple interest, depreciation, present and future value, and yields. Only a few of the available functions are discussed in this text.

Arguments of Financial Functions

When a loan is negotiated, a fee called *interest* is charged for the loan. Interest is computed on the amount owed on the loan. The interest rate and the length of the period to pay off the loan determine the amount of interest to be charged. The monthly payment for a loan is determined by multiplying the Pv (the amount originally owed) by the interest rate by the length of the loan (measured by number of payments).

Functions using built-in formulas to determine amount of interest, amount of payment, and amount of principal paid are completed when variables are entered. Arguments for financial functions include Nper, Rate, Pv, and Per. When they are entered into a function, the result instantly appears in the selected cell.

Nper is the number of payment periods of the loan. A one-year loan with monthly payments has 12 payment periods; a three-year loan with monthly payments has 36 periods. Rate is the interest rate for the loan. The interest rate is determined on a per-period basis. Monthly payments have an interest rate divided by 12 (number of months in a year).

Pv is the present value or amount of the loan. Per is the period for the payment. If this were the first loan payment, Per would be one; if it were the twelfth payment, Per would be 12.

Monthly Payment on a Loan

The function that determines the monthly (or periodic) payment on money borrowed is the *PMT function* (PayMenT). When using financial functions, it is important to have a basic understanding of how to determine interest, principal, and payment.

Let's use the example of a $25,000, 10-year loan with an interest rate of 12 percent. Use the PMT function to determine the monthly payment. Figure 10.11 shows the loan information entered in a worksheet and the completed function.

Figure 10.11 Determining Monthly Payment

	A	B	C	D
1	Amount of Loan	$25,000		
2	Interest Rate	12%		
3	Length of Loan	10		
4				
5	Amount of Payment	($358.68)		

Cell B5: =PMT(B2/12,B3*12,B1)

The PMT function is found in the Financial category of functions. In the PMT Formula Palette, the required arguments are in bold—Rate, Nper, and Pv (Figure 10.12).

Figure 10.12 The PMT Dialog Box

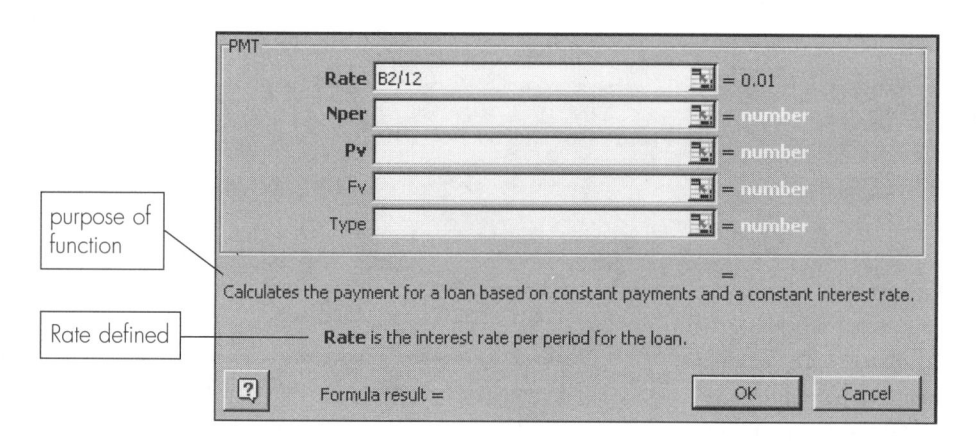

PMT
- Rate: B2/12 = 0.01
- Nper: = number
- Pv: = number
- Fv: = number
- Type: = number

Calculates the payment for a loan based on constant payments and a constant interest rate.

Rate is the interest rate per period for the loan.

[purpose of function] [Rate defined]

The Formula Palette defines the variables; *Rate* is defined as the interest rate per period for the loan (Figure 10.12). In the Rate box, enter B2/12 and then press Tab. This enters the annual interest rate divided by 12 to determine the monthly interest rate.

Nper is defined in the dialog box as the total number of payments for the loan. The loan in this example is a 10-year loan with monthly payments. In the text box, enter the number of years of the loan using the cell reference B3 and multiply by 12 to find the number of monthly payments. The Nper is entered in Figure 10.13 as B3*12.

Figure 10.13 Entering the Number of Payments

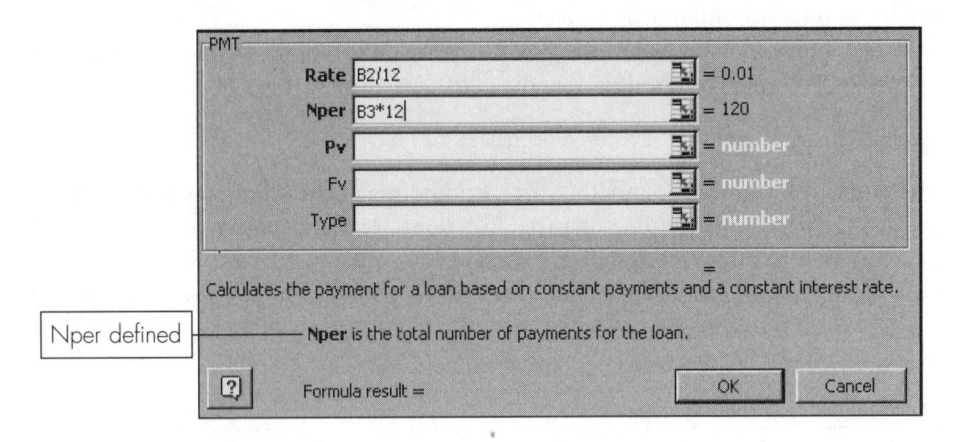

Nper defined — Nper is the total number of payments for the loan.

Next enter the Pv. *Pv* is defined as the present value, or the total amount that a series of future payments is worth now. In the case of a loan, it is the amount borrowed ($25,000, in cell B1). The completed PMT dialog box is shown in Figure 10.14. These three arguments complete the function; notice that the amount of the payment, 358.677371, is shown in the PMT Formula Palette.

Figure 10.14 Entering the Present Value

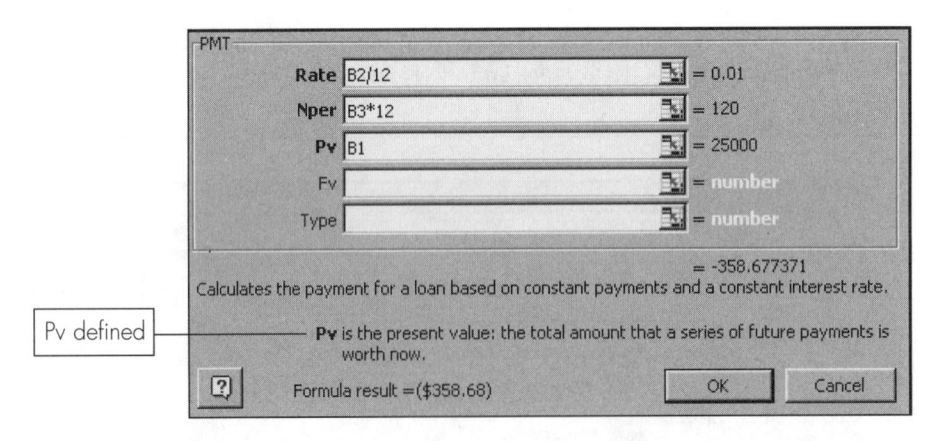

Pv defined — Pv is the present value: the total amount that a series of future payments is worth now.

The completed worksheet is shown in Figure 10.15. The amount of the payment is in parentheses, indicating that it is a negative amount. It is negative because the amount is to be paid from (subtracted from) a bank account. To show the monthly payment as a positive number, place a minus sign (-) in the formula bar before the function syntax. In this case, the formula bar would read =-PMT(B2/12,B3*12,B1).

Figure 10.15 Monthly Payment Result

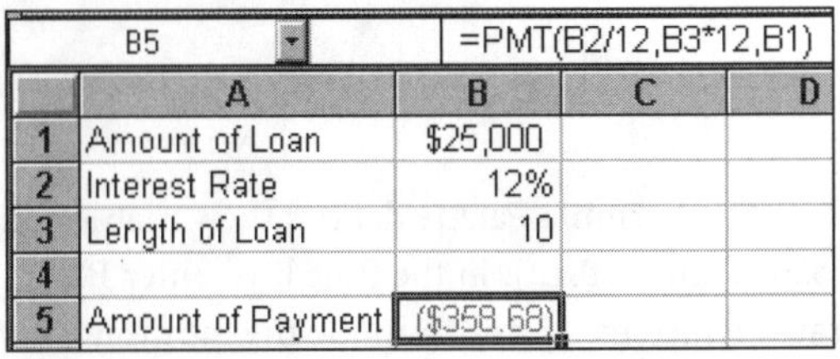

B5 =PMT(B2/12,B3*12,B1)

	A	B	C	D
1	Amount of Loan	$25,000		
2	Interest Rate	12%		
3	Length of Loan	10		
4				
5	Amount of Payment	($358.68)		

One advantage of computer software is in the ability to conduct a What-if analysis. In the case of the loan in the previous example, what if the interest rate were decreased to 10 percent? The resulting worksheet in Figure 10.16 shows that the monthly payment would be $330.38.

Figure 10.16 What-if Example

	A	B
1	Amount of Loan	$25,000
2	Interest Rate	10%
3	Length of Loan	10
4		
5	Amount of Payment	($330.38)

B5 =PMT(B2/12,B3*12,B1)

Exercise 10.2 Using the Payment Function

Determine the amount of the monthly payment on a car loan. The amount borrowed is $8,500 for three years at 11 percent interest.

1 Open the workbook **Exer 10** to the sheet named **Payment**.

2 In cell A2, replace **Student's Name** with your name.

3 In cell B8, access the **PMT** function from the **Financial** category.

4 The collapsible **PMT** dialog box opens. Click on the Collapse Dialog button, and then click in cell B7. Click on the Expand Dialog button.

5 In the **Rate** text box, you need to divide the interest rate by 12 to express the interest on a monthly basis; enter **/12** in the box.

6 Press **Tab** to place the insertion point in the **Nper** box, then collapse the dialog box. Click in cell B6. In the Expand Dialog text box on the screen, enter ***12** after the cell reference since payments are on a monthly basis. Then click on the Expand Dialog button.

7 Press **Tab** to place the insertion point in the **Pv** box, then collapse the dialog box. Click in cell B5, and then restore the dialog box. Click **OK**.

8 The amount of the payment is entered into cell B8 as **($278.28)**. Click in cell B8. In the entry area, place a minus sign (-) just after the equal sign.

9 Save and print the worksheet. At the top write "Print 1."

10 Print a second copy of the worksheet that shows the formulas. Print it on one page, perhaps in landscape mode to make it fit.

Complete a What-if analysis.

11 What if the amount of interest were nine percent? Change the amount in cell B7 to **9%**. Print a copy of the worksheet. At the top write "Print 2."

12 What if the length of time for the loan were four years (and the interest were nine percent)? Change the amount in cell B6 to **4**. Print a copy of the worksheet. At the top write "Print 3."

13 Close the workbook without saving changes.

Interest of a Loan Payment

A payment made on a loan consists of the amount applied to the interest and the amount applied to the principal (or Pv) of the loan. The *principal* of a loan is the amount owed on it. The **IPMT function** (Interest PayMenT) is used to determine the amount of a loan payment that is applied to interest.

In the Paste Function dialog box, access the Financial category and select IPMT. The arguments needed are Rate, Per, Nper, and Pv. The arguments Rate, Nper, and Pv were used in the PMT function. Because more interest is paid at the beginning of a loan than at the end, the *Per* (the period for which the interest payment will be computed) is a factor. If it were the first payment period of the loan, 1 would be entered; if it were the second payment of the loan, 2 would be entered.

To illustrate this function, interest will be determined for a first payment. Use a loan of $25,000 over a period of 10 years at a 12 percent interest rate with payments made monthly. A worksheet using this function is shown in Figure 10.17, with the amount of interest for the first payment being $250.

The completed IPMT Formula Palette is shown in Figure 10.18. Enter 1 (first payment) in the Per text box.

Figure 10.17 Interest on a Loan Payment

	A	B	C	D
1	Amount of Loan	$25,000		
2	Interest Rate	12%		
3	Length of Loan	10		
4				
5	Amount of Interest	($250.00)		

B5 =IPMT(B2/12,1,B3*12,B1

Figure 10.18 Interest on a Loan

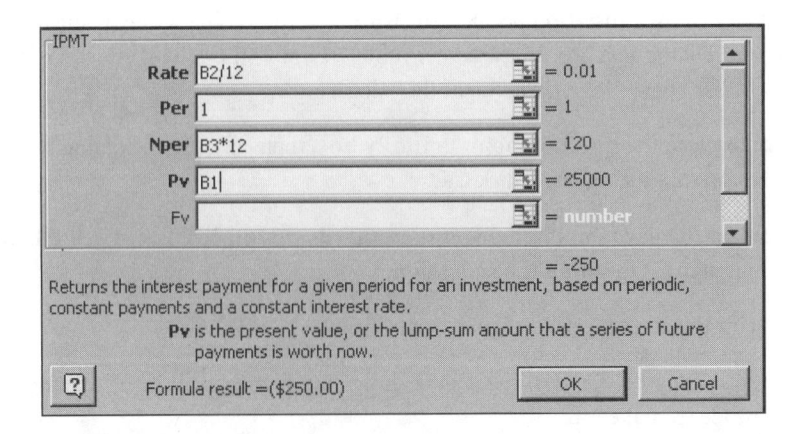

IPMT
Rate B2/12 = 0.01
Per 1 = 1
Nper B3*12 = 120
Pv B1 = 25000
Fv = number

= -250
Returns the interest payment for a given period for an investment, based on periodic, constant payments and a constant interest rate.
  Pv is the present value, or the lump-sum amount that a series of future payments is worth now.

Formula result =($250.00)   OK   Cancel

What if this were the last payment of the loan? The Per (period) for the last payment would be 120, for the 120th payment made (10 years times 12 payments each year). The result is shown in Figure 10.19. The amount of interest for the 120th payment is $3.55.

Figure 10.19 Interest Amount on a Loan

	A	B	C	D
	B5	=IPMT(B2/12,120,B3*12,B1)		
1	Amount of Loan	$25,000		
2	Interest Rate	12%		
3	Length of Loan	10		
4				
5	Amount of Interest	($3.55)		

Again, the amount is negative because it is an amount to be paid.

Exercise 10.3 Determining an Amount of Interest

Determine the amount of the interest on the first payment on a car loan. The amount borrowed is $8,500 over a three-year period at 11 percent interest.

1 Open the workbook **Exer 10** to the sheet named **Interest**.

2 In cell B5 access the **IPMT** function from the **Financial** category.

3 The collapsible **IPMT** dialog box opens. Enter the **Rate** as **B2/12**, the **Per** as **1** (first payment), the **Nper** as **B3*12**, and the **Pv** as **B1**. Click **OK**.

4 The amount of interest **($77.92)** is entered in cell B5.

5 In the entry area of the formula bar, enter a minus sign (-) after the equal sign (=).

6 Save and print the worksheet. Write "Print 1" at the top.

7 Print a second copy of the worksheet that shows the formulas used.

Complete a What-if analysis.

8 What if the rate were nine percent? Change the rate in cell B2 to **9%** and print another copy of the worksheet. Write "Print 2" at the top.

9 What if it were the last payment? Click in cell B5, then click on the Paste Function button. The **IPMT** dialog box opens. Change the **Per** from **1** to **36**. Click on **OK**.

10 Print the worksheet. At the top write "Print 3."

11 Close the worksheet without saving changes.

Using Principal on Loan

The **PPMT function** (Principal PayMenT) is used to compute the amount of the principal paid on a loan. The principal of a loan is the amount owed. When a loan payment is made, part of the payment is for the interest and the rest is applied to the principal.

Let's use the same loan that was used to determine the interest payment. This is a $25,000, 10-year loan with an interest rate of 12 percent. What is the amount of the first payment that applies to the principal? Figure 10.20 shows the worksheet showing this formula.

Figure 10.20   PPMT Function

B5		=PPMT(B2/12,1,B3*12,B1)	
A	B	C	D
1 Amount of Loan	$25,000		
2 Interest Rate	12%		
3 Length of Loan	10		
4			
5 Amount of Principal	($108.68)		

The completed PPMT Formula Palette is shown in Figure 10.21. The four arguments—Rate, Per, Nper, and Pv—are completed.

Figure 10.21   Principal Payment Function

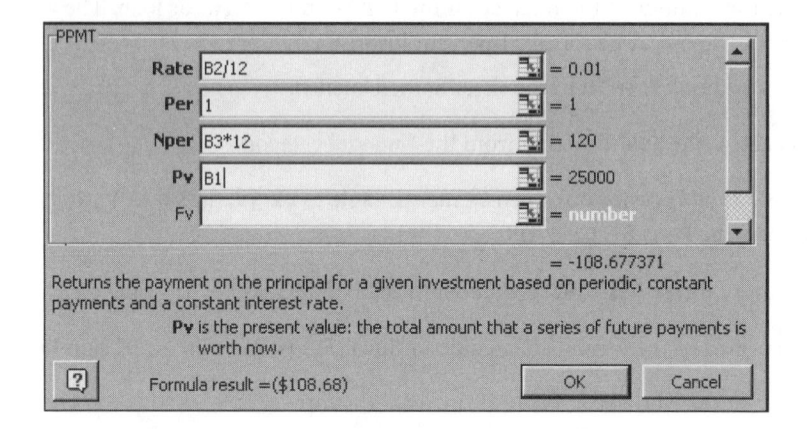

```
┌─PPMT─────────────────────────────────────────────┐
│          Rate  B2/12              = 0.01          │
│           Per  1                  = 1             │
│          Nper  B3*12              = 120           │
│            Pv  B1                 = 25000         │
│            Fv                     = number        │
│                                                   │
│                                   = -108.677371   │
│ Returns the payment on the principal for a given  │
│ investment based on periodic, constant payments   │
│ and a constant interest rate.                     │
│       Pv is the present value: the total amount   │
│       that a series of future payments is worth   │
│       now.                                        │
│ [?]   Formula result =($108.68)   [ OK ] [Cancel] │
└───────────────────────────────────────────────────┘
```

The amount of the principal on the last payment would be entered the same way, except the Per would be 36, for the 36th payment made. Figure 10.22 shows this formula in the formula bar and the result in cell B5. The amount applied to principal for the 36th payment is $153.95.

Figure 10.22   Principal Paid on a Loan

B5		=PPMT(B2/12,36,B3*12,B1)	
A	B	C	D
1 Amount of Loan	$25,000		
2 Interest Rate	12%		
3 Length of Loan	10		
4			
5 Amount of Principal	($153.95)		

Exercise 10.4   Determining an Amount of Principal

Determine the amount of the principal paid on the first payment of a car loan. The amount borrowed is $8,500 for three years at 11 percent interest.

1   Open the workbook **Exer 10** to the **Interest** sheet.

2   In cell A6 enter **Amount of Principal**.

3   In cell B6 access the **PPMT** function from the **Financial** category.

4   In the **PPMT** dialog box, enter the **Rate** as **B2/12**, the **Per** as **1**, the **Nper** as **B3*12**, and the **Pv** as **B1**. Click **OK**.

5   Display the amount as a positive number.

6   In cell A7 enter **Amount of Payment**.

7   In cell B7 enter the function for PPMT as a positive number. Does the interest + principal = payment?

8   Save and print the worksheet. At the top write "Print 1."

9   Display the formulas and print another copy of the worksheet. Print it on one page, perhaps in landscape form so it fits.

Complete a What-if analysis.

10   What are the interest and principal payments for the first payment of the second year? Replace the **Per** with **13** in both the interest and principal functions. Print a copy of the worksheet; at the top write "Print 2."

11   What if the interest rate were nine and a half percent? Change the amount in cell C5 to **9.5%**. Notice that the amounts change in the cells that contain C5 as a cell reference in their functions.

12   Print a copy of the worksheet. At the top write "Print 3."

13   Close the worksheet without saving changes.

Preparing a Payment Chart

When borrowing or lending money, it is informative to have a *payment chart* that shows the amounts of interest, principal, and outstanding balance throughout the life of a loan. This chart is easy to prepare using financial functions. The chart in Figure 10.23 shows a part of a payment schedule created for a $3,000, two-year loan at eight percent interest. The information for the loan is placed at the top of the worksheet.

Notice that the payment amount is the same each month, but the amount applied to interest decreases and the principal applied against the loan increases.

Figure 10.23 Payment Chart

	A	B	C	D	E	F
1	Amount of Loan	$3,000				
2	Interest Rate	8%				
3	Length of Loan	2				
4						
5	Payment No.	Beginning Balance	Payment Amount	Interest Amount	Principal	Ending Balance
6						
7	1	$3,000	$135.68	$20.00	$115.68	$2,884
8	2	$2,884	$135.68	$19.23	$116.45	$2,768
9	3	$2,768	$135.68	$18.45	$117.23	$2,651
10	4	$2,651	$135.68	$17.67	$118.01	$2,533
11	5	$2,533	$135.68	$16.88	$118.80	$2,414
12	6	$2,414	$135.68	$16.09	$119.59	$2,294
13	7	$2,294	$135.68	$15.29	$120.39	$2,174
14	8	$2,174	$135.68	$14.49	$121.19	$2,053
15	9	$2,053	$135.68	$13.68	$122.00	$1,931
16	10	$1,931	$135.68	$12.87	$122.81	$1,808
17	11	$1,808	$135.68	$12.05	$123.63	$1,684
18	12	$1,684	$135.68	$11.23	$124.45	$1,560
19	13	$1,560	$135.68	$10.40	$125.28	$1,434
20	14	$1,434	$135.68	$9.56	$126.12	$1,308
21	15	$1,308	$135.68	$8.72	$126.96	$1,181
22	16	$1,181	$135.68	$7.88	$127.81	$1,054
23	17	$1,054	$135.68	$7.02	$128.66	$925
24	18	$925	$135.68	$6.17	$129.52	$795
25	19	$795	$135.68	$5.30	$130.38	$665

This chart was created by placing function formulas in row 7 and then copying the formulas through the rest of the worksheet. The function formulas are shown in Figure 10.24.

Figure 10.24 Payment Chart Formulas

	A	B	C	D	E	F
5	Payment No.	Beginning Balance	Payment Amount	Interest Amount	Principal	Ending Balance
6						
7	1	=B1	=-PMT($B$2/12,$B$3*12,$B$1)	=-IPMT($B$2/12,A7,$B$3*12,$B$1)	=-PPMT($B$2/12,A7,$B$3*12,$B$1)	=B7-E7
8	2	=F7	=-PMT($B$2/12,$B$3*12,$B$1)	=-IPMT($B$2/12,A8,$B$3*12,$B$1)	=-PPMT($B$2/12,A8,$B$3*12,$B$1)	=B8-E8
9	3	=F8	=-PMT($B$2/12,$B$3*12,$B$1)	=-IPMT($B$2/12,A9,$B$3*12,$B$1)	=-PPMT($B$2/12,A9,$B$3*12,$B$1)	=B9-E9
10	4	=F9	=-PMT($B$2/12,$B$3*12,$B$1)	=-IPMT($B$2/12,A10,$B$3*12,$B$1)	=-PPMT($B$2/12,A10,$B$3*12,$B$1)	=B10-E10
11	5	=F10	=-PMT($B$2/12,$B$3*12,$B$1)	=-IPMT($B$2/12,A11,$B$3*12,$B$1)	=-PPMT($B$2/12,A11,$B$3*12,$B$1)	=B11-E11

Column A is used to number the payments. AutoFill was used to complete this column. The beginning balance, $3,000, is in cell B1 (the cell reference of B1 is used wherever the amount is shown on the worksheet).

Column C is used for the payment amount. The function for the payment amount, PPMT, is entered in cell C7. The minus sign before the function name displays the result as a positive number. This formula is then copied through the rest of the column. Absolute references are used for the Pv, Rate, and Per. Absolute references should be entered in the Paste Function dialog box at the same time the cell reference is entered (by using the F4 function key).

Column D is used for the amount of interest; the IPMT function is entered in cell D7. The minus sign before the function name is used so the result will be a positive number. In the IPMT dialog box, the Per is the first payment (cell reference A7). This is entered as a relative reference so it changes to match the appropriate payment number in column A when the function is copied.

Column E is used for the amount applied to the principal; the PPMT function is entered in cell E7. Again the minus sign is placed before the function name so the result will be a positive number.

Column F is used for the ending balance, which is found by subtracting the amount of principal in column E from the beginning balance in column B.

In cell B8 is the formula for the beginning balance, which is equal to the ending balance of row 7. In this example it is =F7.

After the formulas are entered, copy them through the columns. Notice the relationship of the relative and absolute references as the formulas are copied.

Exercise 10.5   Preparing a Payment Chart

Prepare a payment chart for a six-month, $500 loan at seven percent interest. Payments will be made monthly.

1 Open the workbook **Exer 10** to the **Payment Chart** sheet.

2 Enter the payment numbers in column A beginning with row 8. Enter **1** in cell A8 and **2** in cell A9. Use the AutoFill feature to extend through the number of payments needed (**6**). Format for center alignment.

3 In cell B8 key the beginning balance, **$500**.

4 In cell C8 access the **PMT** function in the **Financial** category.

5 In the **Rate** box, enter **B5** (as an absolute reference) divided by **12** (**$B$5/12**).

6 In the **Nper** box, enter **B4** (as an absolute reference) multiplied by **12** (**$B$4*12**).

7 In the **Pv** box, enter **B3** (as an absolute reference). Click **OK**.

8 Display the amount as a positive number.

9 In cell D8 access the **IPMT** function from the **Financial** category.

10 In the **Rate** box, enter **B5** (as an absolute reference) divided by **12** (**$B$5/12**).

11 In the **Per** box, enter **A8** as a relative reference. As the number of the payment changes, this reference will also change.

12 In the **Nper** box, enter **B4** (as an absolute reference) multiplied by **12** (**$B$4*12**).

13 In the **Pv** box, enter **B3** (as an absolute reference). Click **OK**.

14 Display the total as a positive amount.

15 In cell E8 access the **PPMT** function from the **Financial** category.

16 In the **Rate** box, enter **B5** (as an absolute reference) divided by **12** (**$B$5/12**).

17 In the **Per** box, enter **A8**. As the number of the payment changes, this reference will also change.

18 In the **Nper** box, enter **B4** (as an absolute reference) multiplied by **12** (**$B$4*12**).

19 In the **Pv** box, enter **B3** (as an absolute reference). Click **OK**.

20 Display the total as a positive amount.

21 In cell F8 enter the formula to find the ending balance. The ending balance is the beginning balance minus the principal (**=B8-E8**).

22 In cell B9, enter the beginning balance. It is **=F8**.

23 Copy the appropriate formulas through the worksheet.

24 Format correctly for currency and with two decimals.

25 Adjust the column widths if needed.

26 Save and print the worksheet.

27 Print a second copy of the worksheet showing the formulas in landscape style on one page. Adjust the column widths so all of the functions are visible.

28 Close the worksheet without saving changes.

Depreciation Functions

An asset decreases in value because of obsolescence or wear and tear. This decrease in the value of an asset is called *depreciation*. Accountants use several different methods to determine depreciation; functions for the common methods of determining depreciation are included with Excel.

In this unit, depreciation will be determined using the straight-line method, the declining balance method, and the sum-of-years' digits method.

Depreciation Basics

Cost, life, and salvage value must be known to determine depreciation. The *life of asset* is the estimated time an asset will be usable. The estimated value of an asset at the end of its life, called the *salvage value*, is also needed. The *cost* is the amount paid for an asset.

Straight-Line Depreciation

To use *straight-line depreciation*, select the *SLN function* from the Financial category. The required arguments are Cost, Salvage, and Life.

In the depreciation functions, Life is expressed as the number of periods over which an asset is depreciated. If the depreciation is on an annual basis, the Life is the number of expected years of use. If the depreciation is monthly, the Life is the number of expected years of use multiplied by 12 (the number of months in a year).

The SLN (Straight-LiNe depreciation) Formula Palette is shown in Figure 10.25. When using straight-line depreciation, refer to the definitions presented in the dialog boxes to assist in preparing a worksheet. In Figure 10.25, Cost is defined as the initial cost of the asset.

Figure 10.25 Straight-Line Depreciation Dialog Box

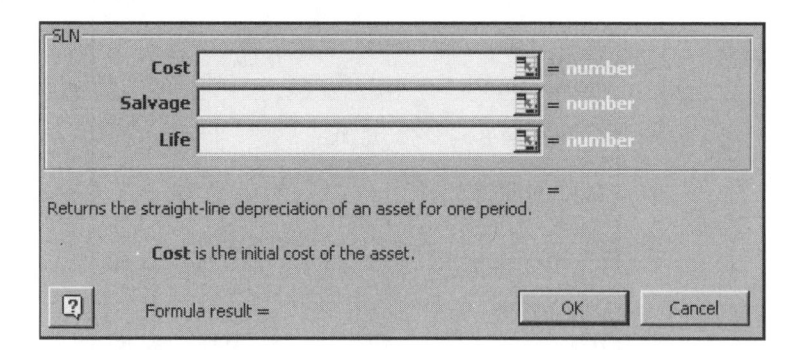

As an example, office equipment is purchased for $5,000. The salvage value is anticipated to be $750 with a life of three years. The worksheet to determine the amount of depreciation using the straight-line method is shown in Figure 10.26.

Figure 10.26 Worksheet for Straight-Line Depreciation

	A	B
1	Purchase Price	$5,000
2	Life of Asset	3
3	Salvage Value	$750

If depreciation is to be determined on a monthly basis, express the life on a per month basis by multiplying the life (number of years) by 12. The completed SLN Formula Palette is shown in Figure 10.27.

Figure 10.27 Completed Straight-Line Depreciation Dialog Box

Depreciation is often placed in a schedule so the value of an asset can be traced over its entire life. Figure 10.28 shows a depreciation schedule using straight-line depreciation. When straight-line depreciation is used, the asset decreases in value an equal amount each period. In this illustration, an asset was purchased for $5,000 with a useful life expectancy of three years. The salvage value is estimated at $750. ***Book value*** is the cost less the current depreciation. When the asset is fully depreciated, the book value should equal the salvage value.

Figure 10.28 Straight-Line Depreciation Schedule

	A	B	C	D
1	Asset A		Straight-Line	
2	Depreciation Schedule			
3				
4	Purchase Price	$5,000		
5	Salvage Value	$750		
6	Life of Asset	6		
7		Annual Depreciation	Total Depreciation	Book Value
8	Year 1	$708.33	$708.33	$4,292
9	Year 2	$708.33	$1,416.67	$3,583
10	Year 3	$708.33	$2,125.00	$2,875
11	Year 4	$708.33	$2,833.33	$2,167
12	Year 5	$708.33	$3,541.67	$1,458
13	Year 6	$708.33	$4,250.00	$750

Figure 10.29 shows the functions used in the above depreciation schedule. Notice that the arguments are expressed as absolute values.

Figure 10.29 SLN Functions Displayed

	A	B	C	D
1	Asset A		Straight-Line	
2	Depreciation S			
3				
4	Purchase Price	5000		
5	Salvage Value	750		
6	Life of Asset	6		
7		Annual Depreciation	Total Depreciation	Book Value
8	Year 1	=SLN($B$4,$B$5,$B$6)	=B8	=$B$4-C8
9	Year 2	=SLN($B$4,$B$5,$B$6)	=C8+B9	=$B$4-C9
10	Year 3	=SLN($B$4,$B$5,$B$6)	=C9+B10	=$B$4-C10
11	Year 4	=SLN($B$4,$B$5,$B$6)	=C10+B11	=$B$4-C11
12	Year 5	=SLN($B$4,$B$5,$B$6)	=C11+B12	=$B$4-C12
13	Year 6	=SLN($B$4,$B$5,$B$6)	=C12+B13	=$B$4-C13

Exercise 10.6   Using Straight-Line Depreciation

Determine the depreciation for an asset that was purchased for $2,000 with a life expectancy of three years. The salvage value is estimated at $250. Determine the annual and monthly amounts for depreciation using the straight-line method of depreciation.

1   Open the workbook **Exer 10** to the sheet **Straight Line**.

Determine the annual depreciation.

2 In cell B10 access the **SLN** function from the **Financial** category.

3 In the **SLN** dialog box, enter cell **B5** for **Cost**, cell **B7** for **Salvage**, and cell **B6** for **Life**. Click on **OK**. The annual amount of depreciation, **$583.33**, is entered into cell B10.

Determine the monthly depreciation.

4 In cell C10 access the **SLN** function from the **Financial** category.

5 In the **SLN** dialog box, for **Cost** enter cell **B5**; for **Salvage** enter cell **B7**; for **Life** enter **B6*12**, since the monthly depreciation is needed. Click on **OK**. The annual amount of depreciation, **$48.61**, is entered into cell C10.

6 Adjust column widths and cell heights if needed.

7 Print and save the worksheet. At the top write "Print 1."

8 Print a copy of the worksheet that shows the formulas. Print it on one page.

Complete some What-if analyses.

9 What if the life of the asset were seven years? Print a worksheet showing this possibility. At the top write "Print 2."

10 What if the salvage value were $1,500? Print a worksheet showing this possibility. At the top write "Print 3."

11 Close the workbook without saving changes.

Declining-Balance Depreciation

The declining-balance method of depreciation uses the theory that an asset depreciates more at the beginning of its life than at the end. To use the ***declining-balance depreciation*** method, select the ***DB function***. The necessary arguments are Cost, Salvage, Life, and Period. In the DB Formula Palette, Period is defined as the period for which you want to calculate the depreciation. The completed DB (Declining-Balance) Formula Palette is shown in Figure 10.30. When the depreciation period is less than a full year, the number of months the asset is used in the first year is entered here.

Figure 10.30 Declining-Balance Dialog Box

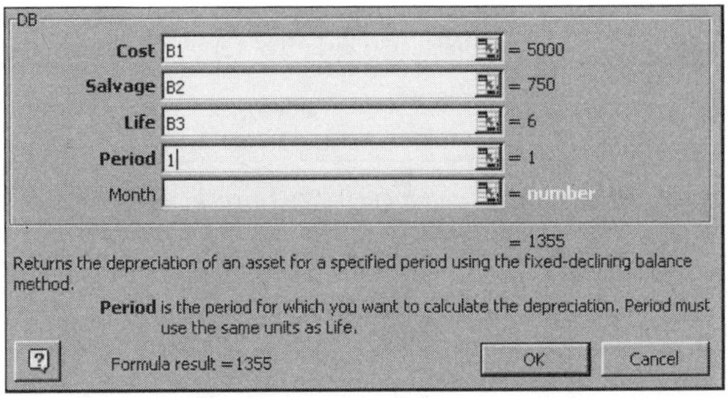

A depreciation schedule using the declining-balance method is shown in Figure 10.31.

Figure 10.31 Declining-Balance Depreciation Schedule

	A	B	C	D
1	Asset A		Declining Balance	
2	Depreciation Schedule			
3				
4	Purchase Price	$5,000		
5	Salvage Value	$750		
6	Life of Asset	6		
7	Year	Annual Depreciation	Total Depreciation	Book Value
8	1	$1,355.00	$1,355.00	$3,645
9	2	$987.80	$2,342.80	$2,657
10	3	$720.10	$3,062.90	$1,937
11	4	$524.95	$3,587.85	$1,412
12	5	$382.69	$3,970.54	$1,029
13	6	$278.98	$4,249.53	$750

The formulas used are shown in Figure 10.32. In this example, the asset depreciates on an annual basis; the first year is entered as Period 1, year 2 is entered as Period 2, etc. In the formula, the Period is entered as a relative reference to match the year in column A.

Figure 10.32 Declining-Balance Functions

	A	B	C	D
1	Asset A		Declining Balance	
2	Depreciation			
3				
4	Purchase Pri	5000		
5	Salvage Valu	750		
6	Life of Asset	6		
7	Year	Annual Depreciation	Total Depreciation	Book Value
8	1	=DB($B$4,$B$5,$B$6,A8)	=B8	=$B$4-C8
9	2	=DB($B$4,$B$5,$B$6,A9)	=C8+B9	=$B$4-C9
10	3	=DB($B$4,$B$5,$B$6,A10)	=C9+B10	=$B$4-C10
11	4	=DB($B$4,$B$5,$B$6,A11)	=C10+B11	=$B$4-C11
12	5	=DB($B$4,$B$5,$B$6,A12)	=C11+B12	=$B$4-C12
13	6	=DB($B$4,$B$5,$B$6,A13)	=C12+B13	=$B$4-C13

Exercise 10.7 Using the Declining-Balance Function

Use the declining-balance method to determine the depreciation of an asset that was purchased for $2,000 with a life expectancy of three years. The salvage value is expected to be $250. Determine the annual and monthly amounts of depreciation over the life of the asset.

Exercise 10.7—Using the Declining-Balance Function

1. Open the workbook **Exer 10** to the sheet **Declining Balance**.

Complete a depreciation schedule on an annual basis.

2. In cell B10 access the **DB** function from the **Financial** category.

3. In the **DB** dialog box, for **Cost** enter B5 as an absolute reference (**$B$5**); for **Salvage** enter B7 as an absolute reference (**$B$7**); for **Life** enter B6 as an absolute reference (**$B$6**); for **Period** enter A10 as a relative reference.

4. Click **OK**. The amount, **$1,000.00**, is entered in cell B10.

5. Copy the formula through the third year. Notice how the depreciation amount decreases each year.

Complete a depreciation schedule on a monthly basis for the first year.

6. In cell C10 access the **DB** function from the **Financial** category.

7. In the **DB** dialog box, for **Cost** enter B5 as an absolute reference (**$B$5**); for **Salvage** enter B7 as an absolute reference (**$B$7**); for **Life** enter cell B6 as an absolute reference and multiply by **12** (depreciation figured on a monthly basis); for **Period** enter A10 as a relative reference.

8. Click **OK**. The amount, **$112.00**, is entered in cell C10.

9. Copy the formula through the appropriate range of the worksheet. Notice how the depreciation amount decreases each month. Click in cells C12, C15, and C20 to see how the formula was copied; notice that the Per value changes with each formula.

10. Save and print the worksheet. At the top write "Print 1."

11. Print a copy of the worksheet that shows the formulas.

Complete some What-if analyses.

12. What if the value of this asset were $8,500 and it had an expected life of eight years? Make the necessary changes and print a copy of the worksheet for the first year. At the top write "Print 2."

13. What if the value of this asset were $2,500 and it had an expected life of two years? Make the necessary changes and print a copy of the worksheet for the first year. At the top write "Print 3."

14. Close the workbook without saving changes.

Sum-of-Years' Digits Depreciation

The *sum-of-years' digits depreciation* method, like the declining-balance depreciation method, recognizes that an asset depreciates in greater amounts during the early years of its life.

To access the sum-of-years' digits function, select *SYD function*. The arguments are Cost, Salvage, Life, and Per. The completed SYD (Sum-of-Years' Digits) Formula Palette is shown in Figure 10.33.

Figure 10.33 Sum-of-Years' Digits Dialog Box

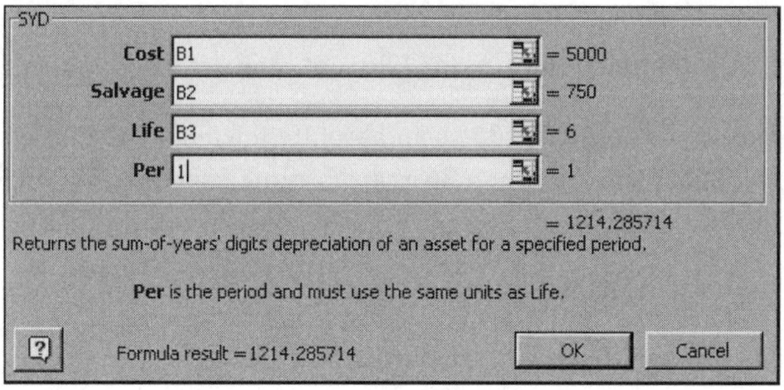

A worksheet illustrating the sum-of-years' digits method of depreciation is shown in Figure 10.34.

Figure 10.34 Sum-of-Years' Digits Depreciation Schedule

	A	B	C	D
1	Asset A		Sum-of-Years' Digits	
2	Depreciation Schedule			
3				
4	Purchase Price	$5,000		
5	Salvage Value	$750		
6	Life of Asset	6		
7	Year	Annual Depreciation	Total Depreciation	Book Value
8	1	$ 1,214.29	$ 1,214.29	$3,785.71
9	2	1,011.90	2,226.19	2,773.81
10	3	809.52	3,035.71	1,964.29
11	4	607.14	3,642.86	1,357.14
12	5	404.76	4,047.62	952.38
13	6	202.38	4,250.00	750.00

The formulas are shown in Figure 10.35. Again, the Period argument equals the corresponding number in column A and uses a relative reference.

Figure 10.35 Sum-of-Years'-Digits Method of Depreciation Formulas

	A	B	C	D
1	Asset A		Sum-of-Years' Digits	
2	Depreciation Sched			
3				
4	Purchase Price	5000		
5	Salvage Value	750		
6	Life of Asset	6		
7	Year	Annual Depreciation	Total Depreciation	Book Value
8	1	=SYD($B$4,$B$5,$B$6,A8)	=B8	=$B$4-C8
9	2	=SYD($B$4,$B$5,$B$6,A9)	=C8+B8:B9	=$B$4-C9
10	3	=SYD($B$4,$B$5,$B$6,A10)	=C9+B9:B10	=$B$4-C10
11	4	=SYD($B$4,$B$5,$B$6,A11)	=C10+B10:B11	=$B$4-C11
12	5	=SYD($B$4,$B$5,$B$6,A12)	=C11+B11:B12	=$B$4-C12
13	6	=SYD($B$4,$B$5,$B$6,A13)	=C12+B12:B13	=$B$4-C13

Exercise 10.8—Using Sum-of-Years' Digits Depreciation

Summary of Financial Functions Used

DB	Calculates the depreciation of an asset using the fixed declining-balance depreciation.
IPMT	Calculates the interest payment of a loan payment.
PMT	Calculates the periodic payment for a loan.
PPMT	Calculates the payment on the principal for a loan.
SLN	Calculates the straight-line depreciation of an asset.
SYD	Calculates the sum-of-years' digits depreciation for an asset.

Exercise 10.8 Using Sum-of-Years' Digits Depreciation

Determine the depreciation for an asset that was purchased for $2,000 with a life expectancy of three years. The salvage value is expected to be $250. Determine the annual and monthly amounts for depreciation. Use the sum-of-years' digits method of depreciation.

1 Open the workbook **Exer 10** to the sheet **Sum Yrs Digits**.

Complete a depreciation schedule on an annual basis.

2 In cell B10 access the **SYD** function from the **Financial** category.

3 In the **SYD** dialog box, for **Cost** enter **B5** as an absolute reference (**$B$5**); for **Salvage** enter **B7** as an absolute reference (**$B$7**); for **Life** enter **B6** as an absolute reference (**$B$6**); for **Period** enter **A10** as a relative reference.

4 Click **OK**. The amount, **$875.00**, is entered in cell B10.

5 Copy the formula through the third year. Notice how the depreciation amount decreases each year.

Complete a depreciation schedule on a monthly basis.

6 In cell C10, access the SYD function.

7 In the **SYD** dialog box, for **Cost** enter **B5** as an absolute reference (**$B$5**); for **Salvage** enter **B7** as an absolute reference (**$B$7**); for **Life** enter cell **B6** as an absolute reference and multiply by **12** to determine monthly depreciation (**$B$6*12**); for **Period** enter **A10** as a relative reference.

8 Click **OK**. The amount, **$94.59**, is entered in cell C10.

9 Copy the formula through the appropriate range of the worksheet. Notice how the depreciation amount decreases each month.

10 Save and print the worksheet. At the top write "Print 1."

11 Print a copy of the worksheet that shows the formulas.

Complete some What-if analyses.

12 What if the price of this asset were $8,500 and it had an expected life of eight years? Make the necessary changes and extend the annual basis amounts through eight years. Print a copy of the worksheet; at the top write "Print 2."

13 What if the price of this asset were $2,500 and it had an expected life of two years? Make the necessary changes and print a copy of the worksheet. At the top write "Print 3."

14 Close the workbook without saving changes.

LOOKUP Functions

Another important feature of spreadsheet software is the ability to look up information contained in a table and transfer that information into a worksheet. Lookup tables may be constructed for FICA deductions, tax tables, and discount rates (if they vary for different categories of customers), for example. In a school setting, an instructor may use a lookup table to determine the final grade for a student.

These tables are often complex and take considerable time to construct properly. They are valuable because they will be used over and over again in a business. Consider a large business payroll. Using a lookup table to determine the amount of withholding tax is much faster than manually looking for each employee's withholding on an individual basis.

When a *LOOKUP function* is used, one specific number is compared with a group of numbers in a lookup table. When a match is found, a value is placed in the original worksheet. For grade records, when a score is 90%, an A is entered in the original worksheet. The match is 90%; the related value placed in the worksheet is A.

Lookup tables can be placed either horizontally or vertically on a worksheet. The LOOKUP functions are VLOOKUP and HLOOKUP. A lookup table may be on any worksheet of any workbook.

Using Vertical Lookup (VLOOKUP)

To illustrate a lookup table, we will use one that assigns a grade to a test score. Figure 10.36 shows a worksheet for the grades of a class. The students are listed in column A with their test scores in column B. The grading scale is presented in columns E and F; the score in column E is required to place the corresponding grade listed in column F. The letter grade, A, B, C, etc., will then be placed in column C.

The *VLOOKUP* Formula Palette is shown in Figure 10.37. The arguments are Lookup value, Table array, and Col index num.

Figure 10.36   Using a Vertical Lookup Table

	A	B	C	D	E	F
1		Score	Grade		Grade Scale	
2	Tom	89			0	F
3	Dick	82			60	D
4	Harry	95			70	C
5	Jane	100			80	B
6	Joe	92			90	A
7	Hillary	76				
8	Jim	56				

Figure 10.37   Dialog Box for the VLOOKUP Function

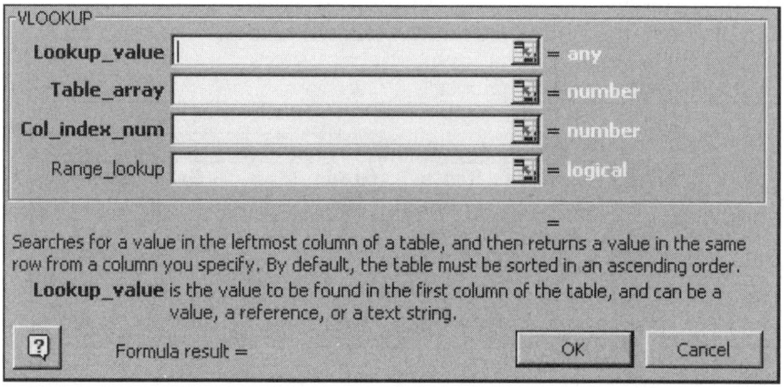

Lookup value "is the value to be found in the first column of the table." The Lookup value is the number that is used to make the match. In Figure 10.38, the Lookup value is the score in column B.

The *array* or *Table array* "is a table of text, numbers, or logical values, in which data is retrieved," and is used to find matching data. In Figure 10.38, the table array is E2:F6. This range contains the entire lookup table. Because the table array remains the same, express the array in absolute references.

The *column index number* (Col_index_num) is defined as "the column number in the table array from which the matching value should be returned." In Figure 10.38, the actual test score is compared with the grades listed in first column (column E). When the grade falls within a certain range, the corresponding number of the second column in the table array will be entered in the worksheet cell. The column index number is the column number of the array that contains the values to be entered in the worksheet. In Figure 10.38, the first column of the lookup table contains the comparison data, and the second column contains the grade to be assigned. Because the values from the second column will be entered into a worksheet cell, the column index number is 2.

The completed worksheet after the LOOKUP function has been completed is shown in Figure 10.38, with the LOOKUP function for cell C2 displayed in the formula bar.

Figure 10.38   VLOOKUP Function

C2			=VLOOKUP(B2,$E$2:$F$6,2)		
	A	B	C	D	E	F
1		Score	Grade		Grade Scale	
2	Tom	89	B		0	F
3	Dick	82	B		60	D
4	Harry	95	A		70	C
5	Jane	100	A		80	B
6	Joe	92	A		90	A
7	Hillary	76	C			
8	Jim	56	F			

Tom has a score of 89; his resulting grade should be a B. Excel obtains this result as follows: The Lookup value is in cell B2, so Excel uses 89 as the Lookup value. Then it moves to the Table array, E2:F6. The exact number 89 is not listed in the array, so Excel looks for the next lower value in the array; the number 80 is the value Excel finds. The second column of the array contains the values that will be placed in the cell containing the formula, so the Col index num is 2. A grade of B corresponds with a score of 80, so a B is entered in cell C2.

This formula is then copied to the rest of the grades, range C3:C8. When copying the formulas, be sure that the lookup table is expressed in absolute values.

Figure 10.39 shows the completed table of student grades.

Figure 10.39 Worksheet for Assigning Grades

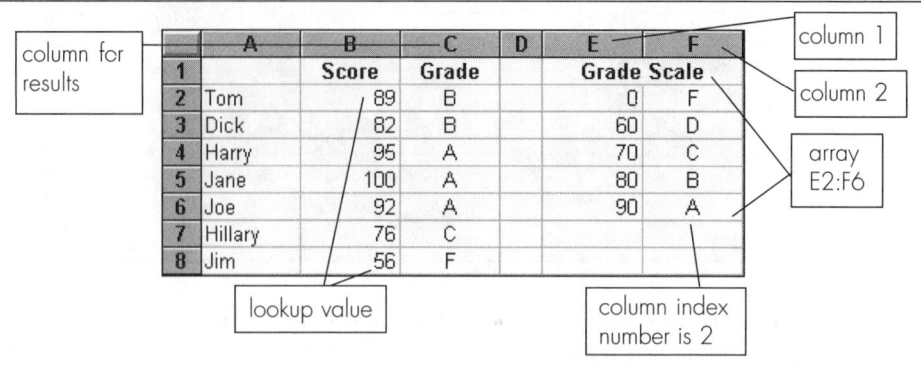

	A	B	C	D	E	F
1		Score	Grade		Grade Scale	
2	Tom	89	B		0	F
3	Dick	82	B		60	D
4	Harry	95	A		70	C
5	Jane	100	A		80	B
6	Joe	92	A		90	A
7	Hillary	76	C			
8	Jim	56	F			

- column for results
- lookup value
- column 1
- column 2
- array E2:F6
- column index number is 2

The LOOKUP functions are located under Lookup & Reference in the Function category section. VLOOKUP is listed in the Function name section.

Exercise 10.9 Using a Vertical Lookup Table

Complete a worksheet that includes a lookup table to determine final grades for a college computer class.

1 Open the workbook **Exer 10** to the **VLookup** sheet.

2 In cell C3 access the **VLOOKUP** function from the **Lookup & Reference** category.

3 In the **Lookup_value** box, enter **B3**, the value of the test score.

4 In the **Table_array** box, click on the Collapse Dialog button.

5 Highlight the range E3:F7; then press the shortcut key for changing cell references to absolute references.

6 Click on the Expand Dialog button.

7 In the **Col_index_num** box, key **2**. The value to be placed in the main worksheet is the corresponding grade in column F. Column F is column 2 of the table array.

8 Click **OK**. The grade of **B** is entered in cell C3.

Copy the function.

9 Copy the function through the appropriate range of the worksheet.

10 Save and print the worksheet.

11 Print a second copy of the worksheet that shows the formulas.

Using Horizontal Lookup (HLOOKUP)

The concept for using the *HLOOKUP function* is identical to that of the VLOOKUP function except that the lookup table is arranged on the worksheet horizontally instead of vertically.

Figure 10.40 shows the grade report with the lookup table at the bottom of the worksheet (A11:E12) in a horizontal arrangement.

Figure 10.40 Using a Horizontal Lookup Table

	A	B	C	D	E
1		Score	Grade		
2	Tom	89	B		
3	Dick	82	B		
4	Harry	95	A		
5	Jane	100	A		
6	Joe	92	A		
7	Hillary	76	C		
8	Jim	56	F		
9					
10					
11		0	60	70	80	90
12		F	D	C	B	A

Cell C2 contains: =HLOOKUP(B2,$A$11:$E$12

The lookup table can be on a different worksheet or in a different workbook. If it is in a different workbook, both documents need to be open when using a LOOKUP function.

Exercise 10.10 Using a Horizontal Lookup Table

You will use a horizontal lookup table to determine the bonus rate for sales employees. The bonus rate depends on the amount of sales, and once the rate is determined, it is used to calculate the amount of the bonus. The bonus rate lookup table is created and saved on a different worksheet in the workbook.

1. Open the **Exer 10** workbook to the sheet named **Hlookup**. The worksheet has been started.

2. Open to the next sheet, **Hlookup Table**. The lookup table on this sheet is used to determine the amount of each bonus. The bonus rate increases as the amount of sales increases.

3. Return to the **Hlookup** sheet. In cell C7, access the **HLOOKUP** function from the **Lookup & Reference** category.

4. In the **HLOOKUP** dialog box, enter the variables. You may want to use the Collapse Dialog and Expand Dialog buttons. For **Lookup_value** enter **B7**; for **Table_array** click in the **Hlookup Table** sheet, drag through the table range A4:G5, and enter the references as absolute; for **Row_index_num** enter **2**. Click **OK**. The amount, **0.0175**, is entered into cell C7.

5. In cell E7 enter the formula to determine the amount of the bonus. This is the amount of sales multiplied by the bonus rate.

6. Complete the total salary. This is the base salary plus the bonus amount.

7 Copy the formulas in row 7 through the rest of the worksheet.

8 Format correctly for currency; format the bonus rate as a percent rounded to two decimals.

9 Save and print the worksheet. Print a copy of the worksheet that shows the formulas used.

Summary

- Functions are available to be used in the preparation of a worksheet. Types of functions include financial, engineering, mathematical, and database functions.
- The sequence of information used in a function is the function's syntax.
- An argument of a function is a variable used in a function to produce a result. Arguments are enclosed in parentheses in the formula bar.
- The result of a function is placed in a worksheet cell.
- In the Paste Function dialog box, function categories are listed on the left side; function names are listed on the right side.
- When possible, use cell references instead of actual values in arguments.
- A collapsible Formula Palette opens with each function. Variables are entered in this dialog box.
- The value of each argument is shown in the Formula Palette. The result is shown at the bottom of the Palette.
- The simple mathematical functions that are available include SUM, PRODUCT, ROUND, EVEN, and ODD.
- The PRODUCT function multiplies arguments.
- The ROUND function is used to round a number to a specified number of decimals.
- The EVEN function is used to enter the next higher even integer.
- The ODD function is used to enter the next higher odd integer.
- Financial functions are used to determine the monthly payment of a loan, the amount of interest or principal on a loan, or the depreciation of an asset using several different methods of depreciation.
- The monthly payment of a loan is determined by using the PMT function.
- Rate is the interest rate; it is expressed on a per period basis.
- Nper is the number of periods a loan will be outstanding.
- Pv is the current amount of a loan.
- The interest paid on a loan is determined by using the IPMT function. It calculates the amount of the interest paid on a loan.
- The principal paid on a loan is determined by using the PPMT function. It calculates the amount of the principal paid on a loan.
- A payment chart is used to show the interest and payments for the life of a loan.
- Functions are available to determine asset depreciation. The methods to calculate depreciation include the straight-line method, the declining-balance method, and the sum-of-years' digits method.
- Cost is the purchase price of an asset.
- Life is the expected useful life of an asset.
- Salvage is the expected value of an asset at the end of its useful life.

- Period refers to the period for which an asset's depreciation will be calculated.
- In the declining balance method, the argument Month will be used for the first year of depreciation.
- Book value is the cost of an asset less the current depreciation.
- The straight-line depreciation method assumes that an asset depreciates at an equal rate each year.
- The declining-balance and sum-of-years' digits methods of depreciation assume that an asset depreciates at a higher rate in the early years of its life.
- LOOKUP functions are used to compare a specific number in a worksheet with a lookup table and assign the corresponding value in the worksheet.
- Lookup value is the value found in the first column or row of an array.
- Table array is the defined table of information in which data is looked up.
- Col index num is the column number of the lookup table from which a matching value will be entered in a worksheet.
- Lookup tables may be either vertical or horizontal. They may be on the same worksheet or in a different worksheet or workbook.

Important Terminology

arguments	interest	PRODUCT function
array	IPMT function	Pv
book value	life of asset	Rate
column index number	LOOKUP function	result
Collapse Dialog button	lookup tables	ROUND function
cost	Lookup value	salvage value
DB function	mathematical functions	SLN function
declining-balance depreciation	Nper	straight-line depreciation
depreciation	ODD function	SUM function
EVEN function	Paste Function	sum-of-years' digits depreciation
Expand Dialog button	Paste Function button	SYD function
financial functions	payment chart	syntax
Formula Palette	Per	Table array
functions	PMT function	VLOOKUP
HLOOKUP function	PPMT function	What-if analysis
	principal	

Buttons to Know

Chapter 10 Using Built-in Functions

Study Questions

True-False

Place a T in the space provided if the statement is true; if it is false, place an F.

_____ 1. A function is a complex formula that automatically completes a series of mathematical calculations.
_____ 2. The syntax of a function is the way a function is written.
_____ 3. An argument in a function is the variable used to calculate the result; an argument is displayed in parentheses.
_____ 4. To use a function, click in the Fast Function button and follow the instructions.
_____ 5. When the Paste Function dialog box opens, all functions are available.
_____ 6. Arguments are entered in a collapsible Formula Palette that opens when a function is selected.
_____ 7. Use an actual value rather than a cell reference when entering an argument for a function.
_____ 8. To determine the amount of interest on a loan, use the IPT function.
_____ 9. The fee that is charged on a loan is called interest.
_____ 10. In a payment chart, the ending balance of one period is the same as the beginning balance of the next period.
_____ 11. In financial functions, Nper is the total number of periods in a loan.
_____ 12. In financial functions, Pv is the total amount to be paid.
_____ 13. In the IPMT function, Per is the period for which interest is paid.
_____ 14. To determine the amount of each payment of a loan, use the PPMT function.
_____ 15. In entering the Rate in the PMT function, divide the rate by 12 if interest is figured on a monthly basis.
_____ 16. The amount of interest paid remains the same throughout the life of a loan.
_____ 17. To use a depreciation function, the cost of the asset, the life of the asset, and the asset's salvage value must be known.
_____ 18. The depreciation functions are in the Depreciation category of the Paste Function dialog box.
_____ 19. Straight-line depreciation takes into account the fact that an asset depreciates at a faster rate at the beginning of its life.
_____ 20. In the declining-balance method of depreciation, the Period argument remains the same as the function is copied.
_____ 21. In using the DB function, the Month argument for an asset purchased in January is different from the Month argument for an asset purchased in August.
_____ 22. In a lookup table, the Table array is the range of the table.
_____ 23. In a lookup table, the Col index num is the row number of the worksheet.
_____ 24. When using the VLOOKUP function, the lookup table must be placed on a different worksheet.

Fill-In

Place the word in the space that correctly completes the statement.

1. For complex formulas like those for depreciation, use a _____ rather than keying in complex formulas.
2. The variables in a function's syntax are called _____ .
3. The function that multiplies arguments is the _____ function.
4. The function that rounds a number to a specified number of digits to the right or left of the decimal is the _____ function.
5. The function that returns the next highest even integer is the _____ function.
6. The ODD function applied to cell B3, [3 | 45.873695], would show a result of _____ .
7. Functions for interest and depreciation are in the _____ function category.
8. The function that enters the next higher odd integer is the _____ function.
9. The function that determines the monthly payment on a loan is the _____ function.
10. An interest rate of 6% resides in cell H10. Payments are monthly. The Rate argument is entered as _____ (assume the function will be copied to additional cells).
11. A four-year loan has biannual payments (two each year). Use _____ for the Nper argument in the PMT function.
12. The function that determines the amount of interest applied to a loan is the _____ function.
13. The function that determines the amount of principal paid on a loan is the _____ function.
14. An asset decreases in value because of wear and tear. This is called _____ .
15. How long an asset will be in use is called the _____ of the asset.
16. The _____ value is an estimate of how much an asset may be worth at the end of its life.
17. The function to determine straight-line depreciation is the _____ function.
18. The function to determine declining-balance depreciation is the _____ function.
19. The function to determine depreciation using the sum-of-years' digits method is the _____ function.
20. A _____ table is useful when information is used several times.
21. The _____ function is the function used for a vertical lookup.
22. The columns in an array are numbered. The third column in a five-column table is number _____ .
23. The column where the results of a lookup will be placed is the column where the _____ is entered.

The Syntax of Functions

Replace the syntax of the following business functions.

Item 1

Determine the monthly payment, interest amount, and principal amount for the following home loan:

	D	E
6		
7	Amount of loan	$75,000
8	Interest Rate	8%
9	Length of Loan	30 years
10	Payments	Monthly

1. Determine the monthly payment. In the space provided, write what will be entered in the Paste Function dialog box in order to complete the function.
   a. Rate _____
   b. Nper _____
   c. Pv _____
2. Determine the amount that is applied to interest for the fifth month. Write what will be entered in the Paste Function dialog box.
   a. Rate _____
   b. Per _____
   c. Nper _____
   d. Pv _____
3. Determine the amount that is paid on the principal for the third month. Write what will be entered in the Paste Function dialog box.
   a. Rate _____
   b. Per _____
   c. Nper _____
   d. Pv _____

Item 2

Determine the depreciation functions for the first year of the following asset. The asset was purchased in June. Be sure to use cell references in the functions and assume that they will be copied to additional cells.

	A	B
4		
5	Cost	$450
6	Life of Asset	8
7	Salvage Value	$75

4. Use the straight-line function. In the space provided, write what will be entered in the Paste Function dialog box in order to complete the function.
   a. Cost _____
   b. Salvage _____
   c. Life _____

5. Use the declining-balance function. Write what will be entered in the Paste Function dialog box.
   a. Cost _____
   b. Salvage _____
   c. Life _____
   d. Period _____
   e. Month _____
6. Use the sum-of-years' digits function. Write what will be entered in the Paste Function dialog box.
   a. Cost _____
   b. Salvage _____
   c. Life _____
   d. Per _____

Assignments

Note: The Ch10 subdirectory may be deleted from the Student Data Disk after completing Chapter 10.

Assignment 10.1

Prepare a chart for making car payments on a car that was purchased for $11,500 at an interest rate of nine percent. The length of the loan is three years, with monthly payments.

1. Open the workbook **Ch10 As1** and save it as **Assig 10-1**.
2. In cell A1, replace **Your Name** with your first and last name; in cell A3, replace **Today's Date** with the current date.
3. In cell B10, enter the formula that shows the balance due as the same as the loan amount (**=B5**).
4. Enter the function for the monthly payment.
   - In cell C10 access the PMT function.
   - In the **Rate** box, enter cell B6 as an absolute value. Be sure to divide the rate by 12.
   - In the **Nper** box, enter the number of periods. The loan is for three years, paid on a monthly basis; use an absolute value for cell B7 and multiply by 12.
   - In the **Pv** box, enter the amount of the loan using an absolute value. Click **OK**.
   - Enter a minus sign (-) before **PMT** to display the result as a positive number.
5. Enter the function for the interest payment in cell D10 and format it for a positive value.
6. Enter the function for the principal payment in cell E10 and format it for a positive value.
   - In the **Rate** box, enter the interest rate. Use an absolute value for cell B6. Be sure to divide the rate by 12.
   - In the **Per** box, enter the number of the period in cell A10.
   - In the **Nper** box, enter the number of periods. The loan is for three years, paid on a monthly basis; multiply the absolute cell reference for B7 by 12.
   - In the **Pv** box, enter the amount of the loan in cell B5 using an absolute value.
   - Place a minus sign (-) before the function name to get a positive result.
7. Complete the formulas for the worksheet.
   - In cell F10, enter the formula to determine the ending balance. The ending balance is determined by subtracting the amount of principal from the balance due.
   - In cell B11, enter the balance due. This is the ending balance of the previous payment.

- Copy the formulas to complete the worksheet. The balance in cell F45 should be zero (**0**).
- In cell A47, key **Totals**. Enter formulas for the totals of the payments, the amount of interest, and the amount of principal. The total paid, **$13,165.09**, includes the amount of the car, $11,500, and $1,665.09 interest.

8. In the **Page Setup** dialog box, select to center horizontally and vertically in portrait style with no gridlines. Create a header and footer, and include your name, the file name, the sheet name, and the page number. Check in Print Preview to see how many pages this worksheet takes to print. If it takes more than one page, continue with Step 9. If it fits on one page, skip to Step 10.
9. Print the column titles.
   - Access the **Sheet** tab in the **Page Setup** dialog box.
   - In the **Print titles** section, enter **$9:$9** in the **Rows to repeat at top** section. This identifies row 9 as the row containing the titles.
10. Save and print the worksheet.
11. Print a copy of the worksheet in landscape style that shows the formulas.
12. Return to portrait style.

What if the interest rate were eight and a half percent?

13. Change the interest rate to eight and a half percent and print a copy of the worksheet.
14. Print copies of the worksheet with interest rates of eight percent, nine and a half percent, and 10 percent.

Checkpoint:

Interest Rate of 9%		
	Monthly Payment	$365.70
	Amount of Interest, Period 1	$86.25
	Amount of Principal, Period 1	$279.45
	Ending Balance, Period 1	$11,220.55
	Balance Due, Period 2	$11,220.55

Assignment 10.2

A truck has been purchased by a company and the appropriate method of depreciation needs to be determined. Prepare a worksheet that compares the different types of depreciation methods available. Depreciation is figured on an annual basis.

The truck was purchased for $100,000. Its expected life is eight years with a salvage value of $2,500.

1. Open the workbook **Ch10 As2** and save it as **Assig 10-2**.
2. Enter the function for straight-line depreciation.
   - In cell B7, access the SLN function.
   - In the **Cost** box, enter the cell reference for the cost of the asset (use an absolute reference).
   - In the **Salvage** box, enter the cell reference for the salvage value of the asset (use an absolute reference).
   - In the **Life** box, enter the cell reference for the life of the asset (use an absolute reference).
   - Copy the formula in cell B7 to the appropriate cells in order to complete the straight-line depreciation section.

3. Enter the function for declining-balance in cell C7.
   - Complete the **Cost**, **Salvage**, and **Life** sections of the dialog box.
   - In the **Period** box, enter the cell reference for the period of depreciation (cell A7).
   - Click in the **Month** box. Read the description in the dialog box. Since this asset was purchased in January, leave the **Month** box empty.
   - Copy the formula in cell C7 to the range C8:C14.
4. Complete a function for the sum-of-years' digits method and copy it to the sum-of-years' digits section of the worksheet.
5. Complete the worksheet.
   - In cell A16 type **Total**. Format it for bold and center alignment.
   - Enter the formula to determine the totals in row 16.
   - Use the Borders palette to place appropriate lines for the totals.
   - Format the worksheet to center on the page both vertically and horizontally without gridlines. Create a header and footer, and include your name, the file name, the sheet name, and the page number.
   - Format numbers for currency.
6. Save and print the worksheet.
7. Print a second copy of the worksheet that shows the formulas. Place it on one page so it is easy to read (perhaps by changing the orientation or adjusting column widths)

   Checkpoint:
Straight-Line, Year 1	$12,187.50
Declining-Balance, Year 1	$36,900.00
Sum-of-Years' Digits, Year 1	$21,666.67
Total Depreciation, Declining-Balance	$97,486.75
Total Depreciation, Straight-Line	$97,500.00

Assignment 10.3

Midvale School Supplies prepares an inventory sheet for each product in stock. You will prepare the worksheet used to inventory three-ring binders. Quantity discounts are given for large orders; the amount charged for the product will be determined in a lookup table. You will also prepare some statistical analysis of the completed data.

1. Open the workbook **Ch10 As3** and save it as **Assig 10-3**.

Complete the discount chart.
2. Click in the **Discount Chart** sheet tab. Enter the following information:

	A	B	C
4			
5	Unit Price	$0.90	
6	Unit Cost	$0.40	
7			
8	Quantity Discounts	Discount Rate	Quantity Price
9	1	12%	
10	30	18%	
11	80	24%	
12	125	32%	
13	175	40%	
14	225	48%	

3. Complete the Quantity Price column. The quantity price is the amount a company will pay per unit of product. The larger the discount rate, the lower the quantity price.
4. Complete the **Sept** worksheet.
   - Arrange the two worksheet windows side by side, one with the **Discount Chart** worksheet and the other with the **Sept** worksheet.
   - Access the VLOOKUP function in cell D9.
   - In cell E9, enter the formula to determine the sales price.
   - In cell F9, enter the formula for the gross profit in dollars.
   - In cell G9, enter the formula for the percentage of gross profit. This is determined by dividing the gross profit by the amount of each sale.
   - Copy formulas through the worksheet as needed.
5. Format the worksheet.
   - Format the percentages and the unit price for three decimal places.
   - Use Currency style where appropriate.

Complete additional statistics and copy to other parts of the worksheet.
6. Complete additional statistical analysis.
   - In the range B22:B24 key **Averages:**, **Maximums:**, and **Minimums:**.
   - In cell C22 access the AVERAGE function. Average the quantity sold. Also include the averages for the sales amount and the gross profit both in dollar amounts and as percentages.
   - In cell C23 access the MAX function. Determine the maximum quantity sold. Also include the maximum sales amount and the gross profit, both in dollar amounts and as percentages.
   - In cell C24 access the MIN function to determine the minimum sale made. Also include the minimum sales amount and the gross profit, both in dollar amounts and as percentages.
7. Format the statistical analyses.
   - Format the statistical numbers for two decimal places. Use the Comma or Percent style.
   - Format the document to print on one page, centered both vertically and horizontally. Do not print gridlines. Create a header and footer, and include your name, the file name, the sheet name, and the page number.

- Place a border surrounding the average, maximum, and minimum sections.
- Adjust the column widths if needed.
8. Preferred customers are those who order more than 200 binders in any one month. Use an IF function in column H to identify the preferred customers.
9. Save and print the worksheet. At the top write "Print 1."
10. Print a copy of the worksheet that shows the formulas.
11. What if the price of each binder increased to $1.00? Change the amount in cell B5. All of the cells containing B25 as a cell reference automatically adjust to reflect the new cost. Print a copy of the worksheet. At the top write "Print 2."

Checkpoint:

P.O. 8375 Gross Profit in Dollars	$11.83
P.O. 8375 Gross Profit Percent	45.799%
Average Quantity Sold	147.30

Assignment 10.4

Prepare a payment chart for a five-year, $15,000 loan at an 11 percent interest rate. Include the monthly payment, the monthly amount applied to interest and to principal, and the ending balance.

1. Open the workbook **Ch10 As4** and save it as **Assig 10-4**.
2. In cell A1, replace **Student's Name** with your first and last name, and place the current date in cell A3.
3. Complete the data in the worksheet.
    - In cell B10, enter the amount of the loan in cell B5.

Note: The numbers in column A extend to 60; monthly payments for five years equal 60 monthly payments.

- In cell C10, enter the function for loan payments.
- In cell D10, enter the function for the amount of interest.
- In cell E10, enter the function for the amount of principal.
- In cell F10, enter the formula for the ending balance.
- In cell B11, enter the beginning balance for the new period.
- Copy the formulas to the appropriate ranges of the worksheet.

4. Format the worksheet.
    - Format to print the worksheet in the center of the page without gridlines. Create a header and footer, and include your name, the file name, the sheet name, and the page number.
    - This worksheet will print on two pages. Determine an appropriate page break. Print titles on the second page as needed for understanding what the numbers signify.
    - Format for currency as needed.
    - Make other formatting decisions in order to present a professional-looking worksheet.
5. Save and print the worksheet.
6. Print another copy of the worksheet that shows the formulas. Print on two pages in landscape style. Adjust the column widths.
7. Return to portrait style.

What if the interest rate changed?

8. Change the interest rate amount to nine percent and print a copy of the worksheet.

9. Change the interest rate amount to 10 percent and print a copy of the worksheet.

Checkpoint:
Interest Rate of 11%   Month 1 Payment $326.14
                        Month 1 Amount of Interest $137.50
                        Month 1 Amount of Principal $188.64
                        Month 1 Ending Balance $14,811.36

Assignment 10.5

Don's Travel Agency wants to compare the various depreciation methods for a recently purchased computer system. Prepare a workbook that can be used to compare the straight-line, declining-balance, and sum-of-years' digits methods of depreciation. Prepare each depreciation schedule on a separate sheet.

The computer system was purchased for $25,000 with a life expectancy of eight years and a salvage value of $3,500. Depreciation will be determined on an annual basis. The first year of depreciation is a full 12-month year.

1. Open a new workbook and enter the following data. (The same information will be entered on three separate worksheets. You may want to to enter and format this information in one step.)

	A	B	C	D	E
1	Don's Travel Agency				
2	Computer System				
3	Depreciation Schedule - Straight Line				
4					
5		Cost	$25,000		
6		Salvage	$3,500		
7		Life	8		
8					
9	Year	Beginning Value	Amount of Depreciation	Total Depreciation	Book Value
10	1				
11	2				

   - Save the workbook as **Assig 10-5**.
   - Use AutoFill to extend the years in column A to **8**.
   - Format the title of the worksheet for bold, one font size larger, and centered over columns.
   - Format the worksheet to print in the center of the page (vertically and horizontally) without gridlines. Create a header or footer, and include your name, the file name, the sheet name, and the page number.
   - Format the column titles in row 9 for bold, center alignment, and wrapped text. Adjust the column widths.

2. Rename the sheet tabs. Name them **Straight-Line**, **Declining-Balance**, and **Sum-of-Years' Digits**. In each sheet, change the title to reflect the depreciation method used. Adjust the title over the columns. You may need to change the font size to fit the text in the space.

3. Complete the worksheets.
   - Complete the **Straight-Line** sheet. Adjust the column widths if necessary.
   - Complete the **Declining-Balance** sheet.
   - Complete the **Sum-of-Years' Digits** sheet.

4. Print the workbook.
5. Print a second copy of the workbook that shows the formulas used.

   Checkpoint:
Amount of Depreciation—Straight Line	$2,687.50
Amount of Depreciation—Declining Balance, Year 1	$5,450.00
Amount of Depreciation—Sum-of-Years' Digits, Year 1	$4,777.78

Assignment 10.6

Midvale School Supplies would like you to prepare an inventory sheet for desk chairs, similar to the one you prepared for three-ring binders in Assignment 10.3. A lookup table is prepared indicating the quantity discount rate. You will use the horizontal lookup table to determine the selling price for each order.

1. Open the workbook **Ch10 As6**, and save it as **Assig 10-6**.
2. Determine the selling price for each desk in the **Pricing Chart** worksheet.
3. Complete the **Sept** worksheet.
   - In cell D9, enter the LOOKUP function to determine the unit price. The unit price is found in the **Pricing Chart** worksheet.
   - Complete the sales amount.
   - Determine the profit in dollar amounts and in percentages. The percentage formula is the gross profit in dollars divided by the sales amount.
4. Format the **Sept** worksheet.
   - Use Page Setup to center the worksheet horizontally and vertically and to print without gridlines. Create a header and footer, and include your name, the file name, the sheet name, and the page number.
   - Format the worksheet in an appropriate style.
5. Save and print the **Sept** worksheet. At the top write "Print 1."
6. Print a copy of the worksheet with the formulas displayed on one page in landscape style. Adjust the column widths if necessary.

What if the price of the chair were $60?

7. Change the unit price of the chair to $60 and return the worksheet to portrait style. Print the worksheet. At the top write "Print 2."

   Checkpoint:
Sept Worksheet with Unit Cost of $45	P.O. 8384 Unit Price	$76.50
	P.O. 8384 Sales Amount	$612.00
	P.O. 8384 Gross Profit in Dollars	$252.00
	P.O. 8384 Gross Profit Percentage	41%

Case Problem 10.1

The Piece Work Company shrinkwraps books. Employees are paid by the number of books wrapped—the more they complete, the more they earn. For instance, the first 50 books wrapped are paid at $0.50 each. The next 25 are paid at $0.75 each, and so on. The payment schedule is provided at the end of this problem. A bonus of $10 is given to any employee completing more than 100 units.

Plan a worksheet to show the number of items completed and the pay rate. Also include the amount of the bonus, if any, and the total earned.

Format the worksheet so it is attractive. Include your name in the header or footer. Be sure to print a copy that shows the formulas. Save the worksheet as **Case 10-1**.

The information needed is shown below:

Name	Amount Completed
Diana Bacha	87
Ruth Anreson	102
Barbara Jones	36
Peter Kendall	92
Robert Hurtado	83
Juan Morta	97
Candace Brown	56

The rate chart is shown below. Use a table array similar to those in Assig 10-3 and Assig 10-6.

1–50	$0.50
51–75	.75
76–90	.80
91–100	.85
101–110	.90
111+	.93

Case Problem 10.2

You are buying a new car and have two cars in mind—a new car and a used car. You have looked at the financing available and have found several different financing solutions.

The used Safari you are considering costs $15,000. You may finance it at 9.05 percent interest for four years or at 8.55 percent interest for three years.

The new Jetway you are looking at costs $18,000. You may finance it at 7.75 percent interest for three years or 8.75 percent interest for four years.

Using Excel functions, determine the following information. You may want to prepare this on several sheets of a workbook
- The monthly payment required for each loan plan.
- The total interest to be paid over the life of each loan.
- The total cost of each car using each financing choice.

Prepare a report that summarizes your findings. You may want to place it on a new sheet in the workbook containing the worksheets for each financing method. Save the workbook as **Case 10-2**.

Checkpoint:

Monthly Payment of Safari, Three-year Loan	$473.86
Monthly Payment of Safari, Four-year Loan	$373.63

Chapter 11

Using Excel to Manage Lists

Objectives

1. Describe a list and a database, and define the components of each.
2. Prepare and sort a list.
3. Query a list.
4. Filter information from a list and prepare reports.

Introduction

Worksheets are often used to store a list of related data, such as a list of clients' addresses and telephone numbers. A list, called a database, is a group of related records that stores similar information. A computer provides quick access to that information.

Information may not only be stored; it may be retrieved or rearranged quickly. Information within a list can be arranged in alphabetical or numerical order.

There are several database programs available, including Access and dBase. Excel's list feature provides the basic functions of a database program. Many businesses use Excel for their database as well as their spreadsheet needs.

At the end of this chapter, you may delete the Ch11 directory from your Student Data Disk.

Basics of List Management

Components of a List

A *list* is a group of related records, also called a ***database***. A ***record*** consists of several categories of information about a single person or topic; each category is called a ***field***. The telephone book is an example of a database; each individual entry is a record, and the four fields of information in the telephone book are last name, first name, address, and telephone number.

In this chapter, a personal address book containing the name, address, and telephone number of several people will be used as an example of a list. The entire address book is the list; each individual entry is a record in the list. Each category of information in the record is a field. The fields required for an address book database are first name, last name, address, city, state, zip code, and telephone number. These fields become column labels.

Building a List

When developing a list, the first step is to determine the type of information needed. It is possible to then determine the fields to be used and identify those fields. In the first row of a database, enter labels, which become the field names. The labels for an address book are shown in row 3 of the worksheet in Figure 11.1.

Figure 11.1   Fields of a Database

	A	B	C	D	E	F	G
1	Address Book Database						
2							
3	First Name	Last Name	Address	City	State	Zip	Tele No.

In the rows below the field names, enter the records; each row consists of one record. Figure 11.2 shows the completed database; it contains seven fields and five records.

Figure 11.2   Completed Database

	A	B	C	D	E	F	G
1	Address Book Database						
2							
3	First Name	Last Name	Address	City	State	Zip	Tele No.
4	Sharon	Andrews	8775 Treetop Lane	Denver	CO	80215	555-3942
5	Kim	Bond	95 Kendall Loop	Lincoln	NE	50349	555-4432
6	Kevin	Carlton	455 NE 23rd	Portland	OR	97332	555-1607
7	Bruce	Jones	943 Charles Ave.	Eugene	OR	97321	555-0391
8	Courtney	King	903 N Queenly	Everett	WA	40593	555-9831

When entering information into a database, use the Tab key to move to the next column. At the end of each row, press Enter. The active cell moves to column A of the next row down. Do not insert extra spaces at the beginning of a cell or leave blank columns or rows between entries.

Exercise 11.1   Preparing a List

Enter the fields and records of a list containing information about employees in a company. The list includes the name (first and last), address, telephone number, and social security number of each employee. For convenience in using the list, the address should be separated into fields for street address, city, state, and zip code.

Note: Before completing the exercises and assignments in this chapter, you will need to expand the Chapter 11 files on your Student Data Disk. In Windows Explorer, locate the Ch11 file and double-click on it, When all the files have been expanded, you will be able to open them in Excel.

1   Open the **Ch11 Exer** workbook and save it as **Exer 11-1**.

2   Insert a new sheet in front of Sheet1. Rename it **Ex 11-1**.

3   In row 2 of the worksheet, enter labels of **First Name**, **Last Name**, **Street**, **City**, **State**, **Zip**, **Tele. No.**, and **Soc. Sec. No.** Use the abbreviations to keep the labels short. Format the labels for bold.

4   Beginning with row 3, enter the following records for the database. Use **Enter** at the end of each record. You may want to adjust the column widths as data is entered.

- Janet Coffey, 3857 So. Dressel Drive, Palo Alto, CA, 94333, 555-5837, 111-22-3333
- Jeffrey Martin, 2306 N.W. Brynwood Lane, Redwood City, CA, 94332, 555-9287, 444-55-6666
- Charng Yeuan, 3857 Maple Lane, Menlo Park, CA, 94312, 555-3859, 222-33-4444
- Farideh Karvandi, 8585 No. Perez Road, Palo Alto, CA, 94333, 555-8283, 777-88-9999
- Kathy Edmondson, 36500 Elm Lane, Menlo Park, CA, 94311, 555-1728, 111-00-2222
- David Perry, 10233 Forest Hill Drive, Palo Alto, CA, 94333, 555-1827, 333-44-5555
- Joan Eisman, 546 Torreyville Drive, Redwood City, CA, 94332, 555-0928, 666-77-8888
- Destiny Eisman, 2983 Alder Circle, Redwood City, CA 94332, 555-8774, 999-00-1111

5   Adjust the column widths as needed.

6   Group all the worksheets in the workbook. Scale the worksheets of the workbook to fit on one page in landscape style, centered both horizontally and vertically. Place your name, the sheet name, and the file name in the header.

7   Save and print the worksheet. The completed database is shown here:

	A	B	C	D	E	F	G	H
1								
2	First Name	Last Name	Street	City	State	Zip	Tele. No.	Soc. Sec. No.
3	Janet	Coffey	3857 So. Dressel Drive	Palo Alto	CA	94333	555-5837	111-22-3333
4	Jeffrey	Martin	2306 N.W. Brynwood Lane	Redwood City	CA	94332	555-9287	444-55-6666
5	Charng	Yeuan	3857 Maple Lane	Menlo Park	CA	94312	555-3859	222-33-4444
6	Farideh	Karvandi	8585 No. Perez Road	Palo Alto	CA	94333	555-8283	777-88-9999
7	Kathy	Edmondson	36500 Elm Lane	Menlo Park	CA	94311	555-1728	111-00-2222
8	David	Perry	10233 Forest Hill Drive	Palo Alto	CA	94333	555-1827	333-44-5555
9	Joan	Eisman	546 Torreyville Drive	Redwood City	CA	94332	555-0928	666-77-8888
10	Destiny	Eisman	2983 Alder Circle	Redwood City	CA	94332	555-8774	999-00-1111

Rearranging a List

Sorting a List

Sorting a list rearranges the records in alphabetical, numerical, or chronological order. When records are sorted, rows are rearranged according to the contents of one or more columns.

Click in any cell in a list, and then select the *Sort* command from the Data menu. Excel automatically highlights the entire list, excluding labels. It is important to have no blank columns or rows in a database. Figure 11.3 shows a selected list.

Figure 11.3   Sort Range

	A	B	C	D	E	F	G
1	Address Book Database						
2							
3	First Name	Last Name	Address	City	State	Zip	Tele No.
4	Bruce	Jones	943 Charles Ave.	Eugene	OR	97321	555-0391
5	Courtney	King	903 N Queenly	Everett	WA	40593	555-9831
6	Kevin	Carlton	455 NE 23rd	Portland	OR	97332	555-1607
7	Sharon	Andrews	8775 Treetop Lane	Denver	CO	80215	555-3942
8	Kim	Bond	95 Kendall Loop	Lincoln	NE	50349	555-4432

Once the list is selected, the Sort dialog box automatically opens, shown in Figure 11.4. The column label of the active cell is automatically entered in the Sort by box and the database's active label moves to the first selected cell.

The list will be arranged in alphabetical order by last name. In Figure 11.4, the column label Last Name is entered in the Sort by section.

The order, or arrangement, of the sort is also selected. The ***sort order*** is either ascending or descending. For numbers, *ascending order* is from the smallest to the largest number, and *descending order* is from the largest to the smallest number. The ascending sort order for text is in alphabetical order from A–Z, and descending order is from Z–A. For chronological order, ascending order is from the earliest to the latest date, and descending order is from the latest to the earliest date.

Figure 11.4   Sort Dialog Box

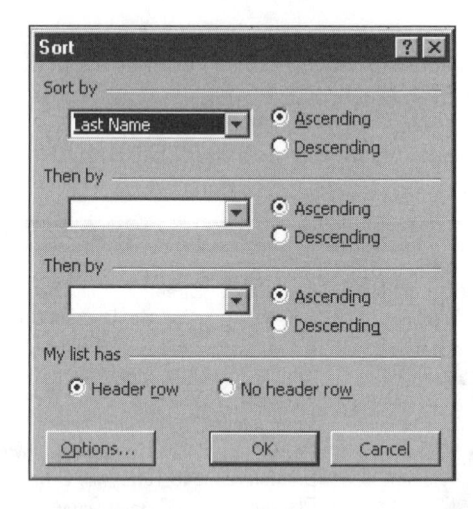

The address book has been sorted by last name in ascending order in Figure 11.5.

Figure 11.5   Sort Completed

	A	B	C	D	E	F	G
1	Address Book Database						
2							
3	First Name	Last Name	Address	City	State	Zip	Tele No.
4	Sharon	Andrews	8775 Treetop Lane	Denver	CO	80215	555-3942
5	Kim	Bond	95 Kendall Loop	Lincoln	NE	50349	555-4432
6	Kevin	Carlton	455 NE 23rd	Portland	OR	97332	555-1607
7	Bruce	Jones	943 Charles Ave.	Eugene	OR	97321	555-0391
8	Courtney	King	903 N Queenly	Everett	WA	40593	555-9831

When there are identical entries in the sorting field, additional sort criteria are needed. For instance, if two or more last names are identical, do a secondary sort by first name. In the Sort dialog box, two additional fields may be used to sort a list. The list shown in Figure 11.6 includes three people with the last name of Smith.

Figure 11.6   Sorting Three Fields that Contain Identical Field Entries

	A	B	C	D	E	F	G
1	Address Book Database						
2							
3	First Name	Last Name	Address	City	State	Zip	Tele No.
4	Kam	Smith	5873 River Road	Denver	CO	81293	555-1829
5	Kim	Smith	895 Grant Avenue	Phoenix	AZ	85303	555-1038
6	Kim	Smith	775 Bristol Rd.	Denver	CO	81223	555-1162

The Sort dialog box for the sort in Figure 11.6 is shown in Figure 11.7. The Sort by section indicates Last Name in ascending alphabetical order as the first sort. The second sort is by first name, the information in column A. The text box of the first Then by section shows this sort, also in ascending alphabetical order. State, in column E, is used as the third sort, in ascending order. If records have identical last names and first names, they are sorted by state.

The down arrow by a sort choice accesses a drop-down list showing the labels of the selected list. The drop-down sort list for the address book database is shown in Figure 11.8.

Always check the results of a sort before continuing. If you do not like the results, the sort can be undone immediately by selecting Undo Sort from the Edit menu or by clicking the Undo button.

Figure 11.7   Three-level Sort Defined

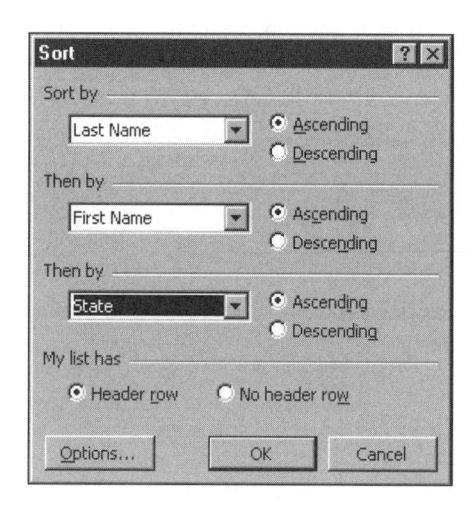

Figure 11.8   Drop-down Sort List

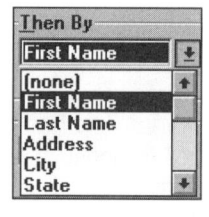

Any Excel worksheet can be sorted using these procedures, not just one containing a list.

Sorting Quickly by One Field

There are two sort tools on the Standard toolbar that can be used when sorting by only one field. To sort in ascending order, select one cell in the field to be sorted, and then choose the ***Sort Ascending button***. To sort a list in descending order, select one cell in the field to be sorted; then select the ***Sort Descending button***.

Returning a Database to Its Original Order

Once a sort has been completed and saved, the list has been altered. However, it may be important to retain the original order of a list. To do this, create and label a column that contains sequential numbers starting with 1 to number each entry in the list. To return the list to the original order, sort by the column containing the number sequence.

Printing a Database

Because lists are often large and take several pages to print, row and column labels should be printed on all the pages.

Headers and footers are useful for providing pertinent information. Using the current date, for instance, is extremely helpful. Most lists change frequently as they are updated; customers are added or deleted, addresses change, etc. By printing the current date in the header or footer, the most recently printed list is easily identified. It is sometimes useful to also include the time in the header or footer.

Exercise 11.2 Sorting a List

You will sort the list of employees created in Exercise 11.1.

1 Open the workbook **Exer 11-1** to the sheet **Ex 11-1**.

2 Copy **Ex 11-1** to a new sheet. Use the shortcut menu to copy the sheet. Move the mouse to the tab of **Ex 11-1** and click the right mouse button; select **Move or Copy**. Select **Ex 11-1** and be sure the **Create a copy** box is checked. Click **OK**.

3 Move the new sheet so it is after the **Ex 11-1** worksheet, and rename it **Ex 11-2**.

4 Select any cell in column B, the column that will be used as the sort criteria. (Do not select the label.)

5 From the **Data** menu, select the **Sort** command. The **Sort** dialog box opens and the entire list is selected.

6 In the **Sort by** section, **Last Name** is entered. Be sure **Ascending** order is selected. Click **OK**. All of the cells are arranged in alphabetical order by last name; however, there are two records with the same last name entry, **Eisman**.

7 Print the worksheet. Write, "Print 1" at the top.

8 To sort the **Eisman** records, select a cell in column B (not the label).

9 Open the **Sort** dialog box by selecting the **Sort** command from the **Data** menu.

10 Be sure the **Sort by** field is **Last Name** in **Ascending** order. In the first **Then by** section, click on the down arrow and select **First Name**. Be sure it is in **Ascending** order. Click **OK** to complete the sort.

11 Save and print the worksheet. Write "Print 2" at the top.

12 Click in any cell in the Zip column (column F). Click on the Sort Ascending button. The entries are sorted by zip code from smallest to largest.

13 Print a copy of the worksheet. Write "Print 3" at the top.

14 Click on any social security number. Click on the Sort Descending button [Z↓]. The entries are sorted by social security number from highest to lowest.

15 Print a copy of the worksheet. Write "Print 4" at the top.

16 Save and close the workbook.

Using a Custom Sort

In addition to sorting by ascending or descending order, a *custom sort* may be required. A *custom sort order* is one in which information is sorted in a predetermined way neither alphabetical nor numerical. Sorting by calendar months (January, February, March) requires a custom sort. The normal rules for alphabetical and numerical order do not apply.

Figure 11.9   Sort Options Dialog Box

To complete a custom sort, select Sort from the Data menu. In the Sort dialog box, click on the Options button to open the Sort Options dialog box, shown in Figure 11.9.

Select a custom sort in the First key sort order box. Click on the down arrow to access the built-in custom choices, shown in Figure 11.10.

The days of the week and months of the year are built-in custom choices. Any custom list that is created by AutoFill is available in the custom sort options.

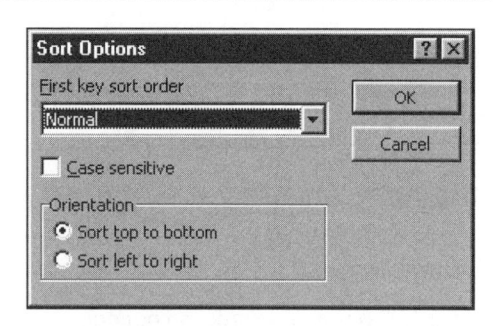

Figure 11.10   Custom Sort Choices

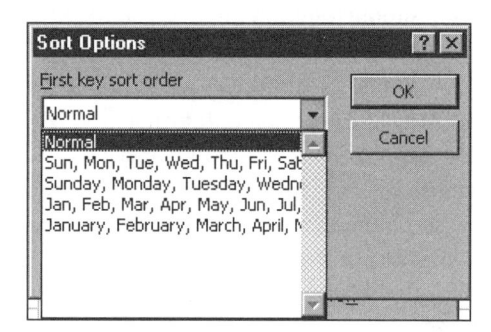

Ascending or descending order can be applied to custom lists. For months of the year, ascending would be January, February, March, etc. A descending order would be December, November, October, etc.

Exercise 11.3   Using a Custom Sort

You will sort a list using the custom sort feature.

1 Open the **Exer 11** workbook to **Sheet1** and rename the sheet **Ex 11-3a**.

2 In column A, select a cell that contains data. From **Data** select **Sort**. Click on the **Options** button.

3 Select a custom sort that lists the full names of the months, and then click **OK** two times. The months are sorted in ascending order.

4 In column C, select a cell that contains data. From **Data** select **Sort**. Click on the **Options** button.

5. Select a custom sort that lists the abbreviated month names. Sort these in descending order. The months are listed from December to January.

6. In column E, select a cell that contains data. Sort by days of the week in ascending order.

7. Select a cell in column G. Sort in descending order.

8. Print the **Ex 11-3a** sheet.

9. Select **Sheet2** and rename it **Ex 11-3b**.

10. Click in any cell. From **Data** select **Sort**.

11. Select to sort by **Month**, then click in the **Options** button. Select to sort by month from January to December. Then click **OK**.

12. In the **Then by** section, select to sort by **Salesperson** in ascending alphabetical order. Click **OK**.

13. Save and print the worksheet.

Maintaining a List

Using Data Forms

After a list is created, records can be added, edited, or deleted using a data form. A *data form* is a dialog box that displays one complete record at a time. The fields of a list match the text boxes on the data form. Although information can be edited in a worksheet list, users often find a data form helpful when working with a list.

Figure 11.11 shows the data form for the first entry of the address book.

A data form displays information from one record (row) of a worksheet. Each field is stored as a single column in a list. A data form displays all the fields in the order in which they appear on the worksheet (from left to right).

The scroll bar to the right of the fields indicates the approximate location of the displayed record in the list; it also enables the user to browse through the records.

The *record number indicator* is in the upper-right corner of a data form. It shows which record is displayed and how many records are in the entire list. The command buttons at the right side of a data form are used when working with a list.

Figure 11.11   Data Form

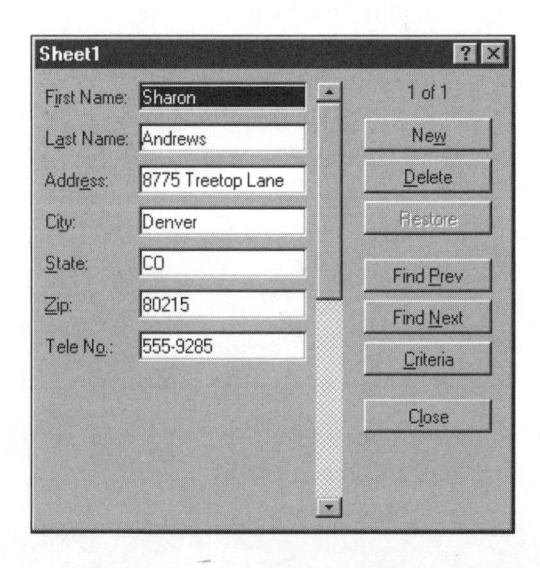

Using a Data Form to Edit a List

To access a data form, select Form from the Data menu. A data form opens with the first record of the list displayed.

The New button opens a blank form so additional records may be added. To delete the current record, use the Delete button. Clicking on Restore erases any changes made and restores the record to its original version.

To select a different record, use the Find Prev and Find Next buttons. Use the scroll bar to move between records. The Criteria button is used to retrieve information or query the list. Criteria are discussed further in the next section. To close the data form, click the Close button.

A data form is usually displayed with edit boxes placed after the field names. These fields are *editable fields*, which means they can be changed. Fields are sometimes included in a data form that cannot be edited; their contents may have been calculated by a formula. These fields are *computed fields*. Computed fields are displayed in a data form but cannot be changed.

Figure 11.12 shows the editable fields Name, Hourly Rate, and Number Hours and the computed field Total Pay. The Total Pay field was computed by multiplying the hourly rate by the number of hours, and it changes when either the hourly rate or the number of hours changes. Because the Total Pay field is a computed field, it cannot be edited in the data form.

Figure 11.12 Editable and Computed Fields

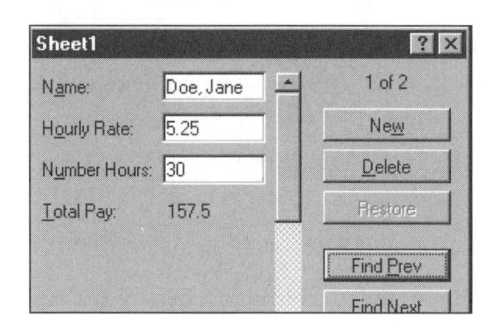

When changes are made in a data form, they are reflected in the original list. Editing existing records, adding new records, or deleting records is often easier and faster in a data form than in a worksheet because only one record is visible.

Exercise 11.4   Using a Data Form

You will access the employee list created in Exercise 11.1 and add and edit records.

1   Open the **Exer 11** workbook. Copy sheet **Ex 11-2** and place it after sheet **Ex 11-3b**. Rename the copy **Ex 11-4**.

2   Select any cell in the list.

3   From the **Data** menu, select the **Form** command. A data form opens to the first record (**Janet Coffey**). The record number indicator in the upper-right corner of the data form shows **1 of 8**.

4   Click on **Find Next**. Another record opens; **2 of 8** is shown in the record number indicator.

Chapter 11 Using Excel to Manage Lists

5   Click on **Find Next**. Another record opens; **3 of 8** is shown in the record number indicator.

6   Click on the scroll box and move it back to the top. Verify that the record number indicator reads **1 of 8**.

Add new records.

7   Click on **New** to open a new form.

8   In the **First Name** field, type **Linda**. Press [Tab].

9   In the **Last Name** field, type **Marten**. Press [Tab].

10 In the **Street** field, type **38572 Pine Avenue**. Press [Tab].

11 In the **City** field, type **Palo Alto**. Press [Tab].

12 In the **State** field, type **CA**. Press [Tab].

13 In the **Zip** field, type **94333**. Press [Tab].

14 In the **Tele. No.** field, type **555-8763**. Press [Tab].

15 In the **Soc. Sec. No.** field, type **222-44-6666**. Press [Enter]. A new form opens.

Enter the next record in the new form.

16 Enter the following records. Press [Tab] between the fields and [Enter] after the last field of each record is entered.
   - Jay Phillips, 8751 Cook Drive, Menlo Park, CA, 94331, 555-5621, 444-66-8888
   - Joseph Petrjanos, 17700 Snyder Drive, Menlo Park, CA, 94331, 555-6713, 333-55-7777

17 Add a record for yourself. Use your name, address, etc., as information for the record.

18 Click on the **Find Prev** button until the record for **Destiny Eisman** is open. Highlight the telephone number and change it to **555-7784**. Highlight the street address and change it to **2873 Parsons Drive**. The remaining fields stay the same.

19 Click on **Close** to exit the data form. Three new records have been added to the list, and one record has been changed.

Sort the edited list.

20 In the Last Name column, select any cell that contains data. From the **Data** menu, select **Sort**. The **Sort** dialog box opens. Sort by **Last Name** in **Ascending** order, then by **First Name** in **Ascending** order, and then by **State** in **Ascending** order. Click **OK** to exit the Sort dialog box.

21 Save and print the worksheet.

Finding a Record

Two advantages of using a computerized list are the speed and accuracy with which information can be found. To access or find information in a list is also called to *search* or *query* a list.

There are three ways to find a record using a data form. Using the Find Prev and Find Next buttons in the data form is one way to browse through the database and view records. Using the scroll bar to browse the database is another method. The Criteria button of the data form can be used to find specific information.

Click on the Criteria button to open the criteria window of the data form so a search can be executed. *Criteria* are the instructions Excel uses to locate records. For instance, to find information about Sam Adams, one criterion to search for is Adams (the last name); another is Sam (the first name).

The criteria view of a data form is shown in Figure 11.13. The record number indicator changes to read Criteria to indicate that Excel is ready to search the database for the criteria entered.

In criteria view, Clear and Form buttons are added. The Clear button clears all existing criteria; the Form button closes criteria view and returns to data form view. The Close button closes the form and returns to the worksheet list.

To search for Smith in Phoenix, enter the name Smith in the text box for the Last Name field. Press Tab to move to the City field and enter the city name, Phoenix (Figure 11.14).

Figure 11.13   Criteria View of a Data Form

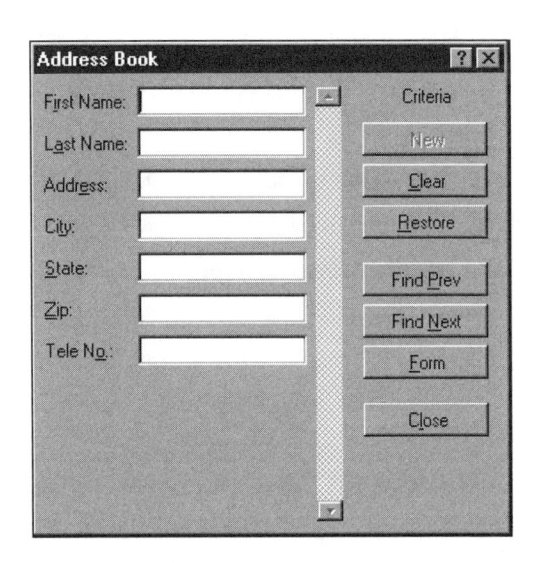

Figure 11.14   Criteria Entered

Press Enter on the keyboard or click on the Form button, and almost immediately the requested record opens. To change the criteria, click the Criteria button to return to criteria view. Then click Clear to clear the previously entered criteria and return to a blank form.

Exercise 11.5 Searching a Database

You will search a list and find records and information.

1   Open the **Exer 11** workbook to the sheet **Ex 11-4**.

Open a data form.

2   From **Data**, select the **Form** command. The first data form opens.

Retrieve information. What is the street address of Ms. Edmondson?

3   Click on **Criteria**. In the **Last Name** text box, key **Edmondson**. Click on **Find Next**. Write the address here. _____ What is the record number? _____

4   Move the scroll box back to the top of the scroll bar.

How many people live in Redwood City? (You will need to search by the city name and count the number of matches.)

5   Click on **Criteria**. Click on **Clear** to begin a new query. In the **City** text box, key **Redwood City**. Click **Find Next**. This retrieves the first matching record.

6   Click **Find Next**. A new record containing Redwood City opens; this is the second matching record.

7   Click **Find Next**. A new record opens; this is the third matching record.

8   Click **Find Next**. The screen flashes or the computer beeps, indicating there are no other records that match the criteria. Three people in the list live in Redwood City.

Find the Martin that lives in Palo Alto.

9   Be sure the scroll box is at the top of the scroll bar and the record number indicator reads **1 of 12**. Click on **Criteria**, then **Clear**. In the **Last Name** text box, key **Martin**.

10 Press [Tab] two times to place the insertion point in the **City** text box and key **Palo Alto**.

11 Click on **Find Next**. The screen flashes or the computer beeps, and a record opens that does not match, indicating there is no matching record.

12 Be sure the scroll box is at the top of the scroll bar.

13 Click on **Criteria**. Change the name entry to **Mart**. Perhaps the spelling was different; enter just a part of the name. Click on **Find Next**. The record for Linda Marten opens. Write the address and telephone number here. _____

14 Click on **Find Next**. The screen flashes or the computer beeps, indicating there are no additional matching records.

Query the database on your own.

15 What is the first name of Mr. Perry? _____

16 What is the record number for Mr. Perry? _____

17 What is the telephone number of Joan Eisman? _____

18 What is the record number for Joan Eisman? _____

19 Who has the telephone number 555-3859? _____

20 What is this record number? _____

21 Exit the data form and close the workbook without saving.

Using Filters

About Filtering

Businesses often prepare reports using only some of the records in a list. For instance, a report may be needed listing all of the customers in one city. Excel will search for all of the customers in that city and display only the matching records. The original list is not affected; all records remain in memory. Gathering specific information from a list is called *filtering a list*.

Using AutoFilter

Using *AutoFilter* is a quick and easy way to filter a list. Cell contents are matched with a criterion; only the rows containing cells that match the criterion are displayed.

With a cell of the list active, select Filter from the Data menu, and then select AutoFilter (Figure 11.15). Drop-down arrows are now placed on the column labels in the list. Click an arrow to display a list of all the entries in a column (Figure 11.16).

Figure 11.15   Selecting AutoFilter

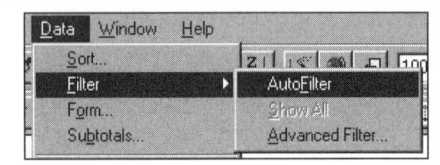

Figure 11.16   AutoFilter List

Select the criterion needed to filter the list. In the example, OR will be selected as the state. Excel automatically displays only the records that match—in this case, all persons in the state of Oregon. The filtered list is shown in Figure 11.17. Notice the row numbers that are displayed; the rows that do not match the criterion are temporarily hidden. Only two records match the criterion.

Figure 11.17   List Filtered to Find Oregon Entries

	A	B	C	D	E	F	G
1	Address Book Database						
2							
3	First Nam	Last Nam	Address	City	Stat	Zip	Tele No
6	Kevin	Carlton	455 NE 23rd	Portland	OR	97332	555-1607
7	Bruce	Jones	943 Charles Ave.	Eugene	OR	97321	555-0391

When a filtered list is displayed on the screen, visual clues remind you that it is a filtered list. The arrow of the filtered criterion displays in color. The row heading is in color when records are not displayed. The status bar displays the number of records in the filtered list (2 of 5 records found), shown in Figure 11.18.

This filtered list can be filtered further by selecting another criterion from another field.

Figure 11.18   Status Bar while Filtering a List

To remove the filter and show all of the records, select Show All from the Filter submenu. To remove the drop-down arrows, select AutoFilter from the Filter submenu.

After a list is filtered, it can be sorted using the same sorting commands used for any Excel list.

Printing a Filtered List

A filtered list can be printed just as it is displayed. Changes for margins and placement can be made in Print Preview or Page Setup. If the filtered list is displaying the drop-down arrows when the Print command is given, the arrows will not print with the worksheet.

Exercise 11.6   Filtering and Printing a List

The employee list from Exercise 11.1 will be filtered and then printed.

1   Open the workbook **Exer 11** to sheet **Ex 11-4**.

2   Copy the **Ex 11-4** sheet and place it before **Sheet3**. Rename the new sheet **Ex 11-6**.

Filter the list to find people living in Palo Alto.

3   Select any cell in the list. From the **Data** menu, select **Filter**, and then **AutoFilter**.

4   Click on the drop-down arrow by **City**. Select **Palo Alto**. Only the records of people living in Palo Alto are displayed.

Format the list.

5   Highlight the range of labels in row 2. Format for bold and centered alignment.

6   Insert two rows above the field names. In cell A1, key **Addresses in Palo Alto**. Format it for bold, italic, a font size of 12 points, and merge and center over the columns.

7 Adjust column widths for all fields, if needed.

Print the list.

8 Save and print the worksheet.

Custom AutoFilter

AutoFilter can be customized to search for two criterion. *Custom AutoFilter* is used for information that matches criteria from two different fields or for a list requiring specific numerical amounts, such as a list of customers who owe more than $250. For instance, preparing a list of all customers who live in Illinois and have purchased more than $500 would require using Custom AutoFilter.

In the drop-down list for filtering a field, Custom is a choice. When Custom is selected, the Custom AutoFilter dialog box opens, shown in Figure 11.19.

Figure 11.19 Custom AutoFilter Dialog Box

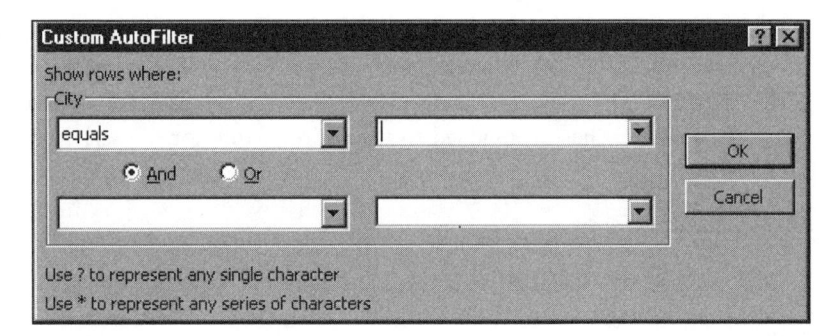

Four text boxes are available, each with a drop-down arrow. The boxes at the left are used to enter the *comparison operators* that specify the type of calculation to perform. The comparison operator shown in Figure 11.19 is "equals." Figure 11.20 shows the drop-down list for comparison operators.

The drop-down text boxes on the right of the Custom AutoFilter dialog box show all data entries in the selected fields. Figure 11.21 shows the entries available in the Last Name field.

Figure 11.20 Comparison Operators

Figure 11.21 Drop-down List of Data Entries for Selected Field

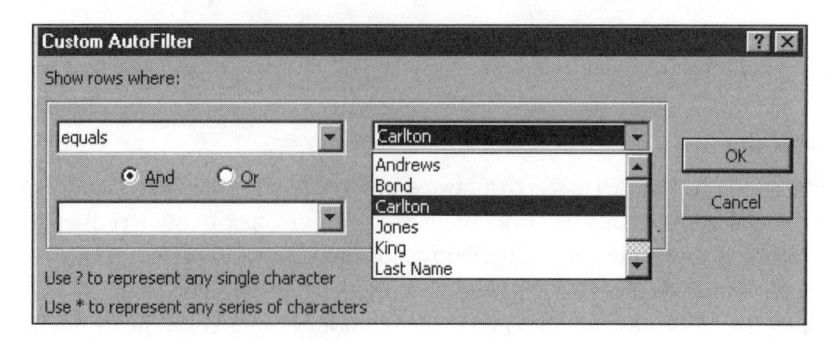

To filter a list, select the comparison operator in the left box and the matching field in the right box. If a listing of all people named Carlton is needed, the comparison operator "equals" would be entered in the text box.

The option buttons between the two lists are And and Or. When filtering for all people named Andrews or Carlton, the Last Name field must match either Andrews or Carlton; select the Or button. If a result is to match both criteria, such as people named Carlton and living in Oregon, select And.

To illustrate, a column has been added to the address book for the salary of each employee, shown in Figure 11.22.

Figure 11.22 Address-book Database with Salaries

	A	B	C	D	E	F	G	H
1	Address Book Database- Employee Salary							
2								
3	First Name	Last Name	Address	City	State	Zip	Tele No.	Salary
4	Sharon	Andrews	8775 Treetop Lane	Denver	CO	80215	555-9285	$ 45,000
5	Kim	Bond	95 Kendall Loop	Lincoln	NE	50349	555-4432	$ 30,580
6	Kevin	Carlton	455 NE 23rd	Portland	OR	97332	555-1607	$ 44,298
7	Bruce	Jones	943 Charles Ave.	Eugene	OR	97321	555-0391	$ 25,837
8	Courtney	King	903 N Queenly	Everett	WA	40593	555-9831	$ 26,389
9	Peter	Nelson	332 E 43rd	Salem	OR	93320	555-9301	$ 21,870
10	Mark	Carlton	10328 NW Ranger	Burns	OR	94432	555-3002	$ 19,383

A report listing all employees earning more than $30,000 will be prepared. This requires use of custom criteria. Using AutoFilter, select the arrow in the Salary field, and then Custom from the drop-down menu. The Custom AutoFilter dialog box opens, shown in Figure 11.23. Because the list will show only those records in which salary is greater than $30,000, use "is greater than" in the drop-down menu and "30000" in the text box.

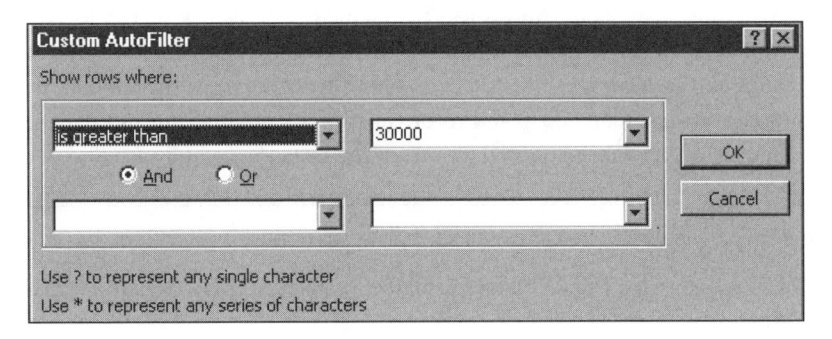

Figure 11.23 Custom AutoFilter for Numerical Criterion

Click OK; the filtered list is shown in Figure 11.24.

Figure 11.24 Numerical Filter Completed

	A	B	C	D	E	F	G	H
1	Address Book Database- Employee Salary							
2								
4	Sharon	Andrews	8775 Treetop Lane	Denver	CO	80215	555-9285	$ 45,000
5	Kim	Bond	95 Kendall Loop	Lincoln	NE	50349	555-4432	$ 30,580
6	Kevin	Carlton	455 NE 23rd	Portland	OR	97332	555-1607	$ 44,298

Immediately after the filter is performed, the status bar reports the number of records meeting the criteria. Figure 11.25 indicates three matches in the eight records.

Figure 11.25 Status Bar after Using AutoFilter

The list can now be sorted in any manner, perhaps from smallest to largest salary or in alphabetical order.

Custom criteria can be applied to meet more specific criteria, such as salaries between $20,000 and $30,000. In this case, the Custom AutoFilter dialog box would look like Figure 11.26. The And and Or option buttons are important in this type of filter.

Figure 11.26 Using Two Comparison Operators

When using two comparison operators, select And if the result is to meet both specifications. For instance "is greater than 30000 And is less than 45000" will display all records with values that fall between 30,000 and 45,000. When the result is to meet one or the other of the specified criteria, use the Or option button. For example, "is less than 30000 Or is greater than 45000" will display records with values that are less than 30000 and records with values that are greater than 45000.

To remove the AutoFilter, choose Filter from the Data menu, and then Show All.

Exercise 11.7 Filtering, Sorting, and Printing a List

You will filter information from a list and print the filtered list. You will then sort and print the filtered list.

1 Open the workbook **Exer11**.

2 Rename **Sheet3** to **Ex 11-7**. You will be using the list for Alpha Corp.

Prepare a list of all women earning more than $30,000.

3 Click in any cell in the open list. From the **Data** menu, select **Filter**, and then **AutoFilter**.

4 Click on the arrow for the field named **Gender**. Select **F** (for female).

5 Click on the arrow for the field named **Annual Salary**.

6 Select **Custom**. In the **Custom AutoFilter** dialog box, enter the comparison operator **is greater than** and the amount **30000**. Click **OK**.

7 Do a quick save. Print a copy of the report. At the top write "Print 1."

Hide columns and print another report.

8 In the worksheet, hide columns C (Street), D (City), E (State), F (Zip), and G (Tele. No.).

9 Print this worksheet in portrait style without gridlines. At the top write "Print 2."

10 Select any cell from the filtered list. From the **Data** menu, select **Sort**. In the **Sort** dialog box, select **Annual Salary** by **Descending** order. Click **OK**.

Print the sorted report.

11 Print the report. At the top write "Print 3."

Restore the list to the full list.

12 From the **Data** menu, select **Filter**, and then **Show All**. Display all columns that were previously hidden.

13 Save and close the worksheet.

Summary

- A list of related records is called a database.
- A record contains several pieces of information about one topic or person.
- A field is a category of a record. A record contains several fields of information.

- A list may be entered in a worksheet. Each row contains one record; each column contains one field.
- Sorting a list is rearranging the information in alphabetical, numerical, or chronological order.
- To sort a list, click in any cell in the list, and then select the Sort command from the Data menu.
- In the Sort dialog box, select each field to be sorted and the order of the sort.
- Ascending order sorts in alphabetical order from A to Z or in numerical order from smallest to largest.
- Descending order sorts alphabetically from Z to A or numerically from largest to smallest.
- To sort quickly by one field, use the Sort Ascending and Sort Descending buttons.
- A custom sort may be days of the week or months of the year. Any list may be sorted by a custom sort.
- A data form is used in entering or editing information and querying a list. One record is shown in each data form.
- The record number indicator in a data form indicates which record is being viewed and the total number of records in the list.
- To open a data form, select the Form command from the Data menu.
- Finding information is also called searching or querying.
- In a data form, criteria define the specific information for the search. The criteria can be text or numerical information.
- Fields in a data form are editable or calculated fields. Editable fields may be altered in the data form; calculated fields cannot be edited.
- Gathering specific information from a list is called filtering the list.
- A filtered list contains only the records that match certain criteria.
- To filter a list, select Data, then Filter, and then AutoFilter. Arrows appear by each field label to aid in filtering data.
- A filtered list may be sorted.
- Custom AutoFilter is used to filter two separate criteria.
- A comparison operator may be used in a custom search to determine criteria based on numerical values.

Important Terminology

ascending order
AutoFilter
comparison operators
computed fields
criteria
Custom AutoFilter
custom sort
custom sort order

data form
database
descending order
editable fields
field
filtering a list
list
query

record
record number indicator
search
Sort
Sort Ascending button
Sort Descending button
sort order

Buttons to Know

Study Questions

True-False

Place a T in the space if the statement is true; place an F if the statement is false.

_____ 1. A list of information, called a database, may be entered into a worksheet.
_____ 2. The main function of database software is to store groups of records that list similar information.
_____ 3. An example of a list is the payroll information of a business.
_____ 4. Information in a list can be located quickly with the use of a computer.
_____ 5. A record contains fields of information.
_____ 6. A field is a single piece of information in a record.
_____ 7. In a worksheet list, each column defines a record and each row defines a field.
_____ 8. Rearranging the information in a list is called filtering the list.
_____ 9. To sort a list, all data needs to be selected.
_____ 10. The Sort dialog box is used to determine which fields to sort by.
_____ 11. A record can only be sorted alphabetically by any field.
_____ 12. The Sort command is used to open the Sort dialog box and is accessed in the Format menu.
_____ 13. In order to list numbers from smallest to largest, select a sort by descending order.
_____ 14. Sorting alphabetical information from A to Z is called sorting in ascending order.
_____ 15. The Sort Descending button may be used to sort by one field in alphabetical order.
_____ 16. Days of the week may only be sorted alphabetically.
_____ 17. When entering a list record by record, it is often easier to use a filter window rather than enter the information directly into a worksheet.
_____ 18. A database may be presented as a worksheet called a data form.
_____ 19. To access a new data form, click on the Next button.
_____ 20. The field names in a worksheet are different from those in a data form.
_____ 21. An editable field is a field that cannot be edited because it contains calculations.
_____ 22. A computed field is displayed in a text box in the data form.
_____ 23. Gathering specific information about a field is called searching the database.
_____ 24. Criteria are the information used to filter a list.
_____ 25. AutoFilter is a quick way to search a list for a set of criterion.
_____ 26. A list may be filtered for only one criterion.
_____ 27. A comparison operator is a math symbol that helps define the range of numbers for a filtered list.
_____ 28. A filtered list cannot be sorted or changed.

Fill-In

Place the word in the space that correctly completes the statement.

1. A _____ is a collection of related information.
2. Each category of information of a record is a(n) _____ .
3. In the worksheet view of a list, a(n) _____ is placed on a row of the worksheet.
4. Rearranging a list in alphabetical or numerical order is called _____ the database.

5. To alphabetize a list, select to sort by _____ (ascending/descending) order.
6. To determine the column by which to sort, use the drop-down list and select the _____ name.
7. To sort by the months of the year, use a(n) _____ sort.
8. To list information one record at a time, use a _____ form.
9. The indicator on a data form that tells how many records the database contains is the _____ indicator.
10. Fields in a data form that cannot be changed are called _____ fields; those that can be altered are called _____ fields.
11. To search for a record in a data form, click on the _____ button.
12. Extracting information from a list is called _____ the list.
13. When the _____ command is selected, drop-down arrows appear by the field names.
14. To select more than one criterion in a filtered list, access the _____ AutoFilter dialog box.

Assignments

After you complete the Chapter 11 assignments, you may delete the Ch11 subdirectory from your Student Data Disk.

Assignment 11.1

You will sort and print a list of employees for Turner Packaging Company. This assignment must be completed before Assignment 11.2.

1. Open the workbook **Ch11 As1** and save it as **Assig 11-1**.
2. Rename **Sheet1** to **Turner, Print 1**.
3. Format the worksheet in Page Setup for landscape style printed on one page, centered both horizontally and vertically. Create a header and footer and be sure to include your name, the file name, the sheet name, and the page number.
4. Enter today's date in the heading (replacing the words **Today's Date**). Remember the shortcut **Ctrl**+;.
5. Sort the list alphabetically.
   - Select any cell in the list. From the **Data** menu, select **Sort**.
   - Sort in alphabetical order, first by last name and then by first name.
   - Print a copy of the worksheet.
6. Sort the list by salary.
   - Copy the **Turner, Print 1** worksheet to a new sheet just after the original. Name the sheet **Turner, Print 2**.
   - Place the largest salary first. If two employees have the same salary, sort alphabetically by last name, and then by first name.
   - Change the label in row 2 to read **Salaries**.
   - Print the list.
7. Sort the list by date of birth.
   - Copy the **Turner, Print 2** sheet to a new sheet. Rename it **Turner, Print 3**.
   - Place the oldest employee first. Click in any cell in the **Date of Birth** field. Use the Sort Ascending button. (Excel recognizes dates and will sort properly.)

- Change the label in row 2 to read **Date of Birth**.
- Print a copy of the worksheet.
8. Sort the database by date of hire.
   - Copy the **Turner, Print 3** sheet to a new sheet. Rename it **Turner, Print 4**.
   - Place the most recent hire first. If hiring dates are the same, sort alphabetically by last name and then by first name.
   - Change the label in row 2 to read **Date of Hire**.
   - Print a copy of the worksheet.
9. Copy the Turner, Print 4 sheet to a new sheet. Rename it **Original**.
   - Restore the list to its original form by sorting by number in column A.
10. Save the workbook.

Assignment 11.2

Turner Packaging Company needs an updated list. You will use a data form to edit the list. Then you will filter the list and print the reports. Complete Assignment 11.1 before this assignment.

1. Open the workbook **Assig 11-1** to the **Original** worksheet. Change the name to **Original 1**.
2. Copy the sheet to a new workbook.
   - On the worksheet tab, right-click the mouse button to access the shortcut menu.
   - Be sure the **Create a copy** box is checked. In the **To book** section, access **New book** from the drop-down list.
3. Save the book as **Assig 11-2**.
4. In the header or footer, enter the assignment number.
5. Use a data form to edit the list.
   - Click in any cell in the list. From **Data** select **Form**. Click on **Criteria**. In the **Last Name** section, key **Hensley**. Click **Find Next**.
   - When the data form for **Jeff Hensley** opens, click on the **Delete** button. A warning box opens. Click **OK**.
   - Click on **New**. Add **Ryan Keller**; date of hire is **4/5/93**; date of birth is **8/28/69**; gender is **M**; salary is **$19,500**.
   - Click on the up arrow of the scroll bar until you return to record 1.
6. Edit the following records:
   - **John Crone** received a **$1,000** raise; **Faye Nelson** received a raise of **$1,500**.
   - Click on **Close** to exit the data form.
7. Ryan Keller is at the bottom of the list. In the Number column, enter **14**.
8. Do a quick save and print the sheet.
9. Make a copy of the sheet just after the original. Rename it **Original 2**.
10. On the **Original 2** sheet, prepare a report for all female employees.
    - From the **Data** menu, select **Filter**, and then **AutoFilter**.
    - Click on the down arrow next to **Sex**. Select **F** (female).
    - Change the label on row 2 to read **Female Employees** and be sure today's date is correct (**Ctrl**+;).
    - Sort the list by salary, beginning with the largest salary. If salaries are the same, sort alphabetically by last name and then by first name.
    - Print the list.

11. Prepare a similar list of male employees on a new sheet named **Original 3**. Change the heading to indicate that this is a list of male employees. Sort by salary, beginning with the largest salary. If salaries are the same, sort alphabetically by last name and then by first name. Print a copy of the worksheet.
12. Prepare a list of employees earning less than $30,000.
    - Copy **Original 3** to a new sheet and name the new sheet **Original 4**. Place it at the end of the workbook.
    - Select a custom filter for **Salary**.
    - In the **Custom AutoFilter** dialog box, select **is less than** as the comparison operator. Enter **30000** in the text box.
    - Sort the list alphabetically by name.
    - Change the second line of the title to read **Employees Earning Less Than $30,000**.
    - Print a copy of the worksheet.
13. Prepare a report of all male employees who earn between $15,000 and $35,000.
    - Copy **Original 4** to a new sheet and name the sheet **Original 5**. Place it at the end of the workbook.
    - Select a custom filter for a salary that **is greater than 15000** and **is less than 35000**. Click **OK**.
    - In the **Gender** field, select **M** (male).
    - Change the second line of the title to read **Selected Men's Salaries**. Be sure today's date is correct.
    - Sort by salary, beginning with the smallest salary. Print a copy of the worksheet.
14. Save the worksheet.

Assignment 11.3

You will maintain a list that keeps track of the amounts owed to Julie Burkes, Optometrist. The list will be sorted, edited, and printed.

1. Open the workbook **Ch11 As3** and save it as **Assig 11-3**.
2. Rename **Sheet1** to **J. Burkes**.
3. Format the worksheet.
    - Create a custom header. In the **Center section** of the header, key **Julie Burkes, O.D**. Format it for bold, italic, and a font size of 12 points. In the **Right section** text box, enter the current date. In the **Left section** text box, enter the file name followed by the sheet name.
    - Format to print centered horizontally and vertically, in landscape style, and on one page.
    - In the **Center section** of the footer, format the page number so it shows the entire number of pages and will read "Page 1 of 1" when printed. Put your name in the **Left section** text box.
    - Print without gridlines.
4. Sort and print the list.
    - Sort the list in alphabetical order by last name. If last names are identical, sort by first name.
    - Print a copy of the list. At the top of the printout, write "Assig 11.3, Print 1."
5. Access a data form. An error was entered in the record of **Robin McGinn**. Change the city to **St. Louis**, the state to **MO**, and the zip code to **64585**. Exit the data form.

6. Complete the formulas in the worksheet.
   - Freeze panes at cell C6.
   - Enter a formula in cell H6 for the late charge. A late charge of two percent of the present balance is assessed.
   - In cell K6, enter the formula to determine the new balance. The new balance is the present balance plus the late charge plus the current charge minus the amount paid.
   - Format columns G–K for Comma style with two decimals.
   - Copy the formulas to the rest of the worksheet.
7. Enter the current charges for Robin McGinn.
   - Access a data form. Click the **Criteria** button.
   - In the **Last Name** field, key **McGinn**. Click the **Find Next** button.
   - When the record for **Robin McGinn** opens, enter **301.59** in the **Current Charge** field.
   - Click on the up arrow of the scroll bar until you return to the first record.
8. Enter the current charges for Chuck Evans.
   - Click the **Criteria** button, then click **Clear**. In the **Last Name** field, key **Evans**.
   - Click the **Find Next** button. When the record for **Chuck Evans** opens, enter **358.05** in the **Current Charge** field.
   - Click on the up arrow of the scroll bar until you return to the first record.
9. Continue in the same way and enter the current charges for the following clients:

Client	Amount
Sam Owen	$100.00
Lorella Henning	125.00
Barbara Metcalf	557.50
Brian Roberts	259.30
Carol Armstrong	150.00
Bryan Byers	203.50
Terry Holcomb	350.00

10. Carol Squire has paid $295.29 on her balance.
    - Click the **Criteria** button. In the **Last Name** field, key **Squire**.
    - Click the **Find Next** button. When the record for **Carol Squire** opens, enter **$295.29** in the **Paid** field.
    - Return to the first record.
11. Richard Gamble has paid $200 on his balance.
    - Click the **Criteria** button. In the **Last Name** field, key **Gamble**.
    - Click the **Find Next** button.
    - When the record for **Richard Gamble** opens, enter **$200** in the **Paid** field.
    - Return to the first record.
12. Continue in the same way and enter the amounts paid for the following clients:

Client	Amount
Lorella Henning	$200.00
Terry Holcomb	147.90
Brian Roberts	259.30
Sam Owen	150.00
Saleh Binjaafar	146.88
Robin McGinn	300.00

13. Add new clients.
    - In a data form, click on **New**.
    - Enter a new record for **Kathy Ross, 3672 Edgecliff Rd., Belleville, IL, 62379**. Enter a current charge of **$350**.
    - Click on **New** to open a new record.
    - Enter a new record for **Roseanne Smith, 13043 Qually Rd., Belleville, IL, 62379, $200**.
    - Enter a record for **Bruce Roberts, 367 W. Powell Rd., St. Louis, MO, 64539, $150**.
    - Close the data form.
14. Adjust the column widths if needed.
15. Unfreeze the panes.
16. Sort the list alphabetically by last name and then by first name.
17. Save and print the worksheet. Write "Assig 11.3, Print 2" at the top.

    Checkpoint:
Late Charge for Chuck Evans	7.57
New Balance for Chuck Evans	744.20

Assignment 11.4

You will retrieve the database prepared in Assignment 11.3, complete some reports, and edit the data.

1. Open the workbook **Assig 11-3** to the **J. Burkes** sheet.
2. Filter and print a list.
    - Filter the list to show all of the customers with a current balance (the new balance is greater than zero).
    - Sort the list by the new balance from largest to smallest. If the same balance occurs for more than one patient, sort alphabetically by last name and then by first name.
3. Format the worksheet.
    - Hide columns C, D, E, and F.
    - Change the first line of the heading to read **Outstanding Balances**.
    - Insert a row between rows 2 and 3.
    - On row 2 enter the current date ([**Ctrl**]+;).
    - Adjust the title so it is centered over the existing columns if needed.
4. Print the list. At the top, write "Assig 11.4, Print 1."
5. Unhide all columns and restore the worksheet to the original list.
6. Filter a list for all patients in MO. Sort first by new balance from smallest to largest, then alphabetically by last name, and then by first name. In the title on row 1, key **Missouri Patients**. Print the list. At the top write "Assig 11.4, Print 2."
7. Restore the list to show all of the records.
8. Prepare a report that lists all of the clients with current charges. Sort it from the smallest charge to the largest. Change row 1 to read **Current Charges**. Print only the columns that include customer names and current charges. Adjust the title if needed. At the top write "Assig 11.4, Print 3."
9. Restore the list to show all records.
10. Prepare a report that lists all clients with new balances over $200 and current charges. Include the name, zip code, complete information about the present balance, late and current charges, amount paid, and the new balance in the printed list. Change row 1 to read **Current Charges with Balance**.

Adjust the title if necessary. Sort the report in alphabetical order. At the top of the report, write "Assig 11.4, Print 4."
11. Restore the worksheet to show all records and columns. Change the title in the first line back to **Patients**.
12. Do a quick save and close the workbook.

Assignment 11.5

E-Z-Way Software Sales keeps its inventory using an Excel worksheet. The beginning inventory is provided for you. You will edit the inventory, filter reports using the inventory, and sort and print reports. The completed list in this assignment will be used for Assignment 11.6.

1. Open the workbook **Ch11 As5** and save it as **Assig 11-5**.
2. Rename **Sheet1** to **E-Z-Way**.
3. Complete the formulas in the list. You may want to freeze panes when working with a worksheet of this size.
   - In cell G6 enter the formula to determine the ending inventory. It is the **Beg Inv** plus **Purch** less **Sales**.
   - In cell I6 enter the formula to determine the value of the inventory. It is the **End Inv** times the **Cost Price**.
   - Copy the formulas to the rest of the worksheet as needed.
4. Sort the database by category.
   - Sort the list in alphabetical order by category and then by product name.
   - Hide columns D, E, and F.
5. In the header and footer, include the file name, the sheet name, the page number, the date, and your name. Print in landscape style, centered vertically and horizontally on one page.
6. Print a copy of the list. At the top of the printout write "Assig 11.5, Print 1."
7. Sort the database by **Total Value**. Sort from largest to smallest. Print a copy. At the top of the printout write "Assig 11.5, Print 2."
8. Unhide all columns.
9. Use a data form to enter the following software purchases and sales:

Purchases	
Quark XPress	13
Lotus 1-2-3	9
Publish It Easy!	17
MS Word	23
MS Excel	17
WriteNow	5
FileMaker Pro	12
Claris Works	7

Sales
	MS Excel	20
	MS Word	25
	FileMaker Pro	10
	WriteNow	13
	WordPerfect Mac	18
	PageMaker	9
	MS Works	3
	Lotus 1-2-3	13
	Quark XPress	15
	MacWrite II	5
	Publish It Easy!	10
	Claris Works	8

Sort the database and print it.
10. Do a quick save.
11. Sort the list first by category and then by product name in alphabetical order.
12. Print a copy of the sorted database. At the top write "Assig 11.5, Print 3."

Assignment 11.6

You will filter an existing list and create reports from that information. Assignment 11.5 must be completed before this assignment.
1. Open the **Assig 11-5** workbook.
2. Prepare a report from this list for all word-processing software programs. In row 3, place a title that identifies the report. Print the report. Write "Assig 11.6, Print 1" at the top of the printed sheet.
3. Prepare a report for products that had purchase quantities of 10 or more. Include the **Product No., Product Name, Category**, and **Purch**. Sort the purchase quantities from largest to smallest. If purchases are the same, sort by product name. Include a title that identifies the report. Print the report. Write "Assig 11.6, Print 2" at the top.
4. For reordering purposes, prepare a report that lists all products with an ending inventory of less than 18. Include the **Product No., Product Name, Category, End Inv, Cost Price**, and **Total Value**. Sort by ending inventory from smallest to largest. If needed, sort identical entries by product name. Include a title that identifies the report. Print the report; write "Assig 11.6, Print 3" at the top.
5. Prepare a report that lists all products with purchases that show an ending inventory above 20 and a total value over $4,500. Sort from the smallest to the largest purchases; use product name in alphabetical order for the second sort field. Include a title that identifies the report. Print the report. Write "Assig 11.6, Print 4" at the top.
6. Prepare a report that lists all spreadsheet and word-processing products. Sort by ending inventory from the largest to the smallest. As a secondary sort, use total value from largest to smallest. Include a title that identifies the report. Print a copy. At the top write "Assig 11.6, Print 5."
7. Save and close the workbook.

Case Problem 11

You are asked to prepare a database for your instructor that includes the students of the current term. You will list the students, their social security numbers, the cities where they live, the courses in which they are enrolled, and their final grades for the current term.

Your instructor has various uses for this list and would like several reports prepared.

The student information is as follows:

Name	Soc. Sec. No.	City	Course	Grade
Jackie Burl	444-77-0000	San Francisco	Excel	B
Peggy Pohl	555-88-1111	Palo Alto	Excel	A
Kitty Landess	666-99-2222	Oakland	Word	A
Missy Tavangari	777-00-3333	Oakland	Word	C
Janice Anderson	888-11-4444	Palo Alto	Word	A
Richard Grave	999-22-5555	San Francisco	PageMaker	B
Elsie Canutt	000-33-6666	San Francisco	Excel	B
Hannah Trapp	111-44-7777	Palo Alto	PageMaker	A
Sue Anderson	222-55-8888	Palo Alto	PageMaker	A
Bruce Charles	333-66-9999	Palo Alto	Word	C
Roland Herandez	444-88-1111	Oakland	Excel	D
Lori Grave	555-99-2222	San Francisco	Excel	C

From this list, prepare the following reports. Be sure each report is properly identified. Your instructor's name should be included in each report. Save the workbook as **Case11**.

- Prepare a report that lists all of the students in alphabetical order.
- Prepare a report for each of the three classes offered. Arrange the report by grade earned.
- Prepare a report of all students who live in San Francisco and have earned a B.
- Prepare a report of all students who have received an A. List only the student's name and the course name.
- Prepare a report of all students living in Palo Alto and Oakland who have earned an A or B.

Chapter 12

Using Macros

Objectives

1. Recognize the need for a macro.
2. Record and run macros.
3. Save macros and create a macro identification system.

Introduction

Although Excel completes many tasks easily, there are times when additional shortcuts could be used. A macro combines a series of commands and keystrokes into one step. When this series of commands is needed, the macro is run by using only one keystroke.

Using Macros

What Is a Macro?

A *macro* is a series of commands, such as selections from menus and dialog boxes, keystrokes, and clicks on toolbar buttons, that are executed automatically with one keystroke. When a command requiring several steps is used over and over, a macro can be created to automate the steps and complete them quickly.

For example, in many of the worksheets that you have already completed in this text, the title has been formatted in bold, increased one or two font sizes, and merged and centered over all of the columns of the worksheet. Completing this formatting takes several steps. By creating a macro for these steps, a title may be formatted with just one click of the mouse.

Another timesaving macro can be created for the formatting choices in the Page Setup dialog box. By creating a macro, you can combine several steps—such as formatting the placement of a worksheet on the page, printing gridlines, and placing the preparer's name in the header or footer—into a single step. Macros add a great deal of power and flexibility to Excel.

Note that at the end of this chapter, you may delete the Ch12 directory from your Student Data Disk.

Planning a Macro

Excel creates a macro by recording every keystroke and mouse click made. All menu and dialog box commands, keystrokes, and other actions needed to complete a task are included in the macro. The steps to record a macro are similar to the steps used to record an audio tape. First determine the steps that will be automated, then turn on the recorder, complete the actions needed in the macro, and turn off the recorder when finished.

Most worksheets created in this text use a consistent formatting style for column labels. They may be bold, wrapped text, and centered both horizontally and vertically within their cells. A border may be placed under or around column labels. Because this formatting style is prepared over and over again, completing a macro to format column labels will save time.

Recording a Macro

In the Tools menu, the Macro command opens a submenu of specific macro commands. To start recording, select Macro and then *Record New Macro,* as shown in Figure 12.1. The *Record Macro dialog box* opens, shown in Figure 12.2.

Excel automatically assigns a name to each macro. The assigned names are numberical, beginning with Macro1, then Macro2, etc. The name of a macro may be changed to a descriptive name, such as ColLabel for a macro that will format column labels. Spaces or punctuation marks are not allowed in a macro name. A more detailed description of a macro can be entered in the Description box.

A macro may be saved in several places; the drop-down list by the Store macro in text box provides a list of choices (Figure 12.3).

A macro may be saved in the current workbook, a new workbook, or a *personal macro workbook.* Macros in the personal macro workbook are always available when Excel is open and reside on a specific computer. In a shared environment, it is

Figure 12.1   Recording a New Macro

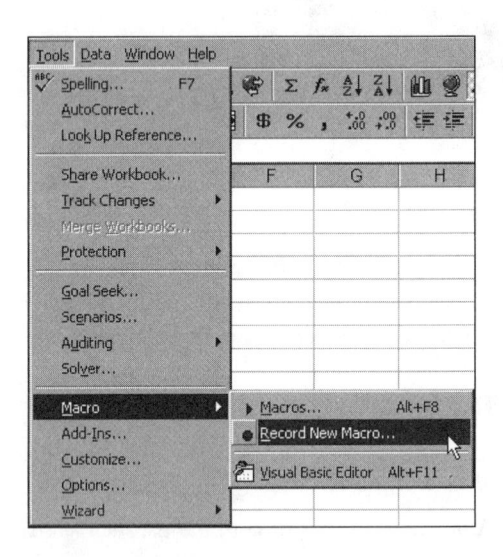

Figure 12.2   Record Macro Dialog Box

Figure 12.3   Store Macro in Drop-down List

practical to create and store your macros on your data disk so they will be available to you at all times.

When a macro is saved with a workbook, it is available only when that workbook is open. In this text, a workbook will be created to store macros created. When it is open, the macros will be available.

Click OK to start recording. The *Stop Recording toolbar* opens, which consists of the *Stop Recording button* and the Relative Reference button, shown in Figure 12.4.

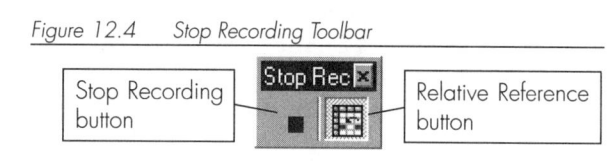

Figure 12.4   Stop Recording Toolbar

When a macro is being recorded, all menu commands, keystrokes, text and data entries, etc., that are entered are recorded as part of the macro.

To complete the column labels macro, use the keystrokes and commands that would be used for formatting the cells. For example, in the Format Cells dialog box, you would change the alignment, font style, and border. As the macro recorder is running, the status bar states Recording, as shown in Figure 12.5.

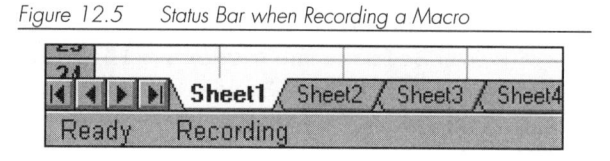

Figure 12.5   Status Bar when Recording a Macro

Stopping Recording

When the macro is complete, click on the Stop Recording button ■. The Stop Recording toolbar automatically closes. (A macro may also be stopped by selecting Macro from the Tools menu, and then Stop Recording.)

Once a macro is recorded it can be used in other worksheets of the workbook.

Warning: Don't forget to stop recording a macro. All keystrokes are recorded until the macro recorder is stopped. Many users forget to stop recording, resulting in large, unwanted macros!

Saving a Macro

Macros may be saved in the current workbook, in a new workbook, or in a personal macro workbook. When creating macros, use the drop-down list shown in Figure 12.6 to determine which workbook they will be stored in.

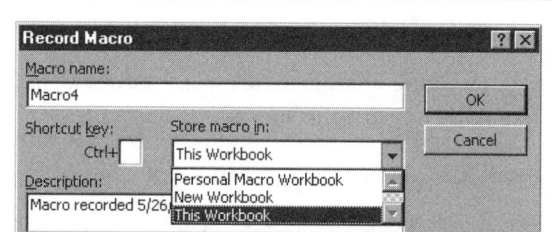

Figure 12.6   Saving a Macro

Macros are stored in a hidden module in the workbook. A *module* stores the Visual Basic code of the macro. *Visual Basic* is a programming language that is read by a computer. Macros are stored in Visual Basic. As a macro is created, the keystrokes and commands are translated into Visual Basic instructions, called code. Figure 12.7 shows part of a module containing the macro and its code in Visual Basic.

Figure 12.7   Viewing a Module Sheet for a Saved Macro

```
End With
With Selection.Font
    .Name = "Arial"
    .FontStyle = "Bold"
    .Size = 10
    .Strikethrough = False
    .Superscript = False
    .Subscript = False
    .OutlineFont = False
    .Shadow = False
    .Underline = xlUnderlineStyleNone
    .ColorIndex = xlAutomatic
End With
Selection.Borders(xlDiagonalDown).LineStyle = xlNone
Selection.Borders(xlDiagonalUp).LineStyle = xlNone
```

Exercise 12.1   Recording a Macro

Record a macro for column titles. They will be bold, set for wrapped text, and centered both horizontally and vertically within the cells and a border will be placed at the bottom.

Note: Before completing the exercises and assignments in this chapter, you will need to expand the Chapter 12 files on your Student Data Disk. In Windows Explorer, locate the Ch12 file and double-click on it. When all the files have been expanded they may be opened in Excel.

1   Open a new workbook.

2   In cell A1, enter your first name and complete the entry. Be sure cell A1 is still active.

3   From the **Tools** menu, select **Macro** and then **Record New Macro**. The **Record Macro** dialog box opens.

4   In the **Macro name** section, replace **Macro1** with **ColLabel**. Do not use a space.

5   Press [Tab] three times. In the **Description** section, key **Format Column Labels**. Click **OK** to close the dialog box. The Stop Recording toolbar opens.

6   From the **Format** menu, select **Cells**. The **Format Cells** dialog box opens.

7   Click on the **Alignment** tab. Select **Wrap text** and center both horizontally and vertically. Click on the **Font** tab. Select bold type. Click in the **Border** tab. Place a bold border at the bottom of the cell. Click **OK**.

8   Click on the Stop Recording button ▪. The Stop Recording toolbar disappears from the screen. Notice that your first name has been formatted.

Save the worksheet as Macro.

9 Select **Save As** from the **File** menu. Name the workbook **Macro**. Save it as a Microsoft Excel Workbook, not another format the Office Assistant may suggest. You will use this file to store all macros used in this class. (If you are using on data disk, save the macro workbook at the root level.)

10 Close the workbook.

Running a Macro

Excel uses the term *run a macro*, meaning to play back a recording. Highlight a cell or range of cells in which to apply a macro. Then select the Macro command from the Tools menu and then Macros in the submenu.

Figure 12.8   Macro Dialog Box

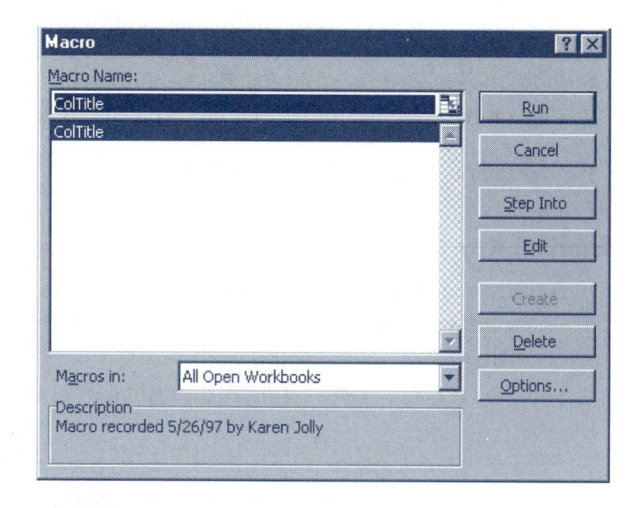

The *Macro dialog box* opens, listing all available macros (Figure 12.8).

Select the macro and click Run, or double-click on the macro name in the window to run the macro. The commands saved with the macro are applied to the selected cell or range of cells.

✎ *Helpful Hint*

Save all open workbooks prior to running a newly created macro.

Saving a Worksheet Containing a Macro

Macros contain code specific to Excel for Office 97. When a workbook that contains a macro is saved, it must be saved as a Microsoft Excel Workbook and not another format that the Office Assistant may suggest.

Exercise 12.2   Running a Macro

Run the macro recorded in Exercise 12.1.

1 Open a new workbook and the workbook saved as **Macro**. If a dialog box opens warning you about macros, select **Enable Macros**.

Run a macro.

2 In the new workbook, key **Monday** in cell A2. Use the AutoFill feature to extend the range through **Friday** (cell E2).

3   Select the range of cells containing the days of the week if it is not still highlighted.

4   From the **Tools** menu, select **Macro** and then **Macros** to open the **Macro** dialog box.

5   Click on the **ColLabel** macro and then click **Run**. (The name of the macro sheet appears before the macro name because it is saved in a different workbook.) The selected cells are formatted. Adjust column widths if needed.

Run the macro again.

6   In cell A4, key **January**. Use AutoFill to extend the months through **June**.

7   Select the range of cells containing the months of the year if it is not still highlighted.

8   From the **Tools** menu, select the **Macro** command and then **Macros**. In the **Macro** dialog box, double-click on the **ColLabel** macro. The selected cells are formatted.

9   Save the new workbook as **Exer 12-2**.

Shortcut Key

A macro may be accessed by a single keystroke. This keystroke is called a *shortcut key*. When a macro is created, a letter can be assigned to it. To run the macro, press the Ctrl key and the letter.

The Record Macro dialog box has a text box for entering a shortcut key. The shortcut is case sensitive; if a capital letter is used, the capital letter must be used when playing the macro back.

Figure 12.9   Entering a Shortcut Key in the Record Macro Dialog Box

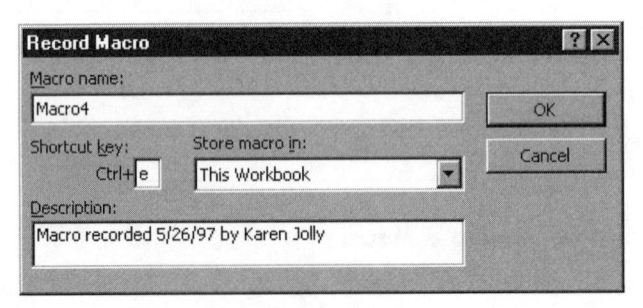

In Figure 12.9, the letter "e" is used as the shortcut key. The macro can be run by holding down the Ctrl key while pressing the e key on the keyboard.

Exercise 12.3   Using Shortcut Keys

You will assign a shortcut key to an existing macro. You will then run the macro using this shortcut key.

1   Open the **Macro** workbook. If a dialog box opens warning you about macros, select **Enable Macros**.

2   Select **Sheet2**.

Assign a shortcut key.

3   From the **Tools** menu, select **Macro** and then **Macros**. Click once on **ColLabel** to select it.

4 Click on the **Options** button.

5 In the **Shortcut key** box, key **d** next to **Ctrl+**. (Shortcut keys are case sensitive; be sure a lowercase "d" is entered.)

6 Click **OK** and then click on the **Close** box.

Run the macro.

7 In cell A1 key **July**. Use AutoFill to extend the months through **December**. Highlight the range if that has not already been done.

8 Hold down the Ctrl key and press **d** on the keyboard. The macro runs and completes the formatting.

9 Adjust column widths.

10 Save the Macro workbook.

Identifying Macros

When only one or two macros are used, it is easy to remember their names and shortcut keys. However, as more macros are created, it is important to remember what macros are named, what they do, and their assigned shortcut keys.

Since macros are stored as part of a workbook, it is helpful to use a sheet in the same book to identify the created macros, the actions they complete, and the assigned shortcut keys. Set up a *library sheet* that lists the needed information. An example of a sheet used to identify macros is shown in Figure 12.10.

Figure 12.10   Macro Library

Sharon's Macro Library

Macro Name	Commands	Shortcut Key
ColTitle	Wrap text, center, bold, underscore	d
Title	Enlarge, change font, bold, center across columns	t
PageSetup	Center horizontally and vertically, no gridlines, header and footer information	p
Totals	Currency, two decimals, bold, underline	l
PrintFrmlas	Show formulas, adjust col width, scale to fit page, print, return to show results	e

Save the Macro workbook on your Student Data Disk and open it each time you use Excel so your macros are always available.

It takes considerable practice at the computer to fully understand recording and running macros. The assignments in this chapter will include preparing several additional macros, saving them, and creating new worksheets using these macros.

Exercise 12.4   Preparing a Library Sheet

You will create a library sheet that describes the macros created and saved. You will include the previously recorded macro.

1 Delete sheets 1 and 2 of the **Macro** workbook.

2 Rename **Sheet3** in the workbook **Library**.

3 Create a worksheet like the one illustrated below. Replace **Sharon** with your name.

	A	B	C
1		Sharon's Macro Library	
2			
3	Macro Name	Commands	Shortcut Key

4 Format the headings as displayed above. For the title, use 16-point bold type and merge and center.

Run a macro.

5 Run the macro to format column labels.

6 Adjust the column width of column B to about **46.00**. Columns A and C will be about **9.00**.

7 Format column C for centered alignment.

8 In cell A4, key the name of the macro you created, **ColLabel**.

9 In the commands section (cell B4), enter the commands of **Wrap text, Merge and Center, bold, and underscore.**

10 In the Shortcut Key column (C4), key the assigned shortcut key, **d**.

11 Do a quick save. Print the Library sheet.

Introduction to Visual Basic

Macros are saved in a module written in a programming language called Visual Basic. Learning this programming language is usually a separate course and cannot be covered in this text; however, some basics will be introduced.

Macro recordings are called modules and use Visual Basic programming language. Figure 12.11 shows the macro that was written to format column titles.

Figure 12.11   Macro in Visual Basic

```
' ColHead Macro
' Format Column Titles
' '
Sub ColHead()
      With Selection.Font
        .Name = "Braggadocio"
        .Size = 10
        .Strikethrough = False
        .Superscript = False
        .Subscript = False
        .OutlineFont = False
        .Shadow = False
        .Underline = xlNone
        .ColorIndex = xlAutomatic
      End With
      With Selection.Font
        .Name = "Braggadocio"
        .Size = 14
        .Strikethrough = False
        .Superscript = False
        .Subscript = False
        .OutlineFont = False
        .Shadow = False
        .Underline = xlNone
        .ColorIndex = xlAutomatic
      End With
      Selection.Borders(xlLeft).LineStyle = xlNone
      Selection.Borders(xlRight).LineStyle = xlNone
      Selection.Borders(xlTop).LineStyle = xlNone
      With Selection.Borders(xlBottom)
        .Weight = xlThin
        .ColorIndex = xlAutomatic
      End With
      Selection.BorderAround LineStyle:=xlNone
End Sub
```

A macro is identified in the first line by its name. Its description is on the second line. Both the name and description lines begin with an apostrophe and are shown in green, indicating they are comments. A comment does not affect a Visual Basic statement.

The first and last lines of code are the *beginning point* and *ending point* for the macro. A *Sub statement* starts and names the macro. An *End Sub statement* ends the macro.

The body of a macro is shown in black and is the script between the Sub and End Sub statements. These Visual Basic commands translate the actions used when recording the macro commands.

The *With statement* and the *End With statement* specify the commands of the macro. In Figure 12.11, the first and second With statements contain information about the font. The last With statement contains information about the borders.

If errors are made in a macro, they can be changed in Visual Basic if the programming language has been learned. However, the fastest way for most users to make corrections is to record the macro again. Any red text in Visual Basic indicates an error that needs to be corrected.

To access the code, select Edit in the Macro dialog box. The module opens in Visual Basic, as shown in Figure 12.12.

Figure 12.12   Visual Basic Module

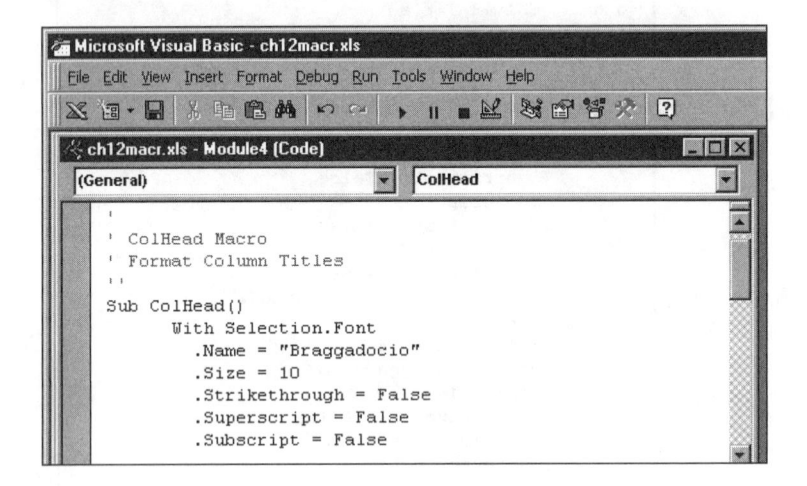

In addition to editing a macro on the screen, you may also print it to make editing easier. To print a macro, select the Print command from the File menu in the Visual Basic application.

Exercise 12.5   Printing a Macro

You will print a module.

1 Open the **Macro** workbook. If a dialog box opens warning about macros, select **Enable Macros**.

2 From the **Tools** menu, select **Macro** and then **Macros**.

3 In the **Macro** dialog box, select **Edit**. Visual Basic opens to the current module.

4 In the **Visual Basic** window, select **Print** in the **File** menu.

Summary

- A macro is a series of commands that uses only one keystroke to instruct Excel to perform a series of actions or calculations.
- To record a macro, select Tools, then Macro, and then Record New Macro.
- Each macro has an assigned name and shortcut key. A description of the macro may also be included.
- A macro may be saved in a personal macro workbook, making it available each time Excel is open. A personal macro workbook resides on an individual computer.
- The Stop Recording toolbar is open while a macro is being recorded.
- To play back a macro is called running a macro. Select Tools, then Macro, and then Macros to open the Macro dialog box and select the macro.
- The Macro dialog box lists all of the macros available on all of the open worksheets.

- A saved macro is available only when the workbook in which it is stored is open. If it is not saved in a personal macro workbook, it may be stored in the open workbook or in a new workbook.
- A shortcut key for a macro is Ctrl plus an assigned letter.
- To assign a shortcut key, select the letter in the Record Macro dialog box.
- Macro shortcut keys are case sensitive. A "K" is different from a "k."
- Store macros in a personal macro workbook saved to your own disk when working in a classroom or other shared environment. By saving it to your own disk, you will have the macro available to you at all times.
- Preparation of a library sheet is helpful for remembering macro names, descriptions, and assigned shortcut keys.
- Macros are written in Visual Basic, a programming language.
- The first and last lines of Visual Basic code are the beginning and end points.
- A Sub statement starts and names a macro; an End Sub statement ends a macro.
- With statements contain the instructions of a macro and are followed by End With statements.

Important Terminology

beginning point
End Sub statement
End With statement
ending point
library sheet
macro

Macro dialog box
module
personal macro workbook
Record Macro dialog box
Record New Macro
run a macro

shortcut key
Stop Recording button
Stop Recording toolbar
Sub statement
Visual Basic
With statement

Buttons to Know

Study Questions

True-False

Place a T in the space if the statement is true; place an F if the statement is false.

_____ 1. A macro is a command that can be executed with one keystroke.
_____ 2. The Macros command is located in the Options menu.
_____ 3. All available macros are listed in the Run Macro dialog box.
_____ 4. In the Record Macro dialog box, a macro can be named and assigned a keyboard shortcut letter.
_____ 5. To run a macro, select Run from the Macro menu.
_____ 6. To stop recording a macro, use the Stop Macro toolbar.
_____ 7. A macro is saved in a sheet of a workbook called the Macro sheet.
_____ 8. Only one macro is available at a time.
_____ 9. Shortcut keys are case sensitive.
_____ 10. Using a library sheet is a way of keeping track of created macros.
_____ 11. Visual Basic is a programming language. In order to create a macro, instructions must be keyed into the module using Visual Basic.

Fill-In

Place the word in the space that correctly completes the statement.
1. To record a macro, first choose the _____ command from the _____ menu. Then select Record Macro.
2. A macro is saved on a(n) _____ sheet.
3. A(n) _____ is assigned to a macro and used to run the macro.
4. After a macro is completed, click on the Stop Recording button in the _____ toolbar.
5. The shortcut key for running a macro is _____ + the assigned letter.
6. To run a macro, select the Macro command from the _____ menu, or use the keyboard command.

Assignments

Assignment 12.1

Prepare macros for formatting worksheets. You will create a library sheet of the macros created and stored on your Student Data Disk. It is important to use the names suggested so you can use the macro throughout the rest of the text. If you name it something else, you may not remember the name when it is next needed. Remember to save macros from this chapter in the root directory of the Student Data Disk if you are deleting subdirectories at the end of each chapter.
1. Open the **Macro** workbook from the Student Data Disk. If a dialog box opens warning about macros, select **Enable Macros**.
2. Create a macro that will format the title of a worksheet.
   - Create a new sheet in the **Macro** workbook. You will use a new sheet to create additional macros. Click in cell A3.
   - From the **Tools** menu, select **Macro** and then choose **Record New Macro**.
   - In the **Macro name** section, replace **Macro1** with **Title**.
   - In the **Shortcut key** text box, key **t** (for title). Select to store the macro in **This Workbook**.
   - Describe the macro as **formatting applied to the title of a worksheet**. Click **OK**.
   - Click on the Bold and Merge and Center buttons. Select cell A1. In the Formatting toolbar, select the **Brittanic Bold** font or the **Tahoma** font. If neither is available, select a font of your choice.
   - In the font size area of the Formatting toolbar, select **18** point. If a bold font was not selected, click on the Bold button.
   - Click on the Stop Recording button in the Stop Recording toolbar.
3. Enter the macro in the library sheet. Click on the **Library** tab of the workbook. On the next available row, enter the information for this macro. Its name is **Title**; its commands include en**large and change font**, **bold**, and **merge and center**. Its shortcut key is **t**.
4. Create a macro for lines 2 and 3 of the title.
   - Click in a sheet of the Macro workbook that is not the Library sheet. Click in cell A2. Create a macro named **Title2**. Use the shortcut key of **r**. Describe it as **formatting row 2 of a title**.
   - In the Formatting toolbar, select the same font and font style used for the **Title** macro. In the Font Size box, select **14** point. Also format for merge and center.

- Click on the Stop Recording button in the Stop Recording toolbar.
5. Enter the macro in the library sheet. Click on the **Library** tab of the workbook On the next available row, enter the information for this macro. Its name is **Title2**; its commands include **enlarge and change font, bold**, and **merge and center**. Include the information that it is **designed for rows 2 and 3 of a title**. Its shortcut key is **r**.
6. Create a macro for Page Setup information and enter the information in the Library sheet.
    - Be sure you are in a sheet of the Macro workbook that is not the Library sheet. Click in an empty cell.
    - From the **Tools** menu, select **Macro** and then choose **Record New Macro**.
    - Name the macro **PageSetup**.
    - Assign it a shortcut letter **p** (for Page Setup). Be sure to save it in **This Workbook**.
    - Describe it as **setting margins and altering header and footer**.
    - Click **OK**.
    - From the **File** menu, select **Page Setup**. Click in the **Margins** tab. Center the page horizontally and vertically.
    - Click in the **Header/Footer** tab. Create a header and footer, and include your name, the file name, the sheet name, and the page number.
    - Click **OK**. Click on the Stop Recording button of the Stop Recording toolbar.
    - Click on the **Library** tab and enter the information that describes this macro in the next available row.
7. Record a new macro and enter it in the Library sheet. This macro will be used to format totals in a worksheet.
    - Name the macro **Totals** and assign it the shortcut letter **l**.
    - Format a cell for bold and Currency style with two decimals. Place a single line above the row and a double line under it. From the **Format** menu, select **Column** and then choose **AutoFit Selection**.
8. Look at the Visual Basic code.
    - Open to the **Macro** dialog box. Select the **Totals** macro, then click on the **Edit** button.
    - The macro should look like the following sample. If your macro is not like this, complete the macro again. (You will get error messages about this macro, but just click **OK**.)

```
Sub Totals()
'
' Totals Macro
' Format Totals
' Keyboard Shortcut: Ctrl+l
'
    Selection.Font.Bold = True
    Selection.Style = "Currency"
    Selection.Borders(xlDiagonalDown).LineStyle = xlNone
    Selection.Borders(xlDiagonalUp).LineStyle = xlNone
    Selection.Borders(xlEdgeLeft).LineStyle = xlNone
    With Selection.Borders(xlEdgeTop)
        .LineStyle = xlContinuous
        .Weight = xlThin
        .ColorIndex = xlAutomatic
    End With
    With Selection.Borders(xlEdgeBottom)
        .LineStyle = xlDouble
        .Weight = xlThick
        .ColorIndex = xlAutomatic
    End With
    Selection.Borders(xlEdgeRight).LineStyle = xlNone
    Selection.Columns.AutoFit
End Sub
```

9. Close Visual Basic.
10. Do a quick save before running the macros.
11. Complete a worksheet using the recorded macros.
    - Open the workbook saved as **Ch12 As1** and save it as **Assig 12-1**. Rename **Sheet1** to **As 12-1**.
    - Center the title (name of firm) over all columns of the worksheet. From **Tools** select **Macro** and then **Macros**. In the **Macro** dialog box, be sure to select **All Open Workbooks** in the **Macros** section. Select the **Title** macro, then click **Run**. The title on the worksheet has been formatted.
    - Highlight row 2 of the worksheet. From **Tools** select **Macro** and then **Macros**. In the **Macro** dialog box, select the **Title2** macro. Then click **Run**. Row 2 on the worksheet has been formatted.
    - Highlight row 3 and use the shortcut of **Ctrl**+r.
    - Highlight the column titles in row 5. Either use the shortcut or from **Tools** select **Macro** then **Macros**. In the **Macro** dialog box, double-click on the **ColLabel** macro.
    - Run the Totals macro for the row and the column containing totals.
    - Run the **PageSetup** macro.
    - Format the numbers in the worksheet correctly for currency. Do not include decimals in the numbers.
12. Open Print Preview. Is the worksheet centered? Are the headers and footers accurate?
13. Print the sheet.
14. Check the format and appearance of the worksheet. If it is not OK, make changes and reprint the worksheet.
15. Print the Visual Basic code for all macros. In the **Print** dialog box, you may need to select **Current Project**.
16. Save the workbook.

Assignment 12.2

You will create an additional macro. You will then prepare a worksheet and run macros to format the worksheet.

1. Open the **Ch12 As2** and **Macro** workbooks. Save the **Ch12 As2** workbook as **Assig 12-2**. If a dialog box opens warning about macros, select **Enable Macros**.
2. Rename **Sheet1** to **As 12-2**.
3. In the **Macro** workbook, create a macro to print formulas. Name the macro **PrintFormula** and provide an appropriate description and shortcut key. This macro will show formulas, adjust the column widths, print in landscape style, print the worksheet with the formulas displayed, and return to the Normal view of the worksheet.
4. Complete the formulas in the worksheet.
    - In cell C7, enter the formula for a 10 percent increase of the current price (column B).
    - In cell D7, enter the formula for a 15 percent increase of the current price (column B).
    - In cell E7, enter the formula for a 20 percent increase of the current price (column B).
    - Copy the formulas in row 7 to rows 8–15 to complete the worksheet.
    - In cell A17, key **Total**.
    - Complete the formulas needed in row 17 (totals of all columns).

5. Format the worksheet. Use the macros prepared to help in formatting (Title, Title2, ColTitle, PageSetup, Totals).
6. Be sure numbers are formatted correctly for currency.
7. Determine whether to print the worksheet in portrait or landscape style.
8. Print two copies, one showing the formulas. Use the **PrintFormula** macro to print the formulas; use landscape style for the formula sheet. Save the workbook.

Checkpoint:
Model TV2003	10% Increase	$192.50
	15% Increase	$201.25
	20% Increase	$210.00

Assignment 12.3

This worksheet shows the results of a proposed increase in pay. You will determine the proposed hourly and weekly pay. Then prepare a summary of the changes that would be made.

1. Open a new workbook and the **Macro** workbook. If a dialog box opens warning about macros, select **Enable Macros**.
2. Enter the following information into a sheet of the new worksbook:

Payroll Analysis Report				
December, 1998				
Employee Name	Current Hourly Pay Rate	Current Weekly Pay	Proposed Hourly Pay Rate	Proposed Weekly Pay
Tom Jorgenson	8.5			
Art Mason	7.75			
Norman Overby	6.35			
Mary Quinn	9			
Paula Schatz	10.5			
Tom Vincent	9.25			
Proposed % Increase	4.50%			
Hours per week	40			
Total Proposed Pay				
Total Curent Pay				
Amount of Increase				

3. Save the workbook as **Assig 12-3**.
4. Complete the worksheet.
   - In column C, enter the formula for the current weekly pay for each employee.
   - In column D, enter the formula for the proposed hourly pay rate for each employee.
   - In column E, enter the formula for the proposed weekly pay.
   - In cell B20, enter the formula for the total proposed pay. It is the sum of the Proposed Weekly Pay column.
   - In cell B21, enter the formula for the total current pay. It is the sum of the Current Weekly Pay column.
   - In cell B22, enter the formula for the amount of the increase. It is the total proposed pay less the current pay.
5. Use macros to format the worksheet.
6. Print the worksheet.
7. Print an additional copy of the worksheet showing the formulas in landscape style. Use a macro to do this.
8. Change the pay increase to five and a half percent and print a copy of the worksheet with the results displayed.

Checkpoint:

Tom Jorgenson	Current Weekly Pay	$340.00
	Proposed Weekly Pay	$355.30
Summary	Total Proposed Pay	$2,146.43

Now that you have completed the exercises and assignments for this chapter, delete the Ch12 directory from your Student Data Disk. Before deleting the Ch12 subdirectory, however, make sure you have saved Chapter 12 macros to the root directory.

Chapter 13

Creating Formulas from Labels

Objectives

1. Use Natural-language formulas.
2. Create and define names for cells and cell ranges.
3. Apply names when creating a worksheet.
4. List names and cell references used in a worksheet.

Introduction

Using cell references is the most common way to enter formulas. Excel also uses column and row labels in formulas. Specific cells and ranges of cells can also be identified by a name. The assigned name, rather than the cell references, is then used in the formula. Using names in a formula actually describes what the formula is doing, making it easier to proofread the worksheet. The names may be labels or other identifying text.

Note that at the end of this chapter, you may delete the Ch13 directory from your Student Data Disk.

Using Natural-Language Formulas

Formulas that are created using the labels of a worksheet are called *Natural-language formulas*. Using the worksheet shown in Figure 13.1, the formula =Salem Hardware will place the value of the intersecting cell, 105, in the cell containing the formula.

Figure 13.1   Using Natural-Language Formulas

	A	B	C	D	E
1		Hardware	Software	Books	Supplies
2	Salem	105	421	124	521
3	Medford	268	235	235	214
4	Springfield	587	541	104	114

The formula =SUM(Software) enters the total of the software column.

To complete the worksheet in Figure 13.1, enter the totals needed in column F and row 5. To enter the total for row 2, enter =SUM(Salem). To total column B, enter =SUM(Hardware). The completed worksheet displaying the formulas is shown in Figure 13.2.

419

Figure 13.2   Displaying Natural-Language Formulas

	A	B	C	D	E	F
1		Hardware	Software	Books	Supplies	Total
2	Salem	105	421	124	521	=SUM(Salem)
3	Medford	268	235	235	214	=SUM(Medford)
4	Springfield	587	541	104	114	=SUM(Springfield)
5	Total	=SUM(Hardware)	=SUM(Software)	=SUM(Books)	=SUM(Supplies)	=SUM(Total)

Cell F5 is used for the total. Since both A5 and F1 contain the same label, Total, Excel cannot determine whether to enter the total of the row or the column and asks you to determine which label to use. The Identify Label dialog box, shown in Figure 13.3, opens so you can identify the label.

There are several restrictions for using labels in formulas. The label must contain a letter as the first character. Spaces are not allowed, so an underline is placed between words, such as in the label tax_rate.

Figure 13.3   Identify Label Dialog Box

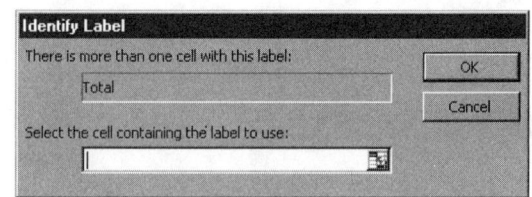

When using Natural-language formulas, it is important to be sure that there are no identical labels in the open workbooks or worksheets. If there were, the formula would calculate the result using all rows and columns with the same label from all the open documents. Therefore, when using Natural-language formulas, it is recommended that only the current workbook is open and that the workbook contains data on only one worksheet.

A worksheet using Natural-language formulas must be saved as an Office 97 workbook; earlier versions of Excel do not recognize Natural-language formulas.

Exercise 13.1   Using Natural-Language Formulas

Sunrise Greens prepares a weekly income report. The worksheet has been started; you will complete it using Natural-language formulas.

Note: Before completing the exercises and assignments in this chapter, you will need to expand the Chapter 13 files on your Student Data Disk. In Windows Explorer, locate the zipped Ch13 file and double-click on it. When all the files have been expanded, you will be able to open them in Excel.

1   Open the workbook saved as **Ch13 Ex1** and save it as **Exer 13-1**.

2   In cell E6, enter the Natural-language formula to add the Sunday income. The formula is **=SUM(Sunday)**.

3   Complete the formulas for the daily totals in column E. (Use a copy command.)

4   In cell B13, enter the Natural-language formula to add the green fees. The formula is **=SUM(Green Fees)**.

5   Complete the formulas for the types of income in row 13.

6   Complete the grand total amount. In cell E13, enter the formula **=SUM(Total)**. The **Identify Label** dialog box opens; select a cell containing the Total label. Use either the row or column label.

7 In cell A15, enter **Highest Day**. In cell B15, enter the Natural-language formula to enter the highest amount of sales. Saturday's total is the highest. The Natural-language formula will be **=Total Saturday**.

8 Place your name in cell A17.

9 Save and print the worksheet.

Using Cell Names in Formulas

A cell or a range of cells may also be assigned a name. Then when a formula is prepared, the name of the cell range is used instead of the cell references. Using names for a single cell, a range of cells, a value, or a formula provides an easy-to-remember identifier when creating worksheets. It also eliminates the need to enter complex formulas using cell references, making formulas easier to proofread.

To illustrate this, the selling price of an item will be determined by adding the cost to the sales tax, which is a percentage of the cost. The cell containing the cost of the item is named Cost; the cell containing the sales tax rate is named Tax_Rate. The formula for the tax amount therefore reads =Cost*Tax_Rate. The meaning is clearer, and the formula is easier to proofread written this way than with the cell references =A4*B6.

Figure 13.4 shows a worksheet created using named cells. The cost, $100, is entered in cell B1 and the cell is named Cost. The tax rate, 5%, is entered in cell B2 and the cell is named Tax_Rate. The amount of the tax is entered in cell B3 and the cell is named Tax Amount. The formula in cell B3 uses the cell names rather than the cell references and is =Cost*Tax_Rate. The result, $5, is entered in cell B3.

The total price is then found by adding the cost to the amount of tax. The formula in cell B4 that determines the total price is =Cost+Tax_Amount. The formula is shown in Figure 13.5.

Figure 13.4   Using Named Cells in a Formula

	A	B	C	D
1	Cost	$100		
2	Tax Rate	5%		
3	Tax Amount	$ 5		
4	Total Price	$ 105		

Tax_Amount =Cost*Tax_Rate

When using cell names, the assigned name of the cell, instead of the cell reference, appears in the Name box. The column and row labels that describe the data can be used as names in any formula, or another descriptive name may be used to represent a cell or range of cells.

Figure 13.5   Formula Using Cell Names

	A	B	C	D
1	Cost	$100		
2	Tax Rate	5%		
3	Tax Amount	$ 5		
4	Total Price	$ 105		

Total_Price =Cost+Tax_Amount

There are advantages to using the naming method to identify cells. By using a name rather than a cell reference, the worksheet is easier to proofread. A complex formula is also easier to create and understand with words rather than cell references. Cost+Sales_Tax is easier to understand than =B1+C2. And when the structure of a worksheet is changed, changing a reference in one place will automatically change all formulas that use the same name.

Defining Names

The process of naming a cell is called *defining a name*. Defining a name for a cell replaces the cell reference with text that identifies the cell. There are two methods used to define names.

To define a name, first select a cell or range of cells. These will be cells that contain data, not labels. Then select the ***Name command*** from the Insert menu. A submenu, shown in Figure 13.6, opens beside the Name command; select Define from the submenu.

Selecting the Define command opens the ***Define Name dialog box***, shown in Figure 13.7.

Figure 13.6 Defining a Name in the Insert Menu

All previously defined names of a worksheet are listed in the Define Name dialog box. If cells are highlighted, they appear in the Refers to text box. If they are not selected, use the Collapse Dialog button in the Refers to section to provide access to the worksheet cells so they can be selected. Then click on the Expand Dialog button to return to the Define Name dialog box.

Click on the Add button to add the cell references of the selected cell or range in the Refers to section.

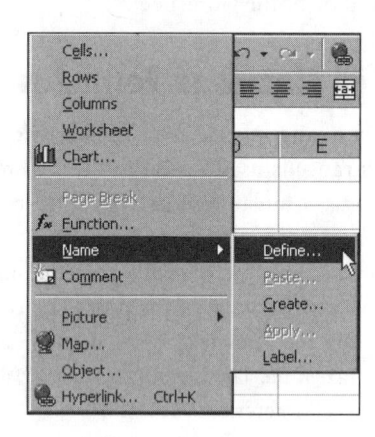

Figure 13.7 Define Name Dialog Box

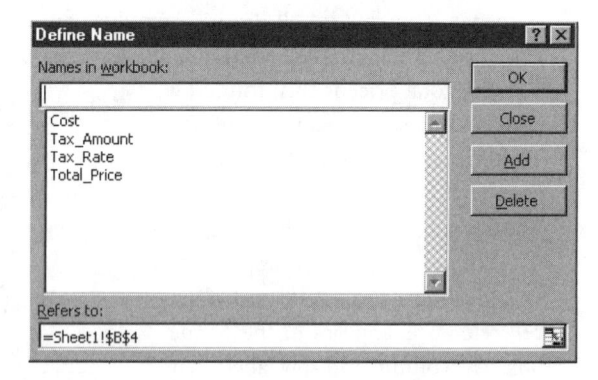

In naming a cell or range of cells, spaces are not allowed; therefore an underscore or a period is used in place of the space between the words. The first character of a named cell must be a letter or underscore.

Excel will suggest a name for the cell, usually the label of the column or row adjacent to the highlighted cell. If Excel's choices are not acceptable, enter your new choice in the dialog box or formula bar.

Power Users

The Define Names dialog box can also be opened by using the shortcut **Ctrl**+**F3**.

Another way to define the name of a cell is in the Name box on the left side of the formula bar. The arrow between the Name box and the entry area is used to access and create names. Click on the arrow to see the names previously used in the worksheet, as shown in Figure 13.8.

Names may also be entered in the Name box by keying them in. Caution must be exercised when naming cells in the Name box. If a name has already been used and is keyed as the new name, the original name is replaced by the new name with no warning.

Figure 13.8   Accessing List of Defined Names

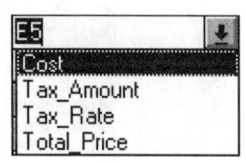

In multiple-sheet workbooks, names defined in one sheet also apply to the other workbook sheets if the labels match. To avoid a formula that contains identical labels from several sheets, include the sheet name as well as the cell name in the formula. Such a reference is called a *3-D reference*. A 3-D reference uses the name of the sheet first, followed by an exclamation mark (!), then the cell location. Examples of 3-D references are Sheet1!$A$3 or Montana!$B$5. 3-D references can also contain names of defined cells, such as Sheet1!Montana_Sales.

Exercise 13.2   Defining Names

Ryan's Craft Center prepares a report of its daily receipts. The worksheet has been started; you will name cells and cell ranges.

1   Open the workbook saved as **Ch13 Exer** and save it as **Exer 13**.

2   Select the sheet named **Exer 13-2**.

Name column B Amount.

3   Select column B.

4   From the **Insert** menu, select **Name**, then choose **Define**. The **Define Name** dialog box opens. In the text box for **Names in workbook** enter **Amount**. Click **OK**.

5   Click in cell C5. Access the **Define Name** dialog box. The suggested name is **Cash_Disc_Rate**. Click **OK**.

6   Highlight the range C9:C15.

7   The Name box currently reads **C9**. Click in the box to highlight the cell reference. Key **Disc_Val**, which is the name of the range. Press **Enter**.

8   Save the worksheet. Keep it open if you are continuing with Exercise 13.3.

Pasting Names in a Formula

Keying a named cell when entering a formula takes more time and provides more opportunities for errors to occur. To eliminate this possibility, Excel pastes previously defined names in the worksheet. First enter the equal (=) sign in a cell. Then from the Insert menu, select Name, then choose Paste. The *Paste Name* dialog box opens listing all defined names, as shown in Figure 13.9.

Figure 13.9   Paste Name Dialog Box

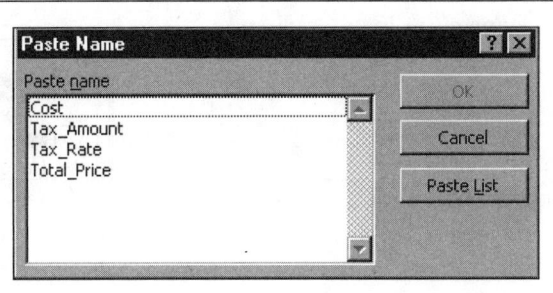

[Paste Name dialog box showing: Paste name list with Cost, Tax_Amount, Tax_Rate, Total_Price; buttons OK, Cancel, Paste List]

Select the name of the cell or range of cells listed and then click OK (or double-click on the name). A name is pasted as a relative reference if it defines a range; a name is pasted as an absolute reference if it defines a single cell.

Power Users

To quickly display the Paste Name dialog box, press **F3**.

Exercise 13.3   Pasting Names in a Formula

The Ryan's Craft Center worksheet has defined cell names. You will complete the worksheet by using those named cells in creating formulas.

1 Open the **Exer 13** workbook to sheet **Ex 13-2** if it is not already open.

Enter formulas using the Paste Name dialog box.

2 Click in cell C9. Enter an **=** (equal sign) to begin the formula. From the **Insert** menu, select **Name**, then choose **Paste**.

3 In the **Paste Name** dialog box, click on **Amount** in the list box. Click **OK**. The **Paste Name** dialog box closes and the name **Amount** is entered in the formula bar and the active cell.

4 With cell C9 active, enter a * (multiplication sign). Press **F3** to access the **Paste Name** dialog box. Select **Cash_Disc_Rate**, then **OK**. This places the name in the formula and completes the formula. Press **Enter**. The amount of the discount, **7.52**, is entered in cell C9.

5 Copy the formula to the rest of the **Cash Discount** column.

6 Click in cell D9. Use the **Paste Name** dialog box to enter the formula **=Amount-Disc_Val**. The amount, **368.40**, is entered in cell D9.

7 Copy the formula to the rest of the Amount Received section.

8 Check to be sure money amounts are correctly formatted.

Complete the worksheet.

9 Select the sheets **Ex 13-2**, **Ex 13-4**, and **Ex 13-6**. Create a header or footer and include your name, the file name, the sheet name, and the page number. Center the worksheet vertically and horizontally on the page.

10 Select the **Ex 13-2** tab.

11 Save and print the worksheet.

12 Print a second copy showing the formulas. (Adjust the column widths so it prints on one page.)

Automatic Features for Naming Cells

Creating Names

Excel is intuitive enough to suggest names from the row or column labels of a selected range. Excel selects the name when the *create names* feature is used.

To create names, first select a range. From the Insert menu, select Name, then choose Create. The *Create Names dialog box* opens, shown in Figure 13.10.

Figure 13.10   Create Names Dialog Box

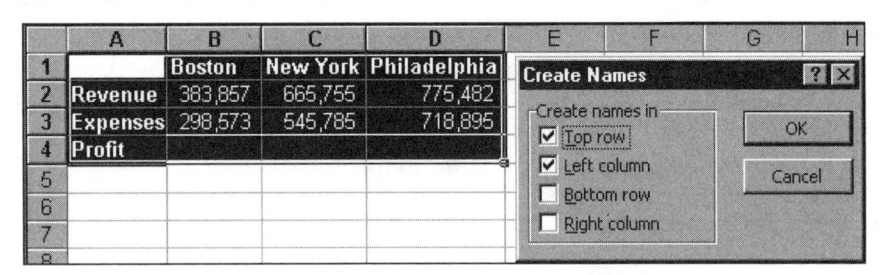

Excel uses the row and column labels for the names. The Create Names dialog box in Figure 13.10 instructs Excel to use the labels in the top row and the left column as the names.

🄿 Power Users

The keyboard command to open the Create Names dialog box is **Ctrl**+**Shift**+**F3**.

When both columns and rows have names applied, it can be confusing to determine which ranges the names correspond with. Figure 13.11 shows the ranges and their assigned names.

Figure 13.11   Range Names and Their Location

Name of Range	Placement of Range
Revenue	B2:D2
Expenses	B3:D3
Profit	B4:D4
Boston	B2:B4
New York	C2:C4
Philadelphia	D2:D4

To place the profit for Boston in cell B6, enter the formula =Boston Profit. Cell B4 is named both Boston and Profit, so the name in the formula will enter the profit from cell B4 in cell B6 (Figure 13.12).

Figure 13.12   Entering a Formula by Creating Names

	A	B	C	D
1		Boston	New York	Philadelphia
2	Revenue	383,857	665,755	775,482
3	Expenses	298,573	545,785	718,895
4	Profit	85,284	119,970	56,587
5				
6		85284		

Cell B6: =Boston Profit

Exercise 13.4   Creating Names

Best View Movie Theater has completed its weekly profits report. Cell references have been used in this worksheet, but the management of the theater would like to use named cells in the worksheet.

You will create range names for the worksheet.

1   Open the **Exer 13** workbook from the Student Data Disk and select worksheet **Ex 13-4**.

2   Click on the worksheet cells to view the formulas used.

3   Highlight the range A5:I15 (it includes column and row labels). From the **Insert** menu, select **Name**, then choose **Create**.

4   In the **Create Names** dialog box, select the boxes by **Top row** and **Left column** if they are not already selected. Then click **OK**.

5   Click in cells B15 and G15. Notice that the formulas still use cell references.

6   Click on the arrow by the Name box to view the list of names used when they were created.

7   Save the worksheet.

Applying Names

A completed worksheet that contains formulas may be converted into one using named cells. This is useful when an Excel user must share the formulas at a later date with someone not familiar with worksheets. The *apply names* feature will convert formulas using cell references to those using named cells and ranges.

In the worksheet in Figure 13.13, the formulas to determine the profit were originally entered using cell references. To use apply names, cells and ranges must have names defined. When the defined names are applied to the worksheet, formulas containing cell references are changed to contain the defined names. Figure 13.13 compares the formulas as originally written with the formulas after the created names were applied.

Figure 13.13   Comparing Formulas with Named Cells

Formulas

	A	B	C	D
1		Boston	ew York	adelphia
2	Revenue	383857	665755	775482
3	Expenses	298573	545785	718895
4	Profit	=B2-B3	=C2-C3	=D2-D3

Names

	A	B	C	D
1		Boston	New York	Philadelphia
2	Revenue	383857	665755	775482
3	Expenses	298573	545785	718895
4	Profit	=Revenue-Expenses	=Revenue-Expenses	=Revenue-Expenses

To apply names to a worksheet, select the entire worksheet range. From the Insert menu, select Name, then choose Apply. The Apply Names dialog box opens (Figure 13.14). Select the entire list (or just those names that will be applied), and click OK.

Figure 13.14   Apply Names Dialog Box

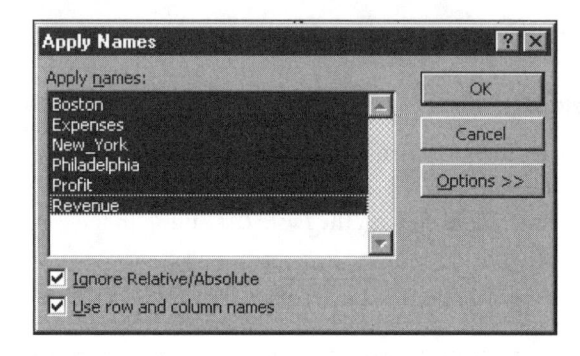

Exercise 13.5   Applying Names in a Worksheet

Names have been created for the worksheet for the Best View Movie Theater. You will apply names in existing formulas to change cell references to defined names.

1. Open the **Exer 13** workbook to worksheet **Ex 13-4**.

2. Highlight the worksheet.

3. From the **Insert** menu, select **Name**, then choose **Apply**. In the **Apply Names** dialog box, all names are selected (or select them all if they are not). Click **OK**.

4. Click in cells B9, B14, and B15 to read the formulas.

5. Click in cells I9, I14, and I15 to read the formulas.

6   In cell A19, key **Weekend Profits**.

7   In cell A20, key **Weekday Profits**.

In cell B19, enter the formula to determine the net profits for the weekend days of Saturday and Sunday.

8   Click in cell B19. Key an **=** (equal sign). Key **Saturday Net_Profit**. Be sure the spaces and underscores are correctly entered.

9   Press ➕ (plus). Then key **Sunday Net_Profit**.

10 Click on the **Enter** button to complete the entry. The net profits for Saturday and Sunday are added together.

11 In cell B20, enter the formula to add the net profits for Monday, Tuesday, Wednesday, Thursday, and Friday.

12 Format money amounts for Currency style with zero decimals.

13 Save and print the worksheet in landscape style.

14 Change the sheet to display the formulas. Adjust column widths and select to scale to two pages wide and one page tall. Print a copy.

15 Close the worksheet without saving changes.

Pasting a List of Names

In order to view the entire list of names used and their corresponding cell references, the entire list can be pasted into the worksheet. Access the Paste Name dialog box from the Insert menu; select Name, then choose Paste. Then click on the *Paste List* button in the Paste Name dialog box, shown in Figure 13.15.

Figure 13.15   Pasting a List of Names

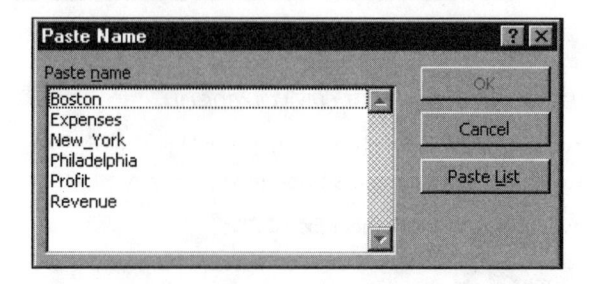

When the list is pasted into the active cell of the worksheet, cell references and related names are entered into the worksheet, beginning with the active cell (Figure 13.16). Be sure the active cell is not located in the main body of the worksheet, as the list will replace existing cell contents. A 3-D reference is used to identify the source of the cells.

Figure 13.16   The List of Names Pasted to the Worksheet

Boston	=Sheet1!$B$2:$B$4
Expenses	=Sheet1!$B$3:$D$3
New_York	=Sheet1!$C$2:$C$4
Philadelph	=Sheet1!$D$2:$D$4
Profit	=Sheet1!$B$4:$D$4
Revenue	=Sheet1!$B$2:$D$2

Pasting the entire list of named cells and their references is another useful tool when proofreading a worksheet and checking for accuracy. It is important to include a list of names used in any workbook that uses named ranges.

Exercise 13.6   Pasting a List of Cell Names

You will paste a list of all the names used in the exercises in this chapter.

1   Open the **Exer 13** workbook to sheet **Ex 13-6**. Click in cell A1 if it is not selected.

2   From the **Insert** menu, select **Name**, then choose **Paste**.

3   In the **Paste Name** dialog box, click in the **Paste List** button.

4   Adjust column widths.

5   Save and print the worksheet.

Summary

- Natural-language formulas use row and column labels in the formula. Simply key a formula that replaces the cell references with the label.
- A cell, range of cells, or formula may be assigned a name.
- When names are defined, those names may be used in formulas rather than using cell references.
- To define a name, select Insert, then Name, then Define, or double-click in the Name box of the formula bar.
- Names for cell references require either a period (.) or an underscore (_) in place of a space.
- Pasting names inserts names into formulas. Names may be pasted from the Insert menu or in the Name box on the formula bar.
- Names that are defined as a range are regarded as relative references. Names that are defined as individual cells are regarded as absolute references.
- Column or row labels are used as names of ranges when using the Create Names dialog box.
- A worksheet created with cell references can be converted to one containing named cells by using the apply names feature.
- To show the names of all cells and their cell references used in a workbook, select the Paste List button in the Paste Name dialog box.

Important Terminology

3-D reference
apply names
create names
Create Names dialog box

Define Name dialog box
defining a name
Name command

Natural-language formulas
Paste List
Paste Name

Study Questions

True-False

Place a T in the space if the statement is true; place an F if the statement is false.

_____ 1. A formula that uses column and row labels is called a normal worded formula.
_____ 2. The formula =SUM(Saturday) will add the range of cells in the column or row labeled Saturday.
_____ 3. A cell or range of cells may be given a name to simplify preparing formulas.
_____ 4. When a formula is prepared using named cells, their names must be keyed in when creating the formula.
_____ 5. The Define Name command is found on the Macro menu.
_____ 6. Names may be defined and accessed in the Name box of the formula bar.
_____ 7. Cells cannot be named after a worksheet is completed.
_____ 8. To name a cell or range of cells, use the Assign Name command.
_____ 9. When defining a name of a cell or range of cells, use a hyphen or period in place of a space.
_____ 10. The Apply Names dialog box is used to apply defined names to a worksheet.
_____ 11. Pasting names can be done only by accessing the Insert menu.
_____ 12. To select column and row labels as cell names, select Choose Names from the Insert Name submenu.
_____ 13. A formula that is created using cell references cannot be altered to one using named cells.
_____ 14. The Paste List button identifies every cell containing data or text in a worksheet.
_____ 15. A cell reference that includes the sheet name is called a Full Reference.

Fill-In

Place the word in the space that correctly completes the statement.

1. Formulas that are created using the labels of a worksheet are called _____ .
2. To name a range of cells, highlight the cells and then select the _____ command from the Insert menu. Then select Define.
3. To place a name of a cell range in a formula, select _____ Name from the Insert menu.
4. Use the _____ dialog box to paste names into a worksheet when entering a formula.
5. Names may be defined and pasted in the _____ box of the formula bar.

6. To enter the amount of sales of books in Auburn using a Natural-language formula, enter the intersecting cell. The formula would be written = _____ .
7. When using a completed worksheet to define names, first select Insert, then choose Name, then select _____ .
8. To apply created names, select Insert, then choose Name, then select _____ .
9. The Paste List button is found in the _____ Name dialog box.

Assignments

After completion of Chapter 13, you may delete the Ch13 folder from your Student Data Disk.

Assignment 13.1

American Computer Sales is a mail order business selling computers and software. Information about their business has been entered into a spreadsheet. You will use Natural-language formulas to create formulas and complete the spreadsheet.

1. Open workbook **Ch13 As1** and save it as **Assig 13-1**. If Chapter 12 was completed, open the **Macro** workbook. If a dialog box opens warning about macros, select **Enable Macros**.
2. Use Natural-language formulas to complete the worksheet in the **Assig 13-1** workbook. You will place totals in the Total column and the Total row.
3. Run the PageSetup macro. Use landscape style. If you didn't complete the assignments in Chapter 12, place your name and the file name in the header and the sheet name in the footer; center the worksheet both horizontally and vertically.
4. Save the worksheet. Print the worksheet in Normal view and in the view that shows formulas.

Assignment 13.2

You have invested in several stocks and want to determine the current value of each stock and the total value of your stock portfolio. The basic worksheet is completed. You will complete the worksheet by naming cells and using cell names in the formulas. Use any macros that have been created to assist in preparing and printing this worksheet.

Stocks are divided into eighths (3⅜) and quoted to three decimals (3.375); however, the prices in the worksheet are formatted for Currency style rounded to two decimal places ($3.38).

1. Open workbook **Ch13 As2** and save it as **Assig 13-2**. Rename **Sheet1** to **Portfolio** and **Sheet2** to **List**.
2. Using column labels as a guide, define the names for the columns in the Portfolio sheet. Do not define the individual names of the stocks.
3. Complete the formulas for the Portfolio sheet using the named cells.
   - In cell D8, enter the formula for the total cost. The total cost is the number of shares times the cost per share.
   - In cell F8, enter the current value. The current value is the number of shares times the current price per share.
   - In cell G8, enter the formula for the net change. The net change is the current value minus the total cost.
   - Copy the formulas in row 8 to the appropriate cells.
4. On the summary row, enter the totals for the worksheet. Total only columns D, F, and G. Format the totals for bold.

5. In the title, replace **Student's Name** with your name; replace **Today's** with today's date.
6. Format the columns containing money amounts for Currency style.
7. Adjust column widths and row heights as needed.
8. Format both the Portfolio and List worksheets identically—to fit on one page in either portrait or landscape style, centered both vertically and horizontally. Place the sheet name in the header the file name in the footer.
9. Save and print the Portfolio worksheet.
10. Place a list of cell references and corresponding names in the sheet named List; print the List sheet.
11. Print the formulas used in the Portfolio worksheet. Make the necessary adjustments so the worksheet will print on one page.
12. Save the workbook.

Assignment 13.3

Susan's Computer Sales is completing the October 18 payroll. The basic structure and format is in place; you will complete the worksheet, name cells, and use those names in formulas. Use macros that have been prepared to assist in formatting and printing the worksheet.

1. Open workbook **Ch13 As3** and save it as **Assig 13-3**.
2. Rename **Sheet1** to **Payroll** and **Sheet2** to **List**.
3. Payroll is a large worksheet; you may want to freeze panes while working with it.
4. Create names for the data area of the Payroll worksheet.
   - Highlight the range of the worksheet that includes the column labels (excluding those merged and centered over colulmns). Do not include the employee names.
   - Select to create names for the **Top row** only.
5. Define the appropriate individual cells as **Fed_Inc_Tax_Rate** and **FICA_Rate**.
6. Enter needed formulas for the worksheet using the cell names.
   - Enter IF statements in columns B and C to determine the regular and overtime hours worked. Overtime includes all hours worked after the first 40 in a one-week period.
   - Complete the Pay Earned column. Overtime is paid at 1.5 times the regular rate.
   - Complete the Deductions column. The federal income tax and FICA rates are given in the worksheet.
   - All employees pay $20 for medical insurance and have other deductions of $15.
7. Complete the totals for the worksheet. Do not total the section for hours worked. Leave a blank line between the main body of the worksheet and the totals. Format totals in bold with a surround border.
8. Format the worksheet for currency.
9. Format the Payroll and List sheets at the same time. Run the PageSetup macro, or place your name and the sheet name in the header with the date and the file name in the footer and center the worksheet vertically and horizontally. Format the worksheet in landscape style on one page.
10. Save and print the Payroll worksheet.
11. Check the format and appearance of the worksheet. Make adjustments as needed and reprint it.
12. Create a list of all assigned names used and their cell references on the List sheet. Then print the List sheet.
13. Save the workbook.
14. Print a copy of the Payroll worksheet with the formulas displayed on one page. Adjust the column widths as needed.
15. Close the workbook without saving changes.

Assignment 13.4

S. George's Clothing has completed its first quarter report for sales in the men's department. They would like to convert the worksheet so it uses named cells in the formulas rather than cell references. Use macros to assist in preparing and printing the worksheet.

1. Open workbook **Ch13 As4** and save it as **Assig 13-4**. Rename the **Sheet1** tab to **First Quarter** and the **Sheet2** tab to **List**.
2. Create names for the **First Quarter** worksheet using the top row and the left column as the names. Do not include the cells containing totals.
3. Apply the names to the worksheet.
    - Highlight the **Total** row and apply names.
    - Highlight the **Total** column and apply names.
4. Format both worksheets identically. Run the PageSetup macro, or format to place your name and the sheet name in the header and the file name and the date in the footer and center the worksheet horizontally and vertically.
5. Save and print the **First Quarter** worksheet.
6. Create a list of named cells with their cell references in the sheet named **List**; print the sheet.
7. Save the worksheet.
8. Print a copy of the **First Quarter** worksheet that shows the formulas used.

Assignment 13.5

Nevin and Ryan's Clothing Store has two outlets. They have entered the data for their quarterly report and would like you to complete the report. They also need summary information about the sales in each location. Nevin and Ryan would like you to name the cells so they can proofread the worksheet easily. Use macros to assist in preparing the worksheet.

1. Open workbook **Ch13 As5** and save it as **Assig 13-5**.
2. Rename **Sheet1** to **Third Quarter** and **Sheet2** to **List**.
3. Name cells and ranges.
    - Create names for the worksheet. Use the names in the top row and left column.
    - Define the cell containing the commission rate individually; it will be used as an absolute reference.
4. Complete the formulas needed in the worksheet. Be sure to use cell names.
    - Complete the formula for the total sales using cell names. It is the total amount of dress clothes plus the total amount of casual clothes.
    - Complete the formula for the commissions. It is the commission rate times the total sales. Use names in the formulas.
    - Copy formulas where needed in the worksheet.
    - Complete the totals in row 14.
5. Prepare the summary report.
    - In cell C17, enter the total sales of dress clothes sold in Ashland. The formula reads:
      =Janice_Johnson Dress_Clothes+Leora_Parton Dress_Clothes
    - In cell C18, enter the total sales of dress clothes sold in Medford using named references.

- In cell C19, enter the total sales of casual clothes sold in Ashland using named references.
- In cell C20, enter the total sales of casual clothes sold in Medford using named references.
6. Create additional cell names for the summary information in rows 17–20.
7. Complete the total summary information.
   - In cell C22, enter the formula to add the total sales in Ashland. Add the total sales of dress clothes in Ashland to the total sales of casual clothes in Ashland.
   - In cell C23, enter the formula to add the total sales in Medford. Add the total sales of dress clothes in Medford to the total sales of casual clothes in Medford.
   - Format the summary for currency with dollar signs in every cell.
8. Format both worksheets in an appropriate style, but use the same settings. Run the PageSetup macro, or include your name and the sheet name in the header and the file name and the date in the footer and center the worksheet both horizontally and vertically. Be sure the money and number amounts are correctly formatted.
9. Save and print the worksheet.
10. Create a list of named cells and their references in the sheet named List. Print the sheet.
11. Print a copy with the formulas displayed in landscape orientation.
12. Change the commission rate to 10%. Print a second copy of the Third Quarter worksheet in Normal view and portrait style.
13. Save and close the workbook.

Case Problem 13

The Pear Computer Store asks you to prepare a worksheet showing the sales of each salesperson and the amount of commission each has earned for the current year. The company sells several different products, and each product uses a different commission rate. You will need to allow room for the sales and commission amounts and for the totals of each.

You have been asked to name the cells when preparing this worksheet. Use macros to assist in preparing, formatting, and printing the worksheet. Create a list of all named cells and their references, and print the list. When you print the report, also print a copy of the worksheet with the formulas displayed. Save the workbook as **Case 13**.

The commission rate for each product is as follows:

Product	Rate
CPUs	13%
Monitors	8%
Keyboards	12.5%
Accessories	5.8%
Software	18%

The sales information is provided in the following list. Include the total commissions for each salesperson in the worksheet. For the date, key **For Year Ending December 31** followed by the current year.

Salesperson	CPU	Monitor	Keyboard	Accessories	Software
Betty Markham	40,593	10,292	345	129	783
Thao Mai Huynh	22,383	18,921	883	228	558
Thomas George	10,293	22,029	215	209	958
Jennie Mendoza	33,295	9,385	338	155	1,039
Mike Carson	50,298	10,299	985	198	978

Checkpoint:

    Total CPU Sales   156,862

    Commission for Betty Markham $6,292

Now that you have completed the exercises and assignments for this chapter, you may delete the Ch13 directory from your Student Data Disk.

Chapter 14

Linking and Embedding

Objectives
1. Link Excel worksheets in the same workbook and in different workbooks.
2. Copy information between applications.
3. Link and embed objects into other applications.
4. Use drag and drop to link objects between applications.

Introduction

Information contained in one worksheet is often used in other worksheets. This information can be entered into all worksheets separately or with the grouped sheets, or it can be copied or linked to another worksheet or file. When information is linked to different worksheets, changes made in one are automatically made in all, thereby saving time and ensuring accuracy.

Information can also be copied or linked between different applications. For instance, an Excel spreadsheet can be displayed in a word-processing document. If the spreadsheet is linked to the document, changes made to either document will automatically be changed in both documents.

Note that at the end of this chapter, you may delete the Ch14 directory from your Student Data Disk.

Linking Excel Data

Data entered in one worksheet can be copied or linked to another worksheet in the same workbook or to worksheets in different workbooks. When data is copied, the information is pasted into the new document, forming a *static link*; changes made in one document will not be made in the other. Linked data forms a *dynamic link*; when a change is made in the data of one document, the data is automatically changed in all linked documents.

Linking Worksheets

Because it is common for the same information to be used in different worksheets, linking provides a way of keeping all worksheets current. For example, sales reports prepared for separate territories may include a summary of the information. Numbers can be entered into each worksheet, or they can be linked. If the cells are linked, they become dynamic; a change made in one automatically changes all the linked cells. Documents that contain a link are called **linked documents**.

Figure 14.1 shows a linked workbook. Notice that the workbook includes a summary worksheet and individual worksheets for three territories: Portland, Eugene, and Corvallis.

The data in each of the individual worksheets is similar; Figure 14.2 shows the Portland data.

Note that the Portland totals are also shown in the summary worksheet. These totals can be copied from one worksheet to another, forming a static link. If they were a dynamic link, a change in the Portland worksheet would be updated in the Summary sheet.

To link data, you would use a copy-and-paste technique. First, access the original worksheet—in this case the Portland worksheet. Highlight the cell or range of cells for the data to be linked, then select a copy command. Move to the summary sheet and click in the cell where data will be entered. From the Edit menu, select Paste Special. The Paste Special dialog box opens, shown in Figure 14.3.

Click on the *Paste Link* button. The data is pasted in the Summary worksheet and is linked to the original. A 3-D reference appears in the linked cell, as shown in Figure 14.4.

The 3-D reference for cell B4 reads =Portland!$B$10, indicating the original worksheet and the cell reference in that worksheet.

When the linked data in the Portland sheet changes, it is automatically updated in the linked document. Figure 14.5 shows the same two worksheets when data is changed in

Figure 14.1   A Linked Summary Worksheet

	A	B	C	D
1	West Coast School Supplies			
2				
3		Pencils	Paper	Paint
4	Portland	135	160	95
5	Eugene	110	110	135
6	Corvallis	115	165	140
7	Total	360	435	370

Figure 14.2   A Linked Worksheet

	A	B	C	D
1		Portland		
2				
3				
4			Pencils	Paper	Paint
5	Mon	25	30	17
6	Tue	26	31	18
7	Wed	27	32	19
8	Thu	28	33	20
9	Fri	29	34	21
10	Total	135	160	95

Figure 14.3   Paste Special Dialog Box

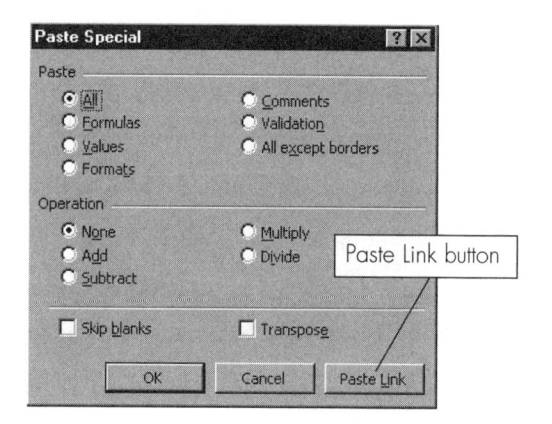

Figure 14.4   3-D Reference for a Linked Cell

B4		=Portland!$B$10

	A	B	C	D
3		Pencils	Paper	Paint
4	Portland	135	160	95

one. The Monday totals have been changed in the Portland worksheet; they are also updated in the Summary sheet because of the dynamic link.

Figure 14.5   Changing Linked Data

	A	B	C	D		A	B	C	D
1	West Coast School Supplies				1	Portland			
2					2				
3		Pencils	Paper	Paint	3		Pencils	Paper	Paint
4	Portland	150	166	100	4				
5	Eugene	110	110	135	5	Mon	40	36	22
6	Corvallis	115	165	140	6	Tue	26	31	18
7	Total	375	441	375	7	Wed	27	32	19
8					8	Thu	28	33	20
9					9	Fri	29	34	21
10					10	Total	150	166	100

Exercise 14.1   Linking Excel Worksheets

West Coast School Supplies does daily sales reports for each branch store. These reports are combined in a weekly report. You will create the weekly summary report from the completed daily reports.

Note: Before completing the exercises and assignments in this chapter, you will need to expand the Chapter 14 files on your Student Data Disk. In Windows Explorer, locate the zipped Ch14 file and double-click on it. When all the files have been expanded, you will be able to open them in Excel.

1   Open workbook **Ch14 Ex1** and save it as **Exer 14-1**.

2   Click on the **Portland** tab.

3   Click in the cell containing the total of widgets. Select a copy command.

4   Click on the **Summary** tab, then click in cell B5, the cell for widgets in Portland.

5   From the **Edit** menu, select **Paste Special**. In the **Paste Special** dialog box, click on the **Paste Link** button. The amount **135** is entered in cell B5; the 3-D reference in the entry area reads **=Portland!$B$10**.

6   Click in the cell containing the total of sprockets in the Portland sheet. Select a copy command.

7   In the Summary sheet, select the cell for sprockets in Portland (cell C5).

8   From the **Edit** menu, select **Paste Special**. In the **Paste Special** dialog box, click on the **Paste Link** button. The amount **160** is entered in cell C5; the 3-D reference in the entry area reads **=Portland!$C$10**.

9   Repeat the process to link the total of doodads in Portland to cell D5 in the Summary sheet.

10   Link the Eugene totals to the Summary sheet. Use the same process as you did for the Portland sheet.

Note: Link each cell separately and not as a range. Linking as a range eliminates the ability to make some editing changes later.

11   Link the Corvallis totals to the Summary sheet. Use the same process as you did for the Portland and Eugene sheets.

12 If Chapter 12 was completed, open the **Macro** sheet and run the PageSetup macro for all sheets of this workbook. Otherwise, create a header and footer to include the file name, sheet name, your name, and the date, and select to print so the sheets are centered both vertically and horizontally.

13 Save and print the workbook. Write "Print 1" at the top.

14 Print a copy of the formulas used in the Summary sheet. If you have completed Chapter 12, you should run the **PrintFormula** macro.

15 Make the following changes. As you make the changes, note that the totals change in the weekly reports and in the Summary sheet.
- Change Portland widgets for **Monday** to **30** and for **Tuesday** to **31**.
- Change Eugene sprockets for **Wednesday** to **32** and for **Thursday** to **33**.
- Change Corvallis doodads for **Thursday** to **41** and for **Friday** to **42**.

16 Save and print the workbook. At the top write "Print 2."

Linking Workbooks

Linking among workbooks is also a useful feature. Large, complex workbooks can be broken into manageable portions through links. For example, instead of placing all the budget data in one workbook, several departmental budgets can be created. Then a "master budget" can be completed that links relevant data from the individual departmental budgets to the master budget.

Linked workbooks can also save recalculation time and computer memory. Errors are reduced because transferring numbers from one workbook to another is done automatically by linking the data. All books are updated when a change is made, ensuring accuracy.

Workbooks are linked in the same way that worksheets are linked. Both workbooks must be open at the same time. However, take care when linking workbooks to be sure that the links are accurate.

A reference from one workbook to another is called an *external reference*. A file link is automatically created when an external reference is used. A file link always contains two workbooks: the destination workbook and the source workbook. The *source document* is the original workbook containing the source cell or cells. The *destination document* is the workbook where information will be pasted.

Before creating links save all workbooks. The link will then refer to the saved name of the workbook and not the generic name *Book1*.

A workbook can be the source or the destination of numerous links. For instance, one source workbook may be linked to several different destination files, and one destination file can have many sources. Workbook 1 can be linked to Workbook 2, which can be linked to Workbook 3, thereby creating a workbook that is both a destination book and a source book. When workbooks are linked to each other, they are considered dependent on one another.

Use caution when opening linked workbooks. Messages sometimes appear regarding the need to update links in workbooks, as shown in Figure 14.6. If in doubt, respond "Yes" to update workbooks that contain links.

Figure 14.6   Update Links Warning Box

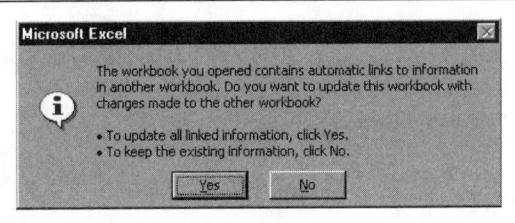

Exercise 14.2   Linking Workbooks

The headquarters of West's Best School Supplies prepares summary worksheets that summarize their stores' sales data by state throughout the western region. Most of the worksheet is completed, except the data for Oregon. You will link the summary data from Oregon that was completed in Exercise 14.1 to the worksheet that summarizes the sales for the western region.

1. Open workbook **Ch14 Ex2** and save it as **Exer 14-2**. Also open workbook **Exer 14-1** if it is not already open. You will link the Oregon figures from **Exer 14-1** to **Exer 14-2**.

2. Arrange the windows so both workbooks are open side by side.

3. Activate the **Summary** sheet in the **Exer 14-1** workbook. Select the cell containing the total widgets. Then select a copy command.

4. Activate the **Sheet1** sheet in the **Exer 14-2** worksheet. In the cell for widgets in Oregon, access the **Paste Special** dialog box, and select **Paste Link**. Note the 3-D reference in the formula.

5. Link the total of sprockets and doodads from Oregon in the Exer 14-1 workbook to the appropriate cells in the Exer 14-2 workbook.

6. Complete the **Exer 14-2** workbook, and format the numbers for commas with no decimals. Run the PageSetup macro if Chapter 12 was completed.

7. Print two copies of **Exer 14-2**, one in Normal view and one that shows the formulas used. Use the **PrintFormula** macro if Chapter 12 was completed.

8. An error was made. There should be **47** sprockets sold on **Friday** in **Corvallis**. Make the change in the Corvallis worksheet, then print another copy of **Exer 14-2**.

9. Save the worksheets.

Copying between Software Applications

Multitasking

Multitasking allows more than one application to be open at the same time and provides an easy way to move between the applications. Multitasking is available in all Windows programs.

The taskbar shows all applications that are currently running (open) on your computer, as shown in Figure 14.7. To move between open applications, click on its title in the taskbar.

Figure 14.7   Using the Taskbar to Access Other Applications

Another method used to move between applications is to hold down the Alt key on the keyboard while tapping the Tab key. In the middle of the screen, a box appears that indicates open applications (Figure 14.8). Holding down the Alt key while tapping the Tab key moves the selection box to another application. Continue tapping the Tab key until the wanted application is selected. Release the Alt key to activate that application.

Figure 14.8   Using Alt and Tab Keys to Access Other Applications

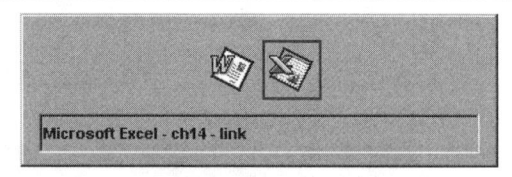

Opening and Viewing Two Applications at Once

All applications that appear on the taskbar are open; however, only one is active at any given time. When working with windows, two or more applications may be viewed at the same time. For instance, side-by-side windows, one containing a word-processing document and one containing a spreadsheet, may appear on the screen as shown in Figure 14.9.

Figure 14.9   Viewing an Excel Spreadsheet and a Word-Processing Document

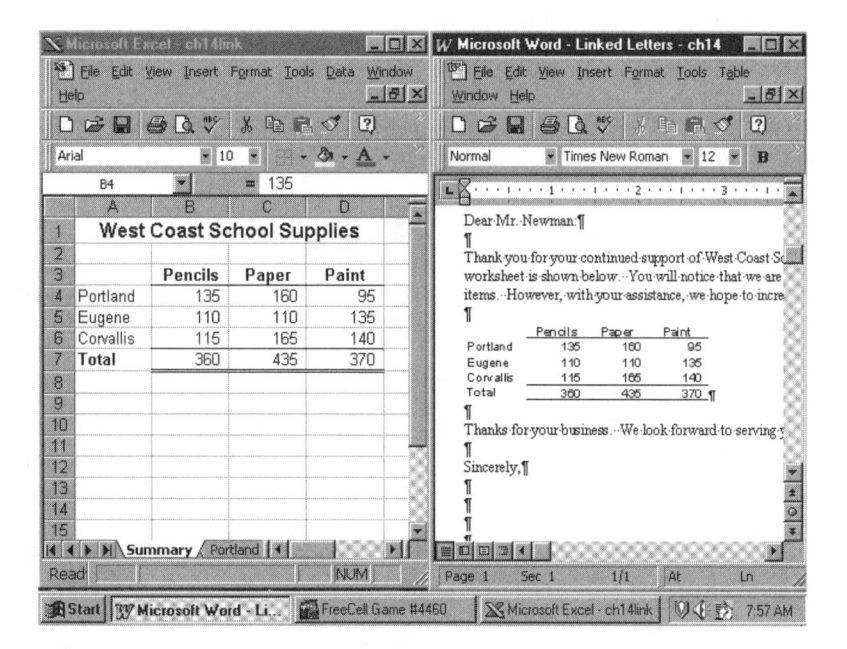

Chapter 14   Linking and Embedding

The letter shown in the Word document on the right is called a *compound document* because it contains data from more than one application. The text was created in Word and the spreadsheet was created in Excel.

Each document must be opened from its application. For instance, to open an Excel spreadsheet, Excel must be the active application. Likewise, to open a Word document, Word must be the active application.

To tile open applications, right-click on the Windows status bar and choose a tile option. This allows you to view documents from more than one application at the same time. When the Maximize button displays in the upper-right corner of an application title bar, you may click on it to make the application window fill the screen. When the Restore button displays, as shown in Figure 14.10, you may click on it to restore the application window to its previous size and location.

Figure 14.10   Maximize and Minimize Buttons on Title Bar and Toolbar

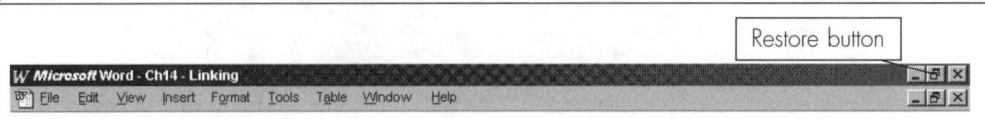

Copying Data between Applications

A picture or part of a document from another software application can be placed in an Excel worksheet. A worksheet may also be placed in a word-processing document. Exchanging data between software applications is common in today's business world.

There are several methods of exchanging data between applications. A file may be saved and then inserted into another application, or the data can be copied and pasted into it. ***Object linking and embedding*** (*OLE*) can be used to create links for information that has been created in one application and copied to a document in another application.

Copy-and-paste techniques used between applications are much like copy-and-paste techniques used within one application. Highlight what is to be copied and select a copy command. Then indicate where the information is to be pasted and select a paste command. Copied data is static and does not change when changes are made in the original.

Exercise 14.3   Copying Data between Applications

You will prepare a memo for the sales manager of West's Best School Supplies that reports the sales for the week. You will copy a worksheet from Excel to a word-processing memo.

1 Open **Excel** and a word-processing application.

2 From Excel, open the **Exer 14-2** workbook. If a warning box opens asking you if you want to update linked information, click on **Yes**. From Word (or another word-processing application), open the **Ch14 Ex3 Memo** document. Save the word-processing document as **Exer 14-3 Memo**.

3 Right-click on the Windows status bar and choose **Tile Vertically**. This tiles the windows so they are side by side on the screen.

4 Select the range of cells containing data in the Excel worksheet, including the title. Select a copy command.

5 Click the mouse in the blank paragraph in the word-processing document. Select a paste command.

6 At the end of the memo, press Enter twice and key your initials, followed by a colon, then the file name (**Exer 14-3 Memo**).

7 Save and print the memo.

8 In the Excel window, change **California** to **Colorado**. Notice that it does not change in the memorandum as it is edited.

9 Close the memo and the worksheet without saving changes in either.

Drag and Drop

Drag-and-drop moving and copying is also available between applications. The source and destination files must be open and visible on the screen, usually arranged side by side. Select the data and drag it to the destination file; the information is moved to the destination file.

To copy information, hold down the Ctrl key while dragging the data. Release the mouse button first, then Ctrl.

When the drag-and-drop method is used, the data is not linked.

Exercise 14.4 Using Drag and Drop between Applications

You will copy a spreadsheet to a sales memo for West's Best School Supplies.

1 Open the **Exer 14-2** workbook. If a warning box appears asking you if you want to update linked information, click on **Yes**. Open the **Ch14 Ex3 Memo** document (a word-processing document). Save the word-processing document as **Exer 14-4 Memo**.

2 Display both documents on the screen so they are side by side.

3 In the word-processing document, scroll so the paragraph marker (¶) between paragraphs is visible on the screen.

4 Select the range of the worksheet that contains data.

5 Hold down **Ctrl**, then click on the edge of the selected range and drag it across the open window to the paragraph marker in the word-processing document.

6 At the end of the memo, enter a blank line and key your initials, followed by a colon, then the file name (**Exer 14-4 Memo**).

7 Save and print the memorandum.

8 Close the Excel document and maximize the word-processing window.

Object Linking and Embedding (OLE)

Microsoft products in Office 97, including Excel and Word, support OLE. This allows information to be linked and/or embedded into another application. When an object is pasted into another application, it is embedded into the application. It is pasted as a complete object and remains constant when the original source file changes. Changes can also be made in the destination file, but they are not reflected in the original.

Information from different applications can also be linked. For instance, when changes are made in the original spreadsheet, the linked spreadsheet in the word-processing document will also change. If you are working in the word-processing document, changes made in this spreadsheet are reflected in both the word-processing and Excel documents because they are linked. The data is dynamic because changes update the data in both documents. Links have been made within Excel; using OLE allows linking between applications.

When using OLE, the document that created the information is considered the source document. The document receiving the information is considered the destination document. These terms are used for both linking and embedding data.

Embedding Information

Embedding is similar to copying information from one application to another. A copy of the information is placed in a new file and saved as part of that file. This method requires more disk space than linking, but it also provides an exact copy in the destination file. If the information needs to be edited in the destination file, simply double-click on the embedded information. The toolbar and menu bar of the source program will replace those of the destination program, and editing can take place in the destination file.

To embed information, first make a copy of the information from the source file. In the destination document, position the insertion point or cursor in the desired location. Then select Paste Special from the Edit menu. The Paste Special dialog box opens, as shown in Figure 14.11.

Figure 14.11   Paste Special Dialog Box

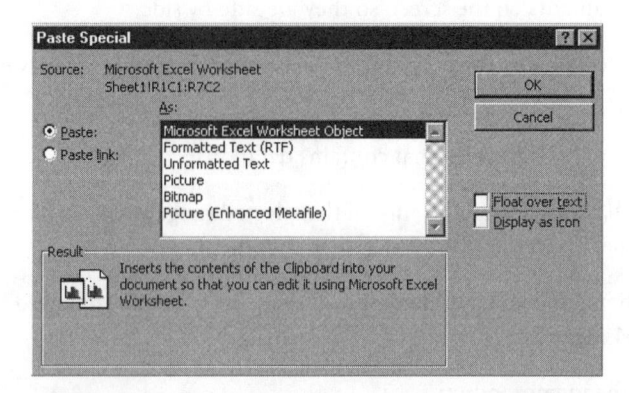

The choices for pasting are Paste or Paste link. Pasting the document embeds the information into the client document. At the bottom of the dialog box the result of the selected action is shown. In Figure 14.11, the definition given as the result of pasting a word document object is that it inserts "the contents of the Clipboard into your document so that you can edit it using Microsoft Excel Worksheet."

If Picture is selected, the result is inserted as a picture and cannot be changed. This provides a better format for working with computer pictures and produces a higher quality printed result. This format also takes less storage space when saved and allows the picture to be redrawn faster on the screen.

Embedded information can be changed in the destination file. However, these changes are made only in the destination file and not in the source file.

Exercise 14.5 Embedding Information

You have selected to embed the information for the sales memo for West's Best School Supplies rather than copy it.

1 Open the **Exer 14-2** workbook and the **Ch14 Ex3 Memo** document (a word-processing document). As the Excel document is opening, a warning box may appear asking if you want to update information links; if so, click **Yes**. Save the word-processing document as **Exer 14-5 Memo**.

2 Arrange both windows on the screen so they are side by side.

3 Select the range of the worksheet that contains data, including the title. Then select a copy command.

4 Click on the paragraph mark in the word-processing memo to place the insertion point in the blank paragraph.

5 From the **Edit** menu, select **Paste Special**. Select to paste the data as a **Microsoft Excel Worksheet Object**, and select **Paste**. Click **OK**. The spreadsheet is embedded into the memorandum.

6 In the memo, place your initials and the file name, **Exer 14-5 Memo**, at the end.

7 Save and print the memorandum.

8 Enter a change in the worksheet. Note that the data in the word-processing document stays the same.

9 Close the documents without saving changes.

Changing Embedded Information

Once information has been embedded into a document, it is part of that document. However, if a change needs to be made in the information, it can be made from within the document.

Double-click on the embedded information. This activates a link to the source program, displaying the toolbar(s) and menu bar of that application. Figure 14.12 shows an embedded active spreadsheet in a word-processing document. When it is selected, bold borders with handles appear around the worksheet, indicating that it is active. An active embedded file may be edited. Changes occur in the destination file, but the source does not change because it is not linked.

Figure 14.12 Making Changes in an Embedded Spreadsheet

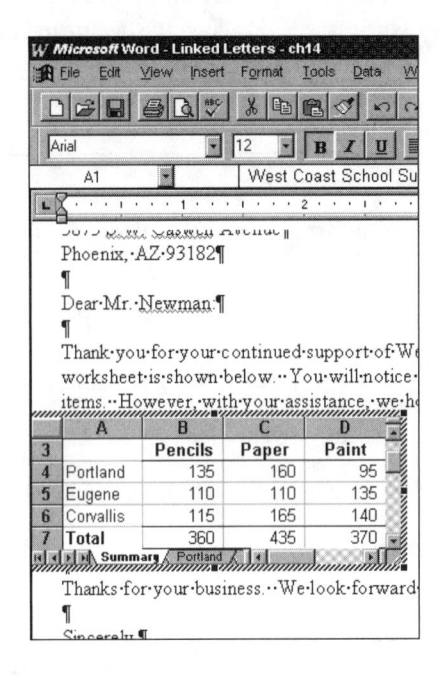

Make the necessary changes in the worksheet. When finished, click again in the word-processing document to return to the word-processing application's toolbar and menu bar.

Exercise 14.6 Changing an Embedded Document

You will change the embedded spreadsheet in the memorandum created in Exercise 14.5.

1 Open **Exer 14-2** in Excel and open the **Exer 14-5 Memo** document in a word-processing program. If a warning box opens asking if you want to update information links, click **Yes**. Save the memorandum as **Exer 14-6 Memo**.

2 Make sure the memorandum is the active document. Double-click on the spreadsheet in the memorandum. Excel's toolbar, menu bar, and formula bar appear. Change the state from **California** to **Colorado**. It is changed in the memorandum document but not in the spreadsheet document.

3 At the end of the memo, change the file name (**Exer 14-6 Memo**).

4 Save changes and print a copy of the changed memorandum.

Linking between Software Applications

Just as a information can be linked between two documents in the same application, information can also be linked between documents created in different programs. When a change is made in one document, it is automatically updated in the documents that contain a link to the edited information.

Object Linking and Embedding 447

Linking a spreadsheet to a Word document is similar to using the copy-and-paste method. First create a spreadsheet, chart, or other information in Excel. Then highlight the worksheet or portion of the worksheet to be copied, and select a copy command.

Activate the source file, then select Paste Special from the Edit menu. The Paste Special dialog box opens, as shown in Figure 14.13.

Figure 14.13 Using the Paste Special Dialog Box for Linking

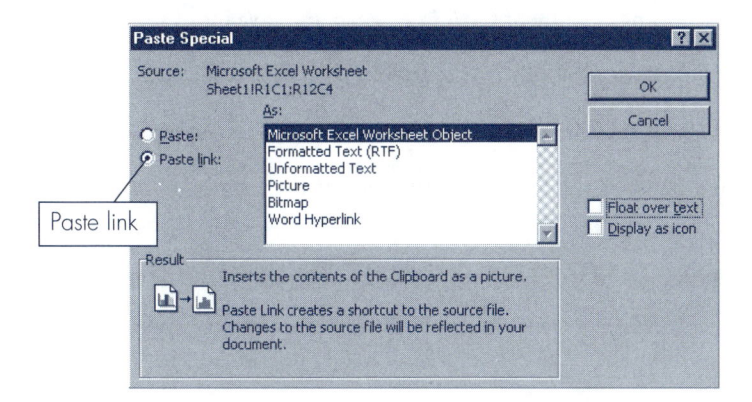

Select Paste link. The information is pasted as an object, picture, or text. A link is created; changes to any of the linked information will be reflected in all locations to which this data is linked. Both the spreadsheet and word-processing documents are shown in Figure 14.14.

Figure 14.14 Linking a Spreadsheet

Figure 14.15 shows the same linked worksheet in both applications after a change was made in Excel and was automatically updated in Word.

Figure 14.15 Changing a Linked Spreadsheet

Exercise 14.7 Linking Information between Two Applications

Kendall & Associates has prepared a sales report and has asked you to link it to a memorandum. You will also link a chart to the memorandum. Then a correction will be made in one document that will be reflected in all links.

1 Open workbook **Ch14 Ex7** and save it as **Exer 14-7**.

2 Open the word-processing document **Ch14 Ex7 Memo** and save it as **Exer 14-7 Memo**.

3 Place the two documents side by side on the screen.

4 In the Excel spreadsheet, highlight the range A1:E11. Select a copy command.

5 Position the mouse between the last two paragraphs of the memorandum; click once to place the insertion point.

6 From **Edit** select **Paste Special**. Click on **Paste link** and **Microsoft Excel Worksheet Object**. Then click **OK**.

7 Save the workbook.

8 Print a copy of **Exer 14-7 Memo**. Save **Exer 14-7 Memo** as **Exer 14-7b Memo**.

9 In the Excel window, click on the tab for **Sheet2**. Select the chart, then a copy command.

10 In the word-processing document, place the insertion point after the worksheet and press **Enter** so a blank paragraph is available.

11 From **Edit** select **Paste Special**. Then link the chart to the memo.

12 Print **Exer 14-7b Memo** and the Excel spreadsheet and chart.

13 In the spreadsheet, change the **CDs** from the **Main Mall** to **78,375**. In the **Area Shopping Center**, change **Tapes** to **30,879**.

14 Print a copy of the three documents again. Notice that the change is reflected in the memorandum and the chart. At the top write "Changes Made."

15 Save all documents.

Summary of Copying, Linking, and Embedding

Method of Integration	What It Does	How It Is Used
Copy and Paste	Places a copy of the information in a document.	The data is static and changes made in one document do not change other documents.
Embed	Information is displayed in both the source and destination files.	Changes may be made in either the source or destination files. However, the changes are reflected only in the document where changes are made and are not entered in other documents.
Link	Information is displayed in the source and destination files.	Data can be changed in either the source or the destination file. When a change is made in one document, it is automatically updated in all linked documents.

OLE is supported by all Microsoft products. The concepts presented in this chapter—copy and paste, linking, and embedding—can be used in PowerPoint and Access just as they are used in Word and Excel.

Summary

- A dynamic link is one where changes made in one document are automatically reflected in the other documents linked to the edited information.
- To link data in a worksheet, select the data in the source file, then select a copy command. Place the insertion point in the destination file. Access the Paste Special dialog box, then select Paste link.
- An external reference refers to a different worksheet that contains the reference.
- The source file contains the data referred to in an external reference; the destination file contains the external reference.
- Multitasking refers to the ability to have more than one application open at the same time.
- A compound document contains data created in more than one application.
- Copying data between applications is completed the same way as copying within an application. Data copied between applications is static and cannot be changed.
- Embedding information from one application to another is similar to copying data within the same application. Changes can be made to either document, but they are reflected only in the document where the changes occurred.
- When documents are linked, changes made in one document are automatically reflected in all other documents containing links to the edited information.
- Changes made to dynamic data change all the documents that contain links to that data; linked data is dynamic.
- Changes made to static data do not automatically change the documents to where the information was copied; information that is copied and pasted is static.

- The document from which information is copied is the source file. The application used to create the information is the source program.
- The document receiving information is the destination file. The application receiving information is the destination program.
- To embed information, select it and choose a copy command. Activate the destination file, open the Paste Special dialog box, and select Paste.
- To link information, select it and choose a copy command. Activate the destination file, open the Paste Special dialog box, and select Paste link.
- Embedded information changed in the destination file is not automatically changed in the source file because a link is not established.

Important Terminology

compound document
destination document
dynamic link
embedding

external reference
linked documents
multitasking
object linking and
    embedding (OLE)

Paste Link
source document
static link

Buttons to Know

Study Questions

True-False

Place a T in the space if the statement is true; place an F if the statement is false.

_____ 1. A dynamic link between worksheets means that a change in linked information in one document changes all documents linked to the edited data.

_____ 2. To link data, select the cell to be linked, then a copy command.

_____ 3. A 3-D reference is used only between an Excel worksheet and a word-processing document.

_____ 4. A chart in an Excel document may be changed; once it is pasted into a word-processing document, it can not be changed.

_____ 5. Linking can be done only between worksheets in an open workbook.

_____ 6. An external reference refers to a document different from the workbook that contains the external reference.

_____ 7. Multitasking is the ability to have different applications open at the same time.

_____ 8. A compound document uses two or more worksheets in a workbook.

_____ 9. When information is copied from a workbook to a word-processing document, it is static.

_____ 10. Changes can be made in a worksheet embedded in a word-processing document. Double-click on the worksheet; the toolbar, menu bar, and formula bar from Excel replace those of the word-processing program, allowing you to edit.

_____ 11. Information in a word-processing document can be moved to a spreadsheet using the drag-and-drop method.

Fill-In

Place the word in the space that correctly completes the statement.
1. A worksheet is updated in both an Excel document and a word-processing document when changes are entered in only one of the documents because the files are _____ .
2. Use the _____ _____ dialog box to link a document.
3. A link establishes a relationship between the destination file and the _____ file.
4. A _____ document contains information from more than one application.
5. Object linking and embedding is also known as _____ .
6. Linked data is _____ ; changes made in the source file are reflected in the destination file.

Assignments

After completion of Chapter 14, you may delete the Ch14 folder from your Student Data Disk.

Assignment 14.1

You have been asked to complete the payroll reports for Helen's Light Industrial. Employees are paid weekly, and individual payroll records are prepared for each employee. You will complete the weekly reports and link the information to the employees' individual records.

This workbook is complex. There are four tabs for the payroll records, one for each weekly payroll date in the month of July. There are individual tabs for each of the four employees. The individual employee records will be linked to the original payroll records.

1. Open workbook **Ch14 As1** and save it as **Assig 14-1**.
2. You may want to open several copies of this document, arrange them on the screen, and work in different tabs in each window. This saves time in switching back and forth to different sheets.
3. Link the Gilliam information.
   - Click on the **July 7** tab and select the information for Gilliam, B9:H9. Then select a copy command.
   - Click on the **Gilliam** tab and select cell B8.
   - From the **Edit** menu, select **Paste Special**, then choose **Paste Link**. The information from the July 7 payroll is entered into the individual record for Gilliam.
4. Link the Hare information.
   - Click on the **July 7** tab and select the information for Hare. Then select a copy command.
   - Click on the **Hare** tab and select cell B8.
   - From the **Edit** menu, select **Paste Special**, then choose **Paste Link**.
5. Repeat the linking process for Holm and Lees.
6. Complete the July 14 payroll.
   - Select the **July 14** payroll sheet.
   - Enter the following hours worked: **Gilliam, 37**; **Hare, 42**; **Holm, 40.5**, **Lees, 36**.
7. Link the July 14 payroll to the individual records.
   - Select the range B9:H9 for Gilliam and select a copy command.
   - Click on the **Gilliam** tab and select cell B9.
   - From **Edit**, select **Paste Special**, then choose **Paste Link**.
   - Repeat the linking process for Hare, Holm, and Lees.

8. Complete the July 21 payroll.
   - Enter the following hours worked: **Gilliam, 38; Hare, 42; Holm, 40.5; Lees, 43**.
   - Link the July 21 payroll to the individual records.
9. Complete the July 28 payroll. Enter the following hours worked: **Gilliam, 42; Hare, 39; Holm, 44; Lees, 41**. Link the July 28 payroll to the individual records.
10. Click on all worksheets to be sure column widths, number formats, and other formatting is accurate.
11. The employees received a pay increase for the July 28 payroll. Enter the following hourly rates: **Gilliam, $5.60; Hare, $7.55; Holm, $8.38; Lees, $6.90**.
12. Format the placement of the worksheets on the page.
    - Print in landscape style on one page, centered both vertically and horizontally.
    - Do not print gridlines.
    - In the header, include the sheet name and your name. In the footer, include the page number and the file name.
13. Save and print the workbook.
14. Print the formulas for the **July 7** and **Gilliam** sheets.

Assignment 14.2

Joshua's Software Sales has completed its spreadsheet summarizing the sales for October. A draft of a memorandum has been prepared regarding the sales data. You are asked to include the spreadsheet information in the memorandum for the president of Joshua's.

1. Open the Excel workbook **Ch14 As2** and the word-processing document **Ch14 As2 Memo**. Use either Word or WordPad as the word processor.
2. Save the Excel worksheet as **Assig 14-2** and the word-processing document as **Assig 14-2 Memo**.
3. In the worksheet, place your name at the right side of the header.
4. Embed the spreadsheet data at the end of the memorandum. Be sure to paste the data as an Excel object.
5. Edit the worksheet in the memorandum. In the title, leave only the name of the firm. Bold the column labels, and shade the total column and row. Change the column widths if necessary.
6. In the workbook, create a chart sheet that shows the revenue by city for each product. Use a column or bar chart.
7. Save and print the entire workbook.
8. In the word-processing document, embed a copy of the chart below the embedded spreadsheet so the data is displayed as a graph as well as a worksheet.
9. Save and print the word-processing document.

Assignment 14.3

Wonder Electronics has completed its quarterly sales report and is ready to send the results to the accounting department. You will link a spreadsheet to a word-processing memorandum.

The president would like the same information in a chart. You will create a chart and link it to the word-processing document.

1. Open the necessary documents.
   - Open workbook **Ch14 As3** and save it as **Assig 14-3**.
   - Open the word-processing program and the document saved as **Ch14 As3a Memo**. Save the memo as **Assig 14-3a Memo**.
   - Place both the worksheet and the memorandum side by side on the screen, if possible.
2. Link the worksheet to the memorandum. Highlight the needed range in the worksheet and select a copy command. In the memorandum, leave two blank lines between the text and the linked worksheet.
3. Print a copy of the memorandum and the spreadsheet.
4. Save both the worksheet and the word-processing document. Close the **Assig 14-3a Memo** file.
5. Prepare a column chart and link it to a memo to the president of the company.
   - Prepare a column chart below the cells containing data. Enhance it as you wish.
   - In the word-processing program, open the **Ch14 As3b Memo** document and save it as **Assig 14-3b Memo**.
   - Link the chart at the bottom of the memorandum.
   - Save both documents.
   - Print the word-processing document and the worksheet.
6. The accounting department found an error in the amount for televisions in January. Change the amount in the worksheet to **$35,987.56**. This will change the information in the chart and in both word-processing documents.
7. Save and print copies of all the corrected documents.

Case Problem 14

Frank Gillard's Honey Bees sells honey to a three-state region. Individual worksheets for March's sales have been prepared. You have been asked to complete the information needed to prepare reports for the president, Frank Gillard. These new reports should reflect the quarterly sales.

The monthly reports have been completed and are saved on the data disk as Case 14. You will need to link the information from each monthly to the Summary sheet, then prepare a chart or charts reflecting the quarterly data. Check the accuracy of the formulas you use.

You will also use a word-processing program to prepare a memorandum to the president of the company. In the memo, include a text summary of the data; of particular interest is the top sales for each month and any area where sales are slipping. You will want to include worksheet data in the memorandum, perhaps by copying or linking the worksheet to the memo.

Submit a complete report to the president, Frank Gillard. Include the formulas used in the worksheet.

After the information is printed, the Alabama firm calls to report errors in their sales report. Make the corrections and print a new copy. The errors are as follows:

Month	Week	Change to
January	Week 1	$5,440
February	Week 2	$5,447
March	Week 4	$5,450

Chapter 15

Using Templates

Objectives

1. Identify and create a template.
2. Use a template to create worksheets.
3. Create and use customized templates from the Spreadsheet Solutions templates.

Introduction

A template is a workbook that has been designed so the basic worksheet structure, including the format and formulas, can be used to create other worksheets. An accurate worksheet is created by entering only the data. Templates are used to plan finances and to add consistency to the appearance of worksheets and the organization of data.

Worksheets that are used over and over, such as expense records or payroll reports, are examples of documents that should be created as templates. Simply entering new variables to templates and saving the templates as worksheets creates new worksheets.

Several built-in templates, called Spreadsheet Solutions templates, can be customized for business or personal needs.

Note that at the end of this chapter, you may delete the Ch15 directory from your Student Data Disk.

Excel Templates

Creating complex Excel worksheets can be time consuming, and often the same types of worksheets are used repeatedly. Rather than create a new worksheet each time one is needed, create a ***template*** that can be used several times. A template is a worksheet that is used as the basis to create similar worksheets. Creating a template saves the styles, formats, formulas, macros, and generic text (such as labels) of a worksheet. When using a template, fill in the data and a new worksheet is complete.

Preparing and Saving a Template

To prepare a template, enter text, formats, and formulas. Then save the worksheet as a template.

At the bottom of the Save As dialog box, select the down arrow by the Save as type. Select Template, as shown in Figure 15.1.

As soon as Template is selected, Excel opens the Templates folder in the Save in section; this is the default directory for saving templates. In a classroom, templates should be saved to the data disk in drive A along with all other Excel worksheets completed in class.

Figure 15.1 Selecting Template in the Save As Dialog Box

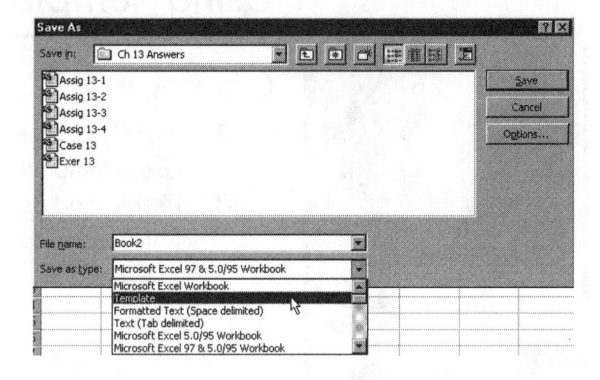

Exercise 15.1 Creating a Template

Kristi Andrews Marketing prepares a sales report each week. They have started a worksheet that they would like to use as a template. You will complete the worksheet and save it as a template.

Note: Before completing the exercises and assignments in this chapter, you will need to expand the Chapter 15 files on your Student Data Disk. In Windows Explorer, locate the zipped Ch15 file and double-click on it. When all the files have been expanded, you will be able to open them in Excel.

1 Open workbook **Ch15 Ex1**.

2 Place the formulas for the needed totals in row 12.

3 Use the Paste Function dialog box to determine the daily averages for column G and row 14. Because there are no amounts entered in the worksheet, error messages will appear.

4 Format the averages for two decimal places and the other numbers for zero decimal places.

5 Place a bold line under the average row.

6 Replace the date in cell B5 with a volatile date.

7 Run the PageSetup macro if you have completed Chapter 12. If you have not, format to center the sheet horizontally on the page. Enter your name and the file name in the header and the sheet name and page number in the footer. Then format for a top margin of 2" and include gridlines.

8 Access the **Save As** dialog box. Click on the down arrow by **Save as type** and select **Template**. Be sure to save the template on your Student Data Disk. Name the worksheet **Weekly Sales**.

9 Close the template.

Using a Template

A template document is opened the same way as any other worksheet is opened.

In Explorer and the Open dialog box, a template document is visually identified by its icon. A template icon has a border across the top; a document icon has a turned-down corner. The top icon in Figure 15.2 is for an Excel document; the bottom icon is for an Excel template.

When a template is listed in Explorer with all its properties showing, the extension of .xlt (Excel Template) displays.

Figure 15.2   Document and Template Icons

Exercise 15.2   Using a Template

You will open the template saved in Exercise 15.1. You will then use it to create a worksheet providing sales information.

1   Open the worksheet template **Weekly Sales**.

2   Enter the following information for the salespeople. As the amounts are entered into the worksheet, the totals are automatically calculated to reflect that the values have been entered in the cells.

	A	B	C	D	E	F
1	H. Gilliam	554	642	471	614	705
2	S. Holm	548	648	567	578	498
3	B. Lees	657	477	800	536	577
4	S. Wilhite	885	501	517	604	608

3   Access the **Save As** dialog box. Name the worksheet **Exer 15-2**. Do not save the worksheet as a template.

4   Print a copy of the worksheet.

Using Spreadsheet Solutions Templates

Several templates, also called *Spreadsheet Solutions templates*, have been built into Excel 97. They include templates for an *Expense Statement*, an *Invoice*, and a *Purchase Order*. In addition, there is an order form for additional software from a vendor (Village Software). Additional templates may be accessed from the World Wide Web. The available templates are displayed in the Spreadsheet Solutions tab of the New dialog box, shown in Figure 15.3. The General tab is used

Figure 15.3   Accessing Spreadsheet Solutions Templates

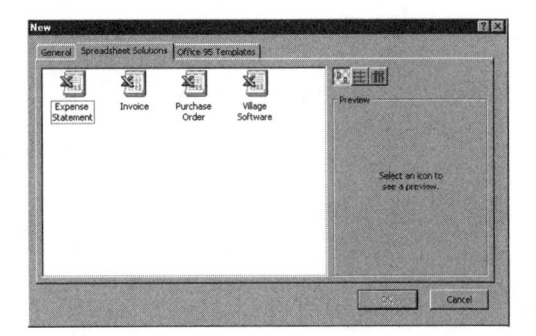

to open a new workbook. The Office 95 Templates tab lists the built-in templates from Office 95 and is available only if your Office 97 software was updated from Office 95.

Note: If a template is not available on the Spreadsheet Solutions tab, run Setup again to install it. Spreadsheet Solutions templates are not installed with a "normal" setup.

Spreadsheet Solutions Templates

Spreadsheet Solutions templates provide templates to prepare an expense statement, an invoice, or a purchase order—worksheets commonly used in business. Only the Expense Statement template will be explained in this text; however, the same procedures are used for customizing and saving any Spreadsheet Solutions template.

The Expense Statement template provides a basic expense statement that can be customized for any business. Formulas are entered. Then, when an expense statement is needed, simply fill in the variable information and print the statement. Figure 15.4 shows a blank Expense Statement.

Figure 15.4   Expense Statement Spreadsheet Solutions Template

Customizing a Template

All Spreadsheet Solutions templates may be customized to personalize worksheets for any firm. Click on the Customize button in the template screen and enter personalized information. When you customize a template, the new information entered automatically becomes a part of the template.

The Customize screen for the Expense Statement template is shown in Figure 15.5.

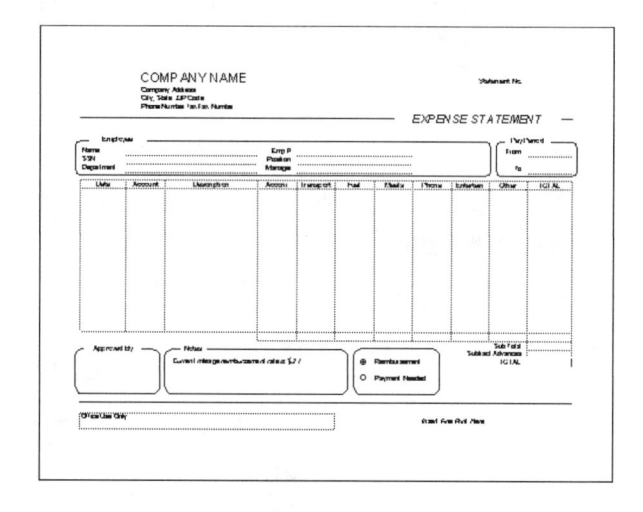

Figure 15.5   Customizing a Template

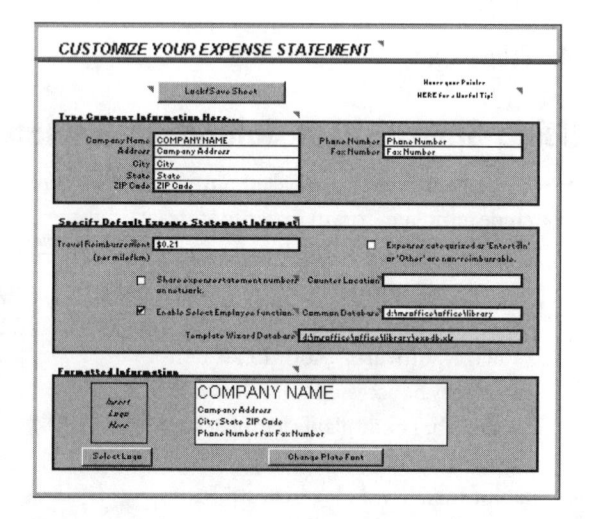

Fill in the blank fields in the template. The red triangles provide comments that explain the sections of the template when the mouse is positioned over them. A logo may be added by clicking in the Select Logo button. A logo is usually clip art or a picture.

A completed Customize screen is shown in Figure 15.6. The logo is the checkmark, a clip art graphic that is included with the Office 97 suite. If a logo is not used, the placeholder for the logo does not appear in the expense statement.

Saving a Template

After customizing a template, lock and save it for future use. As the last step in customizing a template, click on the Lock/Save Sheet button at the top of the Customize screen. The Lock/Save Sheet dialog box opens, as shown in Figure 15.7.

Click OK. The Save Template dialog box opens with Template selected in the Save as type section, as shown in Figure 15.8. Enter the file name of the template and select a subdirectory. For classroom uses, it is advisable to save all work to your Student Data Disk and not the default Templates subdirectory.

When a template is saved in the Templates subdirectory, it is available in the New dialog box along with the Spreadsheet Solutions templates. When it is saved on the Student Data Disk, it is opened in the same way as other documents.

Figure 15.6   Completed Customize Tab

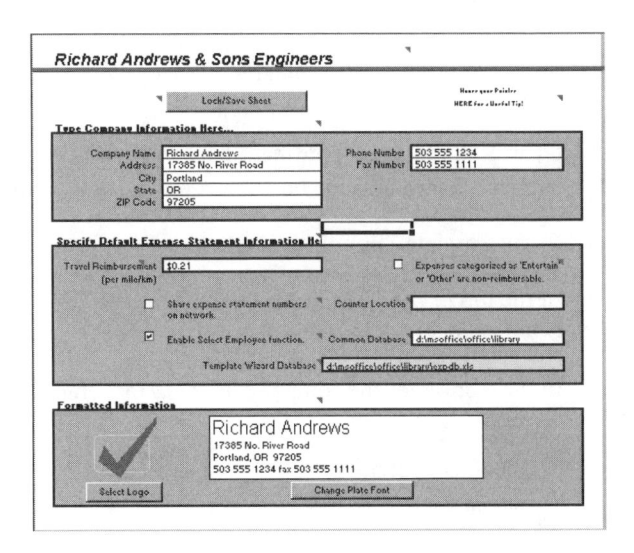

Figure 15.7   Lock/Save Sheet Dialog Box

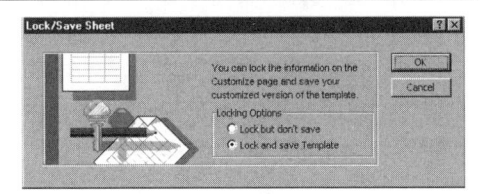

Figure 15.8   Save Template Dialog Box

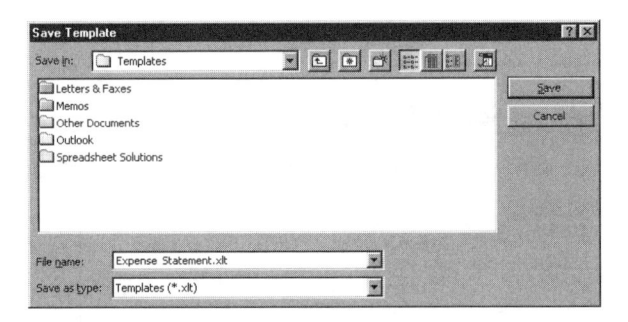

Exercise 15.3 Customizing and Saving a Template

You will customize and save a Spreadsheet Solutions template for a company's expense statement. Spreadsheet Solutions templates take large amounts of disk space. These documents should be saved to the hard drive of the computer.

1 Open Excel to the **Spreadsheet Solutions** tab of the **New** dialog box. Open the **Expense Statement** template. When a dialog box opens warning about macros, select **Enable Macros**.

2 In the template, click on the **Customize Your Statement** tab.

3 At the top of the statement, replace **CUSTOMIZE YOUR EXPENSE STATEMENT** with the company name **G & J Gardens**.

4 In the section for the company information, enter the following information:

   G & J Gardens
   3046 So. Pacific Avenue
   Santa Barbara
   CA
   93110
   (805) 555-1211
   (805) 555-1222

5 At the bottom of the statement, click on the **Select Logo** button. Select the **Flower.wmf** graphic. If Office 97 is running on your system, you will find a **Clipart** subdirectory in the **MSOffice** directory; the flower graphic is located there.

6 Save the template to the **Templates** subdirectory on your computer. From **File**, select **Save As**. In **Save as type**, be sure **Template** is selected. Name the template **Ex15-3 Expense**.

7 Close the template.

8 Click on the **Expense Statement** tab.

Using a Saved Template

When a template is saved on a stand-alone computer, it may be saved so it will appear in the Spreadsheet Solutions tab of the New dialog box. However, you have saved your template on your data disk so you will access it the same way you have opened previous workbooks. When the template opens, enter the variable information for the expenses. The completed expense statement is shown in Figure 15.9.

Figure 15.9 Completed Expense Statement

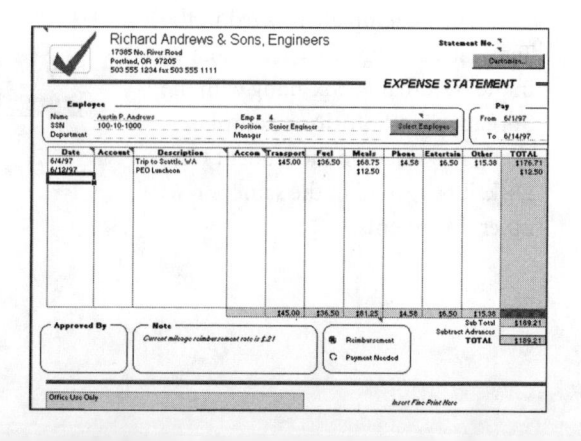

In the Expense Statement template, the shaded cells contain formulas. When the variable information is entered, the shaded cells are completed automatically.

Save the document as an Excel workbook file. The original template remains the same so another expense statement may be completed. Excel 97 has the capability to link the information in a Spreadsheet Solutions template to a summary spreadsheet, if you wish. The Template File - Save to Database dialog box, shown in Figure 5.10, asks if you would like to create a new record or continue without updating. If this dialog box opens, select "Continue without updating" and click OK.

Figure 15.10   Save to Database Dialog Box

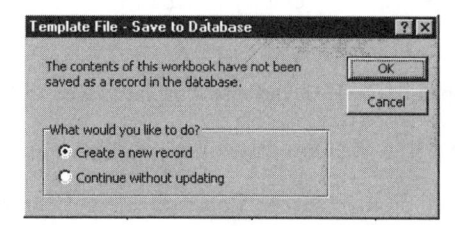

The Template Toolbar

When working with Spreadsheet Solutions templates, a toolbar opens customized for each type of template. The *Expense toolbar* is shown in Figure 15.11.

Figure 15.11   Expense Statement Template Toolbar

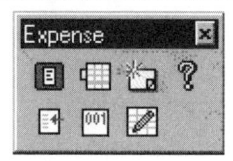

The buttons on the Template toolbars are as follows:

- Size to Screen/Return to Size
- Hide Comments/Display Comments
- New Comment
- Template Help
- Display Example/Remove Example
- Assign a Number
- Capture Data in a Database

Use the Size to Screen/Return to Size button to display the entire form in a reduced size or restored to its full size. Hide Comments/Display Comments shows or hides the comments. The New Comment button is used to add a comment to a cell in the template. Use Template Help to access Help. Display Example/Remove Example shows an example of the template. Assign a Number automatically assigns a tracking number to the form. The Capture Data in a Database button adds the template information to an associated database.

Exercise 15.4 Using a Customized Template

You will complete an expense statement for the first two weeks of this month.

1. Open the **Ex15-3 Expense** template saved in Exercise 15.3. Be sure to enable macros.
2. Save it to the hard drive of the computer as a workbook named **Exer 15-4 Expense**.
3. Click on the **Expense Statement** tab and enter the variable information given below. (There will be several blank fields.) You are the sales manager. Automatically number the expense statement using the Assign a Number button [001] in the statement number field in the upper-right corner. If a warning box opens asking if you want to proceed, click **OK**. Use the first two weeks of this month for the dates in the **From** and **To** fields. All expenses are for account number 001. The expenses are given below:

   - On the second of the month, you took a customer to lunch. You traveled 30 miles at a cost of $0.21 per mile. (The meals cost $18.95.) Enter a formula in the Transport column to determine the cost for transportation.
   - On the fifth of the month, you made a trip to Los Angeles and spent the night. You drove 175 miles (at a cost of $0.21 per mile), your accommodations cost $49.50, your meals cost $68.75, phone calls cost $4.50, and you had other expenses of $11.40.

4. Save the workbook. Do not update the database.
5. Print a copy of the workbook.
6. Delete **Ex15-3 Expense** and **Exer 15-4 Expense** from the **Templates** subdirectory.

Summary

- A template is a worksheet that is used as the basis for other similar worksheets.
- Using a template speeds preparation of a worksheet. Enter only the variable information.
- Templates can be completed and then saved as regular worksheets. This does not alter the template, so it may be used again.
- Spreadsheet Solutions templates are built-in templates that have been created for business needs.
- A Spreadsheet Solutions template can be customized for individuals or businesses. A logo and other information is placed in the worksheet.
- A toolbar provides tools to use with the various Spreadsheet Solutions templates.
- Once a template is created and customized, it can be used many times.

Important Terminology

Expense Statement	Invoice	Spreadsheet Solutions
Expense toolbar	Purchase Order	templates
		template

Buttons to Know

Study Questions

True-False

Place a T in the space if the statement is true; place an F if the statement is false.

_____ 1. A template is a worksheet that is saved so it can be used several times.
_____ 2. To save a template, select File then Save Template.
_____ 3. A template document cannot be opened from the Open button.
_____ 4. A template may be changed only one time.
_____ 5. Built-in templates are called Completed Templates.
_____ 6. Built-in templates may be customized for an individual business.
_____ 7. Built-in templates may be used only once.
_____ 8. Using Spreadsheet Solutions templates is the only way to create templates.
_____ 9. A specific toolbar for the selected Spreadsheet Solutions template opens with each template.

Assignments

Assignment 15.1

Howard's Logging Mill, Inc., prepares its payroll each week. Howard would like to have a template created for future use, and has provided a past payroll report as a model. You will create the template and then complete the payroll worksheets for two weeks. The template will then be ready for the third week, July 28. The third week will not be completed.

1. Open the workbook saved as **Ch15 As1**. Notice that formulas are already entered in the **Payroll** worksheet.
2. Copy the **Payroll** sheet to three new sheets, one for each week in the month. Hold down **Ctrl**, click on the **Payroll** tab, and move to the right one tab. The sheet is copied. Repeat until there are four **Payroll** worksheets.
3. Rename the sheet tabs to match the payroll dates for July. Use names of **7-7**, **7-14**, **7-21**, and **7-28**.
4. Select all of the sheets, run the PageSetup macro, center the worksheets horizontally and vertically, and format for landscape style. If you have not completed Chapter 12, place your name and the file name in the header and the sheet name and page number in the footer. Then center the sheets in landscape style both vertically and horizontally.
5. Save the workbook as a template. In the **Save As** dialog box, click in the down arrow by **Save as type** and select **Template**. Be sure to save on the Student Data Disk and not in the default Templates folder. Name this file **Temp 15-1**. Close the template.
6. Add an employee and save the altered template.
   - Open **Temp 15-1**. Select all of the payroll sheets.
   - One new employee has been hired, **Winona Hastings**. Add her to the template document, keeping the employees in alphabetical order. Her pay rate is **$6** per hour.
   - Check the cells in Winona's record to be sure formulas are included. If they are not, copy them to her record. Ungroup the sheets.
   - In the **Save As** dialog box, use the file name **Temp 15-1**. Choose to save the workbook as a template. If a warning box opens asking if you want to replace the file, select **Yes**.

Chapter 15   Using Templates

7. Close the template.
8. Open the **Temp 15-1** template.
9. Save the template as a Microsoft Excel workbook named **Assig 15-1**.
10. Complete a weekly payroll.
    - Click on the **7-7** tab.
    - Use the following chart to enter the hours worked for each employee in column C:

		Hourly Rate	Hours Worked
7			
8			
9	Dearborn, Andrea	6.28	42
10	Ewert, Bob	7.35	37.5
11	Freeman, Connie	8.29	36
12	Gilliam, Helen	5.25	41
13	Gogham, Daniel	6.39	40
14	Hare, Martha	5.83	44
15	Winona Hastings	6.00	45.5
16	Hinton, Evelyn	8.75	41
17	Holm, Stanley	5.85	35
18	Lees, Beverly	6.75	38
19	Priesner, Andrew	7.25	40
20	Stultz, Richard	8.00	44

   - Print a copy of the **7-7** worksheet.
11. Complete the payroll for 7-14.
    - Click on the **7-14** tab.
    - Use the following chart to enter the hours worked for each employee in column C:

	A	B	C
7		Hourly Rate	Hours Worked
8			
9	Dearborn, Andrea	6.28	47
10	Ewert, Bob	7.35	42
11	Freeman, Connie	8.29	41
12	Gilliam, Helen	5.25	40
13	Gogham, Daniel	6.39	38
14	Hare, Martha	5.83	40
15	Hastings, Winona	6.00	37
16	Hinton, Evelyn	8.75	42
17	Holm, Stanley	5.85	41
18	Lees, Beverly	6.75	40
19	Priesner, Andrew	7.25	45
20	Stultz, Richard	8.00	43

- In the title, change the date to reflect the week of **July 14**.
- Print a copy of the **7-14** worksheet.
12. Complete the payroll for 7-21.
    - Click on the tab for the **7-21** worksheet.
    - Enter the following hours for each employee in column C:

	A	B	C
8		Hourly Rate	Hours Worked
9	Dearborn, Andrea	6.28	44.5
10	Ewert, Bob	7.35	40
11	Freeman, Connie	8.29	39
12	Gilliam, Helen	5.25	42
13	Gogham, Daniel	6.39	37.5
14	Hare, Martha	5.83	41
15	Hastings, Winona	6.00	42.5
16	Hinton, Evelyn	8.75	40
17	Holm, Stanley	5.85	40
18	Lees, Beverly	6.75	43
19	Priesner, Andrew	7.25	44
20	Stultz, Richard	8.00	42

- Change the date of the worksheet title to reflect the week of **July 21**.
13. Save the workbook and print a copy of the **7-21** worksheet.

Assignment 15.2

Charlie's Department Stores is a nationwide chain. They report sales by store and region. You will save the monthly sales report as a template. You will then complete reports for the next two months.

Note: In order to complete this assignment, you must know how to link cells.

1. Open workbook **Ch15 As2**.
2. Save it as **Assig 15-2**. Be sure to save this as a workbook and not as a template.
3. There are two tabs indicating the Western and Eastern divisions. Each worksheet lists information for the malls where the individual stores are located. There are four more worksheets corresponding to the four departments within each store. Click on several of the tabs to see how this workbook is arranged.
4. Select all worksheets in the workbook. Run the PageSetup macro, or format the worksheets so they are centered both horizontally and vertically. In the header include your name and the file name, and in the footer include the sheet name and page number.
5. Link the data in the workbook.

Western Division
- Link the entry for the women's clothes department at the Salem Mall in the **Western Div.** worksheet to the **Women's Clothes** worksheet entry for Salem Mall.

- Link the entry for the women's clothes department at the Crossroads Mall in the **Western Div.** worksheet to the **Women's Clothes** worksheet entry for Crossroads Mall.
- Continue using the Paste link option until all of the entries for women's clothes departments in the Western division are linked to the **Women's Clothes** worksheet.

Eastern Division
- Link the entry for the women's clothes department at the Cherry River Mall in the **Eastern Div.** worksheet to the **Women's Clothes** worksheet entry for Cherry River Mall.
- Link the entry for the women's clothes department at the Crosley Center in the **Eastern Div.** worksheet to the **Women's Clothes** worksheet entry for Crosley Center.
- Continue using the Paste link option until all of the entries for women's clothes departments in the Eastern division are linked to the **Women's Clothes** worksheet.
- The links for the other departments have already been completed.

6. Save the workbook as a template.
   - From **File** select **Save As**.
   - In the **Save as type** box, click on the arrow and select **Template**.
   - Name the worksheet **Temp 15-2**. Be sure to save it to your Student Data Disk.
7. Close the workbook.
8. Open **Temp 15-2**.
9. Save **Temp 15-2** as **Assig 15-2a**. Be sure to save this as a workbook document and not as a template.
10. Select all worksheets by choosing **Select All Sheets** in the tabs shortcut menu.
11. Change the date in row 4 to **January 1999**. Ungroup the sheets.
12. Click on the **Western Div.** tab. Enter the following information. As you enter the information, notice that the totals are automatically calculated because the formulas were already entered in the template document.

	A	B	C	D	E
7		Women's Clothes	Men's Clothes	Women's Shoes	Men's Shoes
8	Salem Mall	$ 36,570.00	$ 47,853.18	$ 68,742.10	$115,780.25
9	Crossroads Mall	48,570.50	56,875.24	20,856.24	156,751.20
10	Floyd's Center	26,478.56	15,678.24	56,701.24	56,587.14
11	Jefferson Square	54,875.21	56,981.24	55,483.24	59,751.25

13. Click on the **Eastern Div.** tab. Enter the following information:

	A	B	C	D	E
7		Women's Clothes	Men's Clothes	Women's Shoes	Men's Shoes
8	Cherry River Mall	$ 45,786.01	$ 48,972.16	$ 67,891.54	$ 56,987.15
9	Crosley Center	56,487.25	57,893.67	84,315.25	64,782.25
10	Jackson Square	56,871.36	59,724.18	79,504.15	84,102.25
11	TriCities Mall	98,514.25	59,735.54	55,678.14	49,605.27

14. Click on the **Women's Clothes, Men's Clothes, Women's Shoes,** and **Men's Shoes** tabs to be sure that the links are accurate. These sheets should be complete.
15. Save and print the workbook.

Use the template to enter information for February 1999.
16. Open the template **Temp 15-2**.
17. Save **Temp 15-2** as **Assig 15-2b**. Be sure to save this as a workbook document and not as a template.
18. Select all sheets and change the date in row 4 to **February 1999**. Then ungroup the sheets.
19. Click on the **Western Div.** tab. Enter the following information:

	A	B	C	D	E
7		Women's Clothes	Men's Clothes	Women's Shoes	Men's Shoes
8	Salem Mall	$ 40,588.25	$ 40,587.37	$ 45,561.25	$ 98,241.25
9	Crossroads Mall	58,742.15	66,581.25	54,785.21	56,423.14
10	Floyd's Center	36,578.15	44,587.25	25,678.24	57,983.10
11	Jefferson Square	54,872.15	168,750.25	54,891.24	25,897.44

20. Click on the **Eastern Div.** tab. Enter the following information:

	A	B	C	D	E
7		Women's Clothes	Men's Clothes	Women's Shoes	Men's Shoes
8	Cherry River Mall	$ 65,784.51	$ 49,874.17	$ 70,485.24	$ 66,870.21
9	Crosley Center	98,562.18	60,785.14	76,315.25	63,482.17
10	Jackson Square	47,985.14	75,648.00	70,562.48	75,319.58
11	TriCities Mall	58,897.15	100,257.67	60,785.25	61,547.55

21. Click on the **Women's Clothes, Men's Clothes, Women's Shoes,** and **Men's Shoes** tabs to be sure that the links are accurate. These sheets should be complete.
22. Save and print the workbook.

Assignment 15.3

DeBord Furniture Company prepares an income statement to report its quarterly income. The owner would like you to prepare the income statement and save it as a template. You will then use the template to prepare quarterly reports for a year (four reports).
1. Open Excel to a new workbook.

2. Enter the following information into the worksheet:

	A	B	C	D	E
6	Item	January	February	March	Total
7					
8	**Revenue**				
9	Sales Revenue	$294,572.38	$387,962.38	$321,953.18	
10	Other Revenue	6,489.28	3,301.73	4,385.33	
11					
12					
13					
14	**Expenses**				
15	Purchases	$162,583.63	$259,857.15	$202,395.53	
16	Advertising	26,385.27	20,378.35	24,371.23	
17	Salaries	90,283.56	98,273.57	92,586.25	
18	Other	5,529.37	4,938.25	3,357.15	

3. Save the workbook as **Assig 15-3**.
4. Insert the title as shown below. Select a WordArt style of your choice.

	A	B	C	D	E
1		DeBord Furniture Company			
2		Income Statement			
3		First Quarter, 1998			

5. Complete the worksheet.
   - Complete the formulas for revenue and expenses.
   - In cell A25, key **Budget Percentages**.
   - Copy the names of the two revenue types to the cells directly below **Budget Percentages**.
   - Copy the names of the four expense types to the cells directly below the two revenue types.
   - Complete the formulas for the **Total** column.
   - In cell A21, key **Net Income**. Complete the formulas to compute the monthly net incomes and the total net income.
   - In cells B26:D27, enter the formulas to determine the percentages of the monthly totals in relation to the quarterly totals. The percentage entered in cell B26 will be the January sales revenue divided by the total quarterly sales revenue. Because formulas will be copied, enter the quarterly totals as mixed references.
   - In cells B28:D31, enter the formulas to determine the percentages of the monthly totals in relation to the quarterly totals. The percentage entered in cell B28 is the monthly purchase divided by the total purchases for the year.

6. Format the worksheet.
   - Use macros and other formatting techniques to format the worksheet.
   - Format money amounts appropriately. Round the percentages to two decimal places.
   - Place appropriate borders.
   - Center the worksheet both horizontally and vertically. In the header include your name and the file name and in the footer include the sheet name and page number, or run the PageSetup macro.
7. Save the worksheet.
8. Print the worksheet. Include a copy that shows the formulas.
9. Save the worksheet as a template.
   - Remove the variables in the worksheet. Leave only the formatting and the formulas. You will have error messages when you delete entries in the percentages section—ignore them.
   - Save the worksheet as a template. Name it **Quarterly Report**.
10. Close the template.
11. Prepare a report for the second quarter.
    - Open the **Quarterly Report** template.
    - Change the text in cell A3 to **Second Quarter, 1998**.
    - Change the column titles to **April**, **May**, and **June**.
12. Save the worksheet as **Assig 15-3b**. Be sure to save it as a workbook and not as a template.
13. Enter the following amounts in the worksheet:

	A	B	C	D
6	Item	April	May	June
7				
8	**Revenue**			
9	Sales Revenue	$294,572.38	$387,962.38	$321,953.18
10	Other Revenue	6,489.28	3,301.73	4,385.33
12				
13				
14	**Expenses**			
15	Purchases	$162,583.63	$259,857.15	$202,395.53
16	Advertising	26,385.27	20,378.35	24,371.23
17	Salaries	90,283.56	98,273.57	92,586.25
18	Other	5,529.37	4,938.25	3,357.15

14. Save and print the worksheet.
15. Prepare a report for the third quarter.
    - Open the template **Quarterly Report**.
    - Change the title to **Third Quarter, 1998**.
    - Change the column titles to **July**, **August**, and **September**.
    - Save the worksheet as **Assig 15-3c** as a Microsoft Excel workbook.

Chapter 15   Using Templates

16. Enter the following amounts in the worksheet:

	A	B	C	D
	Item	July	August	September
6				
7				
8	**Revenue**			
9	Sales Revenue	$223,853.63	$403,985.25	$335,849.25
10	Other Revenue	3,459.72	4,039.25	4,583.10
12				
13				
14	**Expenses**			
15	Purchases	$ 89,385.36	$262,753.25	$203,958.37
16	Advertising	33,852.63	19,385.36	18,758.37
17	Salaries	88,375.35	99,283.54	99,384.26
18	Other	3,958.26	3,396.36	4,438.46

17. Save and print the worksheet.
18. Prepare a report for the fourth quarter.
    - Open the template **Quarterly Report**.
    - Change the title to **Fourth Quarter, 1998**.
    - Change the column titles to **October**, **November**, and **December**.
    - Save the worksheet as **Assig 15-3d** as a Microsoft Excel workbook.
    - Enter the following amounts in the worksheet:

	A	B	C	D
	Item	October	November	December
6				
7				
8	**Revenue**			
9	Sales Revenue	$373,258.36	$448,663.73	$364,254.73
10	Other Revenue	4,593.26	4,582.36	3,485.92
12				
13				
14	**Expenses**			
15	Purchases	$193,554.84	$299,583.83	$207,385.46
16	Advertising	29,305.73	28,573.84	20,736.46
17	Salaries	98,385.82	102,938.58	110,238.65
18	Other	36,495.82	4,382.58	3,395.64

19. Save and print the worksheet.

    Checkpoint:

Assig 15-3 worksheet	Total Revenue	$1,018,664.28
	Total January Revenue	$301,061.66
	Total January Expense	$284,781.83
	January Net Income	$16,279.83
	January Sales Revenue	29.33%
	January Other Expense	40.00%

Assignment 15.4

G & J Gardens would like to have a template created and customized for use as an invoice. You will customize the Invoice template. You will then use the template to create invoices. Because of storage space issues, save the template to the hard drive of the computer.

1. Open Excel to the **Spreadsheet Solutions** tab of the **New** dialog box and select **Invoice**. Be sure macros are enabled.
2. Click in the **Customize Your Invoice** tab.
3. Use a title of **G & J Gardens** in the space that reads **CUSTOMIZE YOUR INVOICE**. Enter the following company information: **3046 So. Pacific Avenue, Santa Barbara, CA 93110**, Phone **(805) 555-1211**, Fax **(805) 555-1222**.
4. The sales tax rate of the state must be entered. Use the California state tax rate of **6%**. The firm accepts Visa and MasterCharge credit cards. Use **$7** as the shipping charge.
5. Insert the **Flower.wmf** graphic as the logo.
6. Move back to the top of the Customize sheet. Click on the **Lock/Save Sheet** button.
7. In the **Lock/Save Sheet** dialog box, make sure that **Lock and save Template** is selected. Then click **OK**.
8. Save the template in the **Templates** subdirectory. Name it **Invoice Template**.
9. Close the template.

You will use the Invoice Template file to create specific invoices for the firm.

10. Open the **Invoice Template** document from the **Templates** subdirectory and save it as **Assig 15-4a** to your hard drive. Prepare an invoice for **Ryan Austin**. Include an invoice number by clicking on the Assign a Number button in the Invoice toolbar. Ryan's address is **3857 So. Williford Drive, Santa Barbara, CA 93102**. His telephone number is **(805) 555-7898**. Use today's date. You are the representative; enter your name in that field. The order number is **3857**. Ryan purchases **6** planters at **$35** each, **1** lilac wreath at **$27.50**, and **2** hose hangers at **$45** each.
11. Save the invoice and print it. Do not update the database.
12. Prepare an invoice for **Delores Jenkins**. Save the invoice as **Assig 15-4b**. For the invoice number, use the next number assigned. Delores lives at **4109 W. Mulberry Lane, Santa Barbara, CA 98120**. Her telephone number is **(805) 555-8273**. Use today's date. You are the representative; enter your name in that field. Delores purchases **1** good grip tool at **$23.50**, **2** hose pots at **$75** each, **2** pot hangers at **$21** each, and **4** garden lights at **$19.50** each.
13. Save the invoice and print it. Do not update the database.
14. Delete **Invoice Template** from the **Templates** subdirectory. Delete **Assig 15-4a** and **Assig 15-4b**.

Assignment 15.5

G & J Gardens would like to have a template created and customized for use as a purchase order. Use the Purchase Order template to create it. You will then use the template to create specific purchase orders.

1. Open Excel to the **Spreadsheet Solutions** tab and select **Purchase Order**. Be sure macros are enabled.
2. Click in the **Customize Your Purchase Order** tab.
3. Use a title of **G & J Gardens** in the space that reads **CUSTOMIZE YOUR INVOICE**. Enter the following company information: **3046 So. Pacific Avenue, Santa Barbara, CA 93110**, Phone **(805) 555-1211**, Fax **(805) 555-1222**.

4. The shipping address is the same as the company address. The company purchases from vendors in two states: California and Oregon. The sales tax rate for California is **6%**; Oregon has no sales tax. Click in the box by **Apply tax on local purchases only** if the box doesn't already have a check in it. The firm accepts Visa and MasterCharge credit cards.
5. Insert the **Flower.wmf** graphic as the logo.
6. Move back to the top of the Customize sheet. Click on the **Lock/Save Sheet** button.
7. In the **Lock/Save Sheet** dialog box, make sure that **Lock and save Template** is selected. Click **OK**.
8. Save the template in the **Templates** subdirectory. Name it **Purchase Order**.

You will use the Purchase Order template to create specific purchase orders for the firm.

9. Using the Purchase Order template, prepare a purchase order for **Garden Wholesalers** (the vendor). Enter the following information for the company: **3875 E. Wilshire Drive, Bakersfield, CA 96712**. The telephone number is **(805) 555-1895**. The order is for **12** planters at **$23.45** each; **6** hose hangers at **$20.25** each, **6** scrolled plant rings at **$9.75** each, and **12** pastel watering cans at **$15.05** each. (In the Units field, enter **ea** for every item.) Save the invoice as a workbook named **Assig 15-5a**. Print a copy of the invoice. Do not update the database.
10. Using the **Purchase Order** template, prepare a purchase order for **Pacific Garden Supplies**. Enter the following information for the company: **58731 Jacksonville Hwy., Medford, OR 97889**. The telephone number is **(541) 555-9382**. The order is for **10** wicker side chairs at **$137.50** each, **4** wicker arm chairs at **$162** each, and **2** wicker tables at **$225** each. Save the invoice as a workbook named **Assig 15-5b**. Print a copy of the invoice. Do not update the database.
11. Delete **Purchase Order** from the **Templates** subdirectory. Delete **Assig 15-5a** and **Assig 15-5b**.

Case Problem 15

Marvel's Dress Shop tracks its daily sales by department and salesperson. Each day Marvel creates a worksheet for this information. She also inserts the daily sales into a weekly summary worksheet. At the end of each week, she transfers the weekly totals to a monthly worksheet. A chart is included with each worksheet. It takes considerable time to complete these tasks.

Marvel has asked you to come up with a better solution for keeping track of this information. She has learned about templates, so she asks you to create some for her. Since you also know how to link information, she wants to have you prepare a template file so that she only needs to enter the daily sales and the rest of the worksheets will automatically be completed.

Plan the necessary template. This template should include worksheets for the daily sales and a worksheet that summarizes the weekly sales. For this assignment, do not include a monthly worksheet.

There are five salespeople: Huong Tran, Jane Pearson, Susan Field, Kelsey Schatz, and Candi Wilson. The clothing departments are dress clothes, casual clothes, and accessories. The cash register provides a summary of the daily sales for each salesperson.

When creating this template, prepare a WordArt title that can be used on all of the reports. Be sure to include a three-line title. Format the worksheets appropriately, using macros if you wish. Be sure your name is placed on the worksheets or in the header or the footer. A bar chart that compares the salespeople within each department is included on the daily and weekly sheets. Save the template as **Marvel's Weekly Sales**. Print a copy of the template formulas so that you and Marvel may look them over. When you are satisfied that the template is accurate, save it. Then close the template.

Open the **Marvel's Weekly Sales** template and enter the following information for Week 1. Save the workbook as **Case 15, Week 1**.

Monday's sales:

	A	B	C	D
6		Dress Clothes	Casual Clothes	Accessories
7	Huong Tran	$675.26	$351.24	$46.20
8	Jane Pearson	485.24	204.54	47.50
9	Susan Field	517.24	104.25	36.00
10	Kelsey Schatz	204.25	84.00	75.50
11	Candi Wilson			

Tuesday's sales:

	A	B	C	D
6		Dress Clothes	Casual Clothes	Accessories
7	Huong Tran			
8	Jane Pearson	578.41	441.54	87.50
9	Susan Field	685.10	389.50	100.50
10	Kelsey Schatz	448.54	507.48	47.58
11	Candi Wilson	620.07	304.58	39.50

Wednesday's sales:

	A	B	C	D
6		Dress Clothes	Casual Clothes	Accessories
7	Huong Tran	$584.25	$401.25	$61.24
8	Jane Pearson			
9	Susan Field	672.14	305.20	31.47
10	Kelsey Schatz	552.14	441.08	12.00
11	Candi Wilson	304.80	198.27	45.00

Thursday's sales:

	A	B	C	D
6		Dress Clothes	Casual Clothes	Accessories
7	Huong Tran	$698.54	$400.15	$56.52
8	Jane Pearson	598.14	357.58	78.25
9	Susan Field			
10	Kelsey Schatz	552.14	480.52	80.10
11	Candi Wilson	400.28	602.85	62.35

Friday's sales:

	A	B	C	D
6		Dress Clothes	Casual Clothes	Accessories
7	Huong Tran	$785.58	$847.25	$100.25
8	Jane Pearson	669.54	443.25	98.56
9	Susan Field	458.20	847.25	42.25
10	Kelsey Schatz			
11	Candi Wilson	907.25	681.25	51.48

Saturday's sales:

	A	B	C	D
6		Dress Clothes	Casual Clothes	Accessories
7	Huong Tran	$852.35	$1,009.68	$125.65
8	Jane Pearson	1,075.28	785.36	89.57
9	Susan Field	998.25	1,527.68	104.67
10	Kelsey Schatz	895.26	996.24	85.65
11	Candi Wilson	1,135.87	687.53	59.60

Save and print the workbook, including the weekly summary sheet.

Prepare the information for Week 2. Save this workbook as **Case 15, Week 2**. The sales information is given below.

Monday's sales:

	A	B	C	D
6		Dress Clothes	Casual Clothes	Accessories
7	Huong Tran	$485.24	$351.24	$146.20
8	Jane Pearson	675.26	285.47	36.00
9	Susan Field	517.24	574.54	47.50
10	Kelsey Schatz	204.25	284.00	75.50
11	Candi Wilson			

Tuesday's sales:

	A	B	C	D
6		Dress Clothes	Casual Clothes	Accessories
7	Huong Tran			
8	Jane Pearson	441.54	578.41	87.50
9	Susan Field	497.25	685.10	93.50
10	Kelsey Schatz	620.07	304.58	47.58
11	Candi Wilson	448.54	807.48	150.50

Wednesday's sales:

	A	B	C	D
6		Dress Clothes	Casual Clothes	Accessories
7	Huong Tran	$985.25	$401.25	$75.24
8	Jane Pearson			
9	Susan Field	592.14	941.08	72.36
10	Kelsey Schatz	324.80	498.27	75.00
11	Candi Wilson	672.14	805.20	31.47

Thursday's sales:

	A	B	C	D
6		Dress Clothes	Casual Clothes	Accessories
7	Huong Tran	$865.54	$485.95	$156.52
8	Jane Pearson	480.28	472.85	62.35
9	Susan Field			
10	Kelsey Schatz	552.14	480.52	85.10
11	Candi Wilson	558.14	357.58	78.25

Friday's sales:

	A	B	C	D
6		Dress Clothes	Casual Clothes	Accessories
7	Huong Tran	$865.54	$485.95	$156.52
8	Jane Pearson	480.28	472.85	62.35
9	Susan Field			
10	Kelsey Schatz	552.14	480.52	85.10
11	Candi Wilson	558.14	357.58	78.25

Saturday's sales:

	A	B	C	D
6		Dress Clothes	Casual Clothes	Accessories
7	Huong Tran	$1,252.35	$899.68	$25.65
8	Jane Pearson	1,135.87	687.53	59.60
9	Susan Field	895.26	1,196.24	85.65
10	Kelsey Schatz	998.25	1,527.68	104.67
11	Candi Wilson	1,075.28	955.36	89.57

Save and print a copy of the workbook.

When you submit this assignment, include the printouts for Week 1 and Week 2 as well as the formulas.

Chapter 16

Additional Worksheet Topics

Objectives

1. Use the Drawing toolbar to enhance the appearance of a worksheet.
2. Insert a map into a worksheet.
3. Complete an organizational chart.
4. Password-protect a document.
5. Lock cells within a document so they cannot be altered.
6. Find and replace text in a worksheet.
7. Place comments in a cell to explain information.

Introduction

Including maps and graphical enhancements as part of a worksheet adds interest and emphasizes certain points. Creating an organizational chart is easy, since this capability is built into Excel. Documents can be protected so changes cannot be made or so that unauthorized users cannot access information. Searching for and replacing cell contents allows you to quickly make corrections or changes in text. Comments can be included in a cell and printed with a sheet.

Note that at the end of this chapter, you may delete the Ch16 directory from your Student Data Disk.

The Drawing Toolbar

The *Drawing toolbar* contains tools that enhance the appearance of a worksheet by adding shapes and color. Only some of the tools are explained in this text, but with exploration at the computer, the others are easy to learn.

The Drawing toolbar is shown in Figure 16.1 with the buttons identified.

Figure 16.1   The Drawing Toolbar

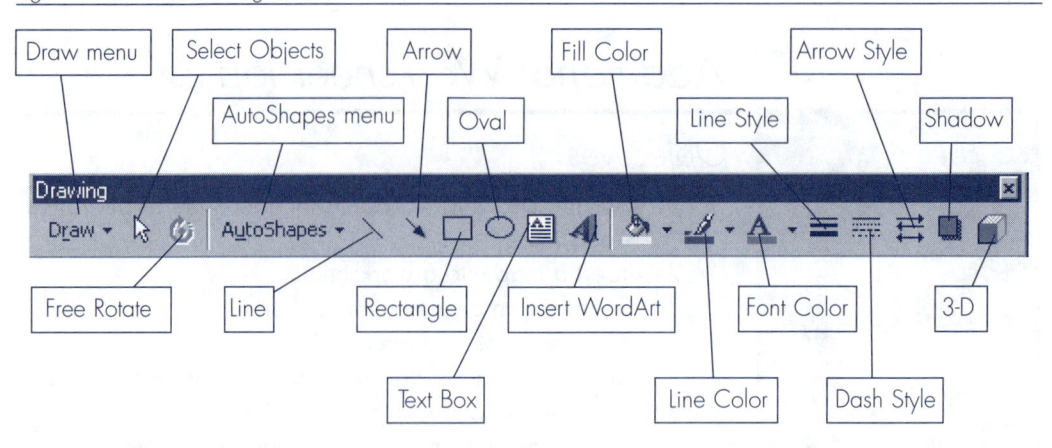

(Labels on the toolbar: Draw menu, Select Objects, AutoShapes menu, Arrow, Oval, Fill Color, Line Style, Arrow Style, Shadow, Free Rotate, Line, Rectangle, Insert WordArt, Text Box, Font Color, Line Color, Dash Style, 3-D)

Using the AutoShapes Menu

The **AutoShapes** selection of the toolbar accesses a group of shapes available to be entered into a worksheet. Simply select a shape and it will be inserted into the worksheet. Figure 16.2 shows the shapes available in the Stars and Banners submenu. An example of a starburst placed in a worksheet is also shown.

Figure 16.2   Selecting an AutoShape

Using the Line and Arrow Buttons

The *Line button* and the *Arrow button* place lines on a worksheet. When either button has been selected, click the mouse at the base of the line and drag to the top. When using the Arrow button, the top is the arrow end. The spreadsheet in Figure 16.3 shows lines drawn using the Line and Arrow buttons.

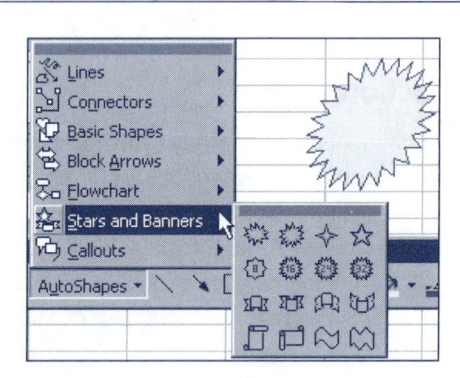

Figure 16.3   Using Lines and Arrows to Connect AutoShapes

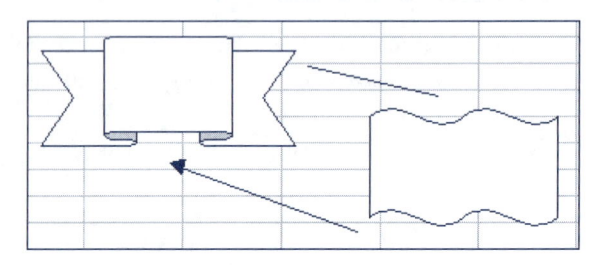

When the Line and Arrow buttons are selected, the mouse indicator takes the shape of a crosshair. To draw an arrow, position the crosshair where the line of the arrow will begin. Click on the mouse and drag to the ending spot for the arrow. The arrowhead appears when the mouse button is released.

Rectangle and Oval Shapes

The *Rectangle* ☐ and *Oval* buttons ○ add the corresponding shape into a worksheet. Click on the shape in the worksheet to make it active; handles appear at the edges of the shape, allowing it to be moved and sized. Rectangles and ovals can be displayed in color and can have text printed within them.

Using Text Boxes

Notes that describe or emphasize parts of a worksheet may be added in *text boxes*. Create a text box, then enter text. A text box may be sized or moved to a new location. Text within a text box can be formatted independently of the rest of the worksheet. Figure 16.4 shows two text boxes on a worksheet.

Figure 16.4   Text Boxes in a Worksheet

	A	B	C	D	E	F
1	Asset	Cost	Estimated Life	Trade-In	Annual Depreciation	Per Month
2	Printer	$18,500.00	5	$500.00	$3,600.00	$300.00
3	Computer	$3,500.00	3	$700.00	$933.33	$77.78
4	Monitor	$4,000.00	4	$550.00	$862.50	$71.88
5	Desk	$1,000.00	12	$100.00	$75.00	$6.25
6	Chair	$150.00	10	$25.00	$12.50	$1.01
7						
8	Total				$5,483.33	$456.92

Annual Depreciation is the amount of depreciation for the firm that is allowed each year.

Per Month is the amount of depreciation that is to be charged as an expense each month. This amount will be reflected on the Income Statement.

Click on the ***Text Box button***; the mouse indicator takes the shape of a crosshair. Click and drag until the text box is the size and shape needed. As the box is created, a solid line indicates its size and shape. A text box is shown in Figure 16.5 with the insertion point in the upper-left corner of the box.

Text automatically wraps to fit into the box. If the box is too small to display all the text, it can be sized later. Its location can also be changed.

Figure 16.5   Active Text Box

WordArt

The ***Insert WordArt button*** accesses the WordArt Gallery dialog box, used previously in this text. This button provides an additional way to quickly access WordArt for enhancing a worksheet.

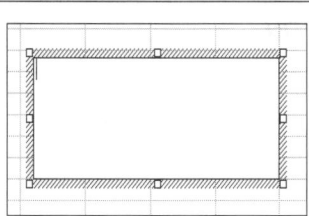

Adding Color

There are three ways to add color to a worksheet: it may be added to the background (fill) of the cell, the border line, or the text. The *Fill Color button* adds color to the background of the selected cell or graphic in a worksheet. The *Line Color button* adds color to the border surrounding the selected cell or image. The *Font Color button* has already been used on the Formatting toolbar to determine text color.

Using color in worksheets and charts adds interest and is a useful way to draw attention to a worksheet. Remember that minimal use of color often creates the most attractive worksheet.

Line and Arrow Style

Several line styles may be used in a worksheet. These include solid lines of differing widths as well as dashed lines. The style of a solid or dashed line may be selected using the *Line Style*, *Dash Style*, and *Arrow Style* buttons. When one of these buttons is selected, a style palette opens showing the styles available. The Line Style submenu is shown in Figure 16.6.

Figure 16.6   Line Styles Available

Using Boxes

The *Shadow* and *3-D buttons* open palettes with choices for the type of shadow or 3-D effect for the selected graphic. Figure 16.7 shows a worksheet with different styles of shadows and 3-D graphics.

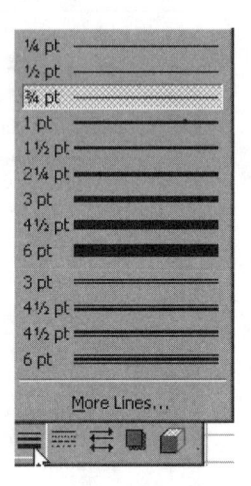

Figure 16.7   Using Shadow and 3-D Effects

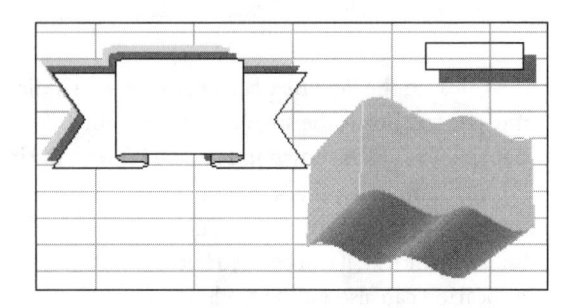

The Draw Menu

The Draw menu at the left side of the Drawing toolbar provides tools used for making changes to shapes on a worksheet. The Draw menu is shown in Figure 16.8.

The *Free Rotate button* is used to rotate a shape. When the shape is active, select the Free Rotate button. Colored handles appear and the mouse pointer takes the shape of a circular arrow. Click on a handle and drag the mouse to rotate the image.

Figure 16.9 shows an image being rotated. Notice the dotted line that indicates the placement of the object.

It is easy to create a visually powerful worksheet with the use of the drawing tools. Caution must be exercised, however, to keep the worksheet simple and attractive. Using too many enhancements will cause a worksheet to become cluttered and the reader may miss the important message of the document.

Figure 16.8   The Draw Submenu

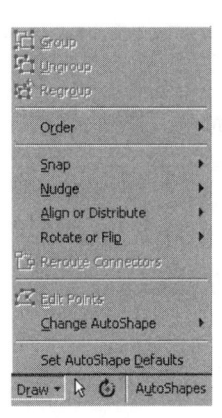

Figure 16.9   Rotating a Graphic

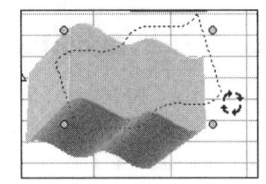

Exercise 16.1   Using Drawing Tools

You will use some of the drawing tools in a worksheet. The style of this worksheet is not intended to be a good example for an actual worksheet; it is designed to make you familiar with the Drawing toolbar. You will need to double-click on the Ch16 file in Windows Explorer to expand files before beginning the exercises in this chapter.

1   Open the **Ch16 Exer** workbook to **Sheet1**.

2   Select all sheets and run the **PageSetup** macro, or place your name and the file name in the header and the sheet name and page number in the footer and center the worksheet on the page both horizontally and vertically.

3   Save the workbook as **Exer 16**.

4   Display the **Drawing** toolbar. Using the **AutoShapes** drop-down menu, place two or three shapes in the worksheet.

5   Use the Line button to place a line between two of the shapes. Use the Arrow button to place an arrow between two of the shapes.

6   Use the Rectangle button to draw a rectangle on the sheet. Use the Arrow button to place an arrow on the worksheet.

7   Click on the Text Box button and draw a text box. Enter your name in the box. Adjust the size of the box so your name fits into it.

8 Click in the rectangle on the sheet to select it. Add a fill color and line color of your choice.

9 Click on the text box on the sheet so it is active. Highlight your name. Choose a different font color.

10 Click on the line between two shapes. When it is active, handles appear at both ends. Click on the Dash Style button and select a dash style.

11 Click on the arrow between two shapes and change its style.

12 Click on the text box containing your name to activate it; select a shadow style.

13 Click on one of the shapes on the worksheet and select a 3-D style. Color this shape (use the Fill Color button).

14 With this 3-D shape selected, click on the Free Rotate button and rotate the image.

15 Resave the workbook. Print a copy of Sheet1.

Using Maps in a Worksheet

Just as charts are used to help visualize a concept, Excel has the built-in capability to place maps in a worksheet. Excel recognizes geographical information in a worksheet. Select a range that includes geographical information. Then select the **Map button** on the Standard toolbar. In the worksheet, drag the mouse over the location where the map will be placed. The *Multiple Maps Available* dialog box, shown in Figure 16.10, opens. Maps may also be inserted in a worksheet from the Insert menu. In this example, Excel lists maps that match the geographic information in the selected cells.

Figure 16.11 shows a map inserted into a worksheet. After a map has been placed on a sheet, the Microsoft Map Control dialog box opens (Figure 16.12), providing choices for formatting the map.

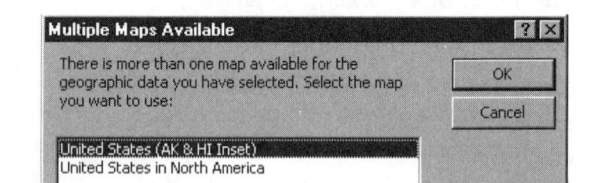

Figure 16.10   Multiple Maps Available Dialog Box

Figure 16.11   The North American Continent

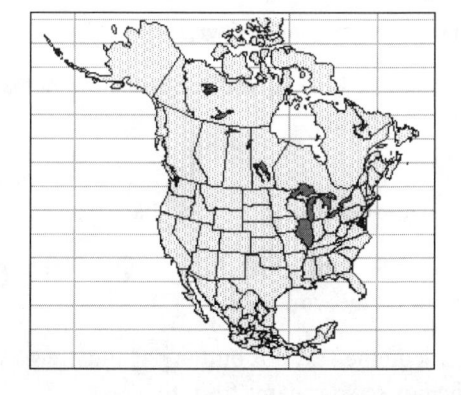

Figure 16.12   Microsoft Map Control Dialog Box

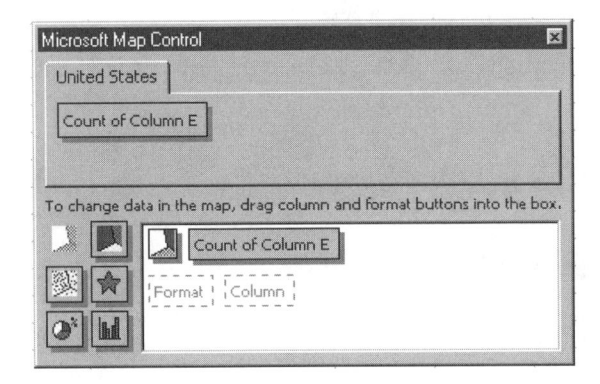

Specific maps may be selected. Double-click on the map to activate it and open the Map Features dialog box, shown in Figure 16.13. Changes to what is mapped can be made in this box; for instance countries, as well as cities and highways, may be displayed on the map.

Figure 16.13   Map Features Dialog Box

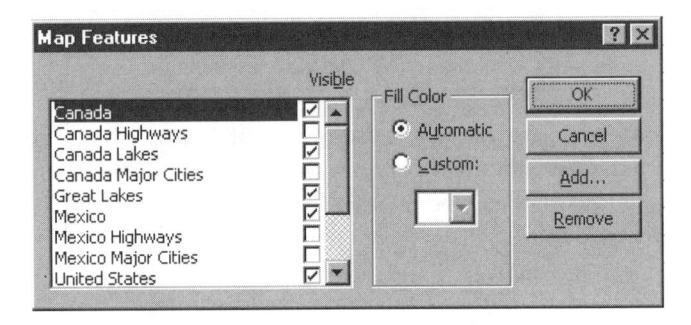

Maps provide another way to add graphics to a worksheet to increase its visual impact.

Exercise 16.2   Placing a Map in a Worksheet

You will insert a map in a worksheet.

1 Open the **Exer 16** workbook to the **Map** worksheet.

2 Highlight a range of the worksheet that contains geographic information, including the labels.

3 Click on the Map button.

4 Move the mouse below the cells containing data and draw a box where the map will be placed. Don't be too concerned about the size of the box because the map can be resized at any time.

5 The **Multiple Maps Available** dialog box opens. Select **United States (AK & HI Inset)** and click **OK**.

6 Close the **Microsoft Map Control** dialog box.

Chapter 16 Additional Worksheet Topics

7 Notice that both the states of Illinois and Missouri are highlighted on the map, identifying the locations of the homes of the employees of A–Z, Inc.

8 Double-click in the map to access the **Map Features** dialog box. Click on the box to view **US Major Cities**.

9 Click **OK**.

10 Save the workbook and print the Map worksheet.

Creating an Organizational Chart

An *organizational chart* is a visual representation of the structure of an organization. Most large companies use this type of chart to view the employees and structure of an organization. An organizational chart is shown in Figure 16.14.

Figure 16.14 Organizational Chart

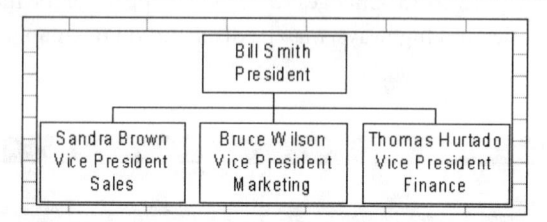

The organizational chart feature is an add-on feature of Excel. An independent software, Org Chart, has been packaged with Excel and designed to work seamlessly with Excel. When Excel was installed, this feature may not have been selected to be included in the installation.

To create an organizational chart, select Picture from the Insert menu, then select Organization Chart. The Org Chart program opens with a sample chart in place, as shown in Figure 16.15.

Figure 16.15 Creating an Organizational Chart

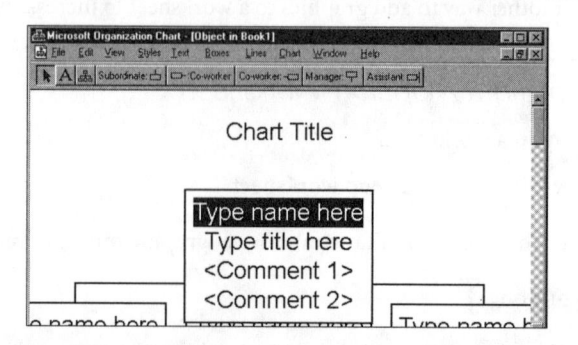

A basic chart with the first two levels of employees opens. Additional employees may be added. There is room for the name and title of each employee, as well as comments. Any field that is not filled in will not print. The unfilled field <Comment 1>, for example, will not print.

Additional formatting choices may be added, as well as graphics and color. When saving an organizational chart, be sure to save it to your Student Data Disk. It may be saved as a separate document or embedded into a workbook.

Exercise 16.3 Creating an Organizational Chart

You will create an organizational chart.

1. Open the **Exer 16** workbook to the **Org Chart** sheet.
2. From **Insert**, select **Picture**, then **Organization Chart**. The Org Chart software opens.
3. Replace **Chart Title** with **Pearson College**.
4. **Paula Pearson** is the **President**.
5. There are two **Deans**: **John Bui** of **Technical Education** and **Margaret Chapman** of **Transfer Program**.
6. Click in the third box at this level and press **Delete** on the keyboard.
7. Add yourself as a subordinate to John Bui. Your title is **Department Chair**. Click on the **Subordinate** button in the menu bar, then click on **John Bui**. In the new box that appears, enter your information.
8. From **File**, select **Exit and Return to Exer 16**.
9. Click **Yes** when a dialog box opens asking if you want to update the object. Excel returns to the worksheet.
10. Save the workbook and print the **Org Chart** worksheet.

Protecting a Worksheet

Excel spreadsheets are usually saved as *read-write documents*. This means they may be read, edited, and resaved. But because Excel spreadsheets can be shared with others, protecting them from changes can be just as important as creating an accurate worksheet in the first place. Excel provides different levels of worksheet protection.

Protecting Your Work

Clicking on the Options button in the Save dialog box opens the Save Options dialog box, shown in Figure 16.16. When selecting a *password*, use one that is easy to remember. Capital and small letters must match exactly each time a password-protected worksheet is opened. As a password is entered, only *** appears on the screen.

Figure 16.16 Save Options Dialog Box for Protecting Worksheets

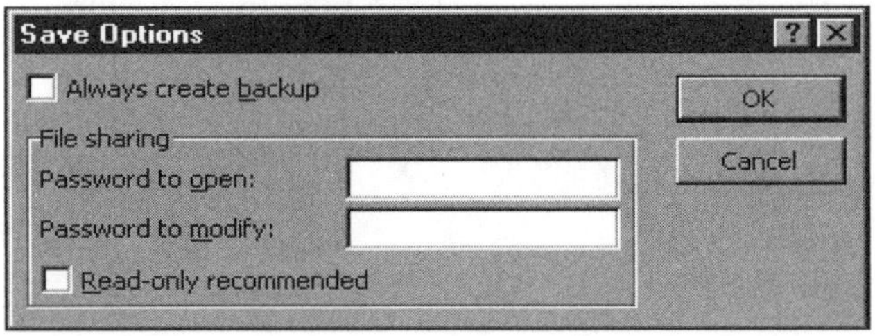

The Read-only recommended check box is used to make the document a *read-only document*; the document can be read but not changed.

After a password is entered, the *Confirm Password* dialog box opens, as shown in Figure 16.17. Reenter the password exactly as it was first entered to confirm it. Note the caution that is printed in the Confirm Password dialog box.

It is important to remember the password at all times!

Figure 16.17   Confirm Password Dialog Box

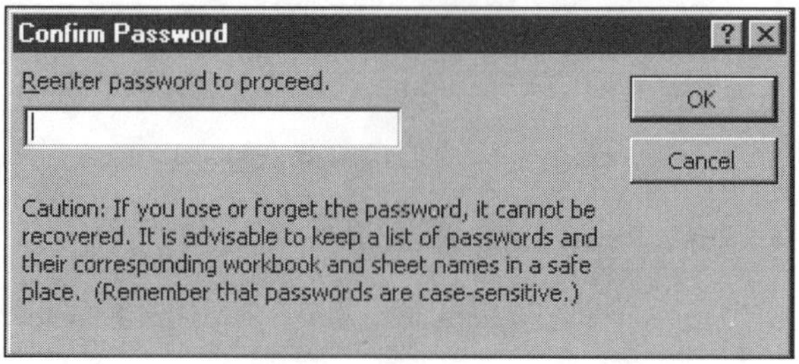

☞ *User's Tip*

Keep a list of your passwords and their corresponding workbook and sheet names in a safe place. A document that is password-protected requires the password before it can be opened or shared.

Click OK to set the password; it can be changed or removed. To remove a password, open the Save Options dialog box, highlight the password in the text box, and press Delete on the keyboard.

Protecting a Worksheet or a Workbook

Figure 16.18   Protection of Worksheets and Workbooks

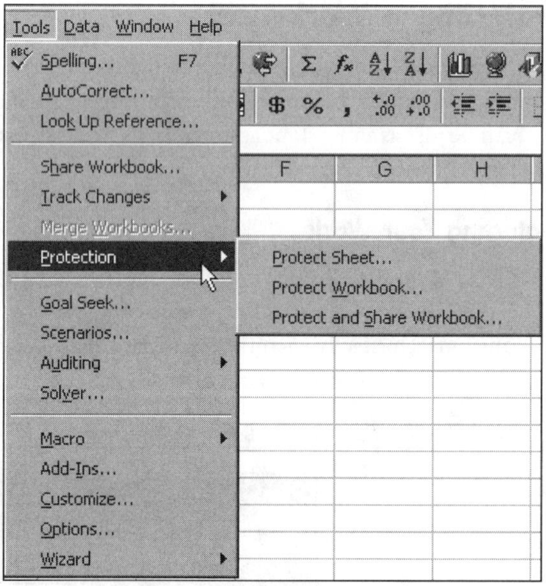

An individual sheet or an entire workbook can be protected. This prevents unwanted changes. All templates should be protected before they are saved. To do this, the sheet must first be active. From the Tools menu, select Protection then Protect Sheet, as shown in Figure 16.18.

The *Protect Sheet* dialog box opens, shown in Figure 16.19. Using a password is optional.

Three levels of protection are available: contents, objects, and scenarios. When Contents is selected, cell contents cannot be changed. When Objects is selected, graphic objects cannot be deleted, moved, edited, or resized. When Scenarios is selected, the scenario cannot be redefined.

To unprotect a sheet, activate the sheet and select Unprotect Sheet from the Protection submenu on the Tools menu.

When Protect Workbook is selected, the *Protect Workbook* dialog box opens, shown in Figure 16.20.

Protecting the structure means that worksheets cannot be moved, deleted, renamed, hidden, or unhidden. Protecting the windows prevents the windows of a workbook from being resized or repositioned.

To unprotect a workbook, select Unprotect Workbook from the Protection submenu on the Tools menu.

Figure 16.19   Protect Sheet Dialog Box

Figure 16.20   Protect Workbook Dialog Box

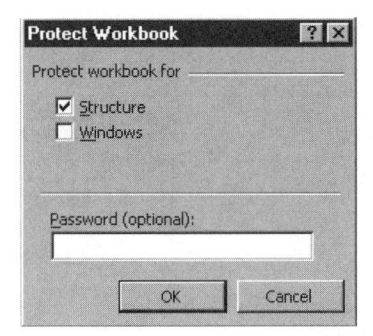

Exercise 16.4   Protecting a Worksheet

West Coast School Supplies has prepared a workbook for their sales and has linked the formulas to a summary sheet. Multiple users will access this worksheet, so it needs to be protected from change.

1 Open the workbook saved as **Ch16 Exer4**.

2 Password-protect the workbook. From **File** select **Save As**.

3 Click on the **Options** button. In the **Password to open** text box, enter your first name. **** appears instead of the letters.

4 Click **OK**. The **Confirm Password** dialog box opens. Reenter your name exactly as first entered. Remember the capital letters used. Click **OK**.

5 Name the workbook **Exer 16-4**, save it, and close it.

6 Open the protected workbook **Exer 16-4**.

7 When prompted, enter the password (your first name). Be sure capital letters are used exactly as they were when the password was assigned. Click **OK**.

8 Now remove the password. From **File**, select **Save As**. Click on the **Options** button.

9 Press `Delete` on the keyboard to remove the password. Click **OK**.

10 In the **Save As** dialog box, click **Save**. A warning box opens asking if you want to replace the original document. Select **Yes**. This replaces the protected workbook with an unprotected workbook.

11 Close the workbook.

Locking Cells of a Worksheet

Cell contents, formulas, or other parts of a worksheet can be protected from change; unprotected parts can still be changed. For instance, protecting formulas allows changes to the data, but the accuracy of the worksheet is still maintained because the formulas remain accurate. Cells, graphics, or window shapes can also be protected from change. In templates, locking permanent cells is important so the basic structure of the sheet cannot be changed.

To protect cells in a worksheet, highlight the cells to be protected. Then select the Cells command from the Format menu. In the Format Cells dialog box, click on the Protection tab, shown in Figure 16.21. Decide if cells are to be *locked* or *hidden cells*. Locking a cell prevents its contents from being changed. Hiding a cell prevents the formula from being displayed in the formula bar; only the results are displayed. Cells can also be unlocked or unhidden in this dialog box.

If cells and objects are to be password-protected, use the Protect Sheet dialog box. When cells or objects are password protected, changes cannot be made unless the password is used.

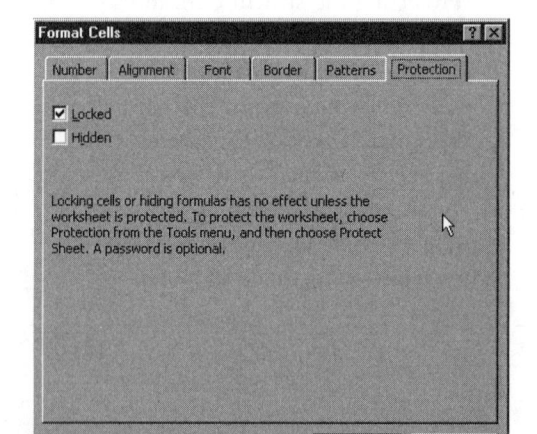

Figure 16.21 Protection Tab of Format Cells Dialog Box

Once a range is protected, the sheet or workbook needs to be protected by using the proper commands in the Tools menu.

Exercise 16.5 Protecting Cells and Worksheets

The management of West Coast School Supplies wants to have a workbook available to multiple users, but wants to protect the formulas and other data from change. You will work with several different methods of protecting worksheets and individual cells within a worksheet.

Protect the Summary sheet.

1 Open workbook **Exer 16-4** and save it as **Exer 16-5**. Click in the **Summary** tab of the workbook.

2. From **Tools**, select **Protection**, then choose **Protect Sheet**.

3. Enter your first name as the password. Be sure all boxes are checked (**Contents**, **Objects**, and **Scenarios**). Click **OK**.

4. Confirm the password in the **Confirm Password** dialog box. Click **OK**.

5. Change **Portland** to **Seattle**. A warning box opens telling you this is a locked cell and cannot be changed. Click **OK**.

6. Click in the **Portland** tab. Change **Mon** to **Monday**. This sheet is not locked and changes can be made.

Unprotect the Summary sheet.

7. Click in the **Summary** tab. From **Tools**, select **Protection**, then **Unprotect Sheet**.

8. Enter the password. Click **OK**.

Protect individual cells in a worksheet.

9. Click in the **Portland** tab.

10. Highlight the column and row labels. (Remember, use **Ctrl** to highlight nonadjacent ranges.)

11. From **Format**, select **Cells**. Click in the **Protection** tab. Click in the box by **Locked** to select it. Click **OK**.

12. Highlight the range B10:D10. From **Format**, select **Cells**. Click in the **Protection** tab. Click in the boxes by **Locked** and **Hidden** to select them. Then click **OK**.

13. From the **Tools** menu, select **Protection** then choose **Protect Sheet**. Enter your first name as the password and confirm it.

14. In the **Portland** sheet, change **Widgets** to **Wookers**. Since it is locked, you cannot make a change. Click **OK**.

15. Click in cell B10. Because the formula is hidden, you cannot see it to make changes.

16. Close the workbook without saving changes.

Additional Editing Techniques

Finding and Replacing Text and Data

There are times when some text must be changed in the original worksheet. Perhaps when the worksheet was edited, it was decided to change terminology from "money" to "finance." Because the term "money" is used throughout the worksheet, it is difficult to scroll through the worksheet and find every place it is used. Excel provides a method of finding and then replacing text or data through the Find and Replace commands.

To find a specific cell, select the *Find command* from the Edit menu; the Find dialog box opens, shown in Figure 16.22.

Figure 16.22   Find Dialog Box

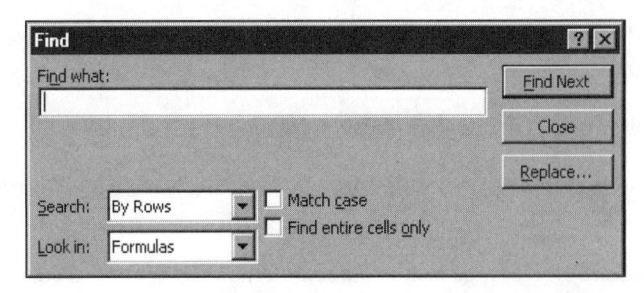

The dialog box opens with the cursor in the Find what box. Key the text or data that is to be located. Click in the check box by Match case to exactly match uppercase and lowercase letters. Excel will then search the worksheet for the text and stop when a match is found. Select Find entire cells only when the entire cell contents must match. If this option is not selected, Excel will find all cells that contain the text as part of the cell contents. For instance, if searching for "B4," select Find entire cells only; cells containing only "B4" are found. When this box is not selected, Excel finds all occurrences of "B4" in any cell, such as "B44" or "AB403." Formulas that contain a reference to B4 will also be located.

The Search area of the dialog box uses a drop-down list to select to search by rows or columns. Searching By Rows searches the first row, then the second, then the third, etc. Searching By Columns searches column A, then column B, etc. The Look in area provides a drop-down list that suggests types of searches—for the formula, the value, or any notes.

Power Users

The keyboard command to open the Find dialog box is **Ctrl**+**F**.

To find and then replace a character or string of characters, select the *Replace command* from the Edit menu. The Replace dialog box opens, shown in Figure 16.23.

Figure 16.23   Replace Dialog Box

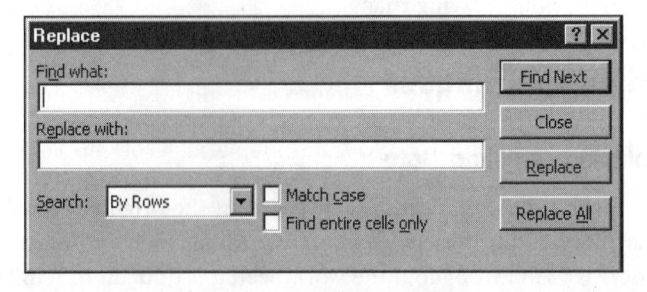

First identify the character or characters to be located. Then indicate the replacement of those characters. If "money" is to be replaced with "finance," key "money" in the Find what text box and "finance" in the Replace with text box.

There are several buttons in the Replace dialog box that provide additional choices. The *Replace All button* replaces every occurrence of the text. The Replace button replaces only the highlighted cell; Find Next matches the next occurrence, which may then be replaced.

While Replace All is faster than looking for individual matches, care must be taken. For instance, when replacing B1 with B3, Excel will replace all instances of B1 with B3. If a cell reference is made to cell B13, Excel will match the B1 of B13 and replace it, changing the reference to cell B33—a reference that should not be changed. An error like this could be very difficult to trace!

Power Users

The keyboard command to open the Replace dialog box is **Ctrl**+**H**.

Using the Find and Replace commands is helpful in making changes in a worksheet and locating a specific cell. These commands are particularly useful when working with large worksheets.

Exercise 16.6 Using Find and Replace

You will use the Find command to find information in a worksheet. You will also replace cell contents.

1 Open workbook **Exer 16**. Click in the **Exer 16-6** tab.

Use the Find command.

2 From the **Edit** menu, select **Find**. In the **Find what** text box, key **Prepared**. Click on **Find Next**.

3 Cell A31 is selected. Click on **Close** to close the **Find** dialog box. Replace **Student's Name** with your name.

Go to cell A1.

4 From **Edit** select **Go To**. Key **A1**. Click **OK**. Cell A1 is active.

This report will be reformatted for another district. Use Replace to make these changes.

5 From **Edit** select **Replace**. In the **Find what** box, key **Oregon**. Press **Tab**.

6 In the **Replace with** box, key **Nebraska**. Click on **Find Next**. The first occurrence of **Oregon** is highlighted. (You may need to move the dialog box so you can see the worksheet better.)

7 Click on **Replace**. The next occurrence of **Oregon** is highlighted. Click on **Replace**.

8 Repeat until all occurrences of **Oregon** have been replaced. Close the **Replace** dialog box and go to cell A1.

9 From **Edit** select **Replace**. In the **Find what** box, key **Washington**. Press **Tab**.

10 In the **Replace with** box, key **Kansas**. Click on **Replace All**. Every time **Washington** appears in the workbook it has been replaced with **Kansas**.

11 Replace **Idaho** with **South Dakota** and **Montana** with **Oklahoma**.

12 Save and print the worksheet.

Using Comments

Comments can be added to any cell in a workbook to document entries, explain calculations, and provide reminders. A comment can be entered either as text or a sound clip. The ability to include comments is especially helpful when workbooks are shared by several users.

To add a comment to a cell, click in the cell and select Comment from the Insert menu. A text box opens. Enter the text, then click outside the box to hide the comment.

A cell that contains a comment is marked with a small red triangle in the upper-right corner of the cell. To read the note, move the mouse to this red triangle; the comment is displayed, as shown in Figure 16.24, or the sound clip is played.

Figure 16.24 Displaying a Comment

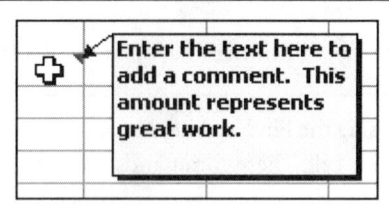

To hide or display comments and their red indicators, access the Options dialog box from the Tools menu. Select the View tab and then select None in the Comments section, shown in Figure 16.25.

Figure 16.25 Displaying Comment Indicators

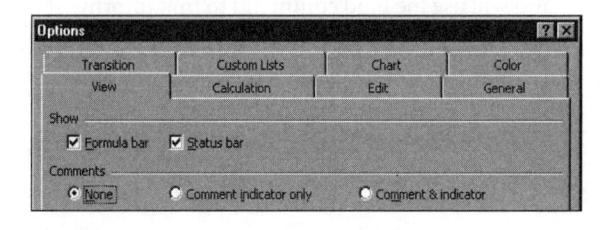

Comments may also be printed. In the Sheet tab of the Page Setup dialog box, select the option to print comments either at the end of the sheet or as they are displayed on sheet.

Comments can be sound clips if the proper recording software and a microphone area available to record and save them. When the mouse is placed over a sound clip comment, the recording plays back.

Sound recordings take a great deal of disk space and should be used sparingly.

Exercise 16.7   Adding Cell Comments

Kendall & Associates is located in several shopping malls in the area. They prepare analysis of their sales by location. They have completed a worksheet and have added cell notes to explain some of the data. You will view the comments, create a comment, and print the comments with the worksheet.

1 In the **Exer 16** workbook, select sheet **Exer 16-7**.

Read cell comments.

2 The red triangle in cell B7 indicates a cell comment. Move the mouse to the cell (do not click in the cell) to read the comment.

3 Read the comment in cell D8.

Add a comment.

4 Select cell E11. Then from **Insert**, select **Comment**.

5 In the comment box, key **This is a 15% increase over last year**. Click in a different cell.

6 Hover the mouse over cell E11 to read the comment.

Print the worksheet and the comments.

7 In the **Page Setup** dialog box, select the **Sheet** tab. Select to print the comments as they are displayed on the sheet. Then click on the **Print** button and print the worksheet.

8 Save the workbook.

Summary

- The Drawing toolbar contains tools that enhance a worksheet. Such enhancements include shapes, color, WordArt, and boxes.
- The AutoShapes menu is used to add lines, shapes, stars, banners, and other shapes to a worksheet.
- Lines and arrows may be added to a worksheet to add emphasis and point out special cells or areas of reference.
- Information may be added to a worksheet in the form of a text box.
- A text box may be resized and moved to any location on a worksheet.
- The text in a text box may be formatted independently.
- The Insert WordArt button is available on the Drawing toolbar.
- Color may be added to the background, borders, or text of a cell or graphic. Color tools are available in the Drawing toolbar.
- Shadow and 3-D boxes can be inserted into a worksheet.
- Graphic objects may be rotated in a worksheet. First select the object, then click on the Free Rotate button. Click in a handle of the active graphic and rotate its orientation.
- The Map button places maps in a worksheet. There are many maps to choose from.
- Excel will place an appropriate map in a worksheet, based on the locations included in the worksheet. Specific maps may also be selected.
- Organizational charts can be created in Excel. They may be saved as a separate document or embedded into a worksheet.
- A workbook may be protected by using a password. A password must be entered before opening the workbook.
- Protect a workbook by accessing the Protection submenu from Tools. Then select Protect Workbook.
- A password is a combination of letters, numbers, and spaces used to protect a document from changes.
- A read-only document may be opened; changes are not allowed.
- Data or text can be located quickly by using the Find command.
- Data or text can be changed throughout a worksheet by using the Replace command.
- A comment is used to provide additional information about a cell.
- The comment indicator is a red triangle that displays in the upper-right corner of a cell and indicates that the cell contains a comment.

Important Terminology

3-D button	hidden cells	Protect Sheet
Arrow button	Insert WordArt button	Protect Workbook
Arrow Style	Line button	read-only document
AutoShapes	Line Color button	read-write documents
comments	Line Style	Rectangle
Confirm Password	locked cells	Replace command
Dash Style	Map button	Replace All button
Drawing toolbar	Multiple Maps Available	Shadow
Fill Color button	organizational chart	Shadow button
Find command	Oval	text boxes
Font Color button	password	Text Box button
Free Rotate button		

Buttons to Know

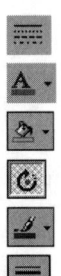

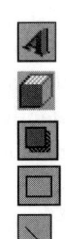

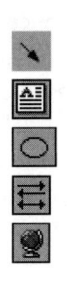

Study Questions

True-False

Place a T in the space if the statement is true; place an F if the statement is false.

_____ 1. The Chart toolbar has buttons on it that add shapes and color to a worksheet.
_____ 2. The AutoShapes menu adds a shadow to an existing text box.
_____ 3. Adding text to a worksheet can be done by inserting a text box.
_____ 4. Text in a text box can be formatted independently of the rest of the worksheet.
_____ 5. A text box cannot be sized or moved.
_____ 6. To adjust the size of a text box, click in a handle of the box and drag to a new size.
_____ 7. To move a text box, click on the handle of the box and drag the box to a new location.
_____ 8. An arrow must be inserted carefully because it cannot be resized, relocated, or removed.
_____ 9. The line style for lines and arrows is always a solid line.
_____ 10. Using the 3-D button places a shadow behind a graphic object.
_____ 11. To change the angle of a shape on a worksheet, use the Turn button.
_____ 12. A map of the United States may be inserted into a worksheet.
_____ 13. The only maps available in Excel are those of the North American continent.

_____ 14. An organizational chart must be inserted into an existing worksheet and is created by increasing the size of the cells.
_____ 15. When a cell is hidden, the formula will not display.
_____ 16. When a cell is locked, it is not visible on a worksheet.
_____ 17. A worksheet may be protected so that it can be accessed only with a password.
_____ 18. When setting a password, it must be confirmed by entering it a second time.
_____ 19. It is possible to search for a specific formula in a worksheet.
_____ 20. If a search is made for references to cell B3 with no check boxes selected, cells containing references to B37 and B302 will be located.
_____ 21. Adding a cell comment provides additional information about specific data in a worksheet.

Fill-In

Place the word in the space that correctly completes the statement.
1. Adding a(n) _____ to a worksheet provides additional information about the data in the worksheet.
2. To change the angle of a graphic, use the _____ button.
3. The Text Box button can be accessed on the _____ toolbar.
4. The _____ toolbar has buttons that change the color of the background, line, and text of a selected cell or graphic.
5. The arrow tool is on the _____ toolbar.
6. The Protect Sheet dialog box is accessed from the _____ menu.
7. Changing all occurrences of a specified text can be done using the _____ command.

Assignments

After completion of Chapter 16, you may delete the Ch16 folder from your Student Data Disk.

Assignment 16.1

The monthly sales report for Ace Paper Supplies needs correction and formatting. You will add graphics and color for attractiveness.
1. Open workbook **Ch16 As1** and save it as **Assig 16-1**.
2. Run the **PageSetup** macro. If you have not completed the macros in this text, format the sheet so it is centered horizontally and vertically. In the header include your name and the file name and in the footer include the sheet name and page number.
3. Correct entries using the Replace command.
   - Replace all occurrences of **Plates** with **Paper Plates**.
   - Replace all occurrences of **Napkins** with **Paper Napkins**.
   - Adjust column widths, if needed.
4. Format the worksheet.
   - Use WordArt to enter the company name, Ace Paper Supplies, in row 1. Adjust the size of the WordArt and the row for attractive placement. Add a 3-D effect.
   - Use a matching color for the rest of the title and the column labels.

5. Add text boxes and format the text.
   - Click the Text Box button and place a text box at the bottom of the worksheet.
   - In the text box, key **% Total Sales is Sales of each item divided by the total sales**. Format **% Total Sales** in bold. Adjust the size and location of the text box.
   - Place another text box to the right of the first.
   - Key **% Total End is the amount of ending inventory for each item divided by the total ending inventory**. Format **% Total End** in bold. Adjust the size and location of the text box.
   - Format the text in a color that complements the WordArt title.
   - Use a shadow box for the text boxes. Format both boxes for the same shadow style.
6. Add arrows for emphasis.
   - Click the Arrow button.
   - Draw an arrow from the top center of the box that reads **% Total Sales** to the bottom of the column showing the **% Total Sales** in column B.
   - Place another arrow from the text box for **% Total End** to the bottom of the column showing **% Total End**.
   - Format the arrow style and line style as you wish.
7. Enter a comment in cell A7 that reads **Calendars are seasonal and need to be sold in three months of the year**.
8. Add a blue ribbon at the bottom of the sheet.
   - Below the cells containing data, insert and center a banner of your choice. Size it so it is an appropriate size for the sheet.
   - Use a blue fill color for the ribbon.
   - Place a text box in the ribbon. In the box, key **Blue Ribbon Month**.
   - Select the text box and format the text in bold, with black as the font color, and centered. If necessary, resize the banner and/or text box so all the text is visible.
   - Be sure the text box is selected. Select a fill color of blue, matching the rest of the ribbon.
9. Save the workbook. Print the worksheet with the comments displayed at the end.

Assignment 16.2

You will protect the quarterly sales report for S & S Office Supplies. You will also hide formulas in the worksheet.

1. Open workbook **Ch16 As2**.
2. Place your name in cell A14.
3. Save the workbook as **Assig 16-2**.
4. Protect the worksheet.
   - From **Tools** select **Protection** then choose **Protect Sheet**.
   - Enter a password and confirm it.
5. Change **District A** to **Eastern**. Since the worksheet is protected, no changes can be made.
6. Open the workbook **Ch16 As2** again, and save it as **Assig 16-2b**.
7. Hide the formulas.
   - Highlight the cells containing formulas.
   - In the **Format** menu, select **Cells**; choose the **Protection** tab in the **Format Cells** dialog box. Select **Locked** and **Hidden**.

- In the worksheet, notice that the formulas are still visible. Formulas are hidden only after a sheet is protected.
8. Password-protect the worksheet. Now look at the cells containing formulas and note that the formulas do not appear in the formula bar.
9. Save and print the worksheet. Then print a copy showing the formulas used.

Assignment 16.3

The quarterly sales report for New England School Supplies is protected. However, cell notes and a text box need to be added. You will unprotect the worksheet, make the changes, and protect the worksheet again.

1. Open workbook **Ch16 As3** and save it as **Assig 16-3**.
2. Below the cells containing data, try to add a text box. Because the workbook is protected, you cannot make changes.
3. Unprotect the worksheet.
   - From **Tools** select **Protection**, then choose **Unprotect Sheet**.
   - The password is **student** (all lowercase letters).
4. Add a text box or other shape that reads **Great First Quarter**. Format it in an eye-catching design.
5. Add comments.
   - For **Paper Products** in **New Hampshire**, enter a comment that reads **Record snowfall for the month**.
   - For **Printer Supplies** in **Massachusetts**, enter a comment that reads **Vendor back-ordered all printer supplies**.
6. Run the **PageSetup** macro, or format the worksheet so it is centered vertically and horizontally on the page. In the header include your name and the sheet name and in the footer include the file name and page number.
7. Protect the workbook again, using the same password (**student**).
8. Save and print the workbook with the comments displayed.

Assignment 16.4

Acme Hardware International has a completed workbook for international sales. However, they have asked you to include maps with the books.

1. Open workbook **Ch16 As4** and save it as **Assig 16-4**.
2. Group all sheets. Then, in the space to the right of the three-line title, use the Map button to enter a map of the world.
3. Ungroup the sheets.
4. At the bottom of each of the sheets, place the map of the area discussed. For instance, place the map of Australia at the bottom of the Australia sheet. You will want to save often; maps are large, requiring large amounts of memory resources.

Note: Maps require large amounts of memory resources. You may be unable to complete them with the amount of memory on your computer. If so, print each worksheet separately, adding maps to the worksheets one at a time.

5. Place your name in the header or footer.
6. Save and print the workbook.

Case Problem 16

Austin's Retailers has decided to report daily sales electronically. You have been asked to design a report that can be completed on a computer. This form will be accessed by all branches and employees in the company. It needs to have explanations within the report and be protected from changes.

Austin's Retailers sells computer supplies. The daily report needs to include the sales for each department, any returns, and the total sales for the entire branch. Include a place for the branch name, the date of the report, each department and its returns, and the branch total. The departments within Austin's are Hardware, Software, and Accessories.

Format the worksheet so it is attractive and eye-catching. While this document will be used only within the firm, it should look professional. If Chapter 15 has been completed, save this as a template and be sure the data is appropriately protected. You may want to hide formulas. Save the template as **Case 16 Temp**. If Chapter 15 has not been completed, save the worksheet in the usual way.

When you have completed and printed the form, submit it along with all supporting documentation, which includes a copy showing the formulas used and any comments.

Using the document, complete yesterday's sales information for the following two branches:

Branch	Hardware Sales	Hardware Returns	Software Sales	Software Returns	Accessory Sales	Accessory Returns
Lane County	$12,038	$785	$3,857	$367	$1,029	$43
Blair County	$20,395	$1,029	$5,873	$229	$1,968	$128

Chapter 17

Excel and the Internet

Objectives

1. Become familiar with the Internet and the way information is organized.
2. Complete Web queries and place retrieved data into Excel spreadsheets.
3. Create a Web page.

Introduction

The Internet, which includes the World Wide Web, has become a popular communication tool. With it, millions of users research information, make travel arrangements, and keep current with the news. These are just a few of the many uses of the Internet.

An intranet is a large, closed network used within a company to store Web pages. An intranet is usually accessible only to employees within the company.

Excel provides direct links to Web sites that offer additional information about Excel and other software components. Information from the Internet can be directly placed into an Excel spreadsheet.

The World Wide Web

What Is the World Wide Web?

The *World Wide Web*, sometimes called the *Web* or abbreviated *WWW*, is a structure of documents that are connected electronically through the Internet. The *Internet* is a very large computer network that links smaller networks and individual computers electronically. An *intranet* is a closed network accessible only to authorized users, usually the employees of a company.

Each document on the Web is called a *Web page*. Web pages store different types of information including text, graphics, sound clips, animation, and video clips. Web pages usually contain links to other pages, helping users navigate the Web. These *links*, short for *hyperlinks*, connect to other documents that contain related information. Each Web page uses a specific address, called a *URL* (*Uniform Resource Locator*). Hyperlinks use URLs to make connections.

In order to connect to the Web, a *browser* program is required. A Web browser usually includes an e-mail package, providing further online communication. *Microsoft Internet Explorer* is a browser program that is included in the Microsoft Office package.

Navigating the Web

The Web contains literally millions of Web pages. Locating information and moving around on the Web can be difficult without the help of a browser. Microsoft Internet Explorer is defaulted to open to the Microsoft home page, shown in Figure 17.1. You may select any Web page or no page to open when you access your browser. Pages change often on the Web, so the look today may be different than it was yesterday.

Web pages have a structure similar to other Windows documents. A menu bar is located across the top of the screen, providing access to the commands used in the application. Below the menu bar is a toolbar that contains buttons for frequently used commands.

Figure 17.1 The Microsoft Home Page

An address (the URL) is located in a text box just below the toolbar. Addresses usually begin with http://. *HTTP* stands for *Hypertext Transfer Protocol* and refers to the way information is transmitted on the Web.

A Web page can provide links to other pages on the Web. In the Microsoft home page shown above, links are presented as both text and graphics (pictures). When the mouse pointer is placed over a link, its shape changes to a hand with a pointing finger. A picture link and a text link are shown in Figure 17.2.

Figure 17.2 Graphic and Text Web Links

Picture Link   Text Link

Clicking on a link carries out the same action as keying the URL of a Web page. When you know a Web address, you can key it into the Address box and press Enter to go to that page, also called a *site*. Likewise, clicking on a link moves you to the page whose address is defined in the link. In either case, you may return to a previous page by clicking the Back button on the toolbar.

The Web is becoming an increasingly important tool for business. Critical information may be located on the Web. Many companies place their home pages on the Web for advertising or sales purposes. A *home page* is generally the first page of a company's or individual's Web site. Most airlines place their schedule and rate information on the Web, allowing reservations to be made from the Web. Current stock prices are available. The amount of data and services on the Web continues to grow each day, making the information available nearly limitless.

Exercise 17.1 Exploring the World Wide Web

You will access the World Wide Web and explore a few sites.

Note: Before completing the exercises and assignments in this chapter, you will need to expand the Chapter 17 files on your Student Data Disk. In Windows Explorer, locate the zipped Ch17 file and double-click on it. When all the files have been expanded, you may open them in Excel.

1. Access the World Wide Web. Your instructor will provide the specific instructions for your computer.

2. Access the Microsoft home page. If your browser does not automatically open to this page, enter the URL **http://home.microsoft.com** in the **Address** section and press **Enter**. You may need to wait for a few seconds while the page is being accessed. How fast this happens depends on the speed of your system or modem and the traffic on the Internet.

3. When the home page appearrs, use the scroll bars to scroll through it. Move your mouse across this home page to find a link. Click the mouse on any link. A new, related page will open.

4. In the toolbar, click on the **Back** button to return to the Microsoft home page.

5. Enter the address **http://www.whitehouse.gov** to access the White House's home page. Spend a few minutes looking at this home page and connecting to the links.

6. Enter the URL to go to the Excel learning page hosted by Microsoft, **http://microsoft.com/excel/learn.htm**. If you have questions about Excel, this is a place to access helpful information.

7. Stock quotes are available through several different locations on the Web. Enter the URL **http://www.stockfind.newsalert.com**.

8. Continue to explore the Web if you have time. To exit the Web, select **Close** from the **File** menu.

Querying the Web

Accessing the Web from Excel

Excel provides tools that link directly to the World Wide Web. From the Help menu, select *Microsoft on the Web*. A submenu opens, shown in Figure 17.3, showing a list of Web sites, mostly those hosted by Microsoft.

When a Web page is selected, the browser opens and the chosen Web site is accessed.

Figure 17.3 Accessing Microsoft on the Web

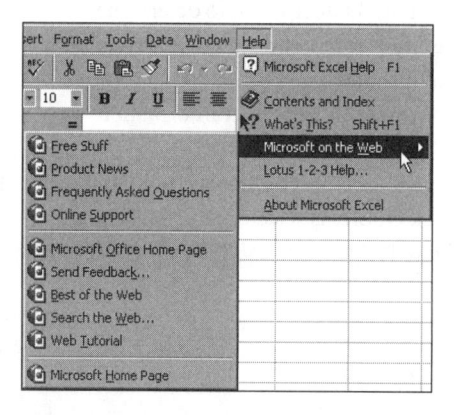

Querying

A benefit of using Excel for Office 97 is the capability to retrieve information from the Web and place it directly into an Excel spreadsheet using Web queries. A *Web query* returns data from the Web, called *external data*, and enters it directly into a worksheet. Excel has four built-in query sites; three of these relate to investment and stock market activities. Access the Web queries from the Data menu. Select Get External Data, then Run Web Query, as shown in Figure 17.4.

The *Run Query dialog box* opens, shown in Figure 17.5, with the built-in queries listed. Three of these are related to stock quotes. The fourth, Get More Web Queries, is a Web site providing additional Web queries for use with Excel. These queries may be downloaded and saved as part of the Excel program. *Downloading* is the process of saving information from an electronic source such as the Internet to your computer. The downloaded queries then become accessible in the Run Query dialog box.

Detailed Stock Quote by PC Quote, Inc provides detailed information about a single stock. Dow Jones Stocks by PC Quote, Inc provides data about the 30 stocks used to determine the Dow Jones Industrial Average. Multiple Stock Quotes by PC Quote, Inc provides current price information for up to 20 selected stocks.

Figure 17.4   Running a Web Query

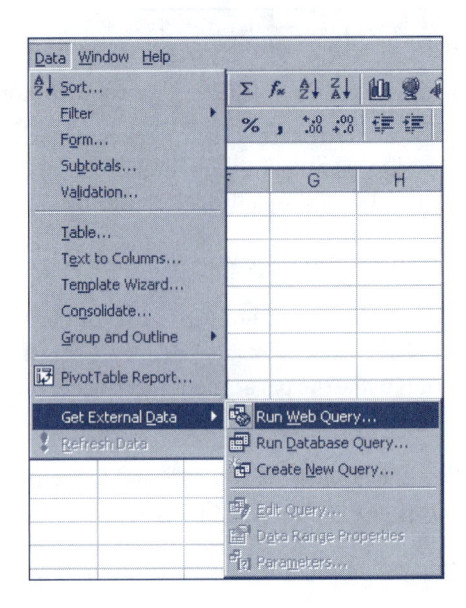

Figure 17.5   Run Query Dialog Box

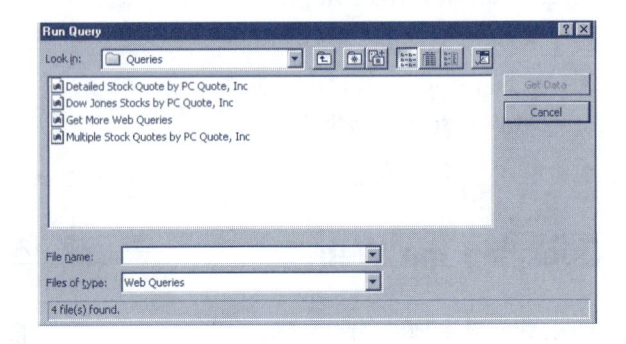

Multiple Stock Quotes is used to illustrate the query feature in the following figures. When Multiple Stock Quotes is selected, the Returning External Data to Microsoft Excel dialog box opens, shown in Figure 17.6.

Data may be inserted in the open Excel worksheet or in a new one. The selected cell in the worksheet is used as the starting place for the data, but this can be changed.

Click OK to open the Enter Parameter Value dialog box, shown in Figure 17.7. This is where specific stock symbols will be entered; up to 20 may be entered in one query. The dialog box is shown in Figure 17.7 with five stock quotes requested. The symbols are for General Motors, Disney, IBM, Coca Cola, and Delta Airlines. In order to access the data, the *stock symbol*, a two- to five-letter abbreviation, must be known.

The Collapse Dialog button allows the symbols to be selected from a worksheet rather than keyed in. When the symbols are entered, click OK; the data is now accessed from the Internet. It may take several seconds to locate the data on the Internet and place it into your worksheet. When the query is complete, a report showing the current stock quotes is entered into the worksheet, as shown in Figure 17.8.

Figure 17.6 Returning External Data to Microsoft Excel Dialog Box

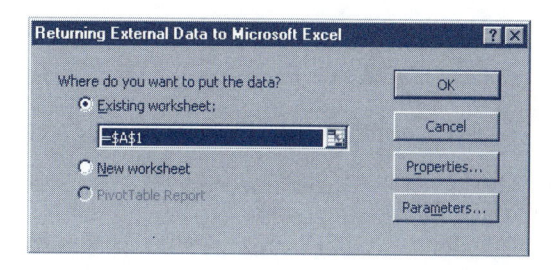

Figure 17.7 Enter Parameter Value Dialog Box

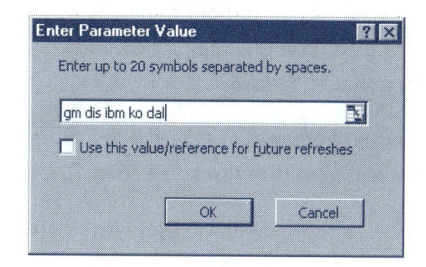

Figure 17.8 Inserting Stock Quotes from the Internet into a Worksheet

This report is entered as a filtered database. The names of the stocks are shown in blue text, indicating that they are hyperlinks. Click on its name to get detailed information about an individual stock.

Exercise 17.2 Querying the Web

You will query the Web to find the latest stock prices on a group of stocks.

1   Open the **Ch 17 Exer** workbook and save it as **Exer 17**.

2   Replace **Student's Name** with your name and enter today's date in cell A3.

3   Click in cell C3 to make it active.

4   From **Data**, select **Get External Data**, then **Run Web Query**.

5   In the **Run Query** dialog box, select **Multiple Stock Quotes by PC Quote, Inc**. Click on **Get Data**.

6   In the **Return External Data to Microsoft Excel** dialog box, check to be sure the range reads **=$C$3**. If it does not, collapse the dialog box and click in cell C3. Be sure the external data will be placed in the existing sheet. Click **OK**.

7   In the **Enter Parameter Value** dialog box, click on the Collapse Dialog button. Scroll through the stock symbols used in the worksheet (B7:B11). Click on the Expand Dialog button.

8   Symbols are entered as a range. Check the box to **Use this value for future refreshes**. Click **OK**.

9   Excel accesses your request and enters the information into the worksheet. Format the information attractively on the page. Print a copy of the worksheet.

10 Save the workbook.

Finding Stock Symbols

The stock symbols used by PC Quote, Inc., are two to five letters long and must be used to download stock information. They are accessed from the URL http://www.pcquote.com/cgi-bin/namelook.exe. The Web page opens with a place to enter the full name of a stock, as shown in Figure 17.9.

Figure 17.9   Finding a Stock Symbol

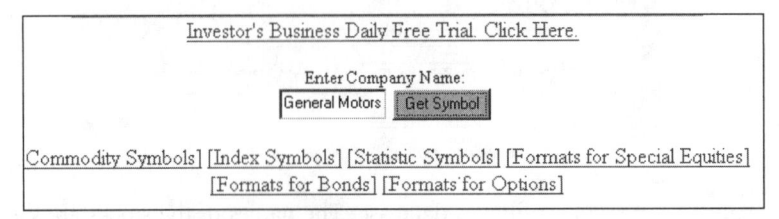

Enter a stock name and click on Get Symbol to access the abbreviation. PC Quote, Inc., moves to an alphabetic listing of the stocks that begin with this name. The listing for General Motors is shown in Figure 17.10. The symbol, GM, is provided in the list.

Figure 17.10 Listing of Stock Symbols

Symbol	Company Name	Exchange
GM	GENERAL MOTORS	New York
GMpD	GENERAL MOTORS CORP	New York
GMpG	GENERAL MOTORS CORP	New York
GMpQ	GENERAL MOTORS CORP	New York
GM.CA	GENERAL MOTORS CORP	Canadian
GM/U.CA	GENERAL MOTORS CORP	Canadian
GMH	GENERAL MOTORS CORP. CLASS H	New York
GMBDX	GENERAL MUNICIPAL BOND FUND INC	OTC Funds
GNMXX	GENERAL NEW YORK MUNI MM FD	OTC Funds
GNYMX	GENERAL NEW YORK MUNI BOND FUND CD C	OTC Funds

Exercise 17.3 Finding a Stock Symbol

You will look for stock symbols.

1 Access the Internet.

2 In the **Address** text box, enter the URL **http://www.pcquote.com/cgi-bin/namelook.exe**.

3 Enter **Microsoft** in the **Enter Company Name** box and click on **Get Symbol**.

4 From the list of stocks, find a symbol for Microsoft. It is _____ .

5 Find a symbol for Intel. It is _____ .

6 Exit the Internet if not continuing with Exercise 17.4.

Refreshing a Query

The External Data toolbar is shown in Figure 17.11; it is used when working with external data in a worksheet.

Figure 17.11 External Data Toolbar

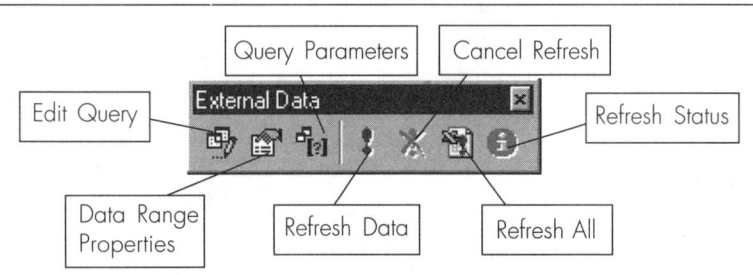

Most queries can be updated periodically. Rather than create the entire listing again, use the External Data toolbar to update it. Each time you *refresh data* you see the most recent version of the information in the database, including any changes that were made to the data.

Select the Refresh Data button ! when only the data in the document should be refreshed. The Refresh All button refreshes the entire workbook including all titles and labels. The Cancel Refresh button cancels the refresh command and leaves the data the same. Use the Refresh Status button to check the status of a query that is running in the background and seems to be taking a long time to return data.

PC Quote, Inc., provides a service for keeping stock prices current on the Internet. With a paid subscription, these stock prices are presented in real time; they are also available to users without paying the subscription and are updated every 20 minutes. With a paid subscription, Refresh will access the current stock prices.

Exercise 17.4   Refreshing a Query

You will refresh the previous query so the stock report is current. Be sure 20 minutes or more has elapsed since you completed Exercise 17.2.

1 Open the workbook **Exer 17** to the **Ex 17-2** tab. This is information from a query for stock prices.

2 Be sure the External Data toolbar is open.

3 Click the Refresh Data button. Your sheet will be updated to show new prices.

4 Save and print the worksheet.

Additional Queries

The queries built into Excel are queries regarding the stock market, stock prices, and the history of stocks. There are additional Web queries that can be downloaded from the Web and used. When programmers develop new queries, the queries are placed directly on the Web. These additional queries are accessed in the Run Query dialog box (shown in Figure 17.12) when Get More Web Queries is selected.

Additional queries provide links to other stock reports and services, currency exchange rates, commodities, money-market reports, consumer interest rates, and mortgage calculations.

These queries can be downloaded onto your computer and run in the same way as the other Web queries.

Figure 17.12   Run Query Dialog Box

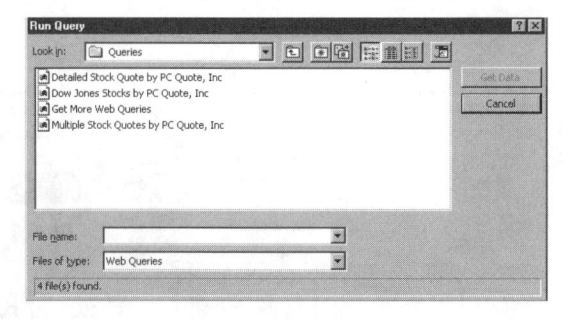

Creating a Web Page

A Web page can be created from an existing document so it is accessible from an intranet or the Internet. Web pages on the Internet are often used for advertising and are being used by more and more businesses. Intranet pages are used to share information within an organization. The Office 97 software makes creating Web pages relatively easy.

Web pages can contain text, graphics, borders, sound clips, and movie clips. An important aspect of Web pages is the ability to create links from one page to another. Web pages are written in *HTML* code (*Hypertext Markup Language*), the programming language used to create Web pages. Recent developments allow Web pages to be written without knowing this programming language.

Links in Excel documents are displayed in blue. To create a link, the URL (address of a Web page) of the link must be known.

To create a Web page, first create an Excel spreadsheet or open an existing one. On the worksheet, highlight the range to be included on the Web page. This is usually just the data, since titles are often added separately. For example, a company places its product catalog on the Web for possible sales. Figure 17.13 shows the portion of the worksheet that will be included on a Web page.

The range will be saved as an HTML file. From File, select Save as HTML. The *Internet Assistant Wizard* opens, providing help in converting and saving information as an HTML document. The Step 1 dialog box of the Internet Assistant Wizard is shown in Figure 17.14.

Specify ranges and charts to put on the Web page in the Step 1 dialog box. All charts in the document will be listed in the dialog box. To exclude anything, click on it and select Remove. To add a range of data, select it and click on Add. When the data range is accurate, click Next to access the Step 2 dialog box, shown in Figure 17.15.

Figure 17.13   Selecting Web Page Text

Figure 17.14   Step 1, Internet Assistant Wizard

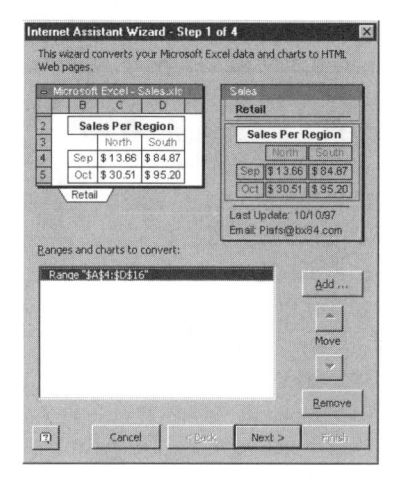

Figure 17.15   Step 2, Internet Assistant Wizard

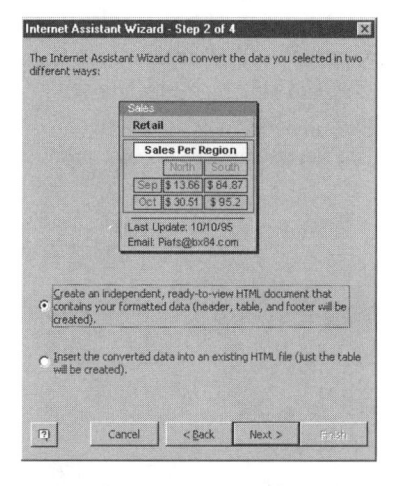

The Step 2 dialog box asks if you would like to create an entirely new Web page or add to an existing page. To edit an existing page, some knowledge of HTML is required. Click on Next to access the Step 3 dialog box, shown in Figure 17.16.

This page is used to add information to a Web page. Specify what information to add above and below the existing Web page. A title and/or a header may be included. The title appears in the title bar of a window; the header appears on the first line of a window. A horizontal line may be placed above and/or below a data table of a Web page. Specific information regarding the Web page and the e-mail address of the creator or firm can be entered.

Click Next to access the Step 4 dialog box, shown in Figure 17.17.

In this step the code page, name, and location for the completed Web page are chosen. Select the code page to use in your Web page. Use the one the Wizard suggests if you have questions. Be sure to save the file as an HTML document. Click Finish; your Web page is saved. It may be viewed with your Web browser.

To view this newly created Web page, open your Web browser and access the document. From File select Open, then locate the document. The completed Web page is shown in Figure 17.18.

Figure 17.16 Step 3, Internet Assistant Wizard

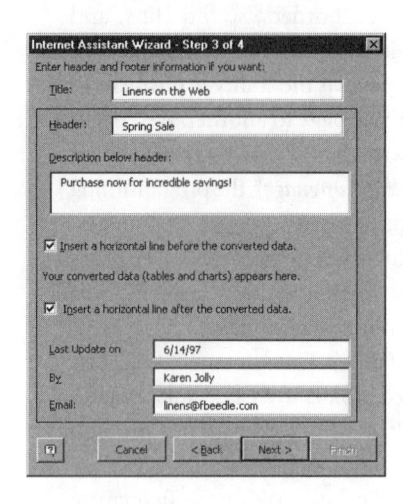

Figure 17.17 Step 4, Internet Assistant Wizard

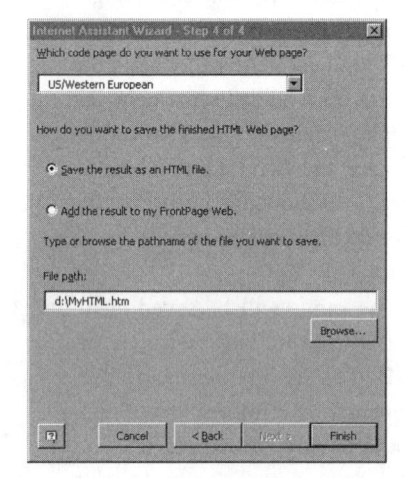

Figure 17.18 Web Page Created in Excel

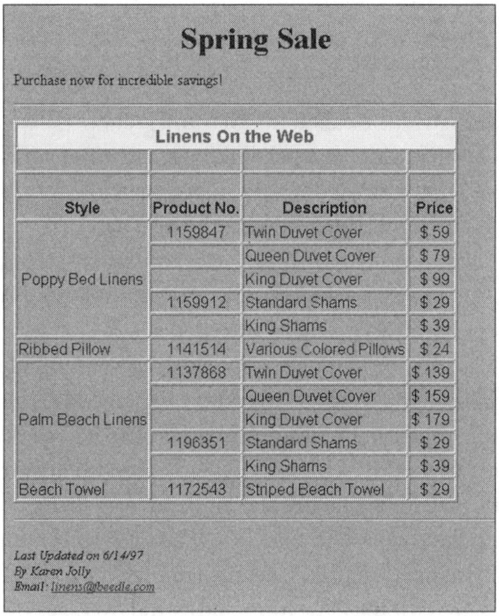

Spring Sale

Purchase now for incredible savings!

Linens On the Web			
Style	Product No.	Description	Price
Poppy Bed Linens	1159847	Twin Duvet Cover	$ 59
		Queen Duvet Cover	$ 79
		King Duvet Cover	$ 99
	1159912	Standard Shams	$ 29
		King Shams	$ 39
Ribbed Pillow	1141514	Various Colored Pillows	$ 24
Palm Beach Linens	1137868	Twin Duvet Cover	$ 139
		Queen Duvet Cover	$ 159
		King Duvet Cover	$ 179
	1196351	Standard Shams	$ 29
		King Shams	$ 39
Beach Towel	1172543	Striped Beach Towel	$ 29

Last Updated on 6/14/97
By Karen Jolly
Email: linens@beedle.com

In order to place your page on the Internet, you must have access to an Internet server. If your instructor would like you to publish your Web pages, specific instructions will be provided for accessing a server.

Exercise 17.5   Creating a Web Page

You will create and print a Web page.

1   Open the workbook **Exer 17** to the **Ex17-5** tab. You will create a Web page using this spreadsheet.

2   Highlight the range of cells containing data, starting at cell A1.

3   From **File**, select **Save as HTML**.

4   In the **Internet Assistant Wizard - Step 1 of 4** dialog box, be sure the range **A1:C12** is selected. Remove all but this one range. Then click **Next**.

5   Create the page as an independent document. Then click **Next**.

6   Title the page **Web Sales**. Insert a border before and after the data. Be sure to include your name as the author and use your e-mail address (or use **astudent@home.com**). Then click **Next**.

7   For the file path, save to your Student Data Disk. Use the name **SalesHTML.htm**. Click on **Finish**.

8   Access your Web browser. When it is running, select **Open** from the **File** menu. Locate your Web page and open it.

9 Print a copy of the page.

10 Close the browser.

Summary

- The World Wide Web is also called the Web and is abbreviated to WWW.
- The Internet is a worldwide network linking smaller networks and individual computers. An intranet is a closed network used within an organization.
- A Web page is an individual document on the Internet.
- Links or hyperlinks are used to connect pages containing related information.
- Each Web page has an address called a URL (Uniform Resource Locator).
- A Web browser provides access to the Internet.
- A home page is usually the first page of a company's or individual's Web site.
- Web pages are written in Hypertext Markup Language, also called HTML. However, Web pages can be created directly from Excel without needing to know HTML.
- Accessing Microsoft on the Web lists frequently used Microsoft Web pages.
- A Web query will place data directly into an Excel worksheet.
- To access built-in Excel queries, access Run Web Query from the Data menu.
- Queries are built in for stock prices, detailed information about a specific stock, or information about the stocks used for the Dow Jones Industrial Average.
- Stock symbols must be known to access the stock quotes. They can be retrieved from the Web.
- Stock prices are updated often. To update a worksheet containing stock prices, use the Refresh Data button.
- Additional queries can be downloaded from the Internet and installed on your computer. They include currency exchange rates, money-market reports, and consumer interest rates.
- A Web page can be created in Excel and saved as an HTML document.
- An Internet Assistant Wizard is used to help create Web pages from Excel.

Important Terminology

browser
downloading
external data
home page
hyperlinks
HTML (Hypertext Markup Language)
HTTP (Hypertext Transfer Protocol)

Internet
Internet Assistant Wizard
intranet
links
Microsoft Internet Explorer
Microsoft on the Web
refresh data
Run Query dialog box

site
stock symbol
URL (Uniform Resource Locator)
Web page
Web query
World Wide Web (Web, WWW)

Buttons to Know

Study Questions

True-False

Place a T in the space if the statement is true; place an F if the statement is false.

_____ 1. The World Wide Web is also known as the Intranet.
_____ 2. Hyperlinks are built into Web pages and allow the user to move quickly to related pages.
_____ 3. A URL is the address of a Web page.
_____ 4. A browser is used in Excel to move quickly between worksheets or workbooks.
_____ 5. A home page is the network page used for a business. Each business is allowed only one home page on the Web.
_____ 6. HTTP is the language used for writing Web pages.
_____ 7. To query the Web means to open worksheets directly on the Web.
_____ 8. Refreshing a query updates information in a worksheet.
_____ 9. Data that is retrieved from the Web and entered into an Excel worksheet is external data.
_____ 10. Additional queries can be downloaded onto your computer.
_____ 11. A Web page can be created only by using Hypertext Markup Language (HTML).
_____ 12. To help create a Web page, Excel uses the Web Page Assistant Wizard.

Fill-In

Place the word in the space that correctly completes the statement.

1. A closed network of Web pages that is available only to authorized users within an organization is called a(n) _____ .
2. The address of a Web page is called the _____ .
3. To access stock quotes and place them in an Excel worksheet, you will _____ the Web.
4. The abbreviations of stock names on the Web are called stock _____ .
5. To save a Web page, select the _____ command from the File menu.

Assignments

Assignment 17.1

Use a Web query to prepare stock reports.
1. Open Excel to a new workbook.
2. Enter and format the title of the worksheet. The first line of the title is **Stock Report**. Enter your name on the second line of the title, and use today's date on the third line.
3. Beginning in cell A9, enter the following information:

	A	B
4	**Stock Name**	**Symbol**
5	Chevron	CHV
6	Dow Chemical	DOW
7	Kroger	KIR
8	McDonalds	MCDpE
9	Sara Lee	SLE

4. Save the workbook as **Assig 17-1**.
5. Click in cell C2. The results will be placed in the worksheet beginning with this cell.
6. Run a Web query to retrieve the stock data from the Multiple Stock Quotes query.
7. Format the worksheet for landscape style.
8. Print the worksheet.
9. At a later time (at least an hour later), open **Assig 17-1** and refresh the query. Print a copy of the worksheet after it has been refreshed.

Assignment 17.2

Use a query to find detailed information about a stock.
1. In an Excel worksheet, select to query the Web.
2. Run a query for a **Detailed Stock Quote** for McDonalds **(MCDpE)**.
3. Place your name in the header.
4. Place a title in the worksheet and print a copy. Save the workbook as **Assig 17-2**.

Assignment 17.3

Use a query to review the Dow Jones Industrial Average report.
1. In an Excel worksheet, select to query the Web.
2. Select **Dow Jones Stocks** and place the data in an Excel worksheet.
3. Place your name in the header.
4. Save the workbook as **Assig 17-3**. Print a copy of the worksheet.

Assignment 17.4

You will create a Web page for a firm that uses the Internet to advertise its products.
1. Open the worksheet saved as **Ch17 As4**.
2. Highlight the range containing data.
3. Create a Web page. In the **Header** section, enter **Baking Supplies Extraordinaire**. Enter **Online Catalog** in the **Description below header** section.
4. Save the Web page on your Student Data Disk. Name it **BakingHTML**.
5. Close Excel and access the World Wide Web. Open your Web page from the Web.
6. Print a copy of the Web page.

Case Problem 17

Complete a stock report for your personal stock portfolio. Select 10 stocks of your choice from the American, New York, or NASDAQ stock exchanges and prepare a worksheet that shows the current stock quotes. Enter today's date on the quote using a dynamic date. Then prepare individual stock reports for each stock selected. Print all reports.

Refresh your stock report at least one day later. Check to be sure the date is today. Print this report.

Appendix A

Managing Documents

It is easy to create and save electronic worksheets and other documents. However, it is not always easy to locate a saved document. It is important to establish an orderly method for saving documents so they can be found later.

This appendix provides a brief overview of the Windows Explorer program and explains how to manage the Excel files created and saved in the exercises and assignments in this text.

Basics

Each saved document is considered a file. Windows 95 allows a file name to contain up to 255 characters, including capital letters and spaces.

Files are stored on disks, either a floppy disk or a hard disk. A floppy disk is inserted into the computer's disk drive, which makes it an external storage method because it can be removed from the computer. Floppy disk space is limited; a 3.5" floppy holds up to only 1.44 megabytes of data.

A hard disk is built into the computer and has more storage space than a floppy disk. Programs (such as Excel or Word) are stored on the hard disk along with user-generated files. Disk drives of one gigabyte or larger are common today. When using a hard disk as the storage device, organization is needed so the programs and data can be easily accessed.

Files are organized in folders on a disk; these folders are also called subdirectories or branches. Folders on a computer are similar to those in a file cabinet because each folder holds additional folders and documents that pertain to the same topic.

Windows Explorer

The Windows 95 operating system provides a program called Windows Explorer to manage files and folders. Windows Explorer helps organize disks by providing commands to copy, move, rename, and delete files.

To access Windows Explorer, click the Start button, select Programs, and then select Windows Explorer, as shown in Figure A.1.

Appendix A   Managing Documents

Figure A.1   Opening Windows Explorer

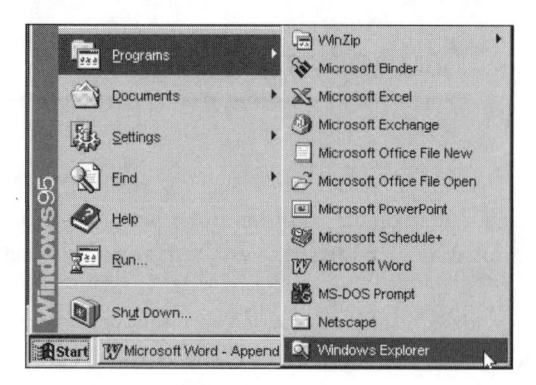

[Screenshot of Windows 95 Start menu showing Programs submenu with entries including WinZip, Microsoft Binder, Microsoft Excel, Microsoft Exchange, Microsoft Office File New, Microsoft Office File Open, Microsoft PowerPoint, Microsoft Schedule+, Microsoft Word, MS-DOS Prompt, Netscape, and Windows Explorer.]

The Exploring window opens, shown in Figure A.2.

Figure A.2   Windows Explorer

[Screenshot of Windows Explorer showing the contents of 3½ Floppy (A:). Left pane shows folder tree with Desktop, My Computer (3½ Floppy (A:), (C:), Disk2_vol1 (D:), (E:), Removable Disk (F:), (G:)), Control Panel, Printers, Dial-Up Networking, Recycle Bin, My Briefcase. Right pane lists folders ch01-03, ch04 through ch17, all File Folders dated 7/17/97.]

The menu bar across the top is used to access commands to move, copy, and rename folders and documents. The left side of the window shows the hierarchical view of objects such as folders; this representation is sometimes referred to as a tree. A plus sign beside an item indicates that it contains folders (branches). Click on an object to view its contents.

The right side of the window displays the contents of the object selected in the left pane. In Figure A.2, the contents pane shows the files and folders on the floppy disk in the A drive. Click on a folder to open it and view its contents.

The Exploring screen in Figure A.2 shows the hierarchical file structure of the Student Data Disk. It is divided into subdirectories (branches), which are identified by folder icons in the contents pane. Each folder stores the documents used in the chapter that corresponds to the folder's name. As you complete the exercises and assignments in this text, you will access and save information within each chapter folder.

Appendix B

Shortcuts

Keyboard Shortcuts

There are several methods to execute a command in Windows. In addition to using the drop-down menus, keyboard commands may also be used.

This appendix lists the frequently used keyboard commands that can be executed either by using a key combination or function key.

Executable Command	Keyboard Command
AutoComplete list, display	**Alt**+**↓**
AutoSum formula, insert	**Alt**+**=**
Bold formatting (apply or remove)	**Ctrl**+**B**
Cancel a cell entry	**Esc**
Cell formulas; alternate between displaying cell values and displaying cell formulas	**Ctrl**+**Shift**+` (left quotation mark)
Chart on a separate sheet, create	**F11**
Close all documents in the active application	**Shift**+**Alt**+**F**; then press **C**
Close the window	**Ctrl**+**F4**
Complete a cell entry	**Enter**
Complete a cell entry and move to the right in the selection	**Tab**
Copy the selection	**Ctrl**+**C**
Currency format with two decimal places (negative numbers appear in parentheses)	**Ctrl**+**Shift**+**$**
Cut the selection	**Ctrl**+**X**
Date format with the day, month, and year	**Ctrl**+**Shift**+**#**
Date; enter the current date (a static date)	**Ctrl**+**;**
Define Name dialog box, access	**Ctrl**+**F3**
Delete the character to the left of the insertion point, or delete the selection	**Backspace**
Delete the character to the right of the insertion point, or delete the highlighted section	**Delete**
Edit the active cell	**F2**
Fill down	**Ctrl**+**D**
Fill to the right	**Ctrl**+**R**
Find dialog box, access	**Shift**+**F5**
	Ctrl+**F**

General number format	**Ctrl**+**Shift**+~
Go To dialog box, access	**F5**
	Ctrl+**G**
Help or the Office Assistant, access	**F1**
Hide columns	**Ctrl**+**0** (zero)
Hide rows	**Ctrl**+**9**
Insert new worksheet	**Alt**+**Shift**+**F1**
Italic formatting (apply or remove)	**Ctrl**+**I**
Maximize or restore the workbook window	**Ctrl**+**F10**
Minimize the workbook	**Ctrl**+**F9**
Move to the beginning of the row	**Home**
Move to the beginning of the worksheet	**Ctrl**+**Home**
Move to the last cell on the worksheet, which is the cell at the intersection of the right-most used column and the bottom-most used row (in the lower-right corner)	**Ctrl**+**End**
New workbook, open	**Ctrl**+**N**
Number format with two decimal places, 1000 separator, and – (minus sign) for negative values	**Ctrl**+**Shift**+**!**
Open dialog box, access	**Ctrl**+**F12**
	Ctrl+**O**
Paste a name into a formula	**F3**
Paste Function dialog box, access	**Shift**+**F3**
Paste the selection	**Ctrl**+**V**
Percentage format with no decimals places	**Ctrl**+**Shift**+**%**
Print dialog box, access	**Ctrl**+**P**
Repeat the last action	**F4**
Restore the window size	**Ctrl**+**F5**
Save As dialog box, access	**F12**
Save command	**Shift**+**F12**
Select entire worksheet	**Ctrl**+**A**
Select the entire column	**Ctrl**+**Space Bar**
Select the entire row	**Shift**+**Space Bar**
Shortcut menu, display	**Shift**+**F10**
Spelling command	**F7**
Standard toolbar (show or hide)	**Ctrl**+**7**
Start a new line in the same cell	**Alt**+**Enter**
Time format with the hour and minute, and indicate A.M. or P.M.	**Ctrl**+**Shift**+**@**
Time; enter the current time (static time)	**Ctrl**+**Shift**+**:**
Undo the last action	**Ctrl**+**Z**
Unhide columns	**Ctrl**+**Shift**+**)**
Unhide rows	**Ctrl**+**Shift**+**(**

Using Keyboard Commands to Select Cells

Executable Command	Keyboard Command
Extend the selection by one cell	[Shift] + arrow key
Extend the selection to the beginning of the row	[Shift]+[Home]
Extend the selection to the beginning of the worksheet	[Ctrl]+[Shift]+[Home]
Extend the selection to the last cell used in the worksheet (lower-right corner)	[Ctrl]+[Shift]+[End]

Using Shortcuts to Access Pull-down Menus

Figure B.1 shows the pull-down File menu. To use the keyboard to access a menu, hold down the Alt key and press the letter that is underlined in the menu name. For instance, to access the File menu, hold down Alt and press F. Then enter the underlined letter in the command name (N for New or O for Open).

Figure B.1   File Menu

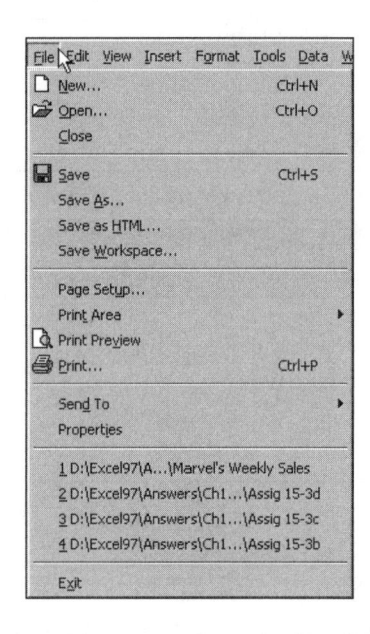

Appendix C

Toolbars

The Standard Toolbar

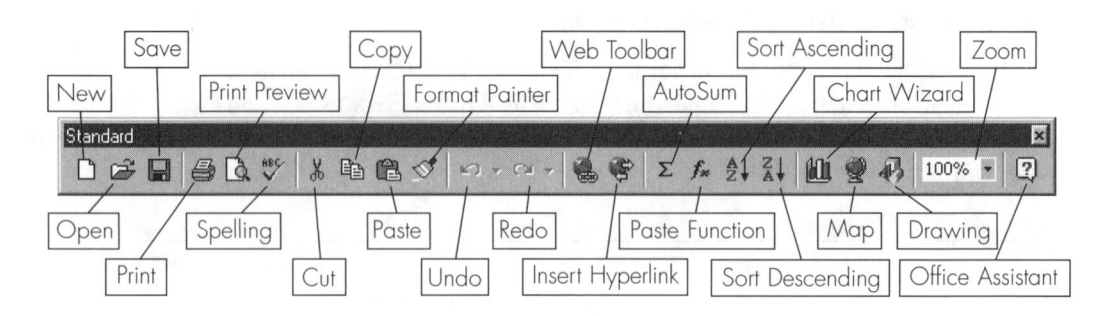

Labels: New, Open, Save, Print, Print Preview, Spelling, Cut, Copy, Paste, Format Painter, Undo, Redo, Web Toolbar, Insert Hyperlink, AutoSum, Paste Function, Sort Ascending, Sort Descending, Chart Wizard, Map, Drawing, Zoom, Office Assistant

The Formatting Toolbar

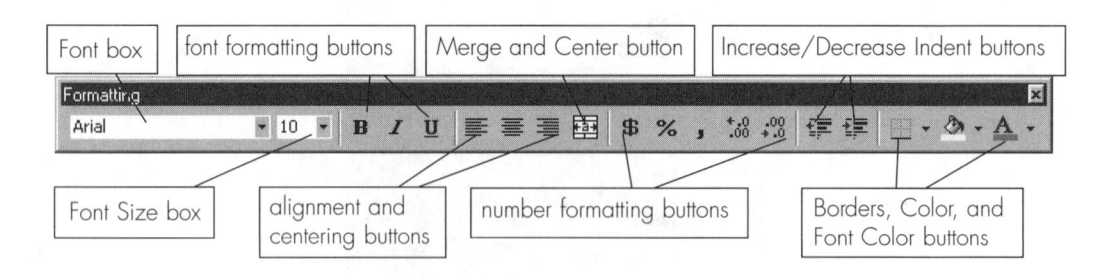

Labels: Font box, Font Size box, font formatting buttons, alignment and centering buttons, Merge and Center button, number formatting buttons, Increase/Decrease Indent buttons, Borders, Color, and Font Color buttons

The Forms Toolbar

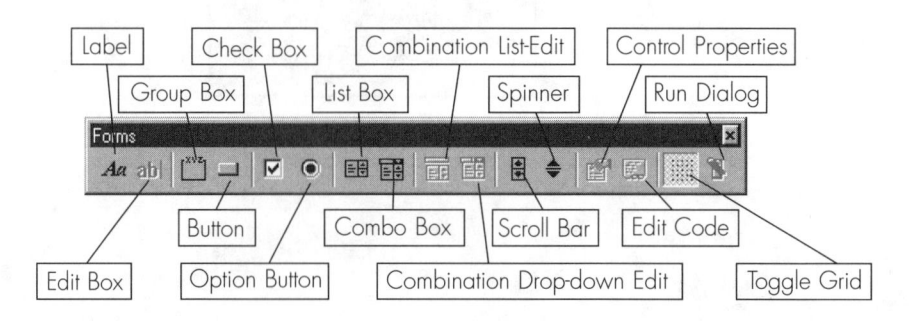

Labels: Label, Edit Box, Group Box, Button, Check Box, Option Button, List Box, Combo Box, Combination List-Edit, Combination Drop-down Edit, Spinner, Scroll Bar, Control Properties, Edit Code, Run Dialog, Toggle Grid

Appendix C Toolbars

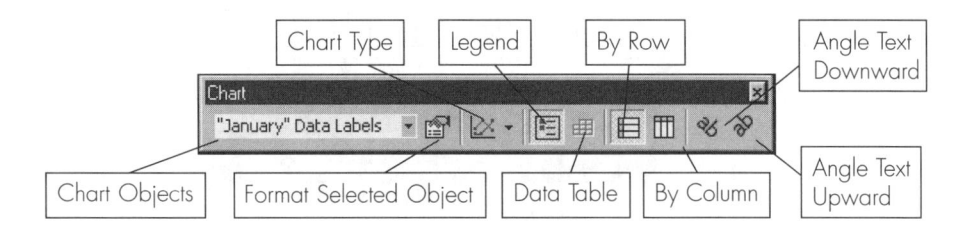

The Chart Toolbar

- Chart Type
- Legend
- By Row
- Angle Text Downward
- Chart Objects
- Format Selected Object
- Data Table
- By Column
- Angle Text Upward

The Control Toolbox Toolbar

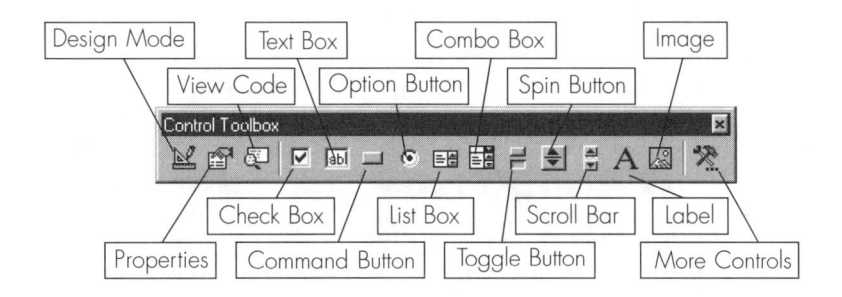

- Design Mode
- Text Box
- Combo Box
- Image
- View Code
- Option Button
- Spin Button
- Check Box
- List Box
- Scroll Bar
- Label
- Properties
- Command Button
- Toggle Button
- More Controls

The Drawing Toolbar

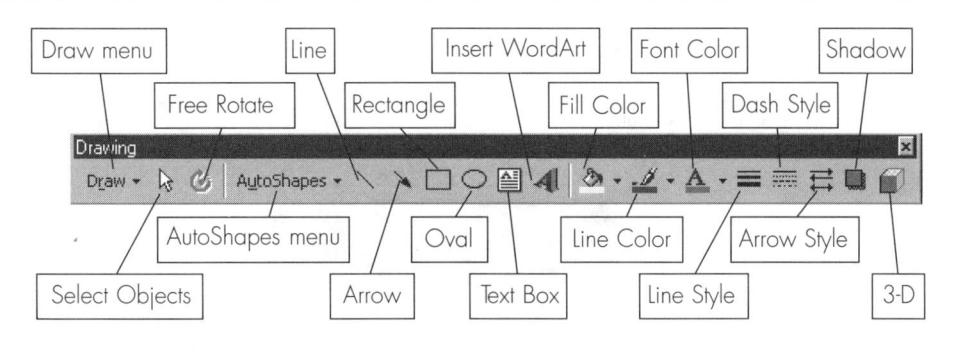

- Draw menu
- Line
- Insert WordArt
- Font Color
- Shadow
- Free Rotate
- Rectangle
- Fill Color
- Dash Style
- AutoShapes menu
- Oval
- Line Color
- Arrow Style
- Select Objects
- Arrow
- Text Box
- Line Style
- 3-D

The External Data Toolbar

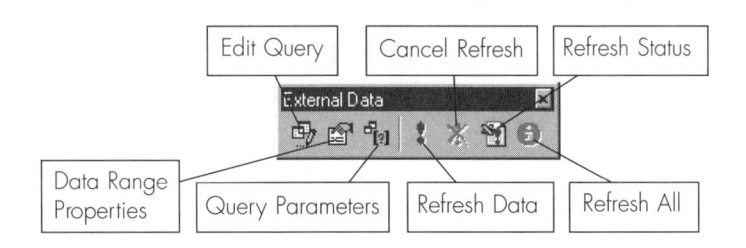

- Edit Query
- Cancel Refresh
- Refresh Status
- Data Range Properties
- Query Parameters
- Refresh Data
- Refresh All

Appendix C Toolbars

The Picture Toolbar

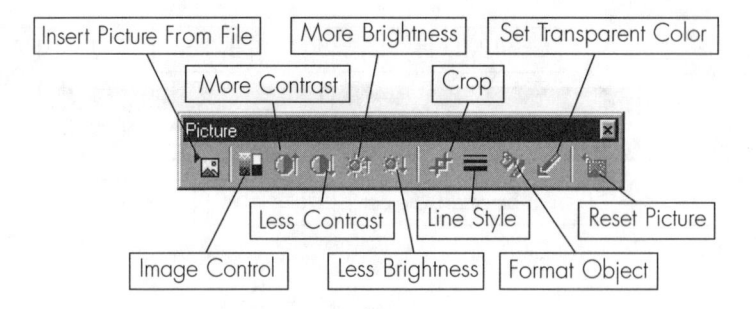

- Insert Picture From File
- More Contrast
- More Brightness
- Crop
- Set Transparent Color
- Image Control
- Less Contrast
- Less Brightness
- Line Style
- Format Object
- Reset Picture

The PivotTable Toolbar

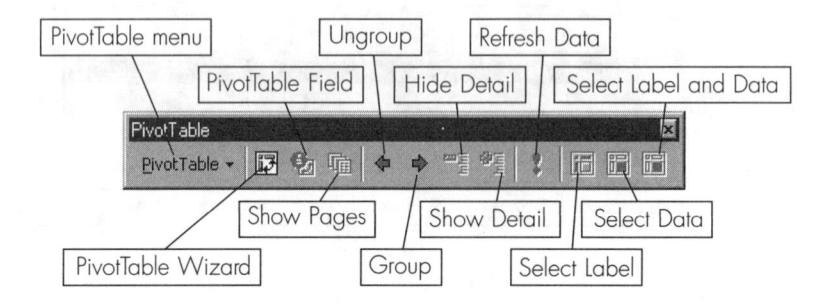

- PivotTable menu
- PivotTable Field
- Ungroup
- Hide Detail
- Refresh Data
- Select Label and Data
- PivotTable Wizard
- Show Pages
- Group
- Show Detail
- Select Label
- Select Data

The Reviewing Toolbar

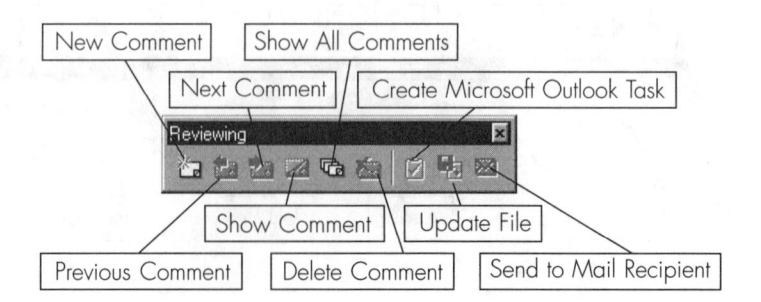

- New Comment
- Next Comment
- Show All Comments
- Create Microsoft Outlook Task
- Previous Comment
- Show Comment
- Delete Comment
- Update File
- Send to Mail Recipient

Appendix C Toolbars

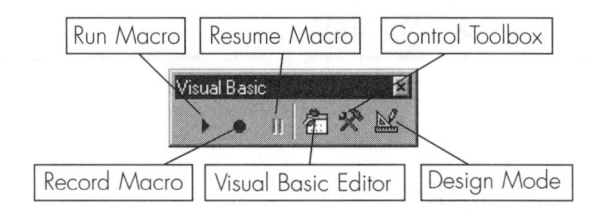

The Visual Basic Toolbar

- Run Macro
- Resume Macro
- Control Toolbox
- Record Macro
- Visual Basic Editor
- Design Mode

The Web Toolbar

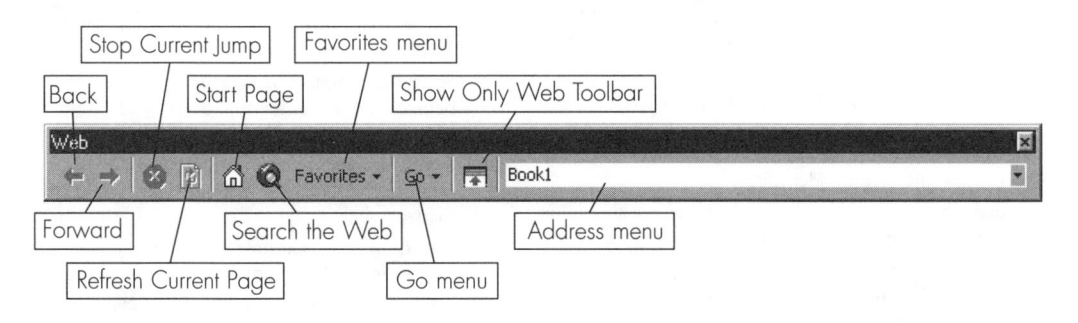

- Back
- Stop Current Jump
- Start Page
- Favorites menu
- Show Only Web Toolbar
- Forward
- Refresh Current Page
- Search the Web
- Go menu
- Address menu

The WordArt Toolbar

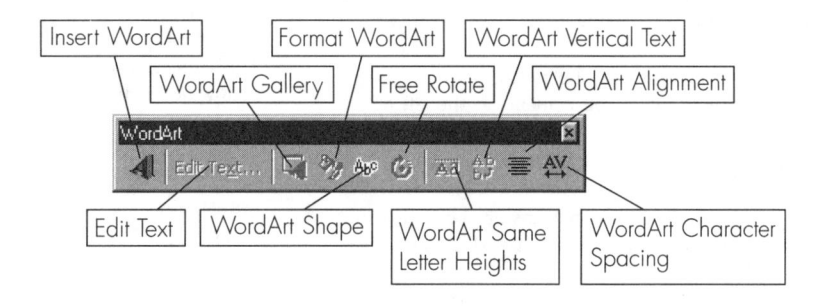

- Insert WordArt
- WordArt Gallery
- Format WordArt
- Free Rotate
- WordArt Vertical Text
- WordArt Alignment
- Edit Text
- WordArt Shape
- WordArt Same Letter Heights
- WordArt Character Spacing

Glossary

#REF! An example of an error message. Error messages begin with a pound sign (#) and briefly describe the type of error-in this case, a cell reference error.

3-D button The button in the Drawing toolbar that adds 3-D effects to graphic images.

3-D reference A reference to a cell not located in the current sheet. It includes the name of the sheet along with the cell coordinates.

absolute reference A cell reference that remains the same if it is copied or moved to a new location. An absolute reference is identified by dollar signs ($) before the row and column identifiers.

active book or **workbook** The book or workbook that is displayed on the computer screen and may have data entered into it.

active cell The cell in which data may be entered. A heavy border surrounding it identifies it. Only one cell is active at a time. An active cell is also called a selected cell.

active sheet or **worksheet** The sheet of a workbook that is displayed. The name in the tab of an active sheet is bold.

Align Left button The button on the Formatting toolbar used to align cell contents at the left of the cell.

Align Right button The button on the Formatting toolbar used to place data at the right edge of a cell.

alignment buttons The buttons on the Formatting toolbar that are used for setting the alignment of cell contents.

Alignment tab The section of the Format Cells dialog box that provides alignment choices.

applying names Converting formulas using cell references to those using named cells and ranges.

area chart A chart that is used to show a change occurring over time. It shows the relationship of each part to the whole.

argument A piece of variable information in a function. It is enclosed in parentheses. It may be a number, text, logical value, cell or range of cells, or reference.

arithmetic operators The symbols used in formulas, usually +, -, *, and /, that specify the operation to be performed.

Arrange Windows dialog box The dialog box used to determine the arrangement of open workbooks on the screen.

array A table used for retrieving information in a LOOKUP function.

Arrow button The button in the Drawing toolbar used to place an arrow on a worksheet or chart.

arrow style A format applied to the ends of an arrow.

Arrow Style button The button in the Drawing toolbar used to select an arrow style.

ascending order The arrangement of a sort in alphabetical order or, in the case of numbers, from smallest to largest.

AutoCalculate Displays the total value of a selected range in the status bar without entering a formula into the worksheet.

AutoComplete Completes a cell entry based on existing entries in the column.

AutoCorrect Automatically corrects common mistakes as text is entered into a cell.

AutoFill Automatically continues a series after only one or two entries have been made.

AutoFilter Filters a list quickly, only displaying records containing certain selected values.

AutoFit Selection A setting choice for column width or row height that adjusts the width or height to accommodate the largest entry.

AutoFormat Formats a worksheet automatically based on several built-in formats.

AutoShapes The menu in the Drawing toolbar used to access shapes that can be placed in a worksheet.

AutoSum A built-in function that adds a range of cells without having specific cell references entered. The keyboard shortcut is Alt+=.

AutoSum button The button on the Standard toolbar used to enter a SUM function into a cell.

AVERAGE function A statistical function that determines the average value of a selected range of cells.

bar chart A chart that displays data markers as horizontal bars. It effectively compares individual figures over a specific period of time.

beginning point The first line of code in a Visual Basic module.

bold A format for an entry that makes it darker than regular type. **This is an example of bold format.** The keyboard shortcut is Ctrl+B.

Bold button The button on the Formatting toolbar used to bold a selected cell.

book A group of worksheets that are saved as a single file, also called a workbook.

book value A value of an asset that equals its cost less the current depreciation amount.

Border tab The section of the Format Cells dialog box used to place borders and determine the size and style of borders.

borders Lines placed at gridlines. They may be at the right, left, top, or bottom of a cell or range of cells. Borders may be of varying styles.

Borders button The button on the Formatting toolbar used to place a border around a cell or range of cells.

Borders palette A pull-down palette that shows the buttons available for quickly applying border styles.

browser A program that accesses the World Wide Web.

buttons The small pictures (icons) on toolbars that are used to communicate commands to Excel.

Cancel box The box in an active formula bar that is used to cancel the current entry and return the cell to the original entry.

category axis The x-axis, located at the bottom of a chart.

category names The labels along a category axis (bottom of a chart) that identify data markers.

cell The space where a row and column intersect and that stores a piece of information.

cell reference The identification of a cell formed by its column letter followed by its row number.

center alignment Formatting of a cell in which contents are centered within a cell.

Center button The button on the Formatting toolbar used to center cell contents.

chart A graphic representation of data.

Chart Location dialog box The dialog box in Chart Wizard that indicates the placement of a chart, either on a new sheet or embedded in an existing worksheet.

Chart Options dialog box The dialog box that is used to make formatting choices in Chart Wizard.

chart range The portion of a worksheet to be charted.

chart sheet A worksheet created for placement of a new chart. Chart sheets may be edited and are linked to the original worksheet data.

Chart Source Data dialog box The Chart Wizard dialog box that identifies the data to be charted and how the data will be ordered.

chart title A title placed in a chart.

Chart toolbar A toolbar that accesses frequently used charting tools.

Chart Type dialog box A dialog box presenting several types of charts to choose from, such as column, bar, and pie.

Chart Wizard Used to create charts. A series of dialog boxes open to guide you through chart preparation.

Chart Wizard button The button on the Standard toolbar used for creating charts quickly.

check box A method of selecting choices in dialog boxes.

Clear command Eliminates a cell's contents, formats, or comments but leaves the cell in the worksheet.

Clippit One of the Office Assistant animated characters that provide assistance with using Excel.

Close button The button in the upper-right corner of a workbook window that is used to close the workbook.

Close command Closes a workbook so it is removed from the screen but does not close the Excel program. The keyboard shortcut is Ctrl+F4.

code buttons Buttons used to customize headers and footers by placing codes that are converted into text, such as the date or time.

Collapse Dialog button The button in a Formula Palette that reduces the Formula Palette so the worksheet can be seen and cells and ranges selected.

color palettes Pull-down palettes accessed from the Formatting toolbar and used to choose a color for a cell, border, or text.

column A range of cells one cell wide that runs vertically through the entire length of a worksheet. Columns are identified by letters.

column chart A chart that displays data markers as vertical bars. It effectively compares individual figures for a specific period of time.

column handles The T-shaped figures at the top of each column in Print Preview used to adjust the column widths of a worksheet.

column headings The letters along the top of the worksheet that identify specific columns.

column index number The column number in a table array from which a matching value should be returned.

column label The identifying text for the values in a column.

column width The distance from the left to the right side of a column. This is adjustable.

Comma style A style of formatting numbers for comma placement and two decimal places.

Comma Style button The button on the Formatting toolbar used to format numbers in the Comma style. The keyboard shortcut is Ctrl+Shift+!.

command An instruction for the computer.

command button A rectangular button in a dialog box used to execute or cancel commands.

comments Notes that are entered in a worksheet that display when the mouse is over them. A note may be text or sound and is used to provide explanations.

comparison operator A math symbol used to compare two values.

completing an entry Finishing an entry. An entry is completed by pressing the Enter key or the Tab key or by clicking on the Enter box in the formula bar.

compound document A document that contains data from more than one application.

computed fields The fields that cannot be changed in a data form.

Confirm Password dialog box The dialog box that opens asking that a password be reentered to confirm its accuracy.

copy area The source cell or range of cells for a copy and paste operation.

Copy button The button on the Standard toolbar used to copy a selected area.

copying cells Copying the contents and/or formulas of a cell to a new location. The copied cells replace the existing cells.

cost of asset The initial cost of an asset.

count all function (COUNTA) A statistical function that counts how many cells in a selected range contain data.

COUNT function A statistical function that counts how many cells in a selected range contain numbers.

Create Names dialog box The dialog box that opens when names are created for cells or ranges of cells for use in Natural-language formulas.

creating names Selecting the names of cells from column or row labels.

criteria Instructions used to locate specific records when querying a list.

Currency format Used for formatting dollar amounts. A dollar sign ($) is placed in the first cell of the list and in the total. A single border is placed above the total and a double border is placed beneath it.

Currency Style button The button on the Formatting toolbar used to format numbers in the Currency style. The keyboard shortcut is Ctrl+Shift+$.

Custom AutoFilter Used to filter a list when the criteria are from two or more fields or are numerical.

custom footer A footer created to contain specific information for the current worksheet.

custom header A header created to contain specific information for the current worksheet.

custom list A list that is created, saved, and available to be entered using the AutoFill command.

custom sort A sort in which information is ordered in a predetermined way that is not alphabetical or numerical.

Customize button The button in Spreadsheet Solutions templates that allows the templates to be personalized.

Cut button The button on the Standard toolbar used to cut selected cells.

Cut command The command used to remove a selection from an active worksheet. The keyboard shortcut is Ctrl+X.

Dash style The style of a dashed line in a worksheet. A dashed line may consist of dots, dashes, or a combination of the two.

Dash Style button The button in the Drawing toolbar used to select the style of a dashed line.

data form A dialog box that displays the information contained in a list one complete record at a time. It is used for editing and creating lists and for finding specific records.

data marker A graphic representation in a chart of a data point.

data point A value in a worksheet.

Data range The section in the Chart Source Data dialog box that identifies the location of source data for a chart.

data series The data in each row or column of a worksheet. Each data series in a chart is identified by a unique color or pattern.

database A group of related records, also called a list.

Date button The code button that is used to insert the current date in the Header/Footer tab of the Page Setup dialog box.

Date & Time The function category used to enter dates and times.

declining-balance depreciation function (DB) The financial function that determines depreciation using the declining balance depreciation method. This method uses the theory that an asset depreciates more at the beginning of its life than at the end.

Decrease Decimal button The button on the Formatting toolbar used to decrease the number of decimal places displayed in a selected cell.

default chart The chart type preset to open when a chart is created; in Excel it is the column chart.

default command The command button that has a dark border surrounding it in a dialog box. It can be executed by pressing the Enter key on the keyboard.

default font The font that is preset to be used in new documents. In Excel, the default font is Arial 10 point.

defaults The format choices that are preset in a software.

Define Name dialog box The dialog box used to list all cell names used in a worksheet and to create additional names for cells for use in Natural-language formulas.

defining a name Replacing a cell reference with text that identifies the cell for use in Natural-language formulas.

Delete command Removes cells, rows, or columns from a worksheet. The remaining cells shift to fill the space.

deleting a worksheet Removing a worksheet from a workbook. The Delete Sheet command is located on the Edit menu.

depreciation The amount an asset decreases due to obsolescence or wear and tear.

descending order The arrangement of a list in reverse alphabetical order (Z to A) or, in the case of numbers, from largest to smallest.

destination The range of cells where data will be moved or copied to, also called the paste area.

destination cell The upper-left cell of a destination range.

destination document A workbook that receives linked data.

dialog box A box that opens to gather additional information related to a chosen command.

dialog box tabs Tabs across the top of dialog boxes, used to access additional topics.

downloading The process of saving information from an electronic source such as the Internet to your computer.

drag-and-drop moving The method of moving cell contents that "grabs" cells in a move area and "drops" them in a new location.

dragging and dropping The method of copying cell contents that uses the mouse to drag cells to a second location.

Drawing toolbar The toolbar that contains tools to enhance worksheet appearance by adding shapes and color.

dynamic link A link formed between documents in which changes made to the data in one document are entered in the other document(s).

editable fields Fields that can be changed in a data form.

editing Making changes in a worksheet.

electronic spreadsheet A spreadsheet that is created with a computer.

embedded chart A chart placed on a worksheet and saved with that sheet. It can be moved, sized, and edited.

embedding Inserting information from one document (the source document) to another (the destination document). Embedded information becomes part of the destination document. Double-clicking on the embedded information opens the application in which it was created.

End Sub statement In Visual Basic, the statement that ends a macro.

End With statement In Visual Basic, the statement that specifies a macro's commands.

ending point The last line of code in a Visual Basic module sheet.

Enter box The button on an active formula bar that is used to complete an entry .

Enter key The key on the keyboard used to complete an entry.

Enter mode The mode Excel works in when data is being entered.

entry area The area of the formula bar that displays the data or formula being entered.

error value A message that appears in a cell when an error in a formula has been made.

Esc key The key on the keyboard used to cancel an entry. It also stops a marquee.

EVEN function The mathematical function that returns a number that is the next higher even integer.

exiting Excel Ending an Excel work session. Exit is selected from the File menu.

Expand Dialog button A button in a collapsed Formula Palette that expands the Formula Palette back to its original form .

Expense Statement A Spreadsheet Solutions template for expense statements.

exploded pie chart A type of pie chart that displays the sections with space between them.

extending a selection Enlarging a block of selected cells. Click in the first cell, press the Shift key, and click in the last cell of the new range.

external data Data that is retrieved from the Web and placed in a worksheet.

external reference A reference in one workbook to another.

field Each category of information in a list. In Excel lists, each column is a field.

file name The name of a saved workbook.

File Name button The code button in the Header/Footer tab of the Page Setup dialog box that is used to insert the file name .

Fill Color button The button on the Formatting and Drawing toolbars used to add background color .

Fill command A command that copies and pastes cell contents in one step.

fill effects The color, background, and gradients used in the background of a chart and in each data marker.

fill handle The small black square at the lower-right corner of an active cell. Click on the fill handle and drag through the desired range to copy an active cell's contents to adjacent cells or to enter a series.

Fill Justify command The command used to distribute a long cell entry into two or more cells, depending on the length of the entry.

fill range An adjacent range of cells to be filled.

filling across worksheets Copying a selection of cells to other worksheets of a workbook.

filtering a list Gathering specific information from a list and only displaying records containing that information.

financial functions Functions for business use, such as to determine simple and accrued interest, depreciation, and present and future values.

Find command Locates data in a worksheet.

floating toolbar A toolbar that is positioned over a worksheet and is not placed in a toolbar dock.

font A type style.

Font button In the Header/Footer tab of the Page Setup dialog box, the code button that is used to format the fonts in a header or footer.

Font Color button The button on the Formatting and Drawing toolbars used to determine text color.

font size The size of a font. The smaller the number, the smaller the text size.

Font tab The section in the Format Cells dialog box used to make decisions about the font used and its attributes.

footer Information that prints at the bottom of each page of a worksheet.

Format Cells dialog box Used to format the contents of a cell. It contains tabs to access different types of choices, such as the Number, Alignment, Font, Border, Patterns, and Protection tabs.

Format Painter button The button on the Standard toolbar used to copy cell formats.

formatting Changing the way a worksheet looks.

Formatting toolbar A toolbar that contains buttons for commonly used formatting commands.

formula A sequence of instructions used to complete a mathematical problem.

formula bar The area near the top of the screen used to enter or edit values and formulas. It consists of the Name box and the entry area.

Formula Palette A collapsible box that opens when a function is selected. It describes the function and its arguments, and it shows the function's results.

Free Rotate button The button on the Drawing toolbar used to rotate a graphic image.

freezing panes Making a section of a worksheet remain visible on the screen at all times while allowing scrolling in the rest of the worksheet. This is useful for keeping row and column titles on the screen at all times when working in a large worksheet.

Function box The box in the formula bar that lists frequently used functions.

function keys The keys on a keyboard that are identified by the letter F followed by a number. They are used for keyboard shortcuts.

functions Complex formulas that are built into Excel to make creating worksheets quicker, easier, and more accurate. Functions are entered into formulas.

General alignment The default format, which aligns data at the bottom of a cell, text at the left, and numbers at the right.

General number format The default format for displaying numbers. The keyboard shortcut is Ctrl+Shift+~.

Go To command Used to access a specific cell located far from the active cell. The keyboard shortcut is F5.

grand total A total of individual totals in a worksheet.

graph A representation of data in a pictorial form. In Excel, a graph is called a chart.

gridlines The lines that separate cells; a worksheet may be printed with or without gridlines.

handles The black squares at the corners and sides of active graphic objects.

header Information that prints at the top of each page of a worksheet.

Header/Footer tab The section in the Page Setup dialog box used to place headers and footers in a worksheet.

Help Used to access information about using Excel. The keyboard shortcut is F1.

hiding columns Adjusting a worksheet so some columns are not shown on the screen or the printed worksheet. Hidden columns are still in the worksheet but are temporarily removed from view. The keyboard shortcut is Ctrl+0 (zero).

hiding rows Adjusting a worksheet so some rows are not shown on the screen or the printed worksheet. Hidden rows are still in the worksheet but are temporarily removed from view. The keyboard shortcut is Ctrl+9.

home page The first page of a company's or individual's Web site.

horizontal alignment The horizontal placement of data within a cell.

horizontal lookup function (HLOOKUP) A LOOKUP function in which the lookup table is arranged horizontally in the worksheet.

hyperlink A connection used in the World Wide Web to link Web sites together, allowing for jumps from one to another.

Hypertext Markup Language (HTML) The programming language used to create Web pages.

Hypertext Transfer Protocol (HTTP) One way information is transmitted on the Web.

icons Small pictures that represent commands.

IF function A logical function that provides a true or false response to a test.

Increase Decimal button The button on the Formatting toolbar used to increase the number of decimal places displayed in a selected cell.

indent alignment The alignment that indents cell contents from the left gridline.

Insert WordArt button The button on the Drawing toolbar used to access the WordArt Gallery dialog box.

inserting cells Adding cells into an existing worksheet. The existing cells shift either up, down, right, or left to make room for the inserted cells. References are automatically adjusted to reflect their new location.

inserting a column Adding a column to a worksheet. The existing columns move to the right to make room for the inserted column.

inserting and copying Copying cells and inserting them between existing cells. The existing cells move to allow room for the copied cells.

inserting and pasting Moving cells and inserting them between existing cells without deleting information.

inserting a row Adding a row to a worksheet. The existing rows adjust to make room for the inserted row.

insertion border A bold, jagged line that indicates an insertion place.

insertion point A blinking vertical line that indicates the placement of new information in a cell entry or the entry area.

inside border Accessed in the Border tab of the Format Cells dialog box, the Inside option places borders between all selected cells.

interest A fee charged for a loan.

interest payment function (IPMT) Used to determine the amount of a loan payment that is applied to interest.

Internet A very large computer network that electronically links smaller networks and individual computers.

Internet Assistant Wizard Provides help converting and saving information as an HTML document.

intranet A closed network accessible only to authorized users, usually the employees of an organization.

Invoice A Spreadsheet Solutions template for invoices.

italic A format for an entry that makes it slanted. *This is an example of italics.* The keyboard shortcut is Ctrl+I.

Italic button The button on the Formatting toolbar used to italicize cell contents.

justifying text Formatting cell contents so the text fills the entire width of the cell.

keyboard Consists of the standard alphabetic and numeric keys, a numeric keypad, arrow keys, and function keys. It is the most frequently used way to communicate with a computer.

keyboard commands The commands that are accessed by using keys on the keyboard rather than the mouse, also called keyboard shortcuts.

label The text that identifies the data within a row or column. Located at the top of a column or the left of a row.

landscape style The page orientation that places a worksheet's top on the long side of the paper.

left alignment Formatting of a cell in which cell contents are placed at the left edge of a cell.

legend A box containing entries identifying the data markers in a chart. The legend shows the pattern and color assigned to each data series in a chart.

library sheet A worksheet that contains the names of created macros, their shortcut keys, and brief descriptions of their uses.

life of asset The number of periods over which an asset is being depreciated. It is the estimated time an asset will be usable.

line chart A chart in which each data marker is plotted on a grid and lines join the markers. It is useful for tracking trends at even intervals over a period of time.

Line Color button The button on the Drawing toolbar used to add color to a border.

line style The style of a border line surrounding a cell or graphic. Line style choices include lines of various widths and double lines.

Line Style button The button on the Drawing toolbar used to select a line style.

link An abbreviation for hyperlink. It is used to connect to other documents on the World Wide Web.

linked chart A chart that changes when worksheet data changes.

linked documents Documents that are connected in such a way that a change to data in one document changes data in the others.

list A group of related records, also called a database.

list boxes In some dialog boxes, list boxes are provided to show additional choices.

logical functions Functions that make a conditional test that can be answered only with true or false.

logical test The item to be determined in an IF function that can be answered either true or false.

LOOKUP function Used to compare a specific number with a group of numbers and determine a related value to enter.

lookup table A table that compares information in order to make a data entry in a worksheet.

lookup value The value in the first column or row of an array that is used to look up information in the lookup table.

macro A series of commands that are executed automatically with one keystroke.

Macro dialog box The dialog box that lists all macros available to use.

manual page break A page break that is set manually, indicated in Page Break Preview by a solid line.

Map button A button located on the Standard toolbar. It is used to insert a map in a worksheet.

margin handles In Print Preview, the boxes displayed at the top and bottom of the page. They can be used to adjust the margins of a worksheet.

margins The amount of white space on the edges of a printed worksheet.

Margins tab The section in the Page Setup dialog box used to adjust the margins of a worksheet.

marquee A moving border that surrounds a selected area when cutting, copying, or pasting. To cancel the marquee, press the Esc key.

mathematical functions Functions used to perform mathematical operations such as determining sum, product, cosine, or matrix determinant.

Maximize button The button in the upper-right corner of a worksheet window that enlarges the worksheet to fill the Excel window. The keyboard shortcut is Ctrl+F10.

maximum function (MAX) A statistical function that determines the largest value in a selected list.

menu bar The first line on the Excel screen below the title bar. It displays choices for working in Excel.

Merge and Center button A button on the Formatting toolbar that is used to merge cells and center the text within the merged cells.

merging cells Combining two or more cells into one cell.

Microsoft Internet Explorer A browser program that is included in the Microsoft Office package.

Minimize button The button in the upper-right corner of a worksheet window that reduces the worksheet. The keyboard shortcut is Ctrl+F9.

minimum function (MIN) A statistical function that determines the smallest value in a selected list.

mixed reference A cell reference in which either the row or the column is absolute. $B5 and B$5 are mixed references. The column or row without the $ sign will adjust while the column or row with the $ sign will remain unchanged.

mode indicator Located at the right side of the status bar, it provides information pertaining to the current working conditions of Excel.

module The location of a macro's Visual Basic code.

mouse A communicating tool used to interact with the computer by pointing at a clicking on areas of the screen.

move area A selected range of cells that will be moved to a new location.

move line A dotted line that indicates the new placement of the gridline when adjusting a column width.

Multiple Maps Available dialog box The dialog box that opens so a specific map may be selected.

multiple paste Pasting to more than one range simultaneously.

multitasking Having more than one application open at the same time to quickly move between applications.

Name box The left side of the formula bar that identifies the cell reference of an active cell.

Name command Found in the Insert menu, it accesses dialog boxes for working with cell names.

naming cells The process of applying a name to a cell or range of cells and using that name in place of cell references in formulas.

Natural-language formula A formula that uses the labels of a worksheet rather than cell references.

New button The button on the Standard toolbar used to open a new workbook.

new workbook A workbook that has not been previously used. The keyboard shortcut to open a new workbook is Ctrl+N.

Nper The function variable for the total number of payments in a loan.

number format buttons The buttons on the Formatting toolbar used to format numbers.

Number tab The section of the Format Cells dialog box that is used to apply number formats to cell contents.

numeric keypad The 10-key data entry pad on the right side of a keyboard.

object linking and embedding (OLE) The process of copying information and creating links between documents created in different applications.

ODD function The mathematical function that returns a number that is the next higher odd integer.

Office Assistant An animated character on the screen that provides assistance with using Excel, answers questions, and offers tips.

online Help Information about working within a program available from the computer.

Open button The button on the Standard toolbar used to access a saved workbook.

Open dialog box The dialog box that is used to open an existing Excel workbook.

opening a workbook Accessing a previously saved workbook.

option button A method of selecting commands in some dialog boxes. Only one option button may be selected at a time.

organizational chart A visual representation of the structure of an organization.

orientation The placement of a worksheet on the page using either the short or long side as the top of the worksheet.

outline border Accessed in the Border tab of the Format Cells dialog box, the Outline option places a border around the outside of a selected range.

Oval button A button in the Drawing toolbar. It is used to place an oval shape in a worksheet.

page break line A dashed line in a worksheet that indicates the place where a new page will begin when the worksheet is printed.

Page Break Preview The view that is used to insert, delete, or move page breaks.

Page Number button A code button in the Header/Footer tab of the Page Setup dialog box. It is used to insert the page number.

Page Setup dialog box The dialog box used to provide Excel with additional information about the way a worksheet should be printed and placed on the page.

Page tab The section in the Page Setup dialog box where choices can be made regarding the orientation and size of the paper and the size of a worksheet on the page.

password A combination of letters, numbers, or spaces used to prevent other users from altering a protected worksheet.

paste area A range of cells where data will be moved or copied to, also called the destination. The keyboard shortcut is Ctrl+V.

Paste button The button on the Standard toolbar used for executing a paste command.

Paste Function button The button on the Standard toolbar that is used to access the Paste Function dialog box.

Paste Function dialog box A dialog box used to access built-in functions. The Paste Function dialog box lists all available functions.

Paste Link button Copies data and creates a link between the copy and the original.

Paste List button A button in the Paste Name dialog box. It pastes a list of named cells and their references in a worksheet.

Paste Name dialog box The dialog box that lists all defined names available to use in creating formulas.

Paste Special dialog box The dialog box that provides choices for pasting information such as pasting only the formula or format.

pasting a list Pasting the entire list of names used in a worksheet and their corresponding cell references.

pasting a name Using a name in a reference by pasting an already created name.

patterns Color, shading, or background styles placed in a cell.

Patterns tab The section of the Format Cells dialog box that is used to apply pattern styles to cells.

payment chart A chart that shows the amounts of interest, principal, and outstanding balance throughout the life of a loan.

payment function (PMT) A financial function used to return the periodic payment on a loan based on a constant interest rate.

Per In financial functions, the period of the loan for which interest is computed.

Percent style The number style that formats a cell for percentages with no decimals. The keyboard shortcut is Ctrl+Shift+%.

Percent Style button The button on the Formatting toolbar used to format numbers for the Percent style.

personal macro workbook A workbook in which macros can be stored so that they are always open when Excel is open. It resides on the hard drive of the computer.

Pick From List A shortcut menu that lists all previous entries in a column so an entry may be repeated without being keyed in.

pie chart A round chart used to show the relationship or proportion of each part to the whole. A pie chart contains one data series; each data marker is a "slice" of the pie.

plot area The area of a chart where values are plotted and represented by bars, lines, or pie slices.

point-and-click method The method of creating formulas by pointing and clicking in a cell to enter the cell reference.

points The units of measurement used for type size.

portrait style The page orientation that places the top of a worksheet on the short side of the paper.

principal The amount owed on an outstanding loan.

principal payment function (PPMT) Returns the amount of the principal paid on a loan.

print area The portion of a worksheet to be printed.

Print button The button on the Standard toolbar used to print a worksheet.

Print dialog box The dialog box that is used to determine specific information about the printing of a worksheet. It asks for the number of copies to print and the range of the workbook to print. The keyboard shortcut is Ctrl+P.

Print Preview A window that allows a miniature version of a worksheet to be viewed prior to printing. This is useful for checking the appearance of the worksheet and making minor changes.

Print Preview button The button on the Standard toolbar that accesses Print Preview.

Print range The section in the Print dialog box that specifies which pages will print.

PRODUCT function A mathematical function used to multiply values.

Protect Sheet dialog box The dialog box that provides options for protecting an individual worksheet.

Protect Workbook dialog box The dialog box that provides options for protecting a workbook.

pull-away palette A group of choices for formatting a worksheet that can be "pulled" away from a toolbar and moved around the screen.

pull-down menu Indicated by a small arrow pointing downward, it displays a list of additional choices for some commands.

Purchase Order A Spreadsheet Solutions template for purchase orders.

Pv In a financial function, the present value of an investment. The present value is the total amount that a series of future payments is worth now.

querying Retrieving a portion of data, also called searching.

range of cells Two or more cells.

rate The interest rate per period for a loan.

read-only document A shared document that allows users to access the information but not to make changes.

read-write document A shared document that allows all users to make changes.

record The information in a list about one subject, broken into several categories. In Excel a row consists of a record.

Record Macro dialog box The dialog box used to name a new macro, assign a shortcut key, and provide a description of the macro.

record number indicator Located in the upper-right corner of a data form, it is used to indicate which record is displayed and how many records are in the entire list.

recording a macro The process of creating a macro.

Rectangle button The button in the Drawing toolbar that is used to place a rectangle shape in a worksheet.

Redo button The button on the Standard toolbar that accesses the Redo command.

Redo command The command that reverses an Undo command.

refreshing data Bringing the most recent version of electronic information to a database, for example upgrading a stock quote to the current price.

relative reference A cell reference that automatically adjusts to its new location when moved or copied.

Repeat command The command that repeats recent actions.

Replace All button Replaces all occurrences of a text string within a worksheet in one step.

Replace command Allows information to be automatically replaced with different information.

Reset All Page Breaks The command that removes manual page breaks and restores all automatic page breaks.

result When using a function, the value that is returned to the worksheet.

retrieving a book Accessing a previously saved workbook.

right alignment Formatting of a cell in which cell contents end at the right edge of a cell.

rotated text Text that is placed at an angle within a cell.

ROUND function A mathematical function used to round a number to a specified number of decimal places.

row A range of cells one cell high that runs horizontally throughout the entire width of a worksheet. Rows are identified by numbers.

row headings The numbers along the left edge of a worksheet that identify specific rows.

row height The distance from the bottom to the top of a row. This is adjustable.

row label Identifying text for the values in a row.

Run Web Query The command used to access queries from the Web.

running a macro The process of applying a macro in a worksheet.

salvage value The estimated value of an asset at the end of its life.

Save As command The command used to save a workbook for the first time. The keyboard shortcut is F12.

Save button The button on the Standard toolbar used to save a changed document with its current file name.

Save command The command used to save changes made to a workbook. The keyboard shortcut is Shift+F12 or Ctrl+S.

scaling Adjusting the size of a worksheet to print on a pre-determined number of pages.

ScreenTip A small reminder that appears on the screen. It provides information about the current operation or provides a description of a toolbar button when the pointer is placed over it.

scroll bars The bars at the bottom and right edges of the screen that allow access to other parts of a worksheet.

scroll boxes Boxes on the scroll bars used to access different parts of a worksheet.

ScrollTip When a scroll box is being moved, the ScrollTip shows the row or column being moved to.

searching Finding information in a list, also called querying.

Select All button Located in the area between the row and column headings. Clicking the mouse button there selects the entire worksheet. The keyboard shortcut is Ctrl+A.

selected cell The cell in a worksheet in which information may be entered. A heavy border surrounding it indicates that it is selected. It is also called an active cell.

Series tab The section in the Chart Source Data dialog box used to alter the order of a series.

Shadow button The button in the Drawing toolbar used to add a shadow to a graphic.

sheet Another term for a worksheet.

sheet name The name of an individual sheet in a workbook. The default names are Sheet1, Sheet2, etc., but they can be changed.

Sheet Name button The code button in the Header/Footer tab of the Page Setup dialog box that is used to insert the sheet name.

Sheet tab The section in the Page Setup dialog box used to provide additional information about the way a worksheet will print, including choices for printing gridlines, row and column titles, or only a portion of the worksheet.

sheet tabs The tabs located at the bottom of worksheets. They display worksheet names. Clicking on a tab accesses that worksheet.

shortcut key A combination of keystrokes by which a macro may be quickly applied.

shortcut menus Menus showing frequently used commands. Access shortcut menus by clicking on the right mouse button. The keyboard shortcut is Shift+F10.

shrink to fit Decreases the size of text within a cell so it fits the existing cell size.

Sort Ascending button The button on the Standard toolbar that sorts a field in ascending order.

Sort Descending button The button on the Standard toolbar that sorts a field in descending order.

sort order The arrangement in which data is sorted.

sorting Arranging records in alphabetical, numerical, or chronological order.

source document The workbook where information that is linked to another document is originally located.

Spelling button The button on the Standard toolbar used to check the spelling in a document.

spelling checker Checks for correct spelling in worksheets and charts. The keyboard shortcut is F7.

split bars The small black rectangles at the top right and bottom left of the scroll bars. They are used to split the window to view different areas of a large worksheet.

spreadsheet A grid of rows and columns used to organize data, also called a worksheet.

Spreadsheet Solutions templates Templates that are built into Excel. They can be customized for individual businesses.

stacked bar chart A bar chart that shows the relationship of individual items to the whole.

Standard toolbar A toolbar used to execute frequently used commands and actions.

standard width The default width of a column before it is altered. The standard width is 8.43 points.

Start button The button on the taskbar used to access programs and files.

static date A date entry that remains the same each time Excel is opened.

static link A link formed when data is copied. The data in the second document does not change when the data in the original changes.

static time A time entry that remains the same each time Excel is opened.

statistical functions Used for statistical analysis.

status bar The area at the bottom of the screen that displays information about the current command or operation of Excel.

stock symbol The two- to five-letter abbreviation for a stock on the New York, American, or NASDAQ exchanges.

Stop Recording button The button on the Stop Recording toolbar that is used to stop the recording of a macro.

Stop Recording toolbar The toolbar used when creating macros. It consists of the Stop Recording and the Relative Reference buttons.

straight-line depreciation function (SLN) The financial function that determines depreciation using the straight-line depreciation method. In this method, an asset decreases in value an equal amount each period.

Sub statement In Visual Basic, the line that starts and names a macro.

SUM function The mathematical function used to determine the sum of a range of data.

sum-of-years' digits depreciation function (SYD) The financial function for determining depreciation using the sum-of-years' digits depreciation method. This method assumes an asset depreciates in greater amounts during the early years of its life.

syntax The sequence of elements in a function.

tab scrolling buttons The arrow buttons to the left of the sheet tabs. They are used to scroll to other worksheets of a workbook.

tabbed dialog box A dialog box that has tabs across the top to access additional sets of commands.

table array A table of information in which data is looked up.

template A worksheet used to create similar worksheets that already contain formulas, formatting, text, and macros.

template toolbars The toolbars that open with the Spreadsheet Solutions templates.

text Letters or words entered into Excel documents.

text box An area in some dialog boxes used to key in information. It is also a box containing text that can be added to a worksheet for emphasis or explanation.

Text Box button The button in the Drawing toolbar used to add a text box to a worksheet.

text orientation The placement of text within a cell vertically or at an angle. It is changed in the Format Cells dialog box.

Time button The code button in the Header/Footer tab of the Page Setup dialog box that is used to insert the current time.

title bar The bar that displays a title at the top of a window or dialog box.

toolbar dock A location at an edge of the screen where a toolbar can be placed out of the way of the main worksheet.

Total Pages button The code button available in the Header/Footer tab of the Page Setup dialog box. It is used to insert the total number of pages of a worksheet.

transposing Changing the arrangement of a worksheet so that the column labels become the row labels and vice versa. Data moves so the worksheet remains accurate.

Underline button The button on the Formatting toolbar used to underline the contents in a selected cell.

Undo button The button in the Standard toolbar that access the Undo command.

Undo command The command used to reverse recent commands.

ungrouping worksheets Removing the grouping of worksheets and accessing an individual worksheet.

unhiding columns Revealing previously hidden columns so they are again visible in the worksheet. The keyboard shortcut is Ctrl+Shift+).

unhiding rows Revealing previously hidden rows so they are again visible in the worksheet. The keyboard shortcut is Ctrl+Shift+(.

Uniform Resource Locator (URL) The address of a Web page.

value axis The y-axis, located on the left side of a chart.

value if false In an IF function, the entry in a cell if the logical test is false.

value if true In an IF function, the entry in a cell if the logical test is true.

vertical alignment The vertical placement of data within a cell.

vertical lookup function (VLOOKUP) A LOOKUP function where the lookup table is arranged vertically on the worksheet.

Visual Basic A programming language used in Excel.

volatile date A date entry that automatically changes to reflect the current date.

volatile time An entry for time that automatically changes to reflect the current time.

warning box A dialog box that opens to warn about a possible error.

Web An abbreviation for World Wide Web.

Web page Each document placed on the World Wide Web. Web pages store various types of information, including text, graphics, sound and video clips, and animation.

Web query Retrieves data from the Web and enters it into a worksheet.

Web site A term for any specific page on the Web.

What-if analysis The process of using a spreadsheet to make business decisions by varying the arguments in a formula or function.

window panes Areas of a large worksheet that can be scrolled independently. A worksheet can be split into up to four window panes. This is useful for viewing different sections of a large worksheet at the same time.

With statement A Visual Basic statement that specifies a series of commands.

WordArt Gallery dialog box A dialog box providing several choices of WordArt styles that can be selected.

workbook A group of worksheets that are saved as a single file, also called a book.

worksheet A grid of rows and columns used to organize data, also called a spreadsheet. A worksheet is saved as part of a workbook.

worksheet group A group of worksheets that may be active simultaneously. When worksheets are grouped, entries can be entered in all sheets at the same time.

worksheet tabs Tabs at the bottom of a workbook that allow access to other worksheets.

worksheet window The portion of a worksheet displayed on the computer screen.

World Wide Web A structure of documents that are connected electronically through the Internet.

wrapping text Allowing multiple lines of text to fit within a cell.

WWW An abbreviation for the World Wide Web.

Index

3-D button, 480
3-D reference, 423, 428–29

A

absolute reference, 137–39
active book, 46
active cell, 7, 10
active chart area, 308
active sheet, 46, 173
adding nonadjacent cells, 83–84
alignment, 42, 238
alignment buttons, 42
Alignment tab, 238
applying names, 426–27
area charts, 323–24
argument, 146, 334, 340
arithmetic operators, 71
arranging windows, 266
array, 359
Arrow button, 478
Arrow Style button, 480
ascending order, 378
AutoCalculate, 86–87
AutoComplete, 199
AutoCorrect, 206–7
AutoFill, 187–91
AutoFilter, 387–88
AutoFit Selection, 220
AutoFormat, 196
AutoShape, 479
AutoSum, 79–80
AVERAGE function, 150–51

B–C

bar charts, 320
beginning point, 411
bold text, 41
book, 36
book value, 351
Border tab, 246
borders, 43–44, 246–47
Borders button, 43
Borders palette, 44, 247
browser, 500
button, 9
Cancel box, 38, 77
category axis, 305, 306
category names, 306
cell, 10
cell reference, 7
Center Across Selection, 239
center alignment, 42
Chart Location dialog box, 313
Chart Options dialog box, 313
chart range, 306
chart sheet, 307
Chart Source Data dialog box, 311
chart title, 307
Chart toolbar, 317
Chart Type dialog box, 311
Chart Wizard, 310–14
charts, 304
    area, 323–24
    bar, 320
    column, 332
    default, 306
    embedded, 313, 315
    exploded, 326
    line, 325
    pie, 336
    stacked bar, 320
check box, 14
Clear command, 230
Clippit, 26
Close button, 7
Close command, 49–50
Col_index_num, 359
Collapse Dialog button, 148, 336
color, 480
color palette, 247
column, 2
column charts, 322
column handles, 57
column headings, 10, 283
column index number, 359
column width, 219–21
Comma Style button, 40
command, 11
command button, 15
comment, 492
comparison operator, 389
completing an entry, 37
compound document, 442
computed fields, 383
confirming a password, 486
copy area, 109
Copy button, 109
Copy command, 109–11, 112–14
copying cell formats, 248–49
copying a worksheet, 175–76
cost, 350
Count All (COUNTA) function, 155
COUNT function, 154
Create Names dialog box, 425
creating names, 425–26
criteria, 325
Currency format, 45, 232–233
Currency Style button, 40
Custom AutoFilter, 389–92
custom footer, 279
custom header, 279
custom list, 193–95
custom sort, 381
Customizing a template, 458–59
Cut button, 103
Cut command, 102

D

Dash Style button, 480
data form, 382–83
data marker, 306
data point, 306
data range, 311
data series, 306
database, 375
Date & Time function, 235
Date button, 280
DB function, 353–54
declining-balance depreciation, 353–54
Decrease Decimal button, 44
Decrease Indent button, 42
default, 41
default chart, 306
default command, 15
default font, 243
defining a name, 421–22
deleting cells, 229
deleting a worksheet, 176

533

depreciation, 350–57
descending order, 378
destination cell, 102, 109
destination document, 431, 444
dialog box, 13–16
download, 502
drag and drop, 103, 106–7, 110
Draw menu, 480–81
Drawing toolbar, 477–81
dynamic link, 436

E

editing a formula, 76
editing text, 38
editable fields, 383
electronic spreadsheet, 2
embedded charts, 313, 315
embedding, 444–45
End Sub statement, 411
End With statement, 411
ending point, 411
Enter box, 37, 75
Entering data by range, 85
Enter key, 3, 37
Enter mode, 71
entry area, 9
error value, 88
Escape key, 77
EVEN function, 338
exiting Excel, 16
Expand Dialog button, 148, 336
expense statement, 457, 458
exploded pie charts, 326
extending a selection, 23
external data, 502
external reference, 439

F

field, 375
file name, 25
File Name button, 280
Fill Across Worksheets dialog box, 186
Fill Color button, 480
Fill command, 182–95
fill effects, 309
fill handle, 184
Fill Justify command, 192
fill range, 183
filtering a list, 387–92
financial functions, 340–44
Find command, 490
finding and replacing text, 489–91
floating toolbar, 203
font, 41, 243
Font button, 281
Font Color button, 480

Font tab, 244
footer, 55, 278
Format Cells dialog box, 231–32
Format Painter, 121–22, 248–49
Format Painter button, 121
formatting, 41–45
formatting alignment, 238–41
formatting currency, 45
formatting dates, 235
formatting a font, 243–45
formatting numbers, 44–45, 232–33
formatting time, 236
Formatting toolbar, 9, 41, 202
formula, 70–79
formula bar, 9, 36
Formula Palette, 147, 335, 341
formulas, printing, 89
Free Rotate button, 481
freezing panes, 273
Function box, 148
function keys, 3
functions, 146–59, 333
 AVERAGE, 150–51
 COUNT, 154
 Count All (COUNTA), 155
 Date & Time, 235
 DB (declining-balance depreciation), 353–54
 EVEN, 338
 financial, 340–44
 HLOOKUP (horizontal lookup), 344, 358, 361
 IPMT (interest payment), 344
 logical, 156–59
 LOOKUP, 358–60
 mathematical, 337–38
 maximum, 152–53
 minimum, 152–53
 ODD, 338
 PMT (payment), 341–43
 PPMT (principal payment), 345
 PRODUCT, 337
 ROUND, 338
 SLN (straight-line depreciation), 350
 statistical, 150–51
 SUM, 337
 SYD (sum-of-years' digits depreciation), 335
 VLOOKUP (vertical lookup), 358–60

G–H

general alignment, 238
General number format, 40
Go To command, 19

grand total, 81–82
gridlines (chart), 307
gridlines (worksheet), 283
handles, 308
header, 55, 278
Header/Footer tab, 278
Help, 26–27
hiding columns, 223
hiding rows, 225–26
HLOOKUP function, 358, 361
home page, 500
horizontal alignment, 238
horizontal fill alignment, 238
horizontal lookup function, 344
hyperlink, 499, 500
Hypertext Markup Language (HTML), 507
Hypertext Transfer Protocol (HTTP), 500

I–K

icon, 3, 9
IF function, 156–59
Increase Decimal button, 44
Increase Indent button, 42
indent alignment, 239–40
inserting
 copying between cells, 112
 pasting between cells, 106
inserting cells, 227–28
inserting columns, 227–28
inserting rows, 227–28
Insert WordArt button, 479
inserting a worksheet, 174
insertion border, 106–7
insertion point, 19, 38
inside borders, 247
interest, 340, 344
Internet Assistant Wizard, 507–8
Internet, 499
intranet, 499
invoice, 457
IPMT (interest payment) function, 344
italic text, 41
justified alignment, 238
keyboard commands, 12

L

labels, 37, 85
landscape orientation, 275
left alignment, 42
legend, 306
library sheet, 409–10
life of an asset, 350
Line button, 477
line charts, 325

Line Color button, 480
Line Style button, 247, 480
link, *See* hyperlink
linked charts, 314
linked documents, 436, 437
linking between applications, 446–47
linking between workbooks, 439–40
linking between worksheets, 436–38
list, 375
list box, 14
logical functions, 156–59
logical test, 157
LOOKUP function, 358–60
lookup tables, 358
lookup value, 359

M

macro, 403
Macro dialog box, 407
manual page break, 287
map, 482–83
Map button, 482
margin handles, 57
margins, 54
Margins tab, 277
marquee, 77, 102
mathematical functions, 337–38
Maximize button, 6
maximum function, 152–53
menu bar, 9, 11
Merge and Center button, 197–98
merging cells, 241
Microsoft Internet Explorer, 500
Minimize button, 7
minimum function, 152–53
mixed reference, 141–44
mode indicator, 11
module, 405
mouse, 3
move area, 101
moving cells, 101–4
move line, 220
moving a worksheet, 175–76
Multiple Maps Available dialog box, 482
multiple paste, 121
multitasking, 440–41

N–O

naming a worksheet, 175
Name box, 9
naming cells, 421–23
Natural-language formulas, 419–20
New button, 51
new workbook, 52
Nper argument, 341

number format, 232–33
number format buttons, 44
Number tab, 232
numeric keypad, 3, 39
object linking and embedding (OLE), 442, 444–49
ODD function, 338
Office Assistant, 26
online Help, 26
Open button, 51
Open dialog box, 51
opening Excel, 5
opening a workbook, 15
option button, 15
organizational chart, 484–85
orientation, 275
outline borders, 247
Oval button, 479

P–Q

page break line, 286
Page Break Preview, 286–88
Page Number button, 280
Page Setup dialog box, 54–56, 274–83
Page tab, 275–76
password, 485
paste area, 102
Paste button, 103, 109
Paste command, 102
Paste Function, 334–36
Paste Function button, 234, 334
Paste Function dialog box, 146
Paste Link button, 437
Paste Name dialog box, 423–24
Paste Special dialog box, 118
pasting a list, 428–29
pasting names, 423–24
patterns, 248
Patterns tab, 248
payment chart, 347–49
Per argument, 341
Percentage Style button, 44
personal macro workbook, 404
Pick From List command, 199–200
pie charts, 336
planning a worksheet, 90–91
plot area, 305
PMT (payment) function, 341–43
point-and-click formula, 76–77
portrait orientation, 275
PPMT (principal payment) function, 345
principal, 344
print area, 288
Print button, 52
Print command, 52–53, 284–86

Print dialog box, 52–53, 284–85
Print Preview, 56–58
printing an embedded chart, 315
printing formulas, 89
printing a workbook, 177
PRODUCT function, 337
protecting a workbook, 486
protecting a worksheet, 485–87
pull-away palette, 247
pull-down menu, 14
purchase order, 457
Pv argument, 342
Querying a list, 384–85

R

range of cells, 21
Rate argument, 341
read-only document, 485, 486
read-write document, 485
Record Macro dialog box, 404–5
record number indicator, 382
record, 375
Rectangle button, 479
Redo command, 116
refreshing data, 505–6
relative reference, 135–36
Repeat command, 116
Replace All button, 491
Replace command, 490
Reset All Page Breaks command, 287
result of a function, 334
retrieving a book, 51
right alignment, 42
rotated text, 240, 481
ROUND function, 338
row, 22
row headings, 10, 283
row heights, 221
running a macro, 407
running a Web query, 502

S

salvage value, 350
Save As command, 49
Save button, 48, 51
saving documents, 46–49
scaling, 275
ScreenTip, 9, 27
scroll bars, 10
scroll boxes, 18
ScrollTip, 18
searching a list, 384–85
Select All button, 24
selected cell, 10
Series dialog box, 189
Series tab, 311

Shadow button, 480
sheet, 1, 7
Sheet Name button, 280
sheet tab, 174, 282–83
shortcut key, 408
shortcut menu, 179–80
shortcuts, 12
Shrink to fit option, 241
site, 500
SLN function, 350
Sort Ascending button, 378–79
Sort Descending button, 378–79
sort order, 378
sorting a list, 377–79
source document, 444
Spelling button, 205
spelling checker, 205–6
split bars, 270
spreadsheet, 1
Spreadsheet Solutions templates, 457–59
stacked bar charts, 320
Standard toolbar, 9, 201
Start button, 5
static date, 235
static link, 436
statistical functions, 150–51
status bar, 10
stock symbols, 503–5
Stop Recording toolbar, 405
straight-line depreciation, 350
Sub statement, 411

SUM function, 337
sum-of-years' digits depreciation, 335
SYD function, 335
syntax, 334

T–U

tab scrolling buttons, 176
tabbed dialog box, 13
table array, 359
tabs, 14
template, 455
template toolbars, 461
templates, opening, 457, 460–61
templates, saving, 455–56, 459
text, 2, 37
text box, 14, 479
text orientation, 240
Time button, 280
title bar, 8, 14
toolbar, 201–4
  Chart, 317
  Drawing, 477–81
  Formatting, 9, 41, 202
  Standard, 9, 201
  Stop Recording, 405
  template, 461
toolbar dock, 203
Total Pages button, 280
transposing a worksheet, 120
Underline button, 44
Undo command, 115
ungrouping worksheets, 175

unhiding columns, 224
unhiding rows, 226
Uniform Resource Locator (URL), 499, 507
unprotecting sheets, 9

V–W

value axis, 305
vertical alignment, 239
vertical lookup function, 358–60
Visual Basic, 405–6, 410–12
VLOOKUP, 358–60
volatile date, 235
warning box, 16
Web pages, creating, 506–9
Web query, 501–6
Web site, 500
Web, 499
What-if analysis, 336
window panes, 270–73
With statement, 411
WordArt, 250–52, 479
WordArt Gallery, 251
workbook, 6, 173
worksheet, 1, 7
worksheet group, 174
worksheet tab, 10
worksheet window, 7
World Wide Web, 499–500
Wrap text option, 241
WWW, 499